Adolf Hitler

Volume I

Adolf Hitler

By JOHN TOLAND

Volume I

Doubleday & Company, Inc., Garden City, New York

Grateful acknowledgment is made for permission to quote portions from the following:

The Young Hitler I Knew by August Kubizek. Copyright © 1954 by Paul Popper and Company. Reprinted by permission of the publisher, Houghton Mifflin Company, Boston.

Hitler's Secret Conversations, 1941–1944, edited by H. R. Trevor-Roper, translated by Norman Cameron and R. H. Stevens. Copyright © 1953 by Farrar, Straus and Young, Inc. Reprinted with the permission of Farrar, Straus & Giroux, Inc., and of George Weidenfeld & Nicolson Ltd., London.

The Testament of Adolf Hitler: The Hitler-Bormann Documents, February–April 1945, edited by François Genoud and translated by R. H. Stevens. Copyright © 1959, Libraire Arthème Fayard; English edition published by Cassell & Co., Ltd. Reprinted by permission of A. D. Peters & Co., Ltd.

Hitler's Interpreter by Paul Schmidt. Copyright © 1951 by Opera Mundi, Inc. Reprinted by permission of Opera Mundi, Inc.

Douze ans auprès d'Hitler: Confidences d'une secrétaire particulière d'Hitler, recorded by Albert Zoller. Copyright © 1949 by Éditions René Julliard. Reprinted by permission of Éditions René Julliard.

Contents

List of Maps & Tables

Foreword

Adolf Hitler was probably the greatest mover and shaker of the twentieth century. Certainly no other human disrupted so many lives in our times or stirred so much hatred. He also inspired widespread adoration and was the hope and ideal of millions. The passage of more than thirty years since his end has done little to alter the perspective of either enemies or true believers. Today we see the other leaders of his era—Roosevelt, Churchill, Mussolini, Stalin—in a different, more objective light but the image of Hitler has remained essentially the same. To the few who remained his faithful followers he is a hero, a fallen Messiah; to the rest he is still a madman, a political and military bungler, an evil murderer beyond redemption whose successes were reached by criminal means.

As one of those whose life was altered by Hitler, I have done my utmost to subdue my own feelings and to write of him as if he had lived a hundred years ago. I interviewed as many as possible of those who knew Hitler intimately—both worshipers and deriders. Many agreed to talk freely and at length about the unhappy past. Gone was the reluctance of past years to discuss the Führer and his actions for fear their views might be distorted. I conducted more than two hundred and fifty interviews with his adjutants (Puttkamer, Below, Engel, Günsche, Wünsche and Schulze); his secretaries (Traudl Junge and Gerda Christian); his chauffeur (Kempka); his pilot (Baur); his doctors (Giesing and Hasselbach); his favorite warriors (Skorzeny and Rudel); his favorite architects (Speer and Giesler); his first foreign press secretary (Hanfstaengl); his military leaders (Manstein, Milch, Dönitz, Manteuffel and Warlimont); the women he most admired (Leni Riefenstahl, Frau Professor Troost and Helene Hanfstaengl). All but a dozen of these interviews were recorded on tapes which presently are stored in the Library of Congress for safekeeping. All those interviewed whose accounts are included in the book read the passages about themselves and not only made corrections but often added illuminating comments.

Significant new documents, reports and studies have also been utilized to help unravel the mystery of Hitler: the dossiers of the U. S. Army Counter-Intelligence Command, including one agent's interview with Hitler's sister Paula; unpublished documents in the National Archives such as a secret psychiatric report on Hitler in 1918; the unpublished documents from the British Government Archives; the recently discovered Göring-Negrelli correspondence of 1924–25 which sheds new light on Nazi-Fascist relations; the secret speeches of Himmler; and unpublished diaries, notes and memoirs including the revealing recollections of Traudl Junge, Hitler's youngest secretary.

My book has no thesis, and any conclusions to be found in it were reached only during the writing, perhaps the most meaningful being that Hitler was far more complex and contradictory than I had imagined. "The greatest saints," observed one of Graham Greene's characters, "have been men with more than a normal capacity for evil, and the most vicious men have sometimes narrowly evaded sanctity." Deprived of heaven, Adolf Hitler chose hell—if, indeed, he knew the difference between the two. To the end, obsessed by his dream of cleansing Europe of Jews, he remained a Knight of the Hakenkreuz, a warped archangel, a hybrid of Prometheus and Lucifer.

Prologue

STAB IN THE BACK

1

In mid-October 1918 a hospital train, the sides of its carriages defaced by revolutionary slogans, slowly wended its way through Germany toward the secure eastern marches of the Empire. Among the hundreds of casualties on the train were blinded victims of a recent poison gas attack in Belgium. It had followed a devastating British artillery assault on the night of the thirteenth, one of a relentless series of hammer blows that the German front, retreating, bending but not breaking, had sustained since the battle turned so decisively three months earlier. The 16th Bavarian Reserve Infantry Regiment, which took the brunt of the attack, was dug in on hills and fields, a spectral battleground churned into a morass of craters. The men, physically exhausted, and dispirited as much by ugly rumors of mutinies along the front as by the unceasing Allied attacks, huddled in trenches while British shells tore up the ground around them. The veterans were numbed, the recruits terrified.

Suddenly, thuds mingled with the explosions and a pungent cloud drifted into the trenches. Someone shouted, "Gas!" It was their first experience with mustard gas. To some it smelled sweet, to others acrid; in every case it clung tenaciously to the nostrils. The men slapped on their masks, then hunched, inanimate, against the sides of the trenches. Hours passed. The air inside the masks became dense and stale. One of the recruits, driven half mad by suffocation, wrenched the mask from his face only to gulp in the deadly poison. "It caught him by the throat and flung him back choking, gurgling, suffocating, dying."

It was dawn before the gas began to dissipate and the shelling resumed. The men tore off the masks and gulped in the morning air. "It was still stinking of the stuff," writes one, "and reeked again of high explosives, but to us it was the very breath of heaven." The relief was short-lived. In that cruel and unpredictable pattern calculated to reduce the enemy to madness, gas bombs again mingled with high explosives. Those too slow in putting on their filthy masks keeled over and died as the young recruit had. Those who escaped with their lives were painfully blinded, all but one who still could see faintly. He suggested to the others that they hang on to each other's coattails as he attempted to lead them to safety. Thus they stumbled in goose file, the half blind leading the blind, until they reached a first aid station. Among the men thus rescued from a choking death was a twenty-nine-year-old *Gefreiter* (corporal) named Adolf Hitler.

Still blinded as the train carried him eastward, Hitler was in a state bordering on collapse. Like the other victims, his eyes were swollen, his face puffed up. The voices of these men were ghostlike, without timbre, and they irritably rejected the care of their nurses. They would not allow their inflamed eyes to be treated; they would not eat. In vain the doctors told them that they would soon regain their vision; these men had been deceived too long. They wanted only to lie still and moan and be delivered from pain, even if by death.

This wounded and demoralized corporal who fifteen years later would be the leader of the Reich was not yet aware of the magnitude of Germany's defeat. Four years earlier, as the first great German offensive rolled over Belgian, French and British resistance, Hitler's regiment had first been bloodied in battle in that same area, losing an almost inconceivable eighty per cent of its personnel in less than a week. To the ardent Hitler these losses, far from discouraging, had been proof of the fighting spirit of German troops. He wrote to his Munich landlord, ". . . with pride I can say our regiment handled itself heroically from the very first day on—we lost almost all our officers and our company has only two sergeants now. On the fourth day only 611 were left out of the 3600 men of our regiment."

Many Germans in those early days shared this exultant view of Teutonic heroism. But as the months passed the war degenerated into deadlocked trench warfare, the armies facing each other across a scarred no man's land, clashing as one or the other tried to effect a breakthrough, counting advances in a few miles or even yards with casualties in the millions. The early mood of enthusiasm faded. Defeatism and despair corroded the morale of the men who lived ratlike in their dugouts and trenches. Hunger and misery stalked the homeland as the British blockade cut off the flow of essentials to the German people. As the war extended into its third and then fourth year the soldiers' thoughts turned from victory to survival; they would assail the stupidities of their high command and the futility of further fighting. Hitler was one of those few who scornfully rejected such defeatist talk. Despite repeated acts of heroism he was still a corporal but was not distressed by this lack of recognition. He railed at his comrades, particularly the youthful recruits who brought with them "the poison of the hinterland," and if anyone argued with him he would, according to one comrade, "become furious, and then jam hands into his pockets and pace back and forth with long strides, abusing the pessimists."

And perhaps the pessimists were wrong after all. As 1918 dawned, the Germans, after nearly four years on the defensive, were poised to return to the attack. For the western front was stalemated. On all the other battlefields German arms had conquered. Serbia, Romania and finally Russia had succumbed, the last one as much to revolution as to the German assaults. The peace treaty with the new Soviet regime had put the Germans in command of the vast Ukrainian plain, the breadbasket of Europe. And over a million men released by the collapse of enemy resistance in the East now streamed into France to bring the deadlocked issue of the western front to a decision. The Emperor's Battle—as General Erich Ludendorff, the junior but dominant member of the German high command, called it—was at hand.

Throughout the spring, in four mighty assaults, the Germans forced first the British and then the French to retreat. The British with "backs to the wall" were ordered to fight to the last man. When the final big battle began on July 15 near the city of Rheims both sides were aware that the outcome of the war was at stake. "If my attack on Rheims succeeds," said Ludendorff, "we have won the war." Marshal Foch, commander-in-chief of the Allied forces, concurred. "If the German attack at Rheims succeeds," he was reported to have said, "we have lost the war." The attack failed. No German reserves were left. The Allies on the other hand were fortified not only by fresh American divisions but by supplies and provisions streaming from the United States.

In the German army desertions multiplied. Everywhere there was talk of mutiny and revolt, and when the British launched a surprise attack near

Amiens in early August the German lines caved in practically without re-sistance. The Kaiser's men surrendered en masse at times to a single enemy infantryman. Retreating men shouted to reinforcements coming up to the front, "Strikebreakers!" Yet it was not the end. The Germans re-treated but the line held. For every defeatist there still were hundreds of soldiers ready to do their duty. But at home faith was fading. There were numerous strikes and everywhere in the cities radical socialists were talk-ing revolution. To stout spirits like Hitler the secure and unmolested home front, its laggards, its profiteers, its malingerers, its traitors, its Jews who had no love or respect for the German Fatherland, had betrayed the fighting front in its gravest hour. In fact, it was Ludendorff who lost his nerve and pressed the civilian government for an armistice.

Even at this late hour, the ardent spirits like Hitler were convinced that some solution, if not victory, was possible so long as resistance contin-ued. The front had not broken and was retreating in an orderly fashion. It was these profiteers, these malingerers, these Jews who would bring defeat from within.

2

The tragedy to which Hitler was a blinded witness, the collapse of the authority which he held in such unquestioning respect, would eventually open the road for his own astounding rise to power. The world he had known was one ruled by the elite, the descendants of ancient royal houses; high state offices, diplomatic posts, army commissions were all held by men of ancient lineage, aristocrats of superior breeding and education. The war had changed all that. In the trenches men of high and of low births fought side by side; the depleted ranks of noble officers were gradu-ally filled with commoners.

Throughout Europe royalty was clinging to hollow power. From the untitled masses were emerging men like Hitler who would come to wield the substance of power, men of common and often vulgar beginnings, rid-ing the relentless wave of popular revolt against a war which had demanded sacrifices for goals no one could define.

As the train took Hitler to a hospital in the Pomeranian town of Pase-walk, his own pain and despair obliterated any such aspiration, but after several weeks of medical treatment he began to regain his sight. Inflammation of the mucous membrane and swelling of the eyelids had receded; "the piercing in my sockets" began to diminish and "slowly I suc-ceeded in distinguishing the broad outlines of things about me." With sight came an end to depression and the mental instability that had required special treatment from a consulting psychiatrist, Professor Edmund Forster, chief of the Berlin University Nerve Clinic. Little was known about mustard gas and Hitler's inexplicable recovery confirmed Dr. Forster in his diagnosis of the blindness as hysteria. In fact, the patient had experienced the usual symptoms of moderate mustard gas poisoning: burning, swelling, moaning, depression—and recovery in several weeks.

Sight also brought Hitler hope and renewed interest in the events of the day. Berlin itself was in a state of virtual siege as the new Chancellor urged the Kaiser to abdicate so that an armistice could be signed. Hitler had heard stories of rebellion throughout Germany but discounted them as rumor until a delegation of Red German sailors burst into his ward early that November in an attempt to convert the patients to the revolution. Hitler's detestation of Bolshevism was heightened by the fact that three of the leaders were young Jews, none of whom, he was sure, had been at the front. "Now they raised the red rag in the homeland." Indignation was followed by shock. Hitler took to his bed. "I lay there broken with great pains, although I did not let on how I felt; for it was repugnant to me to cry out at a time when you could feel that the collapse was coming." A little later, on November 9, a dignified elderly pastor arrived at Pasewalk hospital to confirm news of the uprisings. Revolution had even broken out in Munich.

The patients were gathered in a little hall and the pastor, so Hitler recalled, "seemed all a-tremble as he informed us that the House of Hohenzollern should no longer bear the German imperial crown; that the Fatherland had become a 'republic.'" As the aged speaker eulogized the services rendered by the Hohenzollerns, he "began to sob gently to himself —in the little hall the deepest dejection settled on all hearts, and I believe not an eye was able to restrain its tears." The pastor went on to say that the war must now be ended, that all was lost and they had to throw themselves upon the mercy of the victorious Allies. To Hitler the revelation was intolerable. "It became impossible for me to sit still one minute more. Again everything went black before my eyes; I tottered and groped my way back to the dormitory, threw myself on my bunk, and dug my burning head into my blankets and pillow."

It was the first time he had wept since standing at his mother's grave eleven years earlier (she had died in agony of cancer), in the churchyard of the Austrian village of Leonding. He had borne the fear of blindness "in dull silence," endured the loss of so many good comrades. "But now I could not help it. Only now did I see how all personal suffering vanished in comparison with the misfortune of the Fatherland." Out of his black despair came a decision. "The great vacillation of my life, whether I

should enter politics or remain an architect, came to an end. That
night I resolved that, if I recovered my sight, I would enter politics."
There was no medical reason for Hitler's second blindness and Dr. Forster
was reinforced in his initial conclusion that his patient was definitely "a
psychopath with hysterical symptoms." Hitler, however, was convinced
that he was permanently blind.

The shame of Germany's surrender on November 11 in the forest of
Compiègne overwhelmed him. Life seemed unbearable, but that night,
or the next, Hitler was abruptly delivered from his misery, as he lay in despair on his cot, by a "supernatural vision" (perhaps deliberately induced
by Dr. Forster).* Like St. Joan, he heard voices summoning him to save
Germany. All at once "a miracle came to pass"—the darkness encompassing Hitler evaporated. He could see again! He solemnly vowed, as promised, that he would "become a politician and devote his energies to carrying out the command he had received."

That night in the lonely ward at Pasewalk the most portentous force
of the twentieth century was born. Politics had come to Hitler, not Hitler
to politics.

* The possibility that Dr. Forster induced Hitler's hallucination through hypnotic suggestion is given credence by a novel about Hitler and Forster written by the latter's
friend, Ernst Weiss, a medical doctor turned playwright and novelist. In this book, *The
Eyewitness*, a soldier, "A.H.," arrives at Pasewalk military hospital in 1918 claiming to
have been poisoned by gas. A psychiatrist, the narrator, diagnoses the case as hysterical
blindness and induces a hallucination through hypnosis.

Part 1

I, VISIONARY

Chapter One

DEEP ARE THE ROOTS
1889–1907

1

Hitler rarely talked about his family but to a few confidants he did confess an inability to get along with his father, a dictatorial man. While he revered his mother, a quiet, soft soul, it soon became evident that the former would be the dominating force in his life. Both parents came from the Waldviertel, a rural area of Austria, northwest of Vienna, not far from the present Czechoslovakian border and, according to one member of the family, there was Moravian blood in the line. Hitler was an unusual name for an Austrian and quite possibly it was derived from the Czech names "Hidlar" or "Hidlarček." Variants of these names had appeared in the Waldviertel since 1430 and changed from Hydler to Hytler to Hidler. In 1650 a direct ancestor of Adolf Hitler on his mother's side was called Georg Hiedler. His descendants occasionally spelled their name "Hüttler" and "Hitler." In those days spelling was as unimportant and erratic as in Shakespearian England.

The Waldviertel was a district of modest beauty, hilly and wooded, its graceful slopes covered with orderly forests, broken occasionally by fields cleared by generations of hard-working, frugal peasants. Hitler's father was born on June 7, 1837, in the village of Strones. His mother was a forty-two-year-old unmarried woman, Maria Anna Schicklgruber. Strones was too small to be a parish and so the baby was registered in Döllersheim as Aloys Schicklgruber, "Illegitimate." The space for the father's name was blank, generating a mystery that remains unsolved: he probably was a man from the neighborhood. There is the slight possibility that Hitler's grandfather was a wealthy Jew named Frankenberger or Frankenreither; that Maria Anna had been a domestic in this Jewish household at Graz and the young son had got her pregnant.

When Alois (as his name would be spelled henceforth) was almost five, Johann Georg Hiedler, an itinerant millworker from nearby Spital, married Maria. But her little son continued to have a blighted family life; she died five years later and the stepfather apparently resumed his drifting. Alois consequently was brought up by Hiedler's brother Johann Nepomuk at house number 36 in Spital. This farmhouse and the one next door would play an important role in the life of young Adolf Hitler, for here, in this isolated village, he spent half a dozen pleasant summer holidays.

The situation in Spital became intolerable for Alois and at thirteen he "laced his tiny knapsack and ran away from his home." This is the touching, if accurate, scene later painted by his son Adolf in *Mein Kampf*. "A desperate decision to take to the road with only three gulden for travel money, and plunge into the unknown." He worked his way to the mecca of venturesome youth, Vienna, where he became apprenticed to a shoemaker, but five years later, after learning this trade, he decided to become "something better" so enlisted in the frontier guards. This made him a civil servant, a step above the priesthood. He studied diligently, passed a special examination, and by the time he was twenty-four was promoted to a supervisory rank, an exceptional honor for a boy from the Waldviertel. Promotions came regularly to the ambitious Alois and in 1875 he was made a full inspector of customs at Braunau on the Inn River, just across from Germany.

No one was prouder of Alois' success than the man who had brought him up, Johann Nepomuk Hiedler. No Hiedler had ever risen so high. There was no son to carry on the name of Hiedler and on a late spring day in 1876 Johann decided to do something about it.* On June 6 his son-in-law and two other relatives made the short trip to the town of Weitra where they falsely testified before the local notary that "Hiedler's brother" —they spelled his name "Hitler"—"had several times stated in their presence and before his death [in 1857] as his last and unchangeable will" that

* He may have had other motives. There was village gossip that Alois was his natural son. It has also been suggested by Franz Jetzinger, author of a generally accurate book on Hitler's youth, that Hiedler may have wanted to legitimize Alois as insurance for the young man's career, "a strong motive if his father had been a Jew."

he had fathered an illegitimate son, Alois, and wanted him made his legitimate son and heir.

Perhaps the change of name from Hiedler to Hitler was carelessness, but more likely it was a cunning peasant trick to becloud the issue. The next day Johann Nepomuk Hiedler traveled with his three relatives to Döllersheim where the original birth record of Alois was registered. After examining the document signed by the three witnesses, the elderly parish priest affirmed from the parish marriage book that a man named Georg Hiedler had indeed married a girl named Schicklgruber in 1842. And so he agreed to alter the birth register. But he must have been reluctant or leery. Although he changed the "illegitimate" to "legitimate" and crossed out "Schicklgruber" in the space for the child's name, he failed to write in another name. In the last space, in extremely cramped writing, he penned: "It is confirmed by the undersigned that Georg Hitler whose name is here entered as Father, being well known to the undersigned, did accept paternity of the child Aloys, according to the statement of the child's mother, and did desire his name to be entered in the register of baptisms of this parish." He himself signed the names of the three witnesses and each, in turn, made his mark, a cross.

The amendments on the register were neither dated nor signed. The parish priest had reason to be devious. Not only had he written in the father's name as "Hitler," instead of the "Hiedler" appearing in the marriage book, but he must have known the entire procedure was illegal on two counts: a deceased man could not be recognized as a father except by legal proceedings; moreover, the mother had to corroborate the facts.

There was yet another ambiguity in the matter—the willingness of Alois Schicklgruber to accept the new name. Illegitimacy had been of little embarrassment to him; in lower Austria it was common and in some remote districts ran as high as forty per cent. Children were the lifeblood of any farm community and every healthy worker was welcome. It could even have been more of an embarrassment to change his name once he had achieved a measure of success as a Schicklgruber.

Whatever the motivation, Alois was somehow induced by Johann Nepomuk Hiedler to change his name. (The talk in the village was that he had been persuaded by a promise that the old man would change his will and this gossip was somewhat confirmed six months after Hiedler's death when Alois bought a farm for five thousand florins.) In any case his decision to assume the name of Hitler was momentous. It is difficult to imagine seventy million Germans shouting in all seriousness. "Heil Schicklgruber!"

To the girls of Spital, Alois must have cut a dashing figure in his uniform, close-clipped military haircut, bushy eyebrows, sweeping *Kaiserbart* (handlebar) mustache, and two fiercely jutting tufts of hair on either side of a clean-shaven chin. He too had an eye for the girls. Like his legal father, he had already sired an illegitimate daughter. Nor had marriage to the daughter of an inspector in the imperial tobacco monopoly been much of a restraint to amorous adventures. After all, she was sickly and fourteen years his senior.

One of the most attractive Spital girls was Johann Nepomuk Hiedler's granddaughter, Klara Pölzl, a sweet-faced, quiet sixteen-year-old. She was slim, almost as tall as stocky Alois, with abundant dark brown hair and even features. Whether it was love at first sight or simply a desire to provide his ailing wife with a willing housemaid, he managed to persuade the family to let Klara follow him to Braunau. She was installed with the Hitlers in an inn where Alois was already carrying on an affair with a kitchen maid, Franziska (Fanni to the customers) Matzelsberger.

This situation was too much for Frau Hitler. She left Alois and was granted a legal separation. Now it was Fanni's turn to enter the Hitler ménage and she established herself more as common-law wife than mistress. She was only too aware of how tempting a pretty maid could be to the susceptible Alois and one of her first acts was to get rid of Klara. Two years later, in 1882, Fanni gave birth to a boy, like his father, illegitimate.

The following year Hitler's estranged wife died of consumption and he married Fanni. The ceremony was timely. Within two months a second child, Angela, was born. At last Alois had a legitimate child, even if conceived illegitimately. He also accepted legal responsibility for the boy, who became Alois Hitler, Jr. Fanni, restored to respectability, was no happier since Alois, Sr., once more showed signs of wandering affections. Like her predecessor, she contracted a serious lung ailment and was forced to leave Braunau for the country air of a nearby village. Since this left Alois alone on the top floor of the Pommer Inn with two infants, it was only logical for him to seek help from his attractive niece. Once more the compliant Klara was installed in the Pommer Inn and this time she became housemaid, nursemaid and mistress. Adolf Hitler's mother-to-be was such a goodhearted girl she also did her best to help restore Fanni to health, visiting her frequently. Curiously, Fanni welcomed the ministrations of her rival.

In the summer of 1884 the wretched life of Fanni ended. Predictably, the next lady in waiting in the Hitler household was already pregnant. Alois wanted to marry Klara; she could care for his two children and he was genuinely fond of her. But the Church forbade their marriage since, by the fake legitimization, his own father and Klara's grandfather were brothers. Alois appealed to the local priests for a special dispensation from Rome. It was granted within the month, undoubtedly because of Klara's pregnancy. And at the first possible moment, on the morning of January 7, 1885, Alois and his niece were married at the Pommer Inn. Present were the two children, Alois, Jr., and Angela, and three witnesses: Klara's younger sister, Johanna, and two customs men. Their new maid had taken care of all the arrangements; in her enthusiasm she overheated the parlor and throughout the ceremony Alois teased her for it. There was no honeymoon and after a simple meal Alois returned to the customs station. Before noon, as Klara later wistfully recalled, "my husband was already on duty again."

Remarkably, the untidy private life of Alois had never interfered with his professional duties. He continued to be an efficient and honest public servant, esteemed by colleagues and superiors alike. He held himself in the same high esteem although his local reputation was not good; extramarital affairs in such a small town inevitably became common gossip. Among the ugly rumors was one that he had bought a coffin for his first wife while she was still alive.

Klara flourished in her new role as *Hausfrau*. She was a model housekeeper and completely devoted to Alois, Jr., and Angela, treating them as if they were her own. Four months after the ceremony she gave birth to a son, and within two years to a girl and another boy. The youngest died within a few days of birth and shortly afterward both of the older children contracted diphtheria and succumbed. The tragedy was hard for Klara to bear. Fortunately she had an outlet for her affections in Alois, Jr., and Angela, but relations with her husband were strained. From the first she had regarded Alois as a superior being and the road from housemaid to mistress to wife was so complicated for a simple girl from Spital that she still addressed her husband as "uncle."

The death of three children apparently affected her regular rate of pregnancy and it was not until April 20, 1889,* that the fourth child was born. He was one quarter Hitler, one quarter Schicklgruber, one quarter Pölzl, and one quarter uncertain. In the baptismal registry he was entered as "Adolfus Hitler." Later Klara claimed that Adolf was a sickly baby and that she always lived in fear of also losing him, but their housemaid remembered Adolf as a "very healthy, lively child who developed very well."

In either case, Frau Hitler lavished love and attention on her boy and, as a result, probably spoiled him. Life went on placidly at the Pommer Inn. The father spent more time with his cronies and his hobby,

---

* Crown Prince Rudolf had recently committed suicide at Mayerling.

beekeeping, than he did at home, but he apparently had ceased his sexual wanderings—or at least was becoming more discreet. He was remembered pleasantly by the housemaid, who described him as a "very strict but comfortable man" who treated the help with consideration. One day, for instance, this exalted official actually took off his boots rather than soil the freshly cleaned floor. But to his new customs supervisor Alois Hitler was an unsympathetic figure. "He was very strict, exacting, and pedantic, a most unapproachable person. . . . He took pride in his uniform, and always had himself photographed in it."

When Adolf was three years and four months old his father was promoted and the family moved to Passau, a good-sized city down the Inn on the German side of the river, where the customs inspection office was located. Living in a German city and playing with German children made a lasting mark on the youngster. The distinctive lower Bavarian dialect, for instance, would remain his mother tongue. It reminded him, he recalled, "of the days of my childhood."

Frau Hitler had not became pregnant again and it has been suggested that in overcompensating the "sickly" child she was still nursing him. It was not until Adolf was almost five that the next child, Edmund, was born. At last Adolf was freed from his mother's constant surveillance, and almost complete freedom came shortly after when his father was reassigned to Linz. The family, apparently because of the newborn baby, stayed in Passau and the five-year-old Adolf now could play endlessly with the German children or wander at will for hours, his own master.

For a year he reveled in this carefree life. Then in the spring of 1895 the family was reunited in Hafeld, a small farm community some thirty miles southwest of Linz. They lived in a farmhouse situated on nine acres of gently rolling fields. The property established the Hitlers near the top of local society. A month later the six-year-old Adolf was further separated from his possessive mother by entrance into a small *Volksschule* (primary school) several miles away at Fischlam. The regimentation of education was reinforced within a few weeks by rigorous supervision at the hands of his father, who had just retired, after forty years of service, to a life of modest comfort as a minor country gentleman.

It was a pretty house on a slight rise, almost completely hidden by an orchard of fruit and walnut trees and flanked by a brook, artificially straight, churning with clean water. Despite the new restrictions, Adolf must have led a happy life in such pleasant surroundings, for there was no lack of neighboring children for companionship.

It took Adolf and his half sister Angela more than an hour to walk to school, a rigorous trip for a small boy. The building, "shabby and primitive," was separated into two classrooms, one for the boys and one for the girls. The Hitler children made a good impression on the master, who remembered Adolf as "mentally very much alert, obedient, but lively." Moreover both children "kept the contents of their school bags in exemplary order."

"It was at this time that the first ideals took shape in my breast," Hitler wrote in *Mein Kampf*, an account with the usual exaggeration of an autobiography. "All my playing about in the open, the long walk to school, and particularly my association with extremely 'husky' boys, which sometimes caused my mother bitter anguish, made me the very opposite of a stay-at-home." Even at this age he could express himself vocally and before long he became "a little ringleader."

In the months to come his position at home became increasingly difficult. Retirement was proving to be a drudgery for Alois since he had no talent for farming. To add to the aggravation, another child, Paula, was born in the late fall of 1896. With five children, including a crying infant, in the cramped quarters, Alois probably drank more heavily than usual and certainly became quarrelsome and irritable. His main target was Alois, Jr. For some time the father, who demanded absolute obedience, had been at odds with the son, who refused to give it. Later, Alois, Jr., complained bitterly that his father frequently beat him "unmercifully with a hippopotamus whip," but in the Austria of those days severe beatings of children were not uncommon, being considered good for the soul. Once the boy skipped school for three days to finish building a toy boat. The father, who had encouraged such hobbies, whipped young Alois, then held him "against a tree by the back of his neck" until he lost consciousness. There were also stories that Adolf was whipped, if not so often, and that the master of the house "often beat the dog until the dog would cringe and wet the floor." The violence, according to Alois, Jr., extended even to the docile Klara and, if true, must have made an indelible impression on Adolf.

As for young Alois, life at Hafeld had become unbearable. He felt not only mistreated by his father but neglected by his stepmother and out of this deprivation came a deep resentment of his half brother Adolf. "He was imperious and quick to anger from childhood onward and would not listen to anyone," he told an interviewer in 1948, still resentful after fifty-two years. "My stepmother always took his part. He would get the craziest notions and get away with it. If he didn't have his way he got very angry. . . . He had no friends, took to no one and could be very heartless. He could fly into a rage over any triviality."

Feeling abused and rejected, Alois, Jr., followed in the footsteps of

HITLER'S FAMILY TREE

Paternal Grandfather UNKNOWN
could be Johann Nepomuk Hiedler;
his brother, Johann Georg Hiedler;
or a Jew from Graz named
Frankenberger or Frankenreither.

MARIA ANNA SCHICKLGRUBER,
b. Strones 4/15/1795
m. in Döllersheim to
Johann Georg Hiedler
5/10/1842

FRANZISKA
MATZELSBERGER

ALOIS SCHICKLGRUBER
b. Strones 6/7/1837
(illegitimate; legitimized in 1876
as Alois Hitler)
d. Leonding 1/3/1903

ALOIS
HITLER, JR.
(illegitimate)

ANGELA
HITLER

LEO
RAUBAL

GUSTAV
HITLER
b. 5/17/1885
d. 12/8/1887

WILLIAM
PATRICK
HITLER

ANGELA
("GELI")
RAUBAL

LEO
RAUBAL, JR.

JOHÄNN BAPTIST PÖLZL━━━━━JOHANNA HIEDLER
b. Spital;   b. Spital 1/19/1830
baptized Spital 5/25/1828   d. Spital 2/8/1906
m. Spital 9/5/1848
d. Spital 1/9/1902

(third marriage)━━━━━━━━━━━━━━KLARA
                               PÖLZL
                           b. Spital 8/12/1860
                      m. Braunau am Inn 1/7/1885
                           d. 12/21/1907

IDA   OTTO   ADOLF   EDMUND   PAULA
HITLER   HITLER   HITLER   HITLER   HITLER
b.9/23/1886   b.Autumn 1887 b. 4/20/1889   b. 3/24/1894   b.1/21/1896
d. 1/2/1888   d. several   d. Berlin   d. 2/2/1900   d. 1950s
                days   4/30/1945
                later

Alois, Sr., and ran away from home at the age of fourteen, never to return
in his father's lifetime. His vengeful elder retaliated by reducing the boy's
inheritance to the legal minimum. The departure of his half brother left
Adolf the principal butt of their father's frustrations. The elder Hitler
piled additional chores on the youngster's back and carped at him constantly for failing to come up to expectations. A few months later the
disgruntled country gentleman sold the burdensome farm for the more en-
joyable town life of Lambach half a dozen miles away. For six months the
family lived on the third floor of the Gasthof Leingartner just opposite
the imposing Benedictine monastery. Freed from farm chores, Adolf's existence also became more palatable and he did well at the modern school.
His marks were excellent and in the last quarter of the school year
1897–98 he had twelve 1's, the highest grade. He also had a good natural
singing voice and on certain afternoons attended the choir school at the
monastery, under the tutelage of Padre Bernhard Gröner. On the way he
had to pass by a stone arch in which was carved the monastery's coat of
arms—its most prominent feature a swastika.

At this time he became "intoxicated" with that "solemn splendor of
brilliant church festivals." The abbot became his idol and he hoped to
join the Church himself, one aspiration that curiously met his anti-clerical
father's approval. Adolf later told Frau Helene Hanfstaengl that "as a
small boy it was his most ardent wish to become a priest. He often borrowed the large kitchen apron of the maid, draped it about his shoulders in
vestment fashion, climbed on a kitchen chair and delivered long and fervent sermons." His devout mother would certainly have welcomed such a
career, but Adolf's interest in things priestly ended as quickly as it began.
Before long he was caught smoking.

The family was now living in pleasant quarters on the second floor of
a spacious house connected to a mill. It was an ideal headquarters for the
venturesome boy, providing him with a variety of arenas for his favorite
game of cowboys and Indians. To the couple who owned the mill, Adolf
was a "little rogue," rarely at home but always "where something was happening," usually as the leader in raids on pear trees and other pranks.
When the "wild boy" did come home his trousers were torn, his hands
and legs scratched and bruised from his adventures.

Lambach proved to be as dull as the farm to the restless Alois and in
1899 he bought a snug house across from the cemetery wall in Leonding, a
village on the outskirts of Linz. The house was no larger than usual but
the location was far more to Alois' taste. Leonding had 3000 inhabitants
and took on an air of civilization from its proximity to Linz with the lat-

ter's theaters, opera house and imposing government buildings. The local companionship was more congenial.

With Alois, Jr., gone from home, it was Adolf who bore the brunt of the father's discipline. It was he, recalled Paula Hitler, "who challenged my father to extreme harshness and who got his sound thrashing every day. He was a scrubby little rogue, and all attempts of his father to thrash him for his rudeness and to cause him to love the profession of an official of the state were in vain. How often on the other hand did my mother caress him and try to obtain with her kindness, where the father could not succeed with harshness!"

In a show of rebellion Adolf decided to run away from home. Somehow Alois learned of these plans and locked the boy upstairs. During the night Adolf tried to squeeze through the barred window. He couldn't quite make it, so took off his clothes. As he was wriggling his way to freedom, he heard his father's footsteps on the stairs and hastily withdrew, draping his nakedness with a tablecloth. This time Alois did not punish with a whipping. Instead he burst into laughter and shouted to Klara to come up and look at the "toga boy." The ridicule hurt Adolf more than any switch and it took him, he confided to Frau Hanfstaengl, "a long time to get over the episode."

Years later he told one of his secretaries that he had read in an adventure novel that it was a proof of courage to show no pain. "I then resolved never again to cry when my father whipped me. A few days later I had the opportunity of putting my will to the test. My mother, frightened, took refuge in front of the door. As for me, I counted silently the blows of the stick which lashed my rear end." From that day on, so Hitler claimed, his father never touched him again.

Even at the age of eleven there was something in the thin-faced youngster's look that set him apart from his fellows. In the class picture that year of the Leonding Volksschule he sits in the center of the top row, several inches taller than his comrades, chin up, arms crossed. With his glint of rebellion, his cocky assuredness, he is patently the top boy. He was breezing through school with little effort and had already discovered another talent. He could draw. A picture of Wallenstein dated March 26 of that year, 1900, indicates a budding talent as an artist. In the classroom he would spend some of his study time surreptitiously sketching. A boy named Weinberger once watched in wonder as Hitler recreated from memory the castle of Schaumberg.

At recess and after school he remained the leader. He had already resided in more places than most of his comrades would visit in their lives

and they saw him as a man of the world. In play he was inspired by the
adventure stories he was devouring by James Fenimore Cooper and his
German imitator, Karl May. The latter had never been to America but his
tales of noble Indians and hardy cowboys were accepted as gospel by generations of German and Austrian boys. To Adolf the adventures of old
Shatterhand and his comrades were almost an obsession. He tirelessly led
his schoolmates into violent re-enactments and when the enthusiasm of
the older boys flagged he recruited younger ones and even, on occasion,
girls.

It was about this time that he found more significant stimulation in
two illustrated magazines devoted to the Franco-Prussian War of 1870.
He pored over the words and pictures. "It was not long before the great
historic struggle had become my greatest inner experience," he claimed in
Mein Kampf, which occasionally twisted the truth for political purposes.
"From then on I became more and more enthusiastic about everything
that was in any way connected with war or, for that matter, with soldier-
ing."

The Boer War, which broke out that same year, also inspired him
with Germanic patriotism as well as providing play material. For hours he
led his Boers into "hot battle" against those unfortunate ones who had to
portray the English. Often he would become so involved that he kept
his father waiting an hour or so for the tobacco he was supposed to pick
up at the store. The result, recalled Weinberger, was a "hot" reception at
home. These adventurous days perhaps helped shape the course of Hitler's
career. "Woods and meadows," he once wrote, "were the battlefields on
which the 'conflicts' which exist everywhere in life were decided."

That year six-year-old Edmund died of measles. Four deaths were almost too much for Klara to bear, and—with Alois, Jr., gone—there was
only one son to carry on the family name. Coming as Adolf was completing his last year at the Volksschule, this latest domestic tragedy heightened the conflict between father and son. Alois wanted the boy to follow
his example and tried to inspire him with stories from his own life as a
civil servant. His son yearned to be an artist but for the time kept this revolutionary plan to himself and without argument accepted his father's
plan for the next step in his education. He was eligible to enroll either in a
Gymnasium, which placed emphasis on classical education and prepared a
student for university, or in a *Realschule*, which was more technical and
scientific. The practical Alois decided on the latter and Adolf acquiesced
since such a school also had a course in drawing.

The nearest Realschule was in Linz and on September 17, 1900, he set out for the first time, green rucksack on his back. It was a long trip, more than three miles, and halfway there he could see the city lying below him flanked by the Danube River. It must have been a magic yet formidable sight to a boy raised in villages and small towns. There, on a rise, jutted the famous Kürnberg Castle where the "Nibelungenlieder" were said to have been composed; below stretched a forest of church spires and clusters of impressive buildings. His road wound down a steep hill to the heart of the city and the Realschule, a gloomy four-story building on a narrow street. Utilitarian and forbidding, it looked more like an office building than a school.

From the beginning Adolf did poorly. No longer the leader, the brightest, the most talented, he was overwhelmed by his surroundings. The other students tended to look down on boys from a country suburb; and the personal interest and attention he had received from teachers in the smaller schools were not to be found in such a large institution. In that year's class picture he again was perched on the top row but gone was the cocky Adolf; in his place sat a lost, forlorn youngster.

Retreating into his shell, he showed increasing lack of interest in schoolwork. "I thought that once my father saw how little progress I was making at the Realschule, he would let me devote myself to my dream, whether he liked it or not." This explanation in *Mein Kampf* could be either an excuse or a reason for his failure to be promoted because of deficiencies in mathematics and natural history. His detractors claim his failure was due to inherent laziness but it was just as likely a form of revenge against his father, some emotional problem, or simply unwillingness to tackle uncongenial subjects.

The next year, however, Adolf changed tactics and showed a marked improvement in the classroom. Older than his mates, he once more became the leader. "We all liked him, at desk and at play," said Josef Keplinger. "He had 'guts.' He wasn't a hothead but really more amenable than a good many. He exhibited two extremes of character which are not often seen in unison, he was a *quiet* fanatic."

After school the boys, under the leadership of Adolf, who had learned to throw a lasso, played cowboys and Indians down by the Danube meadows. Hitler also held sway at recess, lecturing his group on the Boer War and passing out sketches he made of gallant Boers. He even talked of enlisting in their army. The war helped arouse in young Hitler a yearning for German nationalism, a feeling shared by most of the boys. "Bismarck was for us a national hero," recalled Keplinger. "The Bismarck song and lots more German hymns and songs of the same character, were forbidden to be sung.* It was a crime even to possess a sketch of Bismarck. Although privately our teachers felt well enough that we boys were in the right, they had to punish us severely for singing these songs and brandishing our German loyalties."

For some reason Adolf took his Germanism far more seriously than the others, perhaps as a rebellion against his father, who was a stout advocate of the Habsburg regime. Once Keplinger accompanied him part of the way home, up the steep Kapuzinerstrasse. At the top of the hill Hitler stopped before a small chapel. "You are not a *Germane* [old German]," he bluntly told Keplinger. "You have dark hair and dark eyes." His own eyes, he noted proudly, were blue and his hair (at that time, according to Keplinger) was light brown.

He was already entranced with the heroic figures of German mythology and at the age of twelve attended his first Wagnerian opera, *Lohengrin*, at the Linz Opera House. He was "captivated at once" as much by the Germanic feelings it aroused in him as by the music. Inspirational words—such as those of King Henry to his knights—wakened in him the primal urge of race and nationalism:

> *Let the Reich's enemy now appear.*
> *We're well prepared to see him near.*
> *From his Eastern desert plain*
> *He'll never dare to stir again!*
> *The German sword for German land!*
> *Thus will the Reich in vigor stand!*

This time he finished the school year successfully, passing all subjects and receiving "good" and "very satisfactory" in conduct and diligence. But almost from the beginning of his Second Form he again began slipping; once more mathematics was too much for him and he dropped to a "variable" in diligence. Then, near the end of Christmas vacation, crisis at school was overshadowed by a major family disaster.

On January 3, 1903, Alois left home for his morning visit to the Gasthaus Stiefler. No sooner had he seated himself at the table for regular patrons than he remarked that he wasn't feeling very well. Moments later he died—of pleural hemorrhage.

He was buried two days later in the church cemetery in sight of the Hitler house. On the gravestone was attached an oblong picture of the former customs official, eyes fixed determinedly ahead. "The sharp word that

* The Austrian and German anthems had the same music by Haydn and the Pan-Germans would rebelliously sing the lyrics of "Deutschland über Alles." They would also greet each other in secret with the German "*Heil!*"

fell occasionally from his lips could not belie the warm heart that beat beneath the rough exterior," read the commendatory obituary notice in the Linz *Tagespost*. "At all times an energetic champion of law and order and universally well informed, he was able to pronounce authoritatively on any matter that came to his notice."

2

Contrary to popular belief, Alois did not bequeath his family a life of penury. At the time of his death he was receiving a pension of 2420 kronen, a sum considerably more substantial than that received, for example, by the principal of a Volksschule. The widow was granted half of this amount as well as a lump sum equivalent to a quarter of one year's pension. In addition, each child would receive 240 kronen annually "until its 24th birthday or until it becomes self-supporting, whichever shall be the earlier."

The remarkable change in the little house was the absence of tension. Gone was the authoritarian shadow cast by Alois. Adolf, almost fourteen, was the man of the family. Klara attempted to carry out the wishes of her husband concerning the boy, but her only weapon was entreaty. Needless to say, this was no deterrent to Adolf's dream; whenever anyone asked what he was going to be, the answer was invariably, "A great artist."

Even the gentle influence of his mother was diminished at the beginning of the spring term when Adolf was permitted to room in Linz so that he wouldn't have to endure the long daily trip to school. He was installed in the home of an elderly lady, Frau Sekira, with five other schoolboys. Here he became known for his reserve, always using the formal *Sie*, not only with the landlady but with his peers. While this change of locale did little to improve his low standing in school, it did give him more time for drawing and reading. According to Frau Sekira, he used an inordinate amount of candles for night work. Once she found him bent over a map which he was decorating with colored pencils. "Why, Adolf, what on earth do you suppose you are doing?" she asked. The curt answer was: "Studying maps."

The desultory school year ended with a failure in mathematics and Frau Hitler was informed that her son would again have to repeat a year unless he passed a special examination in the fall. This cast only momentary gloom on the household, for that summer they were all invited to Spital for a vacation. With two large, old-fashioned trunks filled with clothes and dishes, the Hitlers set off by train for the country. They were met in Weitra by Klara's brother-in-law, Anton Schmidt, who drove them to the tiny settlement of Spital in his oxcart. It was a pleasant summer. Klara found companionship and sympathy in her family, and Adolf, who contrived to avoid work in the fields, would occasionally play with the Schmidt children. Once he made them a large dragon kite "with a long colorful tail from different colored paper" which "rose beautifully in the air." But more often he spent his time reading and drawing. The last two pursuits already had marked him as a peculiar youngster; he preferred living in his own dream world. When it rained Adolf was forced to stay in the children's room. "On such occasions," recalled Maria Schmidt, "he often paced up and down or drew or painted and was very angry if he was interrupted. He pushed me out of the room and if I cried outside, he tried to get his mother to give me some tea or something else. We often teased Adolf Hitler and threw something against the window when he was inside, whereupon he quickly jumped out and chased us."

Shortly after the return to Leonding came another change in the family. Angela, "a jolly person who enjoyed life and loved to laugh," married a Linz tax official, Leo Raubal. Adolf intensely disliked Leo and later claimed he drank too much and gambled; but the youngster probably objected more to the fact that his new brother-in-law, a civil servant, heartily disapproved of art as a profession.

Adolf had succeeded in passing his make-up exam and was now involved in the demanding work of the Third Form. His most difficult subject was French, which he would condemn years later as a "complete waste of time." Professor Hümer, the French teacher, had mixed feelings about young Adolf. "He had definite talent, though in a narrow field," he recalled. "But he lacked self-discipline, being notoriously cantankerous, wilful, arrogant and irascible. He had obvious difficulty in fitting in at school. Moreover, he was lazy; otherwise, with his gifts, he would have done much better. In freehand sketching his style was fluent and he did well in scientific subjects. But his enthusiasm for hard work evaporated all too quickly." Dr. Hümer had more than a passing interest in Adolf since he also taught him German and was the class adviser. "He reacted with ill-concealed hostility to advice or reproof; at the same time, he demanded of his fellow-pupils their unqualified subservience, fancying himself in the role of leader, at the same time indulging in many a less innocuous prank of a kind not uncommon amongst immature youths." There was something about the "gaunt, pale-faced youth" that appealed to Hümer, and he did what he could to guide him. But such efforts were fruitless. Young as he was, Adolf had grown set and stubborn in his ways, withdrawing whenever anyone attempted to pry into his private world.

The history professor—Leopold Pötsch—did manage to make an impression on the secretive youngster. Adolf was fascinated by his lectures on the ancient Teutons, which were illustrated by colored slides. "Even today," Hitler wrote in *Mein Kampf*, "I think back with gentle emotion on this gray-haired man, who by the fire of his narratives, sometimes made us forget the present; who, as if by enchantment, carried us into past times and, out of the millennial veils of mist, molded dry historical memories into living reality. On such occasions we sat there, often aflame with enthusiasm, and sometimes even moved to tears."

Outside of this class, however, Adolf was more often moved by tedium and by the spring of 1904 school had become a dull routine. That May he was confirmed on Whitsunday at the Linz Cathedral. This too was a bore to the young artist. Of all the boys Emmanuel Lugert had sponsored "none was so sulky and surly as Adolf Hitler. I had almost to drag the words out of him. . . . It was almost as though the whole business, the whole confirmation was repugnant to him, as though he only went through with it with the greatest reluctance." As soon as the confirmation party got back to Leonding, Adolf ran off to his playmates. "And then," recalled Frau Lugert, "they started charging around the house, playing at Red Indians—a fearful row!"

That year Adolf failed in French. In the autumn his make-up exam was given a passing mark but only on condition that he not return to the Linz school for the Final Form. The nearest Realschule was some twenty-five miles away in Steyr. Once again Adolf would be forced to live away from home. Frau Hitler and the fifteen-year-old journeyed to Steyr where she found a little room for him at the home of the Cichini family. From the beginning Adolf was unhappy. He detested the new town and the view from his room was sinister. "I often used to practice shooting rats from the window." Adolf spent more time shooting rats, reading and drawing than on schoolwork. As a result his grades for the first semester suffered. While he received an "excellent" in gymnastics and "good" in freehand drawing, he was only "adequate" in two favorite subjects, history and geography, and failed mathematics and German. He would go to ridiculous lengths to avoid schoolwork. Upon arriving in class one morning with a huge scarf tied around his neck, he pretended to have lost his voice and got himself sent home.*

* That spring, while visiting in a nearby town, he wrote a revealing poem in a guest book. Four words cannot be deciphered.

    1. There the people sit in an airy house
       Refreshing themselves with wine and beer
       And eat and drink riotously
       (   ) out then on all fours.

Despite all this, his marks gradually improved and he was informed he could graduate if he returned in the fall for a special examination. Adolf brought this relatively good news to his mother on a sultry day in July 1905. She had sold the farm at Leonding, scene of so much turmoil and unhappiness, and now lived in a rented flat in a dour stone-faced building at Humboldtstrasse 31 in the middle of Linz. The year away from his mother's protective care had brought a marked change in Adolf's appearance. He was no longer a boy but a youth with unruly hair, the rudiments of a mustache and the dreamy expression of a romantic young bohemian. One of his classmates in Steyr, named Sturmberger, caught all of this in a pen-and-ink drawing that could have been entitled "Portrait of the Artist as a Young Man."

He was greeted as a hero by the adoring Klara, and mother and son resumed their warm relationship. Shortly they left with Paula for another summer in Spital. Here the youth was stricken by a lung infection (the family had a history of respiratory diseases). This illness brought mother and son even closer together and the summer, despite its problems, must have been a pleasant change for both of them after Adolf's exile in Steyr.

By the time the Hitlers left the country, the youth was well enough to return to Steyr for his make-up examination on September 16. He passed; and that night he and several comrades celebrated with a secret wine party, which left him dead drunk. "I've completely forgotten what happened during the night." He only remembered being wakened at dawn on the highway by a milkwoman. Never again would he suffer such humiliation. It was the first and last time he got drunk.

Despite the certificate, Hitler could not face his *Abitur*, the final examination for a diploma; in fact, the mere thought of additional schooling at an *Oberrealschule* or technical institute was repugnant. Using his lung condition as an excuse—"suddenly an illness came to my help"—he persuaded Klara to let him discontinue his studies. Detractors later charged that Hitler had lied about his ill-health in *Mein Kampf*, but Paula

---

2. There they climb up high mountains
   (   ) with proud faces
   And tumble down in somersault fashion
   And cannot find their equilibrium.

3. Then they arrive sadly at home
   And then are forgotten the hours
   Then comes (   ) his wife (poor?) man
   And cures his wounds with a beating.

The poem was illustrated by the sketch of a smallish man being beaten with a large stick by a woman with huge breasts. The sketch and poem are remarkable coming from a boy just turned sixteen; it is equally remarkable that he could make such a bizarre entry in a guest book.

testified that her brother did suffer a hemorrhage; a boyhood friend remembered that "he was plagued by coughs and nasty catarrhs, especially on damp, foggy days," and a neighbor testified that he was "in poor health and had to leave his studies because of a lung problem—as a result of which he was spitting blood."

With no father and no school to deter him, the sixteen-year-old was free to drift, his own master, a despiser of authority. It was an escapist existence. Adolf read voraciously, filled sketchbooks with drawings, went to museums, the opera and the waxworks, once saw a movie near the railroad station that shocked his moral sense ("What a horror of a film!"). No longer did he seek out companionship; no longer was he the leader of childhood games. He wandered the streets of Linz, solitary but not lonesome—his mind churning with dreams of the future. The company of others became tedious. Late in the fall of 1905 he finally met someone he could tolerate. August Kubizek, son of an upholsterer, also had a dream: he would be a world-famous musician. Already he could play the violin, viola, trumpet and trombone and was studying musical theory at Professor Dessauer's School of Music. One evening the two young men met at the opera. Kubizek noted that Hitler was reserved, meticulously dressed. "He was a remarkably pale, skinny youth, about my own age, who was following the performance with glistening eyes." Kubizek himself had a sensitive look and with his high forehead, curly hair and dreamy eyes seemed destined for an artist's life.

Together Adolf and Gustl (Hitler refused to call his new friend "August") began attending almost every opera performance. Other nights they would stroll along the Landstrasse, Adolf twirling his ever present black ivory-handled cane. Once Kubizek got up the nerve to ask his uncommunicative companion if he worked. "Of course not," was the gruff reply; a "bread-and-butter job" was not for him.

Since Hitler did not like talking about himself, their conversation centered on music and art in general. One day, however, Adolf abruptly drew out a black notebook to read a poem he had just written; a little later he showed his new friend several drawings and designs, then confessed he was going to be an artist. Determination at such an age impressed Kubizek ("I was thrilled by the grandeur which I saw here"), and from that moment his admiration for Hitler approached hero-worship. Although his recollections, consequently, are often exaggerated and sometimes even fictionalized, no comrade knew the young Hitler so intimately.

While the two had much in common, they were of conflicting temperaments. Kubizek considered himself "adaptable and therefore always willing to yield," while Hitler was "exceedingly violent and high-strung."

These differences only solidified the friendship. Kubizek, a patient listener, relished his own passive role, "for it made me realize how much my friend needed me." Hitler warmed to such a sympathetic audience and would often make speeches "accompanied by vivid gestures, for my benefit alone." These orations, usually delivered when they were walking through the fields or on some deserted woodland path, reminded Kubizek of an erupting volcano. It was like a scene on the stage. "I could only stand gaping and passive, forgetting to applaud." It took some time before Kubizek realized his friend was not acting but was "in dead earnest." He also discovered that all Hitler could stand was approval and Kubizek, enthralled more by Adolf's oratory than by what he said, readily gave it.

On fair days during this seminal period the two young men would occupy a bench on the Turmleitenweg where Adolf read, sketched, and painted water colors, or they would perch themselves on a rock ledge far above the Danube. In such seclusion Hitler poured out hopes and plans, giving his vivid imagination free rein. It was no one-sided relationship. Adolf seemed to know exactly how Kubizek felt. "He always knew what I needed and what I wanted. Sometimes I had a feeling that he was living my life as well as his own."

While Adolf was enjoying the carefree existence of a young bohemian dandy, he occupied humble quarters. The apartment on the third floor at Humboldtstrasse was rather pleasant if restricted. The kitchen, its single window looking out on the courtyard, was small but homey. Paula and Klara slept in the living room, which was dominated by a portrait of Alois, the personification of the dignified civil servant. The third room, hardly larger than a closet, was occupied by Adolf. Unlike the previous homes, this was a peaceful one, run largely for the young master, whose present each Christmas to his mother was, typically, a theater ticket. To Klara he was a young prince with slumbering talent, obviously destined for fame; and she resisted the practical suggestions of relatives that Adolf learn a respectable trade so he could contribute to the family income.

In the spring of 1906 one of Adolf's dreams was realized; his mother allowed him to visit Vienna, the mecca of art, music and architecture. For a month he roamed the romantic old city (he probably stayed with his godparents, Johann and Johanna Prinz) totally enthralled. He kept Gustl posted. "Tomorrow I go to the opera to see *Tristan*, the day after to *Flying Dutchman*, etc.," he wrote on a three-sectioned postcard on May 7. "Even though I find everything very fine, I am longing for Linz again. To the Stadttheater today." A second postcard, sent the same day, pictured the Royal Opera House. Adolf found the interior uninspiring. "Only when the mighty waves of sound roll through space and the whistling of the wind yields to the frightful rushing billows of sound does one feel nobility and forget the gold and velvet with which the interior is overloaded." These lines were typical of the budding artist—atrocious grammar mixed with poetic imagery, grandiose but sensitive sentiments.

Adolf returned to Linz more dedicated than ever to a life of art and architecture. He insisted that Gustl share this dream, finally persuading him to go into partnership on a ten-kronen state lottery ticket. Hitler talked endlessly of how their winnings should be spent. They would rent the entire second floor of a large house across the Danube and work in the two rooms farthest apart so that Gustl's music should not be a distraction. Adolf himself would furnish every room, create the murals and design the furniture. Their apartment, he daydreamed, would become the head-quarters for a circle of dilettantes. "There we would make music, study, read—above all, learn; the field of German art was so wide, said my friend, that there could be no end to the study of it." There was a final delightful and revealing provision: "A lady of exquisite culture would preside over the household as 'chatelaine,' but this educated lady would have to be sedate in temperament and years in order that no expectations or intentions should be aroused of a kind unwelcome to us." This fantasy, like most, was dissolved by reality: their ticket did not win.

After another uneventful summer vacation in Spital, highlighted by his present of a magic lantern to the Schmidt children, Adolf resumed his existence as budding artist and dreamer. In early October he began taking piano lessons from Gustl's teacher. Paula recalled her brother "sitting for hours at the beautiful Heitzmann grand piano my mother had given him." No expense was too great for such a son. It was about this time that Hitler revealed himself to Kubizek in a startling new role. It occurred on the evening they first saw Wagner's *Rienzi*. The story of the hero's rise and fall as tribune of Rome had a curious effect on Adolf. Ordinarily he began criticizing the performers or musicians once the final curtain dropped. This night he not only said nothing but rebuked Kubizek to silence with "a strange, almost hostile glance." Hitler strode into the street, silent, paler than usual, the collar of his black overcoat turned up against the November chill. Looking "almost sinister," he led his puzzled companion to the top of a steep hill. Suddenly he grasped Kubizek's hands tightly. Eyes "feverish with excitement," he began speaking in a hoarse, raucous voice. It seemed to Kubizek as if another being had taken over his friend—"it was a state of complete ecstasy and rapture, in which he transferred the character of Rienzi, without even mentioning him as a model or example, with visionary power to the plane of his own ambitions." Till now Kubizek had been convinced that his friend's true goal was to be an artist or perhaps an architect. This Adolf was a complete stranger, ranting as if possessed of "a special mission which one day would be entrusted to him"—a call from the people to lead them to freedom. This scene may have been one of Kubizek's fictions, but it surely reflected the state of mind of his romantic friend. It was 3 A.M. by the time they descended to Kubizek's house. After the boys solemnly shook hands, Adolf did not head home. Instead he started up the hill again with the explanation: "I want to be alone." His family became the dubious beneficiary of his visionary experience. "Very often," remembered Paula, "he used to give lectures on the themes concerning history and policy to my mother and me in a rhetorical way."

The vision on the hill was followed by a moody period in which he felt as rejected and injured as a Dostoevski hero. He could have stepped out of the pages of *The Adolescent*. The piano lessons stopped within four months. Kubizek felt it was because "those dull, monotonous finger exercises did not suit Adolf at all," but it was more likely occasioned by the ill-health of Klara Hitler. On January 14, 1907, two weeks before Adolf's last piano lesson, his mother called on Dr. Edward Bloch, a Jewish physician known locally as the "poor people's doctor." In a quiet, hushed voice she complained of a pain in her chest; it kept her awake night after night. An examination indicated that Frau Hitler had "an extensive tumor of the breast." Dr. Bloch did not tell the patient she had cancer but the following day he summoned Adolf and Paula. Their mother was "a gravely ill woman," and the only hope, and that but a slight one, was surgery. Bloch was touched by Adolf's reaction. "His long, sallow face was contorted. Tears flowed from his eyes. Did his mother, he asked, have no chance? Only then did I recognize the magnitude of the attachment that existed between mother and son."

The family decided to risk an operation and Klara Hitler entered the hospital of the Sisters of Mercy in Linz on January 17. The next day Dr. Karl Urban removed one of her breasts. By this time Aunt Johanna—a hunchback, irascible but always on hand—had arrived from Spital to keep house for the children. For nineteen days Klara recuperated in a third-class ward at three kronen a day; she could have afforded more comfortable quarters but, typically, economized on herself. The three flights to the apartment on the Humboldtstrasse were too difficult for Klara to climb and late that spring the family moved across the Danube to the suburb of Urfahr into three rooms on the second floor of an attractive stone building at Blütengasse 9. It was a quiet, pleasant neighborhood, a short ride on the streetcar across the long bridge to Adolf's favorite haunts.

The youth had a new preoccupation. He fell in love. Until then his relationship with girls had been trifling. During one vacation in Spital, for example, there had been a brief encounter in a barn with a girl who was milking a cow, but when she showed a willingness to go further, Adolf had rushed off, knocking over a large pot of fresh milk. While strolling the Landstrasse with Kubizek, they had approached a "distinguished looking girl, tall and slim," with thick fair hair swept into a bun, a young Valkyrie. Adolf excitedly gripped his companion's arm. "You must know," he said resolutely, "I'm in love with her." Her name was Stephanie Jansten; and she too lived in Urfahr. He composed numerous love peoms to her, including one entitled *Hymn to the Beloved*, and read them all to his faithful Gustl. Adolf confessed he had never spoken to her but that eventually "everything would be clear without as much as a word being exchanged." Theirs was such an idyllic match, said Hitler, that they communicated by eyes alone. "These things cannot be explained," he said. "What is in me is in Stephanie too." Kubizek urged him simply to introduce himself to Stephanie and her ever present mother. Hitler refused to do this; he would have to mention his profession and he was not yet an academic painter. He was immersed moreover in Norse and German mythology where the women were anything but ordinary, and he probably had a romanticized, knightly concept of all things sexual. No prosaic introduction for this young Siegfried! Fantasy built on fantasy. If all else failed he would kidnap her while Kubizek engaged the mother in conversation.

When Stephanie continued to ignore Hitler's presence he imagined she was angry with him (she was about to become engaged to a lieutenant, and it would come as a complete surprise to learn years later that Hitler had been her devoted admirer). Despondent, he swore he could bear it no longer. "I will make an end of it!" He decided to jump off the bridge into the Danube. But Stephanie would have to go with him in a suicide pact. He devised a plan complete in every detail, with appropriate dialogue for everyone, including Kubizek, who must witness the tragic event.

It was a convenient love affair for a susceptible youth of imagination. Success would have led to marriage and the end of an artistic career; failure only contributed to another pleasurably painful fantasy. More important matters soon put Stephanie in the background. Adolf's creative drive had made a turn from art to architecture. He was still an indefatigable water colorist, but these paintings, while pleasantly executed with a degree of talent, could not satisfy the ideas and emotions seething inside him. "Adolf never took painting seriously," said Kubizek; "it remained rather a hobby outside his more serious aspirations." His architectural designs, on the other hand, gave expression to an irresistible urge to create as well as a sense of order that was almost obsessive. He was driven to alter the shape of Linz. He would stand in front of the new cathedral, praising some features, criticizing others. He redesigned structure after structure in a passion for improvement. "He gave his whole self to his imaginary building and was completely carried away by it." As he ranged the streets with his one-man captive audience, Hitler pointed out features that must be changed, then explained in detail what had to be done. The town hall was uninspiring and he envisioned in its place a stately modern structure. He would also completely remodel the ugly castle, restoring it to its original grandeur. The new museum did please him and he returned time and again to admire its marble frieze, which depicted historical scenes. But even this had to be changed; he would double the length to make it the longest frieze in Europe.

His plans for a new railroad station showed a flair for city planning: to rid the growing Linz of tracks that were ugly as well as a traffic hindrance, he set his station on the edge of town, running the tracks under the city. The public park would spill over onto the old station site. His imagination was boundless. He planned to run a cog railway to the top of the Lichtenberg where he would place a spacious hotel and a three-hundred-foot steel tower which, in turn, would look down upon a magnificent new high-level bridge spanning the Danube.

His life had become one of isolation. Hitler slept late and stayed in the house most of the day reading, painting and designing. The downstairs neighbor, the wife of the postmaster, would see him leave the house after 6 P.M. and, on his return from his adventures with Kubizek, hear him pace around the living room until early morning. One day her husband suggested Adolf enter the postal service but he replied that he was going to be a great artist someday. "When it was pointed out that he lacked the necessary means and connections for this, he replied briefly: 'Makart and Rubens worked themselves up from poor circumstances.'"

Adolf was restless; and Linz had no more to offer him. He yearned for the world outside, specifically Vienna. He tried to convince his mother that he should be allowed to enter the Academy of Fine Arts. Klara was pressed from the other side by arguments from her son-in-law and Josef Mayrhofer, the children's guardian. Both insisted that it was time the boy selected a respectable profession. Mayrhofer even found a baker who was willing to take Adolf as an apprentice.

But Klara could not resist her son's passionate pleas and that summer he was allowed to withdraw his patrimony, some seven hundred kronen, from the Mortgage Bank of Upper Austria. This was enough for a year in Vienna, including tuition at the academy. Adolf's victory was marred by a deterioration in his mother's health and he probably left home with emotions of guilt, regret and exultation. But examinations for the Academy of Fine Arts were held only in early October and if he didn't go to Vienna now his career would have to be postponed another year. On a late September morning in 1907, Kubizek appeared at Blütengasse 9. Both Klara and Paula were weeping and even Adolf's eyes were wet. His suitcase was so heavy it took both youths to carry it down the stairs and to the streetcar.

During Adolf's first trip to Vienna, he had deluged his friend with postcards. But ten days passed without a word. Kubizek conjured up scenes of illness, accident and even death. He decided to find out what had happened from Frau Hitler. Her first words were: "Have you heard from Adolf?" Her face was more careworn than ever; her eyes were lifeless, her voice listless. With Adolf gone, she seemed to have let herself go and become "an old, sick woman." She began repeating all the laments he had heard so many times: why hadn't Adolf chosen a proper profession? he would never earn a decent living painting or writing stories; why was he wasting his patrimony on "this crazy trip to Vienna?" why did he refuse to take any responsibility for raising little Paula?

Adolf was living near the Westbahnhof on the second floor of Stumpergasse 29 in the flat of a Polish woman named Zakreys. He was depressed. He had taken his exam at the academy with confidence. The verdict was shocking: "Test drawing unsatisfactory."* When the stunned young man asked for an explanation the rector assured him that his drawings "showed my unfitness for painting, and that my ability obviously lay in the field of architecture."

It took the downcast Hitler a few days to realize what Kubizek had already guessed—his painting was only a hobby and his true destiny was as an architect. The road ahead seemed insurmountable; entrance in the Academy's School of Architecture depended on a diploma from the building school and to enter this institution he needed a diploma from Realschule. Determined to succeed, yet depressed by the difficulties, he spent the next weeks aimlessly, reading for hours in his little room, attending the opera and wandering the streets to admire the buildings.

In Urfahr, Klara Hitler was dying. The postmaster's wife wrote Hitler and he rushed back. On October 22 he again consulted Dr. Bloch, who revealed that drastic treatment was necessary to save the patient's life. Klara, it seemed, had been operated on too late and "there were already metastases in the pleura." The treatment, continued Dr. Bloch, was not only dangerous—large doses of iodoform on the open wound—but ex-

---

* A contemporary, Marc Chagall, was rejected by the Academy of Art in St. Petersburg.

tremely expensive. Money was no object to Adolf and he agreed to remunerate Dr. Bloch for the iodoform in advance, while promising to pay for the treatment itself later.

Kubizek was startled when Adolf unexpectedly turned up at his home, deathly pale, eyes dull. After explaining what had brought him from Vienna, Hitler burst into a diatribe against doctors. How could they say his mother could not be cured? They simply were incapable of curing her. He was staying home, he said, to help take care of his mother since his half sister, Angela, was expecting a second child. Kubizek was surprised that his friend didn't even ask about Stephanie, nor did Adolf mention her for some time, "so deeply engrossed" was he with his mother.

By November 6 she was receiving an almost daily dosage of iodoform. It was an agonizing procedure. Gauze was saturated with iodoform (which had a nauseating, clinging, "hospital" odor) and then folded around the open wound. Not only did the iodoform burn its way into the tissues but once it entered the system the patient could not swallow. Klara's throat burned and yet she could not quench this burning thirst since all liquids tasted like poison.

Hitler devoted himself to his mother, sharing the household duties with the postmaster's wife, Paula and Aunt Johanna. Klara had been installed in the kitchen since it alone was heated all day. The cupboard had been removed and replaced by a couch. Adolf slept here so he could be in constant attendance. During the day he was part-time cook and Frau Hitler confided to Kubizek with pride that her appetite had never been better. At these words her usually pale cheeks colored. "The pleasure of having her son back and his devotion to her had transfigured the serious, worn face."

In the cold, damp days that followed, Kubizek could not believe the change in Hitler. "Not a cross word, not an impatient remark, no violent insistence on having his own way." Adolf "lived only for his mother" and even took over as man of the house. He would scold Paula for doing poorly at school and one day made her swear solemnly to their mother that she would henceforth be a diligent pupil. Kubizek was deeply impressed by this uncharacteristic behavior. "Perhaps Adolf wanted to show his mother by this little scene that he had meanwhile realized his own faults."

Each waking hour was filled with pain for Klara. "She bore her burden well," recalled Dr. Bloch, "unflinchingly and uncomplaining. But it seemed to torture her son. An anguished grimace would come over him when he saw pain contract her face." On the evening of December 20 Kubizek found Frau Hitler, mouth drawn and eyes sunken, sitting up in bed, supported by Adolf to ease the pain. Hitler motioned his friend to leave. As he started out, Klara whispered, "Gustl." Usually she addressed him as Herr Kubizek. "Go on being a good friend to my son when I'm no longer here. He has no one else."

By midnight it was apparent that the end was near but the family decided not to disturb Dr. Bloch. Klara was beyond his help. In the dark early morning hours of December 21—in the glow of a lighted Christmas tree, according to Hitler—she died quietly. After daylight, Angela asked Dr. Bloch to come to the Blütengasse and sign the death certificate. He found Adolf, face wan, at his mother's side. On a sketchbook was a drawing of Klara, a last memory. Dr. Bloch tried to ease Hitler's grief by saying that in this case "death had been a savior." But Adolf could not be comforted. "In all my career," recalled Dr. Bloch, who had witnessed many deathbed scenes, "I never saw anyone so prostrate with grief as Adolf Hitler."

Chapter Two

"THE SCHOOL OF MY LIFE"
DECEMBER 1907–MAY 1913

1

The morning of December 23, 1907, was damp and foggy. Klara was carried out of Blütengasse 9 in a "hard polished wooden coffin with metal corners" and the hearse headed down the slushy street to a church. After a short service the little funeral cortege—hearse and two carriages—proceeded slowly across the Danube and over the hill to Leonding. She was buried, as she wished, beside her husband, with her own name inscribed on his marker. The family, all in black, stood silently in the misty graveyard, within sight of the snug little house they had once occupied. Adolf in a long black overcoat held a black top hat. He seemed even paler than usual to Gustl, his face "stern and composed."

Christmas Eve was lugubrious for the Hitlers. The family made a formal visit to Dr. Bloch to settle the medical bill. The total was 359 kronen, of which 59 kronen had already been paid on account. It was a considerable sum, representing more than ten per cent of Klara's estate, but it was extremely reasonable since it included seventy-seven home and office visits and forty-seven treatments, most of them with iodoform. The balance was paid with profuse thanks. The sisters talked while Adolf, wearing black suit and loosely knotted tie, stared at the floor, a shock of hair tumbling over his forehead. Finally he grasped the doctor's hand and looked directly at him. "I shall be grateful to you forever," he said and bowed. "I wonder if today he recalls this scene," wrote Dr. Bloch thirty-three years later in *Collier's*. "I am quite sure that he does, for in a sparing sense Adolf Hitler has kept his promise. Favors were granted to me which I feel were accorded no other Jew in all Germany or Austria."

Both Adolf and Paula had been invited to spend the rest of the day with the Raubals and Adolf turned down the invitation. He was becoming increasingly uneasy with brother-in-law Leo, who couldn't resist taking every opportunity to urge him to abandon his foolish dream of becoming an artist. In fact, the youth confided to Kubizek, all his relatives were constantly pestering him and so he was escaping to Vienna. He was bound to become an artist and prove to that narrow-minded clan he was right, not they.

He was equally determined that his friend leave his father's upholstery shop to become a professional musician. The Kubizeks had refused to let Gustl go to Vienna the previous autumn, but Hitler renewed his pleas and arguments, firing the imagination of both Gustl and his mother with tales of Vienna—the operas and concerts, the unlimited opportunities for the study of music. Convincing Herr Kubizek was more difficult. He regarded Adolf as "a young man who had failed at school and thought too highly of himself to learn a trade." But Hitler's power of persuasion even at that age was exceptional and this practical man agreed to let his son go to the capital for a trial period. One of the arguments that had helped sway him was that Gustl would be living with a bona fide art student.

Hitler journeyed again to Leonding to tell his guardian of his decision to return to Vienna for good. This time there was no argument. Herr Mayrhofer readily, if reluctantly, gave his consent—he told his daughter it was his duty to do so—and Adolf spent the next few weeks with Angela and Aunt Johanna, making final family arrangements. By now all bills had been paid to the last groschen, including that for the funeral, which came to the considerable sum of 370 kronen. The neighbors were thanked for their help during Klara's illness. Adolf was so grateful to the postmaster and his wife that he gave them one of his paintings. Even after all obligations were settled, there must have remained at least three thousand kronen from the estate of the economical Klara. Since Angela had assumed responsibility for the eleven-year-old Paula, it is likely she got more than two thirds. Alois Hitler, Jr., later told his elder son that he had persuaded Adolf they should "turn their part of the inheritance over to the girls," since the Raubals were short of funds; Adolf promptly gave his share to Angela, while Alois gave his to Paula. If true, that left Adolf very little with which to start his career in Vienna: an orphan's pension and what was left of his patrimony.

Early in February Adolf received unexpected encouragement from Vienna. A neighbor persuaded Professor Alfred Roller, director of scenery at the Royal Opera, to take a look at young Hitler's paintings and advise him on his career. The offer from Roller helped beat down the family protests, and Adolf made definite plans to leave. On February 10, 1908, he filled out the form for his and Paula's pensions. It was returned three days later with a note that it should have been countersigned by their guardian. Adolf passed on the form to Herr Mayrhofer but was too impatient to wait for an answer from the Pensions Office. He packed his clothes, books and art materials, bade farewell to his family and left Blütengasse 9 for the last time.

Gustl accompanied him to the station—it was probably February 17—and during the wait for his train Adolf spoke of Stephanie. He still had not introduced himself to her but perhaps he would write her. As the train moved out of the station, Adolf called through the open window, "Follow me soon, Gustl." It is doubtful if the young man's reading extended to the inspirational works of Horatio Alger but he certainly would have felt a kinship with Alger's heroes. The third-class fare on the local train was 5.30 kronen and after five hours the eighteen-year-old Adolf Hitler arrived for the third time in the magic city of Vienna. It was only a few minutes' walk from the Westbahnhof to Frau Zakreys' establishment at Stumpergasse 29 but it must have been an arduous one with such bulky luggage. Although the weather was dreary that month, Adolf's spirits were high. On February 18 he wrote an enthusiastic card to Kubizek:

> Dear Friend! Eagerly await news of your coming. Write soon and definitely so that I can get everything ready to receive you in style. All Vienna is waiting. . . . As we said to start with you stay with me. We can see later how we get on. Piano to be had here in the so-called Dorotheum [government pawnshop] for as little as 50–60 florins. Well, many greetings to you also to your esteemed parents from your friend Adolf Hitler. Once again please come soon!

Five days later, on a foggy Sunday, Gustl arrived at the Westbahnhof, a brown canvas bag "overflowing with food." As he stood confused by the bustle of the station waiting room, he saw Adolf coming toward him, already a citizen of Vienna. "In his dark, good-quality overcoat, dark hat and walking stick with the ivory handle, he appeared almost elegant." Hitler was so delighted to see his friend, he kissed him on the cheek. He took one handle of the heavy bag, Kubizek the other, and they emerged into the turmoil of the city. It was already dark but electric arc lights made the station plaza "as bright as day."

They passed through the wide entrance of Stumpergasse 29, an imposing structure, crossed a small courtyard to its humbler annex and struggled up dark stairs to a room on the second floor. Sketches were scattered everywhere. Adolf spread a newspaper over the table and brought out his own sparse food supply—milk, sausage and bread. Kubizek shoved these aside and, like a magician, produced from his canvas bag roast pork, freshly baked buns, cheese, jam and a bottle of coffee. "Yes," Hitler is supposed to have exclaimed, "that's what it is to have a mother!"

After the feast Hitler insisted on conducting his tired friend on a tour of the city. How could Kubizek possibly go to sleep without seeing the Ring? First Adolf introduced him to the grandeur of the Opera House— "I felt as though I had been transplanted to another planet, so overwhelming was the impression"—then came the graceful spire of St. Stephen's, and finally Adolf insisted on "something else special," the delicate St. Maria am Gestade Church. But it was so misty that Kubizek could see little and he was grateful when they finally got home well after midnight and he crawled into the bed the landlady had made up on the floor.

Since the room was too small for two *and* a piano, the persuasive Adolf convinced Frau Zakreys to give up her own large room and move into his. The young men agreed to pay twenty kronen a month, double the original rent. The grand piano took up more space than imagined and, since pacing was a requirement for Adolf, the furniture had to be rearranged to give him a promenade three strides in length.

Within two days Gustl had registered at the Academy of Music and passed the entrance examination. "I had no idea I had such a clever friend," was Hitler's curt comment. Nor was he interested in hearing about Kubizek's progress in the weeks to follow. He made a scene when Gustl was visited by a fellow student, a pretty young girl, and after she left, delivered a tirade, as he paced back and forth, "about the senselessness of women studying." Kubizek had "the impression that Adolf had become unbalanced. He would fly into a temper at the slightest thing." Nothing Gustl did seemed to suit Adolf, "and he made our life together very hard to bear. . . . He was at odds with the world. Wherever he looked he saw injustice, hate and enmity."

The underlying reason was Hitler's own rejection and this came into the open when he suddenly burst into a bitter denunciation of the Academy of Fine Arts. ". . . a lot of old-fashioned fossilized civil servants, bureaucrats, devoid of understanding, stupid lumps of officials. The whole Academy ought to be blown up!" His face was livid; his eyes ("There was something sinister about them") glittered with hatred. Then he finally revealed that he had been thrown out, turned down. "What now?" asked the concerned Kubizek. Hitler sat down at the table and began to read a book. "Never mind," was the calm reply.

Despite his talk of determination to succeed, he had yet to take advantage of Professor Roller's offer of help. Several times, portfolio in hand, he had gone to the studio of the noted stage designer but could never get up the nerve to knock on the door. At last he tore up the letter of introduction "so he would not be tempted again." He could have been afraid his work was not good enough; or been driven by some inner urge for failure; or simply have been overwhelmed by Roller's fame and feared meeting him.

About a week after Hitler left Linz, Herr Mayrhofer was informed by the Pensions Office that the two orphans, Paula and Adolf Hitler, would each be granted three hundred kronen a year until they reached the age of twenty-four. Mayrhofer was authorized to divide the entire six hundred kronen a year as he saw fit and he decided to give each orphan twenty-five kronen a month.

This regular sum, equivalent to some six current American dollars, undoubtedly gave renewed hope to Hitler but, assuming that he still had most of the six hundred and fifty kronen from his patrimony, life would still have been spartan. His roommate later insisted that Hitler often went hungry. "For days on end he could live on milk and bread and butter only." Kubizek never knew how much money Adolf had and assumed he was secretly ashamed of how little it was. "Occasionally, anger got the better of him and he would shout in fury, 'Isn't this a dog's life.' "

The money Hitler saved on food and other economies—he "pressed" his trousers, for example, under the mattress—enabled him to go to the Burgtheater or the Opera several times a week. Nor would Hitler sit in the gallery with girls—"all they were after was flirting." He made Kubizek stand with him in the promenade, where women were not admitted, at the considerable cost of two kronen a ticket. They never saw the end of the longer operas, since they had to leave at 9:45 P.M. in time to get home before the entrance to Stumpergasse 29 was closed. Otherwise they would have to tip the concierge. Back in their own room Hitler would force Kubizek to play on the piano what they had missed.

Hitler never tired of hearing Wagner. Even when Gustl wanted to see a first-class production of Verdi at the Royal Opera, Adolf insisted on dragging his friend to the People's Opera for a second-rate Wagner production. The music would transport him and was "that escape into a mystical world which he needed in order to endure the tensions of his turbulent nature." Together they saw Adolf's favorite opera, *Lohengrin*, ten times. *Die Meistersinger* similarly entranced Hitler, who never tired of quoting the lines from the second act:

> *And still I don't succeed.*
> *I feel it and yet I cannot understand it.*
> *I can't retain it, nor forget it.*
> *And if I grasp it, I cannot measure it.*

Kubizek did manage to inveigle Adolf to several Verdi operas but he only approved of *Aïda*. He objected to the trick theatrical effects. "What would these Italians do if they had no daggers?" One day they heard an organ grinder playing *La donna è mobile* and Hitler exclaimed, "There's your Verdi! Can you imagine Lohengrin's narration on a barrel organ?"

The two young men also spent many evenings at concerts for which Kubizek, as a student at the Academy, got free tickets. Gustl was surprised when Adolf began "developing a taste for symphonic music" and a particular fondness for the Romanticists—Weber, Schubert, Mendelssohn and Schumann. Other favorites included Bruckner, Beethoven and Grieg, whose Piano Concerto in A Minor never failed to move him.

Lack of money did not dim the luster of their Vienna. It was the golden era for opera and music. Gustav Mahler had just quit the Royal Opera for the Metropolitan in New York City but had left behind magnificent productions, many designed by Roller. Particularly notable were their collaborations on *Rienzi* and the first two parts of *The Ring*. The new director, Felix Weingartner, while causing some furor by making cuts in certain Mahler productions, was already carrying out his predecessor's plan to complete *The Ring* with new Roller scenery. Both directors, incidentally, were Jews, as were many Viennese luminaries of literature and the theater, such as Hugo von Hofmannsthal, Arthur Schnitzler, Richard Beer-Hofmann and Hermann Bahr.

Vienna was the capital of an empire in its final years of flowering, a polyglot center with no common tongue and a population gathered from the four corners of Austria-Hungary. It was a brilliant, cosmopolitan city where joy of life ran hand in hand with a sense of impending doom. This seat of the Habsburg dynasty was German in tradition, yet unique among metropolises. It was a capital not only of banking and finance but also of fashion and culture. Unlike Germany, it was a melting pot of incongruous peoples. "Swamped for long centuries by the Slavs, the Magyars, and the Italians," commented one contemporary reporter, "this town, they say, has no longer a drop of German blood." There was a Bohemian theater, an Italian opera, singers from France and clubs for the Polish; and in some cafés there would be Czech, Slav, Polish and Hungarian newspapers but not one in German. You might be "a German of pure breed, but your wife will be a Galician or a Pole, your cook a Bohemian, your nursemaid an Istriote or a Dalmation, your valet a Serb, your coachman a Slav, your barber a Magyar, and your tutor a Frenchman. . . . No, Vienna is not a German town."

Those, like Adolf, who had left the cities and villages of the realm for Vienna fell under its spell despite, perhaps because of, its disturbing contradictions. It was a city of glamor and slums, of cast-iron conventions and radical intellectual experiments, of free thought and violent racial prejudice. Drawn as he had been to this glittering city, "the dubious magic of the national melting pot," as he later described it, began to repel Hitler as the months passed and any kind of success eluded him.

He and Kubizek would leave their room on the Stumpergasse, often with empty stomachs, pass through dingy middle-class streets to the center of the city with its "splendid mansions of the nobility with garishly attired servants in front and the sumptuous hotels." Adolf became increasingly rebellious, railing endlessly at the social injustice of all that unearned wealth. What bothered him more than hunger was the filth of the bug-infested room on the Stumpergasse. Hitler, Kubizek recalled, was "almost pathologically sensitive about anything concerning the body."

His feeling for the city was not unique. "Every outstanding personality brought up in the peculiar intellectual atmosphere of Vienna lived ever after in a dialectical syncretism of love and hatred for the city which offered splendid potentialities for the highest accomplishments, as well as the most stubborn resistance to their realization." So wrote Bruno Walter in his biography of Mahler, whose inspired production of *Tristan*, with its striking orange, purple and gray sets by Roller, Adolf Hitler would see almost monthly for the next five years. Vienna in short was peopled by the *Raunzer* (grumblers) and had a tradition of attacking its most outstanding citizens; it derided Freud's psychoanalysis, hissed at the too modern sounds of Arnold Schönberg and the too bright colors of Oskar Kokoschka, and found much to criticize in the works of Hofmannsthal and Schnitzler.

The youthful Hitler, alternately fascinated and repelled, spent time ferreting out the evils of the gaudy city. According to Kubizek, who saw him as a young Werther with a social conscience, he followed an erratic program of self-education, wandering the Meidling section to "research" the housing conditions of the workers; he haunted the Ringstrasse, inspecting it and adjoining areas by the hour, before returning to his dingy hole of a room to redesign large sections of the capital. The youth was as much city planner as architect and, as he strode up and down the narrow passage between door and piano, he forced Kubizek to listen to endless lectures on "conscientious planning." Once he disappeared for three days, returning with the announcement that the "tenements will be demolished," and proceeded to work all night on designs for a model workers' settlement.

Adolf also would sit at the table until late at night, writing in the uncertain glow of their single source of illumination, a smoky kerosene lamp. Curious, Kubizek finally asked what he was doing and Hitler handed over several scribbled sheets:

> Holy Mountain in the background, before it the mighty sacrificial block surrounded by huge oaks; two powerful warriors hold the black bull, and press the beast's mighty head against the hollow in the sacrificial block. Behind them, erect in light-colored robes, stands the priest. He holds the sword with which he will sacrifice the bull. All around, solemn, bearded men, leaning on their shields, their lances ready, are watching the ceremony intently.

Hitler explained to the puzzled Kubizek that it was a play. Excitedly he described the action which took place at the time Christianity was brought to Bavaria; the mountain men would not accept the new faith and were determined to kill the Christian missionaries. This play was probably never finished and others—such as a drama about the painter Murillo— were envisaged and occasionally started, their plots usually lifted from Germanic mythology or history. Adolf would write until dawn, then toss the results on Gustl's bed or read aloud a page or two. Each of these dramas required expensive productions with scenes ranging from heaven to hell, and Gustl suggested that Adolf write something simpler—for example, an "unpretentious" comedy. This adjective infuriated Hitler and he put his mind to an even more ambitious project. It was inspired by a casual remark of Kubizek's that the outline of a music drama about Wieland the Smith had been discovered in Wagner's posthumous papers.

The following day Kubizek returned from lunch to find Hitler at the piano. "I'm going to work up Wieland into a musical drama," he said. Adolf's plan was to compose the music and peck it out on the piano to Gustl, who would "put it on paper, adapt where necessary and finally write the score." A few nights later Hitler played the overture on the piano, then anxiously awaited Gustl's opinion. Kubizek thought it was secondhand Wagner, but the basic themes *were* good and he offered to put the music into proper metric form. While Hitler was never satisfied with his friend's changes, he continued to compose day after day as well as to design the scenery and costumes and sketch the hero in charcoal. Adolf would spend his evenings on the libretto, keeping one eye on Kubizek, and when he fell asleep over the orchestration would shake him awake and then read out, in a soft voice—because of the late hour—from his manuscript. After several weeks, however, Adolf put aside the opera. Perhaps some problem or other had come up that demanded his attention. Or perhaps the fire of creation that had possessed him had burned out. He talked less and less about their unfinished project and finally ceased mentioning it.

That spring Kubizek went home for the Easter holidays. He wrote back that he had contracted conjunctivitis, probably from studying so much in the kerosene light, and might arrive at the Westbahnhof wearing glasses. It was a lonely, dreary Easter Sunday for Adolf. That year, 1908, it fell on April 19, the day before his nineteenth birthday. His answer to Gustl on mourning paper was filled with heavy humor: "It filled me with deep sorrow to hear that you are going blind; you will hit more and more wrong notes, misread the music and end up blind while I slowly go deaf. Oweh!"

The room on the Stumpergasse seemed more dismal than ever to Gustl after the countryside of Linz and he persuaded Hitler to go on excursions in the open country. In the mild spring sunshine they spent several Sundays in the Vienna Woods and took steamer rides down the Danube. Although it was the season when a young man's fancy was supposed to turn to love, sex played little overt part in their lives. On promenades, girls and women would often slyly glance at them. At first Kubizek thought their interest was directed to him, but it soon became apparent that the reserved Adolf was the object; he coldly ignored their silent invitations. If the two did nothing about sex, they spent hours at night discussing women, love and marriage, with Adolf as usual dominating the conversation. Over and over he insisted that he must keep "The Flame of Life" pure. That is, he believed—in accordance with his Catholic upbringing—a man and woman should keep themselves chaste in body and soul until marriage and thus be worthy of producing healthy children for the nation.

But the dark side of sex also haunted him and he talked "by the hour" about "depraved [sexual] customs." He railed against prostitution, condemning not only the whores and their customers but society. His condemnation approached obsession and one night after attending a performance of Wedekind's *Spring's Awakening* he took Gustl's arm and said, "We must see the Sink of Iniquity once." They turned down a small dark alley—it was the Spittelberggasse—and walked past a row of small houses, so brightly lit that one could see the girls inside. "In their scanty and slovenly attire they sat there," recalled Kubizek, "making up their faces or combing their hair or looking at themselves in the mirror, without, however, for one moment losing sight of the men strolling by." Occasionally a man would stop in front of a house, converse with a girl—and the light would go out. When the two youths reached the end of the alley Adolf maneuvered them in an about-face and they took another long look at the appalling sight. Back in their room, Adolf went into a lengthy tirade on the evils of prostitution "with a cold objectivity as though it were a question of his attitude towards the fight against tuberculosis, or towards cremation."

Gustl finished his competitive examinations with excellent grades and conducted the end-of-term concert. Three of his songs were sung and two movements of his sextet for strings performed. In the artists' room, a proud Adolf at his side, he was congratulated not only by the head of the Conductors' School but by the director of the Academy of Music.

It was early July, time for Gustl to return to Linz. He was spending the summer with his parents but insisted on paying his half of the rent until his return in the autumn. Adolf himself was silent about his own plans and, when Gustl vowed to get a position as violinist with the Vienna Symphony Orchestra so he could pay more than his half of their expenses, Hitler's reaction was irritable. The compliant Gustl, inured to his friend's dark moods and still glowing with his own success, took no offense. At the Westbahnhof, Adolf assured him "for the hundreth time" how dull it would be living in the Stumpergasse room alone but showed no apparent emotion as they parted ("The more anything touched him, the cooler he became"). Then he did something unusual: grasped both of Kubizek's hands, pressed them firmly and made off hastily without looking back.

Gustl wrote from Linz—a postcard and a letter—and received a picture postcard explaining that Hitler had been "working very hard, often till 2 or even 3 in the morning." Adolf promised to write before he went to Spital for his own vacation, adding testily, "Shan't want to at all if my sister is coming." He probably was referring to Angela, who, along with her husband, remained critical of his way of life. A fortnight passed without word from Adolf. Finally a letter arrived about July 20 which, by the things it said and those it omitted, told much of the curious and lonesome life he was leading:

Dear Friend. Perhaps you will already have guessed why I have not written for so long. The answer is very simple, I could think of nothing to tell you or what would have interested you particularly. I am still in Vienna, and here I stay. Alone here for Frau Zakreys is at her brother's. Still I am pretty well in my hermit life. There is only one thing I miss. Up till now Frau Zakreys has always drummed me out of bed in the morning. I have been used to getting up very early, in order to work, whereas now I have to look after myself. Is there no news from Linz?

He asked for a guide to Linz and a timetable of the Danube steamer.

. . . Otherwise I don't know any news, only this morning I caught a murderous stream of bedbugs that soon after was swimming dead in "my" blood, and now my teeth are chattering with "heat." I think such cold days as this year are rare in summer.

Hitler spent the remainder of the month in the stifling, bug-infested room. That his life continued to be dull was indicated in the next letter Kubizek received in August. While replete with Hitler's usual self-pity, mistakes in grammar and spelling, it was "a lovely letter" to the uncritical Gustl—"probably the most revealing letter that he ever sent me." Revealing it was, from its emotional greeting, "Good Friend!" First he asked forgiveness for not writing lately. "There were good reasons, or rather, bad ones; I could not think of any news. That I am suddenly writing to you now after all shows merely that I had to search for a very long time, in order to collect a few items of news for you. So here goes." He passed on their landlady's thanks for the rent money, carelessly calling her "Zakays" and then "Zakrays," although he had correctly spelled her name in a previous letter. He revealed he had just recovered from "a bad attack of bronchial catarrh" and joked heavily about the weather—"It's lovely pleasant weather with us at the moment, i.e. it is raining heavily and in this year of boiling heat that is truly a blessing from heaven." He noted that the Linz authorities, rather than rebuild the theater (one of his own favorite projects), had decided to "patch up the old shack yet again," and charged that they had "as much idea of building a theater as a hippopotamus of playing the violin."

Hitler revealed that he was at last quitting Vienna for Spital and would "probably be leaving on Saturday or Sunday." By the end of August he was enjoying the fresh air of that village. There was little else to enjoy. Increased pressure was being brought to abandon his way of life in Vienna, this time by his aunt Johanna. But, recalled Paula, this "last attempt to persuade him to take up the career of an official was in vain." Even Paula was showing signs of crossing her big brother. Now twelve, she resented his advice, including the reading list he prescribed (one item was *Don Quixote*, which he had sent from Vienna). "Naturally he was a great brother for me, but I submitted to his authority only with inner resistance. In fact we were brother and sister, who did frequently quarrel, but were fond of each other, and yet each spoiled each other's pleasure of living to-gether."

As it had been with Angela and Alois, Jr., so it was now with Paula. There was affection but little understanding or common interest. The un-pleasantness of Spital that summer marked the end of Hitler's youth. His refusal to consider a more practical profession cut him off from his family; never again would Spital, the scene of so much pleasure in his boyhood, be a refuge. For the fourth time he set off for Vienna, this time truly on his own.

In mid-September Hitler once more applied for admission to the Academy of Art. But the drawings he submitted, the labor of a year's soli-tary study, were so lowly regarded that he was not allowed to take the test. Along with the crushing blow of a second rejection, Hitler was faced with the problem of survival. His stay at the Stumpergasse room had probably exhausted his patrimony. Even if he had accepted his share of his mother's inheritance—and this is doubtful—it could have amounted to no more than enough to last another year in Vienna. His first economy was a cheaper room. In mid-November he gave Frau Zakreys notice and paid his share of the rent for the month. Without leaving a note for Kubizek, who was expected momentarily, he moved to the other side of the West-bahnhof to a gloomy building on the Felberstrasse overlooking the rail-road yards.

On November 18 he registered his new address with the police (a reg-ulation in both Austria and Germany whenever one moved), listing his oc-cupation as "student" rather than "artist." Several days later Kubizek ar-rived in Vienna. Adolf had sent him a picture postcard from Spital with a one-line message: "Best wishes for your esteemed Name Day." Though Kubizek had received no word since, he was accustomed to Adolf's long si-lences and, upon arriving at the Westbahnhof, he expected to see his friend on the platform. There was no Hitler. He checked his heavy case and hurried to Stumpergasse 29. He couldn't understand why Adolf had moved without leaving a message, and gave Frau Zakreys his own present address. Week after week passed without word from Hitler. Kubizek was puzzled. Had he somehow offended Hitler without knowing it? But they had parted the best of friends and Adolf's letters had certainly not been cool.

On his next trip to Linz, Kubizek visited Adolf's older sister. When he asked for Hitler's new address in Vienna, Angela crossly replied that she didn't know; he hadn't written. She began criticizing Kubizek for con-tributing to her brother's flight from reality. He defended his friend "vigorously," believing she was only mouthing Leo's prejudices and, when the conversation grew unpleasant, left abruptly.

Adolf had cut himself off from Kubizek, from everything that reminded him of Linz and home. His feeling for Kubizek was not as strong as Gustl's for him; as far as Hitler was concerned their relationship had run its course—at least for the time being. Moreover, Gustl had succeeded and he had failed. He celebrated his twentieth birthday alone on April 20, 1909, in the forbidding building on the Felberstrasse. Month after month he endured the cheerless surroundings, continuing the dream life he had led in Linz. He lived a quiet, solitary existence, rarely breaking out of his isolation. His neighbors remembered only that he was polite and distant. The cashier of a nearby restaurant, the Café Kubata, however, was deeply impressed by Hitler "because he was very reserved and quiet, and would read books, and seemed very serious, unlike the rest of the young men." She esteemed him so highly that she always gave "Dolferl" an extra-large portion of *Mehlspeisen*, a meatless, flour-based dish.

By late summer Hitler had to face another crisis. Except for the twenty-five kronen a month pension he had reached the end of his resources. He moved from the Felberstrasse to a smaller building on the south side of the Westbahnhof. The address was Sechshauserstrasse 58 and he occupied another small room, number 21. It was just about as noisy as the last place with the streetcars running down the narrow street. On August 22 Hitler registered his change of address at the police station, this time listing himself as "writer." But in less than a month he left this last refuge of respectability and disappeared into the underworld of poverty. He left behind no word, and on his police form there was a blank for "future address," and "unknown" marked the question: "When moved out." Without funds and unable or unwilling to work, he wandered for the next three months, a tramp. He slept in parks and doorways. For a time his home was a bench in the Prater, the famed amusement center on the other side of the Danube; and in rain he found refuge under the arches of the rotunda, using a jacket as pillow. Winter came early that year and by late October 1909 he was forced to find refuge indoors. He slept in bars, in dingy rooms, in cheap flophouses, in a coffeehouse on the Kaiserstrasse, in the crowded "warming room" on Erdbergstrasse established by a Jewish philanthropist. Once he found a strange shelter in a laborers' barracks, a dirty refuge that had to be shared with other homeless people. He could not sleep for the fetid air and the constant noise of crying children or of some drunk beating his wife.

"Even now I shudder," he later wrote, "when I think of those pitiful dens, the shelters and lodging houses, those sinister pictures of dirt and repugnant filth and worse still." Vienna, which had once been "an enchantment out of 'The Thousand-and-One Nights,'" had been transformed into a jungle of misery and represented, "I am sorry to say, merely the living memory of the saddest period of my life." He turned to the Church for help and would queue up mornings at nine at the convent near his old room on the Stumpergasse for soup. To tramps this was "calling on Kathie" because it was either the name of the Mother Superior or that of St. Katherine's convent itself.

By late fall he had sold most of his clothes, including his black winter overcoat, and so the snow and cold drove him to further humiliation. Huddled in a light jacket late one afternoon just before Christmas, he trudged all the way to Meidling in the outskirts of town. It took two and a half hours to reach his destination, the Asyl für Obdachlose, a shelter for the destitute, and by the time he arrived he was exhausted, his feet sore. Run by a philanthropic society whose principal supporter was the Epstein family, it was originally constructed in 1870 and had been extensively rebuilt and reopened the year before. Here for a modest fee, the homeless —including entire families—were accommodated. Each physically able occupant was expected to help in the housework or tend the grounds. It was a large, modernized structure, sitting alone in a large open field. Its dormitories were spacious and airy with beds lined in military precision, each with its number above a metal clothes rack. The main dining hall, which served a substantial soup with bread, was a model of efficiency yet had a pleasant atmosphere. There were numerous showers, washbowls and toilets—all spotlessly clean.

On that cold December evening Hitler lined up with the other shivering, dejected ones outside the main gate of the Asyl. At last the door opened and the mob of homeless quietly filed in to be segregated by sex, with children accompanying mothers. Hitler got a card entitling him to a week's lodging, and an assignment to one of the large dormitories. To a young man who cherished privacy it must have been a harrowing experience. First he had to endure the humiliation of showering in public and having his bug-ridden clothes disinfected; then his group was trooped like prison inmates to the main dining hall for soup and bread.

It would be difficult for anyone but another recipient of institutionalized charity to understand the shame suffered by a proud young man on his first day within the gates of such an establishment. Entrance into an institution like the Asyl with its efficiency and protectiveness marks an irrevocable enrollment into the bottom rank of the destitute. The inmate has lost the independence of scrounging on his own and becomes, in a sense, a prisoner. The newcomer, overwhelmed by his surrender, is momentarily at a loss. Hitler, too, must have been a picture of dejection that first night in the Asyl, sitting on his neat cot in a large military-like dormitory, surrounded by jabbering comrades, most of whom were veterans of such community living.

A wandering servant in a nearby cot took charge of Hitler. He showed him the ropes: to stay at the Asyl more than the prescribed week, for example, one had only to buy for a few kreuzer the unused portions of admittance cards of those leaving. The servant—his name was Reinhold Hanisch—also had dreams of being an artist and was impressed by Adolf's facile talk. Hitler, in turn, was fascinated by the tales that Hanisch, who had spent several years in Berlin, spun about Germany. Hanisch ("We met every night and kept up our spirits in spite of our troubles") taught his new friend the words to "Watch on the Rhine," noting how Hitler's eyes sparkled at such words as "We Germans fear God but nothing else on this earth."

More important, Hanisch taught his student that to survive a winter in the lower depths not a step must be wasted nor an opportunity lost: on mornings they left the Asyl—Adolf in his threadbare jacket, "blue and frostbitten"—early enough to negotiate the long walk to "Kathie's" in time for soup; then to a warming room or a hospital for several hours' protection from the bitter cold and a little soup, and back to the Asyl at dusk just as the gate opened. In between the major stops they would occasionally earn a few kreuzer by shoveling snow or carrying baggage at the Westbahnhof. But Hitler was too weak for much physical labor; every step on his sore feet was painful. Once there was a call for ditchdiggers and Hitler wondered if he should apply. Hanisch advised him to forget it. "If you begin such hard work it is very difficult to climb up."

Adolf tried his luck at begging. But he had neither the talent nor the gall for panhandling and become a client of a comrade at the Asyl who made a living by selling addresses of those who were "soft touches." Hitler agreed to split the proceeds fifty-fifty and set off with not only the addresses but specific instructions for each customer; for example, he was to greet an old lady on the Schottenring with a "Praised be Jesus Christ," and then say he was an unemployed church painter or a woodcutter of holy figures. Usually she gave two kronen for such a story, but Hitler only got religious platitudes for his trouble. He had similar bad luck with the other prospects and he again turned to the Church, where he got three meat patties and one kronen from the Mother Superior by greeting her with a "Praised be Jesus Christ," along with a reference to the St. Vincent Association.

Hanisch couldn't understand why a man with such education and talent allowed himself to drift so helplessly and asked what Hitler was waiting for. "I don't know myself," was the listless answer. Hanisch had never seen such apathy in the face of distress and decided to do something about it. His interest was not purely altruistic. Seeing a potential meal ticket in the skinny, woebegone Adolf, he encouraged him to make money painting postcards. Hitler protested that he was too shabbily dressed to sell them on the street or door to door. No problem, said Hanisch; he would do it for fifty per cent commission. But they both might get into trouble with the police without a peddler's license. No problem: Hanisch would sell them in taverns disguised as a blind man or consumptive. Hitler's next argument—that he had sold his painting equipment along with his clothes—was again no problem to the resourceful Hanisch. Didn't Adolf have relatives? Nor was Adolf's final protest that he had no writing materials a deterrent to Hanisch. Together with a salesman from Silesia, Hanisch escorted Adolf to the Café Arthaber, opposite the Meidling station. Following the dictation of the two promoters, and using a borrowed pencil, Hitler wrote a card to a member of his family, probably Aunt Johanna, asking her to send some money General Delivery. A few days later Hitler picked up a letter at the post office. In it was a fifty-kronen bank note ("a nice piece of money in those days"). That evening the exuberant Hitler couldn't resist exhibiting the bill as he stood in line at the Asyl. His crafty companion advised him to keep the money hidden; he'd be robbed or, just as bad, "hit" for a loan.

The first priority was a winter coat for the painter, whose cough was getting worse. Hitler rejected the suggestion that he buy a secondhand coat in the Jewish quarter on the grounds that he had been cheated there when he sold his own. Instead they went to the government pawnshop and found a dark coat for twelve kronen. Hanisch wanted Hitler to start painting at once but he insisted on a week's rest. Moreover, there was no suitable place to work in the Asyl. There were better facilities at the Männerheim, the men's hostel where a man had his own room, tiny to be sure, as well as a common room for hobbies.

On February 9, 1910, he made the long trip to the hostel across the center of Vienna to the other side of the Danube. Hanisch did not accompany him; he had decided to get a job as a servant rather than be a nursemaid to Hitler. The XXth District, Brigittenau, was industrial, with a diverse population, including more Jews than any other section except Leopoldstadt. It was a transient area with many of its inhabitants using it as a stopover on the way up the ladder. The Männerheim, about a half mile from the Danube, was a large building at Meldemannstrasse 25–27 taking up most of a block. It could accommodate five hundred men.

A modern structure, not five years old, its facilities were such that some of Vienna's middle-class citizenry were shocked by its "luxuriousness." On the main floor was a large dining room brightly illuminated by arc lights, the lower half of its walls tiled with a warm shade of green. Food could be picked up at counters and paid for by tokens acquired from a marvel of the day, an automatic machine. The food was cheap but good and the portions generous. Roast pork with one vegetable came to nineteen kreuzer and the complete meal cost an additional four kreuzer.

To those who couldn't afford this much, a dozen or so gas stoves were located in an adjacent room. For no charge any guest could cook up his own modest meal "in the most fantastic cooking utensils." The potato was the basic ingredient; scrambled potato pancakes with or without meat filling was a favorite. Combines were formed; those without jobs stayed at home to do the cooking while others worked and paid for the materials.

Just off this kitchen, up three steps, was a reading room, with a dozen tables. There were a number of other reading rooms and game rooms, as well as a library and a "writing" room where a dozen or so men could carry on private business: a Hungarian cut postcards out of cardboard and sold them in the Prater taverns; one old man copied names of betrothed couples from the newspaper and sold them to stores.

There were several dormitories, as neat as those at the Asyl, but most of the occupants enjoyed privacy in tiny cubicles about five feet wide and some seven feet deep. There was just enough space for a small table, a clothes rack, a mirror, a chamber pot and a narrow iron cot, complete with three-sectional mattress, headrest filled with horsehair, double blanket and, miracle of miracles to any sojourner of the lower depths, two clean white sheets that were changed every week. These were not cheerless cells, for each had its own window in addition to adequate artificial lighting. Every floor had an abundance of washbowls, foot bath troughs and toilets; in the basement were a score of tiled showers.* Here too were tailor and barbershops, a shoemaker and a laundry. In addition there were long rows of clean lockers that could be rented by those who needed to store extra clothing or other possessions.

The director was noted as a disciplinarian. He insisted that certain rules be adhered to strictly: the men were to be out of their rooms during the daytime; only chess, checkers and dominoes could be played in the rec-

---

* Several years ago these showers were dismantled since they were not being used. The standards of cleanliness and neatness—despite efforts of the present administration—have deteriorated since Hitler's time. Today's occupants are similar to the frequenters of the Bowery and other American Skid Rows.

reational rooms; undue noise, whether argument or enthusiasm, led to expulsion; wine and beer could be consumed on the premises (after all, this was Vienna) but not hard liquor; and city property was to be respected ("There will be no standing on the beds"). There were few disciplinary problems. A few hopeless tramps did a little stealing but most of the men were sincerely trying to work their way back to respectability.

It was to this snuggery for the homeless that Adolf Hitler came on that chill February day in 1910. He paid his fee—half a crown a day, cheaper by the week—went through another shower and disinfectant routine and was assigned a cubicle (on the third floor according to its present habitués). Good as the facilities had been at the Asyl, here, where charity was not so institutionalized, he could feel more like an individual.

In less than a week Hanisch appeared at the Männerheim. Four days as a servant had been enough for him. Again he took charge of Hitler and established his protégé with his art materials in the writing room at a long oak table near a window. Before long Hitler was turning out pictures the size of a postcard. He worked slowly, painstakingly copying photographs or paintings of city scenes. Hanisch had little trouble selling these sketches at Prater taverns and pocketing half the proceeds, but he soon realized there was more money in larger works and so Hitler turned to water-color scenes of Vienna, usually double the size of a postcard, completing about one a day.

Within a few weeks the fruits of this partnership, together with the tolerable conditions at the Männerheim, had rescued the two young men from winter and poverty. No longer did they suffer from the cold or go to bed with growling stomachs. Hitler reveled in the cleanliness of the tile showers and, since he had but one shirt, would launder it every few days as he scrubbed himself. Despite his relative prosperity, he still could not afford new clothes and was a disreputable sight in his tattered, disinfectant-streaked clothing, long hair and beard.

Warmth and food inspired an interest in politics and Adolf did much to turn the writing room into a forum for dispute and discourse. Here the intelligentsia of the Männerheim gathered, fifteen or twenty from the upper and middle class, those with some acquaintance with literature, music and art. A scattering of workers were also tolerated if they "behaved decently." Adolf became a leader of this group, holding forth at length on political corruption just as other down-and-outers in Skid Rows throughout the world were doing. These lectures, which occasionally degenerated into shouting matches, were sometimes held during the workday. If a political discussion started in the other end of the room while Hitler was at work he couldn't resist the call of battle and would join in, waving his T-square or brush like a knight bound for combat. If Hanisch returned from his peddling during one of these sessions he would disarm his client and coax him back to his seat. But once Hanisch left, Adolf would be on his feet again, denouncing the villainy of the Social Democrats or praising Karl Lueger, the anti-Semitic Christian Socialist Party leader whose mass appeal impressed Hitler. "When he got excited," Hanisch recalled, "Hitler couldn't restrain himself. He screamed and fidgeted with his hands. But when he was quiet it was quite different; he seemed to have a fair amount of self-control and acted in quite a dignified manner."

Adolf became so interested in politics that he spent hours in the magnificent House of Deputies listening entranced to the colorful debates which often degenerated into a babel of multilingual arguments and even brawls. He would return to the writing room and carry on his own harangues, which involved a hodgepodge of Pan-Germanism, along with denunciations of the Social Democrats for their atheism, their attacks on the state and their efforts to seize total power.

Hanisch never heard his friend rail at the Jews during these tempestuous debates or in private, and he remained convinced that Hitler (most of whose favorite actors and singers were Jewish) was by no means anti-Semitic. On the contrary, Adolf would express gratitude for the Jewish charities of which he had been a beneficiary, along with admiration for Jewish resistance to persecutions, and once denied that Jewish capitalists were usurers. Hanisch remembered only one derogatory comment Hitler made when someone wondered why Jews had remained strangers in the land: his answer was that they were "a different race" with "a different smell."

Two of Hitler's closest friends at the Männerheim were Jewish—a one-eyed locksmith named Robinson who often helped him and a part-time Hungarian art dealer, Josef Neumann, who took pity on Adolf's tattered attire and gave him a long frock coat. Hitler "highly esteemed" the latter and once remarked that he was "a very decent man." He also expressed great regard for the three Jewish art dealers who bought most of his work, and more than once told Hanisch, still his agent, that he preferred doing business with Jews "because only they were willing to take chances."

Hitler himself claimed in *Mein Kampf* that he had become a dedicated anti-Semite in Vienna upon his discovery that the Jew was the "cold-hearted, shameless, and calculating director" of prostitution; that the music and art worlds were controlled by Jews; and, most important, that the Social Democrat press was "directed predominantly by Jews." More likely these revelations came much later and his prejudice was little more than that of the average Viennese. Almost every gentile in the Austrian capital was an anti-Semite. Organized groups worked tirelessly to spread hate against Jews and young Hitler became an avid reader of the trash literature which filled the newsstands.

There is evidence that he was a regular reader of such magazines as *Ostara*, the creation of Lanz von Liebenfels, a mystical theorist who shared many of Hitler's own theories and attitudes. The magazine itself was a concoction of the occult and erotic, its editorial policy "the practical application of anthropological research for the purpose of . . . preserving the European master race from destruction by the maintenance of racial purity." Liebenfels' recurring theme was that Aryans must rule the earth by destroying their dark, racially mixed enemies. The latter were damned as inferiors and yet the pages of *Ostara* abounded in lurid illustrations of Aryan women succumbing to the sexual power and allure of these hairy, apelike creatures.* The magazine appealed simultaneously to superiority and fear, featuring such headlines as:

> ARE YOU BLOND? THEN YOU ARE A CULTURE-CREATOR
> AND A CULTURE-SUPPORTER!
> ARE YOU BLOND? IF SO, DANGERS THREATEN YOU!

Ostara stirred in its readers the primal fear of the limitless power of Jews—their control of money, their ascendancy in the world of art and theater, their strange attraction for women. How the erotic pictures in *Ostara* of blonde beauties embracing dark men must have inflamed Adolf! But as yet all these ideas were unrealized, unfocused—and his anti-Semitism would wane as new ideas and projects pushed it into the background.

Later Hitler would tell Frau Hanfstaengl that his hatred of Jews was a "personal thing"; and his sister Paula that he was convinced his "failure in painting was only due to the fact that trade in works of art was in Jewish hands." One can only guess at the "personal thing" which Hitler claimed motivated his hatred of all things Jewish: perhaps an art dealer or pawnshop operator; perhaps an official at the Academy of Art; perhaps some combination of these things; or even something which lay dormant in the recesses of his mind. There could have been a dawning hatred of Dr. Bloch, even though Hitler sent him cordial New Year's wishes a year after Klara's death and signed it "Your ever grateful Adolf Hitler." It is not at all uncommon for a bereaved son to blame a doctor, consciously or

---

* Embittered by the prejudice he was finding in Vienna, Freud would conclude that at the bottom of anti-Semitism lay castration fears because of the Jewish tradition of circumcision.

unconsciously, for the death of a beloved parent. How much more reason in a case involving a Jewish doctor and a dangerous treatment already in disrepute. (Bloch himself later eliminated all mention of iodoform in his accounts of Klara Hitler's treatment.)

During this seminal period in Vienna, Hitler wrote a letter to a friend, revealing not only the possible physical effects of such a submerged obsession ("I often grew sick to my stomach from the smell of those caftan-wearers") but a disgust with doctors and a feeling of his own destiny.

> . . . It was probably no more than a little stomach colic and I am trying now to cure myself by a diet (fruit and vegetables) since all the physicians are idiots anyway. I find it absolutely ridiculous to speak of a nervous ailment in my case when I am the healthiest of men otherwise. At any rate, I am again working with brush and palette and have great joy in doing so, even if the oil technique is giving me great difficulties.
>
> You know—without exaggeration—I always believe that the world has lost a great deal in that I could not attend the Academy and learn the technical end of the art of painting. Or has fate chosen me for something else?*

By the spring of 1910 Hitler had become so involved with politics and the state of the world that he couldn't fill Hanisch's orders. Reproached, he promised to be more diligent but as soon as Hanisch left the building Adolf would read his newspapers from cover to cover and when he finally sat down to work it wouldn't be long before some discussion lured him from the repetitious painting that was becoming a chore. In desperation, or to get away from Hanisch's nagging, Adolf disappeared on the first day of summer with his Hungarian Jewish friend Neumann. The two had often talked of emigrating together to Germany and so set off in quest of their dream. Somehow they got sidetracked by the wonders of Vienna, particularly Adolf's favorite museums, and never left the city. This spree lasted five days; then, on June 26, with scarcely a kreuzer in his pocket, Hitler returned to the Männerheim. But the brief freedom had its effect. For the next month he worked in spurts, saving only enough to finance another vacation, and before long the partnership with Hanisch ended. Adolf was once more on his own.

In the autumn Hitler made another attempt to enroll in the Academy of Fine Arts. Toting a large portfolio of paintings, he made his way

* This letter—along with other equally extraordinary letters and documents pertaining to Hitler that will appear later in this book—comes from the controversial private collection of Dr. Johannes von Müllern-Schönhausen of Vienna, which he has entitled "H.B.H. Privat Archiv."

to the office of Professor Ritschel at the Hofmuseum. He requested Ritschel, who was charged with the care and restoration of pictures, to help him get into the Academy. Hitler's work did not impress the professor although he admitted it was executed with remarkable architectural precision. Dejected, Adolf returned to the Männerheim and resumed painting in the writing room. But without Hanisch he found it next to impossible to sell anything. Desperate for money, he appealed to his aunt Johanna, either by mail or on a short trip to Spital. They had parted acrimoniously several summers ago, but Johanna was close to death and apparently had misgivings about her harsh treatment of Adolf. On December 1 she withdrew her entire life savings from the bank. It was a considerable sum, 3800 kronen, and she gave her nephew a substantial part of it.

She died a few months later in early 1911, leaving no will. When Angela Raubal learned that Adolf had received a much larger share of Aunt Johanna's money than anyone else, she immediately applied to the Linz court for her half brother's share of the orphan's pension. It was only fair since she was a recent widow and supported not only her own children but Paula. Either through pressure or shame, Adolf agreed to renounce the twenty-five kronen a month that had been keeping his head above water the past few years. He appeared of his own free will at the district court in Linz to state that he was now "able to maintain himself" and was "agreeable that the full amount of the orphan's pension should be put to use for his sister." The court promptly ordered Herr Mayrhofer henceforth to give Adolf's share of the pension to Paula. The children's guardian had already received a letter from Hitler stating that he no longer wanted any part of the money.[*]

Even without his pension Adolf enjoyed a security undreamed of by a resident of the Männerheim. At the same time he maintained the standards of old, cooking his own meals and continuing to wear the disreputable clothes that kept him in trouble with the management. We will never know if the money from Aunt Johanna had gone into splurges at the opera and theater; or if he had lost it in some plan concocted by one of his comrades—the place seethed with schemes that were legal, slightly shady or downright crooked; or if he had made a foolish display of his money as he had done once before at the Asyl and been robbed; or if he had given some of it to his sisters in atonement. More likely, he had hidden away the money and was doling it back to himself; those who set out to be artists or writers must adopt such shifty stratagems to keep afloat.

[*] Mayrhofer told his daughter Johanna that Hitler had behaved decently in the matter and "he had no complaints about him, or had he heard any."

Adolf became his own agent and set to work diligently at his corner in the writing room. His comrades respected him because of the artistic air he had acquired. Invariably polite, he never stooped to familiarity though was always ready to help or advise a fellow worker. Yet once politics became a topic, he would toss aside his brush and leap into the fray, shouting and gesturing, his long hair flying. These outbursts made him increasingly unpopular with his fellow lodgers and one day, while preparing his meal in the kitchen, he was roughed up by two big transport workers. He had called them "idiots" for belonging to a Social Democrat labor organization and been rewarded "for his insulting remarks" with a large lump on the head, a bruise on his painting arm and a swollen face.

A new friend, the successor of Kubizek and Hanisch, warned him that he deserved the beating "because you refuse to heed advice and so nobody can help you." Some months previously Josef Greiner had been attracted to the artist as he hunched over a desk in the writing room daubing at a water color of a church. Greiner was a young man of vivid imagination and he and Adolf would sit for hours discussing economics, religion, astrology and the occult. They also talked at length about the gullibility of people. A case in point was an advertisement currently running in the newspapers. Under the picture of a woman whose hair reached the floor was the text: "I, Anna Csillag, with the very long Lorelei-hair, achieved this beautiful hair with the aid of my secret pomade, which I myself invented. Anyone who wants to have such beautiful hair should write to Anna Csillag and receive free a wonderful prospectus with proof and thank-you letters."

"That is what I call advertising," said Hitler, according to Greiner's account. "Propaganda, propaganda as long as the people believe that this crap helps." The concept excited him. Propaganda, he said, could make believers out of doubters. He was convinced he himself could sell the most preposterous item, such as a salve guaranteed to make windows unbreakable. "Propaganda, only propaganda is necessary. There is no end of stupid people."

During the remainder of 1911 and into the following year Hitler settled into a more stabilized routine. He spent less time in fruitless argument and more at painting. The quality of his work improved. His water color of the Minorite Church of Vienna, for example, was so accurate in every aspect that it could have been traced from a photograph. Technically his pictures were quite professional—surprisingly so for a young man without formal art training. While Hitler was blessed with a natural talent for rendering structures, he had virtually none for the human form.

When he introduced figures into a composition, they were poorly drawn and badly out of proportion. A number of his pictures were pleasant to the eye even if they lacked the artistry that separates competence from professionalism. Hitler, in short, was more technician than artist; more architect than painter. It was apparent by 1912 that he could draw competently with pencil, paint well with water colors and even better in oils.

He worked steadily and sold almost everything he completed to Jacob Altenberg and other dealers. Yet Hitler himself no longer boasted of his accomplishments. His comrades in the writing room would cluster around a finished picture and admire it, but he would reply "in a disdainful way that he was only a dilettante and had not yet learned how to paint." His real talent, he thought, was in architecture. He later confided to a friend that he only painted to make money and those few pictures that he did cherish were of architectural subjects. With modest financial success came improvement in appearance; his worn clothes were clean, gone was the beard. He had grown so respectable, that the director of the Männerheim would chat with him, "an honor seldom granted to an inmate."

In manner too he had become more circumspect and, while he continued to argue politics, he had received a valuable lesson. "I learned to orate less, but listen more to those with opinions and objections that were boundlessly primitive." He had discovered one does not gain control of other men's minds by antagonizing them.

Nowhere was Hitler's measure of maturity more evident than in the writing room. As a mark of respect, no one thought of occupying his favorite seat at the window. If a newcomer tried to take this place someone would say, "This place is occupied. This is Herr Hitler's place!" One newcomer, Karl Honisch, soon recognized his uniqueness. "We all lived pretty thoughtlessly through the days. . . . I believe that Hitler was the only one among us who had a clear vision of his future way." He told Honisch that although he had been refused admission at the Academy of Fine Arts, he was going to Munich soon to finish his studies there.

Hitler was the nucleus of the intelligentsia in the writing room, recalled Honisch, "because he used to sit in his place day by day with almost no exception and was only absent for a short time when he delivered his work; and because of his peculiar personality. Hitler was, on the whole, a friendly and charming person, who took an interest in the fate of every companion." Friendliness notwithstanding, he kept his distance. "Nobody allowed himself to take liberties with Hitler. But Hitler was not proud or arrogant; on the contrary, he was goodhearted and helpful." If someone needed fifty heller for another night at the hostel he readily contributed his share—"and I saw him several times starting such collections with a hat in his hands."

During ordinary political debates, Hitler kept at work, if occasionally throwing in a phrase or two. But once the key words "Reds" or "Jesuits" came up and someone made a remark that "rubbed him the wrong way," he would leap to his feet and give argument, "not avoiding vulgarisms, in a very impetuous way." Then he would interrupt himself and return to his painting with a gesture of resignation "as if he wanted to say: a pity for every word wasted on you, you won't ever understand."

In a sense Hitler had made peace with Vienna and its lower depths. He had achieved success and recognition. But the city had little to offer him now. For some months his thoughts had been turning toward Germany, the Fatherland. In a frame over his bed hung a slogan:

> *We look free and open*
> *We look steadfastly,*
> *We look joyously across*
> *To the German Fatherland!*
> *Heil!*

He had spent five and a half years loving and hating the glamorous capital of the Habsburgs and would entitle this chapter of his life "Years of Study and Suffering in Vienna." It was a period of "hardship and misery," "the most miserable time of my life," but one that had molded him more than any university could have done. It was, he thought, "the hardest, though most thorough, school of my life."

On May 24, 1913, carrying all his possessions in a single small battered bag, he stepped for the last time through the double doors of the Männerheim. His mates were sorry to see him leave, Honisch recalled. "We lost a good comrade with him; he understood everyone and helped whenever he could."

Adolf Hitler turned his back on Vienna and looked to Munich for his future. "I had set foot in this town while still half a boy and I left it a man, grown quiet and grave. In it I obtained the foundations for a philosophy in general and a political view in particular which later I only needed to supplement in detail, but which never left me."

The scene of Adolf leaving the hostel that had been home and refuge for three years and three and a half months was indelibly set in the memory of Honisch. With regret he watched Hitler set off on foot with a companion whose name Honisch never could remember. It would have been the wryest irony if it had been his Jewish friend Neumann, who had long shared the dream of emigration to the Reich.

Chapter Three

"OVERCOME WITH RAPTUROUS ENTHUSIASM" MAY 1913–NOVEMBER 1918

1

He stepped off the train from Vienna and climbed the stairs into the hubbub of Munich's Hauptbahnhof. From that first moment almost everything about the capital of Bavaria struck a responsive note. This was home. Even the chatter of the people was pleasing to his ears after the polyglot noise of Vienna. "The city itself was as familiar to me as if I had lived for years within its walls."

It was a pleasant spring day with the sun shining brightly and the air, washed by winds from the nearby Bavarian Alps, seemed much cleaner than that of Vienna. It was a Sunday—May 25—and, except for sightseers, the streets were almost deserted. He gaped at the buildings, the statues, and was seized by a deep love "for this city more than for any other place that I knew, almost from the first hour of my sojourn there. A *German* city!"

After half an hour's enchanted stroll he came to the Schleissheimerstrasse. Very likely he passed by the Königsplatz and was stunned by the grandeur of the great arch, the Propyläen, and the vast square beyond, and then turned down the Briennerstrasse to the imposing, castle-like restaurant-brewery, the Löwenbräuhaus. Here at the edge of Schwabing, the student district, began the Schleissheimerstrasse heading northward. Within two blocks he came upon number 34, the Popp Tailor Shop. On its window was stuck a handwritten notice: "Furnished rooms to let to respectable men."

It directed him to the third floor where Frau Popp showed him a room containing a bed, table, sofa and chair. On the wall hung two oleographs. "The young man and I soon came to terms," recalled Frau Popp. "He said it would do him all right, and paid a deposit." She asked him to fill out a registration form and he wrote: "Adolf Hitler, Architectural painter from Vienna."

"Next morning my Herr Hitler went out and came back again in no time with an easel he had picked up somewhere. He began his painting straight away and stuck to his work for hours. In a couple of days I saw two lovely pictures finished and lying on the table, one of the cathedral and the other of the Theatinerkirche. After that my lodger used to go out early of a morning with his portfolio under his arm in search of customers."

Hitler had arrived in Munich "full of enthusiasm," intending to study art and architecture for three years, but reality never came up to the dream and he never entered the local Academy of Art. It was even more difficult to make a living as a painter here than in Vienna. The commercial art market was by no means as large and he was forced to undergo the humiliation of peddling his pictures door to door and in beer halls. But he was convinced that despite all obstacles he would in time "achieve the goal I had set myself."

Munich in 1913 with its 600,000 inhabitants was, after Paris, about the liveliest cultural center in Europe, and for some years had been attracting a breed of artists that Hitler himself found decadent: Paul Klee from Switzerland and refugees from the east like Kandinsky, Jawlensky and the Burliuk brothers. All were leaders in the New Artists' Association, which had been founded four years earlier to give its members more freedom. While such a concept repelled the classical-minded Hitler, its exponents brought to Munich an artistic ferment and excitement that must have stimulated the young Austrian. "The nomads, which was how the Munich citizens described those long-haired creatures from the East, from Russia and the Balkans, streamed into Schwabing, the northern district of the city, where the streets seem to run so straight only to insure a perfect light . . . in the countless studios." Despite his distaste for these Eastern refugees, Hitler himself was a bohemian and shared their need for freedom and tradition. Here in Munich his idol had composed *Tristan und*

Isolde, Die Meistersinger, and *Das Rheingold,* and here resided Germany's leading poets, Stefan George and Rainer Maria Rilke. Here Richard Strauss was writing his operas, Thomas Mann had recently finished a novella of dissolution, *Death in Venice,* and Oswald Spengler, in a room as barren as Hitler's, was scribbling away at the first volume of *The Decline of the West.* At a nearby Schwabing cabaret, the Eleven Executioners, a disreputable genius of *Henkershumor,* Frank Wedekind, was singing his own shocking songs; throughout the country his plays about sex and depravity disgusted and enthralled audiences.

The spirit of bohemianism, in which even the most outrageous and ridiculous theories of art and politics were welcome, had existed in Munich since before the turn of the century and had attracted unconventional souls from all over the world. Another political extremist had spent more than a year of his exile from Russia several blocks up Schleissheimerstrasse, at number 106; registered as Herr Meyer, his given name was Vladimir Ilyich Ulyanov and in the underground he was called Lenin. Here a dozen years earlier he had been writing tracts based on the theories of Marx.

Now Hitler was haunting the same Schwabing cafés and restaurants and luxuriating in the same easy atmosphere of free thought. His rebellious nature and air of feisty independence were not deterrents. In this milieu he was just another eccentric and he could always find someone to listen to his complaints and dreams. Despite his rapport with Schwabing's bohemianism, and in contrast to his own fiery nature and political radicalism, there had been no change in his painting style. His handling of material continued to be academic rather than experimental, daring or even forceful.

His fascination with Marxism, however, was revived in such fertile ground and he spent hours in the libraries studying whatever he could find about "this doctrine of destruction . . . I again immersed myself in the theoretical literature of this new world, attempting to achieve clarity concerning its possible effects, and then compared it with the actual phenomena and events it brings about in political, cultural, and economic life. Now for the first time I turned my attention to the attempts to master this world plague."

He would return from the libraries to ascend the three flights of stairs to his little room, a book or two under one arm and sausage and white bread for dinner under the other. Herr Popp noticed that he no longer ate at the Löwenbräukeller or smaller restaurants and several times invited him to "sit down and have a bite." But he never did. To Frau Popp he was "an Austrian charmer," a pleasant, helpful young man, if something of a mystery. "You couldn't tell what he was thinking." Often he would remain at home for days. "He just camped in his room like a hermit with his nose stuck in those thick, heavy books and worked and studied from morning to night." Whenever the concerned landlady insisted he spend an evening in their kitchen he always made an excuse. Once she asked him what all the reading had to do with painting. This brought a smile to his dour face. He took her arm and said, "Dear Frau Popp, does anyone know what is and what isn't likely to be of use to him in life?" After these periods of study he would go to a beer hall or café and without any trouble find a receptive ear, and once he started talking someone else would inevitably object, touching off a vociferous political debate. In such arenas and against such antagonists, Hitler sharpened his ideas and theories.

The winter brought Hitler increased hardship since there were fewer customers for his pictures. Even so this period was "the happiest and by far the most contented" in his life. Where Vienna had turned sour under adverse conditions, Munich would never lose its magical allure. "If today I am more attached to this city than to any other spot on earth in this world," he recollected from a prison cell eleven years later, "it is partly due to the fact that it is and remains inseparably bound up with the development of my life; if even then I achieved the happiness of a truly inward contentment, it can be attributed only to the magic which this miraculous residence of the Wittelsbachs exerts on every man who is blessed, not only with a calculating mind but with a feeling soul."

This rewarding if arduous existence was abruptly threatened on a Sunday afternoon early in 1914. At 3:30 P.M. on January 18 he answered a peremptory rap at his door to find a stern-faced officer of the Munich criminal police. The officer—his name was Herle—produced an official document from Austria: a notice for Hitler to "present himself for military service in Linz at Kaiserin Elisabeth Quay 30 on January 20th 1914." If he failed to comply he was liable to prosecution and a fine. More ominous, he was warned that he would be fined heavily and imprisoned up to a year if found guilty of having left Austria "with the object of evading military service."

Adolf was overwhelmed. Three years earlier, while residing at the Männerheim, he had requested permission to report for service in Vienna and had heard nothing since. Officer Herle demanded that Hitler sign a receipt for the induction notice and the young man was so flustered he shakily wrote "Hitler, Adolf." Then Herle arrested him and took him to police headquarters. Next morning he was taken under guard to the Austrian Consulate General. It speaks for Hitler's state that by then the police were sympathetic. The consul general also took pity on the young artist with pinched face, gaunt frame and shabby clothes, and allowed Hitler to send Linz a telegram requesting a postponement until early February. The reply arrived next morning: MUST REPORT ON JANUARY 20. It was already that date and, moved to further compassion by Hitler's alarm, the consul general permitted him to write a letter of explanation to Linz. It was a plea for mercy, replete with grammatical mistakes and misspellings, revealing the fright and desperation of a young man cornered by fate and circumstances. He complained that the summons gave him an "impossible short interval" to settle his affairs, not even enough time to take a bath.

> I am described in the summons as an artist. This title is mine by right, but only in a limited sense is it correct. I do earn a living as a free-lance artist, since I am completely without private means (my father was a civil servant), I do so only to be able to continue my studies. I can devote only a portion of my time to earning a living as I am not yet past the training stage as an architectural painter. Therefore my income is very small, in fact only sufficient to make both ends meet.

His monthly income fluctuated and was presently very low since the art market in Munich was in its "winter sleep about this time and nearly 3 thousand artists live or at least try to live here." He explained how he had applied in 1910 for permission to report for service in Vienna, then painted a pathetic picture of his struggles in that city.

> I was a young, inexperienced person, without financial help and also too proud to seek assistance from anyone or beg. Without any support, depending only on myself, the kronen and heller received for my work were often only enough to provide a place to sleep. For two years my only girl friend was Sorrow and Need, and I had no other companion except constant unsatisfied hunger. I never learned to know the beautiful word "youth." Today, after 5 years, my memories are still in the form of frost-bitten fingers, hands and feet. And yet I cannot recall those days without a certain joy, now that I have come out of the worst of it. Despite great need, amidst my often very questionable surroundings, I kept my name clean, and am not guilty in the face of the law and have a clear conscience except for the omitted military report, of which I did not even know at the time. That is the only thing about which I feel responsible. And for that a modest fine should be sufficient, and I would not protest the payment of same.

His excuses were flimsy but he so successfully played on the sympathies of the consul general that his letter was dispatched along with a note of the consul's own stating that both he and the Munich police were convinced of Hitler's honesty. Since the young man seemed "extremely deserving of considerate treatment," the consul recommended that he be allowed to report to Salzburg rather than go all the way to Linz. The Linz authorities agreed and on February 5, at the expense of the consulate, Hitler journeyed to Salzburg. He was found "unfit for combatant and auxiliary duties, too weak. Unable to bear arms." His generally run-down condition apparently was sufficient to disqualify him.

Adolf returned to his room on the Schleissheimerstrasse where he continued to eke out a living designing posters and selling pictures but his life as a struggling artist and hopeful architect came to an end on June 28. From his room he heard a hubbub in the streets below. As he started down the stairs Frau Popp exclaimed excitedly, "The Austrian heir, Archduke Franz Ferdinand, has been assassinated!" Hitler brushed past her and into the street. He pushed his way through a crowd clustered around a placard to read that the killer of the Archduke and his wife Sophie had been a young Serb terrorist, Gavrilo Princip. Hitler's rooted hatred of all things Slavic, begun at his first visit in Vienna to the House of Deputies, was resurrected.

In Vienna angry mobs were already converging on the Serbian Legation, yet few political experts felt this tragedy would lead to a European crisis. The Kaiser, however, secretly began pressing the Habsburgs to invade Serbia. Germany was ready for war, he told them, and the first country that would rush to Serbia's aid, Russia, was not. Under such pressure Austria declared war on Serbia on July 28. This was followed by a general mobilization of Russia against Austria; whereupon Wilhelm appeared at the balcony of his palace to proclaim "a state of imminent threat of war." An ultimatum was sent to Russia demanding the cessation of mobilization by noon of the following day. There was no answer and at 5 P.M. on the first of August the Kaiser signed the order for Germany's general mobilization against Russia.

The news of war with Russia was received with enthusiasm by a large crowd in front of Munich's Feldherrnhalle, the Hall of Field Marshals. Near the front of the crowd stood Adolf Hitler, hatless, neatly dressed, mustached. No one wanted war more than he: "Even today," he wrote in *Mein Kampf*, "I am not ashamed to say that, overcome with rapturous enthusiasm, I fell to my knees and thanked Heaven from an overflowing heart for granting me the good fortune of being allowed to live at this time." To him it meant the realization of the Greater Germany he had dreamed of since youth.

War fever swept the country. It was generated by emotion rather than logic; with the people in a state close to hysteria, they were eager to seek justice no matter what the cost. War was envisaged as some kind of magical release. Students roamed Munich's streets singing "Die Wacht am Rhein" and shouting for action. One group demolished the Café Fahrig on the Karlsplatz because the band refused to play the national hymn over and over again. Intellectuals too were caught up in the enthusiasm, for it meant an escape from boredom and an end to bourgeois sham. War would be a liberation from social and cultural abuses. Even the socialists, excoriated by Wilhelm a few months earlier as vermin gnawing at the Imperial Oak, accepted the Kaiser's invitation ("We are now brothers") to join the patriotic crusade.

The adherents of Pan-Germanism needed no invitation to follow the parade. "Heil der Kaiser! Heil das Heer!" the leaders of the movement officially proclaimed. "We must gather all men of German tongues into one Reich and one people. An everlasting master race will then direct the progress of mankind!" They could have been speaking for Adolf Hitler. He saw the Hohenzollerns as heirs to the medieval Teutonic Knights who had established German colonies in the Slavic lands to the east, and was therefore convinced that Germany had to fight for her existence, for "freedom and the future."

Two days later, on August 3, the day war against France was declared, Hitler submitted a personal petition to Ludwig III,* requesting permission to enlist in his army, and that afternoon he stood in the crowd outside the Wittelsbach Palace cheering the old monarch. Finally Ludwig appeared and while he was speaking Hitler was thinking: "If only the King has already read my application and approved it!" The following day he received an answer which he opened with "trembling hands." He was accepted as a volunteer. On August 16 he reported to the barracks of his first choice, the Bavarian King's Own Regiment. A poster outside announced that it was filled; but he was accepted by his second choice, the 1st Bavarian Infantry Regiment.

Two of his most pressing problems were solved: he would never have to join the detested Austrian army nor would he have to endure another hard winter on his own. Besides finding a home with sufficient food, clothing and shelter—he had a purpose. There was no more room for doubt; he knew for the first time in his life exactly where he was going and why. Safe in uniform, his only fear was that the war might end before he saw action.

A few days later he was transferred to the 2nd Bavarian Infantry Regiment and began basic training at the large public school on the Elizabeth Platz. It was a short but intensive course of drilling, route marching and bayonet practice that left the recruits fatigued by the end of the day.

* Bavaria, though a part of the German Empire, retained sovereign independence until 1918.

Within a week Hitler was permanently assigned to the 16th Bavarian Reserve Infantry Regiment. The training continued in Munich at an accelerated pace. One of Adolf's comrades, Hans Mend, noticed that when he first handled a rifle he "looked at it with the delight that a woman looks at her jewelry which made me laugh secretly."

2

On October 7 Hitler told the Popps his unit was leaving Munich. He shook hands with Herr Popp and asked him to write his sister if he died. Perhaps she would like his few possessions. If not, the Popps were to keep them. Frau Popp burst into tears as Hitler hugged the two children, then "turned tail and ran." The next day the regiment was marched to the barracks of the elite King's Own Regiment for a solemn ceremony. In the presence of Ludwig III the men swore allegiance to him as well as to Kaiser Wilhelm. Then Hitler and a few other Austrians were required to swear allegiance to their own monarch, the Emperor Franz Josef. The only record of Hitler's reaction to this memorable occasion was his remark to comrades that October 8 would always remain in his memory because on that day they received double rations as well as a special noonday meal of roast pork and potato salad.

Early next morning the regiment marched out of Munich bound for Camp Lechfeld seventy miles to the west. Carrying packs, the men plodded for almost eleven hours, most of it in the teeming rain. "I was put up in a stable," he wrote Frau Popp, "soaked through and through. There was no possibility for sleep." The following day, a Sunday, they marched thirteen hours and bivouacked in the open. But it was so cold they spent another sleepless night. It was midafternoon of Monday by the time they finally reached their destination. They were "deathly tired, ready to drop" but marched proudly into the camp under the staring eyes of a group of French prisoners of war.

The first five days at Lechfeld were the most strenuous in his life with "lengthy practice sessions," as well as extra night marches, in connection with brigade maneuvers. This was all part of the amalgamation of their regiment with another to form the 12th Brigade and the recruits were kept so occupied that it was not until October 20 that Hitler found time to write all this to Frau Popp and inform her that they were moving out that evening for the front. "I'm terribly happy," he concluded. "After arrival at our destination I will write immediately and give you my address. I hope we get to England." That night the recruits were loaded onto trains and Adolf Hitler, the archpatriot from Austria, was at last on his way to do battle for the Fatherland.

A brigade lieutenant, a professional soldier named Fritz Wiedemann, watched with mixed feelings as Hitler and his comrades loaded into the cars. The regimental commander had not been on active service for years, most of the companies were led by reserve officers, and the men had had only perfunctory training. There were few machine guns, the telephone equipment had been originally manufactured by a Nuremberg firm for the British army, and the men didn't even have iron helmets. Instead they were going off to combat in oilcloth caps as did the volunteers of the 1812–13 wars of liberation. What the brigade lacked in equipment and training it made up for in enthusiasm. As each train pulled out, the occupants laughed and sang. It was as if they were bound for a glorious party. There would be a few weeks of gallant and exciting fighting and then victory by the New Year.

At dawn Hitler's train was running along the Rhine, a sight most of the Bavarians had never seen. The sun, drawing up the mist from the river, suddenly revealed the gargantuan statue of Germania looking down from the Niederwald. All along the train the men spontaneously burst into "Die Wacht am Rhein." "I felt as though my heart would burst," recalled Hitler.

Eight days later Hitler's company was thrown into battle near Ypres. As the recruits started forward in the morning fog to relieve a hard-pressed unit, English and Belgian shells began dropping into the woods ahead. "Now the first shrapnel hisses over us and explodes at the edge of the forest, splintering trees as if they were straws," he wrote an acquaintance in Munich, Assistant Judge Ernst Hepp. "We watch with curiosity. We have no idea as yet of the danger. None of us is afraid. Everyone is waiting impatiently for the command, 'Forward!' . . . We crawl on our stomachs to the edge of the forest. Above us are howls and hisses, splintered branches and trees surround us. Then again shells explode at the edge of the forest and hurl clouds of stones, earth and sand into the air, tear the heaviest trees out by their roots, and choke everything in a yellow-green, terribly stinking steam. We cannot lie here forever, and if we have to fall in battle, it's better to be killed outside." Finally it was the Germans' turn to attack. "Four times we advance and have to go back; from my whole batch only one remains, beside me, finally he also falls. A shot tears off my right coat sleeve, but like a miracle I remain safe and alive. At 2 o'clock we finally go forward for the fifth time, and this time we occupy the edge of the forest and the farms."

The battle went on for three more days. The regimental commander was killed and his deputy, a lieutenant colonel, seriously wounded. Under heavy fire Hitler, now a regimental dispatch carrier, found a medic and the two dragged the deputy back to the dressing station. By mid-November the 16th Regiment, according to Hitler, had but thirty officers and less than seven hundred men. Only one in five recruits remained but still came orders to attack. The new commander, Lieutenant Colonel Engelhardt, accompanied by Hitler and another man, ventured far into the front to observe the enemy lines. They were detected and the area was sprayed with machine-gun fire. The two enlisted men leaped in front of their commander, pushed him into a ditch. Without comment Engelhardt shook hands with the two recruits. He intended recommending them both for the Iron Cross but the next afternoon while he was discussing the citations an English shell smashed into the regimental headquarters tent, killing three men and seriously wounding Engelhardt and the other occupants. Moments earlier Hitler and the three other enlisted men had been forced to leave the tent to make way for four company commanders. It was the first of a series of narrow escapes verging on the miraculous for Adolf Hitler. "It was the most terrible moment of my life," he wrote Judge Hepp. "We all worshiped Lieutenant Colonel Engelhardt."

The unsuccessful attempts to take Ypres ended the German offensive and the battle degenerated into static trench warfare. This meant a relatively quiet existence for those attached to the regimental headquarters, now located in a rest area near the village of Messines. At last Hitler found time to paint. He had brought along some equipment and he finished several water colors, including one of the ruins of a cloister near Messines and another of a trench near the village of Wytschaete. He was called on to do a different kind of painting by Lieutenant Wiedemann, the adjutant of the new regimental commander. The color of the officers' dining room—a small room in a commandeered villa—clashed with a romanticized painting of a dying soldier lying across barbed wire. Wiedemann asked Sergeant Max Amann to find someone on the staff who could repaint the room. Amann brought back Hitler. Wiedemann wondered if the walls should be painted blue or pink. Hitler observed that the sun gave the picture a light violet tone and suggested blue. He fetched a ladder, paints and a brush and, as he worked, conversed with the lieutenant. "What I noticed first," recalled Wiedemann, "was his unmilitary manner and his slight Austrian accent, and most of all, that he was a serious person who obviously had been through quite a lot in life."

Wiedemann and Sergeant Amann now had time to make up the decoration list. They recommended Hitler for the Iron Cross, 1st Class, but since he was on the staff put his name at the bottom of the list. For this reason alone Hitler was turned down and instead given a 2nd Class award. Even so, Hitler was delighted and two days later wrote Herr Popp, "It was the happiest day of my life. Unfortunately, my comrades who also earned it are mostly all dead." He asked Popp to keep the newspapers describing the action. "I want to save them for reminiscences, if the dear Lord spares my life." He was also promoted to corporal, and no longer was called *Kamerad Schnürschuh* (an insulting Bavarian epithet, "Comrade Laced Boots"). He had earned the respect of his comrades and officers. He belonged.

Private Hans Mend hadn't seen Hitler since their recruit days in Munich. There he seemed too slight even to carry a full field pack but now as he slouched around, rifle in hand, helmet askew, mustache drooping, "a lively glow" in his eyes, he was the picture of the front-line fighter. The other messengers respected his apparent fearlessness but couldn't understand why an Austrian should take such risks. "He is just an odd character," one remarked to Mend, "and lives in his own world but otherwise he's a nice fellow."

Despite his lectures on the evils of smoking and drinking, "Adi" was generally liked because of his reliability in a crisis. He never abandoned a wounded comrade or pretended to be sick when it came time for a perilous mission. Moreover, he was a good companion during the long, tedious stretches awaiting action. Being an artist actually drew him closer to his barracks mates. He would draw cartoon sketches on postcards illustrating comical moments of their life. Once, for instance, a man shot a rabbit to take home on leave but left with a parcel containing a brick which someone had exchanged for the animal. Hitler sent the victim of the prank a postcard—with two sketches, one of the soldier unwrapping a brick back home and the other of his friends at the front eating the rabbit.

Unlike the others, Hitler got almost no packages from home and to satisfy his insatiable appetite he was forced to buy extra food from the cooks and kitchen help, thus earning the title of the unit's biggest *Vielfrass* ("glutton"). At the same time he was too proud to share his comrades' packages and would brusquely refuse on the grounds that he couldn't repay the favor. He was almost as brusque in his rejection of Lieutenant Wiedemann's offer at Christmas of ten marks from the mess-hall funds.

The regiment went back to the lines soon after the holidays but there was not enough action for Adolf. "Now we are still in our old position and harass the French and English," he wrote Popp on January 22, 1915. "The weather is miserable. Often for days in water up to our knees under very heavy artillery fire. We are looking forward to a few days of relief. Hopefully there will soon come a general offensive along the whole front. It can't go on like this forever."

It was during this military stalemate that a small white terrier, apparently the mascot of an English soldier, leaped into Hitler's trench and began chasing a rat. Hitler caught the dog, which at first kept trying to escape. "With exemplary patience (he didn't understand a word of German), I gradually got him used to me." Hitler named him Fuchsl (Little Fox) and taught him a variety of circus tricks such as climbing up and down a ladder. Fuchsl never left his new master's side during the day and at night slept beside him.

Late in January Hitler, in another letter to Popp, drew a graphic picture of the static but deadly warfare:

> . . . Because of the constant rain (we do not have winter), the closeness of the ocean, and the low-lying terrain, the meadows and fields are like bottomless morasses, while the streets are covered with slimy mud and through these swamps run the trenches of our infantry, a mass of shelters and trenches with gun emplacements, communication ditches and barbed wire barricades, wolf lairs, land mines, in short, an almost impossible position.

The following month he also wrote Judge Hepp about his battle experiences but then ended the letter, somewhat surprisingly, on a political note:

> I think so often of Munich and each of us has but one wish, that it may soon come to a settling of accounts with the gang, that we'll come to blows, no matter what the cost, and that those among us who have the luck to see our homeland again will find it purer and cleansed from foreign influence, so that by the sacrifice and agony which so many hundreds of thousands of us endure every day, that by the river of blood which flows here daily, against an international world of enemies, not only will Germany's enemies from the outside be smashed, but also our domestic internationalism will be broken up.

Whenever anyone asked where he came from Hitler would reply that his home was the 16th Regiment—not Austria—and after the war he would live in Munich. But first they had to win! On this point he was fanatic and if one of his mates jokingly remarked that the war would never be won he became incensed and would pace back and forth, asserting that England's coming defeat was as certain as the "Amen in the prayer."

As long as his comrades talked of food or women Hitler kept to his reading or painting, but once the conversation turned to serious subjects he would stop and deliver a lecture. His simple comrades were entranced by his fluency and loved to hear him "spout" on art, architecture and the like. His reputation as an intellectual was enhanced by the fact that he "always had a book spread out in front of him." He carried several in his pack, one by Schopenhauer ("I learned a great deal from him"). This philosopher's recurrent affirmation of the strength of blind will, the triumph of that will, must have struck a responsive chord.

By the end of the summer of 1915 Hitler had become indispensable to regimental headquarters. The telephone lines to battalion and company command posts were often knocked out by artillery and only runners could deliver messages. "We found out very soon," recalled Lieutenant Wiedemann, "which messengers we could rely on the most."* He was admired by fellow runners as much for his craftiness—he could crawl up front like one of the Indians he had read about in his boyhood—as his exceptional courage. Yet there was something in Hitler that disturbed some of the men. He was too different, his sense of duty excessive. "It's more important to bring our messages to their destination," he once lectured a fellow messenger, "than for personal ambition or to satisfy curiosity." He was unnaturally eager to get up front and would often, without being asked, deliver messages for the other runners.

The tempo of fighting increased in June and July and the constant duty began to tell on Hitler. His face became wan and more sallow. In the dark hours of the morning when an English barrage started he would leap out of bed and, rifle in hand, stride rapidly back and forth, "like a race horse at the starting gate," until everyone was awake. He became even more impatient with his neighbors' gripes. If one complained about the smaller meat ration, he sharply retorted that the French ate rats in 1870.

On September 25 the English pressed their attack and by nightfall the position of the entire 16th Regiment was endangered. Phone communication to the front abruptly ceased. Hitler and another man went forward to find out what had happened and returned "by the skin of their teeth" to report that the lines had been cut. An enemy attack in force was coming. Hitler was sent out to broadcast the warning and somehow survived the deadly barrage once more.

In the past months he had narrowly escaped death an inordinate number of times. It was as if he led a charmed life. "I was eating my dinner in a trench with several comrades," he told an English correspondent, Ward Price, years later. "Suddenly a voice seemed to be saying to me, 'Get up and go over there.' It was so clear and insistent that I obeyed me-

---

* Fritz Wiedemann, who became Hitler's adjutant in 1935 only to be dismissed four years later for opposing the Führer's foreign policy, stated in his book, *Der Mann, Der Feldherr werden wollte*, that Hitler's memory of his war experiences was excellent. "I never really caught him lying or exaggerating when he told of his recollections."

chanically, as if it had been a military order. I rose at once to my feet and walked twenty yards along the trench, carrying my dinner in its tin-can with me. Then I sat down to go on eating, my mind being once more at rest. Hardly had I done so when a flash and deafening report came from the part of the trench I had just left. A stray shell had burst over the group in which I had been sitting, and every member of it was killed."

Perhaps it was the season of perception. That fall on a night made gray-white with hoarfrost he may have felt the sense of his destiny when he wrote this strange poem:

> I often go on bitter nights
> To Wotan's oak in the quiet glade
> With dark powers to weave a union—
> The runic letters the moon makes with its magic spell
> And all who are full of impudence during the day
> Are made small by the magic formula!
> They draw shining steel—but instead of going into combat
> They solidify into stalagmites.
> So the false ones part from the real ones—
> I reach into a nest of words
> And then give to the good and just
> With my formula blessings and prosperity.

A few weeks later he made a portentous prophecy to his comrades: "You will hear much about me. Just wait until my time comes."

There was no snow that December, only endless rain. Entire sections of the meandering trench lines were flooded. The second Christmas was more dismal than the first. While the others opened parcels and cherished letters from home, Hitler sat on his cot as in a trance. During the three days of holiday he scarcely spoke a word. His comrades tried to cheer him up and offered him the pick of their own parcels. He refused with abrupt thanks, then retreated to his private world. Once the holidays ended, Hitler snapped out of his apathy, becoming so cheerful, in fact, that he could smile at mocking remarks about his "quietly spent holidays."

In the early summer of 1916 Hitler's regiment moved south, just in time to take part in the crucial battle of the Somme. It began with an English attack so relentless that almost 20,000 Allies were killed or fatally wounded on the first day alone. In the Fromelles sector the enemy barrage on the night of July 14 cut all regimental field telephones. Hitler and another runner were sent out "in the face of almost certain death, peppered with shot and shell every meter of the way." They cowered for shelter in watery shell holes and ditches. The other man collapsed from exhaustion and Hitler had to drag him back to their dugout.

By July 20 the Battle of Fromelles was on. It cost both sides many lives—and ended where it had started. For the next two months the struggle lapsed into dull but deadly trench warfare with advances or retreats measured in yards. It was during this time that Hitler lost a close friend; Hans Mend was transferred to the rear to act as interpreter in a prisoner-of-war camp. But he still had two other comrades, Ernst Schmidt and Ignaz Westenkirchner—and, more important, his pet. "How many times at Fromelles, during the First World War, I studied my dog Fuchsl," he reminisced on a winter night twenty-five years later. He told of his fascination with Fuchsl's reaction to a buzzing fly. The dog would quiver as if hypnotized, wrinkle his face like an old man, then suddenly leap forward and bark. "I used to watch as if he'd been a man—the progressive stages of his anger, of the bile that took possession of him." Fuchsl used to sit next to Hitler when he ate, watching each movement. If Hitler gave him nothing after taking five or six mouthfuls, the dog sat up and looked at his master as if to say, What about me? "It was crazy how fond I was of the beast."

After three months the Battle of the Somme still raged. The Allies persistently attacked and, in all, would suffer 614,000 casualties in this one campaign, but it was a useless slaughter, for the German lines did not buckle. For almost a week Hitler continued his charmed life despite a number of dangerous missions. Then on the night of October 7 his luck ended as he slept with the other messengers in sitting position in a narrow tunnel leading to regimental headquarters. A shell exploded near the narrow entrance, knocking the messengers into a heap. Hitler was hit in the thigh but tried to argue Wiedemann into keeping him at the front. "It isn't so bad, Lieutenant, right?" he said anxiously. "I can still stay with you, I mean, stay with the regiment! Can't I?"

3

Hitler was evacuated to a field hospital. His wound, his first, was not serious but in the ward he suffered a curious shock, one that almost made him collapse from "fright." It came as he lay on his cot and suddenly heard the voice of a German woman, a nurse. "For the first time in two years to hear such a sound!" Shortly he was on a hospital train bound for Germany. "The closer our train which was to bring us home approached the border, the more inwardly restless each of us became." At last he recognized the first German house—"by its high gable and beautiful shutters. The Fatherland!"

At a military hospital just southwest of Berlin the comfortable white beds were such a change after trench life that at first "we hardly dared to lie on them properly." He gradually readjusted to such comfort, but not to the spirit of cynicism he found in some men. As soon as he was ambulatory, Hitler got permission to spend the weekend in Berlin. He found hunger and "dire misery"—and "scoundrels" who were agitating for peace.

After two months he was released from the hospital and transferred to a replacement battalion in Munich. Here, according to *Mein Kampf*, he at last found the answer to the collapse of morale. The Jews! They were behind the front line plotting Germany's downfall. "Nearly every clerk was a Jew and nearly every Jew was a clerk. I was amazed at this plethora of warriors from the chosen people and could not help but compare them with their rare representatives at the front." He was also convinced that "Jewish finance" had seized control of Germany's production. "The spider was slowly beginning to suck the blood out of the people's pores."

His comrades at the front never heard him talk like this; he appeared to be no more anti-Semitic than they were. Occasionally he would make an innocuous remark such as, "If all Jews were no more intelligent than Stein [their telephone operator], then there wouldn't be trouble." And whenever Adolf talked about Vienna and the overriding influence of the Jews, he did so, Westenkirchner recalled, "without spitefulness." Schmidt, in fact, never heard him discuss the subject at all nor did Lieutenant Wiedemann ("It really seems impossible for me to believe that Hitler's hatred for Jews dated back to that time").

Hitler became disgusted with Munich. He found the mood in the replacement battalion despicable. No one honored a front-line soldier. These recruits had no conception of what Hitler had suffered in the trenches. He longed to be back with his own kind and in January 1917 wrote Lieutenant Wiedemann that he was "again fit for service" and wished "to return to my old regiment and old comrades." On March 1 he was back with the 16th Regiment, receiving a warm welcome from officers and comrades alike. Little Fuchsl went into paroxysms of ecstasy—"he hurled himself on me in frenzy." For supper the company cook "turned out an extra special mess in his honor, *Kartoffelpuffer*, bread and jam and cake." At last Hitler was back home where he belonged. That night he wandered around for hours, flashlight in hand, spitting rats on his bayonet —until someone threw a boot at him and he went to bed.

A few days later the regiment entrained for the Arras area to prepare for another spring offensive. But there was leisure time for painting, and Hitler completed more water colors, scenes of former battles that had meaning to him.* That Easter his art took a popular turn. He painted egg briquettes with calcium and placed them in the garden of the regimental commander, spelling out: "Happy Easter 1917." A few months later there was a new regimental commander, Major Freiherr von Tubeuf, a young, active man who brought discipline back to the unit. He not only made life difficult for both men and officers but criticized his superiors. To work off his frustrations Tubeuf went hunting. Hitler was one of the beaters and he spent two hours crawling around in the brush just behind the front lines flailing away with a long stick and shouting, while his commander (whom he would promote to general in sixteen years) fired away at rabbits.

Despite long and gallant service Hitler was still a corporal. One reason, according to Wiedemann, was that he lacked "the capacity for leadership." Another was his sloppy bearing. He held his head somewhat lopsided toward his left shoulder and slouched around. Although he bathed whenever possible and called a comrade who didn't "a living dunghill," he disliked polishing his boots. Nor would he snap heels at the approach of an officer. More important, there were no authorized spaces as corporal for a messenger. If promoted, Hitler would have had to give up the duty he preferred; and the regiment would have lost one of its best runners.

That summer the regiment returned to its first battlefield in Belgium and participated in the third battle for Ypres. It was as deadly as the first. In mid-July they were bombarded for ten days and nights. When it slackened they could hear under them the ominous sound of digging—the enemy was boring tunnels. Overhead came the drone of planes, then the crash of bombs. In addition there was the constant threat of gas and the men sometimes had to keep their suffocating masks on for twenty-four hours at a stretch. On the last day of July the defenders were confronted with a new terror—tanks. Fortunately, torrential rains turned no man's land into a quagmire and the tanks were bogged down.

In August the shattered 16th Regiment was relieved. They were sent to Alsace for rest and it was at this time that Hitler suffered two grievous losses. A railroad official, captivated by the antics of Fuchsl, offered Hitler two hundred marks for the terrier. "You could give me two hundred thou-

---

* In his unpublished diary Gordon Craig, the stage designer, described these wartime paintings as remarkably artistic productions. His praise may have been tempered by gratitude; it was Hitler who literally saved him from starvation in Paris during World War II by buying his sketches.

sand, and you wouldn't get him!" was Hitler's indignant reply. But as the troops were disembarking, Hitler couldn't find Fuchsl. His column was already on the move and he had to follow. "I was desperate. The swine who stole my dog doesn't realize what he did to me." At about the same time another "swine" rifled his knapsack and made off with a leather case containing sketches, drawings and water colors. Insulted and injured—first by a civilian slacker and then by one of the new breed of cowardly recruits (no front-line soldier would rob a comrade)—he put aside his paints.

Early that October Schmidt finally persuaded Hitler to take an eighteen-day furlough, his first of the war. Their destination was Dresden, home of Schmidt's sister, but they stopped off at Brussels, Cologne and Leipzig for sightseeing. Hitler particularly enjoyed the last city. It was here that Martin Luther preached his first sermon in St. Thomas' Church—the same church where Bach had played the organ for twenty-seven years and was buried, and where Wagner had been baptized. But what impressed him most was the massive 300-foot monument of the Battle of the Nations, honoring the war dead of 1813, which looked more like a fortress than a shrine. "This has nothing to do with art," he commented, "but it is enormous and beautiful." In Dresden they inspected the famous buildings and visited the art galleries, including the famous Zwinger. He was eager to go to the opera until he examined the program—apparently there was no Wagner—and announced there was nothing worth seeing. Later he visited Berlin by himself and stayed a few days with the family of a front-line comrade. "The city is marvelous," he wrote Schmidt on a postcard. "A real world capital. Traffic is still tremendous. Am gone almost all day. Now finally have opportunity to study the museums a little better. In short: there is nothing lacking."

The unit saw little action for the rest of the year and Hitler had much time for reading. To him novels and magazines were frivolous and he concentrated on history and philosophy. "War forces one to think deeply about human nature," he later told Hans Frank. "Four years of war are equivalent to thirty years university training in regard to life's problems. I hated nothing more than trash literature. When we are concerned with the fate of mankind then one can only read Homer and evangelical works. In the later years of the war I read Schopenhauer and reached for him again and again. [The copy of Schopenhauer's selected works which he kept in his pack was worn out.] Then I was able to do without evangelism—even if Christ was a true fighter. But the turning of both cheeks is not a very good recipe for the front."

Quiet as the western front was, that winter proved the most arduous one yet for the front-line troops. Rations were shorter than ever and the men were forced to eat cats and dogs. Hitler's comrades recalled that he preferred the meat of cat to that of a dog (perhaps because of Fuchsl). His favorite food when he could get it, was toast thickly spread with honey or marmalade. Once he found large crates of zwieback, and to satisfy his hunger he began robbing them systematically, craftily taking packages from the bottom. He shared the loot with his mates and, after getting some sugar on barter, would cook for them the front-line version of an Austrian dessert, *Schmarren.*

At home civilians were also forced to eat dogs and cats ("roof rabbits"); bread was made from sawdust and potato peelings, and there was almost no milk. Germany's allies also suffered. Food supplies were so short in Vienna that the Austrian government was forced to appeal to Berlin for grain. Strikes erupted in Vienna and Budapest, set off not only by hunger but by Germany's failure to make peace with the new Bolshevik government in Russia. They spread to Germany itself, which had been under a virtual military dictatorship for several months, and on Monday, January 28, 1918, workers throughout Germany went out on strike. Peace was their main demand but they also insisted on workers' representation in negotiations with the Allies, increased food rations, the abolition of martial law, and a democratic government throughout Germany. In Munich and Nuremberg only a few thousand workers marched through the streets petitioning for immediate peace without annexation, but in Berlin 400,000 workers walked out of their shops to organize a strike committee. Within a week they were forced back to work but a spirit of rebellion had come alive in the capital and it seemed only a question of time before full-scale revolution would break out.

News of the general strike was received with mixed feelings at the front. Many of the soldiers were as war-weary and disgusted as those back home but almost as many felt they had been betrayed by their own civilians. Hitler called it "the biggest piece of chicanery in the whole war." He was incensed at the slackers and Reds. "What was the army fighting for if the homeland itself no longer wanted victory? For whom the immense sacrifices and privations? The soldier is expected to fight for victory and the homeland goes on strike against it!"

At last Berlin made peace with the Soviets at Brest-Litovsk on March 3 but the terms imposed on the young government were so harsh that leftists in Germany claimed the treaty's real purpose was to crush the Russian Revolution. News of the capitulation of the Bolsheviks exhilarated soldiers like Hitler who remained convinced that Germany must win. Now more than ever total victory seemed in their grasp and the majority of troops responded loyally if not eagerly to the high command's order for a massive offensive. In the next four months Hitler's regiment took part in all phases of the massive Ludendorff spring offensives: on the Somme, on the Aisne and finally on the Marne. Hitler's fighting spirit was higher than ever. On one of his trips out front in June he got a glimpse of something in a trench that looked like a French helmet. He crept forward and saw four *poilus*. Hitler pulled out his pistol—messengers had turned in rifles for side arms by then—and began shouting orders in German as though he had a company of soldiers. He delivered his four prisoners to Colonel von Tubeuf personally and was commended. "There was no circumstance or situation," recalled Tubeuf, "that would have prevented him from volunteering for the most difficult, arduous and dangerous tasks and he was always ready to sacrifice life and tranquillity for his Fatherland and for others." On August 4 Hitler was awarded the Iron Cross, 1st Class, but it was for former achievements and not this outstanding feat and simply read, "For personal bravery and general merit."* It was presented to him by the battalion adjutant who had initiated the award, First Lieutenant Hugo Gutmann, a Jew.

By this time it was evident that the great Ludendorff offensives which had pushed to within sight of the Eiffel Tower had failed miserably. Defeat on the western front came as a shock, particularly after the historic victories in the East where vast areas extending as far as the Caucasus had been conquered. Consequently there was a serious drop in morale even among the older soldiers. Disorders on troop and leave trains approached rebellion. Shots were fired from windows. Men disappeared at every station. Officers attempting to maintain discipline were attacked with stones and grenades. Revolutionary slogans such as "We're not fighting for Germany's honor but for the millionaires," were scrawled in chalk on the cars.

Four days after Hitler received his Iron Cross, an Allied counterattack in the dense fog smashed through the German lines at Amiens. Ludendorff sent a staff officer to the front and immediately moved reserves to the breakthrough area. As these fresh troops moved up, those falling back shouted insults: "Blacklegs! You are prolonging the war!"

It was, Ludendorff wrote, "the black day of the German Army in the history of this war." The Kaiser reacted dejectedly but calmly and remarked, "We must draw only one conclusion: we are at the limit of our capabilities. The war must be ended." A few days later Ludendorff and Hindenburg conferred with Wilhelm at Spa. When the Kaiser ordered his

---

* In addition to this decoration and the Iron Cross, 2nd Class, he had won in 1914, Hitler received the following awards: September 17, 1917, Military Cross, 3rd Class, with swords; May 9, 1918, the *Regimentsdiplom* for outstanding bravery; May 18, 1918, the *Verwundeterabrechnen* (Medal for Wounded); and on August 25, 1918, the *Dienstauszeichnung* (Service Medal), 3rd Class.

foreign minister to begin peace negotiations, Hindenburg protested that the army still held much enemy territory and Ludendorff excitedly exclaimed that there must be discipline on the home front as well as "more vigorous conscription of the young Jews, hitherto left pretty much alone."

In the face of rebellion at home and impending collapse at the front, Hitler became more argumentative and talked at length of the swindle perpetrated by the Reds. But his voice was lost in the chorus of complaints from replacements. At such times, according to Schmidt, Hitler "became furious and shouted in a terrible voice that the pacifists and shirkers were losing the war." One day he attacked a new non-com who said it was stupid to continue fighting. They fought with their fists, and finally, after taking considerable punishment, Hitler beat his opponent. From that day, Schmidt recalled, "the new ones despised him but we old comrades liked him more than ever."

Four years of dehumanizing trench warfare had engendered in Hitler, as in so many other German patriots, an abiding hatred of the pacifists and slackers back home who were "stabbing the Fatherland in the back." He and those like him burned with a zeal to avenge such treachery, and out of all this would come the politics of the future. Hitler was far from the dreamy-eyed volunteer of 1914. Four years in the trenches had given him a sense of belonging along with a degree of self-confidence. Having fought for Germany, he was truly German; and having conducted himself honorably under duress, he had pride in his manhood. He had entered the army a raw youth, remarkably underdeveloped for all his twenty-four years and hardships in Vienna; now he was a man, ready to take a man's place in the world.

Early in September the 16th Regiment was moved back to Flanders. Since they were in reserve, the troops were allowed to take furloughs. With a comrade named Arendt he returned to Berlin where he must have been repelled by the rising spirit of discontent in the capital. He also spent a few days at the family farm in Spital. Several weeks after his return the 16th Regiment marched a third time to the area below Ypres. For the third time they dug into the fields and hills near Comines. Then on the morning of October 14 Hitler was blinded by gas near the village of Werwick. He would recover his eyesight only to lose it again November 9, upon learning that Germany was going to surrender. A few days later he would hear voices and see a vision.

4

It is impossible to know how deep Adolf Hitler's fear and hatred of Jews ran on the day he was gassed in Belgium. Within a year, however, hatred of all things Jewish would become an overt and dominant force in his life. Hitler was only one among millions of other patriots who learned to fear Jews and Reds (almost as a single entity) during this period. For in these months the country was engulfed by a terrifying series of Marxist-inspired uprisings that threatened to destroy the fabric of German existence.

Significantly, the revolutions began while Hitler was suffering the depressing aftereffects of mustard gas. On the day he started east in a hospital train—it was October 16—Prince Max of Baden, the new German Chancellor, received a note from President Woodrow Wilson demanding, in effect, the abdication of Wilhelm before America would agree to an armistice. This quickened the disintegration of the German military and within two weeks open revolt broke out when the fleet was ordered to proceed to sea. The crews of six battleships protested. Mutiny broke out in Kiel as sailors pillaged armories and small arms lockers and took over most of the city. In one barracks a stoker established the Kiel Sailors' Soviet and all but one of the ships still in port ran up the red flag of revolution. The men seized officers, tore off their insignia and escorted them to the prison.

In Munich another insurrection broke out on November 7. It was led by Kurt Eisner, a small elderly Jew wearing a black floppy hat which, large as it was, couldn't contain a shock of wild hair. Epically untidy, he was a living cartoon of the bomb-throwing Red. He had already spent almost nine months in prison for his wartime strike activities. By dusk the revolutionaries, joined by many soldiers, had seized every major military post in Munich and Ludwig III of the House of Wittelsbach had been forced to flee in a car, which ran off the road just south of the city, miring itself in a potato field. It was a fitting end to monarchy in Bavaria.

That evening trucks filled with occupants flourishing red flags rattled through the city. Eisner's men seized the main railroad station and government buildings. No one resisted. Police looked the other way as rebels set up machine guns at strategic corners. The burghers of Munich wakened the next morning to find that their Bavaria had become a republic. Revolution had come, German style, without too much fuss and without a single serious casualty. The people accepted their lot in the same spirit. There was no violent reaction. The Müncheners grumbled and waited.

The flames of orderly revolution were igniting spontaneously throughout Germany. In Friedrichshafen workers at the Zeppelin plant formed a council. The factory workers in the Stuttgart area, including the vast Daimler motor works, struck and, led by socialists with views similar to Eisner's, made similar demands. Sailors engineered revolt in Frankfurt am Main. At Kassel the entire garrison, including a commanding officer, revolted without benefit of bullets. There were a few shots fired in Cologne when the garrison of 45,000 went Red but order quickly settled over the city. A civilian revolt in Hanover succeeded even though authorities ordered troops to use force; instead the soldiers joined the rebels. It was the same in Düsseldorf, Leipzig and Magdeburg.

Government after government throughout Germany collapsed as workers' and soldiers' councils took control. Finally, on November 9, the Kaiser reluctantly abdicated, turning power over to the moderate socialists who were led by a former saddlemaker, Friedrich Ebert. It was the end of the German Empire, begun in France on January 18, 1871, when Wilhelm I, King of Prussia and grandfather of Wilhelm II, was proclaimed the first Emperor of Germany in the Hall of Mirrors at the Versailles Palace.

It was also the end of an era. Forty-eight years earlier Bismarck had achieved his dream of unifying Germany and in so doing had created a new image of Germany and Germans. Overnight the foundation on which rested the security of the Junker landowners in East Prussia and the great industrialists crumbled; and overnight the political philosophy on which the majority of Germans had based their conservative and patriotic way of life had apparently disintegrated with the lowering of the imperial flag.

Perhaps the greatest shock to Germans was to find Ebert sitting in the chancellery. In a single day the Hohenzollern regime had evaporated and a man of the people had taken command. How could it possibly have happened? Ebert himself was uneasy in the seat of power. He realized his presence would be an insult to those raised in imperialism. Moreover, he did not even represent the radical spirit of the streets. In fact, whom did he represent? He was so panicky that when Prince Max appeared at dusk to say farewell Ebert begged him to remain in Berlin as "administrator" for the Hohenzollern monarchy.

At 5 A.M. two days later a representative of the Ebert government, Matthias Erzberger, put his signature to the Allied armistice terms in Marshal Foch's private railroad car. Hostilities would cease at 11 A.M. He had insured peace to a shattered nation at the eleventh hour of the eleventh day of the eleventh month of the year, and in so doing innocently gave birth to the myth of the "November criminals"—that it was the socialists who had sold out the nation. It was the Kaiser and the imperial German generals, of course, who had lost the war but President Wilson had refused to make an armistice with them, insisting he could deal only with democratic elements. And by forcing the socialists to assume the blame for something they had not brought about, Wilson gave Adolf Hitler a political tool that he was destined to wield with devastating force.

5

At the end of November 1918 Hitler was discharged from the Pasewalk hospital as "fit for field service" since the patient "no longer complained of anything but a burning of the membrane." Hitler later testified in court that he could only make out the largest headlines in a newspaper and feared he might never read another book. "The medical records at the hospital," he complained, "were made at a time of revolution. Practically no one got personal attention; we were discharged in hordes. For example, I never even received my soldier's pay-book."

He was ordered to report to the replacement battalion of his regiment. This was located in Munich and on his way he must have passed through Berlin, which was in the hands of the Executive Council of the Workers' and Soldiers' Councils—a coalition not only of soldiers and workers but of Majority and Independent Socialists. This conglomeration had already enacted social reforms which would have seemed impossible a few months earlier. It had established the eight-hour day; granted labor the unrestricted right to organize into unions; increased workers' old-age, sick and unemployment benefits; abolished censorship of the press; and released political prisoners.

While Hitler approved the social reforms, he distrusted the revolutionaries who had effected them: the Executive Council was a tool of the Bolsheviks and the betrayer of the front-line soldiers; and its eventual goal was another Red revolution. When Hitler checked in at the Türkenstrasse barracks of Munich's Schwabing area, he encountered the same spirit of rebellion. This installation had gone over to Eisner earlier in the month and was under the control of a Soldiers' Council. There was no discipline; the place was a pigsty. There was no respect for those who had served in the trenches since the first days of the war. Many were there for food and shelter alone. It was far worse than the Männerheim. What particularly incensed Hitler was the behavior of the council members. "Their whole activity was so repellent to me that I decided at once to leave again as soon as possible."

Fortunately he found an old comrade who experienced the same disgust. "The laziest and most impudent among the men were, naturally, those who had never been anywhere near the trenches," remembered his fellow runner, Ernst Schmidt. "The place was full of laggards and cowards." Some two weeks later, when guards were sought for a prisoner-of-war camp at Traunstein, sixty miles to the east on the road to Salzburg, Hitler suggested to Schmidt that they volunteer. Their group, comprised mostly of so-called "revolution men," was met at the railroad station by an officer. The men treated his order to fall in as a joke: didn't he know drill had been abolished? The next day the contingent, except for a few who had seen service in the trenches, were shipped back to Munich. Hitler and Schmidt remained.

6

In Berlin the Spartacists, a far leftist group named after the slave who led the rebellion against the Romans, had taken to the streets to make revolution with the help of revolting sailors. This was no *gemütlich* Munich uprising. By Christmas Eve the capital was close to anarchy. Other cities followed suit, if not as dramatically, and throughout Germany the structure of the military and police began to crumble.

With their abdication of authority, a new force made an abrupt appearance—a phenomenon known as the Freikorps, bands of idealistic activists from the armed forces who shared Hitler's passion to defend Germania from the Reds. The Free Corps, spawned from the German generation born in Hitler's time, had been prepared for today's action by two previous experiences. First had come the prewar youth movement, the Wandervögel (Birds of Passage). These youngsters tramped around the land, often wearing colorful costumes, in their search for a new way of life. For the most part from the well-to-do middle class, they despised the liberal bourgeois society they sprang from and were convinced that "parental religion was largely sham, politics boastful and trivial, economics unscrupulous and deceitful, education stereotyped and lifeless, art trashy and sentimental, literature spurious and commercialized, drama tawdry and mechanical." They regarded family life as repressive and insincere. They also were concerned that the relations between the sexes, in and out of marriage, were "shot through with hypocrisy." Their goal was to establish a youth culture for fighting the bourgeois trinity of school, home and church.

They would sit around campfires, under the direction of a Führer, and sing "The Song of the Freebooters," while silently gazing into a campfire in quest of "messages from the forest," or listening to someone read hortatory passages from Nietzsche or Stefan George, who wrote: "The people and supreme wisdom yearn for the Man!—The Deed! . . . Perhaps someone who sat for years among your murderers and slept in your prisons will stand up and *do the deed*." These young people, thriving on mysticism and impelled by idealism, yearned for action—any kind of action.

They found it in the Great War. Perhaps that is why they were as convinced as Hitler of the righteousness of the Fatherland's cause. Life in the trenches brought officers and men closer together in a brotherhood of suffering and blood. The men worshiped the one who led them into desperate hand-to-hand combat. "To them he was not their commanding officer; he was their Führer! And they were his comrades! They trusted him blindly and would have followed him into hell itself if it were necessary." Together they formed a front-line relationship of democracy hitherto unknown in Germany. The miles of trenches were isolated from the rest of the world and became, in effect, a "monastery with walls of flame."

These comrades of the front lines, these former Birds of Passage, shared with Hitler the shame of surrender and distrust of a home front degenerating into Bolshevism. Understandably, these veterans responded with enthusiasm to announcements placed by the military in newspapers and on billboards announcing that the Spartacist danger had not yet been removed and calling for soldiers to rise and join the Free Corps to "prevent Germany from becoming the laughingstock of the earth."

While this illegal army was forming, the Spartacists, with the approval of many Berliners, were taking over the capital. They controlled public utilities, transportation, and munitions factories. In desperation, on January 3, 1919, the Ebert government dismissed the chief of police since he was known to sympathize with the Spartacists and had recently supported the sailors' mutiny. In retaliation, the Spartacists, now openly admitting they were Communists, called for revolution. Berlin workers responded with enthusiasm and by midmorning of the sixth, 200,000 workers, carrying weapons and red flags, massed from Alexanderplatz to the Tiergarten. Nor did the fog and cold dampen the spirit of the crowd. Groups seized the officers of the Social Democrat newspaper, *Vorwärts*, and the Wolff Telegraph Agency. The chancellery itself was surrounded by the angry mob. Inside hid Ebert and his associates.

By the following morning the Communists were ensconced in the statuary on top of the Brandenburg Gate, their rifles covering the Unter den Linden, the Königstrasse and the Charlottenburger Chaussee. In addition to strategic railroad stations, the Government Printing Office and the Bötzow Brewery were occupied. Within twenty-four hours the government held only a few of the city's major buildings.

Berlin—eventually all of Germany—would probably have gone Communist but for the Free Corps. Within a week units from outside the city marched in and crushed the Red centers of resistance. The Spartacist leaders, including the diminutive Rosa Luxemburg, were hunted down and cruelly murdered.

Four days after the death of "Red Rose" the first national election under the new Republic was held. It was a Sunday, clear and cold. For the first time in German history women were allowed to participate and 30,000,000 citizens out of an electorate of 35,000,000 cast their votes for 423 deputies to the National Assembly. The results, while surprising, should have been predictable. The two rightist parties, which wanted a return of the Hohenzollerns yet pretended they didn't, got about fifteen per cent of the Assembly seats; the two centrist parties, which favored the Republic, won almost forty per cent as did Ebert's Majority Socialists; and the far left Independent Socialists took only seven per cent. The result, as much a victory against revolution as it was for a republic, doomed socialization.

Since strife-torn Berlin was not considered safe, Weimar, some hundred and fifty miles southwest of the capital, was made the home of the National Assembly. Its selection was a cultural as well as geographical choice, for Weimar had been the home of Goethe, Schiller and Liszt. The Assembly met on February 6 in the New National Theater but the convocation lacked the pomp and ceremony of a Hohenzollern event. There were no bands, cavalry escorts or dazzling uniforms.

After five days a working government was organized with Ebert named first President of the Reich by a large majority. He appointed a Chancellor who, in turn, selected his own cabinet. The most significant choice was a strong-willed man named Noske (he called himself the "Bloodhound") as Minister of Defense. It meant that the illegal Free Corps would now operate with the blessing of the infant Weimar Republic and continue to defend the nation from Reds and riot.

7

Traditionally Bavarians detested Prussia and all things Prussian, and the events in Weimar were largely ignored in Munich. One of the city's leading intellectuals, as yet unrecognized by the world, was contemptuous of the attempts of the Ebert government to establish democracy throughout Germany. The lonely and impoverished bachelor, Oswald Spengler— misogynous and misanthropic—had finally published the first volume of *The Decline of the West* in the spring of 1918 and, though still unreviewed, the book was making an impact throughout the country.

"Like the French in 1793 we must go right through to the end in our misfortune, we need a chastisement compared to which the four years of war are nothing," he wrote a friend, ". . . until finally the Terror has brought to a head such a degree of excitement and despair, that a dictatorship, resembling that of Napoleon, will be regarded universally as a salvation."

Hitler, who considered himself born for and destined to politics, was preparing his return to Munich. The prisoner-of-war camp at Traunstein was about to close and he was being reassigned to the 2nd Infantry Regiment barracks in Schwabing along with his comrade Schmidt. Another young man with similar aspirations was already established in Munich. Alfred Rosenberg, a fanatic anti-Semite and anti-Marxist, had come from his native Estonia by way of Russia to find his true home. Like Hitler, he was artist and architect. Like Hitler, he was more Germanic than a native German, and had left his birthplace "to gain a Fatherland for myself." Moreover, he was determined to warn this Fatherland of the Bolshevik terror that had ravaged the old one, and fight to keep it free from Jewish Communism.

Upon learning that there was a German author named Eckart who shared many of his views, Rosenberg decided to make his acquaintance. Dietrich Eckart—poet, playwright, coffeehouse intellectual—was a tall, bald, burly eccentric who spent much of his time in cafés and beer halls giving equal attention to drink and talk. Son of a Bavarian counselor to the King and former patient at an institution "for nervous diseases," he had entree to aristocratic circles. An original, raffish man with a touch of genius (his brilliant translation of *Peer Gynt* was the standard version), he too was a Pan-German and anti-Semite. With his own money he published a weekly paper that had a circulation of some 30,000.

Rosenberg appeared, without introduction, at Eckart's apartment. The poet was impressed by what he saw in the doorway: an intense, dead-serious young man. Rosenberg's first words were: "Can you use a fighter against Jerusalem?" Eckart laughed. "Certainly!" Had he written anything? Rosenberg produced an article on the destructive forces of Judaism and Bolshevism on Russia. It was the beginning of a relationship that would affect the career of Adolf Hitler. Eckart accepted Rosenberg as a "co-warrior against Jerusalem" and soon his articles on Russia began appearing not only in Eckart's paper but in another Munich weekly, *Deutsche Republik*. The theme of these articles was that the Jew stood behind the world's evils: the Zionists had planned the Great War as well as the Red Revolution and were presently plotting with the Masons to take over the world.

8

To many Bavarians Kurt Eisner was the very model of a revolutionary and it was widely believed that his revolution had been financed by Moscow gold. On the contrary, it had cost him only the eighteen marks in his pocket on that historic day in November, and he was, in fact, the antithesis of the ruthless, pragmatic Russian Bolshevik. He ran the Bavarian Socialist Republic as if he were still installed at the *Stammtisch* of his favorite coffeehouse. What Eisner was attempting to establish was not Communism or even socialism but a unique kind of radical democracy. A poet among politicians whose dream of a reign of beauty, illumination and reason was more in keeping with Shelley than Marx, he was already on the path to oblivion; the January elections had brought a resounding victory for the middle-class parties and an overriding demand for his resignation.

Early in the morning of February 21, realizing his cause was hopeless, he wrote out a statement announcing his resignation, but en route to the Landtag to deliver it, he was assassinated by Count Anton Arco-Valley, a young cavalry officer who had been turned down by an anti-Semitic group since his mother was Jewish. Eisner would have been out of office in an hour, his regime replaced by a middle-of-the-road government. The assassination brought about what Arco-Valley most feared, another surge to the left. Eisner, so recently despised and rejected by almost everyone, became an instant martyr and proletarian saint, and the revolutionary movement was resuscitated. Martial law was declared and a new all-socialist government headed by a former teacher, Adolf Hoffmann, was appointed by the Central Workers' and Soldiers' Council. A general strike was called, a 7 P.M. curfew imposed, and the University of Munich closed since its students were already acclaiming Arco-Valley as their hero.

A fortnight later the first congress of the Third International convened in Moscow and the resolution establishing the Communist International (Comintern) was unanimously adopted. In the ensuing victory celebration Lenin called on workers of all countries to force their leaders to withdraw troops from Russia, resume diplomatic and commercial relations, and help rebuild the fledgling nation with an army of engineers and instructors.

Berlin was already responding to the call for world revolution. The previous day, workers, ignoring orders from the Communist Party, had converged on the center of the city to demonstrate and loot. Joined by the Red Soldiers' League and other radical military groups, they seized more than thirty local police stations. Sailors besieged the main police headquarters on the Alexanderplatz which was defended by several companies of Free Corps infantry. The following day 1500 delegates of the Workers' Councils voted overwhelmingly to call a general strike. The capital was immobilized: no electricity, no transportation.

The revolutionaries concentrated on the eastern part of the city, setting up machine guns at key points. To counter them, Defense Minister Noske, using dictatorial powers recently bestowed on him, brought more than 30,000 Free Corps troops into the city on March 5. The rebels were driven back block by block while Berlin's bars, dance halls and cabarets remained open for business as usual.

After four more days of bitter house-to-house fighting with cannon, machine guns and strafing airplanes pitted against rifles and grenades, Noske announced that anyone "who bears arms against government troops will be shot on the spot." Scores of workers were lined up against walls and executed without trial. It was all over by the thirteenth. More than 1500 revolutionaries were dead and at least 10,000 wounded. The spirit of revolt, however, continued to spread throughout the country. Radicals were in power in Saxony and a state of siege existed in the Ruhr basin. Ben Hecht of the Chicago *Daily News* syndicate cabled: GERMANY IS HAVING A NERVOUS BREAKDOWN. THERE IS NOTHING SANE TO REPORT.

Munich too was on the verge of another revolution, this one inspired by a coup d'état in Budapest. On March 22 news arrived that a popular front of Socialists and Communists had seized control of Hungary in the name of the councils of workers, soldiers and peasants. A Hungarian Soviet Republic was announced under the leadership of an unknown, Béla Kun. A Jew himself, twenty-five of his thirty-two commissars were also Jews, provoking the London *Times* to characterize the regime as "the Jewish Mafia." The triumph of Béla Kun emboldened the leftists in Munich. Early on the evening of April 4 delegates from the councils trudged through streets piled with twenty inches of snow, the heaviest downfall in years. Their destination was the Löwenbräuhaus, only two blocks from Hitler's prewar rooming house. Here a resolution was read aloud: "Elimination of the parties, union of the entire proletariat, proclamation of a Soviet Republic and brotherhood with the Russian and Hungarian proletariat. And then no power on earth will be able to prevent the immediate execution of full socialization."

It was a coffeehouse revolution, an innocent version of the bloody reality. Its spiritual leader was Ernst Toller, the poet, and his platform included a demand for new art forms in drama, painting and architecture so the spirit of mankind could be set free. The Cabinet was a congeries of engaging eccentrics: the Commissar for Housing, for instance, ordered that henceforth the living room in all homes must be above the kitchen and bedroom. But the jewel in this crown of originals was Franz Lipp, selected as Commissar for Foreign Affairs (even though he had spent some time in a mental institution) on the grounds that he was the picture of a diplomat with his neat beard and gray frock coat. Lipp sent an indignant telegram to Moscow charging that Eisner's successor had stolen the keys to the ministry toilet, and declared war on Württemberg and Switzerland "because these dogs have not at once loaned me sixty locomotives."

The end came abruptly on Palm Sunday, April 13, when the former Minister President, the socialist schoolteacher Hoffmann, attempted to seize Munich by force. His *Putsch* never had a chance despite the exploits of soldiers like Adolf Hitler. He, for one, prevented the men at his barracks of the 2nd Infantry Regiment from going over to the Reds by climbing onto a chair and shouting, "Those who say we should remain neutral are right! After all, we're no pack of Revolutionary Guards for a gang of vagrant Jews!" Although Hitler and others held the Munich garrison to neutrality, the Hoffmann Putsch was crushed by nightfall and this time the Red professionals—led by Eugen Leviné, a native of St. Petersburg and the son of a Jewish merchant—took over the government. They had been sent to Munich by the Communist Party to organize revolution and, after arresting the poet Toller, promptly converted it into a genuine Soviet. But they proceeded to violate strict party orders to avoid any armed action, "even when a local or momentary success might be possible," by dispatching, in the name of the Bavarian Soviet Republic, a considerable force to confront an army of 8000 men that Hoffmann had hastily gathered to retake Munich. The Hoffmann army was approaching Dachau, a city ten miles above Munich.

The Red commander-in-chief was the man just arrested by the Communists, Ernst Toller. After release from a cellar he went forth to battle on a borrowed horse, as a knight of old, determined that "the revolution must be cleanly fought." On April 18 this Red knight directed the attack against the Hoffmann forces but, being a humanist and individualist, he persistently ignored orders from Munich. First he refused to shell Dachau and instead attempted to avoid conflict by negotiation. When firing erupted and the issue was forced he led his men to an almost bloodless triumph. The Hoffmann forces retreated in panic. The Soviet leaders ordered Toller to shoot the officers he had captured. Naturally he released them and once more he was imprisoned.

After the debacle at Dachau, Hoffmann was forced to accept help from War Minister Noske's Free Corps units. A tactical plan for the conquest of Munich was drawn up with amazing promptness and executed so effectively that the city was completely encircled by April 27. In vengeful retribution the surrounded Reds hunted down enemies of the Soviet Republic throughout Munich. Sailors captured seven members of the anti-Semitic Thule Society, including its attractive secretary. In all a hundred hostages were imprisoned in the Luitpold high school.

By April 29 the ring around Munich tightened and the revolutionaries were in a panic. A false alarm that the Whites had occupied the main railroad station emptied Red headquarters, except for Toller (who had been released to set up a last-ditch defense) and the commander of the Red Army. He decided to wreak final vengeance on the Whites, whose Free Corps troops had recently executed fifty-two Russian prisoners of war in a stone quarry and shot a dozen unarmed workers; he ordered the execution of the hostages in the high school. The horrified Toller rushed to stop the massacre but by the time he arrived at least twenty people had been slaughtered.

Students slipped through what was left of the Red lines and reported these atrocities to Free Corps commanders who issued orders to march into the city at dawn. The first of May was clear and warm as Free Corps units converged on the city from several directions. They had little difficulty routing scattered revolutionaries despite some opposition in the area surrounding the Hauptbahnhof and in the Schwabing section. On all sides the Free Corps men were cheered by the relieved citizenry. In the Marienplatz an open-air mass for the troops was held as red flags were hauled down and replaced by the blue and white of Bavaria.

While Lenin was boasting to a huge May Day crowd in Red Square of the triumphs of Communism ("The liberated working class is celebrating its anniversary freely and openly not only in Soviet Russia, but in Soviet Hungary and Soviet Bavaria"), Free Corps troops were ranging through Munich extinguishing nests of resistance and arresting Red leaders. The streets of Munich belonged to the Free Corps and soon they were marching down the Ludwigstrasse, goose-stepping as they passed the Feldherrnhalle, with one unit, the Ehrhardt Brigade, wearing swastika-decorated helmets and singing, "Swastika on helmet, Black-white-red band . . ."

By May 3 Munich was secured but at the cost of sixty-eight Free Corps lives. These, of course, had to be avenged. Thirty Catholic workers of the St. Joseph Society were seized at a tavern while making plans to put on a play. They were brought to the cellar of the Wittelsbach Palace where twenty-one of them were shot or bayoneted to death as dangerous Reds. Hundreds were shot under similar circumstances and thousands were "chastised" by cruising Free Corps squads. The repression continued with issuance of a series of harsh edicts, some almost impossible to obey, such as the one to surrender all arms immediately or be shot. In the name of law and order citizens were routed out, insulted, beaten and murdered. The Free Corps had saved Munich from the iron heel of the Soviet Republic and its excesses but these seemed pale compared to the cure.

"It would require a volume to narrate all the atrocities committed by the Whites," reported the French military attaché in Munich; ". . . organized barbarism was given free rein . . . a savage debauchery, an indescribable orgy. . . ." But the British officials saw none of this or else they approved of what they observed. "The result of the Soviet episode at Munich, so far as at present can be seen," reported the Political Intelligence Department of the British Foreign Office, "is to strengthen the cause of law and order throughout Germany, and to discredit Spartacism and Bolshevism with the masses." In all more than a thousand so-called "Reds" were executed by the Free Corps. So many bodies littered Munich in so short a time that they became a health menace and unidentified corpses had to be dumped into shallow ditches.

9

The idealistic youth of the Wandervögel had brought their high hopes into the trenches and now, as Free Corps men, onto the streets of Germany. "This is the New Man, the storm soldier, the elite of Mitteleuropa," wrote their poet laureate, Ernst Jünger. "A completely new race, cunning, strong, and purposeful." These would be soldiers of the battle for German salvation. "New forms must be molded with blood, and power must be seized with a hard fist."

Jünger could have been speaking for Adolf Hitler, whose slumbering antipathies had been reawakened by the Red regimes in Munich, and shortly after the liberation of Munich came the event that would change his life and turn the course of world history. On June 28, 1919, the victorious Allies signed the Treaty of Versailles. With little delay the German government ratified its terms. These were harsh. Germany was forced to accept sole responsibility for causing the war and required to pay *all* civilian damage caused by the conflict. Great chunks of territory were wrested from the Reich: Alsace-Lorraine went to France, the Malmédy area to Belgium, most of Posen and West Prussia to Poland. Germany also lost her colonies. Danzig was to be a free state; and plebiscites would be held in the Saar, Schleswig and East Prussia. Further, the Allies would occupy the Rhineland for at least fifteen years and a belt thirty miles wide on the right bank of the Rhine was to be demilitarized. The humiliation was made complete by a regulation forbidding the Germans to have submarines or military aircraft and limiting her army to 100,000 men.

This new force, the Reichswehr, almost immediately exercised a power far beyond its size. To keep the ranks free from Bolshevik influence, a bureau was organized to investigate subversive political activities among the troops and to infiltrate workers' organizations. Among the recruits selected by Captain Karl Mayr, the officer in charge of this unit, was Hitler. He was particularly qualified for such a task but Mayr picked him because of his "exemplary" war record and, perhaps, out of pity. "When I first met him he was like a tired stray dog looking for a master." Mayr got the impression that Hitler "was ready to throw in his lot with anyone who would show him kindness" and that he was "totally unconcerned about the German people and their destinies."

In truth, Hitler was in a state of ferment and turmoil because of the epidemic of revolution. Never had he been so concerned for the state of his adopted country. Recently he had been handed a racist pamphlet—perhaps one of Eckart's—and it brought to mind similar pamphlets he had read in Vienna. "Involuntarily I saw thus my own development come to life again before my eyes." His simmering hatred of Jews had been activated by what he himself had witnessed on the streets of Munich. Everywhere Jews in power: first Eisner, then anarchists like Toller, and finally Russian Reds like Leviné. In Berlin it had been Rosa Luxemburg; in Budapest Béla Kun, in Moscow Trotsky, Zinoviev and Kamenev. The conspiracy Hitler had previously suspected was turning into reality.

Before embarking on their duties, he and his fellow political agents were ordered to attend a special indoctrination course at the University of Munich with instructors such as Professor Karl Alexander von Müller, a conservative with right radical leanings. "For me," wrote Hitler, "the value of the whole affair was that I now obtained an opportunity of meeting a few like-minded comrades with whom I could thoroughly discuss the situation of the moment. All of us were more or less firmly convinced that Germany could no longer be saved from the impending collapse by the parties of the November crime, the Center and the Social Democracy, and that the so-called 'bourgeois-national' formations, even with the best of intentions, could never repair what had happened."

During the war Hitler had told Westenkirchner that in peacetime he would become either an artist or go into politics and when his comrade asked him which party he preferred the answer was, "None." His circle at the indoctrination course had also come to the conclusion that only an entirely new movement could answer their needs. They decided to call it the

Social Revolutionary Party "because the social views of the new organization did indeed mean a revolution."

Added impetus was given such a movement by one of the lecturers, Gottfried Feder, Professor von Müller's brother-in-law. Founder of the German Fighting League for the Breaking of Interest Slavery, he was an engineer by profession but an economist at heart. He spoke to the political agents about the speculation and economic character of stock exchanges and loan capital. This was a stimulating revelation to Hitler. "Right after listening to Feder's first lecture, the thought ran through my head that I had now found the way to one of the most essential premises for the foundation of a new party." Inspired by Feder's demand to end interest slavery, he restudied Marxism, "and now for the first time really achieved an understanding of the content of the Jew Karl Marx's life effort." At last his *Kapital* was intelligible.

After one of his lectures Professor von Müller noticed a small group in lively discussion. "The men seemed spellbound by one of their number who was haranguing them with increasing vehemence in a strange guttural voice. I had the odd feeling that their excitement was his work. I saw a pale, small face under an unsoldierly flowing lock of hair, with close-cropped mustache, and remarkable large light blue eyes that shone fanatically."

"Do you know you have a natural orator among your students?" Müller told Captain Mayr, indicating the pale-faced soldier. Mayr called out, "You, Hitler, come up here." Hitler approached "awkwardly, with a kind of defiant embarrassment." His talent for oratory led to an assignment in a Munich regiment as a lecturer. "I started out with the greatest enthusiasm and love. For all at once I was offered an opportunity of speaking before a larger audience; and the thing that I had always presumed from pure feeling without knowing it was now corroborated: I could 'speak.'" With each speech Hitler grew more confident and his voice developed to such an extent that his words could be understood in every corner of the squad rooms.

His social life was by no means as successful since many of those to whom he made friendly overtures regarded him as a spy. A small man named Thiele publicly snubbed his advances and, when Hitler insisted on following him down the street and expounding on the true mission of the German artist, suddenly interrupted. "Tell me," said Thiele, "did they shit into your brain and forget to flush it?" According to a witness, "the astonished long-distance speaker made calf's eyes and departed without a word."

Hitler could not even get along with two fellow agents who shared his room at the barracks. They complained to Captain Mayr about his "physical habits." Moreover, he "talked and walked in his sleep and made himself generally a nuisance." He was moved to a private room, a small one on the second floor. Formerly a storeroom, its windows were barred but Hitler "seemed to be happy in his cubicle."

Despite Hitler's social shortcomings, Captain Mayr was impressed enough by his abilities as a speaker to send him on a special mission outside Munich; returning German prisoners of war at the Lechfeld transit camp were evidencing Spartacist leanings, and an Enlightenment Detachment was assigned to transform these men into anti-socialist patriots.

The propaganda team left Munich on July 22 and within five days Hitler himself received an education in practical politics. The returnees were bitter and resentful. Cheated of their youth and hope, forced to live like animals in the trenches, they had come home to chaos and hunger. Hitler offered them targets for their hatred as he spoke eloquently of the "Versailles disgrace," the "November criminals" and the "Jewish-Marxist World Plot." His flair for such work was duly noted in a series of commendatory reports. "Herr Hitler, if I might put it this way," commented one observer, "is the born people's speaker, and by his fanaticism and his crowd appeal he clearly compels the attention of his listeners, and makes them think his way."

He returned to Munich and speeches in the squad room. Another duty was to help investigate the fifty or so radical organizations that had recently sprung up in Munich. These included racists, Communists, rabid nationalists, anarchists, and superpatriots, covering the political spectrum from the Bloc of Revolutionary Students and the Society of Communistic Socialists to the Ostara Bund and the New Fatherland.

Early that autumn Hitler was ordered to attend a meeting of a tiny political group calling itself the German Workers' Party. The evening made so little impression on him that he did not mention it in *Mein Kampf,* even though, according to one of the twenty-three participants present, he addressed the gathering in the discussion period and, indeed, "spoke very well." It is doubtful if he took the trouble to find out that the party had been founded earlier that year by a toolmaker in the Munich railroad works, Anton Drexler. Its program was a bizarre combination of socialism, nationalism and anti-Semitism. Its background was shrouded in mystery, seeded as it was by a small group called the Political Workers' Circle, the brain child of Rudolf Freiherr von Sebottendorff, himself a man of mystery. He was a short, corpulent man with slightly protruding eyes, who was "an artist rather than a pedant, a sybarite rather than a Platonist" and had "a certain predilection for firearms but did not openly exhibit it."

Like Hitler, he believed in the Germanic wave of the future and so threw his considerable energies into the formation of a Bavarian branch of the Teutonic Order. Membership was restricted to Germans who could establish the "purity of their blood" for three generations; and every candidate had to pledge he would join energetically in "the struggle against internationalism and Jewry." The revolutions throughout the country forced Sebottendorff to give his organization the innocent title of Thule Society as a cover. By this time he had decided to implement an idea he had long entertained: to win workers to his *völkisch* cause,* he instructed one of the members of Thule, a down-at-the-heels sports writer, to form a Political Workers' Circle. This man sought out Anton Drexler (he had already organized a small ineffectual group of workers called the Free Labor Committee for a Good Peace) and they joined forces to found a new political organization. The preliminary meeting of the German Workers' Party was held at a little restaurant, the Fürstenfelder Hof, early that January. Some two dozen workers, most of them railwaymen of Drexler's shop, were on hand to hear Drexler outline the dual purpose of the party: to liberate the workers from Marxist internationalism by ending the divisive class warfare and to make the upper classes aware of their responsibility to the workers. All they really wanted, said Drexler, was "to be ruled by Germans." Drexler suggested calling their group the German National Socialist Party (the same name of a similarly motivated party founded a year earlier in Bohemia, whose emblem, incidentally, was the swastika), but there was objection that the word "socialist" might be misinterpreted.

Painstakingly Drexler penned out notes for a program. The skilled worker should not consider himself to be a proletariat but a middle-class citizen. And the middle class itself had to be enlarged and strengthened "at the cost of big capitalism." The program also included a cautiously anti-Semitic declaration that "religious teachings contrary to the moral and ethical laws of Germany should not be supported by the state" or, in fact, even tolerated. Within two weeks a foundation meeting was held in the Thule headquarters. The seedy sports writer, Karl Harrer, was elected chairman with Drexler as his deputy.

It could hardly be called a party since it consisted of little more than a six-man committee. "Our meetings were private because of this Red threat," recalled Drexler, a serious, undistinguished, sickly man. "We

---

* Völkisch is impossible to translate in a single word. Literally meaning "folkish," it had overtones of racism; but to translate it simply as "racist" is to ignore its folk-nationalistic implications. Throughout the book it will remain völkisch.

could do little but discuss and study. I embodied my own ideas in a slight brochure called *My Political Awakening. From the diary of a working-man.*" His dream was to find someone with energy and nerve who could make something out of his pamphlet "and contrive a real driving force behind us. It would need to be an outstanding personality, anyhow, who could even attempt to do such a thing, a man of intense conviction, single-eyed, and absolutely fearless."

On September 12 Hitler was ordered by a Major Hierl to attend another meeting of the little Workers' Party. A "single-eyed" man of conviction if ever there was one, he walked into the Sterneckerbräu, a little beer hall on the Herrenstrasse, early that evening to find forty or so workers. The main speaker was supposed to be the poet Eckart but he was sick and had been replaced by the economist Feder, whose subject was "How and by what means is capitalism to be eliminated?"

Hitler had heard Feder's lecture at his indoctrination course and so could concentrate on the membership. His impression was neither good nor bad. This was apparently another of those groups which "sprang out of the ground, only to vanish silently after a time." Obviously its founders had no conception of how to make their club into a genuine party. The evening was a bore and he was relieved when Feder finished talking. Hitler started to leave at the announcement of a free discussion period, but something "moved" him to remain. A few minutes later he was on his feet belaboring a professor who had just advocated the separation of Bavaria from Prussia. Hitler talked for fifteen minutes so ably and cuttingly that the professor ". . . left the hall like a wet poodle, even before I was finished."

Drexler was so impressed by Hitler's delivery and logic that he whispered to his secretary, "This one has what it takes, we could use him!" He introduced himself but Hitler didn't get the name of the unprepossessing man with glasses. Like a religious fanatic, Drexler pressed a copy of his booklet, a forty-page pamphlet with a pink cover, into Hitler's hand and mumbled that he must read it and please come again.

Hitler returned to his little room on the upper floor of the barracks. As usual he had trouble sleeping and set out crusts of bread and leftovers on the floor for the mice. He had gotten into the habit of passing the hours before dawn "watching the droll little beasts chasing around after these choice morsels. I had known so much poverty in my life that I was well able to imagine the hunger, and hence also the pleasure, of the little creatures."

At about five that morning he was still awake on his cot following the antics of the mice when he remembered the pamphlet that Drexler had forced upon him. Hitler was surprised to find himself enthralled from the first page. "Involuntarily I saw my own development come to life before my eyes." The ideas and phrases of the little book kept intruding into his thoughts the following day. He was struck by the phrases "National Socialism" and "new world order," as well as the prediction that a new political party would capture the disillusioned and disinherited among not only the workers but civil servants and the solid lower middle class.

But his interest waned quickly and he was surprised to receive a postcard informing him that he had been accepted as a member of the German Workers' Party. He was requested to attend a committee meeting the following Wednesday. He had no intention of joining a ready-made party since he wanted to found his own and he was about to send off an indignant refusal when "curiosity won out" and he decided to have another look at the queer little group.

This meeting took place in another run-down restaurant on the Herrenstrasse, the Altes Rosenbad. Hitler walked through a dim, deserted dining room to the back where four people sat around a table. He recognized the too eager author of the pamphlet, who enthusiastically welcomed him as a new member of the Deutsche Arbeiterpartie. ("Now we have an Austrian with a big mouth!" he had told a fellow committeeman.) Drexler explained that they were waiting for the chairman of the national organization, Harrer.

At last the sports writer arrived. He was clubfooted, ungainly and shabby. The minutes of the previous meeting were read and the treasurer reported there were seven marks fifty pfennig on hand. Letters were read and discussed at intolerable length. It was worse than Hitler had imagined. "Terrible, terrible! This was club life of the worst manner and sort. Was I to join this organization?" When they began to discuss new membership, Hitler asked a number of questions about the practical aspects of organization. He learned there was no program, not a leaflet, not even a rubber stamp, only good intentions. He quickly glanced through their few directives. They were unclear or vague.

He left depressed by what he had seen but still undecided whether to join or not. It was the "hardest question" of his life and he debated with himself for the next two days. Reason told him to decline but his feeling argued for acceptance. He had vowed to enter politics and this absurd little club had one transcendent advantage—it had not "frozen into an 'organization,' but left the individual an opportunity for real personal activity." Being so small, it could also be more easily shaped to his needs.

Hitler had already reported his findings to Captain Mayr, who passed them on to a group of high-ranking officers and capitalists who met once a week at the Hotel Four Seasons to discuss means of rebuilding Germany's military power. They had come to the conclusion that this could only be achieved with the support of the workers. The little German Workers' Party could be a start and, according to Mayr, General Ludendorff himself appeared at Mayr's office one day with a request that Hitler be allowed to join the organization and build it up.

It was illegal for members of the new army to join political parties but "to please Ludendorff, whose wishes were still respected in the army, I ordered Hitler to join the Workers' Party and help foster its growth. He was allowed at first the equivalent of twenty gold marks in the current inflation money weekly for this purpose." So, in a sense, Hitler was ordered to do what he had already decided to do. He registered as a member of the DAP and was given a membership card.

Hitler's plunge into practical politics was accompanied by an equally important ideological development which also came to fruition as the result of an order of Captain Mayr. Hitler was instructed to answer a letter from a fellow trainee in the education unit requesting information on the Jewish menace. His lengthy answer, four days after the meeting at the Sterneckerbräu, revealed a surprising progression in his own solution of the Jewish question. It was replete with denunciations of Jews that would become all too familiar: "He burrows into the democracies sucking the good will of the masses, crawls before the majesty of the people but knows only the majesty of money. . . . His activities result in racial tuberculosis of the people." The anti-Semitic program, he concluded, should start with legal attempts to deprive Jews of certain privileges on the grounds that they were a foreign race. "But the final aim must unquestionably be the irrevocable *Entfernung* of the Jews." This word could be translated as "removal" and merely mean expulsion from Germany but it is more likely he meant "amputation," that is, liquidation of Jewry.

This was Hitler's first known political document and for the first time he had succeeded in transforming his hatred of the Jews into a positive political program.

Part 2

IN THE BEGINNING WAS
THE WORD

Chapter Four

BIRTH OF A PARTY
1919–1922

1

"When I entered the circle of these few men, there could be no question of a party or a movement." But what the German Workers' Party did give Hitler that autumn was a platform for his own ideas. Just as the writing room in the Männerheim first released his pent-up hatreds and hopes, so this insignificant group of malcontents gave him needed impetus.

His first task was to turn what was essentially a debating society into a political organization. "Our small committee which in reality consisted of seven heads and represented the entire party was nothing more than the head of a small skat club," recalled an amused Hitler in a serialized newspaper story of those first days. "1919 in Munich was a sad time. Little light, lots of dirt, unrest, poorly dressed people, impoverished soldiers, in short, the picture resulting from four years of war and the scandal of the revolution."

The light at their meeting in the back room of the Rosenbad was a single gas flame that burned poorly. "When we were assembled . . . how did we look? Forbidding. Military pants, dyed coats, hats of undefinable shapes but shiny from wear, our feet in remodeled war boots, and a thick cudgel in our hands as a 'walking stick.'" In those days it was a sign of distinction, a proof that one belonged to the people.

"We were always the same faces. . . . First we received the brotherly greetings, and we were informed that the 'seeds' had been planted in respective places, or even established and we were asked if we could make such a report also, and the necessity was stressed to act as a unit." The treasury was usually about five marks and once it reached the high point of seventeen.

Hitler finally persuaded the committee to increase membership by holding larger meetings. At the barracks he personally typed out on the company typewriter some of the invitations to the first public meeting, others he wrote by hand. On the night of the first meeting the committee of seven waited "for the masses who were expected to appear." An hour passed but no one came. "We were again seven men, the old seven." Hitler changed his tactics. The next invitations were mimeographed and this time a few came. The number rose slowly from eleven to thirteen and finally to thirty-four.

The pittance collected from these meetings was invested in an advertisement in the *Münchener Beobachter*, a völkisch, anti-Semitic newspaper, for a mass meeting in the cellar room of the Hofbräuhaus on October 16.

If only the usual number turned up, the expenses would bankrupt the party. Hitler had insisted in the face of Harrer's pessimism that a crowd would come and by 7 P.M. seventy people had collected in the smoky room. There is no record of the reception given the main speaker but almost from the moment Adolf Hitler stepped behind the crude lectern placed atop the head table the audience was "electrified." He was supposed to speak for twenty minutes but went on for half an hour, spilling out a stream of denunciations, threats and promises. Abandoning all restraint, he let emotion take over and by the time he sat down to loud applause sweat covered his face. He was exhausted but elated "and what before I had simply felt deep down in my heart, without being able to put it to the test, proved to be true; I could speak!"

It was a turning point not only in his career but in that of the German Workers' Party. Three hundred marks had been donated by the enthusiastic listeners, now the organization had funds to advertise more extensively and print slogans and leaflets. On November 13 a second mass meeting was held, this time in another beer hall, the Eberlbräu. More than 130 men (mostly students, shopkeepers and army officers) paid an admission fee of fifty pfennigs, something new in local politics, to hear four speakers. The main attraction was Hitler. In the middle of his speech hecklers began to shout out but he had alerted his military friends and within minutes the agitators "flew down the stairs with gashed heads."

The interruption only spurred Hitler to greater rhetorical heights as he closed with an exhortation to stand up and resist. "The misery of Germany must be broken by Germany's steel. That time must come."

Once more he carried the audience with him. He spoke with a primitive force and unabashed emotion that set him apart from the intellectuals who appealed to reason. A police observer, after describing Hitler as a merchant, reported that he had "held forth in an outstanding manner" and was destined to become "a professional propaganda speaker." His appeals were visceral—love of country and hatred of Jews for bringing about the defeat of 1918. By his manner and use of the language of the streets and the trenches, war veterans recognized that he had shared the democracy of the machine gun, barbed wire and muck and thus represented the sacred comradeship of the front lines.

In two weeks another enthusiastic meeting was held with an audience of more than 170, and on December 10 a larger hall, the Deutsches Reich, was used. When the attendance fell off despite an announcement (which spelled Hitler with two *t*'s) that the place was heated, several committee members protested that the meetings were too frequent. There was violent debate in which Hitler argued that a city of 700,000 inhabitants could stand not one meeting every two weeks but ten every week. The road they had taken, he said, was the right one; sooner or later success was bound to come. His persistence was rewarded. The new hall on the Dachaustrasse was near an army barracks and the influx of soldiers raised the attendance to over two hundred.

Hitler's ascendancy deeply concerned some of the other members, who objected to his volcanic, mercurial style. Moreover, he was changing the entire face of the organization with the influx of his rough-mannered army friends, and they feared it would all end in ruin. While Drexler was equally distressed, he was so convinced that Hitler was the hope of the party that he supported the move to make him the new chief of propaganda. Promotion only made Hitler more critical of the inefficiency of the party's business procedures. How could one administer properly without an office and equipment? On his own he found an office at the Sterneckerbräu, scene of his introduction to the party. It was small and had once been a taproom. The rent was so little, fifty marks a month, that the committee didn't even complain when the landlord removed the wood paneling and left the room looking more like "a funeral vault than an office." Using funds he got from Captain Mayr as well as those from the party treasury, he had an electric light installed along with a telephone, a table, a few borrowed chairs, an open bookcase and two cupboards. Hitler's next step was to insist on a paid business manager who would work full time. He found one in his barracks, a sergeant "upright and absolutely honest," who also brought along his small Adler typewriter.

That December Hitler called for a complete reform of the party's organization from a debating society to a genuine political party. A majority of committee members, content to remain just another extreme rightist group, opposed these changes. They could not see, as Hitler clearly did, that propaganda was not an end in itself, only a means to overthrow the Weimar Republic. Once again the plodding Drexler supported Hitler and the two spent hours in the Drexler apartment discussing plans and programs. Their chief bond was a common distrust and hatred of Jewry. Having lost several jobs, so he said, because of Jews and trade unionists, Drexler had become "a radical anti-Semite and anti-Marxist." He lived in the pleasant Nymphenburg district and Hitler would travel there by trolley car. They would become so involved in work that Frau Drexler usually had to call them to supper several times. "My little girl used to climb on Hitler's knee," remembered Drexler, "she knew she was always welcome." He was Uncle Adolf to her.

One evening in the last days of 1919 Hitler arrived at the Drexlers' "armed with a sheaf of manuscript" on which he had roughly sketched out the official party program. They worked for hours "boiling it down" to make it as pithy as possible. "We cracked our brains over it, I can tell you!" recalled Drexler. By the time they finished it was morning. Then Hitler sprang up and banged his fist on the table. "These points of ours," he exclaimed, "are going to rival Luther's placard on the doors of Wittenberg!"

There were twenty-five points to the program and Hitler wanted to present them to the public at a mass meeting. Predictably there were objections from the committee, not only to a number of the points but to an open meeting. At first dubious, Drexler was finally carried away by the idea and at the next meeting gave Hitler his full support. Those who objected were overruled and a date was set: February 24, 1920.

Leaflets and posters printed in bright red were plastered all over Munich but by this time Hitler himself began to fear he might be speaking to "a yawning hall." The meeting was to start at 7:30 P.M. and when Hitler entered the great Festsaal of the Hofbräuhaus at seven-fifteen he found it jammed with almost 2000 people. His heart "burst with joy." What particularly pleased him was that more than half the crowd appeared to be Communists or Independent Socialists. He was confident that the true idealists among this hostile group would swing over to his side and he welcomed any disturbance they might provoke.

The meeting opened quietly with the main address by an experienced

völkisch speaker named Dingfelder. He attacked Jews but did so obliquely.
He quoted Shakespeare and Schiller and was so bland that even the Communists weren't offended by anything he had to say. Then Hitler got to
his feet. There were no catcalls. He looked anything but an orator in his
worn, old-fashioned blue suit. He opened quietly, without emphasis,
outlining the history of the past ten years. But as he told of the postwar
revolutions that swept through Germany, passion crept into his voice; he
began to gesture, his eyes flashed. Angry shouts came from all parts of the
large hall. Beer mugs flew though the air. Hitler's army supporters—"swift
as greyhounds, tough as leather, and hard as Krupp steel"—eagerly went
into battle armed with rubber truncheons and riding whips. Trouble-
makers were hustled outside. At last some degree of order was restored and
Hitler resumed speaking, undismayed by the continuing chorus of derisive
shouts. His experiences at the Männerheim had accustomed him to such
disturbances and he seemed to draw energy from them. The audience
warmed to his spirit as well as his words and applause began to drown out
the heckling.

He spoke scathingly of the tons of paper money being printed and
how the corrupt Social Democrat government only prosecuted petty
hoarders. "What can such a hoarder do if his name is Hummelberger and
not Isidor Bach?" This anti-Semitic jibe was followed by as much protest
as approval but once he directed his attack at the Jews from the East applause drowned out the hecklers. There were shouts of "Down with the
Jewish press!"

Unaccustomed to speaking to such a large audience, his voice would
be loud one moment, weak the next. But even his inexperience was appealing. A twenty-year-old law student named Hans Frank was struck by
his obvious sincerity. "The first thing you felt was that there was a man
who spoke honestly about how he felt and was not trying to put something across of which he himself was not absolutely convinced." After the
polished phrases of the first speaker his words had an explosive effect.
They were often crude, always expressive. And even those who had come
to hoot him were compelled to listen. He spoke simply and so clearly that
those at the farthest tables could hear. What particularly impressed young
Frank was that he "made things understandable even to the foggiest brain
. . . and went to the core of things."

Finally he submitted to the audience the twenty-five theses of the
program, asking them to "pronounce judgment" on them point by point.
There was something for almost everyone but Jews. For the patriotic,
union of all Germans in a Greater Reich; colonies for excess population;
equality for Germany among nations; revocation of the Versailles Treaty;

creation of a people's army; and a "ruthless battle" against criminals to ensure law and order. For the workers, abolition of all income unearned by
work; confiscation of war profits; expropriation of land without compen-
sation for communal purposes; and profit sharing in large industrial enter-
prises. For the middle class, the immediate socialization of the great department stores and their lease, at low rates, to small tradesmen;
"generous development" of old-age national health standards. For the
völkisch-minded, the demand that Jews be treated as aliens, denied the
right to hold any public office, deported if the state found it impossible to
feed its entire population, and expelled immediately if they had emigrated
after August 2, 1914.

After each point Hitler would pause to ask if everyone understood
and agreed. The majority shouted out raucous approval but there were organized cries of derision and some protesters jumped up on chairs and
tables. Again and again the truncheon and whip brigade went into action
and by the end of Hitler's two-and-a-half-hour tirade there was almost
unanimous support for every word he uttered. The final applause was tumultuous and young Frank was fully convinced that "if anyone could
master the fate of Germany, Hitler was that man."

To Hitler the evening, including its riotous objections, had been an
unalloyed triumph, and as the crowd filed out he felt that the door to his
future had at last opened. "When I closed the meeting, I was not alone in
thinking that now a wolf had been born, destined to burst in upon the
herd of seducers of the people." He was living up to his own name, for
Adolf was derived from the Teutonic word meaning "fortunate wolf."
And from that day on "wolf" would have a special meaning for him—as
nickname among close friends; as a pseudonym for himself and his sister
Paula; and as a name for most of his military headquarters.

There was little notice of Hitler's emergence in the Munich newspapers, but the meeting meant the first major step forward for the German Workers' Party. A hundred new members were enrolled. At Hitler's
insistence a list of members had already been drawn up and proper membership cards issued. To give the impression of size the first card was numbered 501, with the members listed in alphabetical order. Hitler, painter,
was number 555.

2

He began a new life, mixing with an enlarged circle of colorful characters whose common denominator was a love of things German and a
fear of Marxism. There was a Munich physician, a believer in the sidereal

pendulum, who claimed this gave him the power to detect the presence of a Jew in any group of people. Of far more importance was a former company commander, Captain Ernst Röhm, a homosexual. Röhm was an exemplary officer, a comrade to be trusted in peril. He was short and stocky with closely cropped hair and an engaging smile. He was a walking monument to the war; the upper part of his nose had been shot away and a bullet had left a deep scar in one cheek. An officer in the new Reichswehr, he once remarked, "Since I am a wicked and immature man, war and unrest appeal to me more than the orderly life of your respectable burgher." From the moment the two met at a secret meeting of a nationalist group called the Iron Fist, Röhm was convinced that the dedicated corporal was just the man to head the German Workers' Party. Röhm had already changed the working-class character of the Drexler-Harrer organization by bringing in so many soldiers. They were the ones who kept order at rowdy meetings. Between Hitler and Röhm were bonds of blood and suffering since both belonged to the brotherhood of the front-line fighter, and though Röhm had recently replaced Captain Mayr as Hitler's commander he insisted that his subordinate use the familiar *du*, a familiarity which was leading to Hitler's acceptance by other officers.

An even closer acquaintance was the writer Dietrich Eckart, who had once remarked that the new breed of political leader must be able to stand the noise of a machine gun. "I prefer a vain monkey who is able to give the Reds a salty reply, and doesn't run away when people begin swinging table legs, to a dozen learned professors." Moreover their man had to be a bachelor. "Then we'll get the women!" They had become friends, not merely political acquaintances, despite differences in age (twenty-one years) and background (Eckart was a university man of culture). Both were bohemians, both could speak the language of the gutter, both were nationalists and hated Jews. Eckart believed Jews who married German women should be jailed for three years and, if they repeated the crime, executed.

Eckart, a born romantic revolutionary, was a master of coffeehouse polemics. A sentimental cynic, a sincere charlatan, constantly on stage, lecturing brilliantly if given the slightest opportunity be it at his own apartment, on the street or in a café. A drug addict and drunkard, his vulgarity was tempered by vestiges of his social background. Hitler reveled in the company of this warm and voluble intellectual buccaneer who was playing Falstaff to Hitler's Prince Hal in Munich's ribald night world. Eckart became the younger man's mentor. He gave Hitler a trench coat, corrected his grammar, took him to better-class restaurants and cafés and introduced him to influential citizens ("This is the man who will one day liberate Germany"). The two spent hours discussing music, art and literature as well as politics and the association with the tempestuous writer left a lasting mark on Hitler.

Several weeks after the Hofbräuhaus meeting the two men set off together on an adventure in Berlin. Elite Free Corps troops under General Walther von Lüttwitz, ordered to disband by the socialist Weimar government, had instead marched on the capital where they seized control of the city and installed their own Chancellor, a minor civil servant named Kapp. Both Hitler and Eckart saw the potentialities of the right-wing Kapp Putsch and volunteered to go to Berlin and determine whether there was any possibility for joint revolutionary action in Bavaria. Captain Röhm approved the project and they were sent off in an open sports plane. It was Hitler's first flight and the pilot—a young war ace, Lieutenant Robert Ritter von Greim, winner of the Pour le Mérite—would become the last Luftwaffe commander. The weather was so turbulent that despite Greim's skill Hitler kept vomiting. For a time it appeared as if the mission was aborted since the airport at their interim stop was occupied by striking workers, but Hitler snapped on a fake goatee and Eckart posed as a paper dealer, and the party was permitted to proceed to Berlin. When they touched down at Berlin the wan Hitler vowed that he would never, never fly again.

Although Berlin had surrendered to the Free Corps on March 13 without a shot being fired, theirs was a hollow victory. No one of stature would accept a position in "Chancellor" Kapp's cabinet. From the beginning his hastily planned Putsch was a fiasco and what brought it down was not a counterattack or acts of sabotage. Berliners, joining the rest of the nation in a wave of anti-militarist feeling, had apparently concluded that another revolution was too much, and when a general strike was called by the Ebert government the workers responded so wholeheartedly that it was impossible for the Kapp regime to function. Electricity was shut off; trolley cars and subways stopped. There was no water; garbage rotted in the streets; shops and offices were closed.

Only Berlin's night life went on unimpeded, in darkness or candlelight. It was corruption out of an overdone movie with heavily rouged girl prostitutes of eleven competing with whip-toting Amazons in high lacquered boots. There were cafés for every taste and perversion— homosexuals, lesbians, exhibitionists, sadists, masochists. Nudity had become boring and art itself was plumbing the nadir of obscenity, disillusionment and cynicism. Berlin was the center of the Dadaist movement

Birth certificate of Adolphus Hitler.
HOFFMANN

Baby Adolf. BUNDESARCHIV

Hitler's mother. LIBRARY OF CONGRESS

Hitler's father. LIBRARY OF CONGRESS

Alois Hitler with son Aloïs, Jr. HANS HITLER

Angela, Hitler's half sister, and Alois, his half brother, with Granny. HANS HITLER

Angela (Hitler) Raubal and son Leo.
HANS HITLER

Top picture, choir school at Lambach monastery about 1899, Hitler top row, second from right. HARRY SCHULZE-WILDE

Above, Hitler, the leader of his class in a village school. Leonding, 1900. HARRY SCHULZE-WILDE

Right, Hitler, the failure in a city school. Linz, 1901. LIBRARY OF CONGRESS

Paula, Hitler's younger sister, studying family album about 1950. HANS HITLER

Alois Hitler, Jr., about 1950. HANS HITLER

Hitler's best boyhood friend, August Kubizek. HARRY SCHULZE-WILDE

Kubizek about 1960. His doctor is on the right. HARRY SCHULZE-WILDE

Above, Hitler at sixteen as sketched by F. Sturmberger, a schoolmate from Steyr who presently resides in Linz. LIBRARY OF CONGRESS

Below, Dr. Bloch, who treated Hitler's mother for cancer, in his office at Linz. This picture was taken in 1938 by order of Bormann for the Führer's "personal film cassette." The inscription read: "The Führer often sat on the chair beside the desk." BUNDESARCHIV

Water color of old Vienna by Hitler in 1911–12.
U.S. ARMY

Auersberg Palace, Vienna, 1911–12. Architecturally accurate but the figures are far out of proportion. BUNDESARCHIV

Ruins of Becelaere, Belgium. 1917. U. S. ARMY

Above, Hitler, extreme left, in trenches. HOFFMANN

Below, l. to r., two World War I comrades— Ernst Schmidt and Sergeant Max Amann—with Hitler and his dog Fuchsl. HARRY SCHULZE-WILDE

Above, Hitler decorated
with the Iron Cross.

Below, Dr. Edmund Forster, the first
psychiatrist to treat Hitler,
October–November 1918.

and one of its poets, Walter Mehring, was giving Berliners a frightening look into the future in the form of a slangy, satirical verse:

> *C'mon, boys, let's all go*
> *Off to the pogrom with a ho-ho-ho.*
> *Pull in your bellies and throw out the Jews.*
> *With swastika and poison gas*
> *Let's have a go at murder in the mass.*

The general strike of the Ebert government turned into a Franken-stein monster. By crushing the Kapp forces so successfully, it opened the way for another wave of leftist revolt. The Communists stirred up disor-ders throughout Germany to such a degree that President Ebert was forced to beg General von Seeckt, who had walked out on the government a few days earlier, to accept command of all military forces and crush the Red revolt. His first act was to recommission all the Free Corps troops which had just been disbanded. In a wry turn of events, the mutineers of yesterday were called on to enforce law and order today, and in a stroke of black comedy worthy of a Dadaist playwright Ebert paid the Free Corps troops the bonus that the Kapp regime had promised them to overthrow his government.

The task facing the reorganized Free Corps was formidable. In Sax-ony a Soviet republic had already seized power and by March 20 a Red Army of 50,000 workers had already occupied most of the Ruhr. That same day the Communist *Ruhr Echo* announced that the red flag must wave victoriously over the entire nation. "Germany must become a Re-public of Soviets and, in union with Russia, the springboard for the com-ing victory of the World Revolution and World Socialism."

On April 3 the Free Corps troops swept through the Ruhr, wiping out Red strongholds and dealing ruthlessly with any survivors. "If I were to tell you everything," a youthful volunteer of one Free Corps unit wrote his family, "you would say I was lying to you. No pardon is given. . . . We even shot 10 Red Cross nurses on sight because they were carrying pis-tols. We shot these little ladies with pleasure—how they cried and pleaded with us to save their lives. Nothing doing! Anybody with a gun is our enemy."

By the time Hitler and Eckart arrived in Berlin after their sickening plane ride from Munich, the Kapp Putsch was nearing its end. From the airport they proceeded to the Reich Chancellery where they talked with Kapp's press representative, Trebitsch-Lincoln, a Hungarian Jew. An ad-venturer and something of a rascal—he was arrested in New York as a spy for the Kaiser—he informed them that Kapp had already fled and they had better stay under cover lest they be arrested. Eckart, unhappy at finding a Jew in charge, reputedly seized Hitler's arm and said, "Come on, Adolf, we have no further business here."

But the two stayed on in the capital to meet their hero, General Ludendorff, who was preparing to flee south in disguise, and to confer with a number of North Germans who shared their dreams: members of the Stahlhelm (Steel Helmet), a supernationalist group of veterans; and with leaders of völkisch organizations who were getting substantial financial backing from industrialists. Eckart also introduced his pupil to the salon of Helene Bechstein, wife of the piano manufacturer. She was instantly enthralled by "Germany's young Messiah" and promised to present him to others in her influential circle.

Hitler returned to Munich on March 31. That same day he became a private citizen, perhaps of his own accord, more likely because he was ordered to do so. He packed his belongings, received his demobilization pay of fifty marks along with a coat, cap, jacket, pants, a suit of underwear, a shirt, socks and shoes. He sublet a small back room at Thierschstrasse 41, a middle-class district near the Isar River dominated by three- and four-story buildings with shops and offices on the ground floor and small apartments and rooms above. Hitler's was a tiny cell, eight by fifteen feet, not much bigger than his cubicle at the Männerheim. It was the coldest room in the house and, according to the landlord, Herr Erlanger, "Some lodgers who've rented it since got ill. Now we only use it as a storeroom; nobody will have it any more."

It was no accident that Hitler had chosen a room a few doors from the offices of the *Münchener Beobachter*. It had a new name, the *Völkischer Beobachter*; and continued to be the mouthpiece for anti-Semitic and anti-Marxist sentiments. Hitler's opinion of Jews was largely reflected in this newspaper. Recently, for instance, a story on page one had carried this headline: "Do a Real Job on the Jews!" The author recommended that Germany be cleared of all Jews, no matter how ruthless the measures. From such articles, most of them written by refugees from Russia, Hitler absorbed new information concerning the rising peril of Communism.

His own chief targets were Jews and the peace treaties. Next on his list was the fight against Marxism; both he and Eckart had a grudging admiration for the dedication of German Communists and did their best to win them over. In an article entitled "German and Jewish Bolshevism" Eckart had even recommended what he called "German Bolshevism." And once, with Hitler on the platform beside him, he told a party meet-

ing that the German Communists were idealistic men unconsciously working for Germany's salvation.

The Russian exiles resisted such a compromise and their articles and
conversations on the peril of Bolshevism were having an increasing effect
on Hitler. The most persuasive of these apostles of doom from the East
was Alfred Rosenberg, the young architect-artist from Estonia. At their
first meeting, neither was much impressed by the other. "I would be lying
if I said I was overwhelmed by him," recalled Rosenberg. It was only
when he heard Hitler speak in public that he became enthralled. "Here I
saw a German front-line soldier embarking on this struggle in a manner as
clear as it was convincing, counting on himself alone with the courage of a
free man. That was what drew me to Adolf Hitler after the first fifteen
minutes."

The attraction and admiration became mutual in the next few
months with the appearance of Rosenberg's articles in Eckart's weekly
paper and other nationalist-racist publications. What particularly impressed Hitler was Rosenberg's revelations that Bolshevism was but the
first step in a vast global Jewish plot to conquer the world. Final "proof"
of this was revealed the day after the historic Hofbräuhaus meeting with
publication in the *Völkischer Beobachter* of "the Protocols of the Elders of
Zion." This purported to be the verbatim report of twenty-four secret sessions of the Elders of Zion in Basel, Switzerland, in a conspiracy to conquer the world.* This book was supporting evidence of Hitler's own prejudice and fears. It was also a turning point in his relations with Rosenberg.
Hitler began taking his warnings of Bolshevism to heart; and the
Communist issue, till now subsidiary, gradually took on more import in
the party credo.

Hitler was not alone in acceptance of the "Protocols." That May a
long article appeared in the London *Times* asserting that it should be
taken seriously and seemed to be a bona fide document written by Jews
for Jews. The "Protocols"—spreading throughout Europe and into the
Americas—spurred a virulent anti-Semitism which had been inaugurated
by the advocates of Christianity. For centuries Catholics had been instructed that the Jews had killed Christ and the first Protestant, Martin
Luther, had charged that the Jew had not only transformed God into the

---

* The "Protocols" was written in France, a hotbed of anti-Semitism, by agents of the
Czar and published a few years later in Russia, at the end of the nineteenth century; its
first publication in Germany had come a year after the armistice in a Russian émigré
magazine but had caused little stir. An amateurish forgery, it had been accepted as gospel by both Wilhelm II and Nicholas II. A copy was found, along with the Bible and
War and Peace, in the Czar's house in Ekaterinburg, after the murder of the imperial
family.

devil but was "a plague, pestilence, pure misfortune"—a blight on Christianity and the world which had to be dealt with peremptorily.

Hitler's hatred of Jews had come primarily from his own observation in the last days of the war and during the revolutions that followed.* What he learned from Rosenberg, the Thule Society, or from Gobineau, Luther and other famous anti-Semites merely buttressed his own conclusions. He borrowed only what he wanted from such sources. He probably had been much more influenced by pamphlets and freakish right-wing newspapers that breathed venomous anti-Semitism. Since his early days in Vienna he had devoured such gutter literature and its seed came to fruition on Friday the thirteenth of August 1920, at a mass meeting in Munich's famous Hofbräuhaus.

For two hours he expounded on the subject of "Why We Are Against the Jews," and from the beginning made it clear that his party alone "will free you from the power of the Jew!" In great detail he told how the Jews had polluted society since medieval days. While distinguished by neither originality nor rhetoric, his speech was a marvel of propaganda. Although his own anti-Semitism was personal rather than historical, Hitler demonstrated a genius for amalgamating facts with events of the day in a manner calculated to inspire resentment and hate. He was often interrupted by shouts of approval and laughter. Eighteen times the audience burst into loud applause and the reaction was particularly boisterous when he referred to the Jew as a nomad involved in "highway robbery."

His earlier attacks on Jews had been low key in comparison to this carefully prepared denunciation. For the first time in public he charged that the Jewish conspiracy was international and that their advocacy of equality of all peoples and international solidarity was only a scheme to denationalize other races. Previously he had called the Jew despicable, immoral and parasitic; tonight the Jew was a destroyer, a robber, a pest with the power to "undermine entire nations." Hitler called for an all-out struggle to the death. There was no difference between the East and West Jews, the good or bad ones, the rich or poor ones, it was a battle against the entire Jewish race. The slogan "Proletarians of the world, unite" no longer applied. "The battle cry must be 'Anti-Semites of the world, unite.' People of Europe, free yourselves!" Hitler demanded, in short, a "thorough" solution which he vaguely but ominously described as "the removal of Jews from the midst of our people." He had taken a long step forward

* It was ironic that Erlanger, the landlord of the house where Hitler presently resided, was a Jew who had only pleasant memories: "I often encountered him on the stairway and at the door—he was generally scribbling something in a notebook. . . . He never made me feel that he regarded me differently from other people."

on the road of anti-Semitism. Earlier in the year the *Münchener Post* had been amused by his comic impersonations of Jews. "Adolf Hitler behaved like a comedian, and his speech was like a vaudeville turn." But this present speech brought a more sober recognition from the same newspaper of his platform magic. "One thing Hitler has, you must give him credit, he is the most cunning rabble rouser in Munich practising such mischief."

Yet he was far more than a mischief maker whose appeal was merely to racists. His call for active anti-Semitism was also being heeded by those whose ultimate dream was a greater Reich—respectable, middle-class, middle-aged burghers who had subscribed to the words of Heinrich Class, president of the Pan-German League, back in 1913. "The Jewish race is the source of all dangers. The Jew and the German are like fire and water." In time, preached Class, a man would arise to lead them in this fight against Jewry. "We await the Führer! Patience, patience, he will come. Persevere, work and unite!"

Scribbled outlines of other speeches delivered by Hitler during this period indicate the depth of his obsession: "The bloody Jew. Butchering of spiritual leadership of people The Russian funeral parlor." "The Jew as dictator and today's Germany? Battle between democracy and Dictatorship—No. Between Jew and Germanic. Who understands this?" "Hunger in peace (inflation) through stock market and speculation? Need for luxuries etc. who profits? The Jews . . . Genocide Preparation for this mass insanity—can be proven through mass need—hunger—Hunger as a weapon at all times. Hunger to serve the Jews." "The world revolution means subjugation of the entire world under the dictatorship of the world exchange and its Masters, Judai."

As can be seen from these excerpts, Hitler's obsessive hatred was developing into an encompassing political philosophy. At the same time his hitherto obscure concept of foreign policy was taking shape. By September of that year he had reached the point where he told one audience, "We are tied and gagged. But even though we are defenseless, we do not fear a war with France." In addition he was considering the possibility of a foreign ally and recently had declared, "For us the enemy sits on the other side of the Rhine, not in Italy or elsewhere." Also for the first time— perhaps inspired by Rosenberg and the "Protocols"—Hitler publicly assailed the Jews for their internationalism. His equation of Jews and internationalism and his selection of Italy as an ally against France were still tentative concepts but did indicate his striving for a logical and practical foreign policy. He had come out of the war with the conventional beliefs and prejudices of the front-line soldier, and emerged from the traumatic series of Red revolutions with many of the conventional beliefs and prejudices of the man in the street. At last he was putting his own system in order. But his primary goal, hatred of Jews, which had been surfacing and submerging erratically since the days of struggle in Vienna, was not at all conventional.

Adolf Hitler was advancing faster in the field of practical politics. Almost singlehandedly he had broadened the base of the party which now bore the name of *Nationalsozialistische Deutsche Arbeiterpartei* (NSDAP)—the National Socialist German Workers' Party. It was a name he hoped would inspire and incite, that would scare off the timid and attract those willing to bleed for their dreams.

In this same spirit, Hitler insisted upon a party flag that could compete with the flaming red Communist banner. "We wanted something red enough to out-Herod Herod," recalled Drexler, something to outdo the Reds but "quite different." Finally a dentist from Starnberg submitted a flag which had been used at the founding meeting of his own party local: a swastika against a black-white-red background. The swastika—originally a Sanskrit word meaning "all is all"—long a symbol of the Teutonic Knights, had been used by Lanz von Liebenfels, the Thule Society and a number of Free Corps units. For centuries it had represented not only for Europeans but also for certain North American Indian tribes the wheel of the sun or the cycle of life. From now on, and perhaps forevermore, the swastika would have a sinister connotation.

3

The Kapp Putsch and the annihilation of Communist regimes in central Germany had left the cause of socialism in disarray. Ebert and his Majority Socialists had widened the breach between themselves and the left-wing Independent Socialists by the opportunistic use of Free Corps units against the workers of the Ruhr. In early autumn of 1920 the dissidents—who themselves were divided almost equally between pro-Communists and anti-Communists—met for five days in Halle to determine the future course of the Independent Socialist Party and its relationship to the Third International. The most inspiring speaker at the congress—Grigori Zinoviev, president of the Third International—came from Moscow. The Soviets had sent him to swing the almost 900,000 German socialists to the far left. He spoke for hours "in a somewhat broken German which only heightened the effect of his talk." It was received tumultuously by the pro-Communists.

Bitter debates between right and left ensued and some observers felt the former had the better argument, but the idea of world revolution was too exhilarating to resist. Two hundred and thirty-seven voted to join the Third International under the conditions laid down by Lenin. A hundred and fifty-six voted no—and then walked out of the hall in a body. But of those who remained most became Communists.

One delegate who left Halle alarmed as well as disillusioned was Otto Strasser. He had listened to Zinoviev with mounting annoyance and concern. What he said "sounded like a new Messiah-doctrine" with Moscow dominating Germany. Strasser and an elder brother, Gregor, had long followed the socialist dream. Both were prepared to face drastic reforms but not those directed by a foreign power. What they sought was a German-oriented socialism and Otto had thought he would find it among the revolutionary Independent Socialists.

After Halle he was a man without a party. Disgusted, he journeyed to Landshut to consult his brother, who had organized a Free Corps-type private army of his own with infantry and artillery batteries and a machine-gun company. Gregor admitted that nothing was more dangerous than the Russians and that there wasn't a single political party that could successfully oppose them. "Nothing can be done with talking," he said, "only action." Two important guests, he said, were coming to discuss the problem.

The next morning, according to Otto Strasser's account, a large car drew up in front of his brother's chemist shop. Two men stepped out. Otto recognized the first: General Ludendorff, a hero to all nationalists. Behind at a respectful distance, "like a battalion orderly," was a pale-faced young man with a stubby mustache, clad in an ill-fitting blue suit. It was Hitler. "We must unite all nationalist groups," announced the general. The political training was up to Herr Hitler. Ludendorff himself would take over the military leadership of these nationalist organizations. He asked Gregor to subordinate himself and his storm battalions "under my military leadership and also to join Herr Hitler's party."

Otto was not at all impressed with Hitler although he promised to make Gregor the first national *Gauleiter* (party district leader) and give him the *Gau* of Lower Bavaria. The younger Strasser interrupted. What, he asked, was the NSDAP program? "The program isn't the question," said Hitler. The only question was power. Otto objected. Power was only the means of accomplishing the program. "These are the opinions of the intellectuals," said Hitler curtly. "We need power!" It was obvious he did not like Otto and a moment later he accused him of fighting with the Reds against the Kapp regime.

Otto retorted with his own accusation. How could someone calling himself a National Socialist support a reactionary like Kapp? He explained that he had fought as a socialist in Berlin just as he had earlier marched in

Munich against the Soviet regime. Each course seemed to be the right one; *he* was truly a National Socialist.

Ludendorff interrupted. "The politics of the nationalist opposition can't be communistic," he said, "but it also can't be capitalistic." When he was quartermaster general he had fewer problems with workers than with capitalists. This surprising statement cleared the air and the meeting ended amicably but without a definite decision from the elder Strasser. He wanted to think over the proposition. That evening Gregor told his brother that he had made up his mind to join forces with Ludendorff and Hitler, even though he also had not been too impressed with the latter. "The general will use him at the right place," he said. "I trust Ludendorff in this regard."

Hitler's refusal to reveal his political program to Otto Strasser was not because he had none or could not express it but probably because he was too stubborn to discuss it with a "traitor" who had fought against the Kapp forces. Moreover, Hitler had come to win over Gregor and his battalions and he had the definite feeling at parting that both would eventually be in his camp. Gregor Strasser was his kind of man: a front-line junior officer who, like himself, had won the Iron Cross, 1st Class; he was obviously a man of conviction: an ardent nationalist, opposed to both Marxism and capitalism, who recognized that the Jews were "the backbone and the brains" of both.

The winning of Gregor Strasser was but one of Hitler's accomplishments since he had joined the little German Workers' Party. In less than a year he had not only transformed the character of the organization but raised its membership to almost three thousand. All his time was devoted to the NSDAP and he had traveled widely, making himself and the party fairly well known. He had been the main speaker at some eighty mass meetings, traveled to Berlin with Eckart during the Kapp Putsch and addressed an international congress of National Socialists at Salzburg.

Success on the platform had not turned Hitler's head. In fact he would pace up and down in his little room complaining to his personal bodyguard, Ulrich Graf, a former butcher, of his inability to "go out there and tell the people what he knew, and what he wanted to do. 'If I could only speak! If I could only speak!' he used to shout." Dissatisfied not only with his delivery but with the conduct of the mass meetings, he determinedly set about improving both. He attended rival rallies and invariably found that the main speaker delivered his address "in the style of a witty newspaper article or of a scientific treatise, avoided all strong words, and here and there threw in some feeble professional joke." Such tedious meetings taught him what not to do. He made his own lively and rousing. The atmosphere was down-to-earth and genial with free beer, sausages and pretzels, and even, when party funds permitted, concertina music and folk singing. Then at the psychological moment Hitler himself would make a dramatic appearance with band playing and swastika banners flying. Usually he began quietly. Then, feeling out each audience as an actor would, he adapted his manner and speech to its needs, finally rousing it to a pitch of almost uncontrollable enthusiasm.

The success of the mass meetings did not satisfy Hitler. He wanted a wider forum and for that he needed his own newspaper. The *Völkischer Beobachter* was on the brink of bankruptcy because of numerous libel actions. This was the paper Hitler wanted. A financial crisis was the opportunity he had been waiting for. At 2 A.M. on the morning of December 17 Hitler burst into Eckart's apartment excitedly announcing that the *Beobachter* had to be sold because of debts and was "in danger" of falling into the wrong hands. A separatist leader intended buying it as a platform for his program. The party must get it instead. The asking price was reasonable—only 180,000 marks; and Hitler was positive Eckart could raise this from wealthy friends.

At eight the next morning Drexler was at Eckart's door. It was an unspeakable hour for a man of the latter's habits and "at first," recalled Drexler, "he was bad-tempered. Then we started off." By noon they had collected 60,000 marks from General von Epp whose Free Corps unit helped overthrow Munich's soviet government in 1919, and 30,000 more from other contributors including an anti-Semitic doctor. Drexler himself signed a note for the paper's debts of more than 100,000 marks and at four that afternoon the purchase of the *Beobachter* was properly registered. Now Hitler and the NSDAP—thanks primarily to an eccentric author and a toolmaker—were prepared for the next leap forward.

4

A month later, on January 22, 1921, the first national congress of the NSDAP was held in Munich. In little more than a year the party had become a respected force in Bavarian right-wing politics largely because of Hitler's magnetic personality and obsessive drive. His abilities as an orator, moreover, had turned the original organization from discussion to action. Most of the founders, including Drexler, viewed this transformation with growing concern. While they appreciated the vitality Hitler brought to their lethargic group, they were beginning to wonder if it was worth it. In a remarkably short period of time Hitler had become the dominant force, backed by his fervently faithful entourage. These followers—Röhm, the Strassers, Rosenberg—brought with them the undeniable aura of violence. Many of Hitler's private friends and associates were just as repugnant to the old guard, who felt he had too many bohemian comrades. And what genuine socialist would have intimate connections with bankers, industrialists and socialites such as the Bechsteins?

The first congress would seem to have been the logical place for Hitler to stage a revolt and openly seize power that seemed his for the asking. But he restrained himself since only 411 members answered the call to Munich. Nor was the widening split in policy and tactics yet well enough known to rank-and-file members. On the surface there was unity at the congress, obvious as it was to insiders that a confrontation was in the offing, and everyone joined in the effort to make Hitler's first appearance twelve days later at the Zirkus Krone a success.

The winter had been a severe one with food riots rampant throughout Germany. These public disorders were heightened by a demand of the Allied Supreme War Council in Paris for exorbitant war reparations. Germany, close to bankruptcy, was expected to pay 134 billion gold marks. A large segment of the population already lived with little or no heat and went to bed hungry, and the annual payment was believed to hold out a bare subsistence for the workers as well as hardships for the middle class.

The spirit of indignation was so general that all the major political parties considered holding a common protest demonstration on the Königsplatz. This was canceled lest it be broken up by the Reds. On February 1 Hitler demanded a final decision. The inappropriately named action committee put him off until the following day, and he was informed they "intended" to hold the meeting in a week. "With this the cord of my patience snapped and I decided to carry through the protest demonstration alone." That noon Hitler reserved the Zirkus Krone for the following evening—the manager was a party member and he reportedly charged Hitler little or nothing—and then dictated copy for a flashy poster. Many of the party faithful had qualms. The circus arena could accommodate an audience of 6000 and it seemed impossible that even a moderate number could be induced to attend at such short notice.

The posters were not put up until Thursday morning. Moreover, a cold rain mixed with snow was falling. Hitler himself was so concerned that he hastily dictated leaflets and sent them off to the printer. That afternoon two hired trucks covered with red festoons and flying large swastika flags cruised the city. Each vehicle was manned by a score of party members who tossed out the leaflets and shouted slogans. It was the first time that propaganda trucks had been used by non-Marxists in Munich streets and in some working-class sections they were greeted with raised fists and angry shouts.

By seven that night Hitler got a depressing telephone report from the Zirkus Krone: the auditorium was far from filled. Ten minutes later came a more favorable report and at seven forty-five he was informed that three quarters of the seats were occupied with long lines queuing at the box office windows. As he entered the building "the same joy" seized him as it had a year before at the Hofbräuhaus. "Like a giant shell this hall lay before me, filled with thousands and thousands of people." The ring itself was black with humanity.

"Future or Ruin" was his theme, and his heart rejoiced in the conviction that down there before him lay his own future. After the first half hour he had the feeling that contact had been established and the audience was his. Applause began to interrupt him "in greater and greater spontaneous outbursts." This was finally succeeded by a remarkable hush, a solemn stillness. "Then you could hardly hear more than the breathing of this gigantic multitude, and only when the last word had been spoken did the applause suddenly roar forth to find its release and conclusion in the *Deutschland* song, sung with the highest fervor." The man who had released this flood of emotion was himself intoxicated, and he remained on the platform for twenty minutes watching the arena empty. Then, "overjoyed," he went out into the sleet to his dingy, unheated little room on the Thierschstrasse.

Hitler's performance at the Zirkus Krone was pilloried and praised in the Munich press and he was as pleased by the vituperation as by the approbation. It was not only that he thrived on opposition but that the violence of the attacks against him showed he was rousing visceral feelings. Despite the turbulence he generated, Hitler was becoming the darling of the respectable nationalist forces then making Munich their capital and receiving considerable secret support from the police president and his subordinate, who headed the department's Political Division. These two officials did their best to suppress complaints to the police against party breaches of peace and to protect Nazis when police action could not be forestalled. "We recognized that this movement, the National Socialist Party . . . should not be suppressed," they would testify three years later at Hitler's trial. "We did do that, and we refrained deliberately because we saw in the party the seeds of Germany's renewal, because we were convinced from the start that this movement was the one most likely to take root among workers infected with the Marxist plague and win them back into the nationalist camp. That is why we held our protecting hands over the National Socialist Party and Herr Hitler."*

The Bavarian government also gave him a measure of official recognition. Hitler and other party leaders were received by Gustav Ritter von Kahr, the right-wing Minister President, who was devoted to the preservation of Bavaria's peculiar status against encroachment by the Weimar regime. Bavaria still retained much of its autonomy, such as its own postal service, and its citizens continued to resent any directives from benighted northerners. Upon this issue Hitler and Kahr found common ground and although the Minister President disagreed with the "raging Austrian" on many points he felt the leader of the NSDAP could be useful as a propagandist in his own battle with Weimar.

Kahr's friendly reception gave public notice that Hitler was now a political force. Such recognition was welcome since his differences with the old guard in the party were coming to a head. Hitler's transformation into a personality because of his magnetism and crowd appeal indicated that he had not only altered the original purposes of the party but intended to seize complete control. His adversaries, therefore, took advantage of his absence in Berlin (where he was consolidating ties in that area with conservatives, nationalists and right-wing radicals) to engineer an alliance with a group of socialists from Augsburg. It seemed innocent but Hitler realized this was a sly tactical move to weaken his influence. He hastened back home and launched a startling counterattack. On July 11 he announced his resignation from the party. Three days later he put his cause before the general membership in an ultimatum. He would not return to the party unless he was made first chairman and given dictatorial powers. "I make these demands," he said, "not because I am power hungry, but because recent events have more than convinced me that without an iron leadership the party . . . will within a short time cease to be what it was supposed to be: a national socialist German Workers' Party and not a western association." It was the first manifest appearance of the concept Adolf Hitler had brought from the war—the *Führerprinzip*, the leadership principle, absolute obedience to the commander.

Hitler gave the committee eight days to act but Drexler was so incensed that he refused to compromise. The situation was exacerbated by distribution of an anonymous pamphlet to party members. Entitled

* Nor were these the only protectors of the radical right. Even those judges, police, state and local officials, and military who wished to curb Hitler exhibited considerable partiality toward nationalists involved in violence. Out of 376 political assassinations in Germany between January 1919 and June 1922, 22 were committed by leftists and 354 by rightists. Leftists received, on an average, 180 months' imprisonment while rightists got only four months. Ten leftists were sentenced to death; no rightists.

"Adolf Hitler—Traitor?" it was a libelous concoction of fact and fancy but most charges—such as the ones that Hitler called himself "The King of Munich" and wasted large sums of money on women; and that he was in the pay of the Jews—were so ridiculous that it is difficult to believe the author himself took them seriously.

The eight-day deadline passed. Still Drexler and the committee refused to act. It looked as if Hitler's bluff had failed but in a last-hour secret session Eckart persuaded Drexler to compromise. He, in turn, brought around the rest of the executive committee on the grounds that they would still be a minor group but for Hitler. The latter was presented with a formal, flowery notice granting him the dictatorial powers he demanded and offering to make him chairman in recognition of "your exceptional knowledge, your unusual sacrifice and honorable accomplishments for the growth of the movement, and your unusual oratorical abilities."

A special congress was convened for July 29 to formalize Hitler's selection as new chairman. The meeting was opened by a left-wing Bavarian named Hermann Esser, who had become one of the Führer's closest advisers despite his youth. Widely known as a lady's man, Hitler described him as "a greyhound you must keep on a leash." He introduced Hitler, who proceeded to declare that he had fought repeatedly to keep the organization from turning into a tea club. "We do not wish to unite with other organizations," he said, "but insist that they annex themselves to us so that we can retain the leadership. Anyone who cannot accept this can leave." This went for the Augsburg group and any other out-of-towners. "Our movement came from Munich and stays in Munich." In closing, he reaffirmed his friendship for Drexler and said he was prepared to take on the position of chairman. A poll was taken. There were 543 votes for Hitler and one against.

With Hitler and his "armed Bohemians" now in absolute control of the NSDAP, all the traditions of the German Workers' Party were dumped overboard, since the elitists were dedicated to the proposition that a new order could not be built on old foundations. There would be no more parliamentary debate and democratic procedures. Henceforth, they would follow the Führer principle.

At the same time Hitler did his best to placate the old guard by making no display of power. He issued no general orders and refrained from enforcing the strict discipline he might have. Instead he spent the summer consolidating inner-party support in Munich and quietly expanding the rough-and-ready group which kept order at political meetings into a cohesive uniformed, paramilitary unit. It was established early in August under the innocent name of Gymnastic and Sports Division and, according to a party proclamation, was "intended to serve as a means for bringing our youthful members together into a powerful organization for the purpose of utilizing their strength as an offensive force at the disposal of the movement." Two months later it was given a more descriptive name: *Sturmabteilung* (Storm Detachment). To Hitler the SA was merely a political weapon to keep order and to march around in uniform to impress the discipline-loving burghers. But its leader, Captain Röhm, regarded it as a genuine armed force, his private army. The nucleus came from Free Corps units and one of their early battle songs was revised:

> *Swastika on helmet,*
> *Armband black-white-red,*
> *Storm Detachment Hitler*
> *Is our name.*

With the establishment of a private army and the party apparatus under his complete control, Adolf Hitler was now ready to set the NSDAP on a new, more revolutionary course. In the next months he instigated a series of public provocations. The campaign opened with apparently random acts: the assault of a Jew in the street, illegal display of flags and distribution of pamphlets, and a number of minor public brawls. These petty disturbances of the peace were succeeded, on the evening of September 14, 1921, by one of significance. The occasion was a meeting at the Löwenbräukeller of the Bavarian League, a federalist organization which accepted the social program of the Weimar Constitution while deploring its centralism. Its leader, an engineer named Ballerstedt, was preparing to address the crowd just as Hitler, who regarded him as "my most dangerous opponent," marched in. Scores of SA troops sans uniform had been planted in the audience near the podium and they leaped to their feet to give Hitler a raucous demonstration. Hundreds of other party adherents planted throughout the audience joined in. Then Hermann Esser climbed on a chair, shouting that Bavaria was in its present low state because of the Jews. This brought a chorus of demands that Ballerstedt "give the floor" to Hitler. Someone threw the light switches in an effort to prevent a brawl. It only created tumult. When the lights went on again the SA flooded onto the stage, engulfing Ballerstedt. After beating him up, the SA group shoved him off the stage into the audience.

At an examination by the police commission investigating the fracas, Hitler expressed no regrets. "It's all right," was his dogged comment. "We got what we wanted. Ballerstedt did not speak." The matter did not end with an inquiry. Hitler and Esser were both informed they would be tried for violating the peace. The impending trial only inspired violence which erupted on the evening of November 4, during a Hitler speech at Munich's Hofbräuhaus. By the time he entered the vestibule at 7:45 P.M. the hall was overflowing with more than eight hundred occupants. The women were told to take seats near the front, as far from the doors as possible. The warning didn't faze Frau Magdalena Schweyer, proprietor of a vegetable and fruit shop opposite Hitler's dwelling and his faithful adherent. "I was too excited really to be frightened. It was plain there'd be some trouble: half the people in the place belonged to the Reds." In fact, hostile workers from the Maffei factory, the Isaria Meter Works and other shops far outnumbered Hitler's followers. Moreover the party no longer enjoyed the secret protection of the Bavarian government since Minister President von Kahr had been forced to resign in favor of a more moderate man.

When Hitler saw that the Social Democrats had come early and taken most of the places, he ordered the doors closed. He told the SA bodyguard—there were less than fifty on hand—that this was their chance to show loyalty to the movement "and that not a man of us must leave the hall unless we were carried out dead." They were to attack at the first sign of violence on the theory that the best defense was a good offense. "The answer was a threefold *Heil* that sounded rougher and hoarser than usual." This romanticized account by Hitler was mirrored in the recollections of his followers who saw him as he undoubtedly saw himself: the pure man of iron will from the trenches come to lead the Fatherland back to honor and glory.

As Hitler started toward the speaker's platform, workers shouted threats. Hitler ignored them and pushed forward. Hermann Esser was now standing on the front table, calling the meeting to order. He jumped down and Hitler took his place. At first there were boos but even those who had come to jeer listened to his arguments and he was able to talk for more than an hour without interruption. But his opponents were only biding their time as they downed numerous mugs of beer, storing the empty ones under the tables for ammunition.

All at once someone interrupted Hitler and he shouted a retort. There were isolated angry shouts throughout the room. A man jumped on his chair and yelled, "*Freiheit* [Freedom]!" A beer stein hurtled at Hitler's head. Then half a dozen more. "Duck down!" the young monitors up front shouted to the women. Frau Schweyer obeyed. "One heard nothing but yells, crashing beer mugs, stamping and struggling, the overturning of heavy oaken tables, and the smashing of wooden chairs. A regular battle raged in the room." Curious, she looked up to see Hitler still standing atop a table despite the barrage of heavy mugs flying past his head. The

outnumbered SA fought so ferociously that within half an hour the enemy
had been driven down the stairs. It looked as if a shell had exploded in the
hall demolishing chairs, tables and beer mugs. Finally above the din came
the voice of Hermann Esser: "The meeting goes on. The speaker has the
floor."

Hitler resumed his speech even as his storm troopers were bandaged
or carried out of the room. He finished to an outburst of applause, moments before an excited police officer entered and shouted, "The meeting
is dismissed!"

5

The brawl at the Hofbräuhaus was evidence to Hitler that success
comes to one unafraid to use force. Victory that night brought him and
the NSDAP a spate of publicity. But with the rise in membership came a
demand among more solid citizens to put an end to such uncivilized behavior. The new Bavarian government was also eager to curb Hitler but
wanted more definite provocation and in a display of fair play gave him a
pistol permit.

His show of force was a symptom of the rising nationalist and
völkisch resentment throughout Germany. Earlier in the year, after Germany rejected the Allied demand for increased war reparations, French
and Belgian troops had occupied Duisburg and Düsseldorf as sanctions.
Two months later the Allies issued an ultimatum for payment of two bil-
lions annually along with twenty-five per cent of the value of all German
exports. This was accompanied by a threat to occupy the entire Ruhr.

The moderate conservative cabinet answered with resignations but
the Center Party, which now controlled the government, bowed to the Allied demands. This capitulation infuriated nationalists such as Hitler and
set off a series of violent acts, including assassination of Matthias Erzberger, who was not only a leader of the Center Party but the "criminal"
who had signed the armistice. The assassins were hailed as heroes by many
of those Germans calling for law and order.

Before the end of 1921 nationalists had new cause for wrath when the
League of Nations announced that Poland was to receive that part of
Upper Silesia where four fifths of the mines and heavy industries were lo-
cated. Winter and the steady deflation of the mark with its attendant
hardships aggravated German discontent. On Easter Sunday, 1922, the at-
mosphere of violence was heightened by Foreign Minister Walther
Rathenau's startling turn to the East; he signed a treaty with the Soviet
Union at Rapallo. Anti-Bolshevists like Hitler were incensed, not realizing

the benefits of such an alliance to their own cause of a resurgent Reich. They ignored the fact that this emergence of Germany from political isolation was a severe blow to the Western Allies.

Germany and Russia agreed to resume diplomatic relations, to renounce all claims for reparations on each other, and to resume trade. Neither was to enter into an economic agreement affecting the other without prior consultation. Russia was in need of modern technology; Germany was determined to circumvent the restrictive military clauses of the Versailles Treaty without arousing the suspicions of the International Control Commission operating on its territory. Lenin had already requested German assistance in reorganizing the Red Army; General Hans von Seeckt, head of the Reichswehr, readily complied, and the military of the two powers came into close contact. Small German military units began training Russians while gaining expertise in the use of special weapons.

The full extent and impact of this co-operation could not be calculated by Rathenau's critics and, even though German rearmament was given tremendous impetus by his pact, the very Germans who wanted a strong army labeled him a Red for consorting with the Soviets. This was only one more black mark against a man who had undeservedly become the symbol of subservience to the West since he felt obliged to carry out with determination the onerous economic promises of the Versailles Treaty. Moreover, he was a wealthy Jew, accused by the Nazis of secretly plotting for Jewish domination of the world. On the fourth of June this gifted patriot was murdered, gangster style, by two former members of the Free Corps.

By a quirk of fate the most feared activist in Bavaria was imprisoned that same day. Hitler—after telling his followers: "Two thousand years ago the mob of Jerusalem dragged a man to execution in just this way"—was placed in Stadelheim prison for inciting a riot. The warder led him to a cell with a private toilet, "amiably" pointing out that other celebrities had shared these quarters, including Ludwig Thomas, the Bavarian dramatist, and fellow revolutionary Kurt Eisner. Hitler was not particularly pleased by news of Rathenau's murder. Such isolated acts of vengeance seemed petty to him and this one was primarily a lesson in security. Henceforth he would install a searchlight in the back of his car "to blind the driver" of any pursuing vehicle.

As a result of the assassination, the Weimar government hastily passed a Law for the Protection of the Republic, a Draconian decree designed to halt radical right terrorism. Violent opposition came from Bavarian nationalists of all shadings. At the height of this controversy

Hitler was released from Stadelheim. Isolation from the turbulent arena of politics had forced him to reassess his churning ideas. His almost five-week term in jail with nothing to do but read or think had helped mold his obsessive hatred and fear of Jews into a more connected and purposeful polemic. He wasted no time joining the assault of the Law for the Protection of the Republic and on the day of his release he made one of the most trenchant speeches of his career. Entitled "Free State or Slavery," its apparent target was the new law but in fact was a lethal denunciation of Jews and their insidious plans to conquer the world. Never before had he marshaled his material with more dramatic effect or given such a "reasonable" explanation of *how* and *why* the Jews had gained such power.

All over Europe, he told a receptive audience in the Bürgerbräukeller, a great conflict was raging between the ideals of nationalist-völkisch forces and those of international Jewry. It was the Jew who founded Social Democracy and Communism; it was the Jew who controlled the stock exchange and the workers' movement. At this point Hitler made a shrugging gesture in imitation of the stage Jew and drew an appreciative laugh. He went on to claim that the Jew was a destroyer, a robber, an exploiter. Moreover, Bolshevist Judaism was preparing for the decisive battle and had two great aims: "To make the nation defenseless in arms and to make the people defenseless in spirit."* To do so the Jew had to muzzle those who spoke out in protest. This at last, after more than an hour's denunciation of the Jewish menace, was the lead to Hitler's main theme. "We know that the so-called 'Law for the Protection of the Republic' which comes from Berlin today is nothing else than a means for reducing all criticism to silence." But the National Socialists could not be silenced and he was calling directly for physical violence. "So as I come to the end of my speech I want to ask something of those among you who are young. And for that there is a very special reason. The old parties train their youth in

---

* The depth and virulence of Hitler's anti-Semitism in 1922 were revealed during a conversation he had that year with an acquaintance, Josef Hell. When Hell asked what Hitler intended doing if he ever had full freedom of action against the Jews, the latter suddenly lost his poise. "He no longer looked at me," recalled Hell, "but beyond me into emptiness and made his next statement in a rising voice; he was seized by a sort of paroxysm and wound up shouting at me as if I were a large audience: 'If I am ever really in power, the destruction of the Jews will be my first and most important job. As soon as I have the power, I shall have gallows after gallows erected, for example, in Munich on the Marienplatz—as many of them as the traffic allows. Then the Jews will be hanged one after another, and they will stay hanging until they stink. They will stay hanging as long as hygienically possible. As soon as they are untied, then the next group will follow and that will continue until the last Jew in Munich is exterminated. Exactly the same procedure will be followed in other cities until Germany is cleansed of the last Jew!' "

the gift of gab, we prefer to train them to use their bodily strength. For I tell you: the young man who does not find his way to the place where in the last resort the destiny of his people is most truly represented, only studies philosophy and in a time like this buries himself behind his books or sits at home by the fire, he is no German youth! I call upon you! Join our storm troops!"

He warned that their lot would be hard, with nothing to win and everything to lose. "He who today fights on our side cannot win great laurels, far less can he win great material goods—it is more likely that he will end up in jail. He who today is leader must be an idealist, if only for the reason that he leads those against whom it would seem that everything has conspired." His call to sacrifice and idealism sent the audience into ecstasy.

In the following two weeks Hitler continued to assail the new law and on August 16 he was the star performer at a mass demonstration on the Königsplatz. It had been called by the United Fatherland Leagues and every patriotic society in Munich was expected to join in a combined protest against Weimar's decree. Before the arrival of Hitler and his group there was little excitement. Then came the sound of a stirring march from two brass bands, and finally the sight of marching men all wearing swastika armbands. There were six columns of them carrying fifteen National Socialist flags. In minutes the square became jammed with about fifty thousand excited, expectant people.

As Adolf Hitler stepped up to the platform there was little applause. He stood silent for a moment. "Then he began to speak, quietly and ingratiatingly at first," recalled Kurt Lüdecke, an ardent nationalist who was seeing Hitler for the first time. "Before long his voice had risen to a hoarse shriek that gave an extraordinary effect of an intensity of feeling." He seemed to be only one more fanatic—a threatening, beseeching figure with small hands and intense, steel-blue eyes but, before he knew it, Lüdecke fell under Hitler's spell. As if hypnotized, he suddenly saw the "fanatic" turn into a patriot hero, another Luther. "His appeal to German manhood was like a call to arms, the gospel he preached a sacred truth." Hitler had gained another uncritical convert.

That evening Lüdecke heard Hitler again, this time at the Zirkus Krone. Once more Lüdecke was transfixed. After the speech he was introduced to the speaker, who was disheveled and perspiring. A dirty trench coat was flung carelessly over his shoulders. But all Lüdecke saw was a man of character and courage and the next day he offered himself to Hitler and his cause "without reservation." They talked for more than four hours, then solemnly clasped hands. "I had given him my soul."

6

Out of the controversy over the Law for the Protection of the Republic and the widening split between Weimar and Bavaria came plans for another coup d'état. Its instigator was an obscure Munich public health official, Dr. Otto Pittinger, who planned to overthrow the Bavarian government with the support of the NSDAP and other nationalist organizations and replace it with a dictatorship under former Minister President von Kahr.

Hitler's new convert, Kurt Lüdecke, was given the task of relaying final instructions to possible co-conspirators in the Berlin area. He ranged through North Germany, envisaging himself as the "German Paul Revere" rousing nationalists from bed, until he learned that nothing at all was happening in Bavaria itself. He took the train back to Munich—it was late September 1922—and drove at once to Pittinger's headquarters where the doctor was just emerging. "Is this the coup d'état?" said Lüdecke accusingly. But Pittinger, looking "very haughty in his goggles," ignored him and sped off in a Mercedes for a vacation in the Alps. His uprising had fizzled out. Only the National Socialists were ready to march, and their leader had been forced to go into hiding.

Lüdecke found Hitler in a shabby attic room, his only companions a large dog and Graf, his bodyguard. "I was ready—my men were ready!" he angrily told Lüdecke. "From now on I go my way alone." Even if not a soul followed he would go it alone. "No more Pittingers, no more Fatherland societies! One party. One single party. These *gentlemen*, these counts and generals—they won't do anything. *I* shall. *I alone*."

Earlier that year Hitler had confessed to Arthur Möller van den Bruck, who was writing a book called *The Third Reich*: "You have everything I lack. You create the spiritual framework for Germany's reconstruction. I am but a drummer and an assembler. Let us work together." Envisaging a nationalistic, socialist corporate state, Möller refused Hitler's offer, then told a colleague, "That fellow will never grasp it. I would rather commit suicide than see such a man in office."

The lesson learned in the ignominious Pittinger Putsch convinced Hitler that he must act alone as Führer. It was a concept that excited Lüdecke and he suggested the party copy the technique of Benito Mussolini, who was striving to be the leader of Italy. His Fascist movement was nationalistic, socialistic and anti-Bolshevik; his Blackshirts had recently occupied Ravenna and other Italian cities. Lüdecke volunteered to go to Italy as Hitler's representative to see if Mussolini might prove to be a valuable ally.

In Milan Il Duce received Lüdecke graciously even though he had never heard of Hitler. He agreed with Hitler's views on the Versailles Treaty and international finance but was evasive about the measures that should be used against Jews. What impressed Lüdecke most was Mussolini's supreme assurance when asked if he would resort to force in case the Italian government did not yield to his demands. "We shall *be* the State," he said as if he were royalty, "because it is our will."

Lüdecke's report to Hitler was enthusiastic. Mussolini, he said, would probably seize control of Italy within months. He also confirmed that there were remarkable similarities between Fascism and National Socialism. Both were ardently nationalistic, anti-Marxist and anti-parliamentarian, both were dedicated to a radical new order. In addition, the two leaders were alike. Both came from the people and were war veterans.

Hitler was particularly interested in Mussolini's use of brute force to gain political power. "His eyes grew thoughtful," recalled Lüdecke, "when he heard how the Blackshirts marched into Bolshevized towns and took possession, while the garrisons kept benevolently neutral or, in some cases, even quartered the Fascisti." It only proved what could be achieved by nerve.

Inspired by Mussolini's success and reassured by his own growing support throughout Bavaria, Hitler decided to make his show of force that autumn. He selected Coburg, a town in Upper Bavaria more than a hundred and sixty miles north of Munich. The occasion was a "German Day" celebration which had been organized by a group of völkisch societies. The guests of honor were to be the Grand Duke and Duchess of Coburg. Both were openly nationalistic and she was a relative of the late Czar.

Hitler was invited to attend and to "bring some escort." Choosing to interpret this invitation broadly, he left Munich in a special train on Saturday morning, October 14, 1922, with some 600 SA men, many of whom were paying their own expenses. There was a festive air as the storm troopers, equipped with rations for two days, piled into the special train to the music of their forty-two piece brass band.

It was a rollicking party more like an excursion tour and even in Hitler's compartment there was a holiday air. With him were seven men, the brains and brawn of the inner circle: a former sergeant (Max Amann), a wrestler (Graf), a horse trader and ex-barroom bouncer (Christian Weber), a pamphleteer and ex-Communist (Esser), an architect (Rosenberg), an author (Eckart) and a self-styled sophisticate (Lüdecke). To the last-mentioned, the two most interesting were the ebullient Eckart, who "outshone all the others with his wit and common sense," and Rosenberg, a "block of ice!" who gazed toward him with pale lackluster eyes as though he weren't there.

The train stopped for half an hour in Nuremberg to pick up more adherents. The band struck up again and the men shouted as they waved swastika flags from the windows. Curious bystanders gathered to see what kind of a circus train it was. Jews in another halted train jeered at the swastika flags until Julius Schreck, who would later become Hitler's chauffeur, "leapt into the midst of them and started laying about him."

By the time the train pulled into the Coburg station there were 800 storm troopers. Grim-faced, Hitler stepped out to the platform. He had chosen Coburg as a battleground because of its preponderance of socialists and Communists. He would emulate Mussolini and drive them from their own stronghold. The people of Coburg, Bavarians for only two years, were taken aback by the noisy group that piled out behind Hitler onto the platform with their large band and red banners. The brass band struck up a march and then, with military precision, the SA paraded into town. In the van were eight husky Bavarians in leather shorts carrying alpenstocks. Just behind a row of men carrying large red and black flags came Hitler and his entourage of seven, followed by 800 men armed with rubber bludgeons or knives. Some wore faded and mended field-gray uniforms, some their Sunday best; their only common distinction was a swastika band on the left arm. Hitler himself was the epitome of the common man in his belted trench coat, slouch hat and ridiculous calf-high boots.

A mob of workers pressed from both sides shouting "Murderers! Bandits! Robbers! Criminals!" The National Socialists ignored the epithets, never breaking step. Local police guided the line of march to the Hofbräuhauskeller in the very center of town, then locked the gates, but Hitler insisted on quartering his men in a shooting gallery. To the beat of drums the storm troopers marched back through the hostile mob toward the outskirts of town. As cobblestones began to fly at the columns, Hitler signaled with a wave of his whip, and his men turned on the attackers with their bludgeons. The crowd fell back and the storm troopers continued their march, strutting like soldiers after their first battle. One of the proudest was the bon vivant Lüdecke, who felt as if he had been finally accepted by the rank and file. "Seeing that one brawls as well in an English suit as in shoddy clothes, they forgave me my tailor."

The following morning, Sunday, the leftists called a mass demonstration "to throw out the Nazis." Ten thousand protesters were expected to collect at the square but the size of the opposition only spurred Hitler to defiance. Resolved "to dispose of the Red terror for good," he ordered the SA, whose ranks had grown to almost 1500, to march on the Fortress of Coburg by way of the square. At noon the storm troopers with Hitler in the lead paraded into the center of the city but there were only a few hundred demonstrators at the square. Yesterday the citizens had stood on the sidewalks watching the SA pass by with silent disapproval. Today hundreds of imperial flags hung from the windows and friendly crowds lined the way, cheering the National Socialists with their strange emblem. Today they were heroes. They had ended Red domination of the Coburg alleys and streets. "That's typical of your bourgeois world," Hitler remarked to the men marching at his side. "Cowards at the moment of danger, boasters afterwards."

Coburg proved to Hitler that he and his SA could emulate Mussolini. In little more than two weeks the latter set another example. On October 28 Il Duce's Blackshirts marched into Rome (he took the train) and seized control of Italy.

Four days later Esser, in his usual role as introducer of the Führer, dramatically announced at the banquet hall of the Hofbräuhaus: "Germany's Mussolini is called Hitler!"

Chapter Five

"SUCH A LOGICAL AND FANATICAL MAN" 1922-1923

1

By 1922 Adolf Hitler had surrounded himself with a diverse group from every class which embraced a wide spectrum of cultures and occupations. All shared, to varying degrees, his nationalism and fear of Marxism. Two aviators were among them: Hermann Göring, a fighter ace and last commander of the famed Richthofen Flying Circus; and Rudolf Hess, who had started the war as an infantry officer in Hitler's regiment and ended it as a pilot. Although both were convinced Hitler was the answer to Germany's future and both came from well-to-do families, they differed strikingly in appearance, character and temperament.

Göring was buoyant, theatrical, an extrovert, who made friends easily and nearly always dominated them. His father had been a district judge before accepting an appointment from Bismarck as Reichs Commissar for Southwest Africa. He was married twice and had eight children. Hermann, the next to youngest, was an indifferent scholar whose dream was to serve his country in battle. Through the offices of his godfather he was admitted to the Royal Prussian Cadet Corps. He distinguished himself in the war and, after his twentieth air victory, was awarded the highest military decoration, the Pour le Mérite order. After the armistice he became a pilot for the Swedish airline and got engaged to a married woman, Carin von Kantzow, whose father was a member of the Swedish nobility and whose mother came from a family of Irish brewers. They were to get married as soon as her divorce was final.

Göring could have enjoyed a life of comparative ease in Sweden but he felt the urge to return to Germany and help "wipe out the disgrace of Versailles—the shame of defeat, the corridor right through the heart of Prussia." He enrolled at the University of Munich to study history and political science but was more interested in practical politics and once tried to form his own revolutionary party among officer veterans. "I remember a meeting at which they were discussing getting meals and beds for veteran officers. 'You damn fools!' I told them. 'Do you think that an officer who is worth his salt can't find a bed to sleep in, even if it happens to be the bed of a pretty blonde? Damn it, there are more important things at stake!' Somebody got fresh and I banged him over the head. Well, of course, the meeting broke up in an uproar." That ended his attempt to head a revolution and it wasn't until the fall of 1922 at a mass meeting that he found someone worth following. It was a meeting at the Königsplatz protesting Allied demands to hand over alleged war criminals. A series of speakers from various parties took the platform. Then the crowd began calling out, "Hitler!" By chance he was standing near Göring and Carin, who had been married early that year, and they overheard him remark that he wouldn't think of addressing "these tame bourgeois pirates." Something about the man in the belted trench coat impressed Göring so much that he went to a party meeting at the Café Neumann. "I just sat unobtrusively in the background. I remember Rosenberg was there. Hitler explained why he hadn't spoken. No Frenchman is going to lose sleep over that kind of harmless talk, he said. You've got to have bayonets to back up your threats. Well, *that* was what I wanted to hear. He wanted to build up a party that would make Germany strong and smash the Treaty of Versailles. 'Well,' I said to myself, '*that's* the party for me! *Down with the Treaty of Versailles,* God damn it! That's my meat!'"

At party headquarters he filled out a membership application. The appearance of such a war hero in the shabby office must have caused a stir. "Anyway," he recalled, "somebody tells me that Hitler would like to see me immediately." One look at the imposing Göring was enough for Hitler. Here was the ideal Nordic: luminous blue eyes, straight features and pink and white complexion. "He told me that it was a stroke of fate that I should come to him just as he was looking for somebody to take charge of the SA." They agreed to postpone the announcement a month, but

Göring immediately began training the SA as a military organization. "Military! I'll tell the world it was military!"

He may have looked the perfect Germanic type but he was no racist by Hitler's standards and, in fact, had a number of Jewish friends. Göring had joined the NSDAP "precisely because it *was* revolutionary, not because of the ideological stuff. Other parties had made revolution, so I figured I could get in on one too!" A man of action, he was drawn to an organization dedicated to action and he was just the man Hitler needed at that moment. He had invaluable connections with Junker officers and members of society, and was a display piece for parades and meetings. Nor was he squeamish about bashing in a few heads if necessary.

Compared to Göring, Rudolf Hess was colorless. Born in Alexandria, Egypt, he was sired by a well-to-do wholesaler and exporter who persuaded him to enter the family business, although he would have preferred to become a scholar. He attended boarding school in Bad Godesberg before enrolling at the École Supérieure du Commerce in Switzerland. His studies were interrupted by the war, and when it ended he could not bring himself to continue a business career. Like Göring, he entered the University of Munich, reading history, economics and geopolitics. He too felt betrayed by the "November criminals" but, instead of trying to make a revolution of his own, joined the Thule Society. He took part in demonstrations, spoke on street corners (despite his painful self-consciousness), and as a member of a Free Corps unit helped overthrow the Bavarian Soviet regime.

He too was searching for a leader and had won a prize at the university for writing an essay on the theme "How must the man be constituted who will lead Germany back to her old heights?" The man, he wrote, should be a dictator not averse to the use of slogans, street parades and demagoguery. He must be a man of the people yet have nothing in common with the mass. Like every great man, he must be "all personality," and one who "does not shrink from bloodshed. Great questions are always decided by blood and iron." To reach his goal, he must be prepared "to trample on his closest friends," dispense law "with terrible hardness" and deal with people and nations "with cautious and sensitive fingers" or if need be "trample on them with the boots of a grenadier."

Hess found his ideal in Hitler and for more than a year had served as his trusted lieutenant and confidant. At the same time he also gave allegiance to a man married to a Jew. General Karl Haushofer returned to Germany in 1911 after three years in Tokyo as military attaché, speaking fluent Japanese. He brought back an abiding interest in Asian affairs along with a conviction that a nation's existence depended on the space it controlled. The war was proof to him of this theory. An encircled and suffocated Germany had gone down to humiliating defeat because she lacked *Lebensraum* (living space). After the armistice he became professor of geopolitics at the University of Munich, teaching his students that national salvation lay in self-sufficiency and for this Germany must have not only autarchy (national economic independence) but Lebensraum. Hess was almost as enthralled by Professor Haushofer as he was by Hitler and his hope was to bring the two together. One impediment was Frau Haushofer, whose father was a Jewish merchant. And while Hess followed the letter of racist doctrine, he was a man of sentiment as devoted to her as he was to the Herr Professor.

Hess was a retiring man, modest and unassertive. Although he had fought well on the battlefield and in the streets and his prize-winning essay breathed blood and iron, he was far from bloodthirsty. Yet while he preferred books and music to brawling, he was never found wanting in beer-hall battles and had won Hitler's affection by his action in the bloody fracas at the Hofbräuhaus. With his solid square face, bushy black eyebrows, intense and clenched lips, he was the picture of a man "prepared to trample on his closest friends." Only when he broke into a smile was the true Hess revealed—an ingenuous, bucktoothed young idealist. Ilse Hess, then Ilse Pröhl, recalls that "he rarely smiled, did not smoke, despised alcohol and had no patience with young people enjoying dancing and social life after a war had been lost." An enigma, except to those who knew him intimately, Hess was the ideal disciple. Too bashful and unaspiring to strive for power, he was prepared to follow Hitler wherever he led.

Another blind follower was Julius Streicher. Where Hess and Göring lagged far behind their leader in anti-Semitism, Streicher surpassed Hitler in the virulence of his language. A stocky, primitive man with bald head and gross features, he gave off an aura of raw energy. He had excessive appetites alike at table and in bed. He could be bluffly jovial or blatantly brutal, shifting effortlessly from maudlin sentimentality to ruthlessness. Like Hitler, he was rarely seen in public without a whip but where the former draped his from the wrist like a dog leash, Streicher flaunted his as a weapon. In younger days he had "restlessly wandered from place to place with a rucksack full of anti-Semitic books and pamphlets." His speech was glutted with sadistic imagery and he relished attacking personal enemies in the foulest terms. Convinced that the Jew was plotting against the Aryan world, he had an endless catalogue of abuse at the tip of his tongue.

He was made for the NSDAP and, soon after founding the Nuremberg branch of the party in 1922, he spawned a newspaper dedicated to the damnation of Jews. *Der Stürmer* went a long step beyond *Ostara*, the

Viennese magazine that exercised such influence on the youthful Hitler, in filth and virulence and was already a source of dismay to many of those close to Hitler. The Führer himself was repelled by pornography, disapproved of Streicher's sexual activities, and was concerned by the incessant intraparty quarrels this erratic disciple instigated. Yet at the same time he admired Streicher's boundless energy and fanatic loyalty. "More than once Dietrich Eckart told me that Streicher was a schoolteacher, and a lunatic to boot, from many points of view. He always added that one could not hope for a triumph of National Socialism without giving one's support to men like Streicher." Hitler had an unexpected answer for those who reproached Streicher for his gross exaggerations in *Der Stürmer:* "The truth is the opposite of what people say: he *idealized* the Jew. The Jew is baser, fiercer, more diabolical than Streicher depicted him."

Such were the men close to Hitler. His movement cut across all social classes and so all types were drawn to him—the intellectual, the street fighter, the fanatic, the idealist, the hooligan, the condottiere, the principled and the unprincipled, laborers and noblemen. There were gentle souls and the ruthless, rascals and men of good will; writers, painters, day laborers, storekeepers, dentists, students, soldiers and priests. His appeal was broad and he was broad-minded enough to accept a drug addict like Eckart or a homosexual like Captain Röhm. He was all things to many while he himself was ready to accept anyone who offered fealty in the battle for Germany's resurrection against the machinations of Jewish Marxism.

"My happiest memories are of this time," he recalled in a sentimental flood of recollections on a winter evening nineteen years later. He talked fondly of his early supporters. "Today, when I happen to meet one of them, it moves me extraordinarily. They showed a truly touching attachment towards me. Small stallkeepers of the markets used to come running to see me 'to bring a couple of eggs to Herr Hitler.' . . . I'm so fond of these unpretentious fellows."

Never one to underrate a follower no matter how humble, and perhaps remembering the miserable days in Vienna, Hitler opened up the new, more spacious party headquarters on Corneliusstrasse to those down-at-heels followers who needed refuge from the cold. "In the winter time," recalled Philipp Bouhler, "the anteroom was a place to warm up for unemployed party members and supporters who, loud and freezing, played cards there. You often couldn't hear yourself speak, and from time to time Christian Weber, who was in charge, appeared with a long horse whip to clear out the room."

2

In the fall of 1922 the activities of Adolf Hitler began to interest the Allies. At the suggestion of the American ambassador, Captain Truman Smith—Yale man, West Pointer, and now assistant military attaché in Berlin—was dispatched to Munich "to assess the reported developing strength of the National Socialist movement." Smith was instructed to meet Hitler and "form an estimate of his character, personality, abilities, and weaknesses." He was also to investigate the NSDAP's strength and potentialities. Specifically Smith was to find the answer to these questions: "Was there danger that Bavaria would declare itself independent of Germany? Did there exist in Munich danger of a renewed Communist revolt? Did the possibility exist that Hitler's National Socialists were strong enough to seize power in Bavaria? Was the 7th division of the Reichswehr, which was garrisoned in Bavaria, loyal to the Reich or was its loyalty divided between Berlin and Munich? Could it be depended upon to put down disorders or revolts whether staged by the right or left?"

Captain Smith arrived in Munich just before noon on November 15. After settling at the Marienbad Hotel he called on the acting United States consul, Robert Murphy, at the consulate on Ledererstrasse. The twenty-eight-year-old Murphy (later ambassador to Belgium), informed Smith that the new Bavarian Minister President was "not a strong character, being merely a tool" of former Minister President Kahr. The National Socialists, he said, were rapidly increasing in strength and their leader, while "a pure and simple adventurer," was nevertheless "a real character and is exploiting all latent discontent." Hitler understood the Bavarian psychology but it was questionable if he was "big enough to take the lead in a German national movement."

In the next few days Smith talked with generals, civil officials, Crown Prince Rupprecht ("certainly no genius, but still seems to possess considerable political ability"), a liberal newspaper editor, and Max Erwin von Scheubner-Richter, a refugee of German origin from a Baltic state, who had borrowed his wife's title. The last, a close friend of Rosenberg's, was beginning to exert considerable influence on Hitler. Scheubner-Richter assured Smith that the party's anti-Semitism was "purely for propaganda," and then invited him to attend a review of storm troopers before the new National Socialist headquarters.

"A remarkable sight indeed," Smith noted down in his hotel room that evening. "Twelve hundred of the toughest roughnecks I have ever seen in my life pass in review before Hitler at the goosestep under the old

Reichflag wearing red arm bands with Hakenkreuzen. Hitler, following the review, makes a speech . . . then shouts, 'Death to the Jews' etc. and etc. There was frantic cheering. I never saw such a sight in my life."

The next day, Saturday, Smith spoke with Ludendorff at his home. The general confessed that he had "formerly believed that Bolshevism had first to be stamped out in Russia before it could be crushed in Germany. He has now changed his mind, and thinks that Bolshevism must first be crushed in Germany." He asserted that the Allies "*must* support a strong German government capable of combatting Marxism" and that such a government will never "develop out of the existing chaotic parliamentary conditions" but "can only be formed by patriotic men." He was convinced that the "Fascist movement was the beginning of a reactionary awakening in Europe," and that Mussolini had "real sympathy for the national cause in Germany."

At 4 P.M. the following Monday, Smith met Hitler where he had interviewed Scheubner-Richter. The room was "drab and dreary beyond belief; akin to a back bedroom in a decaying New York tenement." The first words Smith wrote down in his notebook after the meeting were: "A marvelous demagogue. I have rarely listened to such a logical and fanatical man. His power over the mob must be immense." Hitler described his movement as a "union of Hand and Brain workers to oppose Marxism," and said that the "present abuses of capital must be done away with, if Bolshevism is to be put down." The parliamentary system had to be replaced. "Only a dictatorship can bring Germany to its feet." He stated that it was "much better for America and England that the decisive struggle between our civilization and Marxism be fought out on German soil rather than on American and English soil. If we (America) do not help German Nationalism, Bolshevism will conquer Germany. Then there will be no more reparations and Russia and German Bolshevism, out of motives of self preservation must attack the western nations."

He discoursed on other subjects but did not even mention Jews until Smith queried him point-blank about anti-Semitism; and then Hitler replied disarmingly that he merely "favored the withdrawal of citizenship and their exclusion from public affairs." By the time Smith left the dingy room he was convinced Hitler would be an important factor in German politics. He accepted a ticket for Hitler's next speech on November 22 and, upon being unexpectedly summoned back to Berlin, passed it on to Ernst Hanfstaengl, a towering lantern-jawed eccentric who had graduated from Harvard. Would Hanfstaengl be kind enough to take a look at this fellow Hitler and pass on his conclusions? "I have the impression he's going to play a big part," said Smith, "and whether you like him or not he certainly knows what he wants."

He was relying on Hanfstaengl's judgment because of the latter's unusual background. His mother came from a well-known New England family, the Sedgwicks; two of his ancestors were Civil War generals, one of whom helped carry Lincoln's coffin. Two generations of Hanfstaengls had served as privy councilors to the Dukes of Saxe-Coburg-Gotha and were connoisseurs and patrons of the arts. The family owned an art publishing house in Munich well known for its excellent reproductions. Hanfstaengl had been brought up in an atmosphere of art and music, the home a rendezvous for Lilli Lehmann, Wilhelm Busch, Sarasate, Richard Strauss, Felix Weingartner, Wilhelm Backhaus, Fridtjof Nansen and Mark Twain. He himself played the piano with verve and his six-foot-four frame hunched over the keyboard like an impish bear was a common sight in the best Bavarian salons. His nickname was Putzi (little fellow).

On the twenty-second Hanfstaengl took a streetcar to the Kindlkeller, a large L-shaped beer hall filled with a conglomerate audience. There were a few ex-officers and minor civil servants, some small shopkeepers and numerous young people and workers. Many wore the Bavarian national costume. From the press table Hanfstaengl searched in vain for someone he knew. He wondered where Hitler was and a journalist pointed to a trio on the platform. The short one was Max Amann, the one with the glasses was Anton Drexler, and the third was Hitler. He wore clumsy ankle-high shoes, a dark suit. His white collar was starched and he reminded Hanfstaengl of a waiter in a railway station restaurant. But after Drexler introduced him to the audience and Hitler strode swiftly and confidently past the press table he was "the unmistakable soldier in mufti."

The applause was deafening. Hitler stood like a sentry, legs firmly stretched, hands folded behind his back, as he began reviewing the events of the past few years in a quiet, reserved voice. Methodically he built up his case against the government, never stooping to histrionics or vulgarisms. He spoke carefully in literary High German, occasionally allowing a Viennese accent to creep in. Hanfstaengl, not a dozen feet away, was particularly impressed with the speaker's clear blue, guileless eyes. "There was honesty, there was sincerity, there was suffering and the dignity of mute entreaty." After about ten minutes Hitler had the audience's complete attention. Now he relaxed his position and used his hands and arms like a trained actor. He began to insinuate with sly malice in Viennese coffeehouse style, and Hanfstaengl noticed that the women nearby were enjoying the performance enormously. Finally one of them called out, "That's right, bravo!" and, as if in acknowledgment, Hitler raised his voice and with a sweeping gesture began condemning war profiteers. There was a roar of applause.

Hitler wiped the sweat from his brow and took a mug of beer from a man with a dark mustache. It was a telling touch of theater for the beer-drinking Müncheners. When he resumed speaking his gestures became more sweeping. Every so often someone would shout out an insult and he would calmly raise his right hand slightly as if catching a ball or fold his arms and spit out a brief rejoinder that would crush the heckler. "His technique resembled the thrusts and parries of a fencer, or the perfect balance of a tightrope-walker. Sometimes he reminded me of a skilled violinist, who, never coming to the end of his bow, always left just the faint anticipation of a tone—a thought spared the indelicacy of utterance." Gone was all caution as he stormed at his favorite enemies—the Jews and Reds. "Our motto shall be—if you will not be a German, I will bash your skull in. For we are convinced that we cannot succeed without a struggle. We have to fight with ideas, but, if necessary, also with our fists."

As Hanfstaengl emerged from his fascination, he looked around and noted with astonishment how the audience's behavior had changed. "The muffled restlessness of the masses who, an hour ago, had shoved against me and uttered all manner of nasty remarks, had become a deeply moved community. People were sitting listening breathlessly, who had long since forgotten to reach for their beer mugs and instead were drinking in the speaker's every word." Nearby a young woman was staring at Hitler "as though in some devotional ecstasy, she had ceased to be herself and was completely under the spell of Hitler's despotic faith in Germany's future greatness." The speech built to a climax that was "an orgasm of words." Suddenly it was over. The audience cheered frenziedly, clapped and pounded the tables. Hitler's exhaustion reminded Hanfstaengl of "a great artist at the end of a gruelling concert." His face and hair were soaked and his starched collar had wilted. ("Whenever I make a speech of great importance I am always soaking wet at the end, and I find I have lost four or six pounds in weight.")

On the spur of the moment, Hanfstaengl approached the committee table where Hitler was receiving compliments with a self-assured smile free of any arrogance. "Captain Truman Smith asked me to give you his best wishes," said Hanfstaengl. Smith's name piqued Hitler's interest and he asked how Hanfstaengl liked the speech. "Well, I agree with you," he said careful not to hurt Hitler's feelings. "About ninety-five per cent of what you said I can set my name to, and five per cent we will have to talk about that." What he particularly objected to was Hitler's blatant anti-Semitism.

"I am sure we shall not have to quarrel about the odd five per cent," said Hitler affably. He seemed modest and friendly as he stood dabbing at his face with a crumpled handkerchief. He cleared his throat, coughed, then held out a hand. It felt "hardboned, rough," like the "grip of a front-line soldier."

That night Hanfstaengl could not fall asleep. "My mind still raced with the impressions of the evening. Where all our conservative politicians and speakers were failing abysmally to establish any contact with the ordinary people, this self-made man, Hitler, was clearly succeeding in presenting a non-Communist program to exactly those people whose support we needed." Hanfstaengl decided to help him.

In Berlin Captain Smith turned in a long detailed report on his visit to Munich and, on December 5, Embassy Counselor Robbins dispatched a personal message to the Under Secretary of State: "My own prognostication on the general attitude of the Bavarian outfit is that sooner or later a serious break is going to come from here. Hitler, the young Austrian Sergeant, who fought in the German army during the war, and who is now leading a Fascist movement, known as the 'Grey shirts', is working very slowly and I should say efficiently along the same lines as Mussolini. I am told by some of our men who have been down there, that he is an extraordinary orator and though not of the highest moral standing, a great leader of men. He is obtaining a great deal of money from the manufacturers just as Mussolini did and is going very slowly. He told Truman Smith, our Assistant Military Attaché, who was down there, that he had no intention of starting any big movement for the next month or so, and probably not before two months, that he is collecting funds and equipment, and that all was going well."

The report caused little stir in the State Department, which was concerned with more pressing matters, and was filed away. But in Germany there was growing concern over the increase in membership in the NSDAP and its private army. In mid-December a police official of the Bavarian State Ministry of the Interior filed a disturbing report charging that the Hitler movement was "without a doubt dangerous to the government, not only for the present form of government, but for any political system at all, because if they really achieve their dark ideas in regard to the Jews, Social Democrats, and Bank-capitalists, then there will be much blood and disorder."

Another urgent warning was received almost simultaneously by the new Reich Chancellor, Wilhelm Cuno. It came from a curious source, the Bulgarian consul in Munich, and concerned a frank conversation the Bulgarian had recently had with Hitler. Parliamentary government in Germany, said the latter, was about to collapse since the parliamentary leaders had no mass support. Dictatorship was inevitable from either the right or the left. The big cities of North Germany were controlled largely by the left but in Bavaria his NSDAP was certain of victory. Thousands were joining every week. Moreover, seventy-five per cent of the secret police in Munich were National Socialists and there was an even higher percentage among rank-and-file city police. Hitler predicted that Bolsheviks would gain control of North Germany. To save the nation, Bavarians would have to organize a counterrevolution and, to do so, they would need an iron-fisted dictator, a man "ready, if necessary, to march across fields of blood and corpses."

It was a terrifying forecast of things to come, particularly its ominous assertion that Hitler's plan for crushing Bolshevism and resisting French occupation of the Ruhr would win applause from most patriotic nation-alists in Bavaria. They had endured a few terrifying days of Red rule and were prepared to act ruthlessly against anyone preaching leftist doctrine.

3

In the first days of 1923 a quarrel between the French and British at the Reparations Commission resulted in the withdrawal of the latter's del-egation. This gave France the opportunity to solve the reparations prob-lem by force. On January 11 French and Belgian troops marched into the Ruhr on the excuse that Germany had failed to fulfill her obligations. This act not only inflamed nationalist spirit throughout Germany but quickened the descent of the mark, which plunged from 6750 to the dol-lar to 50,000 within two weeks (on Armistice Day, 1918, it was 7.45 to the dollar). The last payment of railway expenses by the Weimar government to the Committee of Guarantees for a trip to Berlin had "required seven office boys with huge waste-paper baskets full of [twenty-mark] notes to carry the full sum from the office down to the railway station." Now it would take forty-nine office boys.

The invasion of the Ruhr, along with inflation and increased unem-ployment, broadened the base of nationalism and brought Hitler more ad-herents. Disdaining co-operation with other groups, including the Major-ity Socialists, he organized protest meetings of his own and announced that twelve public rallies would be held on January 27, the First Party Day of the NSDAP.

Although the Bavarian police president informed Hitler that these demonstrations were banned, he defiantly shouted that the police could shoot if they wished but he himself would be in the first row. He was as good as his word and on the assigned day hurried from one rally to another by car. "Neither during the war nor during the revolution have I experienced such hypnotic mass-excitement," recalled historian Karl Alexander von Müller, who attended the rally at the Löwenbräukeller. The audience rose as one man, with shouts of "Heil!" as Hitler strode down the aisle. "I was very close when he marched through and I saw that this was different from the man I had met here and there in private houses: his small pale face expressed an inner fanaticism. His eyes glanced from right to left as if looking for enemies to conquer. Was it the mass which gave him this strange power? Did it flow from him to the mass? I noted down, 'Fanatically hysteric romanticism with a brutal will.'"

The following day, again flaunting a police ban, the trooping of SA colors took place on the Marsfeld with 6000 storm troopers shivering in the snow. Some wore a uniform of ski cap, brown jacket and leggings while others were in business suits. There was a varied array of flags with swastikas of various sizes. It was a motley group but, once called to attention, the men stood as rigidly as if they were elite troops of the Kaiser. Although the police were ready for trouble there were no disorders. In fact the two-day affair turned out to be anticlimax. There was no Putsch, no public disturbance. Only its repercussions were of import. Hitler's defiance of the police brought a number of middle-of-the-road leaders to his side and drove the University of Munich students down a much more radical path. More significantly, it lowered the prestige of the Bavarian government itself. In his first serious confrontation with the establishment Hitler had come out the victor.

"He is an extraordinary person," reported an American writer, Ludwell Denny, after attending a Hitler rally a few days later. "His speech was intense and brief; he constantly clenched and unclenched his hands. When I was alone with him for a few moments, he seemed hardly normal; queer eyes, nervous hands, and a strange movement of the head." His personal life was certainly not normal. He still lived in the dingy building on the Thierschstrasse but had sublet a larger room, not as cold as the first, if as scantily furnished. It was ten feet wide at most and the head of the bed projected above the single narrow window. The floor was covered with cheap, worn linoleum. On the wall opposite the bed there was a makeshift bookshelf. Illustrations and drawings hung on the walls. The upper shelves of the bookcase overflowed with volumes on the World War, German histories, an illustrated encyclopedia, Vom Kriege by Clausewitz, a history of Frederick the Great, Houston Stewart Chamberlain's biography of Wagner, the memoirs of Sven Hedin, a collection of heroic myths, von Wartenburg's world history and something entitled Geographical Char-

acter Pictures. The bottom shelf, according to Hanfstaengl, was devoted to novels, a collection of semi-pornographic works by Eduard Fuchs (a Jew), and A *History of Erotic Art.*

Frau Reichert who sublet to Hitler, found her tenant extraordinarily moody. "Sometimes weeks go by when he seems to be sulking and does not say a word to us. He looks through us as if we were not there." Though he paid his rent punctually and in advance, he was "a real Bohemian type." She forgave him this, since he was so nice, and let him use her hallway, which boasted a small upright piano. He lived in spartan simplicity, his almost constant companion a large dog named Wolf. Ever since his relationship with Fuchsl in the war he had need for the faithfulness he found in dogs, and had a unique understanding of them. "There are stupid dogs and others who are so intelligent that it's agonizing." In this dingy room he must have thought of his mother and her tragic death, for he wrote about it that year in a poem entitled "Think of It!" Stripped of its amateurish sentimentality, it probed revealingly.

> *When your mother has grown older.*
> *And you have grown older,*
> *When what was formerly easy and effortless*
> *Now becomes a burden,*
> *When her dear loyal eyes*
> *Do not look out into life as before,*
> *When her legs have grown tired*
> *And do not want to carry her any more—*
> *Then give her your arm for support,*
> *Accompany her with gladness and joy.*
> *The hour will come when, weeping, you*
> *Will accompany her on her last journey!*
> *And if she asks you, answer her.*
> *And if she asks again, speak also.*
> *And if she asks another time, speak to her*
> *Not stormily, but in gentle peace!*
> *And if she cannot understand you well,*
> *Explain everything joyfully;*
> *The hour will come, the bitter hour*
> *When her mouth will ask no more!*

By his own admission, Hitler was a recluse in his youth and had little need of society, but after the war he confessed that he could no "longer bear solitude." Though his room was a lonely refuge and prison, he lived a second existence in the cafés, salons, coffeehouses, and beer halls of Munich. He became a habitué of the Café Weichard (next to the Volkstheater), the Carlton Tea Room (an elite rendezvous on the Briennerstrasse) and the Café Heck (on the Galerienstrasse). He would sit for hours in a secluded corner of the latter at his reserved table where he would observe the life flowing around him.

Every Monday he would meet with intimates at the Café Neumaier, an old-fashioned coffeehouse at the corner of the Peterplatz and the Viktualien Markt. It was a long room with paneled walls and built-in benches. Here at the table reserved for regular customers he would try out his latest ideas on his adherents, many of them middle-aged couples. Here also they would gossip and joke while eating a frugal supper, some of which they had brought with them.

Other evenings were spent at Dietrich Eckart's apartment on the Franz Josef Strasse. "What a wonderful atmosphere in his home! How he took care of his little Anna." This was his housekeeper, Annerl, with whom he had been living since separating from his wife. Perhaps Hitler's most constant companion these days was his new acolyte, Hanfstaengl, who introduced him to important people such as William Bayard Hale, classmate of President Wilson at Princeton and leading European correspondent for the Hearst papers, and Wilhelm Funk, whose salon attracted wealthy nationalist businessmen. Together Hitler and Hanfstaengl often attended the soirées of Frau Elsa Bruckmann, the wife of a publisher and born a Hungarian noblewoman, who was greatly impressed by the new political leader. Hitler was dazzled by life at this level. After one visit to the Bechstein suite in a Munich hotel he told Hanfstaengl that he had felt embarrassed in his blue suit. Herr Bechstein had worn a dinner jacket, the servants were in livery and nothing but champagne was served before the meal. "And you should have seen the bathroom, you can even regulate the heat of the water."

Hanfstaengl became a frequent visitor to the little room on the Thierschstrasse and one day Hitler asked him to play something on the piano in the hallway "to calm him." Hanfstaengl found the old upright badly out of tune but played a Bach fugue. Nodding, Hitler listened absently. Then Hanfstaengl began the prelude to *Die Meistersinger*, hoping the old piano wouldn't fall to pieces under his assault. He played "with plenty of Lisztian *fioriture* and a fine romantic swing," and Hitler became so excited that he strode up and down the narrow hallway gesticulating as if conducting an orchestra. "This music affected him physically and by the time I had crashed through the finale he was in splendid spirits, all his worries gone."

Hanfstaengl found that Hitler knew *Die Meistersinger* "absolutely by heart and could whistle every note of it in a curious penetrating vibrato, but completely in tune." Almost daily musical sessions took place in the hallway. Hitler had little liking for Bach and Mozart, preferring Schumann, Chopin and some works of Richard Strauss. His favorites were Beethoven and Wagner. He had "a genuine knowledge and appreciation" for the latter and never tired of hearing Hanfstaengl's colorful versions of *Tristan* and *Lohengrin.*

Infatuated with Hanfstaengl's style, Hitler would introduce him to all his social circles as a showpiece. "Whereas he otherwise kept the different groups in watertight compartments and told no one where he was going or whom he had been talking to," recalled Hanfstaengl in his unpublished memoirs, "he dragged me around from house to house as his resident musician, and had me sit down at the piano to perform." Once at the home of the photographer Heinrich Hoffmann he began playing Harvard football marches. When he explained how cheerleaders and marching bands would stir up the crowd to almost hysterial mass shouting Hitler's interest quickened. Whereupon Hanfstaengl demonstrated on the piano how German marches could be adapted to the buoyant American beat. "That is it," exclaimed Hitler, and paraded up and down like a drum major, "that is what we need for the movement, marvelous." Hanfstaengl wrote several marches in this style for the SA band but his most significant contribution was the transference of the Harvard "Fight, Fight, Fight" to "Sieg Heil, Sieg Heil!"

Hitler often visited the small Hanfstaengl apartment in Schwabing across from the large school where he had done his basic training in 1914. Probably the greatest attraction was Hanfstaengl's wife, Helene, an American of German descent who was tall, brunette and strikingly attractive. He came in his best suit, the shiny blue serge. "He was respectful, even diffident," recalled Hanfstaengl, "and very careful to adhere to the forms of address still *de rigueur* in Germany between people of lower rank when speaking to those of better education, title, or academic attainment." From the first it was obvious he was physically attracted to Helene, as much by her warm, quiet charm as by her looks, and he treated her with a respect bordering on worship. In her unpublished memoirs written ten years later, she describes their first meeting on a Munich street in early 1923: "He was at the time a slim, shy young man, with a far-away look in his very blue eyes. He was dressed almost shabbily—a cheap white shirt, black tie, a worn dark blue suit, with which he wore an incongruous dark brown leather vest, a beige-colored trench coat, much the worse for wear, cheap black shoes and a soft, old greyish hat. His appearance was quite pathetic."

She invited the shabby Hitler to come for dinner "and from that day he was a constant vistor, enjoying the quiet, cozy home atmosphere, playing with my son, and talking over his plans and hopes for the renaissance of the German Reich. It seemed he enjoyed our home above all others to which he was invited, for with us he was not constantly bothered with curious questions and introduced to other guests as the 'coming savior,' but could if he wished sit quietly in a corner, reading or making notes. We didn't 'lionize' him." She saw Hitler as a warm man and was moved by his feeling for her two-year-old son, Egon. "Evidently he liked children, or he was a good actor." One day the youngster ran to meet Hitler at the door, bumped his head sharply against a heavy chair, and began crying. "Hitler with a dramatic gesture beat the chair severely, reprimanding it for hurting 'good little Egon.' This was a surprise and delight to the youngster and from that day, each time Hitler came he would have to repeat this act; Egon urging him 'Please, Uncle Dolf, spank the naughty chair.' "

By spring Hitler felt so at ease with the Hanfstaengls that he would amuse them with imitations of other followers (such as the affectionate Görings) and play on the floor with Egon. For hours he could idly gossip as he consumed a cup of coffee sweetened with squares of chocolate or, on occasion, sip a glass of the best dry Johannisberger wine after improving it with "a heaping spoonful of castor-sugar." Often they went out together in public and one evening saw the second part of the movie *Fredericus Rex.* The scene Hitler liked above all was that in which the monarch threatened to behead the Crown Prince. "It is imposing to think the old King would have beheaded his own son to enforce discipline," he remarked on the way home. "That is the way German justice should be handled. Either acquittal or beheading."

The lightning change from sentiment to ruthlessness was disconcerting to the Hanfstaengls and they discussed Hitler's private life at length. What, for example, was his true relationship with women? One day he told them, "The mass, the people, to me is a woman," and likened his audiences to a woman. "Someone who does not understand the intrinsically feminine character of the mass will never be an effective speaker. Ask yourself what does a woman expect from a man? Clearness, decision, power, action. . . . If she is talked to properly she will be proud to sacrifice, because no woman will ever feel that her life's sacrifices have received their due fulfillment." Another time he asserted that he would never marry. "My only bride is my Motherland," he said, referring to a nation commonly known as the Fatherland. In that case, Hanfstaengl jokingly replied, why not take a mistress? "Politics is a woman," replied Hitler. "Love her unhappily and she will bite off your head."

Some of Hitler's associates felt sure that Jenny Haug, sister of one of his drivers, was his mistress. She was devoted to him and reportedly carried a small pistol in an armpit holster in her role as voluntary bodyguard. Helene Hanfstaengl could not take this story seriously. "Putzi," she said, "I tell you he is a neuter."

One of Hitler's closest companions during these days disagreed. "We chased girls together and I used to follow him like a shadow," recalled Emil Maurice, who also served as Hitler's chauffeur. The two would spend time at the art academy and in artists' studios admiring models posing in the nude. Calling himself "Herr Wolf," Hitler would occasionally pass an evening with Maurice roaming the night spots and streets for girls. Since the latter was attractive to women, he would act as go-between. Every so often, according to Maurice, Hitler would entertain one of these conquests-by-proxy in his little room. "He always offered flowers, even when he was penniless. And we used to go and admire the ballet dancers."

The NSDAP became practically a full-time occupation for Hanfstaengl and he freely gave out advice ranging from enlarging Hitler's tiny mustache to a more fashionable style ("If it is not the fashion now, it will be later because I wear it!") to disparaging his adviser Rosenberg for his "humbug philosophy." While Hitler usually rejected advice he did not hesitate to borrow a thousand dollars, interest-free, from Hanfstaengl, who had just received part of his share of the sale of the family art shop in New York City. Converted into depreciated marks, this was a tremendous sum and enabled Hitler to purchase two American rotary presses and turn the weekly *Völkischer Beobachter* into a daily.

Hanfstaengl's generosity turned out to be a stroke of luck for someone he detested. Hitler made Rosenberg editor of the daily *Beobachter*, replacing Eckart, who was often absent from his desk for weeks. This position not only intrenched Rosenberg's position as the party's expert on the East but reinforced the influence of fellow refugees from Russia such as Scheubner-Richter, a mystery man connected with German industrialists, generals and high society who, besides serving as intermediary with Ludendorff, was becoming one of Hitler's leading advisers. All of the Russian émigrés were fanatically dedicated to the destruction of Bolshevism and most of them were imbued with the czarist solution to the Jewish conspiracy—terror and brute force. To such zealots social and economic anti-Semitism were effete and ineffective methods. Only the pogrom worked.

4

The spring of 1923 was a busy season for Hitler. The most pressing need was money and he set out on a series of tours to raise funds for the party. In early April he and Hanfstaengl headed for Berlin in Hitler's rickety Selve with Maurice at the wheel. They drove through Saxony even though much of that area was under the control of the Communists. At the outskirts of a town just north of Leipzig they were stopped at a road block manned by Red militia. The imposing Hanfstaengl flourished his Swiss passport, then announced in a broad German-American accent that he was a paper manufacturer from abroad come to visit the Leipzig fair. The others in the car were his chauffeur and his valet. The ruse worked. Although Hitler said, "They would have had my head," as they drove away, it was apparent that he resented being taken for a valet.

In Berlin they not only begged money but spent a Sunday visiting the War Museum and the National Gallery. At the latter Hitler stopped in front of Rembrandt's "Man in a Golden Helmet" and drew attention to the heroic, soldierlike expression. It proved, he said, that the great painter, "in spite of the many pictures he painted in Amsterdam's Jewish quarter, was at heart a true Aryan and German!" Afterward they watched the women boxers in Luna Park. Hitler looked on without expression but insisted on staying for several matches, remarking that "at least it was better than this duelling with sabres that goes on in Germany."

Next day they left home, making a long detour around Saxony. Hitler beguiled the tediousness of the way by whistling long passages from the Wagner operas and entertaining his fellow passengers with impersonations. He would even mock himself by reciting a poem written in his honor that consisted of a long series of ill-scanning couplets of words ending with "itler." "When he was in a good mood," recalled Hanfstaengl, "Hitler would repeat this with embellishments of his own and have us in tears of laughter."

They stopped in Bayreuth, home of Richard Wagner, and were admitted into the festival theater, by the caretaker. The stage was still set for The Flying Dutchman, which had been playing when war was declared in 1914, and this gave Hanfstaengl the opportunity to point out that the original stage scenery had been designed by his own great-grandfather, Ferdinand Heine. Hitler was entranced by everything, particularly Wagner's study where his instructions to the artists and staff still hung on the wall.

On the last day of the trip, during a picnic lunch, Hitler mentioned the monument they had seen outside Leipzig commemorating the Battle of the Nations against Napoleon, and then made a comment that disturbed Hanfstaengl: "The most important thing in the next war will be to make sure that we control the grain and food supplies of Western Russia." This indicated that Rosenberg and his Russian friends had been propagandizing Hitler again, and Hanfstaengl retorted that a war with Russia would be futile. The country to reckon with was America with its tremendous industrial potential. "If you have them on the other side you will lose any future war before you start it." Hitler grunted and made no reply but it was obvious that the argument "had not really sunk in."

Upon return to Munich, he embarked on a campaign attacking France's occupation of the Ruhr but often did so obliquely, as if more interested in rousing his audiences against Jews. On April 13, for instance, he blamed them directly for the Ruhr takeover as well as the loss of the war and inflation. He charged that "so-called World Pacifism" was a Jewish invention; that the leaders of the proletariat were Jews ("Jews again!"); that the Freemasons were tools of the Jews ("Once more the Jews!"); and that, in fact, the Jews were conspiring to conquer the world! "So," he shouted, "Russia and Germany had to be overthrown in order that the ancient prophecy might be fulfilled! So the whole world was lashed into fury! So every lie and propaganda agency was brutally set in action against the State of the last—the German—idealists! And thus it was that Judah won the World War. Or would you wish to maintain that the French, the English, or the American people won the war?" He concluded in a burst of emotion demanding justice for the two million Germans who had died in the World War and the millions of orphans, crippled and widows who remained. "We owe it to these millions to build a new Germany!"

In his obsessive hatred of Jews, Hitler had gone over the edge of reality. His anti-Semitism, though expressed in logical terms, had passed all boundaries of logic. He had turned the world upside down: France, England and America had really lost the war. Germany was the eventual winner since she was freeing herself from the Jews. If Hitler was deceiving himself, he also had succeeded in deceiving his listeners. Hitler skillfully appealed to primitive emotions and when audiences left meetings they remembered few details, only that they must join Hitler's crusade to save Germany; that France must be driven out of the Ruhr and, most important, that the Jews must be put in their place.

In the past year Hitler's platform technique had improved markedly. His gestures had become as varied and flexible as his arguments. Hanfstaengl was particularly impressed by a soaring upward movement of the arm. "It had something of the quality of a really great orchestral conductor who instead of just hammering out the downward beat, suggests the existence of hidden rhythms and meaning with the upward flick of his baton." Utilizing his knowledge and feeling for music, Hitler's speeches became musical in tempo. The first two thirds were "in march time," quickening until the last third became "primarily rhapsodic." His power of mimicry was also put to adroit use. He would impersonate an imaginary opponent, "often interrupting himself with a counter-argument and then returning to his original line of thought after completely annihilating his supposed adversary."

Despite the complicated structure of his speeches, they were easy to follow, being designed primarily for emotional appeal. Thus he could switch from subject to subject without losing his listeners because the bridge between topics was an appeal to some emotion—indignation, fear, love or hate. Despite twistings and turnings, he drew along the listeners as an accomplished actor will guide his audience through some complicated progression in a play.

Hitler also had the rare ability to involve his listeners in the proceedings. "When I talk to people," he told Hanfstaengl, "especially those who are not yet Party members, or who are about to break away for some reason or other, I always talk as if the fate of the nation was bound up in their decision. That they are in a position to give an example for the many to follow. Certainly it means appealing to their vanity and ambition, but once I have got them to that point, the rest is easy." All men, rich or poor, he said, had an inner sense of unfulfillment. "Slumbering somewhere is the readiness to risk some final sacrifice, some adventure, in order to give a new shape to their lives. They will spend their last money on a lottery ticket. It is my business to channel that urge for political purposes. In essence, every political movement is based on the desire of its supporters, men or women, to better things not only for themselves but for their children and others . . . The humbler people are, the greater the craving to identify themselves with a cause bigger than themselves, and if I can persuade them that the fate of the German nation is at stake, then they will become part of an irresistible movement, embracing all classes."

Audiences were always properly prepared for his virtuoso displays by pagan-military pageantry. In addition to stirring music and flying banners, new features had been added—Roman-type standards that Hitler had designed himself and a Roman-style salute. Perhaps he had borrowed both from Caesar by way of Mussolini but he claimed that the stiff-arm salute at least was German. "I'd read the description of the sitting of the Diet of Worms, in the course of which Luther was greeted with the German salute. It was to show him that he was not being confronted with arms, but with peaceful intentions. . . . It was in the Rathskeller at Bremen, about the year 1921, that I first saw this style of salute." Whatever source, the

salute, the vibrant "Heils!" together with the music and banners did much
to assure the audience that the man they were about to hear was the true
voice of Germany.

On the same day that Hitler spoke out against France and the Jews
he staged another confrontation with the Bavarian government. He called
upon the Minister President and brought along with him a former military officer who was the commander of a private army of the *Arbeits-
gemeinschaft der Kampfverbände* (Working Group of Combat Organizations), a conglomeration of radical right-wing groups. The two delivered
an ultimatum, demanding that the Bavarian government itself demand
nullification of the Law for the Defense of the Republic. If Weimar refused to comply, then Bavaria must defy the law.

This was Friday the thirteenth, and Hitler wanted the answer by Saturday. It did not come and the radical right military group held a "military exercise" on Sunday. It was Easter and Hitler stood in an open car,
arm outstretched as the storm troopers and other followers paraded past.
From the Görings' car Helene Hanfstaengl noticed in Hitler's eyes "a
glow of triumph and satisfaction." After the review he brought "a gorgeous
bouquet of roses" to the Hanfstaengl apartment as her birthday gift. They
all had "a jolly tea hour together," marked by Hitler's vivacity and wit. A
week later on his own birthday he was glumly paranoiac. He warned Hanfstaengl not to eat any of the swastika-decorated cakes which, along with
other gifts, almost filled his little room. "Don't forget," he said, "this
building belongs to a Jew and it is child's play to let poison trickle down
the walls in order to dispose of an enemy."

On Monday the Minister President finally gave his answer to Hitler: he
personally objected to the edict for the Defense of the Republic but since
it was the law of the land he was obliged to enforce it. In protest Hitler
called for a mass demonstration on May 1. The possibilities were explosive
since the day was not only a sacred holiday to labor and Marxists but the
anniversary of Munich's liberation from the Soviet Republic. On the evening of April 30 the forces of the radical right wing began converging on
the Oberwiesenfeld, a military training area several miles north of
Munich's main railroad station. By dawn there were 1000 men on hand.
Guards were mounted in expectation of leftist attacks but hour after hour
passed without action. "At six o'clock," recalled Hitler, "gangs of Reds
gathered to meet us. I sent some men to provoke them but they didn't
react."

By nine all detachments from outside the city had arrived, swelling
the Hitler forces to some 1300. They stood in the warm sun leaning on
rifles, waiting with mixed boredom and anxiety, while a disgusted Hitler

strode around carrying a steel helmet by its chin straps and asking, "Where are the Reds?" Just before noon a detachment of army troops and green-uniformed police appeared and rapidly surrounded the armed demonstrators. With them was a chagrined Captain Röhm. He told Hitler that he had just come from the commanding general of the area who demanded that the arms be turned over immediately or Hitler would have to take the consequences.

Hitler was incensed but still withstood the pleas of Gregor Strasser and others to defy the government and charge the troops. The decision to turn over arms must have been a bitter one. But if Hitler had attacked, his forces would certainly have been repelled and the fruitless carnage might have meant his end as a political leader, perhaps even as a man. He did achieve a success of sorts in the retreat from the Oberwiesenfeld. In Schwabing his troops came upon a detachment of Communists, put them to flight and set fire to their flags and banners. This was Hitler's moment and he boomed out a short speech: this fire, symbolic of Bolshevist world pestilence, he said, was only a modest prologue to the day in which the National Socialists would seize power! It was a rousing address that lifted the spirits of his men and appeared to change a blundering enterprise into a triumph. But their elation was fleeting. By evening it was apparent that Hitler's first revolutionary move was a fiasco. By that failure he lost many adherents of stature. "I reject Hitler completely!" exclaimed one former Free Corps commander. "He failed miserably on the first day of May and he will always fail."

He was not the only loser at the Oberwiesenfeld. It was even more of a defeat and embarrassment for the Bavarian government. When Hitler was called to answer official charges of having endangered public security he replied with an insolent confidence that put the prosecutor general on the defensive. By refusing to be cowed, Hitler made political capital out of disaster. Rebounding from defeat was becoming a pattern.

A number of foreign observers, however, predicted it was the beginning of his end. Robert Murphy, for one, reported that the Nazi movement was now "on the wane." The people, he wrote, "are wearied of Hitler's inflammatory agitation which yields no results and offers nothing constructive; his anti-Semitic campaign made many enemies; the rowdy-like conduct of his youthful following has antagonized order-loving members of the community."

5

Murphy was only reflecting the impressions of local officials throughout Bavaria who misread the resultant political lull after May Day as a definite turn away from Hitler and his movement. This inertia continued except for a brief flurry caused by the execution of a German nationalist, Albert Leon Schlageter, who had blown up railroad tracks near Duisburg as a protest against French occupation of the Ruhr. He was tried for sabotage by the French and shot on May 26.

When Hanfstaengl heard that a number of patriotic organizations were going to stage a protest demonstration in the Königsplatz the following week, he felt that Hitler should return from his holiday in the mountains and participate. He took the train to Berchtesgaden, a beautiful resort town on the border of Germany and Austria near Salzburg where he found Hitler ("I had fallen in love with the landscape") registered under the name of Herr Wolf at the Pension Moritz on a steep hill known as the Obersalzberg. At first Hitler was not enthusiastic about addressing a demonstration with so many diverse speakers, but Hanfstaengl persisted and the two began blocking out a speech.

That night Eckart, who shared Hanfstaengl's bedroom, complained that Hitler would parade around swinging his rhinoceros-hide whip in a swashbuckling manner to impress the wife of the pension manager. "The way Adolf is carrying on now goes beyond me," he said. "The man is plain crazy." He told of overhearing Hitler show off to the lady in question by denouncing Berlin in extravagant terms: ". . . the luxury, the perversion, the iniquity, the wanton display and the Jewish materialism disgusted me so thoroughly that I was almost beside myself. I nearly imagined myself to be Jesus Christ when he came to his Father's Temple and found the money changers." Whereupon, claimed Eckart, Hitler brandished his whip and exclaimed that it was his mission to descend upon the capital like a Christ and scourge the corrupt.

The following day Hitler accompanied Hanfstaengl to the station and, as they descended the Obersalzberg, remarked that Eckart, whom he had recently replaced as editor of the party newspaper, had become "an old pessimist, a senile weakling." Schopenhauer had only turned him into a doubting Thomas. "Where would I get if I listened to all his transcendental talk? A nice ultimate wisdom that! To reduce oneself to a minimum of desire and will. Once will is gone, all is gone. This life is war." He began whistling the Swan Song from *Lohengrin* in "a curious soft tremolo."

Anton Drexler and his wife also disapproved of Hitler's play-acting on the Obersalzberg. They were equally disconcerted by his growing enthusiasm for revolutionary action. Their alarm was shared by others who objected to his associating with industrialists, wealthy socialites and bankers rather than building a solid base of genuine socialists from the working class. Hitler must have been aware that he faced another revolt within the party, one born of discontent and dismay among those who first held highest hopes for him as leader of Germany's renaissance.

Early that September Hitler attempted to bolster his slipping prestige by a public appearance. The occasion was the German Day celebration in Nuremberg which took place the first two days of September, the anniversary of the Battle of Sedan. More than 100,000 nationalists swarmed into the ancient city, parading through the streets and, according to a state police report, generating "such enthusiasm as had not been seen in Nuremberg since 1914." The streets were a sea of Nazi and Bavarian flags as the crowd roared "Heil!" waved handkerchiefs and tossed flowers and wreaths at Ludendorff and the marching units. "It was the unbridled expression of that multitude of defeated, miserable, displaced, and shattered people, who now saw a ray of hope, of freedom from slavery and need. Many women and men cried, so overcóme were they by emotion."

The largest number of marchers came from the NSDAP and after the opening parade Hitler spoke at one of the meetings. He looked more groomed than he had at Coburg, with pressed suit, low-cut shoes and neatly slicked-down hair. "In a few weeks the dice will roll," he declared prophetically. "What is in the making today will be greater than the World War. It will be fought out on German soil for the whole world."

On the second day the German Battle League was formed. Outwardly an association of nationalists, it was a creature of the NSDAP: its secretary-general was Scheubner-Richter, its military leader was another Hitler man, one of its main organizations (the *Reichsflagge*) was dominated by Röhm; and its initial proclamation (written by Feder) sounded as if it came out of Hitler's mouth. It declared opposition to parliamentarianism, international capital, the class struggle, pacifism, Marxism and the Jews.

German Day at Nuremberg and the founding of the German Battle League marked Hitler's public return to revolutionary tactics. This became more apparent a month later when he was officially made political leader of the new organization. Its "action program" called openly for seizure of power in Bavaria and the rumor spread that Hitler was preparing a revolution. He did, in fact, announce openly that he intended to act rather than allow the Reds to seize power again. "The task of our movement, as always is . . . to prepare for the coming collapse of the Reich, so that when the old trunk falls the young fir tree may be already standing."

Although the Minister President of Bavaria, Eugen von Knilling, shared some of Hitler's beliefs, he had been pushed to the edge of patience by his rabble-rousing tactics. On September 26 Knilling told his

Cabinet that the emergency was so grave that a state commissar general should be appointed who, while subordinate to the Cabinet, "would have a free hand in the exercise of the executive power." He proposed former Minister President von Kahr, who had the support of several nationalist groups and was held in esteem by both conservative monarchists and the Catholic Church.

In the name of law and order Kahr accepted this onerous position and his first act was to ban fourteen mass meetings the Nazis had planned for the morrow. This action was both a threat and an opportunity for Adolf Hitler, who had just returned from a trip to Switzerland to solicit funds. If he submitted it could mean ruin. If he successfully resisted, he could become a politician of national importance. He was cautioned to retreat and fight another day; the movement was not yet strong enough for action. But those close to the rank and file urged him to act. "If nothing happens now the men will sneak away," said the head of the SA Regiment Munich. "In order to keep the men together," said Scheubner-Richter, "one must finally undertake something. Otherwise they will become left radicals."

These were the urgings Hitler heeded. This impulse for action set him on the road to revolution and he began searching Munich and its environs for activist allies. His days were filled with interviews and visits to a variety of influential men: military figures, politicians, industrialists and officials. He talked to the party faithful as well as those who wavered— promising, threatening and cajoling. The one sentence he continuously used was "We must compromise these people so that they have to march with us."

"Absolutely no one could ever persuade him to change his mind, once it was made up," recalled Helene Hanfstaengl. "On a number of occasions when his followers tried to coerce him I noticed the faraway, unheeding expression in his eyes; it was as though he had closed his mind to all ideas but his own." That autumn the faraway, unheeding expression in his eyes had a specific meaning. He saw himself emulating Mussolini—and his march would be to Berlin. Nor was this a vision he revealed only to intimates. In a conference with right-wing military men he called for an attack on Berlin with all Bavaria's forces. "Hitler now had definite Napoleonic and Messianic ideas," recalled one of those present. "He declared that he felt the call within himself to save Germany and that this role would fall to him, if not now then later. He then drew a number of parallels with Napoleon, especially with the return of Napoleon from Elba to Paris."

Chapter Six

THE BEER HALL PUTSCH
1923

1

On the last day of September 1923 Hitler received an unsettling letter from "an old member and fanatic member of your movement," who pointed out a startling prediction in the current yearbook of the well-known astrologer, Frau Elsbeth Ebertin. "A man of action born on 20 April 1889," it said, "can expose himself to personal danger by excessively uncautious action and very likely trigger off an uncontrollable crisis." The stars showed that this man was "to be taken very seriously indeed; he is destined to play a 'Führer-role' in future battles." He was destined to *"sacrifice himself for the German nation."*

Although no name was mentioned, it was apparent that Frau Ebertin was referring to Hitler, and while she did not specify any particular date, she warned that acting rashly in the near future would endanger his life. Another astrologer, Wilhelm Wulff (years later he would advise Himmler's SS on astrological matters), also cast Hitler's horoscope late that summer and *was* definite about a date. His prediction was also ominous: "violence with a disastrous outcome" for the subject during the period of November 8–9, 1923.

Such prophecies were seriously regarded in many quarters. Several German psychiatrists and psychologists were already considering the idea of "psychological astrology." Dr. O. A. H. Schmitz—an ardent disciple of the Swiss psychiatrist, C. G. Jung—had recently suggested that astrology might be exactly what psychology needed. But Hitler's comment on Frau Ebertin's prediction was: "What on earth have women and stars got to do with me?"

Whether he believed in astrology or not, Hitler was convinced that his own destiny would eventually lead him to success; and, as Helene Hanfstaengl had noticed, he tuned out all but affirmative voices. By coincidence he found one of them the same day he received Frau Ebertin's astrological warning. It came in Bayreuth at the Villa Wahnfried, Wagner's home, where he was paying homage to Cosima, the eighty-six-year-old widow of the master. Winifred Wagner, the English wife of Wagner's son Siegfried, was already entranced by Hitler and his movement. She welcomed him warmly; her six-year-old daughter Friedelind thought he looked funny in his Bavarian leather shorts, thick woolen socks, red and blue checked shirt and baggy short blue jacket. "His sharp cheekbones stuck out over hollow pasty cheeks and above them were a pair of unnaturally bright blue eyes. There was a half-starved look about him but something else too, a fanatical glow."

Ill at ease, Hitler walked shyly, awkwardly around the music room and library, tiptoeing as if he were in a cathedral. But later in the garden, as he told the Wagners of his plans for the near future, "his voice took on tone and color and grew deeper and deeper until we sat like a circle of little charmed birds listening to the music although we didn't pay any attention to a word he said." After he left, Frau Wagner said, "Don't you feel that he is destined to be the savior of Germany?" Siegfried laughed indulgently. So far as he was concerned, Hitler was an obvious "fraud" as well as an upstart.

Hitler was across the street, making a pilgrimage to the home of the aged Houston Stewart Chamberlain, paralyzed in his wheel chair. This son of an English admiral had been drawn to Germany, seeing in her people the master race. He was talented and neurotic, and widely regarded as one of the leading men of culture of his day. A worshiper of Wagner, he had married his daughter Eva. The English prophet of racism was so taken by Hitler that he had a "longer and more refreshing sleep" that night than any since he had seen stricken in August 1914. He wrote Hitler a few days later: "With one blow you have transformed the state of my soul. That Germany, in the hour of her greatest need, brings forth a Hitler —that is proof of her vitality."

Chamberlain's words must have helped solidify the growing sense within Hitler that he was a man of fate. A week or so later, while motoring in his new car through the Bavarian hills with Rosenberg and the Hanfstaengls, fog unexpectedly enshrouded the highway and the open red Mercedes lurched into a ditch. No one spoke on the way back to Munich, then he turned to Helene. "I noticed you were not at all frightened by our mishap. I knew we would not be injured. This will not be the only accident which will leave me unharmed. I shall pass through them all and succeed in my plans."

2

Another aspect of fate, in the guise of the inflation, also appeared to be working in favor of Hitler and his march on Berlin. By the beginning of October it took 6,014,300 marks to equal a single prewar mark. The price of one egg equaled that of 30,000,000 in 1913. Many municipalities and industrial firms took to printing their own "emergency money" to meet expenses. The Reichsbank could not refuse to accept this emergency money or to treat it as of equal value with their own notes. The printing of government money itself became farcical: a thousand-mark note issued in Berlin the previous December was now stamped over in red: *Ein Milliarde Mark*; and a 500,000,000-mark note printed by the Bavarian State Bank a few weeks earlier was stamped: *Zwanzig Milliarden Mark*. This 20-billion-mark note presumably could be exchanged for more than $800 but by the time the holder of the modest-looking little note with the astronomical figure got to the cashier it would be worth a fraction of that —providing any cashier was willing to surrender hard foreign currency for it. People were frantic. They dared not hold currency for an hour. A missed trolley car to the bank could mean a man's monthly salary was reduced to a quarter or less. A waiter in Baden told a young American reporter, Ernest Hemingway, that he had saved up enough money for a *Gasthaus*. Now the money wouldn't buy four bottles of champagne. "Germany debases her money to cheat the Allies," said the waiter. "But what do I get out of it?"

The burden of inflation naturally fell on those who could not pay with notes—the workers and the elderly. The first were reduced to a near starvation diet and the latter were brought to poverty level overnight. Pensioners and those who lived on interest from bonds and life insurance found themselves destitute. Securities bought with gold marks were paid off in paper money that deteriorated in value in one's hand. In America only Southerners, whose families had suffered a similar fate after the Civil War days, would have understood.

About the sole ones who rejoiced were those deeply in debt who could pay off their obligations with worthless paper. But the greatest beneficiaries were the exchange barons, the profiteers and opportunistic foreigners who bought up jewelry and real estate at ridiculously low prices. Large estates and buildings went to these vultures for a few hundred dollars. Family heirlooms were exchanged for enough to feed a family a few weeks. There were scenes beyond belief: a woman who had left a basket-full of money on the street, returning a moment later to find the money dumped in the gutter and the basket stolen; a worker with a salary of two billion marks a week able to buy his family only potatoes. And when distribution of the most basic food broke down, raids on potato fields in law-abiding Germany became commonplace.*

By mid-October Hitler, after drawing almost 35,000 new members into the party since January, was more than ever convinced that the people were ready for revolution. "I can only take action," he told a Nuremberg audience, "where my fanatical belief and love for the entire German people lead me." Never had his speeches been delivered with more passion. "You cannot imagine how silent it becomes as soon as this man speaks," one ardent follower wrote her family that October. It was as if the entire audience was no longer able to breathe. "Sometimes it almost seems to me as if Hitler used a magic charm in order to win the unconditional confidence of old and young alike." Another fascinated listener got so close he could see the spit fly under his mustache. "For us this man was a whirling dervish. But he knew how to fire up the people, not with arguments, which are never possible in hate speeches, but with the fanaticism of his whole manner, screaming and yelling, and above all by his deafening repetition, and a certain contagious rhythm. This he has learned to do and it has a fearfully exciting primitive and barbaric effect."

In Bavaria the pressure exerted by such rousing, hypnotic speeches made Commissar von Kahr's task, despite his dictatorial power, an impossible one. Called upon to restrain Hitler violence, he was under pressure from a large segment of the Bavarian leadership to go easy on him. The temper of Bavaria was conservative and nationalistic and, while many re-

---

* The most poignant movie of these days was made not by a German but by D. W. Griffith. This was *Isn't Life Wonderful*, with Neil Hamilton and Carol Dempster as a German couple whose future depends on a tiny patch of potatoes. The climax comes when they secretly gather the potatoes at night, then, hitching themselves like horses to their cart, start through the woods. They are set upon by marauders who steal their crop. The best German film was Pabst's *Die freudlose Gasse* (*Street Without Joy*) in which Greta Garbo, in her first major role, portrays the daughter of a bourgeois family in Vienna brought to starvation by wicked stock manipulators. There are realistic scenes of shoppers waiting all night in front of a butcher store. In the finale the frenzied mob attacks the repulsive butcher who has grown rich on their suffering.

gretted Hitler's crude tactics and violent language, they shared his dream of a strong, rejuvenated Germany. "There are decent emotions which lead misguided people to the Nazis," commented a liberal member of the Bavarian Democratic Party, "men who honorably desire to serve their people and their state." Because of this attitude Bavarian police authorities, aggravated as they were, did little to restrain Hitlerian violence. The head of the army in Bavaria, General Otto von Lossow, was also resisting demands from Berlin to curb Hitler and to ban his newspaper. In the face of Lossow's continued defiance, he was dismissed, an act so infuriating to the Bavarian government that it assumed command of all Reichswehr units in the state.

This defiance, tantamount to revolt, was repeated the next day by army men stationed throughout Bavaria. They renounced the Weimar Republic by taking an oath to the Bavarian government "until an adjustment between Bavaria and the Reich has been arrived at, and I renew my obligation to obey my superior officers." It was mutiny, executed legalistically, formally and without violence—but mutiny nonetheless. "There will be no civil war," a Bavarian cabinet member confided to Robert Murphy. "The ship of state had merely listed too far to the left, and it was and is Bavaria's duty to right it."

Commissar von Kahr himself attacked the federal government in print. In the *Münchener Zeitung* he justified Bavarian defiance and called for an overthrow of the new government of Chancellor Gustav Stresemann, a self-made man with liberal faith in freedom and political rights. Stresemann himself was a nationalist; he charged that 33,000 Marxists held official posts in Prussia and that "as a result domestic politics are purely Marxist; that is to say they are directed against the natural order of things and are oriented towards compulsion, agitation, demagoguery and street fighting. Foreign policy is becoming internationalized and those who control it are careful to ensure that Germany never becomes powerful again." Here again were thoughts and words that could have come from Hitler.

A few days later General von Lossow—still in command of his troops despite dismissal by the Weimar Republic—was reported to have made a speech declaring that there were only three possibilities: going on as usual "in the old jogtrot way," seceding Bavaria from the Reich, or marching on Berlin to proclaim a national dictatorship. Hitler was dedicated to the last proposal. The secession of Bavaria from the federal government was as distasteful to him as doing nothing since an independent Bavaria would probably mean a return to a monarchist government with Crown Prince

Rupprecht, the pretender, as King.* Yet could he force Commissar von Kahr and General von Lossow to join him in a march on Berlin without declaring Bavarian independence? The answer was supplied by Rosenberg and Scheubner-Richter. Their plan was to kidnap Prince Rupprecht and Kahr at the ceremony on November 4 celebrating German Memorial Day. Several hundred storm troopers would seal off the alley near the Feldherrnhalle where the dignitaries would assemble. Hitler would then politely inform the prisoners that he had seized the government to prevent a Red takeover and prevent the separation of Bavaria from the Reich. The Putsch would be, according to Rosenberg, "both short and painless," since Kahr and Rupprecht would be impelled to co-operate.

Hanfstaengl thought it was a "crazy plan," arguing that any attack on the Crown Prince would surely force the army to retaliate. Emphasizing the impracticability and senselessness of the operation, Hanfstaengl turned his warning into a personal attack on Rosenberg. If Hitler kept listening to these Baltic plotters, he said, it would mean the ruin of the movement. Hitler agreed to veto the kidnaping but would make no immediate promises concerning Rosenberg.† "We must think first of a march on Berlin," Hanfstaengl remembered him saying. "Once we have dealt with the immediate situation then we can look around and I can find Rosenberg another job."

3

By now the Bavarian government was run, under the supervision of Minister President von Knilling, by a triumvirate of "vons": Kahr, Lossow and Colonel Hans Ritter von Seisser, chief of the Bavarian state police,

---

* To illustrate the cross-purposes within Hitler's inner circle, Captain Röhm had already made two attempts to enlist Prince Rupprecht's co-operation. On the first occasion he fell to his knees and, with clasped hands, begged Rupprecht to work with Hitler; he was summarily dismissed in a "not too friendly fashion." On the second, Röhm suggested that Hitler, Ludendorff and the Crown Prince jointly rule Bavaria, using this state as a base to win over North Germany with an armed invasion consisting of the various patriotic organizations. "I told him that was nonsense," recalled Rupprecht's political adviser.

† Hitler often told differing stories to his confederates. He may have dismissed the kidnap plot out of hand as his remark to Hanfstaengl implied. Rosenberg, however, was convinced the Putsch was on until he discovered on German Memorial Day that there were strong police units in the alley and informed Hitler that the coup de main had to be abandoned.

Helene Hanfstaengl repeatedly noticed Hitler's habit of keeping his advisers at odds with each other and in the dark—"he never confided a single plan, visit or the fact that he made new acquaintances, to more than one or two followers at a time. This often led to uncomfortable situations when different party members suddenly discovered they were not completely in the picture—H's idea of complete personal control of all plans."

who had gathered together a group of bright staff officers too young to challenge his position. The triumvirate resembled a dictatorship in the old Roman caretaker sense and, though the three men represented a variety of ultraconservative and right radical values, they agreed that Hitler's revolutionary tactics were not pro bono publico and should either be channeled properly or outlawed. The breaking point was reached on October 30 when Hitler made it clear to a wildly receptive audience at the Zirkus Krone that he was ready to march on Berlin. "The German problem will be solved for me only after the black-white-red swastika banner floats on the Berlin Palace!" he shouted. "We all feel that the hour has come and, like the soldier in the field, we will not shirk our duty as Germans. We will follow the order to keep in step, and march forward!"

In an effort to split the triumvirate, Hitler requested an interview with Colonel von Seisser. They met privately on November 1 at the home of a veterinary who headed the Bund Oberland, a nationalistic paramilitary organization. Hitler tried to persuade Seisser that Kahr was unfit and only a pawn of the Bavarian government, then proposed, as he had a week earlier, that Seisser and Lossow align themselves with himself and Ludendorff. But Seisser again declared he would have nothing to do with the World War idol, nor would the top officers in the army. Hitler admitted that, while the generals would be against Ludendorff, majors and lower-grade officers would support him in defiance of their own commanders. It was "high time" to take action, warned Hitler. "Our people are under such economic pressure that we must either act or they will swing to the Communists."

While Seisser privately agreed with Kahr that the Nazis were "trash," both did act. On November 6 the triumvirate conferred with representatives of the nationalist organizations. Their most urgent task, said Kahr, was the establishment of a new national regime. They all agreed that the Weimar government had to be overthrown but it must be done in concert and not independently as certain nationalist organizations were planning. He didn't mention any name but everyone knew he was referring to Hitler. It was questionable, said Kahr, if Chancellor Stresemann could be ousted in the normal way. "The atypical way must be prepared. Preparations have already been made. But if the atypical way must be taken, then everyone must cooperate. It must be accomplished according to a united, sufficiently prepared and thought-out plan."

The next speaker, Lossow, supported Kahr and his determination to crush any Putsch by force of arms. "I am ready to support a rightist dictatorship if the affair is likely to succeed," said the general. He would participate if there was a fifty-one per cent chance for success. "But if we are merely to be harassed into a Putsch, which will come to a sorry end in five or six days, I will not cooperate." In conclusion, both he and Colonel von Seisser underlined their warnings to members of the Battle League to co-operate—or else.

That evening Hitler met with his advisers in the apartment of Scheubner-Richter to draft their own plan of action. They agreed to stage a full-fledged Putsch on the following Sunday, November 11. There were two reasons for this date, one historical, one practical. This would be the fifth anniversary of Germany's surrender. It would also be a holiday with all offices deserted and police and military at low strength. The streets would be relatively free of traffic and the storm troopers could march unimpeded.

The next morning the conspirators met again, this time with the sen-ior leader of the Battle League. Probably Ludendorff was present though he later denied it, but Hitler certainly was there and so were Göring and Scheubner-Richter. Final arrangements for the Putsch were adopted: the major towns and cities of Bavaria would be controlled with the seizure of railroad stations, telegraph offices, telephone offices, radio stations, public utilities, town halls and police headquarters; Communist and socialist leaders along with trade union heads and shop stewards were to be arrested. Numerically Hitler's forces in Munich would have superiority with 4000 armed Putschists facing perhaps 2600 state police and army troops.

Early that same evening Hitler called a second meeting, this time with two additional members, ex-Police President Pöhner, and his former assistant, Wilhelm Frick, who had remained with the police and was still protecting Hitler and his followers. The conspirators discussed a develop-ment that called for a drastic change in plan. Commissar von Kahr had unexpectedly announced he was holding a mass "patriotic demonstration" at the Bürgerbräukeller the next night. The outward purpose was to out-line the aims of his regime but it was probably an attempt to forestall any display of unified action by the National Socialists among leading govern-ment officials, military leaders and prestigious civilians. Hitler was asked to attend but it seemed obvious that the invitation was a trap. Perhaps the triumvirate was going to announce Bavaria's break with Berlin and the res-toration of the Wittelsbach monarchy.

Hitler argued that it was a heaven-sent opportunity. The triumvirate as well as Minister President von Knilling and other government officials would be on the same platform. Why not simply escort them to a private room and either convince them to go along with a coup d'état or, if they were adamant, imprison them? Hitler was undoubtedly talking for effect.

He knew very well that he could not mount a successful Putsch without the full co-operation of the triumvirate. He had no real intention of seizing the government of Bavaria, only of attempting to arouse the Bavarians by dramatics and thus successfully defy Berlin. He actually had no long-range program and was willing to trust to luck and fate.

His co-conspirators were not and the argument went on for hours. But Hitler refused to budge and finally, at 3 A.M. on November 8, ever - one accepted, if reluctantly, his proposal: the Putsch would be launched that night at the Bürgerbräukeller. As soon as the guests filed out into the cold early morning air Scheubner-Richter handed his servant a packet of letters addressed to influential publishers—to be delivered as soon as their offices opened.

It dawned bitter and windy. The cold had come early to Bavaria that year and snow was already falling in the hills south of the city. On the most important day of Hitler's life he had a headache and a throbbing toothache. His colleagues had urged him to see a dentist but he said he "didn't have time, and that there was going to be a revolution which would change everything." He must follow his star. When Hanfstaengl asked what would happen to their project if he fell seriously ill, Hitler replied, "If that should be the case or if I should die it would only be a sign that my star has run its course and my mission is fulfilled."

Late that morning orders were issued to SA leaders by phone, letter or in person to alert their men for action. There were no details, no explanations. Moreover, many of those closest to Hitler still had no idea there was a change in plans. Just before noon, in his little whitewashed office, Rosenberg (sporting a violet shirt and scarlet tie) was discussing the morning's *Völkischer Beobachter* with Hanfstaengl. On the front page was a picture of the general who had brought the Prussian army to the Russian side against Napoleon at Tauroggen. The caption was: "Shall we find a second General Yorck in our hour of need?" While these two, who detested each other, were weighing the possible effects of the picture, they heard stamping outside and a hoarse voice: "Where is Captain Göring?" The door was flung open and Hitler, wearing his tightly belted trench coat and gripping his whip, burst in "pallid with excitement."

"Swear you will not mention this to a living soul," he said with suppressed urgency. "The hour has come. Tonight we act!" He asked them both to be part of his personal escort. They were to bring pistols and rendezvous outside the beer hall at seven o'clock. Hanfstaengl hurried home to tell his wife to take their son Egon to the villa they had just built in the country, then informed a number of international journalists, including H. R. Knickerbocker, that they "must under no circumstances" miss the meeting that evening.

By afternoon Hitler had controlled his excitement and was gossiping at the Café Heck with Heinrich Hoffmann, his photographer crony, as though this was just another ordinary day. Suddenly Hitler suggested they visit Esser, who was laid up with jaundice. While Hoffmann waited outside, Hitler revealed to Esser that he was going to announce the national revolution that evening. He needed help. At exactly 9:30 P.M. Esser, carrying a flag, was to rush up to the podium of the Löwenbräukeller, where a nationalist meeting was to be held, and announce the National Socialist revolution.

Hitler emerged to tell Hoffmann that Esser felt much better and the two strolled aimlessly along the Schellingstrasse. Moments later Göring approached and Hitler took him off for a private talk only to return with the announcement that he had a terrible headache and must leave. By now Hoffmann was completely bewildered. What on earth, he asked, was Hitler doing that evening? He answered mysteriously that he would be "very busy on a very important job," then set off for party headquarters.

By now the SA men were getting out of their work clothes and putting on uniforms which consisted of field-gray windbreakers with swastika armbands, field-gray ski cap, and revolver belt. They were bound for various rendezvous. Karl Kessler of the 2nd Company, was instructed to report to the Arzbergerkeller while shoemaker Josef Richter was sent to the Hofbräuhaus. Members of the Bund Oberland were also on the move. Instead of a swastika they wore a sprig of edelweiss and were equipped with steel helmets. One of the key units, the Führer's special hundred-man bodyguard, gathered at the Torbräu. Their leader, a tobacconist, was haranguing them. "Any one of you who isn't going into this heart and soul had better get out right now." It was their task, he said, to bear the brunt of whatever happened that night at the Bürgerbräukeller. "We're going to run the government out."

It was dark when a car stopped in front of Scheubner-Richter's apartment house and General Ludendorff got out. He talked a few minutes with Scheubner-Richter, then left. Moments later Scheubner-Richter and his servant also drove off at top speed. "Hansl," Scheubner-Richter said, "if things don't go right today, we will all be in jail tomorrow." At party headquarters they met Hitler and other leaders. After some discussion the group headed for the Bürgerbräukeller in two cars. It was almost 8 P.M. The beer hall was about half a mile from the center of Munich on the other side of the Isar River. It was a large rambling building, flanked by gardens and containing a number of dining rooms and bars. The main hall, the largest in the city, except for the Zirkus Krone, could hold 3000 at its sturdy round wooden tables. Officials knew there might be trouble and there were on hand 125 municipal policemen to control the crowd. In addition there was a mounted detachment as well as a number of officers scattered in the audience. In case of an emergency, a company of green-uniformed state police had been installed in a barracks only a quarter of a mile away.

By the time the Hitler caravan crossed the Isar River the hall was closed to all but important personages. Every seat was taken and Hanfstaengl wasn't able to bring in his little group of international journalists. A few minutes past eight Hitler's red Mercedes, followed by Scheubner-Richter's car, approached the beer hall. Hitler was disturbed by the milling crowds. Would his trucks be able to get through this mob? The two cars slowly pushed their way to the front entrance, which was blocked by a phalanx of policemen. Hitler persuaded the police to leave and make room for his troops, which were expected shortly, then led the way through the beer-hall door which Hess held open. There was such a crush that the door shut in the face of Hanfstaengl, who was bringing up the rear with an American woman journalist. He warned the police that there would be a scandal if the foreign press was excluded, but what opened the way was the fact that his companion was smoking an American cigarette, a luxury in Germany. At the edge of the anteroom Hitler stood near a large pillar peering into the jammed hall at the platform where Kahr was speaking in a droning voice. He denounced Marxism and called for a resurgent Germany. His manner was pedantic, as if he were lecturing, and the audience listened politely, relieving the boredom with beer.

Hanfstaengl figured that Hitler would fit more naturally into the scene if he too had a beer and so bought three at the serving counter for three billion marks. Hitler occasionally sipped his as he waited impatiently for the special Brownshirt bodyguard unit. Trucks filled with other storm troopers were already outside but they stayed in place until a few minutes after 8:30 P.M. when his helmeted bodyguard finally arrived. This was the signal for action. The trucks emptied and the armed Nazis surrounded the building. Bewildered and outnumbered the municipal police—unprepared for a political battle—did nothing.

Captain Göring and the bodyguard unit, armed with machine pistols, streamed into the building. Ulrich Graf, Hitler's personal protector, was waiting in the cloakroom for their arrival and hurried up to his chief, who had removed his trench coat to reveal a black long-tailed morning coat cut in Bavarian provincial style. Graf whispered into Hitler's ear and it reminded one onlooker of a patron petitioning the headwaiter for a good table. More than twenty police blocked the invaders but the leader of the bodyguard unit shouted, "Out of the way—you there!" and the police obediently did an about-face, like Keystone Cops, and marched in step right out the front door.

Hitler set aside the beer he had been nursing, pulled out his Browning pistol and, as the storm troopers shouted, "Heil Hitler!" he started into the hall with ex-butcher Graf, Scheubner-Richter (who was squinting myopically in the smoke-filled room) and his faithful servant, Harvard-graduate Hanfstaengl, an ex-police spy, business manager Max Amann, and the idealist-activist student of geopolitics, Rudolf Hess. Brandishing weapons, this motley band began pushing its way through the packed humanity toward the platform. By this time one group of Brownshirts had blocked the exit while another group set up a machine gun positioned to rake the audience. Tables overturned in the uproar. A cabinet member scrambled for cover under his table. Some made for the exits in consternation but were warned back and, if they resisted, were beaten or kicked.

The Hitler phalanx was blocked and, amidst the uproar, he climbed onto a chair waving his pistol. "Quiet!" he shouted and when the tumult continued he fired a round into the ceiling. In the shocked silence Hitler said, "The national revolution has broken out! The hall is surrounded!" No one was to leave the hall. Sweat poured down his pale face. He looked insane or drunk to some but a few were struck by the ridiculous sight of a pistol-brandishing revolutionary in such a badly cut morning suit. Comic as he looked, Hitler was dead serious. He ordered the triumvirate to follow him into an adjoining room, guaranteeing their security. But the three men did not move. Finally Kahr took a backward step as Hitler began clambering over a table toward the speakers' platform. Seisser's aide, a major, came forward, hand in pocket as if about to draw his pistol. Hitler jammed his own pistol against the major's forehead and said, "Take your hand out."

Hitler assured the triumvirate and the audience that everything could be settled in ten minutes. This time the three men and two aides followed Hitler to the side room. "*Komödie spielen* [Put on an act]," whispered Lossow to his colleagues. In the private room Hitler was more agitated than ever. "Please forgive me for proceeding in this manner," he said, "but I had no other means." He answered Seisser's accusations of breaking his word not to make a Putsch with an apology: he did it for the good of Germany. He told them that ex-Police President Pöhner was going to be the new Bavarian Minister President and Ludendorff would assume command of the new national army based on the radical right Battle League, and lead the march on Berlin. After the Putschists seized power, Hitler promised, the triumvirate would have even greater powers: Kahr would be made Regent of Bavaria; Lossow Reich Army Minister; and Seisser Reich Police Minister.

When the three failed to respond Hitler drew out his pistol (all in jest, he later testified). "There are five rounds in it," he said hoarsely, "four for the traitors, and if it fails one for me." He handed over the weapon to Graf, who already was armed with a machine pistol. Under such circumstances to die or not to die was meaningless, replied Kahr coolly. What interested him was General Ludendorff's position in the matter. Hitler didn't seem to know what to do. He took several quick swallows of beer, apologized to Kahr, then charged out of the room. The audience outside was getting out of hand. Someone shouted, "Theater!" Another that this was a Mexican revolution. There was a cacophony of whistles and jeers until Göring, emulating his chief, fired a pistol shot into the ceiling. He bellowed out that this display was not directed against Kahr, the Reichswehr or the state police. When argument failed, he tried humor. "You've got your beer," he shouted. "What are you worrying about?"

The uproar did not faze Hitler. He pushed his way up to the platform ignoring the catcalls and insults. He raised his pistol. The din continued and he shouted angrily, "If silence is not restored, I will order a machine gun placed in the gallery!" All of a sudden he was no longer the figure of fun. "What followed then," recalled Professor von Müller, the conservative historian, "was an oratorical masterpiece, which any actor might well envy. He began quietly, without any pathos." He made it appear as if the triumvirate was about to come around as he assured the audience that Kahr had his full trust and would be Regent of Bavaria. He promised that Ludendorff would assume leadership of the army; that Lossow would be Army Minister and Seisser Police Minister. "The task of the provisional German National Government is to organize the march on that sinful Babel, Berlin, and save the German people!"

From the first words, recalled Hanfstaengl, the insignificant man in the comical cutaway, who resembled a nervous "provincial bridegroom" on display in the dusty window of a Bavarian village photographer, became a superman. "It was like the difference between a Stradivarius lying in its case, just a few bits of wood and length of catgut, and the same violin being played by a master." Professor von Müller couldn't remember in his entire life "such a change of attitude of a crowd in a few minutes, almost a few seconds. There were certainly many who were not yet converted. But the sense of the majority had fully reversed itself. Hitler had turned them inside out, as one turns a glove inside out, with a few sentences. It had almost something of hocus-pocus, or magic about it. Loud approval roared forth, no further opposition was to be heard."

"Outside are Kahr, Lossow and Seisser," Hitler said earnestly. "They are struggling hard to reach a decision. May I say to them that you will stand behind them?"

"*Ja! Ja!*" roared the crowd.

"In a free Germany," shouted the impassioned Hitler, "there is also room for an autonomous Bavaria! I can say this to you: either the German revolution begins tonight or we will all be dead by dawn!" The crowd his, he headed back for the private room to bring the triumvirate to heel.

The man who could decide the matter was already approaching the Bürgerbräukeller in Hitler's Mercedes. General Ludendorff was in the back seat with his stepson (an ardent Putschist) and Scheubner-Richter. Despite the fog, their car careened across the bridge from the inner city at reckless speed. The sight of the general at the entrance of the beer hall brought a chorus of Heils! But Ludendorff, seeing how far things had gone, was "amazed and far from pleased." Hitler hurried out of the anteroom to shake hands with him. They conversed briefly and the scowling Ludendorff agreed to help convince the triumvirate. They disappeared into the side room.

Irritated as he was by Hitler's unilateral action, Ludendorff applied the force of his rank and personality on his two fellow officers. "All right, gentlemen," he told them, "come along with us, and give me your hand on it." It was the general who responded first. Lossow extended his hand and said, "Good." Then the colonel gave his hand to Ludendorff. The civilian, Kahr, was the last to submit but the first to speak once the entire group returned to the platform. Ramrod stiff, his face a mask, the commissar declared that he would serve Bavaria as Regent for the monarchy. The applause that interrupted this sober announcement was "fanatic," according to one police official.

As he surveyed the enthusiastic audience, Hitler was in a state of ecstasy. "I am going," he said emotionally, "to fulfill the vow I made to myself five years ago when I was a blind cripple in the military hospital: to know neither rest nor peace until the November criminals had been overthrown, until on the ruins of the wretched Germany of today there should have arisen once more a Germany of power and greatness, of freedom and splendor."

Then Ludendorff, pale and somber, spoke briefly and earnestly, giving Müller the impression that here was a man who realized "this was a matter of life and death, probably more death than life." In complete control of the situation, Hitler went down the line shaking hands to the accompaniment of wave after wave of cheers. Overcome by mass excitement and beer, the audience could hardly contain its delight. Forgotten were earlier derision and even anger. The crowd stood and roared out "Deutschland über Alles." Tears streamed down many a cheek and some people were so emotionally wrought they could not even sing. But someone next to a state police official turned and said, "The only thing missing is the psychiatrist."

4

There was also high emotion across the Isar at the Löwenbräukeller. The main hall, resounding with the blast of two brass bands, was jammed with more than 2000 members of the Battle League and SA. Only a small part of the audience was made up of the scar-faced Captain Röhm's fanatic followers, but he was the main attraction. He called "for revenge and retaliation against the traitors and the despoilers of our people. . . ."

Then Esser, who had dragged himself from a sickbed, mounted the podium. The plan had been changed somewhat and he did not charge up the aisle carrying a flag or immediately announce the revolution. He was to wait for word that Hitler's coup had succeeded. In the middle of his speech, at 8:40 P.M., a cryptic telephone message was received from the Bürgerbräukeller: "Safely delivered!" Röhm purposefully strode up to the platform and interrupted Esser. The Kahr government, he shouted, had been deposed and Adolf Hitler had declared a national revolution. Reichswehr soldiers tore off the Republic cockades from their hats, leaped onto tables and chairs shouting. Storm troopers embraced each other. The band blared out the national anthem. When the pandemonium subsided Röhm shouted for everyone to march on the Bürgerbräukeller. The men piled out of the Löwenbräukeller as if it were on fire and formed up. With shouting and cheers the raucous army started down the street toward the Isar River. A motorcycle courier stopped the procession with new marching orders from Hitler: Röhm's men were to turn toward the university and occupy General von Lossow's headquarters on the Schönfeldstrasse; the storm troopers were to proceed to St. Annaplatz, pick up a cache of 3000 rifles in the basement of the monastery, then take up positions at Giessing. Only the Bund Oberland was to continue on to the Bürgerbräukeller.

As Röhm's force marched down the Briennerstrasse followed by one of the brass bands, gathering crowds cheered them on. Near the head of the column, proudly holding an imperial war flag, was a fervent young nationalist, there because of allegiance to Röhm and Strasser, not Hitler. His name was Heinrich Himmler. The enthusiasm of jubilant onlookers was heady and the men continued like conquerors up the broad Ludwigstrasse to the entrance of the military district building. Röhm halted his troops outside the gates and strode into the building where he had worked for so many years. The guards threatened to shoot but Röhm outfaced them. He marched up to the second floor to the office of the duty officer, who declared that he was bowing only to force, and then gave the order to open the gates to the rioters. Röhm posted guards, emplaced machine guns at windows and strung barbed wire around the building. He did just about everything except take over the telephone switchboard. This, incredibly, he left in charge of the duty officer, who had no revolutionary leanings.

At the beer hall Hess was rounding up "enemies of the people" as hostages. He stood on a chair in the great hall calling out names of officials and officers, including Minister President Knilling, Police President Mantel and Prince Rupprecht's political adviser. They dutifully stepped forward as if they were unruly schoolboys—all except Justice Minister Gürtner, who made a break for freedom but was caught. At first they were incarcerated in a small room upstairs but then it was decided that Hess should transfer them for safekeeping to a house near the Tegernsee, a lake south of Munich.

Others in Hitler's inner circle were off on assignments: Max Amann, the squat but formidable street fighter, led a group to a bank which he seized for the new government's central offices, while Scheubner-Richter, Esser and Hanfstaengl were reconnoitering the city streets to check on the progress of the revolution. They found a city of confusion. Many citizens were enthusiastic, others perplexed, and some indignant. Few knew what was going on, including those involved in the action since conflicting orders kept emanating from the Bürgerbräu.

The man principally responsible for the first successes of the Putschists was Frick of the Munich Police Presidium. He persuaded his colleagues on duty not to launch any counterattack against the Putschists, then hovered near a phone to calm bewildered police officials who called in for information. His advice always was to wait and do nothing. Because of this state of inaction, his former chief, the deposed Police President Pöhner, was able to walk into police headquarters and, without any show of force, take charge. His first act was to make arrangements for a press conference with the leading non-Marxist newspapers.

At the Bürgerbräukeller Hitler was in a state of euphoria with the police under control and district headquarters occupied by Röhm. Then came a report from the engineer barracks: the Putschists were having an argument with the engineers. Hitler made a snap decision to leave his command post to straighten out the matter in person. It was a grave tactical error, followed by a second: placing General Ludendorff in charge. No sooner had Hitler left the building than General von Lossow said he had to go to his office and issue orders. This seemed reasonable to Ludendorff, who allowed Lossow to march out of the beer hall with Kahr and Seisser not far behind. Hitler did no good at the engineer barracks, being turned away at the gate. He returned half an hour later and was appalled to find that the triumvirate had been allowed to escape. He assailed Ludendorff. How could he have done such a thing? Now Lossow could sabotage the revolution! The general looked frostily down his nose at the former corporal. A German officer, he said, would never break an oath!

Hitler's spirits were raised at 11 P.M. by the arrival of a thousand-man military unit. It was almost the entire complement of the Infantry School, an elite group of cadets. Except for a handful of dissidents, they had been persuaded to join the uprising en masse by Lieutenant Gerhard Rossbach, a veteran of the Free Corps movement. The cadets had placed their own commander under house arrest and accepted the flamboyant Rossbach (like Röhm, a homosexual and gallant fighter) as their new leader. To the blare of a brass band the cadets marched smartly up to the beer hall, wearing swastika armbands and carrying National Socialist flags. Standing at attention, former Quartermaster General Ludendorff and ex-Corporal Hitler reviewed them. Then the cadets marched off to occupy the offices of Commissar von Kahr while the leaders of the Putsch set off in their cars for military district headquarters. At Röhm's command post—the office of General von Lossow—the group began discussing the future course of the revolution. Ensconcing himself in an easy chair, Ludendorff demanded that someone get hold of Lossow or Seisser on the phone. A number of calls were made but neither could be reached. Scheubner-Richter expressed the feeling that something was wrong. Lossow had said he was coming here to his own office. Where was he? And where were Kahr and Seisser? Ludendorff again protested that these three gentlemen had given their oath in full view and sound of thousands. They could not possibly have changed their minds.

Major Max Schwandner, an officer on the staff of the commander of army units in Bavaria, was just entering the building. He had heard rumors of a Putsch and sought out the duty officer, who could only say that "the affair was extremely unclean and fishy." "While we spoke," recalled Schwandner, "Captain Röhm stormed into [the room] in full uniform of the old army with all [his] medals and asked for General von Lossow. I immediately told Röhm that this Putsch was in clear violation of yesterday's understanding with von Lossow. Röhm replied in a voice vibrant with sincerity that everything was all right. Von Lossow, Kahr and von Seisser had all declared themselves in accord with everything and would soon come to Hitler in the military district headquarters. I said only that that was something different."

After Röhm left, the duty officer motioned to Schwandner and whispered, "The affair is crooked." Lossow, he said, was with Seisser and the commandant of the Bavarian army at the 19th Infantry barracks and would "definitely not come here." A little later a call came through the still unmonitored switchboard. It was from Lossow at his new command post, safe in the center of the regimental barracks complex. He ordered a counterattack on the Putschists he had recently pledged to support; loyal army battalions in Augsburg, Ingolstadt, Regensburg, Landshut and other surrounding localities were to be transported to Munich by rail. Schwandner promptly called the transport officer, passed on Lossow's orders and agreed to phone instructions to half of the battalions himself. The Putsch was being planned in one room and sabotaged in the one next to it. Finally just before midnight it occurred to the plotters to limit the switchboard to Putschist traffic but by then all of Lossow's counterorders had been transmitted.

Despite the marching troops, the bands and the excitement, most Müncheners had no idea revolution once more had come to their city. One of the Führer's closest friends, Heinrich Hoffmann, spent the evening in the Fledermausbar without learning that anything out of the ordinary had taken place, and only at midnight did he discover that the revolution was on. By that time jubilant gangs of young people were keeping guests in downtown hotels awake with their songs and cries of triumph.

At the American Consulate Robert Murphy, the acting consul, was composing a telegram to the Secretary of State:

> . . . ACCORDING TO HITLER TASK OF THIS GOVERNMENT IS
> TO MARCH ON BERLIN, WAGE TWELFTH HOUR FIGHT;
> ASSERTED THAT THE DAWN WOULD SEE EITHER NEW
> NATIONAL GOVERNMENT OR THE DEATH OF THE SPEAKER. . . .*

It was a night of terror for those opponents of the coup who were dragged from their homes and held hostage; and for some picked out of the phone book if their names sounded Jewish, who were corraled by the

---

* When Murphy was not permitted to send this telegram in code, he indignantly demanded an interview with Hitler himself. "After hours of argument, I finally did get in to see him at 3 A.M., only to be told rather mildly that I could not send my telegram. My protest was only a formality by that time, since I had already sent my colleague, Halstead, in a car to file the telegram from Stuttgart."

Brownshirts. One unit descended on the socialist Munich *Post*, but while it was smashing the presses, orders came from an irate Hitler to desist since he wanted the plant for his own purposes.

At military district headquarters it was becoming increasingly evident that the triumvirate had broken their word (no one seemed to recall that it had been made under duress) and that events were getting out of hand. Scheubner-Richter and his servant Aigner left to bring back Seisser but could not locate him. On their return they found a "somewhat depressed" Hitler.

Aigner was ordered to take Rosenberg to a printing shop to make copies of the announcement of the new government signed by the principal partners. This done, Rosenberg proceeded to the offices of the *Völkischer Beobachter* to write an editorial for the morning edition. Entitled "Call to the German People," it exhorted the public to hand over President Ebert and other Social Democrats "dead or alive to the People's National Government."

Aigner was already back at military district headquarters where he was instructed by his employer to go home for champagne and food, and to tell Frau Scheubner-Richter that "everything was in order and she should not worry." The situation was deteriorating. Röhm had finally become suspicious of what was going on in the next room and arrested the duty officer. He also issued orders to seize all other army officers in the building but not in time to catch the enterprising Major Schwandner, who had accomplished his mission of summoning troops to Munich. Warned by a civilian employee, he slipped out just before the cordon was drawn.

Things were also not going well for the Putschists at the headquarters of Commissar von Kahr. He had gone there after his escape from the beer hall to find that machinery had already been set in motion to crush the Putsch. Understandably, he did nothing to stop these measures (he had just received an indignant message from Prince Rupprecht: "Crush this movement at any cost. Use troops if necessary") and was helping direct the defense of his building against the lively threat of Lieutenant Rossbach and his thousand cadets from the Infantry School. It should have been easy for the revolutionists to carry out Ludendorff's order to take the building "whatever the cost," and it would have been an important victory but it turned into a standoff with cadets and police facing each other at bayonet point, each group waiting for the other to fire the first shot. No one wanted bloodshed. The cadets had no wish to fire at men in uniform and many of the police shared the young men's faith in Hitler. Negotiations went on interminably until the man of action, Rossbach, became impatient and shouted to his cadets: "What? Still negotiating here? You know General Ludendorff's orders. Why the hesitation? Order your men to fire!"

At last the cadets moved into position with skirmishers advancing in a semicircle followed by machine-gun crews. The police countered by inviting three rebels inside to discuss the matter. They accepted the invitation but with the understanding that if they did not appear in ten minutes the attack would begin. The minutes passed and just as the cadets prepared themselves for action a command rang out, "Companies withdraw!"

The cadets pulled back. The siege was over. The battle that might have swung the decision was lost by default, primarily because the Hitler forces were reluctant to fire upon men they wanted as allies. All the cadets had done was keep Commissar von Kahr bottled up for several crucial hours. Now he left the building and joined Lossow and Seisser at 19th Infantry barracks.

The faint hope held at military district headquarters that the triumvirate would not act overtly against the Putsch faded when it was learned that General von Lossow had sent out this message "to all German wireless stations" at 2:55 A.M.:

> State Commissar General v. Kahr, Col. v. Seisser and General v. Lossow repudiate the Hitler Putsch. Expressions of support extracted by gunpoint invalid. Caution is urged against misuse of the above names.
>
> *v. Lossow*

At the 19th Infantry Regiment, Kahr, hunched and brooding on a settee, was being called upon to write a proclamation to be posted throughout the city. He finally composed one that satisfied everyone. Deception, he said, had turned a demonstration for Germany's awakening into sickening violence. "Had the senseless and purposeless attempt at revolt succeeded, Germany would have been plunged into the abyss and Bavaria with it." He dissolved the NSDAP and other right-wing organizations, declaring that those responsible for the Putsch would "ruthlessly be made to suffer the punishment they deserve." It had been a long and bitter evening for the commissar.

It was not until 5 A.M. that confirmation of the repudiation of the Putsch by the triumvirate reached military district headquarters. The informant was the deposed commandant of the Infantry School. He regretfully informed Hitler that the triumvirate did not feel honor bound to their oaths since they were made at pistol point. General von Lossow was going to put down the Putsch with force. If Hitler was stunned, he did not show it. He made a long speech to his fellow conspirators, ending with the declaration that, if need be, he was determined to fight and die for his cause. With Ludendorff's concurrence, he ordered Scheubner-Richter and his servant (who had returned with the champagne and refreshments) to find their own newly designated Minister President and order him to seize the police headquarters with an Oberland unit. Pöhner set off on his mission with gusto and was so confident that he walked into the Police Directory with a single companion. He was escorted to the office of the major in charge and, to his consternation ("It came like a blow from a club"), was arrested. His former assistant, Frick, was already in custody.

By this time Hitler, Ludendorff and the staff were on their way back to the beer hall, leaving Röhm and his followers to hold the military district building. Dismayed as he was, Hitler had not yet given up. "If we get through, very well," he remarked grimly, "if not, we'll have to hang ourselves." It was still dark as word went out to those Putschists not manning strongholds to assemble at the beer hall. A wet, chilling snow was falling as units converged on the Bürgerbräu. The men had the impression that something had gone wrong but knew no details. Even so they proceeded through the empty streets, flags flying, with at least one group of SA men lustily singing Eckart's "Sturmlied": "Germany, awake! Break your chains in two!"

5

It was a dull, overcast dawn with a biting damp chill. The cold wet snow continued to fall spasmodically. The rank and file of Putschists were gathered glumly in the smoke-filled, dank main hall of the Bürgerbräukeller. Unshaven and unwashed, they were eating a breakfast of coffee, cheese and bread. The excitement and exaltation of last night had evaporated. Then someone announced that the triumvirate had publicly denounced the revolution and the army would not participate. Someone else mounted the speakers' platform, recent scene of such high drama, and began raging against all the traitors—the bourgeois and the generals. "March to Berlin!" he shouted. There was some applause but the suggestion struck Hitler's lawyer, Hans Frank, as "highly romantic and very unpolitical."

The leaders were in a private room upstairs where Ludendorff sat "stony-faced and frightening in his unperturbed calm," as he sipped red wine for breakfast. In his old tweed shooting jacket he was still an impressive figure. But his show of confidence cracked upon getting the information that Lossow had publicly denounced the new government. "I will never again trust the word of a German officer," he exclaimed and re-treated into glum silence.

The coup which had seemed so successful at midnight was unraveling in the cold light of day and Hitler's next step revealed his desperation. He ordered a Battle League unit to seize the police station and rescue the in-carcerated Pöhner. Continuing to act as if there was still hope, he then sent a detachment of storm troopers to the Jewish printing firm of Parcus to confiscate stacks of freshly printed inflation money. (This being Ger-many, each revolutionist had to be paid his stipend.) The sum was 14,605 trillion marks and, in true German fashion, the Parcus brothers demanded and got a receipt.

By this time more Putschist units were arriving in trucks from outside localities. Wet, freezing and weary, they knew nothing of the turn of events and were in good spirits. The largest contingent came from Landshut and halfway to Munich they had been overtaken by a truckload of state police who exchanged Heils with them. Their leader was the druggist, Gregor Strasser. He sat in the cab of the lead vehicle and as it rumbled along the peaceful but busy streets someone observed that every-one was going to work as usual. "This is no revolution. Something is wrong."

"We'll see," said Strasser. At the beer hall he was informed by Cap-tain Göring that "those fellows" had broken their word to the Führer but the people were still with him. "We're going to try the whole thing over again." Then a short, stocky man with a shining bald pate—it was Julius Streicher—burst into the main hall to harangue the gathering on behalf of Hitler. Gesturing with his whip, he spoke raucously and obscenely in an effort to work up enthusiasm. Arms were passed out to those who had none and the men were reloaded into trucks and taken to their posts.

By this time the Battle League unit ordered by Hitler to occupy police headquarters was back at the military district building—mission unaccomplished. They had argued with the police for a few minutes be-fore leaving to avoid a fight. Hitler turned the task of rescuing Pöhner over to his faithful bodyguard unit. This hardy group reached the Police Directory at 9:30 A.M., set up machine guns to cover the building and made as if to attack. But again the rebels had no stomach for shedding blood. They returned to the beer hall—mission still unaccomplished— only to be dispatched minutes later on an easier task: arrest of the Marxist city councilors who had refused to fly the swastika flag over the City Hall.

They forced their way into the old Rathaus. Their commander, the tobacconist, flung open the door of the council room. Cocking his weapon, he shouted that all Social Democrats and Communists were under arrest. Outside in the Marienplatz, according to his account, a large crowd "greeted the appearance of the councillors with jeers and insults. As a matter of fact it was we troopers who had to defend them from the onslaught of the people. Otherwise actual fatalities might have occurred. It was quite a job getting them safely loaded into the lorries."

As these trucks started for the beer hall, Putschist speakers began haranguing a crowd which grew so dense that the number 6 trolley cars bound for Sendling were unable to move. The main speaker was Streicher, who proved to be a greater attraction than the famous revolving figures of the Rathaus clock. By now the Platz was festooned with swastika banners and the party flag waved from the top of the City Hall.

The Putsch was marked by confusion and hesitation on both sides. In some parts of the city the municipal police were pulling down Putschist posters and arresting rebels while in the inner city rebels were arresting police for attempting to put up government posters repudiating the Putsch and dissolving the NSDAP. Hitler's men held most of the major downtown bridges over the Isar River, including the most important, the Ludwigsbrücke, connecting the beer hall with the center of the city. At the Museum bridge citizens were chiding the youthful Putschists. "Do you have your mother's permission to play with such dangerous things in the street?" called out one worker. The little ten-man detachment returned sheepishly to the beer hall.

At another Isar bridge rumors were spreading among the men from Landshut that "something had gone wrong and that betrayal was in the cards." Their fears were justified; at 10 A.M. trucks loaded with men in green uniforms arrived. These were the state troopers, who hurriedly set up two heavy machine guns. The Putschists did nothing since their orders were to hold fire. The state police also had orders to stand in place and the two sides simply stared at each other.

At the beer hall the rebel leaders were in dispute. Colonel Hermann Kriebel, who had served in the war on Ludendorff's staff, wanted to withdraw to Rosenheim on the Austrian border where they might win over the local right radicals. Göring seconded this. It was his home town and he assured everyone it was strongly pro-Hitler. Here they could assemble reinforcements and regroup. "The movement cannot end in the ditch of some obscure country lane," was Ludendorff's sarcastic retort. It was up to Hitler. He hesitated briefly but he was a born gambler and the prospect of a lengthy guerrilla campaign was not appealing. He wanted to win or lose on one throw of the dice and he vetoed the Kriebel plan.

The discussion dragged on until late morning while the situation on the streets deteriorated. At military district headquarters Captain Röhm and his men were under siege by army and state police troops. While the older members of the Battle League were not all eager to face such overwhelming odds, the 150 men of Röhm's own group were ready for combat.

Word of the government attack against Röhm brought arguments at the Bürgerbräukeller to a halt. It was evident that the Putschists had to act now or surrender ignominiously. According to Ludendorff, it was he who first thought of marching in force into the heart of Munich to rescue Röhm. "We march!" he said. If it was Ludendorff's idea, it was carried out in Hitler fashion—as a propaganda parade, a display of power designed to arouse support for the Putsch from the citizenry. "We would go to the city," Hitler later testified, "to win the people to our side, to see how public opinion would react, and then to see how Kahr, Lossow and Seisser would react to public opinion. After all, those gentlemen would hardly be foolish enough to use machine guns against a general uprising of the people. That's how the march into the city was decided on."

Ludendorff was convinced that army troops would not impede the march, and recently had assured a friend: "The heavens will fall before the Bavarian Reichswehr turns against me." Hitler was just as confident that neither army nor state police would fire on a war hero like Ludendorff, who would be in the front row. Hitler's decision ("the most desperately daring decision of my life") was made and orders were hurriedly dispatched to units manning the bridges. Outside the beer hall Colonel Kriebel, the professional soldier, began setting up the line of march. Hitler was just leaving the conference room about 11:30 A.M. as Eckart sauntered in. Once they had been the closest friends. Now Hitler "looked very dark and said, 'Good day,' in a hard voice." Outside the affronted author received another rebuff when he greeted Ludendorff respectfully. The general gave him "an indifferent tip of the hat."

The parade formed quickly. There was no band to lead off since the musicians who had reported to the beer hall that morning got neither breakfast nor pay and marched off after playing a dutiful chorus of the "Badenweiler," the march of Hitler's regiment in the war. In the van were picked skirmishers and eight men carrying the swastika and the black-white-red flags. Next came the leaders: Hitler with Scheubner-Richter on his right and Ludendorff on his left. Alongside were Colonel Kriebel, personal bodyguard Graf, the commander of the Munich storm troopers, and Captain Hermann Göring romantically militant with steel helmet decorated with a large white swastika and wearing a smart black leather coat open enough so that his Pour le Mérite could be seen. He was somewhat ruffled because his idea to bring along the captured councilors as hostages had been vetoed. But the Führer had curtly rejected the scheme; he wanted no martyrs.

Behind the leaders were three units marching abreast in columns of four. On the left was Hitler's hundred-man bodyguard, steel-helmeted and armed with carbines and potato masher grenades; on the right the Bund Oberland; and in the middle the battle-seasoned Munich SA Regiment. There followed a motley collection of men, some in uniform or parts of tattered World War uniforms, some wearing work clothes or business suits. The cadets from Infantry School, smart and ultramilitary, were sandwiched between students, shopkeepers, middle-aged businessmen and hard-faced freebooters. The only common mark was a swastika brassard on the left arm. Most of them had rifles and many had fixed bayonets. Others, particularly the SA, held pistols in chilled hands.

Scheubner-Richter, wearing a pince-nez, grasped Rosenberg's hand and said, "Things look ugly," then gloomily prophesied to Hitler that this would be their last walk together. The Führer himself was pale and grave. Against the bitter cold he wore his familiar trench coat and carried his slouch hat. Ludendorff, overcoat over hunting jacket, was impassive, but he turned and ordered his servant to go home so he wouldn't get hurt.

It was almost noon when the straggling column moved off. In fifteen minutes the 2000 men reached the Ludwig bridge and a small force of state police. The police commander stepped forward as the Putschist skirmishers slowly advanced, called out to halt or be fired upon, then turned to his men and told them to load with live ammunition. As he spoke a bugle blasted, and selected Putschists suddenly converged on the police with bayonets leveled, shouting, "Don't shoot at your comrades!" The police hesitated and before a shout could be fired were overrun. The column continued across the bridge and marched straight ahead. The Zweibrückenstrasse was lined with people, many cheering enthusiastically and waving swastika flags. Bystanders began joining the parade. This enthusiasm inspired the marchers to song and, without band accompaniment, they broke into their favorite, "Storm Song." As they approached the Isartor where its author Eckart, who had gone on ahead, stood in the crowd near the ancient gate, he located a grim-faced Hitler in the first row. Their eyes met and "he stared at me as if to imply, 'So where are you?'"

The chilled men, their exhalations visible in the cold, continued unimpeded and in another fifteen minutes flowed into the Marienplatz, still festooned with swastika banners from the rallies. The Nazi flag still waved atop the City Hall and a large crowd was singing patriotic songs. At this point there was confusion among the marchers. Some were under the impression they were to turn around and return to the beer hall, while others assumed they would continue into the city and rescue Röhm. Colonel Kriebel was surprised when Ludendorff led the way to the right into the Weinstrasse and toward the Odeonsplatz but said to himself, "If Ludendorff is marching that way, naturally we'll go with him." The general himself had not planned this move. "At certain moments in life one acts instinctively and doesn't know why. . . . We just wanted to get to Röhm and bring him back."

The impulsive turn to the right by the heavy-set man in the dark brown overcoat was bringing the Putschists face to face with government forces. In moments the column approached one of Munich's most revered landmarks, the Feldherrnhalle. Here a line of city police blocked the way. But the Putschists surged forward singing, "*O Deutschland hoch in Ehren* [O, Germany high in honor]."

Looking down from her hotel room, Frau Winifred Wagner was amazed to see her idol, Hitler, marching down the narrow Residenzstrasse next to Ludendorff. Just ahead in the Odeonsplatz small groups of green-uniformed men were scrambling into a blocking position. There was only room enough in the street for eight abreast. Hitler locked arms with Scheubner-Richter in preparation for trouble but Ludendorff touched no one, still supremely confident that no one would fire on him. Directly ahead was a cordon of state police under First Lieutenant Michael Freiherr von Godin. Faced with an oncoming mob, Godin called out, "Second Company, double time, march." The state police jogged forward but the Putschists did not break, standing off the enemy with leveled bayonets and pistols. Godin used his rifle to parry two bayonet thrusts, "overturning the men behind them with rifle at high port." All at once a shot exploded. Godin heard it zing past his head; it killed a sergeant. "For a fraction of a second my company stood frozen. Then, before I could give an order, my people opened fire, with the effect of a salvo."

The Putschists returned the fire and panic broke out as marchers and bystanders scrambled for safety. One of the first to fall was Scheubner-Richter—shot in the lungs. Another was Graf, who had leaped in front of Hitler to take the half dozen bullets meant for him. In falling, the personal bodyguard clutched Hitler, yanking him down so sharply that his left arm was dislocated. On the other side Scheubner-Richter also helped drag Hitler to the pavement. Ludendorff's faithful servant, who had been ordered to go home, was bleeding on the asphalt. His friend Aigner, the servant of the dying Scheubner-Richter, crawled to him. He was dead.

Someone stepped over Aigner. It was General Ludendorff marching erectly, left hand in coat pocket, into the line of fire.*

As Hitler sprawled on the ground thinking he had been shot in the left side, comrades tried to shield him. Eighteen men lay dead in the street: fourteen followers of Hitler and four state police, all, incidentally, more or less sympathetic with National Socialism. Those in the front of the marching column alone knew what had happened. The crowd jammed up behind only heard firecracker explosions ahead, then a rumor that both Hitler and Ludendorff were killed. The Putschists scrambled to the rear.

Ludendorff marched through the police cordon and into the arms of a lieutenant who placed him under arrest and escorted him to the Residenz. Once inside, the man who moments before had acted like a hero in fiction began behaving like a spoiled child. He petulantly refused an offer by a police colonel to inform his family of his safety and forbade the colonel to call him "Excellency." From now on he was "Herr Ludendorff" and he would never don uniform as long as the offending police officer wore one.

Hitler painfully struggled to his feet, cradling his injured arm. He was in agony as he slowly moved away from the battleground, face pale, hair falling over his face. He was accompanied by Dr. Walter Schultze, chief of the Munich SA medical corps, a towering young man. They came upon a small boy lying at the curb, bleeding profusely. Hitler wanted to carry him off but Schultze called to his wife's cousin (a botany student named Schuster) to take the boy. At Max Joseph Platz they finally reached Hitler's old gray Selve, which had been loaded with medical supplies. An elderly first aid man named Frankel got in the front seat with the driver while Hitler and the doctor got into the rear seat. Schuster stood on the running board holding the wounded boy. Hitler told the driver to head for the Bürgerbräukeller so he could find out what was going on. But at the Marienplatz they came under heavy machine-gun fire and had to change directions several times. They found the Ludwig bridge blocked and turned back. By this time the boy had regained consciousness and Schuster dismounted so he

---

* Most accounts picture Ludendorff as courageous for staying on his feet and Hitler as ignoble for dropping to the street even though Hitler's arm dislocation indicates he was dragged down. Undoubtedly Hitler would have hit the ground on his own since he was a seasoned front-line soldier. Robert Murphy testified that "both Ludendorff and Hitler behaved in identical manner, like the battle-hardened soldiers they were. Both fell flat to escape the hail of bullets." Another eyewitness, a watchman, also saw Ludendorff throw himself to the ground and then find cover "behind a corpse or wounded man." A second watchman corroborated the fact that no one was standing after the volley.

could take the youngster home. The car continued toward the Sendlinger-torplatz. Here they encountered another burst of fire near the old southern cemetery. Since it was impossible to get back to the beer hall, there was nothing to do but keep driving south toward Salzburg.

Göring's display of his Pour le Mérite decoration had not saved him and he lay on the pavement with a bullet in his upper thigh. Frau Ilse Ballin, who had rushed from her home to help the wounded, found him bleeding profusely. With the help of her sister, she dragged the heavy burden indoors. The sisters dressed Göring's wound and were about to summon an ambulance when he weakly asked them to help him get to a private clinic. He could not bear the indignity of arrest. Frau Ballin, the wife of a Jewish merchant, had pity on him and thus he escaped prison.

6

What had started as a battle ended in a frenzied scramble for refuge as if some natural disaster had struck the Marienplatz. One group of Putschists got inside a young ladies' academy and were allowed to hide under beds and in closets. Others burst into a *Konditorei* and hid their arms under ovens, in flour sacks and coffee machines. The state police rounded up hundreds, disarming them on the street. Those left behind at the beer hall to hold the command post were so unstrung by the catastrophe they surrendered without resistance to green and blue police. They stacked arms and went home to brood. At military district headquarters Captain Röhm also surrendered, realizing there was nothing to be gained by further resistance. The Putsch was over but victorious state police marching away from the beer hall were abused by indignant citizens with cries of: "Pfui! Jew defenders! Betrayers of the Fatherland! Bloodhounds! Heil Hitler—Down with Kahr!"

The SA troops from Landshut were still at their post when word came of the debacle at the Feldherrnhalle. Rumor spread that Ludendorff was dead and Hitler seriously wounded. Gregor Strasser assembled his men and they marched off "filled with bitterness and disappointment at Kahr's betrayal." At a forest they found an SA group from Munich smashing rifles against trees. Strasser ordered them to stop such nonsense. The rifles could come in handy in the future. In closed ranks the Landshut unit paraded defiantly to the Hauptbahnhof singing new words to "Swastika and Steel Helmet." They had been betrayed, they sang, but remained true to the Fatherland.

Another group of SA men was on the highway in cars and a truck loaded with the captured Munich councilors. At a woods on the road to

Rosenheim the convoy halted and their commander led the pale prisoners into the woods. They thought that their "last hour had struck" but were only subjected to the indignity of changing clothes with the SA so the latter could return to Munich as civilians. Minister President von Knilling and the other principal hostages were also free. Hess had successfully transported them out of the city to a villa on the Tegernsee but while he was out telephoning Munich to find out what was happening the young man he had placed in charge of the prisoners was persuaded to drive them home. Hess had lost not only his hostages but his transportation.

After hiding his weapons, Scheubner-Richter's servant returned to the scene of carnage in a borrowed civilian coat to find out what had happened to his master. The Feldherrnhalle was barred and Aigner told a police official who he was. "After much pleading he accompanied me inside where, near the entrance, all the dead were lying side by side. I was close to madness when I had to look for him among the bodies." Aigner found his master lying next to his own best friend, Ludendorff's servant. "Sick in my soul and totally shattered I returned to our residence in Widenmayerstrasse." Frau Scheubner-Richter asked where her husband was. Aigner lied but she insisted on the truth. "I can still remember her words: 'That's terrible but that is why one is an officer's wife.'"

Hanfstaengl missed all the action. He was at his apartment when his sister phoned to say that Putschists were marching into the center of Munich. In the street he encountered an SA acquaintance in a state of collapse who told him that Hitler, Ludendorff and Göring were dead and it was the end of Germany. As Hanfstaengl headed back home to prepare for flight an open car screeched to a halt beside him. Inside were Amann, Esser, Eckart and Hoffmann. He went with them to the photographer's apartment where it was agreed to escape singly to Austria.

Hanfstaengl never thought of hiding in his country home at Uffing but a mishap would force Hitler to do so. His car was some ten miles from Munich when he broke a long silence to announce abruptly that he must have been shot in the arm. "Is it warm?" asked Dr. Schultze. It was not. Perhaps a bullet was there or something was broken. They parked in the woods and with difficulty the doctor began removing Hitler's leather jacket, two sweaters, necktie and shirt. Schultze discovered that the left arm was severely dislocated but it would be impossible to set it properly in a car without assistance. He fastened Hitler's injured arm to his body with a kerchief, then suggested they flee to Austria. Hitler vetoed this and they kept driving south. On nearing Murnau Hitler remembered that the Hanfstaengl villa in Uffing was only a few miles away. He ordered the driver to hide the Selve, then started on foot with the doctor and first aid man toward Uffing.

They arrived at the Hanfstaengl villa, a small stone structure near the village church, about 4 P.M. Without comment Helene led the three exhausted men up to her sitting room. Hitler began to lament the death of Ludendorff and his faithful Graf, both of whom he had seen drop. He became more and more excited. It was Ludendorff's trustfulness, he said, which had cost him his life, and Graf's faithfulness which had robbed Hitler of a perfect adjutant. He began criticizing and condemning the triumvirate for their treachery "and swore he would go on fighting for his ideals as long as breath was in him."

Helene suggested that he get some sleep. He would probably be discovered soon and would need all his strength to face capture. Dr. Schultze and the aid man helped Hitler to a bedroom one floor up where they tried to set his dislocated arm. But the first attempt failed since the arm was so swollen. Hitler grimaced as they tried again, this time successfully. Then the aid man began to bind the arm and shoulder. Helene could hear Hitler's moans of pain through the door.

Foreign newspapers were running garbled stories of the Munich Putsch. In New York City it was described as a militarist uprising with Hitler playing a secondary role. In Rome, where Kurt Lüdecke was again conferring with Mussolini on behalf of Hitler, the noon editions declared that Crown Prince Rupprecht had joined the revolutionists.

By the morning of November 10 the Putschists were either in captivity or flight. Hess, stranded in Tegernsee without a car, was finally able to reach his fiancée, Ilse Pröhl, by phone and tell of the fiasco with the hostages. Could she find some transportation and take him to Professor Haushofer's apartment? Ilse set off from Munich on her bicycle. It was a trip of more than thirty miles and the return with Hess was arduous. One would ride the bicycle for some distance, then rest it against a tree and continue on foot; the other would pick up the bike and repeat the process. (It was his idea.) At last they reached Haushofer's home in the Bavarian capital. He agreed to hide the fugitive even though he thought the Putsch was "a ridiculous matter," for he was fond of Hess despite his limitations—"his strong side was not intelligence but heart and character." Hess was despondent; the Putsch might not have failed if he had not lost the hostages. He talked of suicide. But Haushofer argued him out of this, advising him to surrender instead. This was counsel Hess could not take and, after several days, he left the Haushofer home to hide with friends outside the city. Before long he was risking arrest by bicycling back to Munich every so often to look after Ilse, who had fallen sick.

7

It had been a restless, anxious night at Uffing. Hanfstaengl had not come home and Hitler, rolled up tightly in his host's English traveling rug to ease the pain, had been unable to sleep. Hitler sent for Helene Hanfstaengl and told her the aid man was being dispatched to Munich in hopes of persuading the Bechsteins to send out their closed car to take him to Austria. Dr. Schultze was also going to the city. To make sure everything possible had been done for Hitler's arm, he was bringing back a discreet colleague, an assistant to the eminent Dr. Sauerbruch.

The morning seemed interminable, even the maids were too excited to eat. Only Egon, not quite three years old, was normal and had to be kept under strict supervision lest he call over the wall that Uncle Dolf was there. Just before noon Dr. Schultze returned with Sauerbruch's assistant. Together they explored the shoulder. It was all right and they changed the bandage. Then Dr. Schultze was instructed to tell Drexler that he should represent Hitler in his absence. This information was also to be passed on to Hess, several other party leaders, and Ludendorff, if he was alive.

After the departure of the two doctors Hitler tried to reassure his hostess that her husband was safe, then fretted about what might have happened to his comrades. If he got any sleep that night it was shattered early the next morning by the deafening tintinnabulation of bells from the nearby church. It was Sunday the eleventh. Hitler did not appear until lunch. Because of the sling, he could not wear his coat and had draped Hanfstaengl's huge dark blue terry cloth bathrobe around him. It brought a smile to his gaunt face. He felt like a pseudo-Roman senator, he said, and he told Helene the story of how his father had ridiculed him as the "toga boy."

As the afternoon wore on Hitler grew restless and began pacing up and down the sitting room. He became increasingly impatient concerning the Bechstein car. Why the delay? It was only a matter of hours, perhaps minutes, he fretted, before he would be traced to Uffing. At dusk he asked Helene to close the shutters and draw the curtains, then resumed his moody pacing. Just after 5 P.M. the phone rang. It was Helene's mother-in-law, who had a villa nearby, and as the elder Frau Hanfstaengl began to relate that her house was being searched by police, she was abruptly interrupted by some official who firmly but courteously forbade her to speak.

Then he spoke directly to Helene: he and his men would soon be at her villa.

She walked slowly upstairs. Hitler, still in his host's outsized bathrobe, was standing expectantly in the doorway. She quietly told him the police were coming. "He completely lost his nerve for the moment and exclaimed 'Now all is lost—no use going on!'" He snatched his revolver from a cabinet.

"What do you think you're doing?" said Helene. She grasped his hand and took the weapon from him without a struggle. "How can you give up at the first reverses?" she scolded. "Think of all your followers who believe in you, and who will lose all faith if you desert them now." She spoke calmly. "How can you leave all the people you have gotten interested in your idea of saving your country—and then take your own life?" He sank into a chair, burying head in hands. She slipped up to the next floor to hide the revolver. The first thing she saw was a large bin where she had been hoarding flour. She thrust the gun down into the snowy substance and hurried back to find Hitler in the same dejected position.

She told him that the party had to know what to do while he was in prison and offered to write down instructions to each of his closest followers. All he had to do was sign a number of blank sheets which she could fill in later and deliver to his lawyer. Hitler thanked her for helping him remember his duty and began dictating instructions. First he requested that Amann keep business matters and finances in order, then Rosenberg was to "watch over" the party newspaper and—countermanding earlier instructions to Dr. Schultze—"lead the movement from now on." Hanfstaengl was to help build up the *Völkischer Beobachter* through his foreign connections. Esser and others were to carry on the political end. After all instructions were written and signed, Helene hid the papers in the flour bin.

Moments later came the sound of cars, followed by crisp commands and, most startling of all, the yelp of police dogs. After a wait of several moments there was a knock. It was a diffident young state police lieutenant accompanied by two other officers. The lieutenant politely introduced himself and apologetically wondered if he might search the house. Helene led the officers up the stairs and opened the door to the sitting room. There stood Hitler still in pajamas and bathrobe. The unexpected apparition startled the officers and they stopped. She beckoned them on and once everyone was in the room Hitler not only regained his composure but "broke forth in a tirade against the government, its officials, raising his voice more and more." Completely shattered a moment ago, Hitler now was master of himself. Abruptly he cut himself off and curtly asked the lieutenant to waste no time. He shook hands with the young man and said he was prepared to leave.

It was bitterly cold and he had no overcoat but he refused to put on one of Hanfstaengl's outsize garments, instead draped his trench coat over the blue bathrobe. He was allowed to pin his Iron Cross on the coat. As the group started down the stairs Egon scampered into the hall. "What are you bad, bad men doing to my Uncle Dolf?" he demanded. Deeply moved, Hitler patted the little boy's cheek, silently shook hands with Helene and the maids, then turned quickly and strode out the door. Peering out a window, Helene caught a last glimpse of him as the police vehicle turned toward Weilheim, the district seat. His face was deathly pale.

He arrived there about 9:45 P.M. and was formally arraigned at the district office before being hustled to the prison at Landsberg, some forty miles west of Munich. By this time it was raining hard and gusts of wind occasionally rocked the car. Throughout the tiring trip over winding, deserted roads Hitler was depressed and sullen. Except for a single question concerning the fate of Ludendorff (who in fact was now free after assuring authorities he was little more than an innocent bystander), he remained silent.

At Landsberg prison the chief warden was preparing for a possible attempt by Putschists to free Hitler. An army detachment was on its way to stand guard but had not arrived by the time the great nail-studded, iron entrance gate creaked open to admit Hitler. He was brought to the fortress section of the prison and put into Cell 7, the only one with an anteroom large enough for a military guard. Its former occupant, Count Arco-Valley, the assassin of Eisner, had just been transferred to another.

Hitler was left in the charge of Franz Hemmrich, who helped him undress. "He refused a bite or soup, but lay down on the cot. I went away after securely locking him in." From one lonely bunk in northern Germany where he had lain blind until a vision restored his sight, Hitler had come full circle to another in the south, with only the bare walls and ceiling for company.

When Arthur Möller van den Bruck, who had recently published *The Third Reich*, learned of the abortive Putsch he said, "There are many things that can be said against Hitler. But one thing one will always be able to say: he was a fanatic for Germany. . . . Hitler was wrecked by his proletarian primitivism. He did not understand how to give his National Socialism any intellectual basis. He was passion incarnate, but entirely without measure or sense of proportion."

Hitler was already being talked of in the past tense and it was generally agreed that he could no longer be taken seriously as a political force in

Germany. He had cast the dice, lost everything. "Our history has gone astray," wrote Möller. "Nothing of ours is succeeding in the world. Nothing today; nothing yesterday. Nothing—if we think back—nothing for the last generation. . . . Our cause was still-born from the start. . . . Something has gone wrong with everything. And when we try to set anything aright, it breaks to pieces. . . . An evil spell hangs over the Reich."

But in Munich a defiant underground order of the day was already being issued to Nazis: "The first period of the national revolution is over. It has brought the desired clearing [of the air]. Our highly revered Führer, Adolf Hitler, has again bled for the German people. The most shameful treachery that the world has ever seen has victimized him and the German people. Through Hitler's blood and the steel directed against our comrades in Munich by the hands of traitors the patriotic Battle Leagues are welded together for better or worse. The second phase of the national revolution begins."

In his youth Hitler suffered two major depressions: rejection by the Vienna Academy of Art and the death of his mother. Later he underwent two more crises: the surrender of Germany while he lay gassed and the catastrophe at the Feldherrnhalle. It would take a man of extraordinary will to rise above this last shock and, profiting by his own mistakes, resume his ordained path. In the past few months Hitler, the drummer, had given way to Hitler, the Führer.

Part 3

A MIND IN THE MAKING

Chapter Seven

IN LANDSBERG PRISON
1923–1924

1

Early on the morning after Hitler's arrest, Helene Hanfstaengl received a phone call from an American correspondent, Hubert Knickerbocker. Might he come to Uffing for an interview and bring along his wife and Dorothy Thompson? Helene reluctantly agreed, then phoned her mother-in-law, whose father had been a general in the American Civil War.

> She loves, and always has loved, excitement of all sorts, and this opportunity of participation in current events was too good to let slip by. . . .
> So Mama had a thrillingly interesting time, asking questions, and giving her impressions of the situation. By my silence, Dorothy Thompson was probably erroneously led to believe I was the typical "German *Hausfrau*," as she described me in an article soon after.*

Afterward the party returned to the Hanfstaengl villa and, while Knickerbocker was photographing the rooms, Helene surreptitiously retrieved Hitler's revolver and papers. She stowed them in a briefcase and accompanied Knickerbocker back to Munich, where she went to see

---

* Helene Hanfstaengl's reticence, combined with the volubility of her mother-in-law and her sister-in-law, Erna, resulted in a distortion by several historians, who wrote that Hitler was nursed at Uffing by Hanfstaengl's mother and sister.

Hitler's lawyer. "These are the papers," she told him. "Pass them on and let's see what happens."

The small town of Landsberg had not changed outwardly in five hundred years. Nestling in the valley of the Lech River, it was hemmed on both sides by steep and wooded heights. A bulwark against Swabian invasion since the Middle Ages, it was surrounded by ancient walls pierced by watchtowers. To get to the prison from the Munich side, one crossed an old wooden bridge over the Lech, which was scarcely more than a gushing stream. On the hill ahead was the Gefangenenanstalt und Festungshaftanstalt Landsberg, a complex of grayish-white buildings encircled by high stone walls. The prison was divided into two sections, one for ordinary criminals and one for political prisoners.

In the Festung section the man in Cell 7 refused to eat. Hitler brooded in his room but not because of its smallness and discomfort. His room at the Männerheim had been only half the size and the room on the Thierschstrasse was far gloomier. The narrow white iron bed was comfortable by his monkish standards, and the double barred window not only flooded the room with daylight but looked out on trees and shrubbery to a far pleasanter prospect than that in Munich.

The pain in Hitler's arm was so excruciating he could get little sleep. The house doctor, Brinsteiner, had discovered that he "suffered from a dislocation of the left shoulder with a break in the upper arm and, as a result, a very painful traumatic neurosis." He remained under constant medical treatment and would, in Dr. Brinsteiner's opinion, "most likely suffer permanently a partial rigidity and pain in the left shoulder."

But it was not pain alone that accounted for his utter dejection, or even the realization that his hopes for a march on Berlin had ended in disaster. What hurt as much was the feeling that he had been betrayed—by the triumvirate, by the army, by Fate itself. Moreover, the debacle at the Feldherrnhalle was being ridiculed in the newspapers as a "miniature beer hall revolution" and a Redskin raid schoolboy-style. Foreign correspondents were describing him as "Ludendorff's noisy lieutenant," a pawn in a royalist coup d'état, and the New York *Times* printed his political obituary on the front page: "The Munich putsch definitely eliminates Hitler and his National Socialist followers." Ridicule had always cut Adolf Hitler deeply. Beatings and hunger could be endured but not derision.

Visitors were shocked by his appearance. He was thin and pale, almost unrecognizable. "I found him sitting like a frozen thing at the barred window of his cell," recalled Anton Drexler. Hitler had not tasted food for almost two weeks and the doctor warned Drexler that the prisoner would die if the fast continued. Drexler returned to Cell 7, determined to save someone he had once tried to strip of party leadership. "I said he'd no right to give up all for lost, however bad things seemed. The party would look to him to start it all up again someday. But I couldn't make any impression. He was utterly in despair. So I nearly fell into despair myself, but at last I said how we'd all rather die than go on without him." Drexler talked for an hour and forty-five minutes until finally convinced he had "won him around."

Perhaps Hitler had a relapse since several others also claimed credit for saving him from starvation. One, Hans Knirsch, the founder of the National Socialist Workers' Party in Czechoslovakia, was greeted by an emaciated and despondent Hitler. Knirsch too accused him of deserting the cause to which he had won many adherents. Without him the cause was lost and the party would disband. At first Hitler kept shaking his head but finally he "timidly asked who would continue to follow a man with such a fiasco behind him." Knirsch replied that the Putsch had, in fact, raised everyone's enthusiasm. Hitler must not lose faith in himself; most great leaders reached success over their failures. This, said Knirsch, convinced Hitler and on advice from the prison doctor he was served a bowl of rice. He ate it greedily, "then promised that he would remember Knirsch's admonitions."

It could have been Knirsch who saved Hitler, or Drexler or (so said Lüdecke) Frau Bechstein. There is even the possibility it was Helene Hanfstaengl, who wrote Hitler that she had not prevented him from committing suicide in Uffing only to let him starve himself to death in Landsberg; that this was exactly what his worst enemies prayed he was going to do. "Her advice turned the scale," according to her husband, who was hiding out in Austria. "Hitler had a great admiration for her and his whole appearance at Uffing after the Putsch must have been part of some subconscious urge to turn for succor to this woman, who corresponded so closely to his repressed yearnings. Also, amidst the annihilation of all that he had organized, the Uffing house must have acquired the aura of an extra-territorial asylum." There can be no doubt that Helene's words had a telling effect on Hitler as did the visit of Frau Bechstein, who had done so much for him. Thus he was in a mood to be moved by the words uttered by the simple Drexler, and finally convinced by the arguments of Knirsch. In any event, before Hitler agreed to take the first bite of food he was prepared to be saved, if not ready to do so on his own initiative.

Even after Hitler broke his fast he would not give evidence for his trial. At first he insisted on being questioned but as soon as interrogators arrived he refused to say a word. In desperation, the chief prosecutor dispatched his assistant, Hans Ehard, to Landsberg to "see if he would get

anything out of Hitler." Ehard's efforts were as fruitless as his prede-
cessors' but he patiently continued speaking across a table in a "friendly
voice as if to a sick horse." Hitler sat in sullen silence "staring blankly like
a sheep," then abruptly indicated a pile of reports on the table and sarcastically said that all those official records would certainly not "hinder my
future political work!"

"Well, Herr Hitler," replied Ehard after some thought, "you're probably annoyed by the presence of a stenographer." He ordered the secretary, a prison employee, to leave and take with him the offending papers.
Once they were alone, Ehard tried a new tack, pointing out that he was
only doing his job. Wouldn't Hitler please discuss the matter? Taken off
guard by Ehard's unofficial approach, Hitler suddenly poured out words in
a torrent. He not only gave details of how the Putsch was planned and executed but why he had been forced to take such drastic action. His voice
rose and his face turned bluish. It was, thought Ehard, as if he were
addressing a vast audience. Occasionally the assistant prosecutor would in-
sert a question. If it was an embarrassing one, Hitler would subside into
sullen silence, almost immediately broken by another eruption of words.
Ehard returned to Munich and turned over his report to his superior and
to Georg Neithardt, who would be the presiding judge at the trial. The
former was impressed by what he read but the latter said, "Hitler hasn't
told you everything and he'll probably want to do it just at the trial." But
Ehard didn't believe Hitler was saving his best arguments. He doubted
that the man in Cell 7 could possibly reveal anything more than he had
and then, recalling Hitler's volubility, warned the judge that such a man
could not be "stifled."

The resurrection of Adolf Hitler was confirmed early the following
month by his half sister Angela. She came to the prison "on a cloudy
foggy December evening" expecting to find him despondent. "Never in
my life will I forget this hour," she wrote their brother, Alois Hitler, Jr. "I
spoke with him for half an hour. His spirit and soul were again at a high
level. Physically he is quite well. His arm still gives him trouble, but they
think it is almost healed. How moving is the loyalty he is accorded these
days. Just before me, for example, a count visited him and brought a
Christmas package from the Villa Wahnfried from B. That which he has
accomplished is as solid as a rock. The goal and the victory is only a question of time. God grant it be soon." The package had come from the
Wagner home in Bayreuth and several days later Winifred Wagner sent
another containing a book of poetry. Frau Wagner had lost none of her

faith in Hitler. "Believe me," she reportedly told one audience, "Hitler is the coming man in spite of everything, and for all that he will pull the sword out of the German oak."

His racist allies remained confident of eventual triumph and were re-forming their ranks under such innocuous titles as "Völkischer Singing Club," "Völkischer Pathfinder Detachment," "League of True German Women," and "German Rifle and Hiking League." The old Battle League was also resuscitated under a new name, Frontring, by Captain Röhm, who was in Stadelheim prison with another group of Putschists; it was designed as an "umbrella organization" for all paramilitary groups rec-ognizing the leadership of both Hitler and Ludendorff in the racist move-ment. Hitler disliked the idea but Röhm, still regarding himself as Corpo-ral Hitler's superior officer, ignored his protests.

Hitler's party, although disbanded by law, began covert political oper-ations. The underground center was Munich where Rosenberg set up a committee to continue the NSDAP. But progress was impeded by per-sonal squabbles and ideological feuds. While Rosenberg considered him-self Hitler's temporary political heir, an exiled group in Salzburg—Esser, Streicher, Amann and Hanfstaengl—regarded him as an impostor. They neither liked nor respected Rosenberg. But perhaps that was exactly why he was chosen. He was not the type to attempt to take permanent control of the party, nor did he have followers. Moreover no one else was availa-ble. Göring was also hiding in Austria, slowly recuperating from his pain-ful wound; Scheubner-Richter was dead; Eckart, released from Landsberg, was dying in Berchtesgaden; and Drexler disapproved of the direction in which Hitler was taking the party. Of one thing Hitler could be sure: Rosenberg was loyal.

He managed to steal into Austria one night "through a forest deep with snow" to confer with the Salzburg group. "I talked to one after the other of our comrades, trying to give renewed courage and to dispel all senseless rumors." He left a few days later, skiing across the border, under the assumption that he had reassured the dissidents. They were only rein-forced in the conviction that he was an incompetent and continued to make separate plans which ranged from building up the party treasury by counterfeiting or armed holdups, to crossing the border with machine guns for a raid on Landsberg prison. Nothing worked, including the dis-patch of Lüdecke to the United States to get money for Hitler. "I was howled down in derision," he reported, "every time I spoke of him as a coming power."

In Munich Hitler was still taken seriously. That Christmas a group of

Schwabing artists in the movement celebrated the holiday season in the Blute Café with a living tableau, "Adolf Hitler in Prison." The curtain rose on a cell. Snowflakes were falling outside a small barred window. A man sat at a desk, face buried in hands, and an invisible male chorus was singing "Silent Night, Holy Night." Then an angel placed an illuminated Christmas tree on the table. Slowly the man turned and revealed his face. "Many thought it was indeed Hitler himself," remembered Heinrich Hoffmann, who had provided the *Doppelgänger*, "and a half-sob went through the hall." When the lights went up the photographers noticed moist-eyed men and women hurriedly putting away handkerchiefs.

On New Year's Day, 1924, the financial fate of Germany was settled in London at a meeting between Hjalmar Schacht, the new Reich Commissioner for National Currency, and Montagu Norman, governor of the Bank of England. Schacht, who had already abolished emergency money, began with a frank disclosure of Germany's desperate financial situation. Once the Ruhr crisis was settled, he said, it would be "necessary to set German industry going again," and this could only be done with the assistance of foreign credit and the founding of "a second credit bank in addition to the Reichsbank, a bank based entirely on gold." He thought he could raise half of the capital for this *Golddiskontbank* in foreign currency within Germany itself. "The remaining half I should like to borrow from the Bank of England."

Norman, so wrote Schacht in a memoir characteristically entitled *The Old Wizard*, was not impressed until Schacht announced that the new bank would issue bank notes based on its gold capital of two hundred million marks. "I intend," he said, "to issue those notes in pound sterling." While Norman was silently pondering this extraordinary idea, Schacht continued: "And just think, Mr. Governor, what prospects such a measure would afford for economic collaboration between Great Britain's World Empire and Germany. If we desire to establish European peace we must free ourselves from the limitations imposed by mere conference resolutions and Declarations of Congress. Economically, the European countries must be more closely linked."

Within forty-eight hours Norman not only formally approved the loan at the exceptionally low interest of a flat five per cent but convinced a group of London bankers to accept bills far exceeding the loan, "provided they are endorsed by the Golddiskontbank." With a few bold strokes, the self-styled Old Wizard had deprived Adolf Hitler of one of his most potent political weapons—economic disaster.

2

That Hitler was physically able to stand trial was attested by the prison physician, Dr. Brinsteiner, who also stated categorically in a special report to the warden on January 8 that his patient had no symptoms of psychic disorders or psychopathic tendencies. The doctor, who seems to have had some psychiatric training, concluded that "Hitler was at all times in control of himself, and his will and his mental capacity were not impaired by any illness even if the aims and purposes of the Putsch are interpreted as being faulty."

Hitler had profited by brief imprisonment in Stadelheim prison two years earlier. Similarly the enforced confinement at Landsberg obliged him to re-evaluate his past. In the quiet of his little cell he had come to recognize some of his own mistakes. He had intended the Putsch, for example, to be the beginning of a march on Berlin and the abrupt seizure of power after Mussolini's example. "From its failure I learned the lesson that each country must evolve its own type and methods of national regeneration."

He was able to convince himself that Fate had come to his rescue in the guise of crushing defeat. "It was the greatest good fortune for us National Socialists that this Putsch collapsed," he later wrote and listed three reasons: it would have been "absolutely impossible" to co-operate with Ludendorff; the abrupt takeover of power throughout Germany would have led to the "greatest difficulties" since the party had not begun to make the proper preparations; and the "blood sacrifice" of fourteen comrades at the Feldherrnhalle eventually proved to be "the most effective propaganda for National Socialism."

In the past weeks he had done more than face facts. He had leafed through almost everything in print he could lay his hands on: Nietzsche, Chamberlain, Ranke, Treitschke and Marx. He raced through Bismarck's memoirs and a number of recollections of the World War. "Landsberg was my college education at state expense," he told Frank—and without the "pretentious intellectualizing" of professors. "Anyway, will-power is greater than knowledge. If God had only 'known' the world and not 'willed' it, there would still be chaos today."

Hitler entered prison convinced his own destiny had turned on him but now through rationalization he had persuaded himself that it had saved him. Reaffirmation of his own and Germany's destiny came, according to Hanfstaengl, who had found it safe to return to Bavaria, that January with the death of Lenin. He went into raptures and told Hanfstaengl that history was repeating itself. In 1762 Frederick the Great (whom he hoped to emulate) had also been transported by news of Czarina Elizabeth's death. "Now is the time," he said, "when everything will be golden sunshine." The Soviet Union would succumb and the whole structure of Communism tumble down.

In ten weeks Hitler had raised himself from the depths of despair. Confident that he would be the leader of Germany, he spent long hours worrying over the nation's economic problems and even evolved (so he confided to Frank) a clever way of putting many unemployed back to work: he would construct a system of highways binding the nation closer together and would then mass-manufacture a small economical car that the little man could afford. On February 22, when he and his companions were escorted through the prison gates and driven to detention quarters in Munich, he was mentally and physically prepared for the trial that would determine his future. It would begin in four days.

By chance Frau Ebertin, who had predicted failure of his Putsch, was also in Munich writing an astrological tract. She had a new prophecy for Hitler: he would not be crushed by his humiliating defeat but rise as a phoenix. "It will turn out that recent events will not only give this [Hitler] movement inner strength, but external strength as well, so that it will give a mighty impetus to the pendulum of world history."

All Germany, if not the world, was watching Munich on the morning of February 26, for the political significance of the treason charges against Hitler, Ludendorff and eight co-defendants went far beyond their personal fate. The new republic and democracy were as much on trial as one of Germany's most respected war heroes and a fanatic from Austria.

Carin Göring wrote her mother from Innsbruck, ". . . at this very moment the trial is beginning in Munich. . . . Oh, may God help him that all may go well." The object of her concern, dressed in his best suit and wearing the Iron Cross, was seated serenely in a large classroom of an old red brick structure, the abandoned Infantry School. Hitler was prepared to do battle with spirit and determination. He wanted to be Goethe's "anvil or hammer."

General Ludendorff was the first defendant named in the accusation but it was obvious from the beginning that Hitler was to be the center of attention. He was first to be called to the stand and his opening words made it obvious that he intended to be the hammer. He had come not as defendant but as accuser. In a strong baritone voice he described to the court, much as he had to Ehard in prison, what impelled him to launch the Putsch. He spoke of the march, the bloody assault, his escape to Uffing and his admittance to Landsberg prison. He had but one regret—

that he too had not suffered the same fate as his dear slaughtered comrades.

He assumed all responsibility for what had happened ("The other gentlemen have only co-operated with me") and then denied that he was a criminal. How could he be treated as one when his mission in life was to lead Germany back to honor, to its proper position in the world? The effect of his words, delivered with the conviction of the true believer, could be seen on the faces of the little presiding judge and the chief prosecutor. Neither protested Hitler's accusatory manner or attempted in any way to control his rhetoric. Nor had Assistant Prosecutor Ehard much hope that either would keep Hitler in check: Judge Neithardt, an ardent nationalist, convinced as he was that the Putsch was a "national deed," was determined to find Ludendorff innocent; and the chief prosecutor, prodded by student attacks for daring to accept his assignment, felt compelled to proceed cautiously.

If these officers of the court were under Hitler's influence, Oswald Spengler was not. In a lecture that day he ridiculed the Nazis' love of flags, parades and slogans. "These things undoubtedly satisfy feelings, but politics are something else," he said, and described the trial as that "wretched Hitler case." It only confirmed his view that Hitler was a potential Caesar.

Much of the second day was spent in tedious examinations of other defendants, but Hitler once more dominated the proceedings on February 28. In a closed session he described in extravagant terms how both Munich and Berlin had been corrupted by the Red regime. "You have one classic example here in Munich. We should never have freed ourselves from the Red era if recovery had not emanated from the healthy section of the people." His words generated a heated response and he, in turn, vociferously defended his proposed march on Berlin.

As the trial proceeded Hitler continued to dominate the judges and the courtroom with his oratory and shrewd tactics. At the same time Ludendorff had become a minor character in the drama. Moreover his resentment against the principal co-defendant was becoming obvious. "Hitler misled me," he complained to Hans Frank after the trial. "He lied to me. He told me on the evening of his mad Putsch that the army was behind it to a man. . . . He is only a speech maker and an adventurer." Perhaps he resented that the speech maker and adventurer, the despised corporal, was acting more like the traditional officer of honor than the general. While Hitler accepted responsibility Ludendorff consistently avoided it. He conducted himself with arrogance, snapping at the attorneys and judges as if it were a court-martial and he the presiding officer.

He would "bark at the court in *Kommandostimme*, the tone of the parade ground," recalled an English correspondent, G. Ward Price, "every sylla-ble clipped harsh, and when his imperious voice rose, the little Chief Jus-tice in the middle of the Bench would quiver until his white goatee flickered so badly he had to seize it to keep it quiet."

Newspaper objections to the meek judge were growing and some for-eign observers found it difficult to believe they were at a trial. On March 4 a chorus of criticism directed at Neithardt was heard in the Bavarian State Ministers' Council. State Minister Schweyer charged that the public in-sults heaped on the army and state police by the defendants endangered the safety of the state police itself. Another minister expressed doubts of Neithardt's ability to conduct the trial. At this point a third minister de-clared that the manner in which the trial was being conducted was viewed with concern in responsible circles, especially in Berlin, while a fourth revealed that he had personally censured the presiding judge for allowing Hitler to orate four hours at a stretch—and Neithardt's only reply was, "It is impossible to keep Hitler from talking."

After each day's session he would be escorted back to a cell in the same building. Here it was that two antagonists—Rosenberg and Hanf-staengl—visited him. The first brought Hitler unwelcome news: a strong segment of the party's underground movement was bent on participating in the spring elections as part of a united block of völkisch organizations. It was an attractive idea to those like Gregor Strasser, the druggist from Landshut, since it appeared to offer the party the chance to extend activi-ties into North Germany. Strasser had convinced Rosenberg that the party should participate in national politics but Hitler derided the idea. Unifica-tion struck him as particularly dangerous at a time when the NSDAP was illegal and at the point of dissolution. Moreover, Hitler would have to del-egate authority from prison and he was shrewd enough to realize that what one delegated could easily be lost. His safest course was to keep the party in a state of suspended animation until his release. Hitler's opposi-tion took the form of sarcasm: what a comedown for the party to enter the election under the name of *Der völkischer Block!* "I told him," recalled Rosenberg, "that under the name of NSDAP preparations could not have been made in time. We simply had to wait until we could reor-ganize our party on a legal basis." Rosenberg left assuming he had Hitler's reluctant approval, and began paving the way for a dangerous split in the party.

Hanfstaengl's visit was social and he brought along his three-year-old son. "Now pay close attention, boy," he lectured Egon on their way to the former Infantry School building. They were going to visit Onkel Dolf in prison but someday he would be the leader of the nation and free it from its present misery. The boy envisioned Hitler sleeping on a bare earthen floor with only rats for company. But the reality was disappointing. Overlooking a garden-like back yard, Hitler's cell was very ordinary. The boy was placed on a chair in front of a table while the two men talked, but all he could remember of their spirited conversation was that Onkel Dolf's voice was so resonant that the little table vibrated. Hitler then gave the visitors tea after climbing onto a chair and fishing around on top of a huge brown wardrobe for a box of cookies.

Despite official and unofficial protests the trial continued to be a sounding board for Hitler, and he surpassed himself at the closed sessions of March 11 and 14. These were the days when the defendant was allowed by the law, unlike the English adversary system, to go on at length and freely interrogate the witnesses. And so Hitler treated the triumvirate as if they were the guilty parties. When General von Lossow took the stand Hitler jumped to his feet, shouting out questions. The towering, shaven-headed general bellowed back and pointed a long forefinger at the ex-corporal as if it were a pistol. Hitler sank back into his seat, momentarily subdued, but in a minute was on his feet again attacking the three men who had promised to join him.

General von Lossow's contemptuous declaration that Hitler was only fit to play the role of a political drummer brought such rowdy insults that the defendant was cautioned by the judge to lower his voice. He did so, but only until Lossow described him as part sentimental, part brutal. This time Hitler sprang out of his chair like a jack-in-the-box. "And where is your word of honor! Was this the sentimental and brutal Hitler?"

No, replied Lossow coolly, staring down his nose at the defendant, it was Hitler with the bad conscience. This brought a fresh barrage of insults and Lossow turned to the presiding judge. When no rebuke to Hitler was forthcoming, the general bowed and left the courtroom. Only then did Judge Neithardt tardily announce that Hitler's behavior was a personal insult not to be tolerated. "I accept the reprimand," was Hitler's ironic retort.

"I never can think without melancholy and bitterness about this monstrous trial," recalled one German journalist. "What went on there reminded me of a Munich political carnival. A court which time after time gave the accused the opportunity to make lengthy propaganda speeches; a lay judge who, after Hitler's first speech, declared (I heard it myself): 'But he's a colossal fellow, this man Hitler'; a presiding judge who let one man [Hitler] ridicule the highest officials in the Reich, as 'His Highness, Herr Fritz Ebert': . . . an officer who shouted to an American journalist who was chatting in English with a colleague, 'Speak German in my presence!'; a presiding judge who banished a newspaper cartoonist from the courtroom because one of the accused felt he had been the subject of a cartoon—doesn't all this belong in the Munich picture book of a great political carnival?"

The *Fasching* spirit continued to the end with Hitler's oratory reaching its peak in his final speech. One part lecture, another part exhortation, and a third part invective, it was always compelling and particularly effective since, under German law, the defendant had the last word. Hitler stoutly denied that he was only fit to be the drummer of the nationalist movement and that he was motivated by ambition alone. The charge that he wanted to be a minister was ridiculous. "I aimed from the first at something a thousand times higher than a minister. I wanted to become the destroyer of Marxism. I am going to achieve this task, and if I do, the title of minister will be an absurdity." Moments later Hitler revealed his innermost intention. "The man who is born to be a dictator is not compelled; he wills; he is not driven forward; he drives himself forward; there is nothing immodest about this. . . . The man who feels called upon to govern a people has no right to say: If you want me or summon me, I will cooperate. No, it is his duty to step forward."

He told the members of the court that, despite the failure of the November Putsch, they must honor him as the future power in Germany. For it was destined that the army and those who supported the ideals of the Putschists would be reconciled. "I believe that the hour will have come when the masses, who today stand on the street with our swastika banner, will unite with those who fired upon them. I believe that this blood will not always separate us. When I learned that it was the municipal police which fired, I had the happy feeling that at least it was not the Reichswehr; the army stands as untarnished as before. One day the hour will come when the army will stand at our side, officers and men."

"Herr Hitler," protested Judge Neithardt, "you say that the municipal police was stained. I cannot permit that."

Hitler ignored the gentle rebuke and without breaking his rhythm boomed out his final words: "The army which we have formed grows from day to day; from hour to hour it grows more rapidly. Even now I have the proud hope that one day the hour is coming when these raw recruits will become battalions, when the battalions will become regiments and the regiments divisions, when the old cockade will be raised from the mire, when the old banners will once again wave before us; and then reconciliation will come in that eternal last Court of Judgment—the Court of God—before which we are ready to take our stand. Then from our bones, from our graves will sound the voice of that tribunal which alone has the right to sit in judgment upon us. For, gentlemen, it is not you who pronounce judgment upon us, it is the eternal court of history which will make its pronouncement upon the charge which is brought against us."

Hitler won the battle of words and when the court retired to consider the verdict a number of observers were convinced he would be found not guilty. Judge Neithardt was bent on acquitting Ludendorff regardless of the testimony and the three lay judges, including one who had peered grimly at Hitler throughout the trial, were also unanimously for freeing the chief defendant. "On the evidence of my defense," Hitler commented long after the trial, "they were convinced that Kahr, Lossow and Seisser must have been equally guilty. They were informed of the objection that an acquittal might entail the risk of having the affair referred to the court at Leipzig. This made the jury reflect. They decided it was more prudent to have me found guilty, the more so as they had been promised a remission of the sentence after six months."

When Assistant Prosecutor Ehard arrived on April 1 for the sentence announcement he found the room crowded with women bearing flowers for their idol. He ordered the flowers removed. Other female adherents asked permission to take a bath in Hitler's tub. He denied the request. Just after 10 A.M. the defendants posed for a picture in front of the building. Ludendorff, in full military dress complete with pointed helmet, scowled. To his left stood Hitler in unbelted trench coat so neatly cleaned and pressed it looked new, clutching a velours hat in right hand. His mustache was neatly clipped, his hair slicked down, and he looked as calm, assured and well fed as a successful businessman. For the first time in his life he was on the paunchy side—170 pounds.

By the time the accused were escorted to the courtroom, a large crowd clustered outside the building. It took almost an hour to read out the sentence and there was no outburst when Hitler (along with Pöhner, Kriebel and Weber) was sentenced to five years in Landsberg prison. Six months were deducted because of the pretrial detention. As predicted, Ludendorff was set free. Once more he answered the consideration shown his rank by petulance. "I look upon this acquittal as a disgrace which my dress of honor and my decorations have not earned," said the man who had denied responsibility for the Putsch. His heated protest annoyed and embarrassed presiding Judge Neithardt, who was most responsible for the acquittal.

Even in guilt Hitler was honored by the court. It refused to deport him to Austria as an undesirable alien. "Hitler is German-Austrian. In the opinion of the court a man who thinks and feels as German as Hitler, a man who voluntarily served 4½ years in the German army during the war, who earned high war decorations for bravery in the face of the enemy, who was wounded and whose health was impaired . . . should not be subjected to the Republic Protection Law." The court saved its scorn for Hitler's three enemies, declaring that the tragedy could have been prevented if Kahr, Lossow and Seisser "had clearly said 'no' to Hitler's demands for participation [in the Putsch] or if the repeated attempts by the accused on the night of November 8 to clarify the situation had met with a measure of cooperation."

Hitler's sentence was the first announced. While the others were being read out, he was hurried outside to a waiting car to prevent any demonstration. By late afternoon Hitler was back in Cell 7. It had been refurnished in his absence and looked much more inviting. But his earlier confidence was gone and jailer Franz Hemmrich noticed that he "looked more wretched than ever." This depression soon passed. Before long he opened his leather briefcase and brought out an empty diary. On the frontispiece in the upper right-hand corner he wrote: "Motto: When a world comes to an end, then entire parts of the earth can be convulsed, but not the belief in a just cause." Below this he inscribed these words:

The trial of common narrow-mindedness and personal spite is over—and today starts

MY STRUGGLE (Mein Kampf)

Landsberg on 1 April
1924

The trial that only the Putschists wanted was over and, although Hitler had won the battle of propaganda, he was back in prison. For all he knew, he would remain there four and a half years. To a large segment of the German public and to the Western world in general, the sentence was ridiculously mild for treason and armed uprising. "The trial," commented the London *Times*, "has at any rate proved that a plot against the Constitution of the Reich is not considered a serious crime in Bavaria."

3

Hitler had two comrades on the upper floor of the Festung. Colonel Kriebel was in Cell 8 and the leader of the Bund Oberland, Dr. Weber the veterinary, was in number 9. Although Hitler complained daily about the barred windows, life at the fortress was passable. At 6 A.M. the two night warders went off duty and the cell doors would be opened. Invariably Hitler was dressed, washed and waiting ("He took a good deal of care of his teeth and mouth. That came of his having been gassed in the war"). An hour later convict trustees served the political prisoners a breakfast of coffee and bread or porridge in their common room. At eight the doors to the court and garden were opened and the men were allowed to wrestle, box or exercise on the parallel bars and vaulting horse. Because of his injured arm Hitler "had to content himself with the job of referee."

After half an hour the prisoners strolled in the long narrow garden, bordered on one side by the prison building and the other by a twenty-foot wall. A gravel path was Hitler's favorite promenade and here he would stroll back and forth, usually with Emil Maurice, his chauffeur, voicing the political theorems he had jotted down in his diary. "Sometimes," recalled Hemmrich, "those who had formerly belonged to the Storm Troops would start singing party songs as they stamped along. At first we took no notice, or at least we raised no objection to this, but when the convicts on their side took to yelling in unison and disturbed the peace of the whole neighborhood, we put a stop to it."

At about 10 A.M. the men were brought in from their exercise and mail was distributed. Numerous food packages arrived from nationalist organizations and private admirers. Hitler particularly looked forward to poppy seed strudel, an Austrian specialty, which a group of National Socialist women brought every Friday. But, recalled Dr. Weber, the Chief gave the bacon, sausage and ham to his companions, preferably those on the ground floor. "Upstairs with him were the elite. Yes, even behind the wall there existed a class system. They were not equal before the law, nor were they equal as prisoners."

Just before noon the political prisoners were served dinner—usually a one-pot meal—in the common room. The others waited behind their chairs until Hitler strode in, then someone called out, "Attention!" He stood at the head of the table "until every man in turn came forward with his table-greeting." Politics was rarely discussed. Hitler usually chatted about theater, art or automobiles. After the meal they would smoke and gossip for a quarter of an hour while the table was cleared, and then the Chief would retreat to his cell on the top floor to read, write in his diary or try to catch up on his correspondence. This period was interrupted at about four o'clock for tea or coffee, which was brewed in the common room. At four forty-five the gates to the garden were unlocked again and Hitler would walk alone, or with Maurice, for more than an hour. At six each man had supper in his own cell—a herring or sausage and salad. Those who wanted could buy half a liter of beer or wine. After another hour of sport or exercise the men assembled in the common room before returning to their cells. At ten lights went out.

Occasionally Hitler varied his schedule, retreating to his cell as soon as breakfast was over to study or receive visitors. According to Hemmrich, who soon became his enthusiastic admirer, he exercised a great influence over his comrades. Because of his "sense of soldierly discipline," there were none of the usual outbursts of temper of men penned up together. "He was always at their command to be of help or service."

Usually he was "singularly cheerful" but bad news made him "a trifle thoughtful and anxious." He was particularly disturbed by the rancor of party feuds. It was becoming increasingly obvious that the NSDAP was being split in two and that the schism was due in large part to his own vague instructions to his proxy. Rosenberg had joined with Strasser and others to support the völkisch bloc in the Bavarian state elections; more significant, these two, with the help of Ludendorff, had not only formed the National Socialist Freedom Movement but entered a slate of thirty-four candidates in the national elections.

The Bavarian election came first, in April, and the ill-assorted völkisch bloc scored an unexpected triumph, winning 191,862 votes, and finished second to the Bavarian People's Party. The Görings were delighted with the triumph. "Also," Carin wrote her father from Austria, "it means pardon for all of us living in foreign countries. I really can't believe it I'm so happy. It has been a very bad time. In North Germany we are counting on even more votes for Hitler and his movement, and then Hitler can at last come into power. You see, dear Father, I believe so much in him! He is a wonderful man, a genius, such a one, I am convinced, as God seldom gives to the world."

The national election a month later proved to be as successful as predicted, with the newly formed National Socialist Freedom Movement polling almost two million votes. Thirty-two of the thirty-four candidates —including Strasser, Röhm, Feder, Frick and Ludendorff—were elected. It was ironic that Hitler, who had opposed the basic idea, was responsible in large part for their victory. His oratory at the trial had introduced National Socialism to many voters who were impressed by its leader's forceful manner and his effectively enunciated ideas. But other more profound and lasting forces also contributed to the triumph. The tandem appeal of patriotism and racism was growing throughout the nation. Moreover, even though inflation had been ended by the drastic national currency reform, those in the middle class who had lost homes and property were expressing displeasure at the polls along with those in the working class who were still unemployed.

Understandably, Hitler was not overjoyed by the elections. Ludendorff was claiming credit for the victory and, being free, was in a position to capitalize on his claim. Hitler was forced to join in the applause while fearing that the new group might swallow up his outlawed party. Nor was his apprehension groundless. The threat to his political power was illustrated by circulation of a pamphlet to völkisch groups which admitted that the National Socialists were "pioneers and forerunners" of the völkisch movement, then sarcastically declared that "they are not [its] savior." The whole affair was a painful but valuable lesson to Hitler. Never again, he vowed, would he take a stand unless he was sure he had the power to enforce it.

Hitler was being attacked from his own stronghold. At the offices of the *Völkischer Beobachter*, which had been closed down after the Putsch, Drexler and Feder were conducting a campaign against him. "They called Hitler a dictator and a prima donna and proclaimed that he must be brought under greater control if the party was ever to be built up again," recalled Hanfstaengl. One day Drexler cornered Hans Frank in a small Munich park and poured out a stream of complaints against their imprisoned leader. "He intrigued against me and broke all his promises, pushed me out, and now has wrecked the party for all time with this crazy Putsch!" Once Hitler was free the rowdy Brownshirts would take to the streets again. "There are terrible times ahead for Germany. Hitler betrayed me and that is why I oppose him wherever I can."

That May Kurt Lüdecke returned from his money-raising trip abroad to find confusion in the ranks of the underground NSDAP. "The various groups quarreled internally and with each other. Nor were their antagonisms private scandals—enemies clawed each other in public regardless both of the spectacle they were giving the shocked onlookers and of the damage they were doing to themselves." From Hanfstaengl, Amann and Esser he learned that Rosenberg was the cause of party deterioration. But Rosenberg told him a different story. "They attack me," he said, "because I represent Hitler, whom they dare not attack, helpless though he is. If they eliminate me, they move one step nearer the top."

Lüdecke decided to travel to Landsberg to find out from Hitler how the danger could best be dispelled. According to Lüdecke's account, Hitler declared that the party must pursue a new line of action. Its future lay not in armed coups but the ballot box. "I am convinced this is our best line of action, now that conditions in the country have changed so radically." Hitler appeared to be not at all downcast by the party squabbles. "Indeed, he was so confident of final victory that my own misgivings were dispelled, for his mood was contagious." But the party split continued to widen. A few weeks later Strasser joined with Ludendorff in proposing the foundation of the National Socialist Freedom Party, thus creating a single völkisch party of which the NSDAP would be but a part. This raised the intensity of interparty rancor which, in turn, forced Hitler into making a radical decision. On July 7 *Der Völkische Kurier* announced that he had "laid down the leadership of the National Socialist movement, and that he will refrain from all political activity during his term of detention. He requested his adherents not to visit him in prison since he had so much work and was also engaged in writing a book."

In some circles it was deduced that Hitler was pretending to write as an excuse to avoid the internecine political battle. But even before his arrest he had been seriously thinking of composing a history of the Jews. Now he had a better idea, which obsessed him to such a degree that he welcomed a vacation from politics so he could get it down on paper. In addition to jotting down ideas in his diary, he dictated to Maurice. Then, in the privacy of his cell, he would laboriously type out the manuscript with two fingers on the typewriter loaned to him by the warden.

Guard Hemmrich recalled: "As he finished one section of the book after another he would read it aloud to the others in their evening assemblies." The book was not always written under favorable conditions. The window, for instance, leaked during a heavy rain. One day while mopping the floor Hitler burst into laughter. There was the prison cat "perched on top of a stool in the middle of the mess and puddle and licking at it after her own finicky fashion." His most helpful assistant was a newcomer to the top floor. After Hitler's sentence Rudolf Hess had taken Professor Haushofer's advice to surrender. Hess helped Hitler formulate ideas, took dictation and relieved him of typing chores. Frau Wagner also helped by providing quantities of bond paper, carbon paper, pencils, ink and erasers.

At first the book was to have been a general history but the first volume—under the ponderous working title *Four and a Half Years of Struggle Against Lies, Stupidity and Cowardice*—now included an autobiographical account of Hitler's childhood, his years in Vienna, the war, the Red revolution and the beginnings of the party in Munich. It turned out to be the story of a poor boy's political education and gave him the opportunity to discourse not only on his three favorite subjects—Jews, Marxism and racism—but the futility of parliamentary government, syphilis, the decline of the theater, the monarchy, and responsibility for loss of the war.

Writing down his political theories was in itself a process of self-education. "During my imprisonment I had time to provide my philosophy with a natural, historical foundation." The authorities had made a mistake by imprisoning him. "They would have been far wiser to let me make speeches all the time, without giving me respite!"

It was remarkable how Hitler had gained ascendancy over his jailers. He had already converted a majority of the staff to National Socialism and even the warden became so impressed that he permitted Hitler's lights to stay on until midnight. Surveillance was so lax that the prisoners established their own underground newspaper, which was typed and then hectographed. One section was comic, the other serious. Hitler usually wrote the leading article and would often contribute caricatures. The existence of the paper was not discovered until one man thoughtlessly wrote home about it but by the time Hemmrich raided the editorial office in Cell 1 nothing could be found.

It was also Hemmrich's duty to spy on the evening get-togethers in the common room to make sure no revolution was being plotted. But the eavesdropper became propagandized by Hitler's words and soon fell almost completely under his spell. He and his assistants would gather outside the door "all ears, alert for what he was saying about things that concerned our own interests. We were immensely struck by his speaking."

Hitler would close these meetings with a Sieg Heil! and the group would burst out into a revised version of the song composed by Gregor Strasser's group on the day of the Putsch.

> *Even if they betrayed us*
> *Or herded us like mistreated animals,*
> *We knew what we were doing,*
> *And remained true to the Fatherland.*
> *Hitler's spirit in our hearts*
> *Cannot sink,*
> *Cannot sink.*
> *Storm Troop Hitler*
> *Will someday rise again.*

As Hitler became more involved in his book he left his men to their own devices. Out of boredom one evening a dozen of them subjected him to an old-fashioned peasant hazing. They smeared their faces with oven rust and black, wrapped themselves in sheets and marched to Cell 7 armed with pokers and brooms. Brandishing their weapons, they demanded that he subject himself to their tribunal. What followed was a parody of the Munich trial, Bavarian comedy style. Hitler, so wrote

Hemmrich, joined in the fun and solemnly accepted his sentence, an auto tour of Germany, then "laughing still but shaking his head, went back to work."

Hanfstaengl, one of the less reverent visitors, noticed that Hitler was gaining weight and advised him to take part in prison sports and cut down on sweets. Hitler had an answer for each admonition: "A leader cannot afford to be beaten at games" and "I shall always be able to get the extra pounds off by speaking." Hanfstaengl brought him several art books but it was a recent copy of the satirical weekly *Simplicissimus* that did most to cheer him up. On the front page was a cartoon showing Hitler in armor entering Berlin on a white horse as if he were Sir Galahad. "There you are," he said, "they can laugh but I shall get there yet!"

He received many ladies, including a monthly visit from eighty-three-year-old Frau Carola Hoffmann (no relation to the photographer), whom he called "my beloved and devoted *Mütterchen*." Still pretty and petite, she was a retired schoolteacher who had taken it upon herself the past few years to do his laundry and see that he was properly dressed. She fed him on cakes and cream and, like a good mother, made him pay for the sweets with lectures on how to behave in polite society. Once Carin Göring came for financial assistance but had to be satisfied with a picture of the Führer inscribed "To the honored wife of my SA Commander."

Ilse Pröhl, the fiancée of Hess, was a regular visitor. Every Saturday she bicycled to Landsberg from Munich and one time managed to smuggle in a camera. Hitler and Hess would be waiting for her on top of the Festung staircase and the former invariably kissed her hand in his gallant Viennese manner before leading her to the common room for lunch. Once she came by train with her mother, who was not too fond of Hess, particularly now that he was a prisoner. But a kiss from Hitler changed all that. "My mother was totally unpolitical but as soon as she got back to Munich she joined the party—all because of that hand-kiss."

Professor Haushofer also visited Hess to bring him books and articles on political science and geopolitics, including works by Sir Halford Mackinder. He sometimes saw Hitler but never alone. "I avoided it," he later testified. "I always had the feeling that he felt the distrust of a semi-educated person towards a scientifically educated person." Perhaps it sprang from Haushofer's expressed hope that Hess would continue his academic career and not enter political life, or the fact that the professor openly described the Putsch as a tragic mistake. He was aware that Hitler was writing his political autobiography and that he had discussed Lebensraum and geopolitics with Hess "but I received the impression, and I am utterly convinced, that Hitler never understood these things and did not have the right outlook for understanding them." Realizing that neither Hess nor Hitler understood political geography, Haushofer tried to explain the basis, for example, of the second edition of Ratzel's work. But it was useless. Hitler took from geopolitics only what he wanted.

While Hess still revered the professor, he had already decided to become Hitler's personal secretary and devote his life to National Socialism. By now he was the Chief's closest confidant and, from this position of trust, he confirmed not only Hitler's genuine disgust with the wrangles disrupting the party but his preoccupation with the book. On July 16 Hess wrote a university friend that Herr Hitler wanted to know nothing of present-day politics. "For the time being he has withdrawn himself publicly from the leadership [of the party]. The reason is that he does not want to assume the responsibility for what happens outside without his knowledge, and possibly against his better judgment. Nor is he able to smooth out the constant quarrels, at least not from here. He considers it unnecessary to bother with such petty disagreements. On the other hand, he is convinced that once he obtains his freedom, he can steer everything back on the right track."

Determined opposition to the völkisch merger came from left-wing Nazis in North Germany who denounced the racists as "enemies" of the working class. Collaboration with them, warned one student leader, would force "the true National Socialists, especially the workers," to leave the NSDAP. While these northern leftists agreed with Esser on the impossibility of merger, they wanted no part of him and, two days after the Weimar meeting, one of them wrote a letter obviously intended for the Führer's eyes. It expressed a desire for Hitler to come to the north once he left prison but to leave Hermann Esser behind. Such men would not be tolerated in the north. "We will not build a Chinese Wall around Hitler as was done in Munich in 1923. Here live men of northern blood who refute spiritual servitude, who are not cowardly. We are not speakers and mercenaries . . . but only men who ask for contact with the Führer . . . men who want to serve the cause."

The rising crescendo of disagreement among these in basic agreement reinforced Hitler's decision to stay out of politics and on July 29 he sent another appeal for privacy to *Der Völkische Kurier*. "Since I am presently engaged in a work which must not be disturbed" he would from now on refuse all interviews not confirmed in writing. Wearied as he was of politics and visitors, he did take time that day to see a German-Bohemian party member, N. S. Kugler, who asked a crucial question: "Has your position on the Jewish question been somewhat changed?" This was one subject near his heart. "Yes, yes," he told Kugler, "it is quite correct that I have changed my opinion concerning the methods of fighting Jewry. I have come to the realization that I have been far too soft up to now! While working on my book, I have finally come to realize that the harshest methods of fighting must be employed in the future if we are to win. I am convinced that this is not only a matter of life and death for our people but for all peoples. The Jew is a world pest."

4

Throughout the summer Hitler luxuriated in his pleasant quarters, preparing himself for the battle to come. He confined most of his efforts to the book, secure in the expectation of an early parole. It seemed to be assured on September 18 when Warden Leybold dispatched an extremely favorable report to the Bavarian Ministry of Justice. It declared that during his months of imprisonment Hitler had "proved himself to be a man of strict discipline and order," who was "at all times co-operative, modest and courteous to everyone, particularly to the officials of the institution." Leybold concluded with a prediction that Hitler, upon release, would not resort to any violence or illegality. "There is no doubt that he has become a much more quiet, more mature and thoughtful individual during his imprisonment than he was before and does not contemplate acting against existing authority."

At first it seemed certain that Leybold's strong recommendation would bring about Hitler's release in early fall, but on September 22 the Bavarian state police sent a confidential report to the Ministry of the Interior recommending that Hitler not be released on October 1; and if this came about "unexpectedly" he should be deported as a security measure. The moment he was set free, Hitler would generate riots "because of his energy." Penal Chamber I ignored this recommendation and declared Hitler eligible for parole but an appeal from the Minister of Justice on the grounds that the prisoner had flagrantly violated visiting privileges was upheld. Parole was denied.

Hitler's frustration was complete but, as he had done before, he lifted himself out of this depression and returned to work on his book. "All day long," recalled Hemmrich, "and late into the night one could hear the typewriter going in his room, and his voice dictating to Hess." Nor did he neglect his duty as Führer. On the first anniversary of the Munich Putsch he spoke "with deep emotion" to the political prisoners gathered in the common room. While charging himself "with the entire responsibility for the whole affair," he demonstrated how it had failed for historical reasons.

"His hearers were profoundly impressed with the Leader's sincerity and deep morality."

November passed and though there was still no indication that parole was at hand, he remained stoic.

In the meantime one of his most prestigious followers, Göring, was in a Venice hotel attempting to negotiate a badly needed loan from Benito Mussolini. Although still recuperating from his painful wound, which required heavy drug dosage, the former war ace was exerting himself in the Führer's service. He was involved in a frustrating correspondence with Leo Negrelli, an agent of Mussolini, in hopes of getting two million lire from the Fascists as well as a promise from Il Duce to see Hitler once he was out of prison. In return the National Socialists would publicly support Italy's claim to the South Tyrol—an action that would lose numerous supporters, particularly in Bavaria.

But apparently the Fascists doubted they would get their money's worth from a party whose attempt to emulate the March on Rome had ended so disastrously, and Göring's pleading became shrill. "The Fascists were at one time small and laughed at," he argued.* "One should not believe that National Socialists have no future." In a few years they would be in power. He enlarged upon the embarrassment the NSDAP would face because of its support of such an unpopular cause as the South Tyrol; and pointed out what a bargain Mussolini was getting for a mere two million lire. "For this you would have in our press an important speaking-trumpet. Besides you will get your two million back at the *latest* in five years."

A few days later Göring became more insistent. "It would really be good if the greatest national movements would have more understanding of each other. . . . Anti-Semitism must in a certain sense be international. The Jew must be fought in all countries."

But the month of November slipped by with Mussolini still refusing to commit himself (nor is it likely that he ever did loan the two million lire) and the Führer still in prison. A few of his comrades were released by mid-December. "Hitler bore these repeated disappointments about his own return to freedom with equanimity and philosophy," remembered Hemmrich. "The remainder prepared to celebrate the season at Landsberg as best as they could." They put up holiday decorations and set up a Christmas tree in the common room. But before they could decorate it

---

* The 1924–25 correspondence between Göring and Negrelli was recently discovered and translated by Ben E. Swearingen. It sheds new light on this hitherto obscure period of Göring's career, as well as giving new information on the early Nazi-Fascist relationship.

the efforts of the state cabinet to prevent Hitler's parole finally ended. On December 19 the Bavarian Supreme Court—perhaps influenced by a threat from the three lay judges of the Hitler trial to make a public appeal —ordered his immediate release.

Warden Leybold himself brought the news to Hitler, and early the following afternoon, after spending more than a year in prison, Hitler bade farewell to his comrades, gave them all his money (282 marks), then shook hands with Hemmrich and thanked him for all he had done. There followed a tearful parting with Leybold. "When I left Landsberg," recalled Hitler, "everyone wept (the warden and the other members of the prison staff)—but not I! We'd won them all to our cause."

It was a raw, gray day. Hitler tersely greeted the two who had come to take him home, his printer, Adolf Müller, and Hoffmann, the photographer, before stepping briskly into the touring car, its canvas top raised as protection against the cold. He turned to Hoffmann, who had not been allowed to take photographs in the prison, and told him to get his picture. After one was taken at the ancient city gate, which had a fortress atmosphere, Hoffmann wanted to know what Hitler intended to do now. "I shall start again, from the beginning," he said. As they sped toward Munich Hitler reveled in the experience. ("What a joy it was for me to be in a car again!") He asked Müller to go faster. "No," was the reply. "It's my firm intention to go on living for another twenty-five years."

At Pasing they were met by a group of Nazi motorcyclists who accompanied them into the city. Party faithfuls were waiting outside his apartment house. At the top of the stairs, Hitler was almost bowled over by his exuberant dog. He found his room filled with flowers and laurel wreaths. Neighbors had covered the table with food and drink, including a bottle of wine. Prison had not marked him with self-pity. Far from regretting his months in Landsberg, he professed they had been essential for his development. "That period gave me the chance of deepening various notions for which I then had only an instinctive feeling. It was during this incarceration, too, that I acquired that fearless faith, that optimism, that confidence in our destiny, which nothing could shake thereafter."

Hitler left Landsberg hardened by adversity, more settled in his own convictions. Unabashed by the party feuds and the apparent blighting of his political ambitions, he had returned to Munich determined to take a new political road. Never again would he make the old mistakes. He had been a Führer in name only, serving a party that had been founded by others. From now on he would be a true Führer, shaping his own program in his own way toward long-range goals.

His first task was to assess the political situation. The National

Socialist bloc had lost more than half its seats in the December elections with the popular vote slipping from 1,918,300 to 907,300. Moreover the NSDAP itself was still illegal and he would have to operate underground. On the positive side, he was not only free but deportation proceedings against him had been quashed by the man who had recently fought his parole; Justice Minister Gürtner had undoubtedly been influenced by Austrian refusal to take Hitler back. He had come out of prison as a martyred saint to all völkisch groups, and this racist movement, despite the evidence of the December elections, was burgeoning. This growth, ironically, had been unleashed by the Putsch; many people who had wavered between the moderate and radical wings of the patriotic movement swung to extremism as a result of their emotional involvement in the abortive uprising.

In a sense the NSDAP had a stronger base than ever and, while its two warring groups were wide apart, Hitler was confident he could somehow induce both factions to place loyalty to him above their differences. He was to be the program and his followers would have to equate völkisch aims with his personal political success. The image of Adolf Hitler, the national martyr, would become the personalization of flag, freedom and racial purity.

What had been thought out carefully in the peace and solitude of his cell was quite another thing in the unaccustomed freedom of Munich. On that first evening of liberty he didn't know what to do with himself. "I had the impression that any moment a hand would be laid on my shoulder, and I remained obsessed by the idea that I'd have to ask leave for anything I wanted to do!" Shrewd enough to realize that only time would enable him to regain "contact with reality," he decided to remain quiet for several weeks before embarking on the task of "reconciling the enemy brothers."

One of the first steps in his project to regain civilian composure was a visit to the Hanfstaengls on a snowy Christmas Eve. They had moved from their cramped apartment to a spacious house across the Isar River, a pleasant sector near Herzog Park boasting such prestigious neighbors as Thomas Mann. As Hitler entered the studio he looked around nervously, then said, almost pleadingly, "Hanfstaengl, play me the 'Liebestod.'" After Hanfstaengl "hammered out this tremendous thing from *Tristan and Isolde*, with Lisztian embellishments," Hitler began to relax. Helene brought in her new daughter, Herta. Hitler crooned over the baby and apologized for what had happened at Uffing. "You are the most feudal acquaintances I have," he finally said, surveying the studio. Suddenly, in mid-sentence, he darted a glance over his shoulder. "I'm sorry," he explained, "that's what jail does to you. There is always some damn jailer standing behind watching you." In Landsberg, he explained, someone was constantly observing him through the observation hole in the door. "A horrible feeling, that! I am certain they were seeking for some pretext to have me transferred to an insane asylum. You know I went on a hunger strike for two weeks and they tried to make that grounds for an insanity charge." (Perhaps that was why he ended his fast.)

After dinner and the presentation of gifts that lay under the candlelit Christmas tree, Helene, Hitler and four-year-old Egon settled around the piano while Hanfstaengl played piece after piece on the Steinway. A military march seemed to inspire Hitler to stride up and down the room like a soldier, hands clasped behind his back, recalling scenes from the Great War. For the benefit of Egon, he began imitating a battle, reproducing the noise of howitzers, 75s and machine guns, separately and all at once.

This was followed by a lecture on politics which evolved into a tirade against the Jews. His anti-Semitism, thought Hanfstaengl, seemed to have acquired more specific racial undertones; he had become convinced that Wall Street and, in fact, all America was controlled by the Jews. Then his thoughts—and words—abruptly turned to his dearest friend in Landsberg. "Ach, mein Rudi, mein Hesserl," Hitler exclaimed emotionally. "Isn't it appalling to think he's still there!"

Before he left, Hitler managed to have a few moments of privacy with Helene in the studio. She was seated on a large sofa and all at once he dropped to his knees and put his head in her lap. "If only I had someone to take care of me," he said.

"Look, this won't do," said Helene and asked him why he didn't get married. "I can never marry because my life is dedicated to my country." She thought he was acting like a little boy, and perhaps he was. Seventeen years ago, almost to the day, his mother had died. "It would have been awful if someone had come in," recalled Helene. "Humiliating to him. He was taking a chance, he really was. That was the end of it and I passed it off as if it simply had not happened."

Chapter Eight

HITLER'S SECRET BOOK
1925–1928

1

Hitler was invited to spend New Year's Eve at Hoffmann's home. He refused but when the party was under way a girl urged the photographer to phone the Führer and try again. To Hoffmann's surprise Hitler said he would come "but only for half an hour." His arrival was eagerly awaited, particularly by the ladies, none of whom had met him. Nor were they disappointed. "In his cutaway coat he looked very smart," wrote Hoffmann. "He had not yet started to wear the lock of hair hanging from his forehead, and his air of modest reserve only served to enhance his charm." The women were particularly entranced by his little mustache.

One pretty girl maneuvered Hitler under the mistletoe and kissed him. "I shall never forget the look of astonishment and horror on Hitler's face! The wicked siren, too, felt that she had committed a faux pas, and an uncomfortable silence reigned. Bewildered and helpless as a child, Hitler stood there, biting his lip in an effort to master his anger. The atmosphere, which after his arrival had shown a tendency to become more formal, now became almost glacial." Hoffmann tried to laugh it off. "I'm glad that it didn't happen to one of the more elderly among my guests. But then, you've always had luck with the ladies, Herr Hitler!" Not amused, the Führer bade everyone a polite, cool farewell.

Ever since release from Landsberg, he had lived in semisolitude. He was finding it difficult to adjust politically as well as socially. Determined to confine his activities to behind-the-scenes discussions with Esser and Pöhner, he refused to reveal his new plans and put off worshipful delegations who sought his advice and blessing. At the same time he did not make the mistake of discouraging the adulation of rank-and-file followers, and his silence made them more eager than ever to hear his first speech.

Hitler needed this concentrated solitude to become familiar with recent drastic political and economic developments. The regime in France which had been demanding occupation of the Ruhr had been replaced by a more conciliatory group, and a more equitable payment by Germany of war reparations had been recently instituted by the Allies. On the economic front the establishment of a stable mark had stemmed the toboggan slide to economic chaos. The dual prospect of a peaceable settlement with France and economic recovery meant that Hitler had been deprived of political assets.

On the other hand, a social change had come about which now offered him the chance to re-enter politics on a national scale. Rapid technical developments, urbanization, dispersal of the population and the industrialization of the past decade had upended the middle class. The small merchant, the independent businessman and the farmer were in a state of uncertainty and fear. It was the middle class that had suffered most during the inflation. The margin of affluence which had set these people above the working class had been wiped out along with their savings and capital. Many blamed their misfortunes on the Reds and Jews and their bitterness was already turning into hatred, making them receptive to Hitler's message of anti-Semitism.

The new year presented as many opportunities as difficulties and his political future would depend on ability to cope with both. He made his first move on the fourth day of 1925 in the form of a gesture of truce to the new Minister President of Bavaria, Heinrich Held. He spent half an hour alone with Held, pledging his loyalty and offering to co-operate in the fight against the Reds. He promised to confine himself to legal means in his future political struggles and made such a favorable impression that Held reportedly remarked that evening, "This wild beast is checked. We can afford to loosen the chain."

Alfred Rosenberg was not one of the few admitted to Hitler's company in these days of seclusion and preparation. He knew that Hitler was driving around the countryside with Esser, Amann, Hoffmann and Hanfstaengl and he was irked at being excluded from this select company. "He valued me very much, but he did not like me," Rosenberg later complained. Piqued as well as concerned about the party split, Rosenberg persuaded his friend Lüdecke to write an article warning that the party was doomed unless its members stopped sniping at each other.

After sending a copy of this article to Hitler, Lüdecke requested an interview. It took place at the little room on the Thierschstrasse and, after attacking Ludendorff and delivering a lecture on the Jews, Hitler finally got around to the article. Lüdecke, he said, could not possibly know the real facts of the Putsch or the trial since he'd been out of the country. He derided Rosenberg's attempt to separate him from Esser ("That fellow has more political sense in his fingertips than the whole bunch of his accusers in their buttocks"), then sarcastically advised Lüdecke to see that Rosenberg "comes to his senses and stops playing the offended innocent."

Although Hitler seemed to be rejecting Lüdecke's counsel to end party squabbles, he took it—intending to effect it in his own way. This decision to heal party wounds, combined with his promises to Minister President Held, soon bore fruit. On February 16 the Bavarian government canceled the state of emergency and removed its restrictions on the NSDAP. Ten days later the *Völkischer Beobachter* was back on the stands with a lengthy editorial by Hitler entitled "A New Beginning." He promised to confine himself henceforth to organization and policy, not personal and religious differences, and called for peace among all völkisch elements within the party. They must unite, he said, to defeat the common enemy, Jewish Marxism. It was the new Adolf Hitler in action, determined to operate legally and willing to compromise for the sake of a party unity. At the same time he was going to run the party *his* way, and despite a pledge to work within the governmental framework, he had not tempered his attack on his primal enemy—the Jew.

On the following day, February 27, Hitler made his eagerly awaited return to public life at a party convention in the Bürgerbräukeller where he had launched the Putsch. His speech was scheduled to begin at 8 P.M. but at midafternoon lines were already forming in front of the beer hall. By the time the police closed the doors at 6 P.M. the large hall was jammed with 4000 people. Another thousand were turned away. National Socialists from all over the nation were on hand—with three important exceptions: Röhm, Strasser and Rosenberg. "I won't take part in that comedy," the latter told Lüdecke that afternoon. "I know the sort of brother-kissing Hitler intends to call for." Rosenberg was proud and refused to shake hands with a man he felt had forsaken him.

There was almost as much excitement in the hall as there had been on the night of the Putsch, and as Hitler marched down the aisle wildly enthusiastic adherents waved beer mugs, cheered and hugged each other.

Lifting his eyes above the party leaders, he appealed to the multitude beyond. While his words were fervent, they were not designed to antagonize either faction. He didn't make the mistake of going into the details of the squabbles of 1924; he ignored them. He called Ludendorff "the most loyal and selfless friend" of the movement and urged all those who "in their hearts remained old National Socialists" to join together behind the swastika flag and crush their two greatest enemies: Marxism and Jews. The first was an appeal to revolutionaries like Esser, the second to Drexler and his more conservative völkisch followers.

After an inspirational appeal for national regeneration ("It is madness to believe that a great people of sixty or seventy million cannot be destroyed. It perishes as soon as it loses its drive for self-preservation") he turned his attention to the party officials at the front tables. He neither asked for their loyalty and support nor offered any compromise. He ordered them to join the crusade or get out. "If anyone comes and puts conditions to me, then I say to him: 'My friend, wait and see what conditions I will put to you.' I am not out to get the great masses. After a year you can judge, my party comrades, if I have acted correctly and that it is good; if I have not acted correctly, then I will place my office back in your hands. Until that moment, however, I alone lead the movement and no one makes conditions for me so long as I personally assume all responsibility. And I unconditionally assume responsibility for everything that happens in the movement."

The frenzy in his manner was communicated to the audience. Cries of "Heil!" rang out. Women wept as the crowd pressed from the rear, climbing onto chairs and tables. Men who had been bitter enemies surged to the platform and shook hands, some of them unable to restrain tears. Then Max Amann shouted, "The wrangling must stop! Everyone for Hitler!" Rudolf Buttmann of the German Nationalist Party came forward to make an emotional announcement that all his doubts had suddenly "melted away within me as the Führer spoke." Buttmann's use of this title, hitherto uttered only in private, underlined Hitler's overwhelming success. From now on he would be the Führer in public. He had not only unified the NSDAP but established the leadership principle, the unquestioned rule of one man.

Drained emotionally as well as physically, Hitler left Munich that evening with Winifred Wagner. He and a few aides stayed overnight at her home in Bayreuth, but their presence was such a secret that the younger children of the family would not learn about it for years.

The resurrection of Hitler was followed the very next day by a political development of significance. In the national elections occasioned by

the death of Ebert, seventy-eight-year-old Field Marshal von Hindenburg
became the second President of the Republic. It was obvious that the sympathies of this hero of the right did not lie with the Republic and, while
he attempted to remain neutral, he did little to strengthen the republican
forces. There continued to be frequent cabinet crises, often over trivial issues such as the conservative proposition to award a large financial indem-
nity to the Hohenzollerns. When this was carried over vigorous socialist
protest, a new bill was introduced to indemnify all dispossessed princes.
This, too, was passed despite a socialist referendum to override it. Even the
question of the colors of the German flag produced a cabinet crisis and
Chancellor Hans Luther was forced to resign over it.

It seemed inevitable that this change in national politics should add
impetus to Hitler's rise in power. But his return to the politics of the beer
hall had been too sudden and triumphant to suit the Bavarian government. It only proved how dangerous his gift of oratory was to the state.
He had injected new life into the party too fast, too excessively and the
police forbade him to address five mass meetings set for early March on
the grounds that he had inflamed the Bürgerbräu audience with such violent phrases as "Fight Marxism and Judaism not according to middle-class
standards but over corpses!"

Hitler protested the ban in person. "Those who want to have a fight
with us can have one," he told police officials. "Whoever attacks us will be
stabbed from all sides. I will successfully lead the German people in their
fight for freedom, if not peacefully, then with force. This sentence I repeat
emphatically for the benefit of police spies so that no erroneous reports
will be circulated." These were strong words for a man on parole and the
end result was a ban on speaking in public throughout Bavaria. Open
NSDAP meetings could be held, but not if their Führer spoke. Before
long the proscription extended to almost every German state; Hitler had
been deprived of his major political weapon. He was forced to transfer his
platform to the homes of his wealthy supporters. He spoke—recalled
Heinz Haushofer, whose father took him to a Munich salon—as if he were
at the Zirkus Krone, except that he remained seated. "It was terrible . . .
shouting and arm waving. He was not interrupted. He just spoke and
spoke, like a record running in a groove, for an hour or an hour and a half
until he became absolutely exhausted . . . and when he was finished and
breathless, he just sat down once more a simple and nice man. . . . It was
just as if he switched into another gear. And there was no in-between."

The ban obliged Hitler to confine himself to rebuilding the party and
he tirelessly went from one closed meeting to another in Munich, exhorting audiences much as he had done in the Bürgerbräukeller. By grass-roots

technique—shaking hands with men, kissing the hands of women and holding innumerable intimate conversations—he came into contact with the entire metropolitan membership. He succeeded not only in solidifying his magnetic attractions to the commonalty but in winning complete organizational control of the city party. At the same time Esser and Streicher roamed Bavaria duplicating Hitler's tactics as they rallied local organizations behind the Führer.

By the end of March Hitler controlled almost all Bavarian locals but he was forced to turn over the fate of the party in North Germany to Gregor and Otto Strasser. The first was a good organizer and a gifted speaker and could, as a delegate to the Reichstag, travel free on railroads. After the inspiring speech in the Bürgerbräu, he pledged his allegiance to Hitler but Otto, already a clever journalist despite his youth, had reservations. How long, he wondered, would the honeymoon with Hitler last?

Hitler accepted his enforced retirement from public life much as he had his imprisonment and took advantage of its opportunities. He utilized his free time to establish a solid party apparatus with the help of two colorless but efficient bureaucrats: Philipp Bouhler and Franz Xaver Schwarz. The first became executive secretary of the party. An owlish-looking individual who invariably bowed to Hitler before addressing him, he was obsessed with details. Schwarz, formerly an accountant at the Munich City Hall, was party treasurer. He brought to his job the talents of an adding machine and the spirit of a miser. Together the two men, by subordinating themselves completely to the Führer, became indispensable to the party machinery.

The efficient depersonalization of the party's internal organization by Bouhler and Schwarz enabled Hitler to concentrate on long-range political strategy, write articles and travel extensively in the north to make personal appearances at closed party meetings. He also had the leisure to repair broken friendships, chastise recalcitrants, bring opponents together and attend to personal problems. He reinstated Rosenberg as editor of the refounded *Völkischer Beobachter*, then wrote him a letter praising his integrity and calling him "a most valuable collaborator."

A few days later Hitler wrote another letter and solved a nagging personal problem—deportation to Austria—by facing it directly. He requested the city officials in Linz to cancel his Austrian citizenship since he intended to become a citizen of Germany. Three days later the provincial government of Upper Austria issued an emigration permit absolving him "from allegiance to the Austrian State." For a fee of 7.5 schillings Hitler was freed of the threat of deportation. And though he was not yet a

German citizen, and consequently unable to vote or hold elective office, he was confident that this matter could be resolved when it became necessary.

Of more immediate concern were the rebellious actions of the contumacious and egocentric Captain Röhm. From the beginning he had attempted to make the SA his private army rather than Hitler's political instrument, and while the Führer was in prison he had formed a new organization from storm troop remnants under the name of Frontbann. Convinced that everything he had been working for since the Putsch would be lost if he subordinated the Frontbann to the party, Röhm presented Hitler with a memorandum on April 16 that the 30,000 men of the Frontbann could be the foundation of a national political organization but it must be under Röhm's absolute authority. His request was accompanied by appeals to their past friendship and a vow of personal loyalty.

Hitler had learned how disastrous it was to be dependent on an organization he did not control. Determined to make the new SA solely his instrument, he demanded that the Frontbann accept his personal authority at once. In an apparent effort to apply pressure, Röhm tendered his resignation from the Frontbann and requested a written acknowledgment of this action from the Führer. After waiting for an answer in vain he again wrote Hitler on the last day of April. "I take this opportunity," he concluded, "in memory of the fine and difficult days we have lived through together, to thank you [he used the familiar *Dir*] for your comradeship and to beg you not to exclude me from your personal friendship." There was still no reply and the following day Röhm announced formal resignation of his offices and withdrawal from politics. By maintaining silence, Hitler had forced Röhm to become a man without party or a Frontbann, and was himself free to set up a revitalized SA tailored for his own purposes.

Röhm was shocked and hurt. He complained bitterly, according to Lüdecke: "Though he often does what we advise, he laughs in our faces at the moment, and later does the very thing as if it were all his own idea and creation. I've never seen a man so magnificently unaware that he is adorning himself with borrowed plumage. Usually he solves suddenly, at the very last minute, a situation that has become intolerable and dangerous only because he vacillates and procrastinates. And that's because he can't act as clearly and logically as he can think and talk. . . . Hitler wants things his own way and gets mad when he strikes firm opposition on solid ground. And he doesn't realize how he can wear on one's nerves, doesn't know that he fools only himself and those worms around him with his fits and heroics. But nobody is perfect, and he has his great qualities. Apparently there's nobody else who would do better than he." Röhm, who had so freely bestowed upon the humble corporal the gift of his *"Du,"* was caught between admiration and contempt.

2

That spring at least two of Hitler's personal dreams were realized. First, he managed somehow to acquire a new red Mercedes in which he spent many pleasant hours touring the Bavarian countryside with his bosom companions. He also established an auxiliary headquarters in the mountain village of Berchtesgaden. In this breath-taking scenic area he always found refreshment and mental stimulation. He reveled in the simple life and would wander the hills wearing *Lederhosen.* "Having to change into long trousers was always a misery to me. Even with a temperature of ten below zero I used to go about in leather shorts. The feeling of freedom they give is wonderful."

At first he stayed at the Pension Moritz on the Obersalzberg in a small cottage above the main building. Here in privacy he finished writing the first volume of his book. His principal sounding board was Hess, who had become private secretary at three hundred marks a month, but he also sought editorial advice from Father Bernhard Stempfle, the former editor of an anti-Semitic newspaper, and Hanfstaengl, who set to work crossing out superlatives. Hitler almost always reinstated what the latter eliminated as well as his efforts to "wean him away" from the provincial views of men like Hess and Rosenberg. "You cannot have a *Weltanschauung,*" said Hanfstaengl, "unless you have viewed the world." He suggested Hitler travel abroad during the lull enforced by the speaking ban. In three or four months he could visit America, Japan and India as well as France and England.

"What would happen to the movement if I did that?" The party structure had fallen apart while he was in prison and had to be rebuilt. Hanfstaengl's observation that he would return "full of new plans for the future" nettled Hitler. "What curious ideas you have," he said. "What do you think I can learn from them? And why should I try to learn anyone else's language? I am too old and have no interest and no time."

Hanfstaengl offered to teach him English so he could read British and American newspapers and understand something of the broader world outside Germany. While never refusing the offer, Hitler could never make up his mind to accept it. And even the influence of Helene Hanfstaengl was waning. In hopes of instilling in him some of the social graces, she suggested he learn to waltz. He refused on the grounds that it was an unworthy preoccupation for a statesman and, after her husband noted that Washington, Napoleon and Frederick the Great all enjoyed dancing, retorted that it was "a stupid waste of time and these Viennese waltzes are too effeminate for a man to dance. This craze is by no means the least factor in the decline of their Empire. That is what I hate about Vienna."

Perhaps this rejection of Helene had something to do with her rejection of him the previous Christmas Eve. He was turning to other women for solace. Just across the street from his new rooming house in the town of Berchtesgaden (where he lived, in his own words, "like a fighting cock") was a boutique run by the Reiter girls, Anni and Mitzi. If one can believe Maurice, Mitzi caught the Führer's eye while he was walking his Alsatian in the Kurpark. A friendship between Prinz and Mitzi's police dog led to a flirtation between the owners. Hitler invited Mitzi to a concert, but her older sister protested on the grounds that Hitler was twenty years older than her sixteen-year-old sister. Hitler left in mortification but soon returned with an invitation to both sisters to attend a party meeting. Years later Mitzi claimed that Hitler went beyond flirtation: he called her Mitzerl, compared her beautiful eyes to his mother's and asked for a kiss. When she refused the Führer declared that they must not see each other again. But before long he was walking her around the lake. At a secluded spot he put his hands on her shoulders and suddenly kissed her. "He said, 'I want to crush you.' He was full of wild passion." Before long they were lovers; and while she had visions of marriage, he only talked of renting an apartment in Munich where they could live together.

Hitler found feminine stimulation of a different nature from Winifred Wagner, who accepted him uncritically. He became a hero in the household and delighted in playing the role of the mysterious figure fleeing from enemies bent on assassinating him. In the dead of night he would steal into the Villa Wahnfried. "Late as it was," recalled Friedelind Wagner, "he never failed to come into the nursery and tell us gruesome tales of his adventures. We . . . listened while he made our flesh creep, showing us his pistol which, of course, he carried illegally—a small one that he could hide in his palm, but it held twenty bullets." Then it was that he told the children that the bags under his eyes had been caused by poison gas in the war.

At Wahnfried he was called Wolf. Everybody liked him, even the new schnauzer, which snarled at strangers, but the children were particularly attracted to him. "He drew them quite effortlessly with his hypnotic power. . . . His life was fascinating to us, because it was completely unlike ours—it all had a story-book quality."

On July 18 the first volume of his book was published in Munich by

Eher. At Amann's suggestion the title had been changed to *Mein Kampf*, the name he had given his diary. Sales were good, a little under 10,000 by the end of 1925, but it was criticized then and later as abominably written, pompous and turgid. It read like a Horatio Alger novel grafted onto a political tract. Even its subtitle, *A Reckoning*, was novelistic. Even so, the detailed subjective portrayal (self-serving as it was) of the development of a young man's personal and political convictions gave insight into the nationalistic völkisch wave sweeping across Germany.

Since his release from prison Hitler's anti-Semitic diatribes had been overshadowed by preoccupation with party politics. The book was the channel for these feelings and here he developed the theme to new heights. He made it clear that his hatred and fear of Jews was the center of his private life as well as his political career. At the end of the chapter describing his blindness at Pasewalk he flung down the gauntlet: "We can not bargain with the Jews, only present them with a hard 'either-or.' But I was now resolved to become a politician." And in his role as politician it would be his mission to solve the Jewish question with radically harsh methods—and in the name of God. "Therefore, I am now convinced that I am acting as the agent of our Creator by fighting off the Jews, I am doing the Lord's work." To the growing army of racists in Germany, the pages of *Mein Kampf* were an inspiration and their author the personification of their struggle against all enemies at home and abroad.

3

Hitler must have known that giving Gregor Strasser full power to reorganize the NSDAP in North Germany would be risky and the more successful he became the more dangerous he would be as a political rival. While anti-Semitic, Strasser was no reactionary. His political philosophy could be traced to Spengler and the front-line socialism of the war, based on the elitist principle that leadership of the proletarians must come from the military. He was a typical left-wing National Socialist and this made him particularly useful in bringing party revolutionaries back into line. A husky, outgoing man, he would move crowds as well as individuals and by late summer helped bring more prosperity to the cause than Hitler had expected. The number of cells in some sections doubled and even tripled. This increase came largely through Strasser's appeal to the working class and his freedom from the autocratic control of the Munich leadership.

In early September the struggle against the south became an open issue at a party conference in Hagen. Gregor Strasser had called the meeting to form a coalition against Munich bureaucracy. The conferees naïvely

"In the Beginning Was the Word," a painting by H. O. Hoyer. BUNDESARCHIV

Hitler making a street talk. IMPERIAL WAR MUSEUM

Sterneckerbräu in Munich where NSDAP was founded in 1920. HOFFMANN

Early picture of Hitler in full SA (Brownshirt) uniform. LIBRARY OF CONGRESS

Early party meeting at Hofbräuhaus in Munich. Gregor Strasser is at Hitler's right. To his left, Franz Xavier Schwarz, party treasurer, Max Amann, the party's publisher and the Führer's former sergeant; and Ulrich Graf, the bodyguard. The Beer Hall Putsch would start here in 1923. STADTARCHIV, MUNICH

Leaving party meeting, circa 1922. IMPERIAL WAR MUSEUM

The Beer Hall Putsch, November 9, 1923. LIBRARY OF CONGRESS

The Beer Hall Putsch, November 9, 1923. HAUPTSTAADTARCHIV, MUNICH

Julius Streicher addresses crowd in the Marienplatz, November 9, 1923. HAUPTSTAADTARCHIV, MUNICH

Left, Hitler's cell at Landsberg prison. STADTARCHIV, MUNICH. Right, Hitler returns fifteen years later and tells Max Wünsche, his ordnance officer (who took picture), that his time in prison gave him the opportunity to write *Mein Kampf*. Over the cell door was a large plaque: "In this room lived Adolf Hitler from 11 November 1923 to 20 December 1924." MAX WÜNSCHE

Two previously unpublished letters. Left, Winifred Wagner encloses a book of poetry which she hopes will help Hitler over the long hours. "The poetry is to be interpreted in the frame of reference of Richard Wagner as a drama that can only be understood in connection with the music." EDWARD WHALEN. Below, Hitler's half sister Angela writes their brother about her visit to Adolf in prison and ends the myth that his family did not enthusiastically support his political career. "His spirit and soul were again at a high level.... The goal and victory is only a question of time. God grant it be soon." HANS HITLER

Common room of Nazi prisoners at Landsberg. Behind Hitler, Emil Maurice, early companion and chauffeur. To left, Colonel Hermann Kriebel, military leader of the Putsch. Ilse Pröhl, later Frau Hess, smuggled in the camera that took this and other prison pictures. LIBRARY OF CONGRESS

Hitler in prison with Maurice, Kriebel, Hess and Dr. Friedrich Weber of Bund Oberland. IMPERIAL WAR MUSEUM

Release from prison, 1924. LIBRARY OF CONGRESS

hoped to pry the Führer from his reactionary Bavarian advisers so he could lead Germany toward a revolutionary völkisch millennium. Strasser's program was endorsed. The delegates voted to unite for greater efficiency in organization and propaganda, and approved publication of a series of articles expressing programmatic policies that included economic reforms verging on national Bolshevism. Their editor was to be a brilliant twenty-nine-year-old who had replaced the methodical Himmler as Strasser's secretary. Josef Goebbels was just over five feet tall and weighed not much more than a hundred pounds. Moreover, his small frame had been wracked by infantile paralysis, leaving him with a deformed foot. Goebbels was compensated by a variety of talents: he was a facile writer and, despite an appearance of frailty, was a commanding figure on a platform with his magnetic baritone voice, expressive hands and appealing dark eyes.

Son of a Rhenish petty bourgeois Catholic family, he was molded by academia rather than home or church. His character was most significantly shaped by the University of Munich to which hundreds of disillusioned soldiers had flocked after the armistice. He had been exempted from service because of his clubfoot, but his hero was a tall, strikingly handsome veteran named Richard Flisges—pacifist and anarchist—who instilled in him ideals that would color the rest of his life. Flisges also introduced him to Dostoevski, whose emotional mysticism inspired young Goebbels.

He transferred to Heidelberg and left in 1921 with a Ph.D. in literature. The next few years he spent writing a romantic autobiographical novel entitled *Michael*, several plays and numerous lyric poems. To support himself he worked at a bank, as floorman of the Cologne stock exchange, as tutor, as part-time bookkeeper. It was during this frustrating period that he split with Flisges, for he had come to loathe the internationalism of Marxism. He moved to a völkisch socialism and in Hitler ("the incarnation of our faith and idea") he found a second Flisges to worship. At the same time he was bound to Gregor Strasser. It was this split fealty and its inevitable denouement that helped determine the course of the NSDAP.

This struggle was complicated by an ideological dilemma. In many respects Goebbels was still a Marxist and he persistently attempted to convert Communists to National Socialism. He was determined to evolve a theory which would erect "the bridge from left to right over which those willing to sacrifice came together." He, along with Gregor Strasser, believed that the party should champion the cause of workers in general and trade unionism in particular. This was one of the main points of difference between Hitler and Goebbels. He hoped to influence Hitler on his next trip north; then he could prove that the only thing separating the Communists and Nazis was the Reds' dedication to internationalism.

At last on November 4 the two met in Braunschweig, and when Hitler shook his hand Goebbels was in ecstasy. "Like an old friend," he wrote in his diary. "And those big blue eyes. Like stars. He is glad to see me. I am in heaven." The personal encounter was the beginning of Goebbels' enchantment with the Führer, an enthrallment intensified at a second meeting several weeks later in Plauen. "Great joy! He greets me like an old friend. And looks after me. How I love him!"

Yet within twenty-four hours Goebbels was participating in an open revolt against the central party organization at a meeting of northern Gauleiters. He had been delegated to help Strasser draft a new party program aimed at liberating the Führer from the "reactionary" Munich group and turning him to the left. This program called for state ownership of all land, division of large agricultural estates among landless farmers and nationalization of corporations. It was presented to the Gauleiters at a two-day conference in Hannover on January 24–25, 1926. The sessions were stormy, largely due to the surprise appearance of Gottfried Feder, Hitler's proxy. To Goebbels he was "the servant of capital and interest, the revaluation shit and principal program drafter of the movement." According to Strasser's younger brother, the Gauleiters, with the lone exception of Robert Ley, voted for the new program point by point. Finally Feder, who had objected to almost everything, said, "Neither Hitler nor I will accept this program." He was reminded that he was only a guest but he persisted. As he was announcing that Hitler opposed the Marxists' request for confiscation of crown property as a "Jewish swindle," he was shouted down. Goebbels leaped to his feet, furiously attacking the Munich leadership. He demanded Hitler's expulsion from the party unless he freed himself from their influence. This ultimatum seemed strange coming from someone who had recently written, "How I love him!" but it could have been a product of that adoration, since he was convinced that the Munich bureaucrats were leading Hitler to ruin.

Whatever the case, Feder's report of the fractious meeting finally roused Hitler to action. He summoned all party leaders to Bamberg on Sunday, February 14. There was an uneasiness among the northerners as they took their seats for the secret meeting. They were far outnumbered by the southerners and from the moment Hitler stepped to the rostrum he dominated the proceedings. He had come to Bamberg aware of the problem that faced the party and the threat to his leadership, but his first ringing words made it clear that he was the Führer and the nucleus of the movement. There were to be no more parliamentarian debates, no more democratic procedures in the NSDAP. He would tolerate no splinter groups. Each Gauleiter, each member, was to pledge allegiance to the Führer, and to the Führer alone.

He did not make the mistake of assaulting either Strasser or Goebbels. Perhaps his intuition told him the truth—that both really were loyal to him and merely wanted to guide him away from the likes of Streicher and Esser. He had come to Bamberg not to humiliate the northerners but to bring them back into the fold. He launched his oblique attack on the leftists in purely leftist rhetoric, then offered as an alternative to the two conflicting views a new concept. He took the party out of politics and into the mythology of the leader. The original party program, he said, "was the foundation of our religion, our ideology. To tamper with it would [constitute] treason to those who died believing in our idea." In other words, National Socialism was a religion and Hitler was its Christ. Crucified at the Feldherrnhalle and risen after Landsberg, he had returned to lead the movement and the nation to salvation.

The unexpected thrust of his speech took the northerners completely by surprise. Goebbels had come to Bamberg confident that Hitler could be wooed to the left yet he neither endorsed their position nor debated the issues. Rather he faced the party leadership with a choice: to reject or accept him as the Führer. To have denied him would have meant the end of the party. Strasser replied briefly and nervously. He was a beaten man. And Goebbels, except for shouting out several slogans, remained silent, except in his diary: "My heart aches!"

Convinced it was only a matter of time before the wounds of Bamberg healed and the party arose stronger and more united than ever, Hitler took to the road for financial support. On the last day of February he was allowed to speak to the National Club of 1919 at Hamburg's prestigious Atlantic Hotel since it was not a public rally. His words, which indicated how much he had learned in Landsberg prison, were directed not to the lunatic fringe but to the solid German citizen. He abandoned the style of the Zirkus Krone, opening the address with calm persuasiveness. He told how Germany had lost the war because of Marxism, how the Reds had attempted to take over the country and how they continued to dominate the politics of Germany. Within an hour he had won the audience, not by pyrotechnics or emotion but by logic, not by appeals to racism but to patriotism, property and prosperity.

Once he began to talk of Marxism, however, his style became more forceful. "In a struggle, one side must succumb—either Marxism will be abolished or we shall be abolished." He called for a mass movement dedicated to a relentless attack on the Reds. "Such a movement can only rely upon men's fists just as one can only eradicate poison with a poisonous antidote. This movement must act in exactly that resolute manner. Victory will be decided solely by the stronger skull, greater resolution and greater idealism." This was strong meat for an upper-class audience but it brought forth "stormy applause."

To win, he said, this movement had to be as intolerant as Marxism. "There should be no doubts about it: we recognize clearly that if Marxism wins, we shall be destroyed; we cannot expect a different end. But if we win, we shall destroy Marxism, and down to the roots, without any tolerance. We shall not rest until the last newspaper is destroyed, the last organization dissolved, the last training center closed and the last Marxist converted or eradicated. A middle course does not exist for us!"

It was a remarkable speech, one indicating that he was at last looking for the broadest base of support in a vigorous but legal campaign to gain control of the nation. Nor had he forgotten that he had not yet gained complete control of his own party despite Bamberg. He began directing his charm on the two leaders of the opposition—Gregor Strasser and Goebbels. By early March the first capitulated, despite serious reservations, and sent out a letter to his adherents recalling all copies of his own program.

It took a special trip to Munich early in April to win the second but by the end of Goebbels' second day as the Führer's personal guest he was so excited he had difficulty getting to sleep. The next day Hitler gave him a conducted tour of party headquarters followed by a three-hour monologue ("Brilliant"), rehashing the Bamberg arguments. Captivated, Goebbels came over to Hitler's beliefs one by one, and finally surrendered in a gush of hyperbole.

> We ask. He gives brilliant replies. I love him. Social question. Quite new perspectives. He has thought it all out. . . . He sets my mind at rest on all points. He is a man in every way, in every respect. Such a firebrand, he can be my leader. I bow to the greater man, the political genius!

He left Munich in a state of ecstasy ("Farewell Munich! I love you very much!"), not only forgiven for his past sins but confirmed as co-Gauleiter of the Ruhr area.

With Goebbels and Strasser apparently converted, Hitler once more headed north to get financial support and also to solidify his position with leftist party members. On May Day he addressed an enthusiastic closed meeting at the City Hall in Schwerin, some sixty miles east of Hamburg. By 2 P.M. the large hall was packed with National Socialists from Altona, Hamburg, Bremen, Lübeck and Lüneburg. Hundreds were turned away. The *Hamburger Nachrichten* reported that Hitler's arrival was preceded by "wall-shattering" music.

He had developed body gestures which were, according to Müllern-Schönhausen, the result of lessons from one of the most renowned seers and astrologists in Europe, Erik Jan Hanussen. The two reportedly met that year in Berlin at the home of a wealthy socialite and Hanussen's first words were: "If you are serious about entering politics, Herr Hitler, why don't you learn how to speak?" A master of body language, Hanussen explained that Hitler was not taking advantage of movements to emphasize his words. In the next few years, so Müllern-Schönhausen claimed, they continued to meet briefly and Hanussen not only taught him the tricks of elocution but also advised him on the selection of his associates. Not until the end of 1932, however, would he cast Hitler's horoscope—and seal his own doom.

4

By mid-spring of 1926 Hitler had gained complete control of the NSDAP with establishment of the principle that the Munich local was the hub of the entire movement and should provide the leadership of the national party. This was confirmed at a general membership meeting at the Bürgerbräu on May 22. Here, as supreme Führer, Hitler was invested with the power to select and dismiss any Gauleiter or subleader. This meant termination of all democratic procedures and complete subservience to the Führer principle. As a final precaution, Hitler insisted that the twenty-five points of the original party program be declared unalterable. He got his way—and was now in sole charge of the party's ideology.

In his heart Goebbels had already gone completely over to Hitler but he kept up the façade of loyalty to Strasser, who still had doubts about the Führer. On June 10 Goebbels assured his diary that he would only go to Berlin as Hitler's representative if he could remain "absolutely independent" but two days later was eager to accept any invitation. "Then I would be away from all the muck. Now all depends on his decision. Does he want me?" By the time they met again Goebbels had worked himself into a state of exultant hero-worship.

> Hitler is the same dear comrade. You cannot help liking him as a man. And on top of it that overriding mind. You always discover something new in that self-willed head. As a speaker he has developed a wonderful

harmony of gesture, histrionics and spoken word. The born whipper-up! Together with him you can conquer the world. Give him his head and he will shake the corrupt Republic to its foundations. His best epigram yesterday: "For our struggle God gave us His abundant blessing. His most beautiful gift was the hate of our enemies whom we too hate with all our heart."

Early the next month Hitler all but conciliated the warring factions at the party congress in Weimar. The site had been chosen because Thuringia was one of the few states where Hitler was allowed to speak in public. His major address on the last day of the congress, July 4, was more emotional than political. "Deep and mystical," wrote Goebbels. "Almost like the Gospels. Shuddering we pass together with him along the edge of life's abyss. Everything is being said. I thank providence for having given us this man!" As Hitler walked off the stage the audience exploded into applause and the cheers continued for several minutes. Later Hitler, wearing an ill-fitting field jacket and puttees, stood in the back seat of an open car to review 3500 (the enthusiastic Goebbels put the number at 15,000) storm troopers who marched past, a bit out of step, with right arms raised in salute.

It was an impressive end to a memorable congress despite complaints that there were still fewer than 40,000 members in the NSDAP. Numbers did not concern Hitler at the moment. The party was one of the smallest in Germany but it was an iron fist, his iron fist. He returned to Berchtesgaden to complete the second volume of *Mein Kampf* and to recharge himself for the final task in the reconstruction of the party: conversion of the spell he had cast at Weimar into bureaucratic control of all party locals.

One man he intended to use in this endeavor was Josef Goebbels, who came to visit Hitler's mountain retreat and fell deeper under his spell. "He is like a child: kind, good, merciful. Like a cat: cunning, clever, agile. Like a lion: roaring and great and gigantic. A fellow, a man." And on July 25, his last full day in Berchtesgaden, came the ultimate conversion. "Farewell, my Obersalzberg!" Goebbels wrote that night. "These days have signposted my road! A star shines leading me from deep misery! I am his to the end. My last doubts have vanished. Germany will live. Heil Hitler!"

Hitler kept him in suspense for several months and when Goebbels finally received confirmation that he was going to Berlin he excitedly scribbled: "Berlin signed and sealed. Hurray!" It was more of a victory for Adolf Hitler. Outwardly he had made his peace with Gregor Strasser by admitting him to the party hierarchy but Strasser's talents and energy remained a slumbering threat to the Führer principle. By sending Goebbels to Berlin, where Strasser also had his headquarters, Hitler converted Strasser's former private secretary into his rival.

On November 7 Goebbels set off for Berlin and access to the corridors of power. He was heading for a new life, personally as well as politically, for he had broken his engagement with a girl named Else with whom he had been carrying on a tempestuous affair. How could a rising star in the National Socialist constellation be married to, or even sleep with, a half Jew?

There were almost 50,000 party members by the end of the year, as well as an efficient party directorate with Hess as secretary, Schwarz as treasurer and Bouhler as secretary-general.* The directorate had started with three automobiles and a staff of twenty-five but was growing rapidly. It was a quasi state within a state with departments for foreign policy, labor, industry, agriculture, economy, interior, justice, science and press. Party auxiliaries were either formed or envisioned: a Hitler Youth and leagues for women, teachers, law officers and physicians.

The most important arm of the party was the SA. Eight new units had been installed at the Weimar party congress as demonstrable proof that they were an integral part of the NSDAP. At the same time local and regional storm troop units were co-ordinated with the Führer in direct control. To fit in with his new policy of legality, Hitler chose Franz Pfeffer von Salomon, "a born organizer" and disciplinarian, to preside over a legitimate, non-military organization. "In order to prevent the SA from taking on any sort of secret character from the start," Hitler wrote Pfeffer, "it should not be hidden and should march under a bright sky to destroy all myths that it is a 'secret organization.' . . . Thus the fight against today's state will not take on the atmosphere of a society out for vengeance but a great world-wide movement and war against Marxism, its structure and its wire-pullers. We do not need a hundred or two hundred dedicated conspirators but hundreds of thousands of fanatic fighters for our *Weltanschauung*. . . . We must show the Marxists that the future boss of the streets is National Socialism, just as one day National Socialism will be boss of the state." The official SA uniform was brown shirt with brown tie. The color was purely accidental; a large consignment of brown shirts, originally intended for German troops in East Africa, was available at wholesale.

The end of 1926 was also marked by publication of the second vol-

* The official membership figures for this period are unreliable. Schwarz deliberately numbered all members consecutively to obscure losses caused by resignations or expulsion. Moreover, Gauleiters and local leaders consistently turned in misleading reports so they wouldn't have to send headquarters its full share of the dues.

ume of *Mein Kampf*. Subtitled *The National Socialist Movement*, it was based on the history of the party from the day the twenty-five points of the program were presented to the Munich Putsch. History of a sort had replaced autobiography. Since Machiavelli there had rarely appeared such pragmatic instructions on politics, and Hitler's precepts on propaganda and organization were practical for those operating on street level. His analysis of crowd psychology indicated he had read Freud's *Group Psychology and the Analysis of the Ego*, published a few years earlier in Germany. "A group is extraordinarily credulous," wrote Freud, "and open to influence; it has no critical faculty, and the improbable does not exist for it. The feelings of a group are always very simple and very exaggerated, so that it knows neither doubt nor uncertainty." Similar principles had been expressed by William McDougall and Gustave Le Bon but their works had not yet been translated into German. Ironically it took a Viennese Jew to instruct Hitler that the orator who wished to sway a crowd "must exaggerate, and he must repeat the same thing again and again." And it was Freud too who pointed out that the mass was "intolerant but obedient to authority. . . . What it demands of its heroes is strength or even violence. It wants to be ruled and oppressed and to fear its masters." Typically Hitler took what he wanted from his compatriot, combining Freudian theory with his own ideas to forge a formidable weapon.

The book also indicated that Hitler had drastically altered his foreign policy. He had come out of the war convinced that France was Germany's chief foe and in a speech in July 1920 even considered the possibility of an alliance with the Soviet Union once their Jews were expelled. Now, six years later, in the next to the last chapter of this second volume, he admitted it had been a mistake to look upon France as the main enemy, and completely rejected a war of revision. National Socialist foreign policy must be altered, he said, namely (and the stress is his), "*to secure for the German people the land and soil to which they are entitled on this earth.*" Several pages later he was more explicit. "*We take up where we broke off six hundred years ago. We stop the endless German movement to the south and west, and turn our gaze upward toward the land in the east.*" And by the east he meant primarily Russia which, he charged, had fallen under "the yoke of the Jew." And Fate had chosen Germany to help bring about conquest of this vast Jew-ridden territory.

Expansionism had long been a German dream. In 1906 Klaus Wagner wrote that "every great people needs new territory. It must expand over foreign soil. It must expel the foreigners by the power of the sword." Combining it with anti-Semitism was Hitler's contribution. No longer were the borders of nations decided by royalty, he said. Today it was "*the inexorable Jew who struggles for his domination over the na-*

tions. No nation can remove this hand from its throat except by the sword." And so by the sword he would eliminate the Jewish menace, France, Russia and Marxism, while thrusting Germany and the Germanic ideal to the fore. This conclusion, the result of seven years of probing, had come to him since his vision at the hospital in Pasewalk, by his individual, unsystematic, almost inspirational method.

Hess took a copy of the book to Professor Haushofer. Would he review it in his periodical? Haushofer was "quite unhappy" with what he read, particularly (since his wife was Jewish) with Hitler's racial diatribes. He also saw no relationship between his own theory of Lebensraum and Hitler's conquest of the East. He refused to write a review. "For me at that time," he later recalled, "it seemed to be one of the many ephemeral publications for purposes of agitation. It is self-evident that I had no part in its origin."

Hitler himself had second thoughts about the entire book and later admitted to Frank that he was no author. "Thoughts run away from me when I write." *Mein Kampf,* he admitted, was merely a collection of lead articles for the *Völkischer Beobachter.* "Of one thing I am sure, if I had known in 1924 that I would become Chancellor, I would not have written the book."

A few days after publication of the second volume Hitler turned a Nazi Christmas celebration at the Hofbräuhaus into another virulent attack on Jews. "Christ," he said, "was the greatest early fighter in the battle against the world enemy, the Jews."* He was not the apostle of peace. His life's purpose and life's teaching was the battle against the power of capitalism, and for this he was crucified on the cross by his archenemy, the Jews. "The work that Christ started but could not finish, I—Adolf Hitler—will conclude."

A few months later the self-proclaimed Messiah's greatest political weapon was restored. The public-speaking ban in Bavaria was lifted on March 5, 1927. Four nights later he addressed a large, excited throng at the Zirkus Krone. At 8:30 P.M. there was a shout from outside of "Heil Hitler!" and the band struck up a rousing march. Hitler entered, wrapped in trench coat, followed by his entourage. He quickly strode down the aisle as the audience cheered, feet stamped. Once Hitler reached the platform there was abrupt silence. Then 200 Brownshirts marched in preceded by two drummers and the flag. The audience broke into thundering Heils and held out arms in Fascist salute. On the stage, Hitler stood stern-faced, his right arm out. The music mounted, flags passed by the stage, glittering

---

* Hitler did not consider Jesus a Jew but a *Mischling* (a half Jew who did not adhere to the Jewish religion and therefore was free of the Jewish virus) on the grounds that, with immaculate conception, he only had two Jewish grandparents.

standards with swastikas in wreaths with eagles, patterned after the banners of the Roman legions. The SA men took position below the stage except for flag- and standard-bearers riveted at attention behind the speakers.

At first Hitler spoke slowly, deliberately, then the words began tumbling out in a torrent. According to one police reporter, his gesticulations as he jumped excitedly back and forth fascinated "the spell-bound thousand-headed audience. When he is interrupted by applause, he extends his hands theatrically. The word 'no,' which appears repeatedly in the latter part of the speech, is deliberately and theatrically emphasized." This was oration Hanussen-style. For two and a half hours Adolf Hitler talked of Germany's crisis, concluding that in such chaos the Jews alone were winners. It was an inspirational exhibition, notable not for what he said but how he said it. Of one thing alone he was certain. He planned to attain his goal this time, legally and by utilizing to the utmost the magnetic forces within himself.

During a major speech such as this Hitler would drink as many as twenty small bottles of mineral water and his shirt would be wringing wet. Sometimes, especially in warm weather, he also insisted on having a piece of ice on the rostrum so he could keep his hands cool. After a speech he would leave at once for a nearby room—provided by the sponsors of the meeting—and take a bath.

5

In this and subsequent orations Hitler seemed to be following the socialist line of Gregor Strasser; he even used the terminology of the leftists in attacks on capitalism and the decadent bourgeoisie. But the brunt of the battle to win urban workers over to National Socialism he left to someone more qualified. Josef Goebbels had set off for Berlin in a third-class railroad compartment with a worn satchel containing two suits, several shirts, a few books and a pile of manuscripts. He arrived to find the Berlin Gau in complete disarray and later would write that "what went as the party in Berlin in those days in no way deserved that description. It was a widely mixed collection of a few hundred people with National Socialist ideas." Although much of his account was more fictional than his diaries, this was no exaggeration. Meetings in the capital often degenerated into shouting matches and slaps in the face were commonplace. One quarrel between Gregor Strasser and a man named Hagemann became so acrimonious that it ended in a challenge to a duel.

Goebbels was faced with an apparently impossible task. Besides being at odds with one another, the thousand party members under his jurisdiction were opposed on the streets by overwhelming numbers of Communists and Social Democrats. Gau headquarters were located in a "filthy basement" of a building in the Potsdamerstrasse. "There was complete confusion. The finances were a mess. The Berlin Gau then possessed nothing but debts." This state of affairs inspired rather than depressed Goebbels. He moved his headquarters to a better area, set up regular office hours and established a sound accounting system under his personal control. By February 1927 the Gau owed nothing while owning almost 10,000 marks' worth of office equipment as well as a used car.

Goebbels decided it was now time to broaden the base of membership and to do that he had to attract the attention of a jaded public. "Berlin needs its sensations as a fish needs water," he wrote, "this city lives on it, and any political propaganda not recognizing this will miss the mark." His speeches and articles took on a crisp, graphic style attuned to the Berliner; his SA troops deliberately sought physical combat with the Reds—preferably when the odds were in their own favor—on his theory that "He who can conquer the streets can also conquer the masses; and he who has conquered the masses has thereby conquered the state."

He rehearsed his speeches before a full-length mirror and, according to his landlady, would practice body movements by the hour. Once on the podium he was a brilliant improviser, and soon perfected a variety of styles. Before a meeting he would ask what audience he would face. "What record must I use—the national, the social or the sentimental? Of course, I have them all in my suitcase."

He appealed directly to the masses in graphic, aggressive language. A consummate actor, he could switch from humor to sentiment and then to invective. Often he deliberately provoked the Reds into vocal protests which he would twist to his own advantage. "Making noise," he once said, "is an effective means of opposition." To him propaganda was an art and he was, by all accounts, including his own, a genius at it—and he sold National Socialism with American-style showmanship as if it were the best soap in the world.

He entered the lists of battle in the working-class district of Wedding by announcing in glaring red posters that "The Bourgeois State Is Approaching Its End," and inviting workers to a mass meeting on February 11, 1927, at the Pharus Hall, a center commonly used for Communist Party gatherings. It was an open declaration of war. No sooner did the chairman open the meeting than a Marxist worker shouted out that he wanted to clarify a point in the agenda. The chairman ignored him and when the worker repeated his request he was thrown out by storm troopers. This touched off a brawl in which eighty-three Reds were beaten up. A dozen Nazis were also injured and Goebbels showed his talent as

propagandist by bringing these men on stage where their moaning was
more effective. The Battle of Pharus Hall brought the party to the front
pages of the newspapers, and Berliners who knew little or nothing about
Hitler and his movement were made aware of a new political force in
town. The publicity was meant to be derogatory but in the next few days
2600 applications for membership were received, and 500 of these appli-
cants also wanted to join the SA.

With every meeting the size of the audience increased and by the
time Hitler appeared at the Clou restaurant center there were 5000 present. The occasion was a closed celebration of the Marxist holiday, May
Day, and the Führer began like a Lenin: "We are socialists, we are enemies of today's capitalistic economic system for the exploitation of the
economically weak, with its unfair salaries, with its unseemly evaluation
of a human being according to wealth and property instead of responsibility and performance, and we are determined to destroy this system
under all conditions." This was followed by a long dissertation on
Lebensraum, in Hitler's continuing effort to pound this concept into the
membership. Sixty-two million Germans, he said, were crowded into an
area only 450,000 kilometers square. "This is a ridiculous figure when one
considers the size of other nations in the world today." There were two so-
lutions: either decrease the population by "chasing our best human material out of Germany" or "bring the soil into consonance with the population, even if it must be done by war. This is the natural way which
Providence has prescribed."

Goebbels had hoped for another Red disturbance but all was peaceful
and the speech wasn't even reported in the major newspapers. Determined
to keep the party in the public eye, Goebbels organized another meeting,
three days later, in the Veterans Association Hall. He made up a provoca-
tively anti-Semitic poster ("A people in distress! Who will save us? Jakob
Goldschmidt?") and had thousands of copies plastered throughout Berlin.
Goldschmidt, a leading German banker, was invited to attend the meeting
but at the last minute his board of directors persuaded him to send his private secretary instead.

Goebbels was in good form, delighting his audience with his irony.
"Welcome, workers of Berlin!" he began. "Welcome also to a charming
young lady, the secretary of Jakob Goldschmidt. And please don't bother
to take down every word I say. Your boss will read it all in tomorrow's
papers." He went on to speak scornfully of "Jew journals" and "press syna-
gogues" until a heckler called out, "You don't look so good yourself." The
man, an elderly pastor, kept interrupting until Goebbels finally signaled
his Brownshirts to evict him. In the process the minister was so badly
beaten he had to be taken to a hospital. The newspapers described the vic-

tim as a "white-haired and respectable" pastor of the Reformed Church (he was, in fact, an alcoholic who had been removed from the pulpit and was destined to become an active member of the NSDAP), and this aroused such public indignation that the police commissioner declared the Berlin party illegal.

The ban came as an unpleasant surprise to Goebbels and he did his best to alleviate the situation with slogans such as "Banned but not Dead." With the party forced underground, he had to rely on cover organizations with innocent names such as "The Quiet Lake," "The Beautiful Acorn" and "Hikers of 1927." The Police Department countered with still another ban, this one on Nazi speechmaking throughout Prussia.

Goebbels still had his wit and he was inspired to publish a weekly paper. He gave it an appropriate name, *Der Angriff* (*The Assault*), and brought it out on the day dedicated to American independence. But the reality fell far below his dream and he was shocked by the first issue. The venture seemed doomed to failure. "What a miserable provincial sheet!" he admitted. "Baloney in print!" Only several hundred party members subscribed and few copies were sold at the stands. But Goebbels was convinced that the basic idea was good and gradually transformed it into a going concern by copying the make-up and content of the Communist Party paper.

The problem of Berlin, aggravated by the bitter feud between Goebbels and Strasser, created an atmosphere of sober realism at the annual party meeting in Munich late that July. The expected rate of growth in the urban areas was disappointing. Rather than address the meeting on this crisis, Hitler spoke only in generalities, his heat directed at a target no one in the Bürgerbräu would defend—the Jew.

It was almost as if he were not concerned with the party doldrums and had more important things on his mind. His speeches of the last few months indicated that he was obsessed with his personal ideology, his Weltanschauung. Again and again he hammered at race and the fact that Germany's future lay in conquest of eastern territories. Over and over he preached his pseudo-Darwinist sermon of nature's way: conquest of the weak by the strong.

This program was carried a step forward at the third Party Day in Nuremberg. Almost 20,000 members, 8500 of them in uniform, flooded into the ancient city and there was the usual pageantry—a march with flags and standards to the strains of rousing military airs. It was on the last day of the celebration, Sunday, August 21, that Hitler connected the concept of Lebensraum with anti-Semitism but few realized the significance of this misbegotten marriage, for his terms were too vague. He reiterated his demand for more living space for the German people, then pointed out that power and power alone was the basis for acquisition of new territory. But, he said, Germany had been robbed of her power factors by three abominations: internationalism, democracy and pacifism. Hitler then linked this evil trinity with racism. Were not internationalism, democracy and pacifism all creations of the Jew? Surely if obscurely Hitler had joined Lebensraum with anti-Semitism. His unsystematic search for a Weltanschauung was close to realization.

Hitler was still living at his little room on the Thierschstrasse, and although he was received as a hero in some of the best homes in Germany, his standard of living remained monastic. It was common talk in the neighborhood that he even shared some of his short supply of shirts and socks with the needy. In his modest room he received admirers rich and poor, from all over Germany, exhibiting a willingness and aptitude for making himself agreeable. Many a hand-kiss insured lifelong devotion from women; men were reassured by his firm handshake, his down-to-earth, man-to-man approach.

His speeches also became models of political acumen. During one in Hamburg that autumn Gauleiter Albert Krebs noted that he was conforming strictly to the outline on which there were written a number of catchwords. "Even entire sentences and phrases, which seemed spontaneous and improvised, had been written down. Hitler was not an intuitive speaker as many people, particularly his opponents, believed; he built his speeches systematically and he knew exactly what effect he wanted and how to get it. While Krebs did not realize that Hitler was going through the process of testing his personal world view in public, he did get an insight into the momentous development taking place in the mind of the Führer. "It was clear to him that he could only win the attention of the mass by avoiding the usual terminology and working with new words and new conceptions. His train of thought was of such generally compelling nature that people of different political directions could agree with it. So during his first public appearance in Hamburg, he was able within a single hour, to persuade a suspicious and reserved audience to applaud, and this applause increased until it became, at the conclusion, an enthusiastic ovation. Later the most level-headed listeners declared that, though they were still against the speaker and his party, Hitler himself was obviously much more reasonable then they had imagined."

He was learning how to appeal to the basic needs of the average German. No longer was he the völkisch fanatic, the frightening revolutionary of the Munich Putsch, but a reasonable man who sought only the welfare of the Fatherland. His "basic values and aims" were as reassuring as they were acceptable. His listeners could not possibly know that the "reasonable" words were a mask for one of the most radical programs in the history of mankind, a program that would alter the map of Europe and affect the lives, in one way or another, of most of the people on earth.

That fall Hitler stopped off in Berlin to settle the Goebbels-Strasser feud in person. According to Otto Strasser's account, Hitler appeared at his office with a demand to end the quarrel. "Then tell it to Goebbels," was the feisty answer. "He is the aggressor." Otto Strasser's show of independence by no means reflected his older brother's attitude toward Hitler. The Führer had gone out of his way to demonstrate his trust in Gregor. In addition to bringing him into the party hierarchy, he was grooming him for even higher positions. It was Gregor who had appeared on the same platform with Hitler in his first public appearance in Bavaria; it was Gregor who chaired the last annual party meeting. He would not listen to his brother's warnings that Hitler was becoming dangerously powerful. "Look," he argued, "you know as well as I do that Hitler is no leader but only a popular tribune of the people. He is manageable." Hitler was like a stubborn horse. "We shouldn't let him throw us off but must try to break him in and lead him in the right direction."

Hitler was no horse, said Otto, but a tiger, "and once he throws you off, he'll get rid of you for good." Gregor protested. He could manage the Führer, who was, after all, "a weak, good-natured and honest person. You don't know how much weight he gives to my words and how often he has said to me, 'Gregor, you're right once more. What would I be without you?' Do you think he says such things to Streicher?"

6

By the end of 1927 Hitler had demonstrated that he could handle people as individuals and in groups. It was also evident that his interest in rebuilding the party was long-range. Further, he realized something his advisers did not: before launching an all-out campaign to broaden the base of the movement he must have a burning public issue on which he could mobilize support from worker and burgher alike. Just as important, he would need a clearly defined world outlook to give him direction. This Weltanschauung would come in a year but the issue would not arise for two years and would originate in New York City's Wall Street.

The spring of the new year brought a revocation of the ban against the party in Berlin, followed by a burst of political energy on the part of Goebbels in an effort to win substantial gains in the Reichstag during the coming elections. While his appeal was directed largely at the worker, he called on nationalists and socialists to bury their differences. "Socialism and nationalism are things which supplement, not contradict, each other.

Against each other they are destructive; with each other they are revolutionary and progressive."

The national elections of May 20 were a personal triumph for Goebbels, who was sent to the Reichstag, but defeat for the Führer since the party elected only eleven other delegates. The Nazis had lost 100,000 votes and two seats over the past two years. The loss could be laid neither to Hitler nor to poor organization but to the healthy state of the economy and the absence of a crucial issue. No longer could mere mention of the Versailles Treaty and the "November criminals" win a voter. Politicians are often the last to sense a new trend and the Nazi elite who had gathered at party headquarters in Munich that evening to celebrate a major political breakthrough were deep in gloom at the succession of dismal returns brought in by messengers on bicycles.

Hitler arrived about midnight. Ignoring the atmosphere of dejection, he surprised his followers with a philosophical, almost detached speech. The old politicians expected the usual remarks of a defeated leader. But Hitler dwelt mostly on the healthy gains made by the two working-class parties—the Social Democratic and the Communist. He neither minimized their victory nor treated it as a National Socialist defeat and, in fact, seemed curiously pleased that the two "enemy" parties had defeated the German moderate middle and rightist parties. Unlike his comrades, the Führer felt that a bright political future lay ahead.

After the election Hitler returned to Berchtesgaden, his fount of inspiration. At last he had a place of his own, the Haus Wachenfeld on the Obersalzberg. It was a simple country house in Upper Bavarian mountain style, surrounded by a wooden veranda, with heavy rocks on the pitched roof to prevent the shingles from being ripped off in a storm. The first time he looked through the villa he had been "completely captivated." Luckily for him the owner, the widow of an industrialist, was a party member and she rented it to him for a hundred marks a month. "I immediately rang up my sister in Vienna with the news and begged her to be so good as to take over the part of mistress of the house." Angela brought along her two daughters, Friedl and Angela Maria. The latter, usually called Geli, was a twenty-year-old vivacious girl with light brown hair. "It was not that she was so very pretty," recalled Ilse Pröhl, who had recently married Hess, "as that she had the famous Viennese charm." There were a few critics, including Hanfstaengl, who characterized her as "an emptyheaded little slut, with the coarse bloom of a servant-girl, without either brains or character," but most people liked Geli, including Helene Hanfstaengl, who considered her "a nice, rather serious girl," by no means a flirt. And the photographer Hoffmann described her as "a lovely young

woman who, with her artless and carefree manner, captivated everybody."
On the other hand, his daughter Henriette considered her "coarse, provoc-
ative and a little quarrelsome." At the same time, Henriette was convinced that the "irresistibly charming" Geli was the Führer's only true
love. "If Geli wanted to go swimming . . . it was more important to
Hitler than the most important conference. Picnic baskets were packed,
and we drove to the lake." Not even Geli could get the Führer into the
water. No politician, he argued, should ever allow himself to be photographed in swimming trunks.

Their difference in age, nineteen years, was about the same as that between Hitler and Mitzi Reiter, the former object of his affection. By her
own account, Mitzi in a fit of jealousy had tried to commit suicide the
previous summer. In a bizarre attempt to choke herself, she tied one end
of a clothesline on a door, the other around her neck, but her brother-in-
law freed her after she lost consciousness.

In the discreet love affair with Geli (which most likely was never con-
summated), it was Hitler who was the jealous partner. One day, recalled
Frau Hess, Geli sketched the costume she wanted to wear at the next
Fasching carnival and showed it to him. "You might as well go naked if
you want something like that," he said indignantly and sketched his idea
of a proper costume. "Then she got angrier, much angrier than he had
been. She picked up her drawing and ran out the door, slamming it shut.
And Hitler was so contrite that within half an hour he was looking for
her."

His frustrated love life was overshadowed by a new book which embodied a philosophy of life, a unification of his political and personal convictions. While outwardly unsystematic, his intuition had its own relentless symmetry; and for the past four years, as seen from his speeches and
private conversations, he had been methodically chopping a path through
the jungle of his mind in search of the idea.

From the first words he dictated to Max Amann ("Politics is history
in the making") it was obvious that he was embarked on a venture of
significance. An essential of Hitler's conclusions in this book was the conviction drawn from Darwin that might makes right. It led to a vital link
between self-preservation and Lebensraum. "The compulsion to engage in
the struggle for existence lies in the limitation of the living space; but in
the life-struggle for this living space lies also the basis for evolution." The
consequence was an eternal battle between nations which could only be
won by a people dedicated to strict racial, folk and blood values. Once
standards were lowered and pure blood was mixed with inferior blood the
end was in sight. "Then the Jew can make his entry in any form, and this
master of international poisoning and race corruption will not rest until he

has thoroughly uprooted and thereby corrupted such a people." This was the first time Hitler not only defined his terms but interwove race, folk and blood values with his hatred of Jews.

In *Mein Kampf* he had simply drawn up charges against Jews as enemies of the world and effectively stated the case for a drive to the East to attain living space. Now at last he was ready to bring all the threads of his political and personal convictions together into a consistent (if twisted and paranoid) Weltanschauung, and he waited until the last few pages of his new book to do it. "It is not my task here to enter into a discussion of the Jewish question as such," he began tentatively. Jewry had "special intrinsic characteristics which separate it from all other peoples living on the globe"; it was not a religious community with a "territorially bounded state"; and it was parasitical rather than productive. He had stated all this many times before in far stronger terms but at this point he abruptly explored a new idea. "Just as every people as a basic tendency of all its earthly actions possesses a mania for self-preservation as its driving force, likewise is it exactly so with Jewry too."

Hitler's continued use of non-polemic language was surprising. The Jew, he wrote, was merely impelled by the same motives as everyone else in this deadly struggle for life; the only difference was a different purpose. But then Hitler abruptly turned shrill. "His ultimate goal is the denationalization, the promiscuous bastardization of other peoples, the lowering of the racial level of the highest peoples as well as the domination of his racial mishmash through the extirpation of the folkish intelligentsia and its replacement by the members of his own people." This different goal, expressed in such comparatively calm terms, was what made the Jews the threat of mankind. And since their ultimate aim was conquest of the entire world, Hitler's battle against the Jews was for the good not only of Germany but of the entire world.

By the end of the summer of 1928 Hitler had finally come to the realization that his two most urgent convictions—danger from Jews and Germany's need for sufficient living space—were entwined. If the Reich failed to acquire essential living space it would perish. If the Jewish menace were not stemmed there could be no struggle for Lebensraum, no culture, and the nation would decay.

This, in all likelihood, marked Hitler's point of no return and was the essence of his Weltanschauung. Now a dual task lay before him: to conquer new living space in the East and to annihilate the Jews. What had seemed to be two separate if parallel courses was a single road. It was as if for months he had been observing the twin mountain peaks from his villa on the Obersalzberg, both of which he wanted to climb—and only now realized that the *same* trail led to both. He had seen the light. Martin Luther and all the other anti-Semites before Hitler merely talked of eliminating the Jews but with his new blueprint for the future he hoped to materialize their dream—and become Haman II.

He himself forbade publication of what became known as *Hitler's Secret Book* and appeared for the first time thirty-two years later. Perhaps he feared it was too philosophically heavy for his adherents, too flimsily transparent for the more sophisticated; perhaps he did not want to reveal the ultimate mass-murder plan that hid behind its terminology. Within the pages also lay clues to his motivation for genocide. They were replete with revealing references: the Jew was a "master of international poisoning and race corruption," as well as the instigator of the "evil pacifist liquid manure [which] poisons the mentality favoring bold self-preservation." He referred to the flood of "disease bacilli" now breeding in Russia; and called the crowded working-class districts of Germany (the result of inadequate Lebensraum) "abscesses in the national body" as well as "breeding grounds of blood mixing and bastardization, and of race lowering, thus resulting in those purulent infection centers in which the international Jewish racial-maggots thrive and finally effect further destruction."

This obsession with Jewish poisoning and corruption twice took on a startling personal nature in the book. He referred to the hated Erzberger, who signed the 1918 armistice, as "the bastard son of a servant-girl and a Jewish employer." He could have been talking of his own father. And then he must have been thinking of his mother when he wrote: "If a man appears to have cancer and is unconditionally doomed to die, it would be senseless to refuse an operation, because the percentage of the possibility of success is slight."

Fear that his father may have been part Jewish (which could be a substantial part of why he wanted no children); anguish, anger and guilt at his mother's painful death from cancer along with mixed feelings about the Jewish doctor who, with Hitler's consent, treated her *drastically* with iodoform—all this would seem to permeate *Hitler's Secret Book.* And perhaps it was no coincidence that shortly after finishing this work he made a voluntary visit to a psychiatrist. He sought help from a party member in Munich, Dr. Alfred Schwenninger, to allay a "fear of cancer." There is no record of the treatment but it was soon evident that the psychiatrist missed a golden opportunity to turn Hitler from his awful goal; Dr. Schwenninger also failed to remove his patient's fear of cancer which, along with the obsession to eliminate all Jews, would persist to the last day of his life.

Chapter Nine

A DEATH IN THE FAMILY
1928–1931

1

Hitler's first efforts to implement his Weltanschauung were made by proxy. In Berlin Josef Goebbels was doing his utmost to rejuvenate the party after defeat at the recent elections. During the summer of 1928 he wrote three articles for *Der Angriff* in an attempt to woo those workers who had voted leftist. In language that could have come from a Communist, he charged that the worker in the capitalist state was "no longer a living human being, not an originator, not a creator. He is changed into a machine. A number, a robot in a factory without sensibility or goal." Only National Socialism would bring him dignity and make his life meaningful. In a surprisingly short period Goebbels had replaced Strasser as the chief recruiter of workers in the north, and in so doing apparently removed him as a political rival to the Führer. That Hitler was pleased with Goebbels and approved his socialist line became clear when he permitted *Der Angriff* to become a biweekly and made its editor propaganda chief of the party.

In politics Hitler could be forgiving. If a former opponent was contrite the Führer was likely to reward him. It was his way of turning a liability into an asset. After crushing Gregor Strasser's attempt to change the direction of National Socialism, he had put him in charge of reorganizing the party; and Strasser had so successfully centralized administration that he was becoming one of the most powerful men in the NSDAP. Due primarily to his and Goebbels' efforts party membership rose to some 100,000 by the end of the year.

To solidify his gains in the north, Hitler came to Berlin on November 16, 1928, to speak at the huge Sportpalast on racial and national regeneration. Since it was likely Reds would try to break up the meeting, Hitler's personal bodyguard was present in force. This was a small select group of young men, ranging in age from eighteen to twenty, pledged to protect the Führer with their own lives. They called themselves *Schutzstaffel* (guard detachment) or SS for short. Most of the audience of more than 10,000 had never before heard Hitler and his first words made little impact. The problem was the new loudspeaker system. Standing at the back of the hall, the British journalist Sefton Delmer had trouble making out what Hitler was saying. Delmer did hear him urge Germans not to eat oranges and, putting him down as a "crackpot," left the hall. The cacophony was such that Hitler himself turned off the microphones and shouted. In a few minutes he quieted the Red hecklers and completely dominated the vast audience. "Whoever shows his fist to the German people, we will force to be our brother," he said and then raised the bogy of racial degeneration. "The bastardization of great states has begun. The negroization of culture, of customs—not only of blood—strides forward. The world becomes democratized. The value of the individual declines. The masses apparently are gaining the victory over the idea of the great leader. Numbers are chosen as the new God."

Hitler felt a strain in his throat. For over an hour he had been forcing his voice and, realizing he was "about to fall down from exhaustion," he brought the speech to a close. "We fight against the idea of numbers and the delirium of the masses. We want to see those who are superior take the reins of government in their hands. There are 100,000 among us for whom voting is of no consequence—only the authority of the leader. And these 100,000 know that democracy in itself is a deception." It was a triumph of magnetism over matter. "When Hitler speaks," commented Goebbels about this address, "all resistance collapses before the magic effect of his words. One can only be his friend or his enemy . . . this is the secret of his strength: his fanatical faith in the movement, and with it in Germany."

An American journalist, Louis Lochner, witnessed the same phenomenon a month later at a talk to the students of Berlin University. "My first impression of him was that of a consummate showman. As movie cameras were turned upon him, he pretended not to notice them, spoke earnestly to his shadow, Rudolf Hess, and, as the cameras continued to click, began to write as though he were drawing up an outline of his remarks. It was good acting." Lochner noticed that Hitler's young adherents were hypnotized. "I came away from that meeting wondering how a man whose diction was by no means faultless, who ranted and fumed and stamped, could so impress young intellectuals. Of all people, I thought, they should have detected the palpable flaws in his logic."

One of these fascinated young intellectuals was Albert Speer, an assistant at the Institute of Technology. He had come with some reluctance at the urging of his students and expected to see Hitler in military tunic with swastika armband. "But here he was wearing a well-fitted blue suit and looking markedly respectable. Everything about him bore out the note of reasonable modesty." What struck Speer was that he spoke hesitatingly and somewhat shyly as if he were delivering a historical lecture. "To me there was something engaging about it—all the more so since it ran counter to everything the propaganda of his opponents had led me to expect: a hysterical demagogue, a shrieking and gesticulating fanatic in uniform. He did not allow the bursts of applause to tempt him away from his sober tone." As Hitler's shyness disappeared, he began orating with hypnotic persuasiveness and, along with the rest of the audience, Speer was carried on a wave of enthusiasm which he could almost feel physically. "It swept away any skepticism, any reservations."

2

Hitler's personal approach would have been ineffective without an efficient party organization, and while the 1929 party congress in Nuremberg was outwardly a rally, an emotional testimony of dedication to the Führer and his ideals, the organization of the party was being buttressed in the working sessions. By the end of that summer Hitler had succeeded in setting up a functionary corps in line with an appeal to the German middle class by admitting university graduates and other representatives of the bourgeoisie into the party bureaucracy. While allowing Goebbels and Strasser to win over the workers, he directed his opening campaign primarily to militant veterans and capitalistic businessmen, for he realized he would never get into power without them. He dramatized his new thrust by publicly joining with the Stahlhelm, rabidly nationalistic veterans, and Alfred Hugenberg, the nation's leading film and press lord and head of the völkisch right-wing German National People's Party, in a fight against acceptance of the new American liberalized formula (the Young Plan) for reparations payment. On the surface it seemed a suicidal move that would lose all the new adherents from the left. But Hitler was convinced that he could keep both sides in line and he was counting on success in the forthcoming national plebiscite on the Young Plan to reaffirm his judgment.

In the meantime he and the party were enjoying the financial benefits of their *mariage de convenance* with industry. Hitler bought the Barlow Palace, a three-story building on the Briennerstrasse, as national party headquarters; then early that September moved from his monastic room to one of the most fashionable sections of Munich across the Isar, where he took a nine-room apartment covering the entire second floor of 16 Prinzregentenplatz. He brought along Frau Reichert, his landlady from the Thierschstrasse, and her mother, Frau Dachs.

His sister Angela remained in charge of the Berchtesgaden villa (now his property), but she allowed her daughter Geli, now twenty-one, to take a room in Uncle Alf's new apartment while pursuing her medical studies in Munich. His feelings for her had not altered but their relationship changed. While maintaining the role of uncle, Hitler began overtly, if discreetly, to act more like a suitor. They were occasionally seen together in public at the theater or at his favorite table in the garden of the Café Heck where he often held court late in the afternoon.

Hitler was so enthralled, according to Hanfstaengl, that "he hovered at her elbow with a moon-calf look in his eyes in a very plausible imitation of adolescent infatuation." She inveigled him into going shopping even though he confessed to Hoffmann "how he hated it when Geli tried on hats or shoes, or inspected bale after bale of material, engaging the shopgirl in earnest conversation for half an hour or more, and then, finding nothing that suited her, walked out of the shop." Hitler knew that this would happen on every shopping expedition—yet "always followed her like a faithful lamb."

At the same time Hitler remained the stern uncle, restricting the high-spirited girl's social life to restaurants, cafés and an occasional visit to the theater. Even when she nagged him into letting her go to a Shrovetide ball it was under rigid conditions: her escorts were Max Amann and Hoffmann and they were instructed to bring her back at 11 P.M. Hoffmann warned that these restraints were making her extremely unhappy but the Führer replied that he felt bound to watch over his niece. "I love Geli, and I could marry her." At the same time he was determined to remain a bachelor. What Geli regarded as restraint, he said, was wisdom. "I am quite determined to see that she does not fall into the hands of some unworthy adventurer or swindler."

That Hitler was sexually frustrated seems borne out by an inept attempt to kiss the seventeen-year-old daughter of Heinrich Hoffmann. One day he found Henriette alone at home. "Won't you kiss me?" he said quite seriously, according to her account. Usually he addressed her with the familiar "thou." Today it was "you." ("I liked him because he always was considerate, he always helped me when I wanted something from Father, money for tennis lessons, for instance, or for skiing expeditions. . . . But kissing him?") She politely refused and after a moment's silence Hitler struck the palm of his hand with his whip and slowly walked away.

Of more significance was his meeting with another pretty seventeen-year-old who worked in Hoffmann's photo shop. Eva Braun, the daughter of a teacher and the product of a convent, was—like Geli—a modern girl, athletic and lively. She preferred jazz to opera and American musical comedies to the dramas of Kaiser and Wedekind. Unlike Geli, she was on the plump side and had fair hair. "She was a terror, it's true, the trouble-maker of the class," recalled a teacher, Fräulein von Heidenaber, "but she was intelligent and quick to seize the essential aspects of a subject, and she was capable of independent thought."

They met late on a Friday afternoon in early October. Eva had stayed in the shop to catch up on filing and was on a ladder reaching for the files on the top of a cupboard. "At that moment," she later told her sister, "the boss came in accompanied by a man with a funny mustache, a light-colored English-style overcoat and a big felt hat in his hand. They both sat down on the other side of the room, opposite me." She sensed that the newcomer was examining her legs. "That very day I had shortened my skirt and I felt slightly embarrassed because I wasn't sure I'd got the hem even."

After she climbed down Hoffmann introduced her to the stranger. "Herr Wolf. Our good little Fräulein Eva." A few minutes later they were all sitting down to beer and sausages. "I was starving. I gobbled my sausage and had a sip of beer for politeness' sake. The elderly gentleman was paying me compliments. We talked about music and a play at the Staatstheater, as I remember, with him devouring me with his eyes all the time. Then, as it was getting late, I rushed off. I refused his offer of a lift in his Mercedes. Just think what Papa's reaction would have been!" But before she left, Hoffmann took her aside and asked, "Haven't you guessed who that gentleman is? It's Hitler! Adolf Hitler!" "Oh?" replied Eva.

In the days to come Hitler would quite often drop in at the studio with flowers and candy for "my lovely siren from Hoffmann's." On the rare times he took her out, he avoided his usual haunts for tea in an obscure corner of the Carlton Café or a movie in Schwabing. But by the end of the year his visits to Hoffmann's studio had become a rarity. Perhaps it was because of Eva's boast to several fellow employees that she was Hitler's mistress and he was going to marry her. Hoffmann, who was sure she had never even visited Hitler's apartment, summoned her to his office. Eva broke into tears, confessing she had lied and he threatened to fire her if she repeated the story.

3

The Young Plan plebiscite late in 1929 turned out to be a triumph for Chancellor Stresemann and his liberal program, although he died before the vote was counted. The uneasy alliance of Hitler and Hugenberg's National People's Party needed 21,000,000 votes to defeat the measure and got less than 6,000,000. While this was a crushing defeat for Hugenberg, Hitler cleverly turned it into a victory of sorts. Never one to espouse a lost cause, he turned on Hugenberg with a vengeance, breaking their alliance as unpredictably as he had made it. He was already confidently preparing his forces, enlarged by the publicity of the plebiscite issue, for the coming national elections even though it was a rare observer who now rated the Nazis highly. In his memoirs the former English ambassador to Berlin, Lord D'Abernon, mentioned the Führer once in a footnote. Hitler, he wrote, had been "fading into oblivion" ever since 1924. Both Dr. Arnold Wolfers, director of studies at the Berlin Hochschule für Politik, and the historian Arnold Toynbee concurred with this obituary.

Hitler was thinking of victory and felt it was possible if he could win new workers to his cause. To do this, there must be a dramatic new propaganda ploy. The opportunity came early in 1930, with the death of a law student in Berlin. Horst Wessel, the twenty-one-year-old son of a preacher and a Freemason, had rebelled against his bourgeois upbringing to become a dedicated Brownshirt in the bloody street battles against the Reds. He wrote a poem, "Raise High the Flag!" immortalizing comrades who had sacrificed their lives—"shot dead by Red Front and Reaction," which was published in *Der Angriff* and later set to music.* Wessel fell in love with a onetime prostitute named Erna and moved in with her. In an effort to eject the couple her landlady sought help from the Communists. A Red gang burst into the lovers' room. Their leader, an intimate of Erna's, reportedly shouted, "You know what that's for!" and shot Wessel. In an attempt to make political capital out of the sorry affair, the Communists

---

* Hanfstaengl wrote that the melody was "exactly that of a Vienna cabaret song of the turn of the century," to which the words originally ran more or less like this:

> And as your eye met mine
> And as my lips kissed yours
> Then did love enshroud us.

Wessel merely "hotted up the tune to march time."

called Wessel a pimp, which he was not. On his part Goebbels publicly transfigured the lover into a working-class Jesus, which he was not. "Leaving home and mother," wrote Goebbels, the novelist manqué, "he took to living among those who scorned and spit on him. Out there, in a proletarian section, in a tenement attic he proceeded to build his youthful, modest life. A socialist Christ! One who appealed to others through his deeds."

While Wessel lay dying in a hospital, Goebbels turned a private feud into political assassination by having Wessel's song sung at the conclusion of a meeting in the Sportpalast: "The banners flutter, the drums roll, the fifes rejoice, and from millions of throats resounds the hymn of the German revolution, Raise high the flag!" At last, on February 23, Wessel died. "His spirit has risen in order to live on in all of us," wrote Goebbels. He is "marching within our ranks." To cap the propaganda campaign Goebbels decided to stage an extravagant funeral with Hitler delivering the final oration. But the Führer had reservations about such showmanship. So did Göring, who had returned from Sweden after a cure for drug addiction to win election to the Reichstag. The situation in Berlin, he argued, was already tense enough and the Führer's safety could not be guaranteed. "If anything goes wrong," he said, according to Hanfstaengl's recollection, "it would be a catastrophe. After all, there are only twelve of us in the Reichstag, and we simply haven't enough strength to make capital out of this. If Hitler comes to Berlin it will be a red rag to the Communist bulls and we cannot afford to take the consequences."

Hitler pleaded illness and the funeral had to proceed without him. Göring was right. The procession turned into a battle march with the Reds assaulting the mourners, and even as Goebbels stood at the graveside and dramatically called the roll: "Horst Wessel?" and the storm troopers shouted back "Present!" stones flew over the cemetery wall into the grave. Nothing could have pleased propagandist Goebbels more. "As the coffin came to rest in the cool ground," he wrote, "there went up outside the gates the depraved cry of the subhuman. . . . The departed, still with us, raised his weary hand and beckoned into the shimmering distance: Forward over the graves! At the end of the road lies Germany!"

From such words one would never guess at the true relationship between ordinary Reds and Nazis. While they fought each other relentlessly, they felt a unique comradeship, and it was no rarity for them to unite if one of their brawls in a bar or beer hall was interrupted by the police. Both groups were driven by fervor for a cause, both believed that the end justified the means. They shared similar socialist goals and had the same contempt for parliamentary procedures. On the previous May

Day they had paraded down the streets of Berlin arm in arm, in joint protest against suppression of marching demonstrations, shouting their common slogan: "Freedom, Work and Bread." Moreover, they both hated the Jewish police commissioner, Bernhard Weiss (renamed "Isidor" by Goebbels), and alike regarded the police as "Isidor's" army, a brutal enemy of all revolutionaries.

Two months after Goebbels had squeezed the last drop of propaganda out of Horst Wessel, the Hitler-Otto Strasser feud came out in the open. Since his brother's departure for Munich and party eminence, Otto had become the leading editorial writer of the three newspapers Gregor had founded. While they still carried the National Socialist emblem on their mastheads, they had become a platform for Otto's iconoclastic views, which often ran contrary to those of Hitler. Their differences were brought to a head that April by Otto Strasser's full support of the Saxon metalworkers' strike. Industrialists such as Fritz Thyssen of the United Steel Works insisted that Hitler repudiate Strasser if he wanted more subsidies.

At first Hitler tried threats but these failed and he came to Berlin to exert the force of his personality. The two men met twice at the Hotel Sanssouci. For almost seven hours Hitler flattered, cajoled, promised and threatened but the two meetings only revealed their differences. Neither made a single concession and Otto Strasser rejected a tempting offer to be party propaganda chief. Despite their inability to come to terms, Strasser and his circle did not break at once with the party "because there was still hope that Hitler had been impressed by the discussions" and might even abandon the "Rosenberg line." They were also unwilling to make a public issue of the break, which might hurt the party's chances in the forthcoming provincial elections in Saxony. Otto Strasser, however, realized that he and his socialist followers could not remain in the NSDAP; not after Hitler had professed his intention to follow Mussolini's Fascist principles and deal with industrialists. The talks also revealed Hitler's determination to keep his Weltanschauung so vague and "infinitely interpretable" that he could exercise complete control by means of absolute authority. He knew instinctively that the moment National Socialism was pledged to a concrete program the Führer principle would be compromised.

Hitler must have felt humiliated that young Strasser had contradicted him so flagrantly and openly, but he drove back to Munich without much comment and upon arrival made no public attack. Nor did he carry out a threat to proceed against Otto "with all the means at my disposal." He did nothing except proclaim in the press, as did Gregor Strasser, that no dispute had taken place in Berlin and he and Otto were in agreement.

Rather than punish the rebel openly, Hitler began expelling from the party those who contributed to his papers; and at the end of June he finally gave Goebbels veiled instructions to purge Otto Strasser and his followers. "The National Socialist Party, as long as I lead it," he wrote, "will not be a debating club for rootless men of letters and chaotic salon Bolshevists, but will remain what it is today, an organization of discipline created not for doctrinaire foolishness or political Wandervögel but dedicated to fight for the future of Germany in which class distinction will be broken and a new German people will decide its own destiny!" Goebbels consequently was instructed to "*ruthlessly clean up* the party of all those elements in Berlin." He did so within a few weeks, and Strasser's subsequent call for a general exodus of socialists from the party brought only twenty-four followers. Otto's own brother rejected him, signing a declaration with two other left-wing party members that "they were united behind the leadership of Adolf Hitler and submitted themselves to the strict discipline of the party organization." To a mutual friend, Gregor characterized his brother as the eternal dissident. "The departure of my brother and his fight against the party is pure madness."

While Otto Strasser's split with Hitler caused a sensation in the newspapers, it had little effect within the party. During the long bitter factional struggle between north and south, Hitler had done his best to act as arbiter. He was intent only on conciliation and compromise, and in victory he had been magnanimous. He had rewarded Gregor Strasser with a high party post; and even when Otto embarrassed him in front of witnesses he had done his best to minimize their differences. He made it appear that it was Otto himself who forced his own explusion from the party. Now at last the internecine battle was over and Hitler could concentrate all his energies on the national elections in September.

4

Hitler offered something to almost every German voter in 1930—the farmer, the worker, the student, the patriot, the racist and the middle-class burgher. The common denominator of his wide appeal was the world depression which had followed the Wall Street crash of 1929 and abruptly ended Germany's remarkable recovery. By late summer there were almost three million unemployed in the nation and Chancellor Brüning's policy of economic retrenchment was making matters worse. Here at last was the burning issue that could bring him political control of Germany, thought Hitler. His appeal to workers was couched in Communist terminology. "Working Germany, awake! Break your chains in two!" proclaimed Goebbels' *Der Angriff*. To farmers, whose recent profits were being wiped out by the world-wide decline of agricultural prices, Hitler offered tax adjustments and import duties. The lower middle class, with no trade unions to fight for them, were offered hope; to those just above them in the social hierarchy to whom poverty was a stigma—self-respect; and to the young idealists in and out of universities—an idealistic new world.

This last group was not large but it provided Hitler with a militant, dedicated cadre for the future. They listened entranced as he preached against materialism and selfishness, promised to establish social harmony and a front rank in his crusade for social justice and a revitalized Germany. Convinced that Hitler would create a genuine socialist regime, these young people roamed the streets of the large cities chanting the slogan they shared with their Communist adversaries, "Freedom, Work and Bread!" The rising generation "felt something was moving and the terrible stagnation was over," recalled one follower. "You had to live through it to really understand it." It was a chance to serve that attracted most of these young idealists and Hitler was the only politician of his day who understood the power of such an appeal.

A number of intellectuals, the social elite and royalty itself were also drawn to him. That spring the Kaiser's young son, August Wilhelm ("Auwi"), wrote his dear battle comrade Hitler that it was his "heart's desire" to inform him personally that he had just been admitted to the party. "It was for me a very emotional moment and my thoughts turned to you in loyalty." The Prince feared the spread of Communism and his conversion influenced Prince Philip von Hessen, a nephew of the Kaiser and grandson of Queen Victoria, to join in support of Hitler.

In 1930 he was offering Germans something new—a feeling of unity. He welcomed everyone to join in the crusade. There was no class distinction; the only requirement was willingness to follow Hitler without hesitation in his fight to the death against the Jews and the Reds, in his struggle for Lebensraum and the glory and the good of Germany. "What we felt," wrote an early party member, "what our hearts compelled us to think, was this—Hitler, you're our man. You talk like a human being who's been at the front, who's been through the same mess we were, and not in some soft berth, but like us an unknown soldier." It was these transcendental appeals which roused the emotions of such divergent voters. Nor did Hitler press his anti-Semitism—particularly the "removal" of Jews—except with völkisch groups and the workers. To the more educated and the idealistic this issue was discussed either in whispers or an offhand manner.

That summer Hitler campaigned tirelessly with his omnibus program, delivering twenty major speeches in the final six weeks. A born politician, he found it not only natural but inspiring to mix with crowds, shaking hands, kissing babies and bowing to women. He would eat with the working-class and middle-class adherents more often than with the elite, and his man-to-man approach appealed to the clerk and small businessman as well as the laborer.

Although he approached each group with a separate message, Hitler never forgot the lesson he had learned in Landsberg: that he must win the masses. Consequently he never allowed himself to take an aggressive stand on minor issues. Over and over he hammered at the money barons, the Reds, the Marxists and the "system" that had brought unemployment, lowered farm prices and wiped out the savings of the middle class. He did not pit class against class. He could embrace them all.

Never had Germany—or the world for that matter—been subjected to such persuasion. Goebbels organized six thousand meetings—in large halls, in tents that could hold ten thousand, in the open air. There were torchlight parades; towns, cities and villages were plastered with glaring red posters. The entire Nazi press blanketed the country with special campaign editions that ran into millions of copies; and those that couldn't be sold were given away.

In a final admonition to party workers on the morning of the election Goebbels gave them cynical but practical advice on how to electioneer. "Do it jokingly, do it seriously! Treat your dear fellow creatures as they are used to being treated. Stimulate their rage and their fury, direct them to the proper course." That day long lines queued up at polling places throughout the country. A record 35,000,000 ballots were cast, 4,000,000 more than in 1928. Hitler arrived at the election center in Munich just after midnight to be greeted by an excited Adolf Müller, the party printer: "I think we've won. We may get sixty-six seats!" This would have meant an amazing increase of fifty-four seats since 1928 but Hitler replied that if the German people could think correctly the figure would be higher. "Within myself I was saying: 'If it could be a hundred!'" A hundred and seven seats were won. "How to express what I felt at that moment? We'd gone up from twelve seats to a hundred and seven!"

What surprised the National Socialists came as a sickening shock to their opponents. Officials checked and rechecked for errors before announcing that the Nazis had won 6,371,000 votes, more than eighteen per cent of the total vote. In two years the Hitler movement had risen from 810,000 votes to become the second largest party in the Reich. After pronouncing Hitler dead politically, the Social Democrats had made the mistake of concentrating their attacks on the Reds.

The Communists also made a substantial gain of 1,326,000 votes and the Social Democrats lost fewer than 60,000 votes, an indication that Hitler's gains had come mainly at the expense of the middle-class parties. The most sensational Nazi increase was among the farmers and lower middle class in the rural and Protestant areas in the northern half of the country, but considerable gains were also made among Catholics. In the days before the Beer Hall Putsch Hitler had sought almost exclusively for the dissident, disenchanted, desperation vote. Now he had received support from people who expected him to bring them better lives. It was Hitler's elastic appeal and forceful oratory which had attracted the new voters but it was the tireless work of thousands of cell leaders and cell foremen in the party's efficient vertical organization that got them to the polls.

For the past year or so Hanfstaengl's acid remarks had alienated Hitler but astonishing election victory brought him back to favor. Hess phoned that the Führer was most anxious to see him. Half an hour later Hitler was at the Hanfstaengl home with a proposition: would he take over the post of foreign press chief of the party? "Great things are before us. In a few months, or at the most in a couple of years, we must irresistibly sweep to power. You have all the connections and could render us a great service."

Hanfstaengl accepted and a few days later accompanied Hitler to Leipzig for the trial of three young officers accused of spreading Nazi propaganda in the army. Hitler himself took the stand on September 25 and made a clever, paradoxical speech which managed to appeal to almost everyone. After assurances that he would come to power peacefully through the ballot box, he pledged allegiance to the army and promised to fight against the shameful Treaty of Versailles even if he had to do so "with illegal means." He ended with a vow to the revolutionaries in his party that once he came to power there would be a National Socialist Court of Justice. "Then the November 1918 revolution will be avenged and heads will roll!" Once again Hitler had demonstrated his political agility by satisfying both burgher and revolutionary almost simultaneously, reassuring the first of his peaceful intentions and promising the second bloody vengeance. The effect of his words went far beyond Germany, for he was spokesman of the second largest party in the land and his inflammatory remarks about treaties were no longer the meaningless polemics of a minor politician.

Hanfstaengl was besieged by foreign correspondents who wanted interviews with Germany's new phenomenon. Hitler hurriedly composed an article for the London *Sunday Express*. "The election, so to speak," he wrote, "took the temperature of the German people. The world was shocked to discover Germany in a fever—a high fever. That fever is bound to continue—to rise against existing conditions and unbearable burdens." He demanded not only the revision of the Versailles Treaty and the Young Plan but "the return of the Polish Corridor, which is like a strip of flesh cut from our body." He denied, however, the accusation that Germany was guilty of causing the war, and accused President Wilson of betraying solemn promises to the Reich. "If the German people must suffer as they are suffering today and will be suffering tomorrow," he warned in conclusion, "then let us have suffering that may come from saying 'No' rather than that laid on us by saying our 'yes.'"

A few days later Hitler changed his pace by assuring a reporter for the London *Times* that he would operate in a strictly legal manner. "Don't condemn us, therefore, if we should act as yourselves would act in our place. I hope that England will never find herself in a position like that of Germany, but if she were in such a position and if, in her darkest hour, she was stabbed in the back, what would be the attitude of England when on her feet once more? What would be the attitude of English patriots towards those among their own nation who had sought to destroy their country?"

Two weeks later, on October 13, the 107 Nazi deputies marched into the Reichstag for the opening session clad in brown shirts, each one answering the roll call with a resounding "Present, Heil Hitler!" Socialist member Toni Sender was appalled. "This was the élite of the 'Aryan' race! —this noisy, shouting, uniformed gang. I looked at their faces carefully. The more I studied them, the more I was terrified by what I saw: so many men with the faces of criminals and degenerates. What a degradation to sit in the same place with such a gang!"

The words of delegate Gregor Strasser to the Reichstag were relatively reassuring—"Let us leave it at that and go along with the old system as long as democracy still exists . . . we are now for the democratic Weimar Republic as long as it suits us"—but action on the streets of the capital cast an ominous shadow of things to come. Hundreds of SA men in civilian clothes were already smashing the windows of Jewish shops, cafés and department stores.

5

The international publicity which followed the September elections was a mixed blessing to Hitler. Along with the prestige came an unwelcome visit from his nephew, William Patrick Hitler, who lived in England with his mother. In 1919 Alois Hitler, Jr., then working as a waiter in Dublin, had married an Irish girl, Brigid Elizabeth Dowling. Their life was hectic because Alois kept changing his way of earning a living. He opened a small restaurant in Liverpool, sold it to buy a boardinghouse, turned hotel owner, went bankrupt, and finally became a razor blade salesman. It was an unhappy existence for Brigid and several times she left home. Their quarrels intensified after the birth of William Patrick because Alois shared his father's doctrine that children should be disciplined at an early age; several times while Brigid was out of the house Alois beat the baby, and by the time William Patrick was three the family broke up. According to Brigid Alois deserted them and returned to Germany but Alois told his relatives that his wife had run away with an engineer, taking the boy with her.

When Brigid and her son read about Hitler's electoral success they saw it as "an opportunity of making some money by giving an interview to the Hearst press." After all, Alois had never sent them anything for support. Negotiations were started with a Hearst representative in London and early that October pictures of William Patrick began appearing in the American press under the caption: "This young London office worker, William Patrick Hitler, is a nephew of Adolf Hitler, Germany's new political leader. He was born in Liverpool and knows little of his uncle's aims." He knew so little, in fact, that he wrote his father asking for further details about the life of the new political wonder. "The reply," William Patrick told an OSS interviewer years later, "came in the form of a demand from Adolf for a conference, tickets for the passage were enclosed." Upon arrival in Munich, mother and son found Hitler "in a perfect rage." At a family meeting, also attended by Angela Raubal and Alois, Hitler said he was "gaining some importance and the family need not think they could climb on his back and get a free ride to fame." Release of family information to the Hearst newspapers, he claimed, would destroy his chances of political success in view of his half brother's remarriage without bothering to divorce Brigid. "How carefully I always kept my personal affairs out of the press!" he said according to an article William Patrick wrote nine years later in *Paris Soir*. "These people must not know who I am. They must not know where I come from and from what family . . . even in my book I did not say a word about such things, not a word, and now accidentally my nephew is discovered. Investigations are made, and spies are sent to dig up our past." At this point, in the *Paris Soir* account, Hitler angrily declared that William Patrick was not even a relation, since his father, Alois, Jr. (who was listening to all this without comment), had been adopted by Alois Hitler, Sr. He and his mother (according to the OSS interview) should go back to London and tell the Hearst people that they had discovered the leader of the Nazi Party was another Adolf Hitler and no kin of theirs. This solution "pleased" Hitler and, after urging the two to get back to England "as quickly as possible and disclaim all relationship in the present and in the future," he handed over to Alois two thousand dollars to cover the expenses of mother and son in Munich as well as passage home. Alois paid the expenses, bought the tickets and promised to

send the rest by mail because it would be "much safer." William Patrick
swore it never arrived. (Curiously, a story about Adolf Hitler soon appeared in the New York *American*, a Hearst publication, under the by-line
of Alois Hitler, Jr. In it Alois described his younger brother as a very lika-
ble and generous boy, a dreamer as far removed from reality as the sun
from the moon. On his mother's death Adolf took his younger sister Paula
to Vienna where they endured a grim struggle against pitiless poverty.
Adolf, so Alois wrote, had to sweep streets and perform other menial jobs
to get food for Paula and himself. Then he went to Munich where he got
work as a house painter and decorator.)

Not long after William Patrick and his mother returned to England
Hitler summoned his lawyer to the apartment on Prinzregentenplatz.
Hitler pointed to a letter before him and said "it concerned a 'disgusting
blackmail' plot in connection with one of his most loathsome relatives
with respect to his own ancestry." As Hans Frank recalled it, Hitler was
referring to William Patrick Hitler, who had "hinted" that the press was
very interested in a certain aspect of Hitler's ancestry, namely that he was
part Jewish. The Führer, consequently, ordered Frank to investigate the
matter confidentially.

His report, gathered from "all possible sources," was most disconcerting: Hitler's father, it seemed, was "the illegitimate child of a cook
named Schicklgruber from Leonding, near Linz, employed in a household
in Graz." This cook "was working for a Jewish family named Frankenberger
when she gave birth to her son. And Frankenberger—this happened in the
late 1830s—paid a paternity allowance on behalf of his nineteen-year-old
son from the birth of the Schicklgruber woman's son until he was 14."
There was also a long correspondence between the Frankenbergers and
the cook (Hitler's grandmother), "the general trend of which was the
unexpressed common understanding of the participants that the Schicklgruber woman's child had been conceived in circumstances which rendered the Frankenbergers liable for the paternity allowance." Frank's report concluded regretfully that the possibility could not be dismissed that
Hitler's father was half Jewish.

The Führer heatedly challenged Frank's deduction with the embarrassed explanation that his grandfather, who was impoverished, had successfully blackmailed the Frankenbergers on the false charge of paternity.
Hitler swore that this information came directly to him from both his father and grandmother. He must have been truly shaken by Frank's evidence to tell such a patent lie: his grandmother had died forty years before his own birth. More important was the admission that his
grandmother *had* received money from a Jew, for this allowed the terrible
possibility that his own blood might be tainted. The chance that Adolf

Hitler was part Jewish was minimal.* The important point was that he *feared* so and he would instigate at least two subsequent investigations to reassure himself. A physician named Schuh, who had known Hitler since 1917, recalled he "suffered all his life from painful doubts: did he or did he not have Jewish blood? And he often told us this." Hitler's inability to produce the documentary proof of his own Aryan background, something he demanded from others, could explain why he told William Patrick Hitler: "These people must not know from where and from what family I come."

Despite this distressing personal matter, 1931 augured well for Adolf Hitler. He had suddenly become a best-selling author. *Mein Kampf* had sold an average of little more than 6000 copies annually until the last year when the amount rose to 54,086. This got him a respectable personal income which promised to continue indefinitely. Furthermore, the Brown House, the new party headquarters, was opened on the first of the year. Purchased and renovated by special contributions, profits from Hitler rallies, gifts and dues, it represented the substance and reliability of the NSDAP as a party. On the second floor were the offices of Hitler, Hess, Goebbels, Strasser and the SA. The Führer's office was large and attractively decorated in reddish brown. Ceiling-high windows overlooked the Königsplatz. There was a large bust of Mussolini, and among the pictures on the wall were a painting of Frederick the Great and another of the first attack of the Führer's old regiment in Flanders. "Hitler was not often there," recalled Frank. His method of working was totally unsystematic. He would "breeze in" but before he could be pinned down "just breeze out again." Once cornered, he would hastily finish the business, then launch into "an hour-long monologue."

He preferred to spend his time downstairs in the small refreshment room where he would sit in a corner at the "Führer" table over which hung a picture of Dietrich Eckart. But even this soon palled. The sedentary existence of the Brown House was not for him. He was driven by an urge to move, to win mass support for himself and the party among the people, or to hold high-level conversations with those who could give him either political or financial assistance. The problems he faced at the beginning of 1931 were truly formidable, largely due to the NSDAP's phenomenal membership growth which, in turn, brought an expansion of bureau-

* The research of Nikolaus Preradovic, University of Graz, casts some doubt on Frank's evidence. He found no record of either a Frankenberger or a Frankenreither in the books of the Jewish congregation in Graz, Austria. These books, it is true, begin in 1856, nineteen years after Hitler's father was born, but that was because Jews had been driven out of the Steiermark in 1496 and were only allowed to return in 1856. Before that time, according to Preradovic, there was "not one single Jew" in Graz.

cracy in every department of the party with the resultant frictions and jealousies.

Most troublesome was the SA, many of whose members refused to take Hitler's avowals of legality seriously. The storm troopers had always boasted of their tradition of violence and saw no reason why they should knuckle under to the civilian leaders in Munich. These men were among the most idealistic and many were socialists at heart, sharing with their Communist rivals a revolutionary zeal that was becoming an embarrassment to the Führer. From the first he had trouble with its leaders, who wanted to make the SA the military arm of the party, whereas he had insisted that its main function was to protect rallies and mobilize political loyalty. First had been Captain Röhm, whose violent disagreement with Hitler led to voluntary exile in South America; then came Pfeffer von Salomon, whose similar demands for a stronger SA had led to his recent resignation.

The dissatisfaction of the leaders was shared by their men. Recently dissident Brownshirts in Berlin had revolted on the grounds that they were hungry, overworked and constantly exposed to injuries as well as arrest in their battles with the police and Reds. They refused to act as mere bodyguards for party rallies and, after their seven demands, including a reasonable one for more funds, were turned down by Goebbels, one troop went berserk and raided a local party headquarters guarded by the SS. It took Hitler's personal intervention to put down the revolt. He toured the various SA meeting places, accompanied by armed SS troops, calling for reconciliation. Like a patient and forbearing father, he pleaded, promised and scolded. He spoke little about the seven Brownshirt demands but kept the matter on a personal level, calling for allegiance to himself. Then he announced that he himself would become the new commander of the SA. The wild cheers that followed signaled an end to the brief rebellion and Hitler could return to the election trail.

His promise to head the SA personally was an empty one. He had neither the time nor the inclination to take on such an assignment and by the beginning of 1931 the Brownshirts were still without effective leadership. Then on January 4 it was announced that Captain Röhm (recently recalled from Bolivia where he had helped the Republic fight one of its wars with Paraguay) would become the new chief of staff of the SA. What attracted Röhm back to Germany was Hitler's willingness to give him a fairly free hand in the internal structure of the 60,000-man organization. Resigned to keeping the storm troopers as a disciplined marching unit for the time being, this capable organizer and inspiring leader began reshaping the SA in his own image.

But efficiency was no cure for the deep-seated complaints within the organization, and it soon became evident that another serious revolt was brewing in the capital. The basic grievances of the Berlin Brownshirts remained. Their leader, Captain Walter Stennes, was incensed by the inequities within the organization and once more demanded a system based on "what you know," not "who you know." He openly complained that Hitler "changed his mind every few months with new orders" and that it was impossible to operate under such conditions. Stennes' men were perplexed and perturbed. While agreeing with him, they felt irresistibly drawn to the Führer.

The issue surfaced on February 20, 1931, after Hitler issued orders to both the SA and SS to cease fighting the Reds and Jews in the streets. "I understand your distress and rage," he told the Brownshirts, "but you must not bear arms." They grumbled but did nothing until late the following month when the Führer bowed to a Weimar government decree requiring all potential rallies to be approved by the police. The indignant Stennes denounced this capitulation to the establishment, then called a secret conference of SA leaders at midnight of March 31. All those present declared themselves in favor of Stennes and against Hitler.

In an attempt to settle the matter without bloodshed and publicity, the Führer ordered Stennes to report to Munich for a desk job at the Brown House. Stennes refused and Hitler loosed the SS on the rebels. Open resistance ended within twenty-four hours. It had been a puny rebellion. All Stennes wanted was to bring about pure National Socialism, to serve a party, not an individual. "Whoever goes with me has a hard road," he told his men in a farewell speech. "I recommend, however, that you stay with Hitler for the sake of the National Socialist idea which we do not want to destroy."

On April 4 both *Der Angriff* and the *Völkischer Beobachter* printed articles by Hitler condemning the Stennes "Putsch." He reaffirmed that socialism had always been a major part of the NSDAP but criticized "the buffoons of salon-bolshevism and salon-socialism" who had drifted into the party. He claimed that Stennes was one of these and that he had tried "to introduce into the SA a series of concepts that, accurately, belong to the continuously seditious requisites of the Communists."

These articles only created more furor among the dissident Berlin Brownshirts and Hitler once more rushed to the capital in his role as conciliator and middle-of-the-road revolutionary. This time he took along Hanfstaengl, who wrote: "Hitler had to go around from suburb to suburb and beseech them with tears in his eyes to rely on him to see that their interests were protected." He managed to restore order and spent the next day in a commercial travelers' hotel with Stennes. The latter impressed Hanfstaengl as more the victim than the leader of the revolt. "I found him a very decent fellow, a nephew of Cardinal Schulte of Cologne, and he took me over to one of the open windows, where our conversation was drowned by the noise of traffic, and said: 'Does Hitler realize that the real instigator of this revolt is standing by him?'—and that was Goebbels. 'He has been egging them on to demonstrate in the streets in spite of Hitler's orders that we were not to get into fights, and now they blame it all on me.'"

As usual the appearance of Hitler (backed up by his faithful SS force) brought unity to the SA and this time it was lasting. The dismissal of Stennes and a handful of followers caused no reverberations. Goebbels managed to emerge safely from the farrago, even though many besides Stennes felt he had played an insidious part in the revolt. The Führer himself had suspicions and at an informal gathering of Gauleiters a little later made allusion to them. "When a mother has many children and one of them goes astray," he said, "it is the wise mother who takes the child by the hand and holds on to him."

Hitler also realized that it had taken the force of the SS to bring his straying children back into the fold and, recognizing this, he replaced Stennes as leader of the Berlin-run SA with an SS man. The SS was exultant with its expanded role as protector of the Führer principle. "We were not loved everywhere," their chief, Heinrich Himmler, told a conference of SS leaders a few weeks later. "When we have done our duty we may be stood in the corner; we should expect no thanks. But our Führer knows the value of the SS. We are his favorite and most valuable organization because we have never let him down."

At the same time Hitler the mediator was ready to welcome back into the fold all those storm troopers who had strayed or hesitated—with the exception of those too independent spirits who had to be purged and replaced by loyal adherents. The response to Hitler's gesture of amnesty was almost unanimous. While many Brownshirts were disappointed in Hitler and his insistence on legality, such logic dissolved before his nearly Christlike declaration: "I am the SA and SS and you are members of the SA and SS as I am within you in the SA and SS."

No sooner had the SA been brought into line than their leader, Captain Röhm, came under heavy attack for alleged homosexuality. Earlier Hitler had brushed aside similar charges, "The SA is a collection of men for a particular political goal. It is not a moral institution for raising young girls, but an association of rough fighters." A man's private life, he added, was his own so long as it did not interfere with the National Socialist mission.

The scandal was already becoming a party issue. There were whispers that many of the officers purged in the Stennes Putsch had been replaced by Röhm's homosexual friends. Röhm appeared to act as unconcerned about such accusations as he was about those that his storm troopers committed atrocities. "I know the SA people have been a rough and ready lot in the past, my dear Herr Delmer," he told the correspondent of the London *Daily Express* late in April at the Reichs Restaurant in Berlin. "But from now on, you just watch! My men will be quiet and disciplined and orderly. My job is to prevent the millions of German unemployed from coming under Communist influence as they easily might. I want to turn them, instead, into an orderly citizen force for the defense of Germany against the internal and external Bolshevik enemy." Delmer protested that the rowdy shouts of "Germany, awake!" and "Perish, Judah!" didn't sound much like discipline and good order.

"Oh, don't take those slogans at their face value. That is all only half as serious as it sounds." Then he said something that roused the newsman's interest. "I am removing the rowdy undisciplined from the SA. A little cleansing is good for all such armies." That was why he was presently in Berlin. He explained that there had been a mutiny in the capital under Captain Stennes, a "madman" who had challenged his and Hitler's authority. But Röhm assured Delmer that the mutineers had been quelled and all was in order.

A week later, at Röhm's suggestion, Delmer journeyed to the Brown House to interview the Führer. Hitler admitted he had two demands: cancellation of the war reparations debt and a "free hand in the East." While he was not interested in restoration of the old frontiers or even the return of lost colonies, he demanded that the surplus millions of Germans must be allowed to expand into the Soviet Union. How, asked Delmer, could Hitler get into Russia without violating Polish territory? Hitler's only answer was a cryptic "A way can be found for everything."

Just then Prince August Wilhelm burst into the room with the dramatic announcement that 2400 Brownshirts had been wounded or killed in fights with the Marxists in the first four months of 1931. "*Mein Führer*," he exclaimed, "this is civil war!" "Yes," said Hitler offhandedly. "Undoubtedly this is civil war." Convinced Hitler was a completely ruthless man, Delmer began his article, which was published on May 3, with a prediction: "Germany is marching with giant strides to join the Fascist nations of Europe."

6

Hitler spent the summer of 1931 in consolidating the party and revamping the SA in light of the weaknesses made evident by the Stennes revolt. At the same time he was profoundly disturbed by a personal crisis.

He learned that his chauffeur and companion, Maurice, had become secretly engaged to his niece Geli, who had been living a restricted life in the Prinzregentenplatz apartment. Ironically it was the Führer himself, the perpetual matchmaker, who had given the idea to Maurice. "I'll come and have supper with you every evening when you are married," he urged the young man. "Following his advice," Maurice told an interviewer, "I decided to become engaged to Geli, with whom I was madly in love, like everybody else. She gladly accepted my proposal." For some time the inner circle had known they were lovers; Maurice had openly lamented about "his unhappy love" to Goebbels. Finally he steeled himself to confess. Hitler flew into a rage, accused Maurice of disloyalty and dismissed him as chauffeur.

Some of those close to the Führer were convinced he was only a concerned relative. "His affection was that of a father," Frau Anny Winter, the housekeeper, insisted years later. "He was concerned only with her welfare. Geli was a flighty girl who tried to seduce everybody, including Hitler, and he merely wanted to protect her." In a sense Geli had become a captive. Hitler gave her everything she wanted except freedom and insisted that she have an escort he trusted even when she went to her singing lessons. She complained to a relative that "her life was very hard; that Hitler insisted that she accompany him wherever he went and it was very embarrassing for her, particularly since she knew that Gregor Strasser was opposed to Hitler's being seen with her and furthermore, because it · prevented her from meeting any other young people."

One evening the Hanfstaengls met the couple at the Residenz Theater and they all had late supper at the Schwarzwälder Café. Hanfstaengl noticed that Geli "seemed bored, looking over her shoulder at the other tables, and could not help feeling that her share in the relationship was under compulsion." Frau Hanfstaengl also got the feeling that the girl was repressed, as if "she couldn't do with her life what she wanted." But Frau Winter persisted in her belief that it was Geli who was the chaser. "Naturally she wanted to become Gnädige Frau Hitler. He was highly eligible . . . but she flirted with everybody, she was not a serious girl."

There was no doubt that Geli was impressed by her uncle's fame. Every time they had tea at the Café Heck their table would be besieged by admirers, many of them women who kissed his hand and begged for souvenirs. It was equally evident that the Führer's fondness for her went far beyond that of an uncle. "He loved her," averred Maurice, "but it was a strange affection that did not dare to show itself, for he was too proud to admit to the weaknesses of an infatuation."

There were others who claimed that the two were having a love affair, and Otto Strasser publicized a sensational hearsay story of their aberrant sexual relations that was given credence only by those who wanted to believe the worst of Hitler. He deeply loved his niece but it was unlikely that they had sexual relations. He was too reserved to openly court any woman and too cautious to ruin his political career by taking a mistress into his own apartment—particularly the daughter of a half sister.

By September Geli was involved with another young man, an artist from Austria who had become so enamored on first sight, according to Christa Schröder (Hitler's secretary), that he proposed to her. Once she started to tell Frau Hoffmann of the unhappy romance but, after admitting she was in love with an artist from Vienna and was miserable, cut herself off with: "Well, that's that! And there's nothing you or I can do about it. So let's talk about something else." As soon as Hitler learned of the liaison he forced her to break with the artist, apparently with the connivance of his half sister Angela.

In mid-September Geli phoned her voice teacher that she was taking no more lessons and was leaving for Vienna, then set out for Berchtesgaden to see her mother. No sooner had she arrived than she got a phone call from Uncle Alf urgently requesting her to return to Munich at once. She felt obliged to do so but, upon learning that he was about to leave Munich to attend a meeting of Gauleiters and major SA leaders, she "reproached him for having made her come for nothing." Her indignation turned to fury when he forbade her to leave for Vienna during his absence. The argument continued at a spaghetti lunch for two on September 17. From the kitchen Frau Winter heard their voices loudly raised in argument and, as Geli rushed out of the dining room, the cook noticed her face was flushed.

Geli stayed in her room until she heard her uncle start down the stairs to join Hoffmann, who was accompanying him on the trip, then she followed Hitler to the hallway. She held something in her left hand but Frau Reichert couldn't see what it was. "*Servus*, Uncle Alf!" she called down. "*Servus*, Herr Hoffmann!"

At the outside door Hitler stopped, looked back, and mounted the stairs. He fondly stroked Geli's cheek and whispered something. But Geli remained stiff, resentful. "Really," she told the housekeeper moments later, "I have nothing at all in common with my uncle."

As the new chauffeur, Julius Schreck, drove the Mercedes along Prinzregentenstrasse, Hitler was silent. Suddenly he turned to Hoffmann. "I don't know why," he said, "but I have a most uneasy feeling." Hoffmann, whose unofficial duty was to amuse and cheer up the Führer, told him it was probably just the *Föhn*, a south wind peculiar to the Alps which caused a strange depression. Hitler didn't answer and they drove on toward Nuremberg.

From the kitchen of the apartment, Frau Reichert heard something smash and remarked to her mother, "Geli must have picked up a perfume bottle from her dressing table and broken it." This may have been when she rummaged in the pockets of Hitler's jacket and found a letter written on blue paper. It was from Eva Braun. Hitler had renewed his liaison with her some months previously but so discreetly that Geli had not known about it. Later in the day Anny Winter saw Geli angrily tear this letter in four parts. The prying housekeeper pieced them together and read something like this:

> Dear Herr Hitler,
>   Thank you again for the wonderful invitation to the theater. It was a memorable evening. I am most grateful to you for your kindness. I am counting the hours until I may have the joy of another meeting.
>   Yours,
>   Eva

Geli locked herself in her room with instructions not to be disturbed. But her show of temper did not disturb Frau Winter and so the housekeeper left the apartment as usual that evening and went home. Frau Reichert and her daughter slept in and they both heard a dull sound during the night but thought nothing of it. They too were used to the "capricious" girl.

But next morning Frau Reichert became alarmed when she found Geli's door still locked. She phoned Max Amann and Franz Schwarz. These two summoned a locksmith. Geli was lying on the floor next to a couch, a 6.34-caliber pistol beside her. She was shot in the heart.

That morning Hitler and Hoffmann left the Deutscher Hof Hotel in Nuremberg to continue their journey to Hamburg. As the Mercedes left the city Hitler noticed a car was following them. Fearing this might be an attack, he was about to tell Schreck to speed up. Then he realized the other vehicle was a taxi and a pageboy from the Deutscher Hof, who sat next to the driver, was gesticulating to stop. Upon learning from the boy that Herr Hess had telephoned from Munich and was holding the line, Hitler rushed back to the hotel, flung hat and whip onto a chair and went into a phone booth. He left the door open and Hoffmann could hear him say, "Hitler here. Has something happened?" After a short pause he cried out, "Oh, God, how awful!" Then his voice rose almost to a scream. "Hess, answer me—yes or no—is she still alive?" Apparently the line was cut or Hess had hung up.

"Hitler's frenzy was contagious," recalled Hoffmann. "With its accelerator jammed to the floor boards the great car screamed its way back to Munich. In the driving mirror I could see the reflection of Hitler's face.

He sat with compressed lips, staring with unseeing eyes through the windscreen." By the time they reached the apartment Geli's body had been removed. Since it was Saturday the newspapers didn't carry the story until the following Monday. There were innuendoes that the Führer himself had done away with his niece and allegations that Minister of Justice Gürtner had destroyed the evidence. The Munich *Post*, a socialist daily, gave a long account filled with circumstantial detail about the frequent arguments between Geli and Hitler. It also alleged that the bridge of her nose had been broken and there were other signs of maltreatment.*

Depressed and humiliated, Hitler told Frank that "he could not look at a paper any more since the terrible smear campaign would kill him. He wanted to step out of politics altogether and not appear in public any more." In desperation, he fled with Hoffmann to the empty country house of his printer, Adolf Müller, on the Tegernsee. Upon arrival their driver, Schreck, whispered to Hoffmann that he had hidden the Führer's gun, fearing he might use it on himself. The moment Hitler got to his room he clasped hands behind his back and began pacing. Hoffmann asked what he would like to eat. Hitler shook his head. Hour after hour he paced without pause. It went on all night. At dawn Hoffmann knocked softly at the door. There was no answer. He entered but Hitler continued pacing, hands still clasped behind his back, staring into the distance.

Hoffmann phoned home and got a recipe for spaghetti, a favorite dish of Hitler's. But he still refused to eat. He paced relentlessly two more days without food. Once he came to the phone to hear that Frank had taken the necessary legal steps to stop the scurrilous press campaign. In a tired and weak voice he said, "I thank you. I will get myself back together again. I will never forget you for this."

At last word reached the Müller villa that Geli had been buried in Vienna; present at the ceremony in the Central Cemetery were Röhm, Müller, Himmler and young Alfred Frauenfeld, the self-appointed National Socialist Gauleiter of Vienna. Although Hitler was banned from

---

* Hitler could not have killed Geli since he was in Nuremberg nor is it likely that he or one of his associates ordered her done away with to prevent scandal. If that had been the case, murder would certainly have been committed somewhere else than in the Führer's own apartment. Some of Hitler's adherents claimed that the death was accidental: she was probably frightened by some noise and shot herself in fright. There was also the theory that she was playing theater with the gun and it went off. From the evidence, however, the most logical conclusion is that she shot herself—perhaps in desperation, perhaps in jealousy, perhaps for an unknown reason. William Patrick Hitler's mother told Hanfstaengl that the "immediate family know very well that the cause of Geli's suicide was the fact that she was pregnant by a Jewish art teacher in Linz." In a 1971 interview Hans Hitler, a second cousin of the Führer, speaking for the family, denied this categorically.

entering his homeland because of his politics, he decided to risk arrest and that night he got into the front seat of the Mercedes next to Schreck. Hoffmann sat alone in the back as they drove silently to the Austrian border, followed by bodyguards in another large car. By the time they arrived it was dawn.

Outside of Vienna Frauenfeld was waiting for Hitler in a small car since the Mercedes would have been too noticeable. They drove without a word to the Central Cemetery. Hitler placed flowers on the grave. On the marble slab was this inscription:

> Here Sleeps Our Beloved Child
> Geli
> She was Our Ray of Sunshine
> Born 4 June 1908—died 18 September 1931
> The Raubal Family

While en route to Frauenfeld's apartment, Hitler suddenly broke his long silence. He asked if, by chance, they passed the Opera. Frauenfeld said it would take a slight detour. "Ach, please do so," said Hitler. "At least drive by even though I cannot go in." At Frauenfeld's Hitler ate a good breakfast, then began speaking quietly, not of the tragedy, but of the political future of Germany and himself. His voice was firm and confident as he assured Frauenfeld that he would take over power in Germany by 1933 at the latest, before the Poles seized Danzig. Once back in his own car, Hitler gazed fixedly ahead. Finally he said, as if thinking aloud, "So. Now let the struggle begin—the struggle which must and shall be crowned with success."

A day or two later he drove north to attend the Gauleiter conference. The party stopped at an inn overnight and at breakfast the following morning he refused to eat a piece of ham. "It is like eating a corpse!" he told Göring. Nothing on earth would make him eat meat again.*

In Hamburg he addressed a large, sympathetic audience. He spoke as forcefully and brilliantly as ever. Twice before—at the hospital in Pasewalk and in Landsberg prison—he had emerged from suicidal depressions. Perhaps these were a form of regeneration, for each time he had bounced back from the depths with renewed vigor and a new sense of direction. This was his third resurrection.

---

* He had made such remarks before and had toyed with the idea of vegetarianism but this time, according to Frau Hess, he meant it. From that moment on, she said, Hitler never ate another piece of meat except for liver dumplings. "Suddenly! He ate meat before that. It is very difficult to understand or explain."

Part 4

THE BROWN REVOLUTION

Chapter Ten

"IT IS ALMOST LIKE
A DREAM"
1931–JANUARY 30, 1933

1

Hitler recovered sufficiently from the death of Geli to attend the leadership meeting in the north that was already in session. It was of such import that only Gauleiters and major SA leaders were present and so successful that it marked the end of the party's reorganization. "The movement," he said a few days later, "is today so united that the Gauleiters and political leaders instinctively make the right decisions." As a result, there followed purges of "all lazy, rotten, useless" elements and a thinning of ranks that strengthened the party structure and buttressed Hitler's personal control.

With his own house in order, Hitler felt free to re-enter national politics. On October 14, 1931, an interview was arranged with President von Hindenburg through General Kurt von Schleicher, who had been one of the Old Gentleman's closest advisers. Hitler was visibly ill at ease in the presence of Hindenburg, an overwhelming figure with his six-foot-five-inch height and deep, booming voice. Hitler's lengthy remarks irritated the field marshal, who later reportedly complained to Schleicher that Hitler was a queer fellow who would never become Chancellor; the best he could hope for was to head the Postal Department. Disappointing as the meeting was, Schleicher still had hopes for Hitler; he had been impressed not only by the Führer's success at the last elections but by his nationalistic program. "An interesting man with exceptional speaking abilities," was his judgment. "In his plans he soars in the clouds. You then have to hold him by the coattails in order to keep him on the ground." Schleicher, whose name in German meant "intriguer," was a brilliant improviser but impetuosity tended to lead him into dangerous waters. Privately he felt quite able to handle any former corporal.

Hitler was used to being underestimated. For the next few months he contented himself with building a base of mass support among those Germans who had become disillusioned with the government's failure to cope with rising unemployment. He also made an unprecedented attempt to win foreign approval by talking directly to the American people. He was scheduled to make a radio broadcast on Friday night, December 11, over CBS to explain the "course, meaning and aims" of his party. The German government canceled the speech at the last moment but a translation was published in the Hearst newspapers which were noted for their extreme anti-Communist policy. In it Hitler expressed the hope that Americans, out of an inner impulse for self-preservation, would join him in the "struggle against this world pest" known as Bolshevism.

On the first day of 1932 Hitler told a Munich audience that God was on his side in the battle for a better world. Didn't the Bible say that the lukewarm was condemned to be spewed out? A victory of sorts seemed to offer itself almost immediately in the form of an invitation to Berlin from Hindenburg's advisers. They urged him to help prolong the field marshal's presidency but this went against Hitler's scruples, he said, since it would more or less force him to support Chancellor Brüning's policies. The refusal indicated that Hitler might be prepared to risk his entire political future in a presidential election even though an open contest with Hindenburg was a gamble. The Old Gentleman was a legend. His conservatism would draw many votes from the right and his defense of the Weimar Republic against an extremist like Hitler was sure to attract moderates and democrats alike.

Goebbels wrote in his diary, ". . . the chess game for power begins," and urged Hitler to take the chance. His chief concern was getting enough money to run a campaign. Hitler helped solve this particular problem with a single speech at the Park Hotel in Düsseldorf, center of the German steel industry. In line with a recent decision "to work systematically on the influential personalities of business," and under the auspices of Fritz Thyssen, he addressed an influential group at the Industry Club on January 17.

In confidential conversations prior to the Düsseldorf speech, Hitler had already drastically revised his economic program. He was now for elimination of unions and for managerial freedom as well as a program of public works and rearmament to be directed by the leaders of big business in the interest of economic recovery. Within an hour he had the rapt attention of his audience, for he spoke of matters that directly concerned these hardheaded businessmen. He asserted, for example, that private property was justified and then drew a frightening picture of the growth of Communism. "Bolshevism, if unchecked, will change the world as completely as Christianity once did. . . . If this movement continues to develop, three hundred years from now Lenin will be regarded not only as one of the revolutionaries of 1917, but as the founder of a new world doctrine and he will be worshiped as much perhaps as Buddha." Millions of unemployed and deprived Germans made desperate by the depression, he said, were already looking to Communism for the answer to their distress. That was Germany's most pressing problem of the day and it could be solved not by economic decrees but by political power. The NSDAP alone was prepared and willing to stem the Red tide. Without National Socialism there would no longer be a middle class in Germany, and only with it could the nation be united and revitalized.

Rarely had Hitler spoken so effectively, alternating between emotion and logic. In one moment he shook his listeners with terrible visions of Bolshevism and the end of the system that had brought them security; in the next he appealed to their selfishness: if they wanted their industrial complex to survive and expand they would need a dictator at the helm of government, one who would eventually lead Germany back to its position as a world power. His listeners could visualize fifty years of accomplishment and wealth dissipating and many went home prepared to contribute considerable sums to the man who promised to save them.

2

In mid-February Hindenburg announced he would stand again for President. This forced Hitler to make his own decision. It was apparent that the NSDAP had to run a presidential candidate and no one but Hitler had a realistic chance. Even so he hesitated. "I know that I shall come to power, all others will fail," he once told Frank. "I see myself as Chancellor and I will be Chancellor. I do not see myself as President, and I know I will never be President." His reluctance was genuine and he wavered for almost two weeks before Goebbels finally persuaded him to run. Then he acted with dispatch to make himself eligible. He hastily became a citizen of Germany through the machinations of the Nazi

Minister of Interior in Braunschweig, who made him a councilor of that state. The following day, February 27, Hitler formally announced his candidacy for elections to take place in fifteen days.

The economic depression and political rancor had already turned Germany into a quasi battlefield. "Berlin was in a state of civil war," wrote Christopher Isherwood. "Hate exploded suddenly without warning, out of nowhere; at street corners, in restaurants, cinemas, dance halls, swimming-baths; at midnight, after breakfast, in the middle of the afternoon. Knives were whipped out, blows were dealt with spiked rings, beer-mugs, chair-legs or leaded clubs; bullets slashed the advertisements on the poster-columns, rebounded from the iron roofs of latrines."

Hate scourged the land as the victims of the depression turned on those more fortunate than themselves. Shopkeepers driven out of business cursed the great department stores; the millions of unemployed envied those with jobs and hated the "bosses"; thousands of university graduates found the future barred to them and turned their despair on the establishment. The depression had hit almost every level. Peasants, burdened with taxes and faced with low prices, despised city people while the masses of white-collar unemployed envied the peasants their crops. Those without work camped in hordes on the outskirts of the larger cities. Beggars haunted every street corner and by the time of the election campaign there were six million registered unemployed in the land—with millions of others working only part time or too proud to register as jobless.

To multitudes of these casualties of economic collapse Adolf Hitler was the answer. They cared little about the rumors of his deals with industrialists since he had never compromised with the Weimar government and had remained outspoken in his opposition to the Versailles Treaty and the Red menace. His call was simple: "For Freedom and Bread." Amid the confusion of the nation he seemed to stand like a rock, insisting only on what was best for Germany. Hindenburg countered with posters urging voters to remember his past services: "He hath kept faith with you; be ye faithful unto him." Goebbels answered with: "Honor Hindenburg: Vote for Hitler."

The Führer's appeal was to both the defeated middle-aged and the idealistic youth, and as he toured the country speaking tirelessly he called upon both to join him in his battle against the establishment. The campaign, masterminded by Goebbels, was a marvel of inventiveness. It was the rare wall in the nation that wasn't plastered with glaring red Nazi posters; leaflets were showered on the populace from planes. Fifty thousand small propaganda records were mailed to those well enough off to own a phonograph; "talking pictures" of speeches by Hitler and Goebbels were projected at night in public squares. The heart of the program, however, was a backbreaking speaking schedule. In the first eleven days of March Hitler and Goebbels each made at least one major speech daily and usually two or three.

In the meantime the Hindenburg camp was disordered. Split from the beginning, it was staggered by a whispering campaign alleging that the President's son Oskar had secretly become both a Catholic and a member of the Social Democratic Party. Even more ridiculous was the charge that Hindenburg's two middle-aged daughters were leaders in the Socialist Students League. More time was spent in denying rumors than in attacking Hitler's policies and each denial helped give the fiction more of an appearance of fact. Hindenburg's supporters began arguing and he did little himself to get votes. He made but one public appearance, three days before the election, when he asserted that he had consented to run only because so many Germans of all political hues urged him to stay in office to prevent a takeover by either left or right.

By early evening of election day, March 13, the results showed that Hindenburg was pulling ahead of Hitler. The party militants like Goebbels had been confident that he would sweep into the presidency and, as the returns widened the margin, they grew despondent. An hour after midnight there was no doubt that Hindenburg was winning by more than 7,000,000 votes and was only about 350,000 votes short of the necessary majority. Though there would have to be a runoff election between the two leaders, Goebbels for one was sure that "the dream of power was temporarily over."

Not so Hitler, who had waited stoically at the Café Heck with intimates. He hurried to the Brown House and dictated a statement exhorting the party to begin the battle for the runoff without delay. "The first election is over, the second begins today. I will also lead this one personally!" In the space of a week he and Goebbels, roused from his depression, addressed meetings of Gauleiters, Reichstag deputies and party editors so inspirationally that those present were convinced that Hitler would win next time.

Success in the runoff election was suddenly threatened by publication in the Social Democratic *Münchener Post* of incriminating letters between Röhm and a doctor specializing in psychology. It seemed they shared two interests—homosexuality and astrology. When Hans Frank, after reviewing the evidence, refused to handle a libel suit against the paper, Röhm—with much embarrassed twisting and turning—confessed he was a "bisexual." Hitler's lawyer was flabbergasted, for he had always thought homosexuals were effeminate thrill seekers. "And here," recalled Frank, "was actually the prototype of a brave, aggressive soldier, who gave the impression outwardly, with his scarred face, his upright soldierly posture, that he was very much the whole man."

Hitler had long tolerated Röhm's homosexuality—a remarkable attitude for those days—but his first reaction upon reading the documentary evidence was to lose his temper. Finally he calmed down. "This is a terrible blow," he told Frank. "Such a horrible mess! It's not human, it's bestial, worse, even animals would not do such a thing." He asked if Röhm had "abused" young men or boys. There was nothing in the records to indicate this, said the lawyer, and Hitler became calmer. "That would be utterly intolerable. As long as it is between grown men—what Röhm does. Children are not his victims?" Frank assured him that there was not a single instance. "Well, then we can at least consider whether to keep him or not, but God help him if he abuses young boys! Then he must go!"

If the Röhm scandal distracted Hitler, he certainly had put it behind him by the time the runoff campaign began. He was full of his usual vigor and optimism. This time there was only a week to campaign and Hitler decided to use an airplane so he could make three to four speeches daily.

He invited Sefton Delmer to accompany him on the tour and the British correspondent was impressed that the rigorous schedule was maintained despite bad weather. In almost every city Hitler was besieged by adoring women. In Coblenz two girls cornered him in the corridor of his railway car. From the Führer's compartment, Delmer could hear a series of sobs and hysterical cries from the girls but not a sound from Hitler. He seemed to be in a trance as the correspondent entered the compartment. Ignoring Delmer, he flung aside the window curtain and gazed out at the people on the platform "with his mesmeric stare turning in an arc like a searchlight from left to right, exposing everyone within sight to the emotion the two girls had inspired in him and which he was now throwing back into the crowd."

Only rarely in the rigorous campaign did Hitler's spirits noticeably flag. One of these moments was witnessed by Albert Krebs, Gauleiter of Hamburg. Upon arrival at Hitler's suite in the Hotel Atlantic with a printed copy of a speech made by the Führer the night before, Krebs was greeted with a rhythmic call of *"Mei Supp! Mei Supp!"* (Bavarian for *Meine Suppe*), first from Hitler and then, rather disrespectfully, from his entourage. By the time Krebs was admitted to the Führer's presence the breakfast soup had arrived. Hitler hunched over it, looking tired and melancholy. He glanced up at Krebs and "in a tone of undisguised alarm" asked what he thought about vegetarian diets, then, without waiting for an answer, began a long impassioned lecture which revealed "hypochondriacal fears for his health."

It was the first time Hitler had ever revealed himself as a human being to Krebs—his name in German meant cancer—and the Gauleiter was shaken to hear him explain in detail the reasons for his reformed living habits; outbreaks of perspiration, states of extreme excitement, trembling of limbs and stomach cramps. The last, Hitler insisted, were the forerunner of cancer and this gave him only a few years to finish his work. "I do not have the time to wait," he announced over his plate of soup. "If I had time I wouldn't have become a candidate. The Old Gentleman [Hindenburg] won't last much longer. But I cannot lose even a year. I must come to power quickly in order to solve the gigantic problems in the little time remaining to me. I must! I must!" All at once Hitler ended the discussion. "One can say," commented Krebs, "that he pulled himself together and it was immediately noticeable in his physical bearing, facial expression and voice. The depression was over; the human being Hitler once more became the Führer."

While he gave the public a picture of youthful energy, the Hindenburg forces ran another desultory campaign. This time Hindenburg did not make a single speech, spurring rumors that he was dying. There were also whispers that pensions and salaries would be cut and unemployment relief would be ended if he won re-election. By election eve it appeared that Hitler would win. Even Spengler, who had been deriding him, decided to vote National Socialist on the grounds that "Hitler is a fool but one must support the movement." On Sunday, April 10, Hitler got an additional 2,000,000 votes, raising his total to 13,418,051. The old field marshal increased his total by less than 700,000, yet this gave him a solid majority, fifty-three per cent. The Communist vote had slipped badly. More than a quarter of their voters had either listened to Goebbels' appeals or gone over to Hindenburg to keep Hitler out of the presidential palace.

In London, the *Daily Telegraph* predicted the end of Adolf Hitler while in Munich the iconoclastic Spengler and his sister hung swastika flags out of their windows. "When one has a chance to annoy people," he said, "one should do so."

3

A few days after the election Brüning was persuaded to enact a decree outlawing the SA and SS. The effect of this act was to ruin the politically naïve Chancellor, for it was not only ineffective but brought a concerted storm of protest from the right. This was the opportunity that the politically ambitious General von Schleicher had been waiting for. His dream was to establish a government of the right that would include the Nazis but not give them control. After all, Corporal Hitler and his people were, in Schleicher's words, "merely little children who had to be led by the hand."

He met secretly with the Führer that May and promised to remove the ban on the SA and SS if Hitler agreed not to attack the new rightist government. The deal was made and late that month Schleicher chose as figurehead Chancellor for his regime a wealthy, polished gentleman jockey, Franz von Papen. An ex-General Staff officer, he was also a member of the Prussian Landtag. The astounded Papen's first reaction was "I very much doubt if I am the right man," but it took only a few minutes to persuade him that he might be. Before Papen knew it he was standing, somewhat dazed, before Hindenburg.

"Well, my dear Papen," said the field marshal with paternal kindliness, "I hope you are going to help me out of this difficult situation." He knew only that Papen was a former cavalry officer, financially independent, well known on the racecourses, and had some experience in foreign affairs. But he was pleased with his military bearing and gentlemanly appearance. Again Papen protested that he was not the right man but this time was persuaded in even shorter order by Hindenburg's words: "You have been a soldier and done your duty in the war. When the Fatherland calls, Prussia knows only one response—obedience."

Hitler was spending the weekend at Mecklenburg when Goebbels phoned that Hindenburg wanted to see him that same afternoon. The Führer hastened back to the capital where he was informed by the President that he was going to appoint Papen (no news to the Führer thanks to Schleicher) and asked if Hitler was going to support him. "Yes," was the answer and the brief interview was over.

Undoubtedly Schleicher thought he was acting in the best interest of the people. Convinced that Brüning was too weak to handle Hitler, he was confident, like so many other military men, that the army itself could deal properly with such a radical—and utilize him to help establish a strong nationalist Germany. Schleicher had at last achieved his first aim but as so often happens with those attempting to outdo Machiavelli he was too clever for his own good. He soon learned that Hitler's pledge to support the new government was provisional. He could not consider the matter, he said, until Papen showed his good faith by dissolving the Reichstag and abolishing the repressive measures against the National Socialist movement. Papen did so but Hitler still withheld his support. Instead he sanctioned resumption of street battles with the Reds. A new wave of violence swept over Germany. In July alone eighty-six died in the fighting, including thirty Reds and thirty-eight Nazis. Both sides were equally belligerent. Skirmishes turned into battles in the summer heat. On Sunday, July 10, eighteen police were killed and the following Sunday a Nazi march under police escort through the working-class district of Altona was broken up by a volley of shots from roofs and windows. The marchers fired back. Nineteen people were reported killed and 285 wounded.

Three days later Papen invoked the President's emergency powers— Article 48 of the Weimar constitution. This article had already been invoked a number of times, by Ebert in the economic crisis of 1923 to abolish the eight-hour day, and several times by Brüning to suspend newspapers. Using the argument that the Prussian government could no longer deal with the Reds, Papen made himself Reichs Commissioner of Prussia. This meant the end of parliamentary government in that state and foreshadowed what could be done in every state by a man resolute enough to use the emergency authority granted by the constitution.

4

Elections for the Reichstag were set for the last day of July. It was another whirlwind campaign and Hitler's second "Flight over Germany." Once more Hitler chartered a plane and the same pilot. Hans Baur had proved so competent in all kinds of weather—several times they had made forced landings in storms and fog—that Hitler now refused to fly with anyone else. He also had a second private chauffeur, twenty-one-year-old Erich Kempka. He would meet Hitler's plane in the western part of Germany while Schreck would be on hand in the east. In this election the two drivers covered more than fifty thousand kilometers, most of it over unpaved highways. Hitler treated Kempka as a member of the family. He was equally familiar with Baur. While resting in Weimar after a week of strenuous campaigning, Hitler took him on a tour of the park near their hotel, the Belvedere. For an hour Hitler queried Baur about his World War experiences as a fighter pilot while the rest of the entourage lagged behind. Then Hitler turned and told Gauleiter Sauckel to drive into town and get fifteen young ladies for partners at afternoon coffee. By this time word had gone out that Hitler was at the Belvedere dining room and women began to appear singly and in couples for a look at him. The Führer excitedly poked Baur, who sat at his right. "Just look, Baur, there is a beautiful little lady, a beauty!" Baur sympathized that it was too bad the Führer could only see women at a distance, not at close range. "You're right, Baur," said the amused Hitler. "Now if you make a little side trip, no rooster will crow about it, but with me the ladies advertise and I can't afford that. Women can't keep their mouths shut. So I like them all."

Finally the fifteen girls from town arrived and they were so entranced by Hitler that they ignored their own partners and kept staring worshipfully at him. Embarrassed, he suggested they all move to the Artists' Café. The group piled into cars with everyone but the Führer having at least one girl on his lap. In moments almost every woman in this restaurant was crowding around Hitler. Harassed, he told Hanfstaengl to play the piano but after listening to two pieces he excused himself on the ground that he had to prepare for tomorrow's speeches.

Hitler appeared in some fifty cities in the last two weeks of the campaign, generating rabid enthusiasm wherever he went. Once he kept an open-air crowd of 10,000 in Stralsund waiting in the rain for six hours while Baur was looking in vain for a place to make a forced landing in the dark. An economic paralysis extended throughout the nation and that was one reason Hitler's audiences listened to his lengthy speeches as if hypnotized. Eleven-year-old Egon Hanfstaengl heard him address a large crowd in a vast tent on the outskirts of Munich. "He ran the gamut of emotions, and a wave of frenzied enthusiasm swept the mass." There were rich and poor in the audience, professors and workers. At the beginning they were uneasy in one another's presence but soon all were shouting and applauding wildly as a single entity. Egon noticed one incongruous couple—a professor and a charwoman—leaving the tent "amid the tumultuous acclamation, talking together excitedly, fraternizing in fact. Such was the power of Adolf Hitler." Afterward Egon was taken by his father to the Brown House. "All right, boy," said Hanfstaengl, "sit down somewhere, keep quiet and learn something." A messenger handed a ream of typed pages to Goebbels. "It was the transcript of Hitler's speech, which had apparently just been completed. The Führer left the group and sat down behind his desk, with Goebbels standing behind him, looking over his shoulder. They seemed to run through the speech to groom it for publication. Hitler appeared to be talking to himself as he marked things with a pencil. 'That was good . . . this was effective . . . this must be cut . . .' Not more than an hour ago he had finished one of the most emotional speeches of his career. He had preached, entreated, thundered, and shrieked. Yet, here he was, as cool and rational as any man I've seen."

During the campaign anti-Semitism never was an issue. It was well known that Hitler detested Jews but many voters were ready to overlook this as long as he kept his prejudice on a sensible level. The majority of Germans agreed that there were too many Jewish lawyers and objected to their monopoly of department stores and the entertainment industry. Many Jews themselves deplored the postwar flood of Jews from the East who brought with them the costumes and customs of the ghettos. Two well-known Jewish bankers, in fact, had already requested the new Minister of Labor, Friedrich Syrup, to stop further immigration of these Eastern Jews since their presence increased latent anti-Semitism. Jews regarded themselves as Germans first and then Jews. They had become so integrated into the German economy that they were willing to overlook the social prejudice that remained. After all, even in enlightened Britain and America Jews were excluded from the best clubs and hotels. Nor was toleration of National Socialism confined to German Jews. A group of Palestinian extremists had recently announced that, except for Hitler's anti-Semitism, the NSDAP movement was acceptable and would save Germany.

On July 31 (despite a special edition of a Vienna newspaper revealing Hitler's antecedents under the banner headline HEIL SCHICKLGRUBER)* the Nazis won 13,732,779 votes, half a million more than the combined total of their closest rivals—the Social Democrats and Communists. Encouraged by a victory giving him 37.3 per cent of all the votes, Hitler proposed to his own party that he run for Chancellor.

Göring protested. So did Strasser, for it wrecked his entire policy of seizing power by a coalition with other right-wing parties. But Hitler was too impatient for power to be dissuaded. A messenger immediately was dispatched to Berlin informing Schleicher of Hitler's demand. The general could not take it seriously, so sure was he that Hindenburg would balk at bestowing such an honor on an ex-Gefreiter. He invited Hitler to a meeting in Mecklenburg under the illusion that he could "talk him out of his plans." The two met on August 5 at the Fürstenberg barracks near the capital, and Hitler demanded not only the chancellorship but passage of an enabling bill which would give him power to govern the nation by decree—in effect, to establish a dictatorship. The meeting went so well that Hitler was convinced Hindenburg would also be brought around and, in elation, he proposed that a tablet be fastened to the wall in commemoration of such a historic conference.

Although he brought his euphoria back to the Obersalzberg it was not

---

* Early in 1932 Austrian Chancellor Dollfuss urged the owner-editor of the *Wiener Sonn-und-Montags Zeitung* to investigate Hitler's ancestry. Documents revealing the illegitimate birth of Hitler's father were found and the above-mentioned special edition was brought out in hopes of influencing the German elections.

shared by Goebbels, who doubted they would gain power so easily. He was all for action, not dubious compromises, and his zeal permeated the Nazi ranks. "The whole party is ready to take over power," he wrote in his diary on August 8. "The SA men are leaving their places of work in order to make themselves ready." By August 10, when Hindenburg left his own country home for Berlin, the capital was in a state of semi-siege. To end the crisis Papen offered to resign but Hindenburg was enraged at the thought of making Hitler Chancellor. The upstart Austrian had already broken his promises to Schleicher; besides, Hitler had no governmental experience and couldn't even control the hotheads in his own party. The President even refused to invite him to a meeting.

The next morning, August 13, Hitler checked in at the Hotel Kaiserhof, which had become his Berlin headquarters. It was more like a military command post with the telephone in the anteroom ringing almost constantly. The revolving doors of the Kaiserhof itself never seemed to stop and the lobby seethed with activity. On the main floor, in the emergency office set up for the Führer's adjutants and staff officers, portable typewriters clattered without interruption as representatives of the native and foreign press besieged Otto Dietrich, Hitler's press chief, and Hanfstaengl for the latest pronouncements from the man of the hour.

At noon Hitler saw Schleicher, who informed him that Hindenburg could only offer him the vice-chancellorship. Understandably irate, Hitler attacked the general for breaking his promise and stormed out. Moments later he was in Chancellor Papen's office berating the administration for its leniency with the old system. Papen was taken aback by his caller's aggressive attitude. "The President is not prepared to offer you the post of Chancellor," he said, "as he feels he does not yet know you well enough." Hitler was in no mood for half a loaf. He had dedicated himself to wiping out the Marxist parties, he said, and this could not be done unless he took over the government and ran things his own way. One could not shy away from bloodshed, he added ominously. That was a lesson of history. Had the King of Italy offered Mussolini a vice-chancellorship after the march on Rome?

He left the chancellery in a black mood, driving directly to Goebbels' apartment. Here he waited, irritated and frustrated, for a summons from Hindenburg. At last, at three in the afternoon, Papen's state secretary phoned. Hitler was interested in but one thing: was Hindenburg making him Chancellor? The state secretary would only reply that the President wished to speak with the Führer. The meeting in the study of the presidential palace was short and formal. Hindenburg had made up his mind not to appoint a man like Hitler to such a responsible post but would "make one more appeal to his patriotism" to co-operate with Papen. He opened cautiously by stating that he welcomed the participation of the National Socialists in the government. Hitler just as politely replied that this was out of the question; as head of the largest party in the nation, he would have to insist on a new cabinet with himself as Chancellor.

"Nein!" exclaimed Hindenburg. Never could he "before God, his conscience, and the Fatherland bear the responsibility of entrusting all governmental authority to a single party." Hitler regretted that he could accept no other alternative. "You are going into opposition, then?" "I have no other choice," said the Führer.

With some feeling, Hindenburg complained of the recent clashes between the Nazis and the police. Such incidents, he said, strengthened his conviction that there were wild uncontrollable elements in the NSDAP. He was ready, however, to accept Hitler in a coalition government. The invitation was followed by a lofty rebuke, from field marshal to corporal. "Then I must warn you to carry on your opposition in a chivalrous manner and to remain conscious of your responsibility and duty toward the Fatherland. I do not doubt at all your love for the Fatherland. But I am going to proceed very harshly against any acts of terror or force, such as have been regrettably perpetrated by members of the SA."

The severity of this lecture was somewhat mitigated by Hindenburg's closing words: "We are both old fellow soldiers and want to remain so since our paths may be crossing again. Thus I extend my hand to you as a comrade-in-arms." Hitler emerged from the study overwhelmed by the personality of the marshal but, once the door closed, he turned on Papen for maneuvering him into such a humiliating scene. Out of all this, warned Hitler, would possibly come the downfall of the President. He would not be responsible for what happened next.

When Hitler entered the Goebbels apartment Hanfstaengl noted that he was "as white as a sheet. He said practically nothing and was very moody for a time." Then, curiously, he abruptly brightened up and began to speculate on accepting the vice-chancellorship. "I can imagine that to work with Papen would, in a way, be quite good fun. Somehow you feel that he was a soldier during the war and quite a reckless fellow." The Chancellor, he mused, looked as though he would act like a true comrade. "Mind you, if it amuses his vanity to go on living with his wife in the Chancellor's palace and they confide the real power to me, I would not mind."

Newsboys in the street were shouting out headlines from extras:

SHOCKING PRETENSION—HITLER'S BREACH OF FAITH—HITLER REPRIMANDED BY THE REICH PRESIDENT." The stories, which stated that Hitler had demanded complete power, were based on a government communiqué issued so soon after the interview that it must have been prepared ahead of time. This infuriated Hitler and broke the spell Hindenburg had cast over him. He felt he had been "deceived" by the military and the politicians. A hostile biographer agreed. "Now that the National Socialists had reached the ante-chamber of power," wrote Rudolf Olden, "and were taking part in political parleys, they encountered a measure of haughtiness, contempt and trickery which, if they had not come out victorious, would have earned their just indignation. For all the doors that were thrown open to them, for all the hands that shook theirs, there was not one of the 'respectable people' who received them, who did not want to exploit them, and usually to trick them."

Schleicher was almost as dismayed by the Papen communiqué as Hitler, since he was still convinced that the best solution was to get the Nazis into the government. He hastily sent word to the Führer that there was still a chance to work out an agreement and asked for a meeting. Hitler's brusque refusal to see him sent the ordinarily self-possessed general into a state of shock. That evening a friend found Schleicher pale and frightened, incoherently muttering to himself. Finally his words could be made out: "The decision was right, one could not have given the power to Adolf Hitler."

Throughout the city embittered Brownshirts, long held in check by party leadership, were clamoring for action. By this time Hitler had regained his composure. He summoned SA commanders to the Goebbels apartment and such were his powers of persuasion that they accepted his argument that it was not yet time to seize power, and that a Putsch at this time would be disastrous. All units were sent on a two-week furlough.

Later that night Hitler started south for his retreat on the Obersalzberg. As Schreck wound his way along the dark roads there was silence in the car. Finally Hanfstaengl heard the Führer muttering to himself "in a sleepy and fatalistic baritone from which the metal was almost gone, '*Wir werden ja sehen. Es ist vielleicht besser so* [We shall see. Perhaps it is better so].'" The Führer was more philosophical than his followers and he began to encourage them with words like "Only we ourselves can finish what we have begun," "I would rather besiege a fortress than be a prisoner of it," and "Later on we will say that everything had to happen this way." Perhaps it was because the others could see only the present and he had eyes only for the future. The gamble to outbluff Hindenburg had failed but he was convinced that his fate would see him through.

5

Within a few days Hitler had made another of his remarkable recoveries from adversity but each of those who saw him at Berchtesgaden in those critical hours had a different impression. Joachim von Ribbentrop, a friend of Papen's, had arrived to patch up matters between Chancellor and Führer, and within an hour became a disciple of the latter. "There was room for neither discussion nor contradiction," he recalled. "He simply stated facts that his listeners were expected to accept. He was clearly monomaniacal; a man hard to influence and not given to compromise." Ribbentrop, come on a mission of persuasion, left so convinced that Hitler alone could save Germany from Communism that he joined the NSDAP.

Three American correspondents saw the Führer several days later, on August 17. Louis Lochner, H. V. Kaltenborn and Karl von Wiegand were scheduled for a joint interview but the last, who represented the Hearst press, insisted on seeing him alone. After fifteen minutes Wiegand returned in an angry mood to the little hotel, which stood just above the Haus Wachenfeld. "That man is hopeless," he told his two colleagues. "He gets worse every time I see him. I got nothing out of him. Ask him a question and he makes a speech. This whole trip has been a waste of time."

Hitler came out the front door of his villa just as Kaltenborn and Lochner were climbing up to the open porch. Kaltenborn began with an embarrassing question: "In your attitude of antagonism towards the Jews, do you differentiate between German Jews and the Jews who have come into Germany from other countries?"

Hitler's clear blue eyes seemed to bore into Kaltenborn. "We believe in a Monroe Doctrine for Germany," he exclaimed. "You exclude any would-be immigrants you do not care to admit. You regulate their number. You demand that they come up to a certain physical standard." He had no concern with the Jews of other lands, only any anti-German elements in his own country. "And we demand the right to deal with them as we see fit."

Lochner brought the subject back to the immediate political situation. Was it true that Herr Hitler had asked Hindenburg for the creation of a National Socialist government with power equivalent to that of Mussolini? Hitler heatedly denied making any such deal, then asserted that he did have "the right to complete control." He began talking as if he were already at the helm and gave a candid preview of the kind of rule he

would bring to Germany. It had to be some kind of authoritarian government. Parliamentarianism was not native to continental Europeans, nor
did it belong to their tradition. "Yet we cannot substitute brute force." A
government must have the support of the masses. "You cannot establish a
dictatorship in a vacuum. A government that does not derive its strength
from the people will fail in a foreign crisis."

At the opening session of the new Reichstag the National Socialist
delegates behaved correctly, sitting in silence during opponents' speeches
and co-operating in the election of parliamentary officers. Such exemplary
conduct was rewarded by support of the Center Party for Göring as president of the Reichstag. Several days passed in peaceful and constructive activity. Political stability had at last returned to Germany—thanks to Adolf
Hitler. But within a week he abruptly changed course, apparently on the
spur of the moment. He ordered his delegates to make no objections to a
Communist motion of no confidence in the Papen government.

The session erupted into a wild shouting match and when Papen,
who had rushed out to get Hindenburg's signature on a document to dissolve parliament, tried to get the floor, President Göring pretended not to
see him. Ignoring the decree which the infuriated Papen had flung onto
the presidential desk, Göring called for a vote. It was an overwhelming defeat for Papen—512 to 42.

Hitler was elated by the success of his unexpected coup and prepared
for the national election with confidence. On the platform he exercised
his usual magic. One witness to this was an enemy—the son of the last
Emperor of Austria-Hungary. At a large open-air meeting in Berlin, Otto
von Habsburg stood on the fringe of the crowd with a group of Communists who had been abusing Hitler. Then the Führer made his appearance
and before he opened his mouth those who had just been berating him all
at once were enthralled. "He had them before he even spoke. He had
some sort of magnetic gift." By the end of the speech, to young Habsburg's amazement, the Reds around him were cheering along with the rest
of the enraptured crowd.

Despite Hitler's crowd appeal, his campaign was sluggish since the
financial and physical resources of the party had been severely strained to
the breaking point. Too, Germany had been emotionally drained by the
seemingly endless elections. Goebbels could not stir up the enthusiasm
of the previous campaign and attendance at rallies and meetings slacked
off. Spengler, for example, was so exasperated by the continual elections
that his halfhearted support of Hitler turned to sarcasm. There was no

real Caesar in Germany, he wrote that fall, and a true Führer must be "a hero, not a heroic tenor."

In the midst of Hitler's attempts to generate life in the campaign he was once more beset by personal misfortune. On the first of November Eva Braun, his mistress of some months, shot herself with a pistol as Geli Raubal had done. While she had fallen desperately in love, he had become so involved with elections that he could spend little time with her. He would send her brief messages and even these became less frequent as the political situation intensified. To add to her misery, at least one malicious rival for the Führer's affections showed her photographs of the electioneering Hitler posing with beautiful women.

A little after midnight on All Saints' Day she wrote a letter of farewell to Hitler, then shot herself in the neck, severing an artery. She got to the phone and gasped out to a surgeon, Dr. Plate, that she had shot herself through the heart.

Hitler left the campaign trail and, carrying a bunch of flowers, hastened to the private clinic where she was recovering. "Do you think," he asked Dr. Plate, "that Fräulein Braun shot herself simply with the object of becoming an interesting patient and of drawing my attention to herself?" The surgeon assured the Führer that it appeared to be a genuine case of attempted suicide. She had felt so neglected that she wanted to end it all. When the doctor left, Hitler turned to his companion, Hoffmann. "You hear," he said, "the girl did it for love of me. But I have given her no cause which could possibly justify such a deed." As he paced in agitation he muttered, "Obviously I must now look after the girl." Hoffmann objected. Who could possibly blame him for what happened? "And who, do you think, would believe that?" said Hitler, who knew more about human nature. Nor was there any guarantee that she might not try again.

This incident distracted Hitler from a campaign that was showing signs of deteriorating, and two days later he was presented with another embarrassing problem. On his own, Goebbels joined the Reds in a wildcat strike of Berlin transport workers asking for a pfennig or so an hour increase in pay. It was not the first time that the two parties, with many goals in common, had fought together; and for the next few wet, raw days the Communists and the National Socialists ate communally on the picket line. Side by side they pelted rocks at strikebreakers, tore up streetcar tracks and built barricades.

Hitler could not publicly disavow the actions of his impetuous disciple but he was privately angry at alienating so many middle-class voters and sent orders to end the strike. "The entire press is furious with us and calls it Bolshevism, but as a matter of fact we have no option," explained Geobbels in his diary. "If we had held ourselves aloof from this strike our position among the working classes would have been shaken."

Goebbels' impetuous act also put a crimp in the flow of bourgeois money for the campaign and on Sunday, November 6, Hitler lost more than two million votes along with thirty-four seats in the Reichstag. No longer could a simple alignment with the Center Party give him a majority. More significant, it indicated that the Hitler flood tide had ebbed and the strategy of gaining power through the ballot box had reached a dead end.

There was talk that Hitler once more threatened to commit suicide and it is quite possible that he said as much in his despair. But the pattern of defeat followed by renewed vigor was repeated and in a few days he began to emerge from depression. By the time he granted another interview to Sefton Delmer he seemed to have completely regained his confidence. During their talk in the back room of the Hotel Zum Elefanten in Weimar he surprised the Briton by changing the subject from politics to a rumor that the British government wished to re-establish monarchy in Germany. Delmer said it was the first he had heard of such a story. "The British government is interested only in such measures as are consonant with order and stability in Germany."

"Quite right. Quite right," exclaimed Hitler. "Germany would go up in flames, if anyone tried to put the Hohenzollerns back. Nor have I the slightest intention of becoming a race horse for a royal jockey to jump on my back just as I am about to pass the winning post." This bitter remark may have been prompted by a recent insult from the Crown Princess Cecilie at their meeting in Potsdam; as he was leaving, a member of his entourage heard the Crown Princess exclaim, "Open the windows quickly, it smells here!" The Führer's uncontrollable flatulence would continue to embarrass him.

6

His defeat was of little consolation to Papen, who was still badly out-numbered in the Reichstag. Putting personal distaste aside, he wrote Hitler that the recent elections provided a new opportunity for uniting the country. "We must endeavor to put aside the bitterness of the election campaign and place the good of the country, which we both seek to serve, above all considerations." The memory of their August meetings was too bitter and the response was a letter of accusation. The Führer refused the Chancellor's invitation to a conference on the grounds that discussions led to misconceptions. After their last conference hadn't Papen publicly announced that Hitler demanded total power when he had only requested leadership? Moreover, he was not ready "under any circumstances to repeat the proceedings of August 13" when Papen had insisted on sharing responsibility with Hindenburg. "Unfortunately you could not be persuaded to assume your part of this responsibility. I assumed mine. Instead your chancellery, through trickery—against my wishes and my explanations—successfully lured me into a colloquy with the Reich president. . . . I do not want to have a repetition of this game."

Thwarted, Papen reported to Hindenburg on the afternoon of November 17 that he was unable to negotiate with other parties and that any coalition under his leadership was impossible. The President accepted his resignation and the following day asked Hugenberg what he thought of Hitler as Chancellor. The latter no longer trusted the Führer. "His entire manner of handling political affairs makes it very difficult, in my opinion, to give him leadership. At any rate, I have grave doubts." The marshal then turned to his adviser, Meissner, and wondered if it was true that Hitler had been a house painter in Munich. Without waiting for an answer he turned back to the gray-haired Hugenberg. "My dear young friend, you have spoken out of my own heart!" he said and proceeded to help perpetuate the myth that persists to this day. "One can't put a house painter in Bismarck's chair."

The next morning, at Hitler's insistence, the two men had a private talk. It began poorly with Hindenburg reproaching his visitor for the rude behavior of youthful Nazis in East Prussia. "Not long ago, at Tannenberg, they shouted out so that I could hear: 'Wake up, wake up!' And yet I'm not asleep!" Hitler explained that his followers had not meant to be offensive; they were merely chanting the National Socialist slogan, "Germany, awake!"

After about an hour Meissner entered and the talk became more pointed. Hitler refused to join a non-partisan cabinet unless he was made Chancellor. "In the interest of the Fatherland," he said, "my movement must be preserved and this means that I must have the leadership." Why then did the Nazis join the Reds in the recent transportation strike? "If I had tried to restrain my people," explained Hitler frankly, "the strike would have taken place nonetheless, but I would have lost my following among the workers; this would not have been in Germany's interest."

Much as he distrusted the "house painter," Hindenburg did his utmost to gain his co-operation. "I can only repeat my request: Give me your help." It was an open call for personal allegiance. "I do appreciate the great idea which inspires you and your movement, and I would like to see you and your movement join the government." At the same time he could not give Hitler the chancellorship. Of course, Hitler was free to form a National Socialist government once he had a majority.

With clenched fists on knees, Hitler exclaimed, "Herr Feldmarschall! In order to negotiate with other parties it is only logical, Herr Feldmarschall, that I first have a mandate from you!" He could not conceal his irritation.

Hindenburg smiled ironically.

There was an awkward pause. "Herr Feldmarschall," Hitler finally said, "I have no intention of ruling as dictatorially as the Feldmarschall seems to assume. If you insist that I produce a Reichstag majority, then I cannot desist from putting before the Reichstag a kind of enabling act for special and urgent matters." He alone could get passage of such a decree and that would solve the problem.

This was unacceptable to Hindenburg and once more he tried the personal approach, appealing to Hitler's sense of duty as a soldier. It invoked the "old comradeship-in-arms" which had brought them together in the war. "Meet me half-way in this matter so that we can work together." Hitler departed, intransigent as ever, but Hindenburg must have thought he had made an impression on the ex-corporal when he remarked to Meissner, "Well, well, it seems as if this Hitler is getting sensible little by little."

Petitions for Hitler's appointment as Chancellor deluged Hindenburg and two days later he felt compelled to see him once more. This time Hitler brought with him a carefully prepared statement. Parliamentary government, it read, had failed and was not an expression of the will of the people. The National Socialists alone could prevent Communism and he requested Hindenburg to appoint him leader of a presidential cabinet.

Hindenburg would only repeat his suggestion that Hitler find a majority in the Reichstag to support his chancellorship. Hitler's response was visibly cool but the President ended the ten-minute talk with another offer of friendship.

In the next few days Hitler and Meissner exchanged long letters but the endeavor to reach agreement was fruitless since the former kept insisting on being made a presidential Chancellor with the same sweeping powers as those granted Papen. This impasse so concerned an influential group of business leaders that they decided to apply direct pressure on the field marshal. They had been contributing to the NSDAP under the impression that once the party came to power they would be able to influence its economic policy. Hitler, for example, had assured I. G. Farben that his government would definitely support production of synthetic gasoline; and in a private speech to a group known as the Circle of Friends at the Kaiserhof earlier in the year he had promised to abolish all trade unions along with all other political parties.

Late that November, thirty-nine prominent businessmen (including Hjalmar Schacht, former Chancellor Cuno, and tycoons like Krupp, Siemens, Thyssen, Bosch, Wörmann and Vögler) signed a letter petitioning Hindenburg to appoint Hitler Chancellor of Germany. These pragmatic men were placing a bet on the NSDAP. They were confident Hitler's socialism was a fraud and that, once in power, he would be the tool of capitalism.*

The machinery of parliamentary government had brought Germany to a political standstill. Hindenburg was finding it impossible to form a new cabinet which could operate with a deadlocked Reichstag. "I am ready to leave at any time," he complained to the chairman of the Center Party, who was urging him to drop Papen, whose style pleased him. "If I don't have the confidence at home or abroad which I must have, I don't want to force myself on the country; for this I am too proud." Frustrated on all sides, Hindenburg summoned Papen and Schleicher, the new Minister of Defense, to his office on the first day of December. They arrived about 6 P.M. and, along with Meissner and Oskar von Hindenburg, ranged themselves in a semicircle around the President's desk. Papen pointed out that Hitler would accept responsibility only as head of another presidential cabinet, and suggested that his government remain in office for the time being. He realized he would not get the support of the Reichstag and that body would have to be suspended for a short period. This procedure involved a breach of the constitution by the President but the situation was grave enough to warrant such action. Then if the police could not keep order the army could step in.

"You can do a lot with bayonets," cut in Schleicher sarcastically, "but one thing you cannot do—sit on them for a long time." Papen's plan would not work, said the Minister of Defense, and suggested one that would: replacement of Papen as Chancellor by himself. This would split the Nazis into two factions and he would get a majority in the Reichstag. He would simply offer Gregor Strasser and one or two of his close supporters posts in the new government and thereby get the votes of sixty Nazi delegates. Other support would come from the Social Democrats and bourgeois parties.

* Hitler was not as yet a major beneficiary of German industry. "After weighing all the facts," writes H. A. Turner, "we must recognize that the financial subsidies from industry were overwhelmingly directed *against* the Nazis." The bulk of the funds in the party treasury came from membership dues.

For weeks Papen had noticed that Schleicher was "no longer as frank and open" as previously and their "relationship had become distinctly cool." Even so the Chancellor was amazed that the general who had helped him into office was now proposing to get rid of him. Schleicher had always seemed to support Papen's policies and had even initiated some of them. Resentfully, Papen argued that his Minister of Defense's scheme meant the abandonment of the President's long-range policy of striving for a more satisfactory relationship between administration and parliament.

Exhausted by almost uninterrupted discussions since early morning, Hindenburg sat in silence until the argument finally ended. Then he rose and turned to Papen. "Herr Reichskanzler," he said, "I desire you to undertake immediately the necessary discussions to form a government, to which I shall entrust the carrying out of your plan."

Schleicher was dumfounded. As he left the office with Papen the latter suggested staying in office for a few months until the constitution was amended and parliamentary peace restored. "Then I can resign and you will be able to take over the government with every hope of a good start."

Schleicher's icy retort was that made to Luther as he was leaving the Diet of Worms: "'Little monk, little monk, you have chosen a difficult path.'"

This was painfully apparent the next morning at a cabinet meeting. After Papen had given an account of the previous night's conference with the President he called upon Schleicher, who got to his feet and declared that any attempt to form a new government under Papen would reduce the country to chaos. Nor could the police and the armed services ensure law and order in the event of civil war. After a study of the matter, he said, the General Staff had concluded that local units such as the police and the technical emergency service were so infiltrated with Nazis that the army could not control a Hitler Putsch.

When no minister challenged the army study, Papen hastened to the President's office. Hindenburg, drained by the events of the past day, listened to his complaints in silence. "My dear Papen," he said in a voice that had lost its confident ring, "you'll consider me a cad if I change my mind now. But I am now too old, at the end of my life, to take the responsibility for a civil war. We'll have to let Herr von Schleicher try his luck in God's name."

Rising with the help of his cane, Hindenburg slowly approached Papen and shook his hand. Papen was moved to see "two great tears" roll down the Old Gentleman's cheeks. A few hours later he sent a photograph of himself to Papen as a parting gift. On it was written: "I had a comrade!" the title of a famous soldier song.

When Schleicher appeared before the President and was requested to form a government he made a show of protest: "I am the last horse in your stable and ought to be kept in reserve." Only the threat of resignation by Hindenburg brought Schleicher to accept the appointment. So he said and perhaps he was truly reluctant. He greeted congratulations with a thin smile and another quotation, this one in Latin: "We who are about to die salute you."

And so on December, 2, 1932, Kurt von Schleicher became the first general to be appointed Chancellor since the man who replaced Bismarck in 1890. One of his first acts was to invite Gregor Strasser to his home (they had met previously in a dentist's residence) and offer to make him Vice-Chancellor and Minister President of Prussia. The proposition appealed to Strasser but he was loyal to Hitler and said he must first check with his chief. What he didn't add was that the problem was getting through the protective circle of sycophants and adulators which had formed around the Führer and seemed to control him. "Along comes Hindenburg," Strasser had recently complained to Frank, "a man of honor, who honestly and decently offers him a place in the government, and there stands the *'wahnfriedische'* Lohengrin-Hitler with his darkly menacing boys. Frank, I see black: Göring is a brutal egotist who cares nothing for Germany as long as he becomes something. Goebbels is a limping devil and basically two-faced, Röhm is a pig. This is the Old Guard of the Führer. It is terrible!"

Someone in Papen's office learned about the secret Schleicher-Strasser meeting and told a correspondent, who informed Hanfstaengl, who in turn passed the story on to Hitler. Thus Papen—or a Papen associate—paid back Schleicher in his own coin. The immediate victim, however, was Strasser, who had been dealing with Schleicher in good faith on the Führer's behalf, with the conviction that the best way to keep the party from disintegrating was to get into power at once—even at the price of coalition.

While Hitler, whose suspicions of Strasser had been inflamed by Goebbels, understandably took it as a betrayal, more moderate advisers were inclined to consider Schleicher's latest offer—this time of the vice-chancellorship to the Führer. At a stormy conference of party leaders at the Kaiserhof on December 5 Strasser begged Hitler to accept. But Goebbels and Göring vehemently opposed such a deal and Hitler went along with them. Strasser gave warning that Schleicher would merely dissolve the Reichstag if NSDAP support was not forthcoming. But Hitler, still rankled by Strasser's "betrayal," refused to discuss the matter further.

Two days later Strasser again saw the Führer at the Kaiserhof. This time Hitler openly accused him of treason. Reportedly Strasser replied, "Herr Hitler, I am no more a traitor than any other willing messenger. My plan is to prevent a further deterioration of the party, not to bring it about." Too angry to find the right phrase, Strasser turned, slammed the door and took a taxi to the Hotel Excelsior. Alone in his room he fumed with indignation but he waited until the next morning, December 8, to pen a letter resigning his party offices on the grounds that the Führer no longer trusted him. No call for open revolt, it urged all party officials to remain in their posts. Strasser could not bring himself to deliver the message to Hitler in person but sent it by mail, then waited next to the telephone for a call.

The letter landed at the Kaiserhof, in Goebbels' words, "like a bombshell." Hitler went into such shock that he was momentarily unable to make any decisions. Nor could he pick up the phone and plead with Strasser, who had certainly left the door open for discussion by neither surrendering his seat in the Reichstag nor revoking his party membership. When no message came from the Kaiserhof, Strasser packed his bags and set off for the railroad station. After drinking beer with a friend he took the night train to Munich.

Hitler spent the evening in the Goebbels apartment. "It is difficult to be cheerful," Goebbels noted in his diary. "We are all depressed, above all because of the danger of the whole party falling apart, and all our work having been in vain." At 2 A.M. Robert Ley phoned to report that there was a marked feeling of uncertainty and agitation in party circles. He urged the Führer to return to the Kaiserhof at once. Hitler did so but the arrival of the early morning paper with headlines on Strasser's resignation, set off a tempestuous scene. Hitler was convinced that Strasser had leaked the story to the "Jewish newspapers." He stammered that Gregor had "stabbed him in the back five minutes before the final victory," then was silenced by his own tears.

"Such contemptible behaviour eludes the understanding of us all," wrote Goebbels. "Treason! Treason! Treason! . . . For hours the Führer paces anxiously up and down the hotel room. . . . Once he stops and says: 'If the party should ever break up, I will make an end of things in three minutes with a pistol.'"

Finally someone suggested that the most sensible course was to summon Strasser and patch up the quarrel. Whereupon Hitler ordered his chauffeur, Schreck, to find Strasser "at any price." But he was already at his apartment in Munich, hastily packing to leave for a holiday in Italy. To a friend, who happened to drop by, Strasser said in a resigned voice: "I am a man marked by death." He warned his friend to stay away from the apartment. "Whatever happens, mark what I say: From now on Germany is in the hands of an Austrian, who is a congenital liar, a former officer, who is a pervert, and a clubfoot. And I tell you the last is the worst of them all. This is Satan in human form." Although it was at least the second time Strasser had used such words to damn the Hitler inner circle, he still revered the Führer. Only recently he had told Rosenberg, "I fought as one of Hitler's men and as one of Hitler's men I want someday to go to my grave."

That same day party leaders and Gauleiters assembled in the palace of the president of the Reichstag to hear a declaration attacking Strasser. Still in an emotional state, Hitler stammered with a sob that he had been shocked by Strasser's treachery. According to Goebbels, the assemblage "burst into a spontaneous ovation for the leader. All shake hands with him, promising to carry on until the very end and not to renounce the great Idea, come what may. Strasser now is completely isolated, a dead man."

Strasser's drastic action was no revolt, only a personal attempt to save the Führer from men such as Goebbels. He represented no faction and no important party member followed him into oblivion. Nor was any purge necessary. Hitler merely announced that Strasser had started an authorized three-week sick leave, and once it was known that the Führer had withdrawn his confidence in the traitor the general membership withdrew theirs.

Even so Hitler remained shaken by the desertion of one of his paladins and did his utmost to wipe out the memory of Strasser. In mid-December he issued two long memoranda designed to decentralize the latter's administrative empire. Never again would he allow one man to hold such power in the party. Most of Strasser's political functions went to Hess since he was "most familiar with [Hitler's] basic ideas . . . and his intentions."

While the Führer had regained control of the party, the membership remained uneasy and demoralized. Their political future was bleak. "It is hard to hold the SA and the party officials to a clear course," Goebbels confided to his diary on December 15, and on the twenty-fourth, "I sit here all alone and worry about many things. The past is difficult and the future is cloudy and dark. The terrible loneliness overwhelms me with hopelessness. All possibilities and hopes have disappeared."

Hitler too had fallen into a depression that was undoubtedly intensified by his usual Christmas season despondency. (Later Hitler confided to his valet that he could not abide Yuletide decorations. His mother, he explained, had died near a lighted Christmas tree.) "I have given up all hope," he wrote to Frau Wagner after thanking her for a present. "Nothing will ever come of my dreams." He had no hope left, his opponents were too powerful. "As soon as I am sure that everything is lost you know what I'll do. I was always determined to do it. I cannot accept defeat. I will stick to my word and end my life with a bullet."

Enemies were already celebrating his political demise on the assumption that he had at last overreached himself. "Hitler is finished—not as an agitator or as a leader of an aggressive minority, but as a possible dictator." So wrote William Bullitt in an eleven-page report to President-elect Franklin Roosevelt. "Hitler's influence is waning so fast that the Government is no longer afraid of the growth of the Nazi movement."

At the same time, according to Müllern-Schönhausen, Hitler once more sought help from Hanussen. The famous seer cast a concise horoscope indicating that, although Hitler's constellation was favorable for the near future, there were still a few hindrances to his rise to power. Only one thing, Hanussen reportedly told Hitler, would remove these hindrances—a mandrake (a root in the shape of a man) found in a butcher's yard in the town of Hitler's birthplace by the light of the full moon. Hanussen himself volunteered for this bizarre mission and is said to have reported back to the Haus Wachenfeld in Obersalzberg on New Year's Day, 1933. With appropriate ceremony he presented the mandrake to the Führer that morning along with a rhymed prediction that Hitler's rise to power would begin on January 30:

> The way to the goal is still blocked,
> The right helpers not yet gathered,
> But in three days—from three countries,
> Through the bank everything will change!
> And then on the day before the end of the month,
> You stand at your goal and a turning point!
> No eagle could carry you on your path,
> The termites had to gnaw your way!
> To the ground falls what was rotten and withered.
> It already creaks in the beams!

If Hitler gave credence to this prediction—which was publicized and ridiculed—he would not have been the first famous European to take such matters seriously. The astrologer Louis Gauric had informed Pope Leo X that he would succeed to the pontificate; Nostradamus correctly predicted the death of Henri I; and Pierre Le Clerc reportedly convinced Napoleon that he would be emperor. In any case, the Führer must surely have been startled by the third and fourth lines in the Hanussen poem—for he had recently accepted an invitation to meet secretly in three days with former Chancellor von Papen, at the home of a banker, Baron Kurt von Schröder, one of those wealthy men who had earlier petitioned Hindenburg to appoint him Chancellor. A logical explanation of this explicit forecast is that Hanussen (as his more cynical contemporaries believed) was a clever fraud who based his predictions on information from reliable sources. It should be noted that "through the bank" is a literal translation of *Durch die Bank*, which is also an idiom, meaning "across the board," and the line could be read: "Everything will change radically." Perhaps the wary Hanussen was using this ambiguous term deliberately, to cover several possibilities.

That evening Hitler attended a performance in Munich of *Die Meistersinger* with the Hesses and Eva Braun. Later they all had coffee at the Hanfstaengl home. "Hitler was in his most benign mood," wrote Hanfstaengl. "It took us right back to the twenties when we had first met him. The conductor that evening had been Hans Knappertsbusch and Hitler had not liked his *tempi* and interpretation and was expatiating on the subject. He could really do so with good sense and would hum or whistle many of the passages, the words of which he knew by heart, in order to show what they meant." The Führer continued to reminisce about the old days in a charming manner and then, before leaving, signed his name in the guest book, pointedly adding the date. Then he looked up to Hanfstaengl and, with suppressed excitement, said, "This year belongs to us. I will guarantee you that in writing."

7

Hitler's meeting with Papen at Baron von Schröder's home in Cologne took place as scheduled on January 4. It was supposed to be secret but despite elaborate precautions by all parties a reporter from a Berlin newspaper (he had bribed a member of Hitler's bodyguard) was on hand to take pictures of Hitler and Papen separately entering the Schröder mansion. At the outset of the two-hour conference the latter suggested that the Schleicher regime be replaced by a Hitler-Papen government in which both would be equal. Hitler replied to this startling proposition at length: If he were made Chancellor he would have to be the actual head of government; he would accept some Papen men as ministers but only if they agreed to his policy of eliminating Social Democrats, Communists and Jews from leading positions in the nation. The two men, according to Schröder, "reached agreement in principle" and while leaving the house cordially shook hands.

When Schleicher was shown a picture of this handclasp he stormed to the presidential palace to charge Papen with treachery. He asked Hindenburg never to receive the former Chancellor again except in his presence. But the Old Gentleman was too fond of the dashing ex-cavalryman to believe him capable of deceit. Instead he authorized Papen to continue to meet with Hitler informally while instructing his secretary to keep these negotiations secret from Chancellor von Schleicher.

A few days later Hindenburg further reduced Schleicher in stature. Instead of supporting his proposed confiscation of bankrupt estates in eastern Germany, the President backed his own fellow Junkers. While it is true that Schleicher had been treated like a subordinate, he committed a grievous political mistake by overreacting. He refused to have any more dealings with the rebellious Junkers and in declaring open war on them not only filled Hindenburg's anterooms with angry representatives of the Junker families demanding dissolution of the Schleicher government but brought upon himself the ire of the military caste. The general should have kept in mind that the Junkers and the officer corps had been bound in common cause for two hundred years.

The beneficiary of his ineptitude was Adolf Hitler and he used the rising tide of discontent to good advantage in his appeals to the voters of Lippe. He was throwing all the weight of the party into this minor campaign as though it were another national election. His purpose was to win a victory of such proportions that he could negotiate with Hindenburg and Papen from strength. Gambling that he could come back from the November defeat and regain his mass popularity, Hitler spoke in practically every Lippe village and town. Wherever he went he was greeted with enthusiasm and on January 15 the power of his personal appeal was evident when he won 39.6 per cent of the popular vote, a gain of 17 per cent. Hitler was in Weimar on election day, "his face beaming like that of a small boy," and he termed the victory "a success whose importance it is not possible to overestimate." He felt so confident that the following day he brought the conflict with Strasser (who had returned from vacation in Italy) into the open. In a three-hour speech to his Gauleiters he charged Strasser with treason and wanted it known publicly that he was not only through with him but was now prepared to "break the necks of all party defeatists." The audience responded with "delirious ovations." Although a group of party dissidents were prepared to follow Strasser in a showdown with the Führer, he himself had no relish for a fight. Broken, Strasser resigned his seat in the Reichstag and drove back to Munich.

With Strasser's final exit from the political scene, Hitler felt so secure that he was in a mood to compromise when he saw Papen again on the evening of January 18. This time they met at the home of Joachim von Ribbentrop in the fashionable Berlin suburb of Dahlem. To ensure secrecy Papen was brought to the meeting by the Ribbentrop chauffeur and Hitler's car was driven into the garage so he, Röhm and Himmler could surreptitiously enter the house through the garden.

"Hitler insists on being Chancellor," wrote Frau von Ribbentrop in her notes of this conference. "Papen again considers this impossible. His influence with Hindenburg was not strong enough to effect this. Hitler makes no further arrangements for talks. Joachim tentatively suggests a meeting between Hitler and Hindenburg's son." The discussion ended inconclusively and if Papen was disconcerted by Hitler's inflexible manner, their hostess was not. She was by now as impressed with him as her husband and thought he was "a marvelous man, a true gentleman."

8

With each day Schleicher's position was becoming more untenable and by January 20 he had succeeded in antagonizing almost every party from right to left. His extremity was Papen's opportunity. Ever since his resignation the ex-Chancellor had regularly visited his neighbors—Hindenburg and son—bringing gaiety and frivolity into their dour household. But today he took the short walk through the snowy gardens of the chancellery for a definite purpose. Instead of amusing the President he informed him in detail of the meetings with Hitler and the possible amalgamation of conservative parties. Why not, he suggested persuasively, make Hitler Chancellor—so long as policies were dictated by himself?

The greatest obstacle to this was not the President but his son, who openly disliked the Führer. But Oskar's feelings were apparently based more on snobbery than ideology and he accepted an invitation to discuss their differences at the luxurious Ribbentrop villa on Sunday evening, January 22.

It was decided that Oskar should bring along his father's state secretary, Meissner, and to keep the parley secret from Chancellor von Schleicher, these two started the evening in a box at the Prussian State Opera House where an early work of Wagner's, *Das Liebesverbot*, was being performed. An icy wind was blowing down the Unter den Linden as the party arrived at the theater. One of the main topics of conversation before the curtain went up was the Nazi demonstration held a few hours earlier in front of Communist headquarters. Schleicher had permitted a parade of 20,000 Brownshirts while banning a counterdemonstration by the Reds, and then was forced to send out police to protect the marchers with armored cars and machine guns.

During the intermission Oskar and his wife made themselves conspicuous by greeting many acquaintances. But when the lights went down for the final act Hindenburg and Meissner left by a side entrance, leaving their wives behind. They hailed a taxi, giving their destination only when inside. They saw no car following them and assumed they had tricked Schleicher's spies but to be on the safe side they got out some distance from the Ribbentrop home and trudged through the snow. After some difficulty they located the Ribbentrop gate.

In the salon they found Papen, Hitler, Göring and Frick. The atmosphere was stiff and, after some awkward small talk, Hitler abruptly suggested to Oskar that they retire into the next room. Before Meissner could say anything the two were out of the room and Ribbentrop had closed the door behind them. According to young Hindenburg, Hitler dominated the conversation: he alone could save Germany from the Reds; he alone could be a strong Chancellor since no other government could operate without National Socialist support.

After an hour the two men returned, solemn-faced and the entire company moved into the dining room where a simple one-pot meal of peas and bacon was served from a silver bowl by a gloved servant. Hitler drank mineral water, the others champagne. Hindenburg and Meissner, the last to come, were the first to go and as their taxi plunged into the swirling snow Meissner noticed that his companion was "extremely silent, and the only remark which he made was that it could not be helped—the Nazis had to be taken into the government. My impression was that Hitler succeeded in getting him under his spell." It may have been simpler than that. Hitler could have threatened to make a public scandal of an open secret in high places: the Eastern Aid Fund had been put into effect six years earlier to help the Junkers retain their properties. President von Hindenburg had not only profited handsomely by this act (one reported figure was 620,000 marks) but had already turned over his estate to Oskar to avoid death duties. Nor had conveyance fees been paid. These were grounds for impeachment, and even if no conviction ensued, the name of Hindenburg would be besmirched.

Papen had noticed the impression Hitler had made on Oskar and after the latter's departure pledged his allegiance to the Führer. He promised to support him for Chancellor, vowing he would under no circumstances accept the appointment himself. The clandestine meeting ended with the Hitler party furtively disappearing into the garage. But Schleicher's spies had not been fooled. The next morning the Chancellor phoned Meissner with a sarcastic question: how had he liked last night's one-pot supper? Being a master of intrigue, the general knew he must act quickly. He told Hindenburg that he needed a "military dictatorship" to control the Nazis and tried to persuade him to dissolve the Reichstag and suspend elections. But Hindenburg, weary of Schleicher's interminable schemes, refused to authorize any such emergency measures.

When word of the proposed military dictatorship leaked out, both the Social Democrat and Center parties branded Schleicher as an enemy of the people. His plan was not only unconstitutional but "open high treason." In a futile attempt to placate these dissidents he made another blunder by stating publicly that he had no intention of violating the constitution. This only succeeded in incensing Hugenberg and his Nationalist Party, who promptly abandoned Schleicher.

The sudden turn of events in Hitler's favor brought him back to Berlin on January 27, but then almost immediately he became so frustrated by the intrigues in the capital that he told Ribbentrop he was going to leave. "Joachim proposes link-up with Hugenberg for a national front," Frau von Ribbentrop noted. "Hitler declares that he has said all there is to say to the field marshal, and does not know what to add. Joachim persuades Hitler that this last attempt should be made, and that the situation is by no means hopeless."

Hitler reluctantly agreed to talk with Papen that evening but, as soon as the meeting was arranged, changed his mind on the grounds that he was in no position to talk freely. He announced testily that this time he was really leaving the capital but did agree to let Ribbentrop see the ex-Chancellor on his behalf. That evening Ribbentrop somehow convinced Papen that a Hitler chancellorship was the only solution; and the next morning Papen passed on this conviction to Hindenburg. The field marshal wavered. For months he had been inundated with requests to appoint Hitler, and lately his own son had come to the same conclusion. Though his own distaste for the "Czech corporal," as he persisted in calling him, was as strong as ever, it was apparent that the Old Gentleman was at last in the mood to accept Hitler.

At the moment Schleicher was convening with his cabinet members: he told them that he proposed asking Hindenburg once more for an order to dissolve the Reichstag and if this failed he would be forced to resign. He temporarily adjourned the meeting to see the President. It was a short interview. Would Hindenburg grant a dissolution decree? "Nein!" In that case, said Schleicher, the only alternative was a Hitler government. Hindenburg muttered that the Schleicher government hadn't been able to win a majority but perhaps he himself could find one that could stabilize Germany. He accepted the resignation of the cabinet and, in an exasperated aside, muttered that he didn't want to argue any more about it.

Hindenburg's mind seemed to be wandering. "Whether what I am going to do now is right, my dear Schleicher," he said, "I don't know; but I shall know soon enough when I am up there." He pointed heavenward. "I already have one foot in the grave and I am not sure that I shall not regret this action in heaven later on."

"After this breach of trust, sir," was the bitter answer, "I am not sure that you will go to heaven."

Before the day was out, Papen was back in the presidential office along with Oskar and Meissner. Once again the elder Hindenburg suggested Papen take the chancellorship but all three advisers reiterated that Hitler was the only possible choice. "It is my unpleasant duty then to appoint this fellow Hitler as Chancellor?" grumbled the Old Gentleman. But he insisted that the new government include General Werner von Blomberg (whom he described as a "nonpolitical passionate soldier with pleasant manners") as Minister of Defense and Papen as Vice-Chancellor. The problem was to get Hitler to accept these appointments.

The next morning, a Sunday, Papen saw Hitler. He was agreeable— but had his own demands: new general elections and an enabling law which would give him as Chancellor authority exceeding that of a former Kaiser. It was early afternoon by the time Papen finally reported to Hindenburg that all parties were agreed on the new government. Only then did he mention Hitler's demand for new elections and he made it sound reasonable. He clinched the point with Hitler's promise that these would indeed be the *last elections*. Out of relief that the constitutional crisis was at last ending, neither the President nor his protégé was at all struck by the implications of this promise.

When Göring got the good news he rushed off to be the first to bring it to the Führer, who was having coffee at the Goebbels apartment. For a long time, according to the Goebbels diary, the three men were in such ecstasy that they said nothing. Then they rose and shook hands emotionally. A homey touch was added by Magda Goebbels, who entered with a tray of freshly baked nut cakes just as the three men formed a circle by grasping hands. The celebration was brought to an abrupt end by the appearance of a messenger from Schleicher who warned of a possible military uprising if Hindenburg named the Führer. Hitler and Göring reacted with alarm. Neither thought of checking with trusted adherents at the Potsdam and Berlin barracks to find out if the troops were actually on alert. Instead, Hitler telephoned the commander of the Berlin SA, ordering him to alert all local Brownshirts. Who else had to be warned? asked Hitler and gave the answer himself: Papen, Oskar von Hindenburg and Meissner. While Goebbels and Göring tumbled out of the apartment to carry out these missions, Hitler phoned a Nazi police major, instructing him "to prepare for a sudden seizure of the Wilhelmstrasse by six police battalions." Finally he sent word to the Defense Minister-elect, General von Blomberg, who was taking the night train from Geneva, to proceed at once from the Berlin railroad station to the presidential palace to be sworn in—and thus be prepared to suppress any Putsch.

The rumor of a military coup spread rapidly through government circles, causing considerable panic in the capital throughout the night. The next morning—Monday, January 30—panic was succeeded by a monumental argument in Papen's residence. Hugenberg, the Nationalist Party leader, violently objected to Hitler's demand for new elections and it appeared as if the new government was already doomed. Hugenberg wrangled on at such length that Papen finally exclaimed in desperation, "If the new government is not formed by eleven o'clock, the army is going to march. Schleicher may establish a military dictatorship." And to the query where he got this intelligence, Papen impatiently shouted, "From Hindenburg, Jr.!"

Just then there was a loud cry of "Heil!" from the crowd outside the Papen villa and Hitler entered with Göring. It was 10:35 A.M. and Papen suggested they all follow him to the chancellery. They paraded through the snow-covered chancellery garden and up to Meissner's office. Here they met other ministerial candidates and while they all were waiting to be brought into the President's office Papen raised the question of elections.

"Elections?" Hugenberg testily declared that he thought the question had been settled. Hitler drew him aside but the Führer's considerable powers of persuasion only provoked Hugenberg to vociferous objections. Hitler tried to pacify the old man by seizing his hand and promising to make no changes in the cabinet no matter how the elections came out. The answer was still no.

At that moment Meissner appeared. "Gentlemen, it is five minutes past the appointed time," he said. "The President likes punctuality." Papen saw his coalition breaking up at the threshold of success. "Herr Geheimrat," he begged, "do you want to risk the national unity which has finally been achieved after so many difficult negotiations? You cannot possibly doubt the solemn word of a German man!"

Hugenberg continued to argue bitterly until the harried Meissner rushed out again, watch in hand. "The President requests you not to keep him waiting any longer," he announced. "It is now eleven-fifteen. The Old Gentleman may retire at any moment!"

Once more Hitler seized Hugenberg's hand and this time promised to consult the Center and Bavarian People's parties to ensure the widest possible basis for parliamentary majority. The threat of Meissner's watch probably helped induce Hugenberg to say that he would leave the decision to Hindenburg. Hitler hastily agreed to this and Göring boomed out, "Now, everything is in order!" and they all filed into the President's office.

Hindenburg was so irked he didn't personally offer the post of Chancellor to Hitler—the only Chancellor so slighted. Nor did he greet the new cabinet with a welcoming speech or even outline what tasks lay before them. The swearing-in ceremony was finished rapidly in the style of a shotgun wedding. But Hitler could not let such a historical moment pass in silence and, to everyone's surprise, began a speech. After solemnly vowing he would observe the Weimar constitution, he promised to find a majority in the parliament so that the President would no longer have to sign emergency decrees. Further, he would solve the economic crisis and unite a Germany torn by bitterness and debate. There was a pause for an appropriate response from Hindenburg but the field marshal would only say, as if dismissing the troops, "And now, gentlemen, forward with God!"

Hanussen's prediction, if it was one, had come true. The man who had failed to graduate from high school, who had been refused admission to the Academy of Fine Arts and who had lived as a tramp on the streets of Vienna was Chancellor of Germany on the thirtieth day of January 1933. As he left the room in a daze, Hitler caught sight of Hoffmann, whom he had brought along to take pictures of the ceremony. Clapping his head, he exclaimed, "Good God, I forgot all about you, Hoffmann! And now, I'm afraid, it's too late!" In his haste to get back to the Kaiserhof, Hitler left his new governmental colleagues with scarcely a word. He stood up in his car as it crept slowly through the mass of delirious adherents who were shouting themselves hoarse.

"We've done it!" he announced triumphantly to the party faithful waiting for him at the hotel. All crowded around and he shook the hands of maids and waiters as well as those of rank and wealth.

The news was received throughout Germany with mixed feelings. The liberals were horrified but to the average German anything was better than the parliamentary shambles of the past year. And for many young idealists, the dispossessed, the embittered patriots and the racists there was unrestrained joy. Their dreams were coming true. In Munich Egon Hanfstaengl rushed into his classroom, bursting with the news. "Kurt!" he shouted to a friend. "We've done it! We're in power!" Then he remembered that Kurt was a Jew. Kurt smiled a little thinly before replying: "I'm glad for you. I wish I could be one of you."

No group was more surprised at the sudden ascension of Adolf Hitler than the Berlin Brownshirts. They had been living in poverty for years, risking their lives on the streets of the capital, often in opposition to their Führer's wishes. Now at one stroke their dream was realized but it was only through the newspapers that most of them learned there would be a torchlight parade that evening.

Every able-bodied SA and SS man was out in uniform. Those who expected the usual trouble with the police were surprised by smiles from their old enemies, some of whom now wore swastikas. Carrying torches, the storm troopers started from the Tiergarten at dusk, joined by thousands of Stahlhelm men, and passed under the Brandenburg Gate in disciplined columns to the blare of martial music. Hour after hour they marched down the Wilhelmstrasse shouting the "Horst Wessel Lied" and other fighting songs. First they paid homage to Hindenburg, who stood at a window of the presidential palace and, moments later, to Hitler, who looked down fondly from a window of the chancellery.

Young men perched in trees along the Wilhelmstrasse; boys clung to the iron fences like "bunches of grapes." The excitement was intensified by the winter darkness as the stream of flares glowed hypnotically and the drums beat thunderously. It had all been staged by the master showman, Goebbels, and Hitler himself was so impressed that he turned and asked, "How on earth did he conjure up all these thousands of torches in the space of a few hours?" The little doctor had also managed to take over the radio stations and the country was being treated to a running eyewitness account of the procession.

Papen watched the marchers over Hitler's shoulder. He noticed that as they approached Hindenburg there were respectful shouts but the sight of Hitler brought frantic acclaim. "The contrast was most marked and seemed to emphasize the transition from a moribund regime to the new revolutionary forces. . . . It was an extraordinary experience, and the endless repetition of the triumphal cry: 'Heil, Heil, Sieg Heil!' rang in my ears like a tocsin." As Hitler turned to speak to Papen, his voice was choked. "What an immense task we have set ourselves, Herr von Papen—we must never part until our work is accomplished."

Hans Frank, the lawyer, also stood behind Hitler on that intoxicating night. "God knows our hearts were pure that day," he stated not long before he was hanged, "and if anyone had told us of the events to come, no one would have believed it, least of all I. It was a day of glory and happiness." Tears of joy ran down the cheeks of the celebrants down below.

"Everyone felt the same—that things will get better," remembered one Brownshirt who had revolted with Stennes. "Although realistically there was no reason for them to believe things would improve, they believed it. They had hope again. It was remarkable. I don't think that Germany will ever again find another man who could inspire as much hope, trust and love as Hitler did at that moment."

"Some of the uncanny feeling of that night remains with me even today," wrote Melita Maschmann, who had been taken to the parade by her parents. "The crashing tread of the feet, the sombre pomp of the red and black flags, the flickering light from the torches on the faces and the songs with melodies that were at once aggressive and sentimental." To most foreign observers it was an ominous sight. "The river of fire flowed past the French Embassy," wrote Ambassador François-Poncet, "whence, with heavy heart and filled with foreboding, I watched its luminous wake."

Hitler had a late supper with Hess, Göring, Goebbels, Röhm and Frank in a small private room. Compulsively he talked on and on. "Some foreign source today called me 'anti-Christ,'" he said. "The only kind of anti I am is anti-Lenin." According to Frank, Hitler went on to say he hoped Hindenburg could be won over to his side. "The Old Gentleman liked it very much when I said to him today that I would serve him as Chancellor as loyally as in the days as a soldier when he was my hero." Without respite the talk switched to Communism. "This evening marks the end of the so-called 'Red Berlin.' People are only Red when they have no other way. Those who count on the so-called intelligence of a people are always caught short with the masses. The emotions of a people are like those of a woman, more or less, I would say." Hitler was still talking as they strolled through the garden. "This chancellery," he said, "is like a cigar box. A very unimpressive place for a reception. We will change all that."

That night an exultant Goebbels wrote in his diary: "It is almost like a dream . . . a fairy tale. . . . The new Reich has been born. Fourteen years of work have been crowned with victory. The German revolution has begun!" Few Germans that evening realized this, and perhaps none recalled the prophetic words written by Heinrich Heine, a Jew, not quite a century earlier: "German thunder is truly German; it takes its time. But it will come, and when it crashes it will crash as nothing in history crashed before. The hour will come. . . . A drama will be performed which will make the French Revolution seem like a pretty idyll. . . . Never doubt it; the hour will come."

Chapter Eleven

AN UNGUARDED HOUR
1933–JUNE 1934

> "Neither a nation nor a woman is forgiven for *an unguarded hour* in which the first adventurer who comes along can sweep them off their feet and possess them."

KARL MARX

1

The next morning Frau Goebbels brought flowers to Hitler. He was looking out the window of his room in the Kaiserhof. Slowly he turned and, "with an almost solemn gesture," took the bouquet. "These are the first flowers, and you are the first woman to congratulate me," he murmured, according to her reverent account. After moments of silence he said as if continuing a monologue, "Now the world must realize why I couldn't be Vice-Chancellor. How long my own party members did not understand me!" After another long silence she started for the door. "Yes," she heard him softly exclaim, "now I must remain by myself for some time."

He regarded what had happened as fate, another step on a path long since mapped out. But those who had put him in power were convinced he was merely their dupe. Papen, for one, boasted to his circle: "We have hired him for ourselves," and then reassured a critical friend: "What do you want? I have Hindenburg's confidence. Within two months we will have pushed Hitler so far in the corner that he'll squeak."

The junkers, as embodied by Papen, thought they had bought a restitution of authoritarian rule but Hitler had no intention of being their puppet and at once began laying the foundation for a dictatorship. First he dismissed out of hand a list of questions and demands submitted by the Center Party with the comment that, since negotiations with that party had failed, new elections were necessary. Then, through Papen, he persuaded Hindenburg to dissolve the parliament.

Few realized the import of these first steps. Editorials in the liberal bourgeois papers foresaw no revolutionary changes. After all there were only two other Nazis in Hitler's cabinet—Göring and Frick. "The make-up of the cabinet shows that Herr Hitler had to accept significant restrictions," pontificated the *Frankfurter Zeitung* that day—and forty-eight hours later remarked that "it has become all too evident that the government revolves around Hugenberg, not the Chancellor." Even the Social Democrats were not alarmed since it was widely believed that Hitler could never get the two-thirds majority to change the Weimar constitution.

A similar view was held by the New York *Times*: "The composition of the Cabinet leaves Herr Hitler no scope for the gratification of his dictatorial ambition." And the British ambassador reported: "On the whole the press has taken the appointment of Herr Hitler to the chancellorship with almost philosophic calm," and the "populace took the news phlegmatically."

While all these observers were assuring the world of Hitler's impotence, he was hiding his revolutionary intentions behind a flow of inspirational but conservative phrases in a radio address to the voters on the first of February. He made it clear that he wanted only a return to the old virtues of the past. He said nothing of his plans for the Jews, said nothing, in fact, that offended or alarmed the average citizen.

During the speech the American chargé d'affaires in Berlin was dining with one of those kingmakers who had helped put Hitler in power. Hjalmar Schacht, president of the Reichsbank, revealed that he was the Führer's court financial and economic adviser, and then assured the American that the Nazis would "make no attempt to carry out their well-known demagogic reforms" and that consequently "all big business viewed the new regime with sympathy."

While the last remark was an exaggeration, Hitler would not have been Chancellor without the support of industrialists and the military. The majority in the officer corps agreed with Karl Dönitz, a rising man in the navy, who felt it was simply a choice between Hitler and the Reds.

The support of the military was as self-serving as that of the industrialists, and Hitler knew it. His opinion of generals was not high. "Before
I became Chancellor," he admitted years later, "I thought the General Staff
was like a mastiff which had to be held tight by the collar because it
threatened all and sundry." His experiences with generals to date had not
been happy ones: Lossow had "betrayed" him in Munich and Schleicher
had tried to keep him out of the chancellery. But now that he was in
power he was determined to make his peace with the military and enlist
them in the regeneration of Germany.

He took the first step on the evening of his fourth day as Chancellor
by accepting an invitation to dine at the home of General von Hammerstein, who had been outspoken in his contempt for the Nazis. The party
had been arranged by the new Minister of Defense, General von Blomberg, and its purpose was to introduce the Führer to leaders in the armed
forces. After dinner he rose to speak. At first he was stiff before such company, as he told of the disastrous economic problems facing the nation.
The answer was not a renewed export drive since production exceeded
demand throughout the world and Germany's former customers had developed their own markets. Unemployment and depression, he concluded,
would continue until Germany recovered her former position in the world.

Interest in the room was aroused. It was a solution most of them
cherished. Hitler went on to say that pacifism, Marxism and that "cancer-
ous growth, democracy," must be eradicated. Rearmament was the first requirement for a resurgent Germany and once the Fatherland had regained
its power there would come "the conquest of the land in the East and its
ruthless Germanization." Lest this revelation of his blueprint for the future cause apprehension, Hitler promised that his listeners need not concern themselves over the domestic or foreign policy. The army would not
be used to deal with unrest at home and should devote itself for the next
few years "to the operation of its main objective, training for the defense
of the Fatherland in the case of aggression." As reassurance regarding the
SA, he added that the army would be "the sole bearer of arms, and its
structure would remain unaltered."

Admiral Erich Raeder was favorably impressed and assumed everyone
else present shared his feeling. But Generals Werner von Fritsch and Friedrich Fromm were apprehensive of the talk of aggression and General Ritter
von Leeb had the impression Hitler was trying to bribe them. "A businessman whose wares are any good," he later observed sarcastically, "does not
need to boost them in the loudest tones of a market crier."

The response was mixed, but Hitler had won over a number of new
adherents. Those who hoped to transform the new government into a mil-

itary dictatorship as the first step to a restored monarchy were ready to sanction the National Socialist reforms and many of those with qualms were inclined to go along out of respect for Field Marshal von Hindenburg.

Using the emergency powers of the constitution that had once felt his scorn, Hitler next pushed through a decree, "for the protection of the German people," controlling political meetings and restricting the press. Neither Papen nor any of his colleagues in the cabinet protested regulations that enabled Hitler to paralyze rival parties and to control public opinion. Faced by such unanimity, Hindenburg also succumbed and signed the decree. This was followed shortly by an emergency decree replacing the political regime in Prussia with one of his own choice. The first protests were answered by reason—Papen as the newly appointed Prussian Minister President could surely control the new Minister of the Interior, Göring—but the fact remained that Hitler had accomplished his second step toward dictatorship.

There was a new elite in Germany. The borough president of Hamburg came from a notions shop, one of hundreds who had risen overnight from the lower middle class. Teachers, lawyers and businessmen were also among the leaders. Never before had so many men of modest means been thrust into political prominence. These were the old Nazi fighters whose dedication to the movement and Hitler was now drawing dividends.

Perhaps no other German Chancellor had been so well prepared for assumption of leadership as Hitler, who had regarded himself as Führer for some time. The same could not be said for the party. It had been held together by his magnetism and the dream of power and jobs. This new elite did manage to carry out a National Socialist revolution on the local level but only because of the complacency of the conservatives and the confusion among liberal and leftist opponents.

While the rank and file were clumsily organizing the villages, towns and provinces, their Führer was establishing authority over his disarrayed opponents. At first many misread his diffident, somewhat embarrassed manner with strangers as a sign of weakness. But in short order he gained the upper hand over those who underrated him. "In cabinet meetings," recalled Finance Minister Count Lutz Schwerin von Krosigk, who had been a Rhodes scholar, "one could not but recognize and admire the qualities which gave him mastery of all discussions: his infallible memory, which enabled him to answer with the utmost precision questions on the remotest problems under consideration; his presence of mind in discussions; the clarity with which he could reduce the most intricate question to a simple—sometimes too simple—formula; his skill in summing up concisely the results of a long debate; and his cleverness in approaching a well-known and long-discussed problem from a new angle."

Schwerin von Krosigk and other governmental officials had never before been subjected to such a dynamic personality and it was no wonder they succumbed. His ascendancy over these men of substance was portrayed by a picture in the *Illustrierte Beobachter* that month. No longer was he clad in an ill-fitting suit, no longer did he slouch in wrinkled trench coat, whip in hand. Now smiling and confident, clad in a soft overcoat of good cut and quality, he was the picture of radiant confidence.

2

Despite his personal success, the fate of the Brown Revolution was still in doubt at the end of the first six weeks of power. The emergency deposition of the Prussian government was causing grave concern in other states. By the middle of February Göring had drastically purged the Prussian police of men he could not rely on and issued an order instructing his police force "to avoid at all costs anything suggestive of hostility to the SA, SS and Stahlhelm, as these organizations contain the most constructive national elements. . . . It is the business of the police to abet every form of national propaganda." This was followed by an ominous note to the effect that the police should act decisively against "organizations hostile to the state" and should not hesitate to use their firearms. On the contrary, they would be punished if they failed "in their duty." He was declaring open season on Communists, Marxists and their sympathizers.

Seven of the smaller states were already as hamstrung politically as Prussia, but the larger states—including Bavaria, the home of National Socialism—refused to bow to the Hitler government. This rebellion was accompanied by a Communist campaign calling for resistance to the Nazis. On February 21 the Union of Red Fighters exhorted the Young Proletarians to disarm the SA and SS. "Every comrade a commander in the coming Red Army! This is our oath to the Red soldiers of the Soviet Union. Our fight cannot be broken by machine guns or pistol-barrels or prison. We are the masters of tomorrow!" A few days later the official Communist organ, *Red Sailor*, openly called for violence: "Workers, to the barricades! Forward to victory! Fresh bullets in your guns! Draw the pins of the hand-grenades!"

These revolutionary appeals may have been mere verbiage but Göring took them at face value—or professed to—and raided the Karl Liebknecht House in Berlin on February 24. An official announcement proclaimed that the police had discovered plans for a Communist uprising. On the evening of February 26 Hanussen predicted that this revolution would soon literally burst into flames. At a séance attended by some of the most influential people in the capital he claimed to see smoke . . . an eagle rising from flames . . . and then a large Berlin building engulfed in fire. Those of his listeners who were aware that there had been three attempts the previous day to set fire to governmental buildings must have been particularly impressed.

The arsonist, a twenty-four-year-old native of Holland, Marinus van der Lubbe, had in fact also made up his mind to burn down the Reichstag. A strong, lumpish young man, his protest against capitalism was setting buildings on fire. Four years earlier he had resigned in disgust from the Communist Party to join International Communists, a tiny splinter group which opposed Moscow policies. He had come to Berlin a week earlier under the impression that great things were about to happen there. But attendance at Social Democratic and Communist demonstrations convinced him that the German workers would start a revolution only under the impetus of some startling event. He hoped the sight of governmental strongholds going up in flames would inspire the lethargic German masses to revolt.

Not discouraged by the three abortive fires, on Monday noon—it was February 27—he bought four packages of fire lighters at a shop on the Müllerstrasse and then set off on foot for the Reichstag. Shabbily dressed in pitifully short trousers and peaked cap, he kept circling the ornate gilt- and glass-domed building until he found the best way to enter was from the west—the door least often used. It was a freezing day, heightened by a sharp wind. To warm up he stayed in the post office for half an hour, then walked some more and at about nine that evening was back at the Reichstag. The western approach was deserted and in moments he had scaled the wall and was on the balcony of the first floor.

At 9:30 P.M. a theology student on his way home heard breaking glass inside the parliament building. He saw a figure with a burning object in his hand and ran to alert a police sergeant at the northwestern corner of the Reichstag. The sergeant found the broken window and a glow behind it but watched in astonishment and it was some minutes before he summoned the fire brigade. The first engines arrived just before ten and by then the Session Chamber was in flames.

At his Berlin quarters opposite the Reichstag, Hanfstaengl was awakened from a sickbed by the screams of the housekeeper. He looked out the window at the fire and telephoned the Goebbels apartment where a party for the Führer was in mid-career. When Goebbels heard the news he thought it was a joke. "If you think that, come down here and see for yourself," retorted Hanfstaengl and hung up. A moment later his phone rang. It was Goebbels. "I have just talked to the Führer and he wants to know what's really happening. No more of your jokes now." The annoyance and suspicion in Goebbels' voice seemed genuine and Hanfstaengl lost his temper. He said the place was in flames and the fire brigades were already there. He was going back to bed to nurse his fever.

After Hitler saw the red sky above the Tiergarten he shouted. "It's the Communists!" and set off with Goebbels for the scene of the fire. They found Göring inside the burning building, brown hat turned up in front and looking immense in a camel-hair coat. He had been one of the first to reach the conflagration, and his first order was characteristic: "Save the tapestries!" He told Hitler that it was the work of the Reds. "A number of Communist deputies were present here in the Reichstag twenty minutes before the fire broke out. We have succeeded in arresting one of the incendiaries." And to Goebbels' excited question, "Who was it?" Göring replied complacently, "We don't know yet, but we shall squeeze it out of him, have no fear, Doctor."

"Are the other public buildings safe?" asked Hitler.

"I've taken every possible precaution. I've mobilized all the police. Every public building has been given a special guard. We are ready for anything."

The party began a tour of the destroyed area across pools of water and charred debris. As they entered a lobby filled with foul-smelling smoke a policeman held up his arms to warn Hitler that a candelabrum might crash at any moment. The Chancellor (after remarking contemptuously, "Good riddance to that trashy old shack") fell back to join Sefton Delmer, who had arrived to cover the fire. "God grant that this be the work of Communists," he said—a sign to the correspondent that he was not yet absolutely certain it was a Red plot but only hoped so. "You are now witnessing the beginning of a great epoch in German history, Herr Delmer. This fire is the beginning." He tripped over a fire hose but lost neither his balance nor the thread of his speech. "If the Communists got ahold of Europe and had control of it six months—what am I saying!— two months—the whole continent would be aflame like this building."

After they had climbed the stairs to the next floor they were approached by Papen, who had rushed from a dinner at the Herrenklub in honor of Hindenburg and was immaculate in gray tweed overcoat and black Homburg. "This is a God-given signal, Herr Vice-Chancellor!" Hitler exclaimed. "If this fire, as I believe, is the work of the Communists, then we must crush out this murderous pest with an iron fist!" Papen was relieved that the Gobelin tapestries had been saved and the library was untouched and, when Hitler invited him to attend a conference in Göring's office to decide on what should be done, politely but pointedly declined. He thought he should first report to Hindenburg.

The fire seemed to fascinate Hitler and after arrival at the office of the Reichstag president he leaned over the stone parapet overlooking the holocaust as if magnetized by the flames. By this time the conference room was filling with cabinet ministers as well as other officials and dignitaries including Prince Auwi, the Lord Mayor of Berlin, the police president and the British ambassador. Then the man who had undertaken the initial investigation entered. Rudolf Diels, chief of the political police in the Prussian Ministry of Interior, had come to inform the Führer and Göring that the arsonist, a Dutch national named van der Lubbe, had been found, bare to the waist, inside the Reichstag. When an enraged interrogator yelled, "Why did you do it?" the young radical had replied, "As a protest."

Göring began shouting slogans and orders. "This is the beginning of a Communist uprising. Not a moment must be lost. . . ." He was cut off by Hitler: "Now we'll show them! Anyone who stands in our way will be mown down!" His face was scarlet from excitement and heat. "The German people have been soft too long. Every Communist official must be shot. All Communist deputies must be hanged this very night. All friends of the Communists must be locked up. And that goes for the Social Democrats and the Reichsbanner as well!"

Diels finally managed to tell Hitler that the arsonist denied any connection with the Communist Party and swore he alone had set all the fires inside the Reichstag. Diels added that the confession rang true and that the fire was undoubtedly the work of a single madman.

"This is a cunning and well-prepared plot," scoffed Hitler and resumed his irrational diatribe. "The only thing is that they have reckoned without us and without the German people. In their ratholes, from which they are now trying to crawl out, they cannot hear the jubilation of the masses."

Diels tried to say that it was ridiculous to think the Communists were about to stage a Putsch. Countless Red turncoats had told him it was all talk. But Hitler would not listen. He flew into another outburst, vilifying these "subhumans" and shouting that he needed no more proof to be convinced that the Communists, by "shamefully setting fire to a German palladium, had wished to give the signal for their loudly heralded mass action."

The tempestuous conference ended about 11 P.M. and, after another meeting at the Prussian Ministry of Interior to discuss security measures, Hitler set out for the local offices of the *Völkischer Beobachter* to see how the paper was covering the fire. "It took half an hour before I could find anyone to let me in. Inside there were a few compositors sitting around, and eventually some sub-editor appeared very heavy with sleep." Hitler sent for Goebbels and the two worked until dawn preparing the next edition, which would accuse the Reds of a plot to seize power amid the "general panic."

In the meantime Göring was raging at the man who had been assigned to draw up the report for the official Prussian press service. After a glance at a twenty-line draft which mentioned one arsonist, Göring shouted, "That's sheer rubbish! It may be a good police report but it's not at all the kind of communiqué I have in mind!" Grabbing a blue pencil, he changed one hundredweight of incendiary material to one thousand and, when the author protested that it would be impossible for a single man to carry such a load, retorted: "Nothing is impossible. Why mention a single man? There were ten or even twenty men! Don't you understand what is happening? The whole thing was a signal for a Communist uprising!" After Göring wrote an entirely new communiqué, indicating that van der Lubbe's accomplices were two Communist members of the Reichstag, the original author asked him to sign it, since it was not an official report but a political document. "The news agencies," he explained, "will only accept it from me if you sign it officially." Grudgingly Göring scrawled a large "G." By this time all police radio stations were issuing calls for the arrest of Communist members of the Reichstag, the provincial diets and town councils. Communist functionaries were also to be apprehended and all Red newspapers suppressed.

The stimulation of that night emboldened Hitler to throw off his last inhibitions, for late the next morning he flung himself into an open battle for power. It started incongruously at a cabinet meeting as the Chancellor politely greeted each minister according to rank. After this traditional beginning he took over in dictatorial fashion. The crisis was such, he said, as to warrant "a ruthless settling of accounts" with the Communists which "must not be dependent on legal considerations." He proposed, therefore, an emergency decree to protect the nation from the Reds but made it sound purely defensive and innocuous, referring almost casually to a "special measure to safeguard all the cultural documents of the German people." But when Frick read off his draft it should have been obvious that the decree canceled most rights expected by a democratic society. First it suspended the civil liberties granted by the Weimar constitution—free speech, free press, sanctity of the home, secrecy of mail and telephone conversations, freedom to assemble or form organizations and inviolability of private property. Next it authorized the Reich Minister of Interior to seize control temporarily of any state government unable to maintain order. Not a single minister opposed the deprivation of civil rights but Papen did protest that the threat to intervene with states would be deeply resented, particularly in Bavaria. Papen's dissent was short-lived; he approved a minor change that was a modification in name only. That evening Hitler and he reported to Hindenburg. The Führer argued that the decree was necessary to put down the Red revolution and, when neither Papen nor Meissner expressed disapproval, the President signed without comment.

A civil state of emergency had been substituted for the military measure sought by the conservatives, with the cabinet holding those powers usually bestowed on the commander-in-chief in a military dictatorship. On the surface such power was not so ominous since the cabinet was still overwhelmingly non-National Socialist. The decree was passed so hastily and under such emotional circumstances that no one was sure exactly who had originated the idea to abolish civil rights rather than curtail them as previous chancellors had done. Possibly it was not an underhanded plot of Hitler's in his avowed move toward dictatorship but an accident of history. The fire had obviously brought Hitler to the edge of hysteria and he truly feared a Red revolution. Certainly his erratic actions as well as those of Göring and others close to him were not those of conspirators with a levelheaded plan. Nor did Hitler react so much in panic as in utter faith in his mission. So far as he was concerned the fire was proof of all he had been saying about Reds and Jews for years.

The emergency measures that followed, designed primarily to put down a non-existent revolt, turned out to be a leap forward in Hitler's drive for total power. Truckloads of SA and SS men hastily sworn in as auxiliaries were helping the police enforce the decree. They descended on the rooms and taverns of known Reds and carted them off to prison or interrogation cellars. More than three thousand Communists and Social Democrats were taken into protective custody by the regular police. Airdromes and ports were under strict surveillance while trains were searched at frontiers.

Göring was in his glory and the following day, as Prussian Minister of Interior, he spoke to the nation by radio about the insidious plans of the Reds, groups of whom planned to don Brownshirt and Stahlhelm uniforms and carry out terrorist acts in an effort to destroy the unity of the nation. The burning of the Reichstag, he predicted, was only the first of many other fires that would distract the police and leave the people at the mercy of the revolutionaries. But, he concluded, the nation need not fear. "I may say to the Communists that my nerves have not yet collapsed, and I feel myself strong enough to give the knockout blow to their criminal plans!"

While his explanation was widely accepted in Germany, the outside world was not so gullible. "The assertion that German Communists had any association with the fire is simply a piece of stupidity," stated the London *News Chronicle* and this view was generally shared in diplomatic and foreign press circles. There was a growing feeling that it was the Nazis themselves who had burned the Reichstag as a pretext for crushing the Communists.

Next day, March 2, Sefton Delmer went to Hitler for the answer. He railed at foreigners for making such accusations when they should be grateful for his courageous acts against the common Red foe. Delmer finally broke in to say that the mass arrests were spreading the fear that Hitler planned a bloody reprisal upon his enemies. "I need no St. Bartholomew's night," retorted Hitler. Tribunals had been set up to try enemies of the state and put an end to conspiracies. Delmer took this to mean that he was going to slaughter his foes legally and wondered if the suspension of civil rights would be permanent.

"No," said Hitler. "When the Communist menace is stamped out the normal order of things shall return. Our laws are too liberal for me to deal effectively and swiftly with this Bolshevik underworld. But I myself am only too anxious for the normal state of affairs to be restored as quickly as possible. First, however, we must crush Communism out of existence."

With each day the belief grew throughout Europe that the Nazis were responsible for the Reichstag fire. This theory was strengthened by the startling revelation that there was a tunnel running from Göring's palace to the Reichstag, and the resultant outcry from abroad helped spur Hitler to insist on a trial of van der Lubbe and his purported Red associates despite an objective police report that there was "no doubt" that he had "committed the crime entirely by himself." It was a foolish decision, for it soon became obvious that the quick trial Hitler hoped to clear the air would drag on for months and provide considerable fuel for his enemies both home and abroad.

3

The short-term advantages of the fire did work to the Führer's advantage. Coming so close to the elections, it played on the fears of revolution shared by most Germans. Few objected when squads of Brownshirts ripped down the Red election posters and replaced them with their own. Hitler did not make the political mistake of outlawing the Communist Party but decided to wait until after the elections lest the working-class vote swing over to the Social Democrats. Instead the Nazis inundated the country with terrifying stories of the bloodbath that the Reds had planned to follow the harsh methods that would have to be installed and called on the voters to give the NSDAP a mandate. Göring was blunter: "Fellow Germans, my measures will not be crippled by any judicial thinking," he told a Frankfurt audience on March 3, just two days before the elections. "My measures will not be crippled by any bureaucracy. I won't have to worry about justice, my mission is only to destroy and exterminate. This struggle will be a struggle against chaos, and I shall not conduct it with police power. A bourgeois state might have done that. Certainly I shall use the power of the state and the police to the utmost, my dear Communists, so don't draw any false conclusions; but I shall lead the Brownshirts in this struggle to the death and my claws will grasp your necks!"

It was a confession that brute force would be applied outside the law, and it could have been made only in the charged atmosphere of the Reichstag fire. Fortunately for the Nazis, the Papens, Hindenburgs and industrialists were not at all concerned by alarming words and gave substantial, if occasionally tacit, support to the Hitler campaign. As the Prussian Minister of Finance assured a visiting Austrian, there was no possibility of Nazi excesses so long as "pragmatic, decent" men like Schwerin von Krosigk were in the cabinet. The violent words of buffoons like Göring and Goebbels should not be taken seriously, for "the conservative element would actually run things and Hitler would just be on the sidelines."

The industrialists were so sure of their ability to handle him that some twenty-five of them had decided at a recent meeting to underwrite the election financially. After Krupp von Bohlen expressed the unanimous feeling of the industrialists in support of Hitler, Göring made an appeal for funds: "The sacrifice we ask is easier to bear if you realize that the elections will certainly be the last for the next ten years, probably for the next hundred years." This threat of an end to democratic procedures was taken as a promise by banker Schacht, who said: "And now, gentlemen, cash on the counter." The industrialists conferred in whispers. The elder Krupp pledged 1,000,000 marks (about $250,000) for the Ruhr combine and the representative of I. G. Farben promised 400,000 marks. Other contributions brought the total up to 3,000,000.

With all this money at their disposal, the National Socialists and their two coalition partners were able to blanket the nation with publicity.

All major party speeches were broadcast and, to those without radios, loudspeakers on streets and squares blared out the promises and threats of the new government. Hitler made frequent use of Hindenburg's name as proof of his own legitimacy. Months earlier the same speakers had pictured the old man as a senile fool; now he was transformed into a heroic figure of towering strength.

With the prospect of consolidating power after an overwhelming victory, the party members threw themselves enthusiastically into a campaign that had governmental blessing. No longer were the SA and SS repressed by the police, who now looked upon them as auxiliaries and turned their backs on excesses committed in the name of patriotism.

In his speeches Hitler criticized opponents for having no program yet presented none of his own. All he wanted was four years in office to prove himself. Election eve was turned into a semi-holiday by Goebbels, who labeled it "Day of the Awakening Nation." It seemed that almost everyone was for Hitler. He was the hope of the young idealists and carried the same banner as the patriots. Those who feared a Moscow-inspired revolution saw only two alternatives, a Red or Brown Germany, and the latter seemed more palatable. Many of his former critics, like Theodor Heuss, who would become the first President of the German Federal Republic, claimed to see signs of moderation in Hitler. "He rants much less. He has stopped breathing fire at the Jews and can make a speech nowadays lasting for four hours without mentioning the word 'Jew.'" Hitler even had some Jewish support; the Jewish National Union not only advocated the Führer's ban on entry of Eastern "peddler Jews" but supported his new government.

Despite outer appearances and the vast amounts of money and energy expended on the campaign, the National Socialists received only 43.9 per cent of the votes, and it took those of his nationalist allies to give him a bare majority in the parliament. Narrow as was the margin of victory, it was enough for Hitler to claim a clear mandate from the people and resume his attempt to take control of those states not under his rule. Assured of support from Berlin, the Nazis in Bavaria decided to force the issue. The SA in Munich was mobilized and at noon, March 9, Gauleiter Adolf Wagner, accompanied by Captain Röhm in full SA regalia, appeared at the office of Minister President Held. They demanded that Held immediately appoint a general state commissar, General Ritter von Epp, who had helped crush the Soviet Republic of 1919.

Held wired protests to Berlin but received the answer that Epp had been appointed commissar. Another protest to Hindenburg brought a definitive reply indicating how powerless the Old Gentleman had become:

he requested Held to address all further complaints directly to Adolf Hitler. Bavaria was at last legally in the hands of the National Socialists. The same procedure—threats of violence from below and telegraphic intervention from Berlin—summarily brought all the remaining free states into subjection.

On the day of the takeover in Bavaria Hitler flew to Munich where he was greeted tumultuously. He was euphoric. "Munich is *the* city of Germany closest to my heart," he said. "Here as a young man, as a soldier and as a politician I made my start. The city is also baptized in the blood of those who died in 1923." He instructed the local party leaders to set up a stable Bavarian government even at the expense of admitting non-party members. "Your assignment, gentlemen," he said, "is difficult. But it is important for the political stability of the nation that the power of the Reich no longer be disturbed by special movements or even separatist disturbances in Bavaria. I must finish the work of Bismarck: states are states only as long as they are useful for the good of the Reich."

Later someone asked what should be done with Dr. Ehard, the only effective state prosecutor at the Hitler trial of 1924. "He was severe but he also was objective and polite," said Hitler. "Leave him in the Ministry of Justice."

Many foreigners erroneously believed that Hitler had already consolidated control throughout Germany. Consummate politician that he was, he was assuming power gradually and with the people's consent. "Authority," he remarked to Frank, "is only a springboard, a step to the next step," consequently conciliation with all levels of German society was his present byword. Out of respect for both the Hohenzollerns and Hindenburg, he selected the Potsdam garrison church for the opening of the new Reichstag on March 21. The ancient town, founded by Frederick Wilhelm I and containing the grave of Frederick the Great, was also steeped in Prussian military tradition. It was gaily decorated with swastika banners and the black-white-red flags of the former empire. Guns boomed. Army, Stahlhelm and SA troops formed ranks. Bells pealed out as the official motor caravan headed down the road to the little church in the bright spring sunlight.

Once the towering form of Hindenburg appeared in the field-gray uniform of a Prussian field marshal, the audience rose. Leaning with one hand on his cane and carrying his field marshal's baton in the other, he advanced slowly with dignity. At the imperial gallery he turned, raised his baton and saluted the empty seat of the Kaiser and the royalty lined up behind it. The marshal completely dominated the much smaller man beside him. Ill at ease in his cutaway, Hitler looked to Ambassador François-Poncet "like a timid newcomer being introduced by an important protector into a company to which he does not belong."

The two sat down facing each other. Then Hindenburg took out a pair of tortoise-shell glasses and began to read his speech. The tasks facing the new government, he said, were varied and difficult and he called for a revival of the disciplined and patriotic spirit of old Prussia.

Hitler's speech was directed to those in the crowded church rather than to the people at home listening to their radios. The war had been forced on the Kaiser and Germany, he said and summarized the legacy of economic depression and unemployment he had inherited. After outlining a program for the future he turned to Hindenburg as if he were still his commander and paid him extravagant homage as military and civilian leader. "We consider it a blessing to have your consent to the work of the German rising."

Hitler walked to Hindenburg's chair, bent low to grasp his hand. The old man, visibly moved, slowly descended into the crypt of Frederick the Great and Frederick Wilhelm I, followed by his son and an adjutant who laid wreaths on the two tombs, to the well-timed accompaniment of cannon salutes.

The ceremony, stage-managed by Goebbels made its expected impression. All those present—the military, the Junkers and the monarchists—were convinced Hitler was subservient to Hindenburg and would follow the Prussian ideal. But two days later Hitler made it clear to any objective observer that he was subservient to no man. The setting was different—Berlin's Kroll Opera House, temporary site of the Reichstag—and so was the atmosphere: SA and SS men patrolled the corridors and behind the stage hung a huge swastika flag as a reminder of who was going to be master of Germany. At 2:05 P.M. President Göring opened the session. After a brief speech, including recitation of the song "Germany, Awake!," he turned over the floor to Hitler, who had entered in the simple uniform of a Brownshirt.

There was a momentary silence, followed by a single shout of "Sieg Heil! Sieg Heil!" This set off wild applause as the Führer strode up to the podium through a forest of raised arms. It was his first appearance before parliament and he began reading off a speech that was remarkable for its prudence and moderation. He vowed to respect private property and individual initiative; promised aid to peasants and middle class alike. He would end unemployment and promote peace with France, Britain and even the Soviet Union. But to do all this he needed enactment of the Law for Alleviating the Distress of People and Reich. This so-called enabling act gave him overriding if temporary authority in the land but he made it sound moderate and promised to use its emergency powers "only in so far as they are essential for carrying out vitally necessary measures."

After giving reassurance to parliament, President, the states and the Church that none of their rights would be infringed, Hitler concluded on a firm note that should have canceled out these reassurances. If the Reichstag refused this "opportunity for friendly co-operation," the new regime was prepared to fight for its principles. "It is for you, gentlemen of the Reichstag, to decide between war and peace."

During the recess the foes of the measure mobilized and when the session was resumed the leader of the Social Democrats made a courageous if poorly delivered protest despite chanting in the corridors from the Brownshirts: "We want the bill—or fire and murder!" Hitler himself responded, even though Papen tried to restrain him, in a style reminiscent of the early beer-hall days in Munich, by attacking the Social Democrats with sarcasm and invective. "I do not want your votes. Germany will be free, but not through you. Do not mistake us for the bourgeoisie. The star of Germany is in the ascendant, yours is about to disappear, your death knell has sounded."

Hitler's assault not only crushed the futile revolt of the Social Democrats but intimidated the Center Party. The vote was taken and when Göring announced the results—far beyond the required two-thirds majority with 441 for the bill, 94 against—the National Socialists leaped to their feet cheering as if their team had scored a winning goal in the final seconds of play. Then with hands outstretched they sang the "Horst Wessel Song":

> *Raise high the flags! Stand rank and rank together,*
> *Storm troopers march with steady, quiet tread. . . .*

Democracy was expunged from the German parliament with scarcely a protest. Only the Social Democrats voted against the bill. The other parties handed over to Hitler powers that he privately vowed never to relinquish. And powers surrendered to a man who has use for them are seldom relinquished.

The Center leader got a letter from Hindenburg commending his support of Hitler. "I wish to assure you that the Chancellor has expressed his willingness, even without formal constitutional obligations, to take measures based on the Enabling Act only after consultations with me." These words, honestly meant, momentarily reassured the betrayed Centrists. The majority of Germans were eager to be reassured and many of

ve him overriding if temporary authority in the land but he
nd moderate and promised to use its emergency powers "only in
they are essential for carrying out vitally necessary measures."
After giving reassurance to parliament, President, the states and the
ch that none of their rights would be infringed, Hitler concluded on
. note that should have canceled out these reassurances. If the Reichs-
fused this "opportunity for friendly co-operation," the new regime
repared to fight for its principles. "It is for you, gentlemen of the
stag, to decide between war and peace."

During the recess the foes of the measure mobilized and when the
n was resumed the leader of the Social Democrats made a coura-
if poorly delivered protest despite chanting in the corridors from the
nshirts: "We want the bill—or fire and murder!" Hitler himself re-
ed, even though Papen tried to restrain him, in a style reminiscent
e early beer-hall days in Munich, by attacking the Social Democrats
sarcasm and invective. "I do not want your votes. Germany will be
out not through you. Do not mistake us for the bourgeoisie. The star
rmany is in the ascendant, yours is about to disappear, your death
has sounded."

Hitler's assault not only crushed the futile revolt of the Social
ocrats but intimidated the Center Party. The vote was taken and
Göring announced the results—far beyond the required two-thirds
ity with 441 for the bill, 94 against—the National Socialists leaped
eir feet cheering as if their team had scored a winning goal in the
seconds of play. Then with hands outstretched they sang the "Horst
el Song":

> Raise high the flags! Stand rank and rank together,
> Storm troopers march with steady, quiet tread. . . .

Democracy was expunged from the German parliament with scarcely
est. Only the Social Democrats voted against the bill. The other par-
anded over to Hitler powers that he privately vowed never to relin-
And powers surrendered to a man who has use for them are seldom
uished.

he Center leader got a letter from Hindenburg commending his
rt of Hitler. "I wish to assure you that the Chancellor has expressed
illingness, even without formal constitutional obligations, to take
res based on the Enabling Act only after consultations with me."
words, honestly meant, momentarily reassured the betrayed Cen-
The majority of Germans were eager to be reassured and many of

act
it so
far a

Chu
a fir
tag
was
Reic

sessi
geou
Brow
spon
of th
with
free,
of G
knel

Dem
whei
majc
to th
final
Wes

a pro
ties
quisl
relin

supp
his
meas
Thes
trists

side him. Ill at ease in his cutaway, Hitler looked to A
Poncet "like a timid newcomer being introduced by a
tor into a company to which he does not belong."

The two sat down facing each other. Then Hinc
pair of tortoise-shell glasses and began to read his speec
the new government, he said, were varied and difficult
revival of the disciplined and patriotic spirit of old Prus

Hitler's speech was directed to those in the crov
than to the people at home listening to their radios.
forced on the Kaiser and Germany, he said and summ;
economic depression and unemployment he had inheri
a program for the future he turned to Hindenburg as
commander and paid him extravagant homage as n
leader. "We consider it a blessing to have your consent
German rising."

Hitler walked to Hindenburg's chair, bent low to g
old man, visibly moved, slowly descended into the cry
Great and Frederick Wilhelm I, followed by his son ar
laid wreaths on the two tombs, to the well-timed acco
non salutes.

The ceremony, stage-managed by Goebbels made
sion. All those present—the military, the Junkers and
were convinced Hitler was subservient to Hindenburg ar
Prussian ideal. But two days later Hitler made it clear
server that he was subservient to no man. The sett
Berlin's Kroll Opera House, temporary site of the Rei
the atmosphere: SA and SS men patrolled the corrid
stage hung a huge swastika flag as a reminder of wl
master of Germany. At 2:05 P.M. President Göring
After a brief speech, including recitation of the song "
he turned over the floor to Hitler, who had entered in
of a Brownshirt.

There was a momentary silence, followed by a si
Heil! Sieg Heil!" This set off wild applause as the Füh,
podium through a forest of raised arms. It was his firs
parliament and he began reading off a speech that wa
prudence and moderation. He vowed to respect private
vidual initiative; promised aid to peasants and mid
would end unemployment and promote peace with I
even the Soviet Union. But to do all this he needed ena
for Alleviating the Distress of People and Reich. Thi

them were rushing to join the NSDAP. Others gave their support in less overt ways. Civil servants and bureaucrats (no different from civil servants and bureaucrats in other lands) stayed at their posts to keep the machinery of government running as smoothly as if the most conservative party had won.

The victory in the Reichstag also brought into the open a number of industrialists who had secretly supported Hitler. The steel magnate Krupp openly heiled acquaintances on the street. He wrote Hitler a letter of congratulations stating that he and his colleagues were convinced that Germany at last had "the basis for a stable government." He was rewarded by being chosen as czar of German industry, thus sanctifying the marriage between big business and National Socialism. It was also no accident that Hitler chose Hjalmar Schacht as president of the Reichsbank. This brilliant financier had helped bring Hitler into industrial circles and shared his detestation of democracy and parliamentarianism. (Hitler's Finance Minister approved the choice since he regarded Schacht as a genius in his field. "At the same time he was one of the most apt liars I ever knew," recalled Schwerin von Krosigk. "He stretched the truth until he was right.")

Before his selection Hitler asked Schacht how much the banks could contribute to his public works and armament program. Schacht refused to mention a specific sum but declared the Reichsbank should furnish whatever money was needed "to take the last unemployed off the streets." He got the job and his first act in office was to invent the system of "Mefo" bills—so called after Metall-Forschungsgesellschaft A.G., a dummy corporation formed by four armament firms, the state assuming liability for its debts. The Mefo bills were drawn chiefly by government contractors and were, in effect, not unlike promissory notes that could be extended to five years as a sort of short-term credit. The original feature of Schacht's scheme was to give unlimited credit to the regime and thus allow Hitler to rearm Germany on a large scale.

It was not only bureaucrats and industrialists who were finding it possible to serve the Führer. A number of intellectual and literary figures were espousing the regeneration of Germany. These included the philosophers Krieck and Bäumler, the poets Bluck and Binding, and Germany's most distinguished dramatist, Gerhart Hauptmann, who refused to renounce his honors no matter what government was in power. "I am delighted that Hauptmann should agree with me," wrote Rudolf Binding early that spring, "that we serve the nation to which we belong and have no reason to leave the Academy when the regime changes. The Academy has to safe-

guard the freedom of artistic creation, not the freedom of political observations." In this spirit of co-operation, Hauptmann several weeks later
hung a swastika flag out his window; and some months later assured
Harold Nicolson that Germany would "liberate itself" as Italy had done.

4

A revolution was going on but since it was almost bloodless on the
surface many Germans did not—or chose not to—realize it. This preliminary stage of the Brown Revolution was given an innocuous name,
Gleichschaltung (co-ordination). It appeared to be an efficient process of
unifying the nation and was received with little alarm. What it did was
bring the political, economical and social life of the nation under the control of the NSDAP and plant the seeds of a faceless dictatorship. There
was little resistance primarily because Hitler kept within the law. Consequently his opponents believed he wanted a government similar to the
Weimar Republic. A set of instructions issued to Social Democratic locals
on the day of the enabling law enactment illustrates that party's ob-
tuseness. It was filled with advice on filling out questionnaires and other
mundane matters and but one paragraph mentioned the Nazi revolution
in progress. While their leaders were being searched at night for weapons,
while thousands of Communists and suspected Communists were being
jailed, the Social Democratic Party, which should have been the bulwark
of democracy, was exhorting its followers to stop making bookkeeping errors.

"The whole city lay under an epidemic of discreet, infectious fear,"
Isherwood wrote of Berlin that spring. "I could feel it, like influenza, in
my bones." The city was "full of whispers. They told of illegal midnight
arrests, of prisoners tortured in the S.A. barracks, made to spit on Lenin's
picture, swallow castor-oil, eat old socks. They were drowned by the loud,
angry voice of the Government, contradicting through its thousand
mouths."

Outside the capital, particularly in the smaller towns and cities, a
series of mass meetings, parades and pageantry distracted the people. Voluntary organizations were "co-ordinated" into the National Socialist fabric. Gradually every citizen found himself involved with the regime. Old
familiar street names were changed. In Herne, for example, Rathausplatz
was now Adolf Hitler Platz and Bebelstrasse became Hermann Göring
Strasse. Almost every week there was some new organization: the Country
School for Mothers, the Mother and Child Welfare Organization,
Childrensland Camps, the Food-Supply Welfare Organization.

A month after Hitler had failed to persuade a majority of the electorate to vote for him, he had won the temporary confidence of most Germans by his gradual process of co-ordination. Isherwood watched these solid citizens smile approvingly at the young storm troopers "in their big, swaggering boots who were going to upset the Treaty of Versailles. They were pleased because it would soon be summer, because Hitler had promised to protect the small tradesmen, because their newspapers told them that the good times were coming . . . And they thrilled with a furtive sensual pleasure, like schoolboys, because the Jews, their business rivals, and the Marxists, a vaguely defined minority of people who didn't concern them, had been satisfactorily found guilty of the defeat and the inflation, and were going to catch it."

Jews and Marxists had been systematically persecuted since the takeover. Albert Einstein's bank deposits were seized when a bread knife—categorically a lethal weapon—was found in his house. In Germany such stories were branded as foreign propaganda while in the United States Secretary of State Cordell Hull was assuring leaders of American Jewry that the physical mistreatment of German Jews had "virtually terminated." Even so the outcry of liberals from abroad increased to Hitler's annoyance and he announced that Jewish business in Germany would suffer until the Jews in England and America ceased their atrocity propaganda.

They did not and on April 1 Hitler instituted a boycott with these words: "I believe that I act today in unison with the Almighty Creator's intention: by fighting the Jews I do battle for the Lord." It was only a tentative step, almost as if Hitler were testing to see how far his countrymen would let him go. On the eve of the boycott Italian Ambassador Cerruti had urged him in the name of Mussolini to soften his attitude toward the Jews. Hitler replied that there were few Jews in Italy and Il Duce did not understand the Jewish question which he himself had studied "for long years, from every angle, like no one else." He predicted "with absolute certainty" that in five or six hundred years the name of Hitler would be honored in all lands "as the man who once and for all exterminated the Jewish pest from the world."

Brownshirts were posted before the doors of most Jewish stores and offices. There was little violence and the young SA men were, for the most part, polite when reminding shoppers that they were about to patronize a Jewish business. "Little knots of passers-by collected to watch the performance—interested, amused or merely apathetic." In fact a good number went into the department store Isherwood was watching. He too entered, bought the first thing he saw, a nutmeg grater, and walked out twirling his parcel. This act of defiance was greeted by a wink from one of the young SA monitors. Although the boycotters got support from organizations which called upon farmers to support them, it was ineffective against the large department stores and banks and ended after three days.

Hindenburg himself protested further anti-Semitic measures and wrote the Chancellor a strong letter condemning discrimination against Jewish war veterans. "If they were worthy of fighting and bleeding for Germany, they must be considered worthy of continuing to serve the Fatherland in their profession." But the Old Gentleman was no match for a man whose secret goal in life was Jewish extinction. Hitler replied that the Jews, who monopolized up to eighty per cent of the professions of law and medicine, were now pushing their way into government posts. "One of the major reasons why the old Prussian state was such a clean one was that the Jews were granted only a very limited access to the civil service. The officer corps kept itself almost entirely pure." It was an argument that could not fail to impress the field marshal. This, coupled with a vague promise to give some consideration to Jewish veterans, was enough to permit enactment of decrees on April 7 removing all Jews from civil service posts and restricting the freedom of the legal profession. That same day Hitler told the Doctors' Union that he was aware of their present distress, especially among the young members, and in so doing subtly revealed his two-pronged Weltanschauung. "It is precisely for these young Germans that a Lebensraum and possibilities for the exercise of their profession must be created by a vigorous repression of an alien race. . . . This work of cleansing through racial hygiene now being undertaken will perhaps take centuries. The important thing is to lay a firm foundation today for future political development."

Several weeks later, under the Law Against Overcrowding of German Schools, the number of Jews in higher institutions was reduced. Hitler defended his action in a talk with Bishop Berning and Monsignor Steinmann. After reminding the priests that the Church had banished Jews into ghettos and forbidden Christians to work with them, Hitler explained that he regarded the Jews as "nothing but pernicious enemies of the State and Church, and therefore he wanted to drive the Jews out more and more, especially from academic life and public professions." He was only going to do more effectively what the Church of Rome had been attempting for so many centuries.

Many Jews did leave the country but others did not feel the anti-Semitic program was directed against them personally. For centuries the Jews had survived similar decrees by swimming with the current. What could happen to them in a nation that had produced Goethe and Beethoven? Besides, Hitler's real target was the Eastern Jew.

With all its outward appearance of success, the NSDAP was neither unified nor organized. It had come to power with a weak cadre structure and too many inept "old fighters" in key positions. The party grew rapidly and there were already more than a million and a half members with another million applications awaiting approval. But Hitler was not pleased to see the party become so unwieldy and ordered Schwarz to halt applications on the first of May.

This also marked the beginning of his attack on labor unions. He declared a Day of National Labor and treated it as a celebration of unity between workers and government. The main rally was held that evening at Tempelhof airfield where several hundred thousand workers and their leaders gathered to hear the Führer expound on the dignity of labor and the need for national unity. All lights were extinguished except those beating on the orator and the vast crowd listened in awed silence. He spoke in generalities but with such passion that when he finished the workers cheered as if he had promised them the world, and before they could emerge from the magic of his words they were singing the national hymn and the "Horst Wessel Lied." And as the last strains died down the sky exploded with fireworks. "It was indeed a brave, a magnificent fete," recalled the French ambassador. "The German participants and the foreign guests left with the conviction that a wave of reconciliation and of concord had swept over the Third Reich."

The next morning the SA and SS, with the help of police, seized union offices throughout the nation. Labor leaders who had yesterday pledged allegiance to the government were arrested in their homes; union files and bank accounts were confiscated and labor newspapers shut down. Before nightfall organized labor in Germany was obliterated. But Hitler promised the workers they would be better off than ever in the new German Labor Front and their rights would be fully protected. There was no uprising, no organized protest, and by the end of the month the vast army of workers was marching obediently behind the swastika. They had changed from red to brown without breaking step.

Success did not turn Hitler to excess. To the dismay of the party radicals he became cautious and prudent, as illustrated by his answer to Franklin Delano Roosevelt's plea for world peace in mid-May. Germany, Hitler replied, would welcome the possibility suggested in the President's proposal of bringing the United States into European relations as a guarantor of peace. Absent were the bellicose demands of the first days of office. "The German government wishes to come to a peaceful agreement with other nations and all difficult questions. Germany knows that in any military action in Europe, even if completely successful, the sacrifice would be out of all proportion to any possible gains."*

Only a man completely in control of his party could have changed course so radically. "The speech was the best thing I have heard Hitler do," Lochner wrote his children. "I often wonder how the Nazis would have mobbed their opponent—like Stresemann or Brüning—if he had dared hold such a conciliatory speech! That's the interesting thing about dictatorship, anyway: when it comes to foreign policy, they are tame as lambs (witness Mussolini, Hitler, Stalin, Pilsudski), for they know they have so much trouble consolidating their power at home that they want to avoid everything possible that might look like trouble with foreign nations. It is quite obvious that Hitler doesn't want war."

The speech not only placated the West but was further proof to Hindenburg that the new Chancellor could be trusted. By this time Hitler had succeeded in ingratiating himself with the Old Gentleman. Always polite and deferential, the force and apparent logic of his arguments had torn down the last vestige of the President's distrust. "Within three weeks," Hitler recalled, "we had progressed so far that his attitude toward me became affectionate and paternal."

With Hindenburg under his influence, there was little to impede the gradual assumption of total power and by early summer a series of new decrees entrenched the NSDAP as the ruling force in Germany. First came the subjugation of agrarian organizations under the Entailed Farm Laws "for the preservation of the insoluble bonds of blood and soil." Combined with a settlement policy "based on race," this gave Hitler the foundation for settlement of the Eastern regions by pure Germans after the conquest of that area. While governmental control of the land was being solidified by the political organization of peasants under local, district and state National Socialist leadership (incongruously named Reich Nutrition Estate), Hitler was applying himself to the subjection of Germany's economy. On May 3 the Reich Estates of Trade and Handicraft was established and within a month it had assumed the functions of the

---

* Hitler had genuine admiration for the decisive manner in which the President had taken over the reins of government. "I have sympathy for Mr. Roosevelt," he told a correspondent of the New York *Times* two months later, "because he marches straight toward his objectives over Congress, lobbies and bureaucracy." Hitler went on to note that he was the sole leader in Europe who expressed "understanding of the methods and motives of President Roosevelt."

German Chamber of Industry and Commerce. More significantly, the Adolf Hitler Foundation of German Business was set up on the first of June to the mutual benefit of both the industrialists and the NSDAP. Thus organizational supervision, together with control of market and price policies, put German industry on the road to complete subservience to the government.

Hitler was now prepared to make the next and perhaps most important step: the elimination of political opposition. The Communists had already been eliminated and on June 22 the Social Democratic Party was outlawed as "hostile to the nation and state." Its members were expelled from the Reichstag and many of its leaders joined other dissidents in the newly formed concentration camps. Within a few days the State Party voluntarily disbanded; and two weeks later—while Hitler was telling his Reich governors, "We must now eliminate the last remnants of democracy" —the German People's Party also disbanded.

By this time Hitler had added five more Nazis to his cabinet and so there was little opposition when he proposed that Germany become a one-party state. The new proposal ignored not only the constitution but the enabling law itself, for it stripped the Reichstag of all its powers and made a travesty of the parliamentary system. "When we discussed the measure in the cabinet, there was practically no opposition," recalled Papen, and by the time Hitler called for a vote it passed without dissent. It became the law of the land on Bastille Day, July 14.

Germany, like the Soviet Union, was controlled by a single party and that party was controlled by a single man who, in turn, was possessed by a dream.

5

In every German village and town the red and black swastika waved side by side with the black-white-red flags of the old Reich. Hitler's concept of revolution by absorption was working in a nation that wanted its uprisings orderly and legal. The Führer's storm troopers were now accepted almost as an arm of government; and nearly every important post was held by Nazis or someone controlled by the party. In the classroom and the church, the Brown Revolution was receiving commendation and blessing.

Hitler continued to say that the upheaval was temporary. "The revolution is not a permanent state of affairs," he told the state governors just before the nation was declared a one-party state. "The stream of revolution released must be guided into the safe channel of evolution." Ability must be the only authoritative standard, not membership in the party.

Hitler wanted no bloody uprising, no sweeping reforms to repel the average citizen or industrialist, and he laid down guidelines to his own Gauleiters. "To gain political power we had to conquer rapidly with a single blow; in the economic sphere other principles of development must determine our action. Here progress must be made step by step without any radical breaking up of the existing conditions which would endanger the foundations of our life." Such words deliberately courted physical defiance from his strongest supporters, the Brownshirts, who had waited long years to enjoy the fruits of the spoils system. But he carried off the extraordinary feat of dampening the revolution from below by the sheer force of his personality.

He proclaimed the end of the economic revolution and replaced the party's economic specialist with a representative of big business. Hitler's socialism was his own and subordinate to his secret aims. His concept of organized economy was close to genuine socialism but he would be a socialist only so long as it served the greater goal. He had the bohemian's rather than the revolutionary's disdain for private property and wanted only enough capital to rebuild the army and restore the economy so that he could lead Germany to its proper destiny. He was a Caesar rather than a Lenin, using socialism to get the masses moving. If he had believed they could have been propelled by capitalism it is likely he would have carried that banner. To Hitler, saving Germany justified any means.

It appeared as though he was creating a society of workers. To them he was the soldier-laborer, and they helped propagate this image. Thus millions of Germans humiliated by defeat in war and brought to the edge of economic disaster in peace readily identified with the warrior-worker hero. In ever increasing numbers Communists, whose leaders were in concentration camps, found a home in National Socialism. It was not at all difficult to accept Hitler's definition of the difference between socialism and Marxism: "German socialism is directed by Germans; international socialism is an instrument of the Jews."

By mid-1933 the majority of Germans supported Hitler. The bourgeoisie and the workers, the military and the civil service, the racists and some of the best brains in the country swelled the Nazi ranks. It has long been a political principle that power corrupts. It can also sanctify. Hitler the street ruffian a year earlier had been made respectable by the power of his office. Some Germans were seduced by expediency but more by a wave of idealism. Reform seemed to be sweeping the Reich. Moreover, the economy had taken a turn for the better, and the streets of the large cities were no longer filled with beggars.

An increasing number of intellectuals and artists followed the lead of playwright Gerhart Hauptmann in paying homage, if in varying degrees, to the Führer. Spengler spent an hour and a half with him that July; they agreed about German policy toward France and shared the same disdain for the mediocre leadership in the Evangelical Church. On parting, Hitler assured the author that he "considered it of great importance for people outside the party to be won over to a German policy." Spengler agreed and left with a feeling that the Führer, while insignificant, was a "very decent fellow." Richard Strauss, scarcely Hitler's favorite composer, was even more forthcoming and announced that he was quite satisfied with the change in Germany and, when the Führer attended a new performance of *Der Rosenkavalier* in Berlin, was happy to be received in his box during the intermission.

The princes of the Church were more eager to curry his favor. "Hitler knows how to guide the ship," announced Monsignor Ludwig Kaas, leader of the recently outlawed Catholic Party after an audience with the Pope. "Even before he became Chancellor I met him frequently and was greatly impressed by his clear thinking, by his way of facing realities while upholding his ideals, which are noble. . . . It matters little who rules so long as order is maintained." Pius XI subscribed to the same principles, as was proved on July 20 when a concordat between the Vatican and Hitler was signed. The Church agreed to keep priests and religion out of politics while Hitler, among other things, granted complete freedom to confessional schools throughout the country, a notable victory for German Catholics. His Holiness welcomed Hitler's representative, Franz von Papen, "most graciously and remarked how pleased he was that the German Government now had at its head a man uncompromisingly opposed to Communism and Russian nihilism in all its forms."

The Vatican was so appreciative of being recognized as a full partner that it asked God to bless the Reich. On a more practical level, it ordered German bishops to swear allegiance to the National Socialist regime. The new oath concluded with these significant words: "In the performance of my spiritual office and in my solicitude for the welfare and the interest of the German Reich, I will endeavor to avoid all detrimental acts which might endanger it."

On every level of society Germans were finding a reason to support the new government. The Führer's fantastic popular appeal was evident from the crowds that flocked to Spital to honor the birthplace of his mother. They descended on the farmhouse where the boy Hitler had spent his summers. They climbed on the roof to take pictures, found their way into the courtyard to wash at the wooden trough as if it contained holy water, chipped pieces from the large stones supporting the barn, and carried off everything portable as souvenirs. When the present owners of the farm returned from the fields they would be engulfed by tourists. "It was like a country fair," recalled Johann Stütz. "They painted swastikas on the cows and would parade around singing Hitler songs. Before long the place looked like a ruin."

Late in July 1933 Hitler took time off to make another pilgrimage to Bayreuth. He laid wreaths on the graves of Richard and Cosima Wagner and their son Siegfried. He also attended the annual festival. It was the first time he had seen the Wagner family since becoming Chancellor and he wandered around the library at Wahnfried with undisguised satisfaction. "It was right here that you received me ten years ago," he told Winifred Wagner and then became dejected. "If the Putsch hadn't failed everything would have been different; I would have been the right age. Now I am too old. I have lost too much time and must work with double speed." The moment of depression passed as quickly as it had come and he predicted he would stay in power for twenty-two years. "Then I'll be able to retire, but first I must get more power into my hands so I won't have to bother with the cabinet. Just now they think they have a perfect right to meddle in things that are none of their business." During a vegetarian lunch he confided that once he had full power he would dissolve the monasteries and confiscate their property.

That summer Hitler spent much of his time at his mountain villa on the Obersalzberg. He invited the Hanfstaengls for a holiday at Haus Wachenfeld. Hanfstaengl was busy but sent Helene and Egon, who was twelve. Hitler offered them a ride from Munich and sat in the front seat with the chauffeur. At a lonely stretch of road near Rosenheim their car spluttered and came to a stop. In moments seven bodyguards, automatics in hand, surrounded the car. Kempka examined the motor as Hitler held a flashlight. "It's the old trouble again, my Führer," explained the chauffeur. "Some Reds must have dumped sugar lumps in the gas tank." Hitler warned the bodyguards to keep a sharp lookout, then watched with interest as Kempka unscrewed part of the mechanism, sucked and blew through it, spitting gas and sugar on the road.

Like any other proud householder, Hitler showed Helene and Egon through Haus Wachenfeld. His room on the first floor, which faced directly toward Salzburg, was modest, in keeping with the rest of the villa.

"He had a small writing table, and a number of simple bookshelves," recalled Egon. "I especially looked to see what kind of literature the Führer had chosen for relaxation." Surprisingly, the majority of the books were the wild West novels of Karl May, more suitable for Egon himself than a Chancellor.

The Hanfstaengls were the only house guests but other party members who were staying at nearby boardinghouses and inns would visit. "Göring was constantly around. He and Hitler used to walk on the narrow tile paths in the garden, talking confidentially. Round and round the same plot of grass. If you sat on the veranda in front of the house you could catch bits of conversation as they went by. Göring did most of the talking: 'I have just signed twenty death warrants. . . .' That's about the only utterance I remember for sure. Mother heard it too and both of us were surprised at this grim glimpse behind the scenes of glorious statecraft."

They all had meals together in the pleasant but modest dining room downstairs. Egon couldn't stand the Austrian cooking that was prepared by Angela Raubal, particularly string beans served in a sauce made of milk, flour and quantities of sugar, but he was fascinated by the free and easy table conversation. "They talked about music, and politics, and Chinese art—in fact, about anything. Hitler was rather gracious, for his standards. I mean he didn't make you remember all the time that he was the Führer. As a rule, Hitler never converses, he either listens, or—more commonly—preaches, making his utterances as though they were endowed with the authority of revealed religion. But here, in his '*Landhaus*' he frequently appeared wholly in the becoming guise of an ordinary host, an average man. He talked a lot about motorcars, engines, the size and performance of different ships, and technical things of that sort."

By this time it had become known that the Führer was at Haus Wachenfeld and tourists from all over Germany began congregating on the Obersalzberg. He stayed indoors to avoid being seen and one day the crowd called Egon over and asked whether Hitler was likely to appear. The twelve-year-old went to the Führer and said in stilted German: "Herr Hitler, a devoted multitude is eagerly awaiting your appearance at the gateway."

Hitler burst into laughter and followed Egon outside to greet his admirers. "They nearly swooned. After he went back in, they thanked me profusely, and one hysterical woman picked up some pebbles on which Hitler had stepped and put them in a little vial which she crushed ecstatically against her breast." Later, after another crowd had gathered, Egon collected a stack of postcards, photos and pieces of paper from the group, then wordlessly placed the stack in front of Hitler along with a pen. "My God, boy," he exclaimed with a smile, "you don't give up either, do you!"

By the time Hitler came down from his mountain and returned to Berlin he had decided to present a similarly affable face to the world. That August he allowed Egon's father to publish a book of anti-Hitler caricatures from German and foreign magazines and newspapers. Entitled *Fact vs. Ink*, the jacket showed a good-natured Führer laughing indulgently at his critics. Hanfstaengl cannily picked excellent cartoons, some satirical, some savage, covering the past ten years. In his foreword, prefaced by a quotation from Hitler's hero, Frederick the Great ("Pamphlets are to be hung lower"), Hanfstaengl explained that the book was an attempt to differentiate between the real and the fictional Adolf Hitler.

This kind of propaganda appalled Goebbels but Hitler was swayed by Hanfstaengl's reasoning that British and Americans would be impressed. There was already a feeling among many foreign observers that Hitler was an object more of fun than fear. "While the myth of the leader is growing by leaps and bounds in Germany," observed the *Literary Digest*, "certain independent European dailies and weeklies are stressing the comic aspects of Germany's dictator. They picture Hitler as a comedian, all the more laughable because of his seriousness." The traditional English compassion for the underdog was also working to Hitler's advantage in his dealings with France over reparations and boundaries. Lord Lothian argued that National Socialist brutality at home was "largely the reflex of the external persecution to which Germans have been subjected since the war." British attacks on the Treaty of Versailles were second only to those in Germany.

With this good will Hitler set about revising his nation's foreign policy. It was dominated by his dual doctrines of race and space and, though he occasionally made a detour, he always returned to Germany's Lebensraum in the East. Hitler's hope was to inveigle England to join him as a silent partner in the crusade against Communism. To do that he must convince the English that the Reich had renounced world trade and global naval ambitions. Briefly, Germany would control the continent of Europe and be a bulwark against Communism while England ruled the seas. To further strengthen himself before launching his drive to the East, Hitler sought support from Italy, which was sympathetic to Nazi principles and shared a common hostility toward France because of Mussolini's ambitions in the Mediterranean.

The diplomats Hitler had inherited from the Weimar Republic came from a different class and abhorred his methods, but the majority agreed with most of his basic aims—for entirely different reasons—and persuaded themselves that they could use him and his brand of socialism for their own purposes. "It was generally believed and hoped," recalled career diplomat Herbert von Dirksen, "that the incurable revolutionaries would be eliminated in time and that their successors, after having tasted the wine of power and the comforts which it brought, would turn to productive work, and to a more conservative mentality." And so Dirksen and likeminded colleagues "felt it to be our duty to assist in this process of normalization."

Hitler was as astute in his manipulation of the diplomatic service as he was with the industrialists and militarists. He allowed all the leading officials to remain at their posts, including one Jew and one married to a Jew. He also declared that the Reich desired to establish friendly relations with the Soviets so long as they did not intervene in German internal affairs. His campaign against home-grown Reds did not represent any hostility to Russia and to show his good faith he secretly allowed the Soviet Union to postpone payments on a long-term credit agreement negotiated before his takeover.

By the fall of 1933 Hitler felt the cautious international game had been played to the end. He decided to walk out on the League of Nations, which, among other things, had a confused policy toward rearmament. "We must make a break," he told Papen in a state approaching exaltation. "All other considerations are completely irrelevant." When Hindenburg questioned the wisdom of leaving the League, Hitler argued that it had to be done to affirm Germany's full equality. Against his better judgment, the Old Gentleman gave grudging consent. A gift of two large properties—along with Hitler's and Göring's oral promises to contribute 400,000 marks apiece from Reich and Prussian funds for their improvement—may have influenced him.

On October 14 Hitler formally announced to the world by radio that Germany was withdrawing from the conference and the League. "To be written down as a member of such an institution possessing no such equality of rights is, for an honor-loving nation of sixty-five million folk and for a government which loves honor, an intolerable humiliation."

There was justification in this charge and, in a sense, his withdrawal from a body that discriminated against the losers was more of a symbolic rejection of the Treaty of Versailles than a challenge to the West. He went out of his way to reassure the French of his peaceful intents by including a hope for German-French reconciliation.

Hitler's shock tactic was a gamble—and yet, with its protestations of peace, a fairly safe one. The British predictably felt more sympathy than condemnation. Lord Allen of Hurtwood told the House of Lords: ". . .

we are compelled to admit that we and other nations during the last fifteen years have not handed out to Germany that full measure of wise and fair play which the country merited when it threw out from its own land the regime which made the war."

Hitler characteristically faced the problem of gaining wide approval at home by announcing that he was submitting his decision to a plebiscite to take place by month's end. Within hours his office was flooded with congratulatory messages, including a telegram from Catholic Action "unanimously" supporting their Führer. "It is not ambition which made the Führer leave the League of Nations," Martin Heidegger, one of Germany's greatest living philosophers, told his students, "nor a passion, nor blind obstinancy, nor a desire for violence; it is nothing but the clear wish to be unconditionally responsible for assuming the mastery of the destiny of our people." (Heidegger, then a Nazi, left the party a few months later.)

Hitler had by no means abandoned his two-faced foreign policy. On October 18 he spoke reasonably and temperately to *Daily Mail* correspondent Ward Price. Although the Germans would "put up with no more of this persistent discrimination" against their country, they certainly wanted no second World War.

Reassuring words to a reporter mean little in the world of diplomacy. The German ambassador in Italy wired his foreign office that Mussolini was "very much upset over our step and deplored it extremely." Il Duce not only regarded withdrawal from the League as a severe blow to his own prestige but "saw no way out of the situation and did not know how Germany intended to make any further progress."

Concerned as he was by Mussolini's irritation, Hitler concentrated his attention on winning a convincing mandate in the forthcoming plebiscite. He campaigned as if for an election, utilizing the resources of the party to convince the people to back his withdrawal from the League of Nations. The Church again gave enthusiastic support. Every bishop in Bavaria approved a statement by Cardinal Faulhaber requesting a Ja vote: "In this way the Catholics will profess anew their loyalty to people and Fatherland and their agreement with the farsighted and forceful efforts of the Führer to spare the German people the terror of war and the horrors of Bolshevism, to secure public order and create work for the unemployed." It reflected public resentment at the lost war and the repressive Treaty of Versailles. That was why Hitler had set the date of the plebiscite for November 12, the day after the anniversary of the armistice.

He appealed to all classes as if they were a unified group. "You cannot afford internal conflict in the fight to regain your position among nations," he told the workers at the Siemens plant. "If Germany does not wish to remain as an outcast, it must insist on equal rights, and that can only be accomplished if all Germans hold together as one man. Accept me as your Führer. I have shown that I can lead, and I do not belong to any class or group, only to you."

On election eve Hindenburg identified himself with Hitler, from whom he had accepted such liberal gratuities. "Tomorrow show your national honor and identify yourself with the Reich government," he advised the nation in a broadcast. "Speak up with me and the Chancellor for the principle of equality and for peace with honor and show to the world that we have restored German unity and with God's help shall preserve it."

It was an invocation that few patriots could resist. When the votes were counted the next day 95.1 per cent approved Hitler's foreign policy; and in the Reichstag election 92.2 per cent voted National Socialist, the only party on the ticket. Although some foreign observers scoffed at these results (2154 out of 2242 inmates at the Dachau concentration camp voted for the Führer), the results were a true barometer of German feeling. Adolf Hitler had won his gamble on foreign policy while solidifying his position at home. His mandate was so overwhelming that he was able, within weeks, to pass a law unifying party and state. It stated that the NSDAP was to be "the representative of the German state idea and indissolubly linked to the state."

With the entire population of Germany incorporated into the new regime, Hitler's policy of Gleichschaltung was officially completed. While the Führer had gained considerable power by consent (and threat), he was not yet a true dictator since resistance was still possible from the military and even from the failing Hindenburg. Hitler had led Germany onto the road to dictatorship. They needed no whip to follow a Siegfried who was bringing them out of economic depression and wiping out the dishonor of Versailles.

This could not have been accomplished, of course, without repression. The concentration camp (a term borrowed from the British of Boer War days) had become an accepted part of the national scene and was as much a threat to those on the outside as punishment for those inside. Nor was there any serious protest in the press after confiscation of Marxist and Social Democratic newspapers and publishing houses. Editors and publishers were brought under control and the last vestiges of independence were obliterated with establishment of the Reich Press Chamber. Along with freedom of the press also went that of literature, radio, theater, music, films and fine arts.

By December of 1933 Germany stood on the threshold of totalitarianism, brought there more by the needs of the time and the wish to conform than by terror. Nor was the spirit of conventionality a matter of class. It existed among scientists as well as workers. "We wish thus to conform to the spirit of the total state and to co-operate loyally and honestly," the president of the German Mathematical Association told his colleagues. "Unconditionally and joyfully we place ourselves—as is a matter of course for every German—at the service of the National Socialist movement and behind its leader, our Chancellor Adolf Hitler."

And so came totalitarianism and conformity to every profession on every level of society. Although other nations and races were congratulating themselves that such compliance was peculiarly Germanic and the repressiveness of this regime was typically Teutonic, both were a result of the intolerable demands of economics, geography and the times. These Germans marching to the tune of National Socialism were not unique in their love of order and militarism, or in their cruelty and arrogance.

6

One sour note among Hitler's successes was the delay in the Reichstag fire trial. It did not get under way until the first day of autumn and by that time the German Communists had convinced most of the world that the conflagration had been started by the accusers. First they published in Paris a book purporting to be an exposé of the Hitler terror and the burning of the Reichstag, which was based on fancy. "We had no direct proof, no access to witnesses, only underground communications to Germany," Arthur Koestler later confessed. "We had, in fact, not the faintest idea of the concrete circumstances."

The expatriate Communists followed this success with their own trial. It began in London on September 14, 1933, and was presided over by an international committee of jurists including D. N. Pritt of England and Arthur Garfield Hays of the United States. The illustrious audience included George Bernard Shaw, whose work, particularly *St. Joan*, was admired by Hitler. Shaw had declined a place on the jury and was present in his usual role as dissenter: "Whenever a prisoner is used as a stick with which to beat a Government," he said, "his fate is sealed in advance." After six days the kangaroo court published its predictable findings: "grave grounds exist for suspecting that the Reichstag was set on fire by, or on behalf of, leading personalities of the National Socialist Party."

The next day the German trial opened in Leipzig. Göring took a personal hand in the prosecution and was made to look like a fool by the four Communist defendants. Finally Göring lost his temper and shouted at

Georgi Dimitrov (later Prime Minister of Bulgaria), "You wait until we get you outside this court, you scoundrel!" Göring had the last word but the victory went to the Communists, all of whom were acquitted by the court. Van der Lubbe, who had testified over and over that he and he alone was guilty, was sentenced to death and executed.

The outside world preferred to believe that the Dutchman was only a tool of the Nazis who had set fire to the Reichstag as an excuse to crush the Reds. So did many historians, including Bullock and Shirer, but their judgment was reached before publication of a detailed book by Fritz Tobias which concluded that neither the Nazis nor the Communists were involved in the fire and that van der Lubbe *was* the sole arsonist. While the Tobias book was questioned by some historians, including Bracher, its findings have been corroborated by Hans Mommsen in an authoritative article published by the Institut für Zeitgeschichte, a body not at all likely to favor any Nazi interpretation. Further, examination of van der Lubbe's history and the trial transcripts indicated he was of above-average intelligence and that his action was a lone-wolf attack on the establishment.

While the verdict of the judges of Leipzig was obviously swayed by foreign opinion, it was also an indication that the court system still maintained a measure of independence. Hitler's reply to a Göring complaint that the judges behaved disgracefully ("You would think we were on trial, not the Communists") was revealing: *"Mein lieber* Göring, it is only a question of time. We shall soon have those old fellows talking our language. They are all ripe for retirement anyway, and we will put in our own people. But while the Old Gentleman is alive, there is not much we can do about it."

Hanfstaengl claimed he overheard this pronouncement at a chancellery luncheon, and that autumn he made another attempt to turn Hitler on a course more acceptable to the West. He phoned Martha Dodd, the attractive daughter of the American ambassador, and announced: "Hitler should have an American woman—a lovely lady could change the whole destiny of Europe. Martha, you are the woman!" (Like so many others in the Führer's intimate circle, Hanfstaengl was unaware that Hitler already had a mistress, Eva Braun, if a neglected one.)

Martha Dodd was "rather excited by the opportunity that presented itself" and agreed to meet the Führer and attempt "to change the history of Europe." At the Kaiserhof tearoom Hitler kissed her hand and murmured a few embarrassed words. She found it difficult to imagine that she was face to face with one of the most powerful men in Europe. "He seemed modest, middle class, rather dull and self-conscious—yet with this strange tenderness and appealing helplessness." When she described her impressions at dinner her father was "greatly amused at my impressionableness" and advised her not to wash the hand that had been kissed by the great man.

If Ambassador Dodd was unimpressed by Hitler, his British colleagues were taking him most seriously. They were willing to make considerable concessions to his rearmament demands and their eagerness to secure some sort of agreement was revealed by a visit to Berlin early in 1934 of the Lord Privy Seal, Anthony Eden. Hitler impressed Eden as much more than a demagogue. "He knew what he was speaking about and, as the long interviews proceeded, showed himself completely master of his subject." All Germany asked as a precondition to any international guarantee was the possibility of self-defense. If such a convention were concluded, Hitler promised to guarantee that the SS and SA would be deprived of arms. As if to underline his desire for conciliation, Hitler made an exceptional gesture the following day, February 21, by coming to the British Embassy for lunch. It was the first time the Führer had ever entered a foreign embassy. He showed little interest in food or drink but "thawed materially" once they began discussing their personal experiences in the war. When Eden remarked that ex-soldiers should be the last ever to wish for another war Hitler "assented heartily."

After lunch Hitler was prepared to make more detailed proposals. He asked for 30 per cent of the combined number of military aircraft possessed by his neighbors and was prepared to agree that the number of German aircraft should never exceed 60 per cent of those in the French air force. He also pleasantly surprised Eden by offering to trim down the SA and SS, adding "that his own common sense and political instinct would never allow him to sanction the creation of a second army in the state. Never, never!"

It was a season for concessions and Hitler made another gesture of amity, this time to the United States, on March 14. Foreign Minister von Neurath cabled his consul general in New York to communicate orally the following note to Ambassador Dodd, who would soon arrive there on the S.S. *Manhattan*:

THE REICH CHANCELLOR REQUESTS MR. DODD TO PRESENT HIS GREETINGS TO PRESIDENT ROOSEVELT. HE CONGRATULATES THE PRESIDENT UPON HIS HEROIC EFFORT IN THE INTEREST OF THE AMERICAN PEOPLE. THE PRESIDENT'S SUCCESSFUL STRUGGLE AGAINST ECONOMIC DISTRESS IS BEING FOLLOWED BY THE ENTIRE GERMAN PEOPLE WITH INTEREST AND ADMIRATION. THE REICH CHANCELLOR IS IN ACCORD WITH THE PRESIDENT THAT THE VIRTUES OF SENSE OF DUTY, READINESS FOR SACRIFICE, AND

DISCIPLINE MUST BE THE SUPREME RULE OF THE WHOLE NATION. THIS
MORAL DEMAND, WHICH THE PRESIDENT IS ADDRESSING TO EVERY SINGLE
CITIZEN, IS ONLY THE QUINTESSENCE OF GERMAN PHILOSOPHY OF THE
STATE, EXPRESSED IN ITS MOTTO "THE PUBLIC WEAL BEFORE PRIVATE
GAIN."

The message fell far short of its purpose, being not only offensive in
wording but ill timed. A week earlier the American Jewish Congress had
held an effective mock trial at Madison Square Garden entitled "Civilization against Hitlerism, a presentation of factual record of laws and acts
of the Hitler regime." Samuel Seabury, a well-known attorney, acted as
counsel for Civilization and the witnesses included Mayor Fiorello
LaGuardia, Al Smith and Raymond Moley. Civilization was unanimously
pronounced the winner.

7

Hitler's promise to hold in check the SS and SA reassured France to a
certain extent but their leaders could not be persuaded that Hitler's rearmament program was designed for defense alone. "The British were eager
to get it all over with," recalled Ambassador François-Poncet. "They sent
us note upon note urging us to state what guarantees seemed to us to
strengthen security sufficiently to gain our consent to a relative rearmament of the Reich." The British themselves were privately concerned, particularly by the rapid growth of the German air force, but there was still
considerable public sympathy for the plight of the new Reich, with many
ridiculing the notion that Hitler was driving toward war.

Ambassador François-Poncet shared the view that concessions should
be made to Germany. "Better a limited and controlled armament than unlimited, uncontrolled and unrepressed armament of the Reich!" He felt
any agreement, even a mediocre one, was better than none and did his utmost to win over his superiors. Early that April he journeyed to Paris to
present his views in person but, in an interview with Premier Doumergue,
"was not permitted to breathe one word" and was cut short every time he
attempted to broach the subject. The French decision was to check German ambitions by setting up an anti-Nazi bloc in the East: Poland, the
U.S.S.R. and Czechoslovakia would be the links in this security chain
under the aegis of Mother France.

When France and the Soviet Union approached agreement that
spring, Hitler understandably feared that this was the beginning of an en-
circlement of the Reich. To counter the proposed bloc, Hitler needed a

strong ally. The best prospect was Italy, whose leader had shown little desire for such a union since 1924 when he refused to lend the Nazis a few million lire. It grated on Hitler to be a supplicant but pride gave way to necessity and he made another effort. Controlling his resentment, he wrote Mussolini, ". . . admiration for the historic efforts of Your Excellency is linked with the desire for co-operation in a spirit of true friendship for our two ideologically related nations which can contribute immeasurably to the tranquilization of Europe through suitable attention to identical interests." He argued that since Germany had disarmed it had the right to demand the disarmament of other states, then listed in detail all the usual arguments. To accent the import of the message, Hitler had the letter delivered by Hermann Göring.

Several weeks later Hitler's foreign press secretary and unofficial court jester, Hanfstaengl, also visited Mussolini and suggested that he meet the Führer. "You are both admirers of Wagner and that will give a common starting point," Hanfstaengl remembered saying. "Think what it would mean if you invited him to the Palazzo Vendramin in Venice where Richard Wagner died. He would gain the benefit of your long experience and obtain much-needed insight into the problems of Europe as seen from outside Germany." Mussolini was not averse to the idea and in his good time sent an invitation which, after a show of reluctance, was accepted.

The historic meeting was doomed from the start. According to Filippo Bojano, Italian press representative in Berlin, Mussolini was motivated primarily by curiosity to see the politician all Europe was talking about. "Hitler is simply a muddleheaded fool," he confided to Bojano. "His head is stuffed with philosophical and political tags that are utterly incoherent. I can't make out why he waited so long to take over power, and why he played the buffoon, with his ridiculous electoral contests, in order to take legal possession of the reins of power. Either he is a revolutionary or he is not. Fascist Italy would never have come into being without a march on Rome. We are dynamic, and Signor Hitler is just a prater."

This contemptuous attitude was so publicized that the Italian press turned out en masse, directors and all, "to see this strange freak, Hitler." When he stepped out of his Junkers at Lido airfield on June 14 he looked like a struggling salesman in his worn trench coat over a blue serge suit. He was met by a Duce wearing black shirt, jack boots and glittering gold braid, backed up by Italian troops in full dress. Mussolini flung his arm out in Roman salute so vigorously that correspondent H. R. Knickerbocker thought "he might lose his hand."

Hitler sidled forward uncertainly, his hand almost apologetically responding with a feeble Nazi salute. He was obviously embarrassed by the show Mussolini had staged and, after blinking in the sunlight, awkwardly descended the steps to shake hands with his *beau idéal*. "They were not over three yards from me," wrote Knickerbocker, "and I was fascinated to watch the expressions on their faces. Beneath the obligatory cordiality I found I could see an expression of amusement in Mussolini's eyes and of resentment in Hitler's." Nor did the Führer's embarrassment ease when his host led him down the line of troops. He acted like a schoolboy at his first formal party. He didn't know what to do with his new fedora. First he took it off to salute the Italian flag, then started to put it back on but stopped himself and clutched it in his right hand. Then as he walked alongside Mussolini, who was chatting away in his voluble but eccentric German, he kept shifting the hat from hand to hand as if it were a hot potato.

There was another bit of comedy when the flustered Hitler tried to get Mussolini to precede him in boarding the launch which was to carry them to Venice. But Mussolini, the perfect host, maneuvered himself behind the Führer and waved him down the gangplank as if he were shooing a chicken into a coop. At the hotel landing, Hitler leaped out and jogged forward with bent head. "Mussolini stepped forth superbly. He was aware of being the cynosure of all eyes. His glances flashed, his figure was upright; he was—histrionically—the Duce."

Once inside his suite, Hitler began loudly abusing his advisers for allowing him to arrive in civilian clothes when Mussolini was so effectively attired. He was so upset that the first conversation with his host, despite a glowing official report, was another disaster. Il Duce dominated the talk, which centered on Austria, speaking in a bravura German which was sometimes incomprehensible to Hitler, while Mussolini in turn misunderstood much of Hitler's Austrian German.

The next morning the two men reviewed a parade of Fascist troops in the Piazza San Marco. At one point two columns had an argument about right of way directly in front of the rostrum. Neither unit would give in and when both plunged straight ahead the musicians began caterwauling. Later Hitler asked his new personal adjutant, Lieutenant Fritz Wiedemann, what he thought of the military value of such troops. Wiedemann, adjutant of Hitler's regiment during the war, replied that fighting ability had nothing to do with parading. "This remark, however, made no impression at all on Hitler, especially since, at the very moment, he glanced out the window at an Italian warship and saw to his amazement an array of sailors' shirts and underwear flying from the masts instead of the usual fleet flags."

Only a fool or a master of comedy would have staged the concluding and most important meeting of the dictators at the Lido golf course. "I noticed," recalled Bojano, "that Hitler was speaking all the time in a very excited way, while Mussolini listened, silent and with a scowl on his face." During the two-hour talk Bojano rarely saw Il Duce open his mouth. "He was so bored by Hitler's drivel that that very evening, in the middle of the official reception, he decamped in a hurry, and left the lagoon, stating that he did not want to see anybody."

Hitler left Venice stung by the realization that he had been not only snubbed by Mussolini but outmaneuvered diplomatically. The Führer had agreed to the full recognition of the independence of Austria which he felt belonged within the Reich, while receiving in turn no definite promise of support on the disarmament question. It was thus with amusement that those diplomatic officials who had been present read Foreign Minister von Neurath's circular to foreign missions:

> . . . THE REICH CHANCELLOR'S VISIT TO VENICE WENT OFF WITH EXCEPTIONAL CORDIALITY AND MOST HARMONIOUSLY, AND MADE A GREAT IMPRESSION ON THE PUBLIC AS WELL. . . .
>
> HITLER AND MUSSOLINI GOT ON EXTREMELY WELL TOGETHER AND CONCEIVED FEELINGS OF PERSONAL FELLOWSHIP OVER AND ABOVE THEIR MUTUAL ESTEEM.
>
> THE CONVERSATIONS, WHICH WERE DETAILED AND WERE HELD IN AN ATMOSPHERE OF INTIMACY, RANGED OVER ALL THE QUESTIONS ARISING FROM THE AFFINITY BETWEEN THE TWO CONCEPTS OF THE STATE, AND FAR-REACHING AGREEMENT WAS ESTABLISHED. FORMAL AGREEMENTS HAD NOT BEEN ENVISAGED AND WERE, IN CONSEQUENCE, NOT CONCLUDED. . . .

State Secretary Ernst von Weizsäcker of the Foreign Office confided to a Swiss official that he "could not foresee any closer collaboration between the two men."

Hitler and two friends outside Haus Wachenfeld, the modest villa he bought on the Obersalzberg which grew into the Berghof. HANS HITLER

Hitler confers with Captain Pfeffer von Salomon, head of the Brownshirts, prior to his replacement by Röhm in 1930. Alfred Rosenberg, who introduced "The Protocols of Zion" to the Führer, on right. LIBRARY OF CONGRESS

The depression. One-man demonstration in Berlin, August 1930. BUNDESARCHIV

Hitler learns to use his hands; his teacher, reportedly, was the famous seer Hanussen. BUNDESARCHIV

Geli Raubal, the only true love of Hitler, commits suicide in his Munich apartment during the 1931 presidential campaign. HANS HITLER

Geli with mother, left, and Paula Hitler. TOLAND COLLECTION

Hitler in February 1932, autographed to Egon Hanfstaengl. EGON HANFSTAENGL

Tenant strike in Berlin. Reds join Nazis. BUNDESARCHIV

Chapter Twelve

THE SECOND REVOLUTION— "ALL REVOLUTIONS DEVOUR THEIR OWN CHILDREN" FEBRUARY–AUGUST 1934

1

Hitler's promise to reduce the number of storm troopers was sincere. For years the SA had shown an independence that troubled him and for months its commander, Captain Röhm, had been demanding a military role for his men. The army, naturally, opposed it.

Hitler knew that his best chance for survival was to back the military leaders since he could never achieve his ultimate aims without their full support, and so had announced: "The Reichswehr is the sole bearer of arms of the nation; the SA is responsible for the political education of the people." These words stirred up old resentments among the four million Brownshirts, who recalled the long struggle between the northern and southern factions of the party. While remaining loyal to Hitler as their spiritual leader, many felt he had betrayed the Brown Revolution and was selling out to the right. They regarded themselves as the symbol of party radicalism and were not at all satisfied with the reforms of the first year of power. For months Röhm ("Only he who is without pessimism has ideals") had been calling for a Second Revolution that would bring them the social and material benefits they had fought for. "Anyone who thinks that the tasks of the SA have been accomplished," he told eighty thousand Brownshirts at Tempelhof airfield, "will have to get used to the idea that we are here and intend to stay here, come what may." While the majority of party members shared this anti-capitalistic, anti-conservative sentiment, it was the SA that was most radical and ardent. Over and over Röhm let it be known that he and his men were the true guardians of the National Socialist idea ("We are the incorruptible guarantors of the fulfillment of the German revolution").

Hitler sympathized with the radicals but his head told him that further revolution was not feasible until Germany had recovered from economic disaster and rebuilt her armed forces; and this could not be done without the full support of industry and the military. At the same time, in his continuing role as conciliator, he made Röhm minister without portfolio in his cabinet, promised to appoint him Minister of Defense and sent him a rare commendation on the first day of 1934, remarkable for its use throughout of the familiar second person singular. Hitler meant to praise Röhm while subtly warning him to leave the defense of the country to the military, but Röhm missed the point. Emboldened, he dispatched a memorandum to the Defense Ministry claiming that national security was a prerogative of the SA.

This brought the conflict to a head and General von Blomberg asked Hitler to make a definite ruling. It was thus with regret that the Führer invited SA and Reichswehr leaders to a conference in the marble-pillared lecture hall of the ministry on the last day of February 1934. In a "moving, gripping" speech Hitler urged both sides to compromise. The party, he said, had solved unemployment but within eight years an economic recession would ensue and the only remedy was creation of living space for the surplus population. This might necessitate short, decisive military action in the West and then in the East. But a civilian militia, as suggested by Röhm, would not be the "least bit suitable for national defense." The solution was a people's army, rigorously trained and equipped with the most modern weapons. The SA must confine itself to internal political matters.

At this point Hitler forced Blomberg and Röhm to sign an agreement in his presence. The SA was granted two paramilitary functions: certain units were to operate as a police force along the nation's borders; the premilitary training of youths age eighteen to twenty-one was to be undertaken by the SA while those from twenty-one to twenty-six not serving in the armed forces were to be trained in "SA sport," a code name for organized military training.

It was a blow to Röhm but afterward he invited everyone to a luncheon of reconciliation in his home, formerly a millionaire's mansion. "Hitler did not take part," recalled General von Weichs. "The food was good—the atmosphere frosty. At any rate it seemed as if peace was restored. One certainly believed that the authority of Hitler in the party was so great that his decision would remain binding on the SA."

Once the army men left, Röhm's true feelings, liberated perhaps by drink, exploded. "What that ridiculous corporal says means nothing to us," he told his followers. "I have not the slightest intention of keeping this agreement. Hitler is a traitor and at the very least must go on leave. . . . If we can't get there with him, we'll get there without him." At least one listener was shocked. It sounded to SA Obergruppenführer Viktor Lutze like treason and he reported it to Hess. When the Führer's deputy hesitated to act, Lutze took it upon himself to travel to the Obersalzberg and inform Hitler himself of the dangerous discontent within the highest ranks of the SA. Here again he met with an apparent lack of interest. "We must let the matter develop," said the Führer and closed the discussion as if unwilling to admit that his beloved Brownshirts were in a state of discontent approaching revolt. A few weeks later, however, he flatly refuted Röhm's comment, "The grey [army] rock must be submerged by the brown flood," with the statement that "the new army would be a grey one not a brown one."

Röhm countered by calling a press conference in Berlin that April for the diplomatic corps and foreign journalists. He was an imposing figure, squat, powerful, intense, and he spoke in the flat but authoritative tones of someone who expects to be obeyed. "The SA is the heroic incarnation of the will and thought of the German revolution," he told the foreigners but his next words were obviously intended for Hitler. Those in the party who opposed the Brownshirts, he said, were reactionaries and bourgeois conformists. "The SA *is* the National Socialist Revolution!"

Secretly enemies of Röhm in the SS were already deeply involved in a plot to destroy him. At first it seemed curious that the prime mover was Reinhard Heydrich, head of the SD (*Sicherheitsdienst*, Security Service), and not the SS chief himself. For some time Himmler was reluctant to support the intrigue, perhaps out of fear that an open conflict with the SA would cause a fatal breach within the party. But he was tempted to forget this upon learning that Göring had also joined the conspirators. Göring was not only one of the Führer's closest associates but could give Himmler a post he coveted, chief of the Prussian Secret State Police Office

(*Geheimes Staatspolizeiamt*).* No sooner had Himmler allied himself with the cabal than he was made head of the Gestapo and he reciprocated by dropping hints to all the SS units that an open struggle with the Brownshirts was on the horizon. This seemed a certainty when Heydrich reported he had collected evidence that Röhm was plotting treason. The truth was that Röhm had not the slightest intention of launching a Putsch. He wanted only to force Hitler to give the SA its proper position in the Reich, by setting the Führer "in a golden cage" as it were, to isolate him from evil advisers. He was waging a war of nerves, not treason, but his threatening words were cause for alarm. On June 4 Hitler summoned Röhm to the chancellery and, according to the former's account, their conversation lasted almost five hours. "I implored him for the last time to oppose this madness of his own accord—let him at the same time use his authority so as to stop a development which in any event could end only in catastrophe. . . . The Chief of Staff left this interview after assuring me that the reports were partly untrue and partly exaggerated, and that moreover he would for the future do everything in his power to set things to rights."

Although one witness in the anteroom, Papen's adjutant, swore he heard them "bellowing at each other," there was no indication in Hitler's account that this discussion was a stormy one. It is probable that Röhm left at midnight with the impression that the Führer was sympathetic but under pressure from the military to curtail SA activities. It was also likely that Hitler himself imagined he had just made a genuine truce with Röhm since the SD was almost immediately informed that the Führer had come to agreement with the SA chief on several points.

It was agreed that a monthlong leave for the entire SA would start as scheduled. This was announced by the *Deutsches Nachrichtenbüro* (German News Bureau) on June 7. The following day the DNB published an intriguing "Order of Chief of Staff Röhm," stating: "I have decided to follow the advice of my physicians and take the cure, in order to fully restore my health which has been severely impaired the last few weeks by a painful nervous complaint."

The two announcements reassured the military leaders, who felt that it signaled Röhm's decline, but appalled Heydrich, who had only three weeks to complete his dossier against the SA and thus force Hitler to act decisively. Röhm's sister-in-law, among others, warned him about rumors

* Some post office officials made up an abbreviated stamp for the new organization— Gestapa. Colloquial usage soon turned this into Gestapo, a name that would soon be a synonym for terrorism.

of a Göring-Goebbels-Himmler plot against him. "He had some feeling that there was something wrong," she recalled, "but still did not take it seriously. He never had any doubts whatsoever about Hitler."

2

Discontent from an entirely different quarter descended on Hitler hours after his return from the humiliating visit with Mussolini in Venice. On June 17, a pleasant Sunday, Franz von Papen was preparing to make an address at the University of Marburg. There was considerable interest in what the Vice-Chancellor would say since he had delivered a controversial speech six months earlier at the Bremen Club warning of the growing unrest in Germany over the new regime's assaults on the principles of law and the restrictions placed on the Church. As Papen entered the great auditorium, which was packed with students, professors and a scattering of uniformed party members, there was an air of expectancy. He began with a direct attack on the controlled press in general and Goebbels in particular.

The audience was stunned by such words coming from the official who held the second highest position in the government but this was only the beginning. After criticizing Nazi bigots and doctrinaires along with the single-party system, he urged Hitler to break with those calling for Röhm's Second Revolution. "Have we gone through the anti-Marxist revolution in order to carry out the Marxist program? . . . No people can afford to indulge in a permanent revolt from below if it would endure in history. At some time the movement must come to a stop and a solid social structure arise."

The few shouts of protest from party members were drowned out in tumultuous applause. Only the *Frankfurter Zeitung* managed to print a few extracts from the speech in its afternoon edition. Goebbels ordered all copies of this paper impounded and forbade a scheduled replaying of the speech over the radio. But the text was smuggled out of the country and published, causing a sensation not only abroad but throughout Germany, and when the Vice-Chancellor appeared at a Hamburg race track he was greeted by shouts, "Heil Marburg!"

For the first few days Hitler made no public comment. It was Papen who forced the issue by threatening to resign unless Goebbels' ban on his speech was lifted. Hitler tried to calm his Vice-Chancellor. He admitted Goebbels had blundered, then berated the insubordination of the SA as if he approved that part of the speech. He promised to lift the ban and requested Papen to withhold his resignation until the two of them went to Neudeck to see Hindenburg.

Papen agreed to wait but Hitler broke his word. The next day, June 21, he hastily set out for Neudeck alone and without removing the ban on the speech. His announced purpose was to report to the President on the recent meeting with Mussolini, but it is more likely he wished to see the Old Gentleman without the inhibiting presence of Papen. He may also have wanted to check on Hindenburg's health and find out how much time he had left to make arrangements to be his successor. To accomplish this he would need the support of the military and it was significant that the first person he met on the steps of the Hindenburg estate was Defense Minister von Blomberg in full uniform despite the sweltering heat.

The President had his own reasons for seeing the Führer. He wanted to be enlightened on the turmoil caused by Papen's speech, but he left most of the talking to Blomberg, acting stiff and Prussian, who made it clear that internal peace was the first priority. If Hitler could not remove the present intolerable tension, he said, the President would declare martial law and turn over the job to the army. No mention was made of Röhm and the Second Revolution, nor was any necessary. The Old Gentleman, who had left Berlin in a wheel chair—purchased over his protest that it was too expensive—rallied himself and in a somewhat shaky voice reaffirmed Blomberg's words. It was all over in four minutes and soon Hitler was in his plane winging back to Berlin. During that silent journey his thoughts probably centered on Röhm. "If during these months I hesitated time and again before making a final decision," Hitler would explain to the Reichstag in several weeks, "it was due to two considerations: First I could not easily convince myself that a relationship which I thought to be founded on loyalty could be a lie; second, I still cherished the secret hope that I might be able to spare the movement and my SA the shame of such a disagreement and that it might be possible to remove the mischief without serious conflicts."

Sometime that night Hitler made up his mind to take action. In the morning he phoned Viktor Lutze, who months earlier had warned him against Röhm, and instructed him to report to the chancellery at once. "He led me into his study," wrote Lutze in his diary, "and, taking me by the hand, swore me to secrecy until the whole matter was settled." The Führer revealed with some emotion that Röhm had to be removed because of a determination to arm the SA and set it against the army. "The Führer said that he had always known I would be no party to such matters. Henceforth I was to accept no orders from Munich and take instructions only from him."

In the meantime Heydrich and Himmler were doing their utmost to entrap Röhm and that same day the latter summoned one of his SS commanders, Freiherr von Eberstein, and told him that Röhm was plotting a Putsch. Eberstein was to pass the word on to the military district commanders and put his own troops on "unobtrusive alert," confining them to barracks for emergency action. Within hours the warning was passed through army channels: the chief of the General Army Office informed his officers that an SA coup d'état was imminent and that the SS, which supported the army, should be given any weapons they needed.

By now Hitler had become so convinced that Röhm was plotting an uprising that he told Defense Minister von Blomberg he was summoning all SA commanders to Bad Wiessee, a spa on the Tegernsee where Röhm was taking his rest cure. When they had assembled, continued Hitler, he would personally arrest them and "square accounts." The army was prepared for action. First, Colonel General Freiherr Werner von Fritsch, commander-in-chief of the Reichswehr, passed on the order to place all troops in a state of alert. Leaves were canceled and the men confined to barracks.

Almost simultaneously Hess broadcast a remarkable speech over a nationwide radio hookup that was both a warning and a plea to Röhm: "Woe to him who breaks the faith, and thinks to serve the revolution through rebellion!" he said and then referred to such plotters as "credulous idealists." The entire speech could have been spoken by Hitler himself, for it urged Röhm to abandon his Second Revolution and return to the fold. The following day a blunter warning came from Hermann Göring: Anyone who eroded confidence in Hitler would "pay with his head." Secluded as he was at Bad Wiessee, Ernst Röhm should have been aware of these portents. Another came on June 28 when the German Officers League formally expelled him from its ranks.

Rumors of an imminent showdown were circulating in Berlin and that same day Sefton Delmer got firsthand information about the dilemma Hitler faced from the assistant to Papen's press counselor. "Now we are in the middle of the war for Hindenburg's succession," he explained, with Hitler on one side and the Vice-Chancellor and his fellow conservatives on the other. The showdown, he predicted, would take place at the next cabinet meeting when Papen would force Hitler "to suppress the terrorist anarchy" of Röhm and his Second Revolution gangsters. If the Führer refused the Papen group would resign and Hindenburg would dismiss Hitler and hand over executive power to the army. "Whichever way things go, my boss reckons he has got Hitler by the short hairs. If he accepts, he is shorn of power. If he refuses the army takes over. I only hope Hitler refuses. Even though that might mean a shooting war!"

At the moment the Führer was in Essen, visibly enjoying a vacation as a guest at the wedding of the local Gauleiter. Another guest, Lutze, was concerned. "I had a feeling," he wrote in his diary, "that it suited certain circles to aggravate and accelerate 'the affair' just at this moment when the Führer was absent from Berlin and could therefore neither see nor hear things himself, but was dependent on the telephone."

It was the telephone, indeed, which played a major role in the developing intrigue. No sooner had Hitler arrived with Göring at the wedding breakfast than he was interrupted by a call from Himmler in Berlin, who read off a series of alarming reports. Göring nodded his head in confirmation as he learned of the supposed SA machinations and Hitler became so wrought up that he returned at once to his local quarters. "Here in the hotel room," according to Lutze, who was one of those hastily summoned, "the telephone was going almost uninterruptedly. The Führer was deep in thought but it was apparently clear that he would now have to take action."

The conference was enlivened by the arrival of Göring's secretary with further information from Himmler of an imminent Brownshirt revolt. This report, along with another from an agent of Heydrich that Röhm's Brownshirts had just insulted a foreign diplomat, was too much for Hitler. "I've had enough," he said. "I shall make an example of them." He ordered Göring to return to the capital and be prepared to act upon receiving the code word (it was *Kolibri*, hummingbird), then made a call of his own. He phoned Röhm in Bad Wiessee and complained about the alleged molesting of foreigners. This could not be tolerated, he said with some heat, and told Röhm he wanted to speak to the top SA leaders gathering at the Tegernsee two days later at 11 A.M.

The conversation either did not perturb Röhm or he pretended it didn't, for when he returned to the dinner table he seemed "very well pleased." He informed his guests, one of whom was General von Epp, that Hitler was going to attend the congress of SA leaders on June 30, adding with relish that this would give him the opportunity to "tear the mask from Goebbels." He knew that he could count on his SA and the army. Such an unrealistic comment meant Röhm either was fantasizing or was unaware of the extent of the intrigues swirling around him.

These gathered momentum with Göring's return to Berlin. The following morning, Friday, June 29, he alerted the Prussian police unit along with the Führer's faithful SS bodyguard unit, recently christened *Leibstandarte-SS Adolf Hitler*. More significant, he gave himself plenary powers in

Prussia based on Hitler's declaration of a state of emergency, and then delegated authority in Silesia to the commander of the SS Southeast Region with orders to arrest a number of Brownshirt leaders, disarm all SA headquarters guards and seize the Breslau police headquarters.

By this time the general army alert was in effect even though many of its senior officers were still not convinced that Röhm intended to stage a revolt, and that morning one of them flew to Berlin to express such doubts to Army Commander-in-Chief von Fritsch. This skeptic was General Ewald von Kleist, head of the army in Silesia, and he told Fritsch, in the presence of General Ludwig Beck, that he had been assured by the SA leader in Silesia (a close friend of Röhm's) that Brownshirt preparations for action were only a reaction to army alerts aimed against them. Kleist was convinced that a third party—he mentioned Himmler—was attempting to set the SA and army against each other. Concerned, Fritsch summoned General von Reichenau, head of the Army Office and a loyal Nazi even before 1933. This urbane officer, the very model of a Prussian general with his ever present monocle and imperturbable manner, listened to Kleist repeat his story before commenting: "That may be true, but it's too late now."

A flood of new evidence—consisting of rumors, fake reports and doctored documents—was already being directed into army channels to convince the doubting Thomases that after the Putsch Röhm would execute or dismiss all senior army officers beginning with Fritsch. Fictitious death lists were passed around from so many sources that they began to seem real. An article in the day's *Völkischer Beobachter* by Defense Minister von Blomberg appeared to reinforce this illusion. He proclaimed that the army stood loyally behind the Chancellor.

If Röhm read this article he apparently didn't take it as a personal warning. Enjoying the beauty of Bad Wiessee, he calmly greeted arriving SA dignitaries at his pension and expressed satisfaction at the morrow's meeting with the Führer. Nor was he at all perturbed when a general, a comrade of the war, warned him that he was "making a fatal error" if he believed that the army would not open fire on revolting SA troops. Röhm's actions that evening were hardly those of a man planning an uprising. After a leisurely session of *Tarok*, the three-handed Bavarian card game, he received an injection for neuralgia from his doctor, then turned in for a peaceful sleep.

Not so Hitler. His suite at the Hotel Dreesen in Bad Godesberg was like a military headquarters on the eve of battle and he acted like an irresolute general with his first command. Just before midnight he ordered Gruppenführer Josef (Sepp) Dietrich, commander of his SS bodyguard, to descend on Bad Wiessee with two companies, but a few moments later two phone calls, one from Berlin and another from Munich, forced a drastic change in plans. The first, from Himmler (who had just told the Ribbentrops, "Röhm is as good as dead"), was that the Berlin SA was planning a Putsch which would start at 5 P.M. with the occupation of the government buildings. During the conversation Hitler answered only in monosyllables but once he put the receiver down he shouted, "It's a Putsch!" It seemed that Karl Ernst, head of the Berlin storm troopers, instead of going to Bad Wiessee as planned, had remained in Berlin to direct treasonous operations! (He was in Bremen preparing to take a honeymoon cruise.)

The Führer's stream of denunciations was interrupted by the second call, this from Adolf Wagner, the Gauleiter of Bavaria, who reported that rowdy Brownshirts were already in the streets of Munich shouting, "The Reichswehr is against us!" (Certain units had been alerted by a pamphlet of mysterious origin: "SA, take to the streets, the Führer is no longer for us!")

Hitler's rage turned to panic. Here was proof positive that Röhm was mutinying. "It was at last clear to me," he later said, "that only one man could oppose and must oppose the Chief of Staff [Röhm]. It was to me that he had pledged his loyalty and broken that pledge, and for that I alone must call him to account."

He made a sudden decision, which caught his comrades by surprise: he was going to Bad Wiessee and personally face the "nest of traitors." He ordered his private plane to be prepared for take-off, then paced between terraces and hall pouring out his feelings. How could Röhm have done such a thing? How could he have betrayed his Führer?

3

It was a shaken Hitler who climbed into the three-motored Junkers 52, a replacement for the regular plane, which had engine trouble. It was about 2 A.M. He slumped into his seat, stared fixedly ahead into the darkness. Otto Dietrich, his press chief, "had no idea what was up," until an adjutant instructed everyone to release the safety catch on his gun.

Lutze, who knew, was thinking of Röhm. He hummed to himself:

> *Red of the morning, red of the morning,*
> *Thou lightest us to early death.*
> *Yesterday mounted on a proud street,*
> *Today a bullet through the breast.*

It was a cloudy night with spits of rain. In the gray light preceding dawn Baur landed the plane on the drenched runway at Oberwiesenfeld, the military exercise field where Hitler had had his first humiliating confrontation with police and army twelve years earlier. The airport director was distressed. He had been instructed by Chief of Staff Röhm to alert the entire SA leadership as soon as the Führer's plane, D-2600, approached. But with the last-minute change in aircraft there was only a small group—party personages and several army officers—on hand to greet Hitler. "This is the blackest day in my life," he told them. "But I shall go to Bad Wiessee and pass severe judgment."

Hitler was driven to the Bavarian Ministry of the Interior where he leaped out of the car, followed by a rattled Gauleiter Wagner, who was also Minister of Interior. The Führer strode into the building, the skirt of his leather coat flying, and up the stairs toward Wagner's office. As he burst into the anteroom the head of the Upper Bavarian SA started to salute but Hitler rushed at him, shouting, "Lock him up!" He began cursing all traitors in general and the SA leaders whose men had been lured to the streets of Munich by pamphlets in particular. "You," he yelled, "are under arrest and will be shot!"

It was 6 A.M. when the Führer, still in "a terrifying state of excitement," emerged from the building. A second plane with armed reinforcements had not yet landed but he was too impatient to wait. He got into Kempka's car, taking his usual place beside the chauffeur, and instructed him to head for Bad Wiessee. They started off, followed by another car driven by Schreck. In the entire party there were only eight or nine men and the Führer's secretary, Fräulein Schröder. From the back seat Goebbels talked incessantly of the Brownshirt plot but Hitler only stared ahead. The sun was just breaking through clouds on the horizon. It was going to be "Hitler weather."

In less than an hour they reached the Tegernsee, nestling at the gateway to the Alps, its pure waters steaming with early morning mist. "We are now going to the Pension Hanselbauer," Hitler told Kempka. There was "some dirty work afoot" and they had to surprise the Hanselbauer's occupants. It was almost seven and church bells were calling the faithful to early morning mass when Kempka slowly, cautiously pulled up at the pension. Kempka noticed that some of the windows were closed, others open; there was no guard at the door. Hitler was first to enter. The ground floor appeared to be deserted; there was no one in the dining room, which was set for the midday banquet. Then the landlady appeared, understandably shocked to find herself face to face with the Führer. She started to express the honor she felt but he brusquely asked to be taken up to Röhm.

While the others in the party took positions in front of other rooms, a plainclothes detective knocked on Röhm's door. Then Hitler, revolver in hand, went in. Kempka, peering from behind his Führer, glimpsed a sleep-drugged Röhm blinking with genuine amazement and shock. He was in bed alone.

"Ernst," said Hitler, and then used the familiar *Du*, "you are under arrest." There was none of the fury Hitler had shown at the Ministry of the Interior. He was "somewhat tense but not visibly excited." Briefly and curtly he accused Röhm of being a traitor and told him to get dressed. Protesting vigorously, the SA chief began pulling on civilian clothes but Hitler had already gone and Röhm's words were wasted on the detectives left behind.

The Führer was banging at the opposite door. It opened and an Ober-gruppenführer named Heines stared out drowsily. Behind him stood his bed partner—an attractive young man who doubled as his chauffeur. "A disgusting scene, which made me feel like vomiting," wrote Goebbels.

Hitler went immediately to the next door, leaving Lutze behind to search for weapons. "Lutze, I've done nothing!" exclaimed Heines. "Can't you help me?"

"I can do nothing," said Lutze, more in embarrassment than self-righteousness, and repeated the phrase. Either from indignation or shock Heines refused to get dressed and would not do so until Hitler returned and told him to obey or be shot on the spot. Heines obeyed and was locked in the laundry with Röhm and his colleagues. With them were ten or so SA guards who had slept through the break-in, as well as Heines' chauffeur and several other good-looking youths taken in *flagrante delicto*.

While Hitler was discussing what should be done next, Kempka was sent to a nearby pension to apprehend Max Vogel, Röhm's cousin, who also served as his chauffeur. Vogel was in bed with a girl—the only such case that morning. Kempka, a good friend of his fellow chauffeur, apolo-getically announced he was under arrest. As they went to the garage for the Röhm car, Vogel made a curious last request: could he drive it just once more? Kempka understood and let him make a few slow turns in the driveway as he himself stood on the running board.

Just as Kempka and his prisoner got back to the Hanselbauer a truck filled with about forty armed Brownshirts of Röhm's "Headquarters Guard" arrived from Munich. Their commander was still locked up in the laundry and they were unhappy about it. One of Hitler's adjutants, Wilhelm Brückner, shouted an order to return to Munich at once. They did nothing except stare back sullenly, and a pitched battle seemed likely.

Then Hitler strode forward. "Didn't you hear what Brückner said?"

In a tone of command that managed to be charming, he ordered the guardsmen to return to Munich. "On the way you will meet SS troops and they will disarm you." His manner more than his words took all the fight out of them and the truck drove off.

The prisoners were loaded into two commandeered buses and the caravan started off. Hitler's Mercedes led the way and SA men bound for the lunch banquet at the Hanselbauer would be stopped and interrogated by Hitler. Those whose names appeared on a list hastily drawn up by Goebbels were disarmed and instructed to sandwich their own cars in the cavalcade.

It was about 9:30 A.M. by the time the growing procession reached the Brown House. It had been cordoned off by army troops and Hitler took time to thank them for coming to his aid and give assurances that he had never intended using them against the SA. Once inside party headquarters, Hitler told Goebbels to telephone the code word to Göring. The purge was on. "I gave the order to shoot those who were the ringleaders in this treason and I further gave the order to *burn out down to the raw flesh the ulcers of this poisoning of the wells* in our domestic life and of the poisoning of the outside." The use of words dredging up memories of his mother's cancer and Dr. Bloch revealed the depth of his emotional upheaval.

The cells of Stadelheim were already filled with SA leaders put there by the SS. Those still in the Brown House, such as Röhm, demanded to see the Führer and when he refused asked for Goebbels. He was too occupied with the phone conversation with Göring and, before he finished, the last prisoners were on their way to Stadelheim in an armored car. Their leader was put in a solitary cell, not far from the one he had occupied after the Beer Hall Putsch.

At the Brown House, General von Epp was demanding a court-martial for Röhm. This upset Hitler's equilibrium and he reverted to his early morning rage. Röhm, he exclaimed, was a proven traitor and deserved to die. The general was so taken aback by this outburst that he could not reply but, as he walked away, muttered to his aide, "Crazy!"

A little later, at 11:30 A.M., a conference of SA leaders began in the spacious council chamber. Hitler had not yet regained his composure and his address to his apprehensive audience was a series of disconnected complaints about the SA. Throughout the hourlong tirade Hitler's listeners stood in discomfort. One was fascinated by the foam that kept spewing from his mouth. "In a voice frequently choked with emotion," he accused Röhm of planning to kill him in order to hand Germany over to her enemies. Röhm and his conspirators, he promised, would be shot.

The killings had not yet started since Hitler was waiting for Sepp Dietrich, commander of the elite Leibstandarte, to do the job. He appeared shortly and explained to the exasperated Führer what had kept him so long: his trucks, for one reason, could not travel fast over wet roads on worn tires. For all his show of annoyance at the delay, Hitler had no orders to give. He told Dietrich to wait while he and his advisers argued the fate of the accused. Three hours passed without a decision.

While the Führer vacillated, his associates in Berlin were already carrying out executions. The Himmler-Heydrich-Göring triumvirate needed only the code word Kolibri to set their long-laid plot into action. When Papen reported to Göring's office he was annoyed to see the area "full of SS guards armed with machine-guns." The next surprise was to learn that Hitler had given Göring power to deal with the insurgents in the capital. Papen protested on the grounds that he was the Chancellor's deputy and in his absence such authority could be granted only to him. He insisted that Hindenburg declare a state of emergency and bring in the Reichswehr to restore law and order. Göring refused. He and Himmler's SS had complete control of the situation. He cut short Papen's protests and ordered the Vice-Chancellor to return home immediately for his own safety. Before Papen got there police cars were careening through the streets of Berlin rounding up enemies of the regime. One unit surrounded Papen's office, shot to death his press officer and arrested other members of his staff. The Vice-Chancellor might as well have been incarcerated; for as soon as he entered his own house it became a prison. Papen found his telephone wire cut and a police captain in the reception room who informed him that he was to have no contact with the outside world.

Few Berliners noticed that anything at all unusual was going on that hot Saturday morning. To the many strollers in the Tiergarten and on the Unter den Linden the greatest concern was the increasing heat as the sun climbed. Correspondent Delmer, however, had such a nagging worry that he interrupted his morning sculling session and drove back to his office. "I have stuck my neck right out on that 'Hitler dictatorship in peril' report," he kept saying to himself. What if nothing happened? But when his taxi was held up by a cordon of municipal police his fears were allayed. "Something *had* happened." The police, wearing steel helmets and armed with rifles and submachine guns, were surrounding Röhm's opulent Berlin residence on a corner of the Tiergartenstrasse.

In a suburb, two Gestapo agents were being ushered into General von Schleicher's study by his cook and when one of the visitors asked if that was Schleicher at the desk the former Chancellor looked up and said, "Ja." The men opened fire. Frau von Schleicher, in a corner listening to the radio, rushed toward her stricken husband and was cut down by bullets. He died instantly and she succumbed shortly at the hospital.

In Munich, Hitler still hesitated about passing final judgment on Röhm and his colleagues. The discussion in the meeting room grew so loud that Sepp Dietrich, waiting in the outer office, could hear voices through the double doors of the meeting room. At last this portal opened about 5 P.M. and Martin Bormann, Hess's assistant, emerged. He escorted Dietrich back to Hitler. "Return to the barracks," instructed the Führer, and gave an order that Dietrich felt was wrung out of him: "Select an officer and six men and have the SA leaders shot for treason."

Dietrich examined a list handed over by Bormann. It contained the names of all those taken to Stadelheim but Hitler had checked off only a dozen. They included Heines and the chief of the Upper Bavarian SA— but not Ernst Röhm. Hitler could still not bring himself to make that decision.

When Hans Frank, the Bavarian Minister of Justice, learned that many SA leaders were jailed at Stadelheim he decided to go there in person and take charge. Upon arrival, he ordered the SA prisoners placed in the custody of a detachment of state police, then had himself admitted to Röhm's little cell.

"What does it all mean?" asked Röhm. "What is going on?"

Frank could give little information or assurance. He hoped that everything would proceed legally. Röhm replied that he was prepared for the worst. "I am not concerned about my own life but please take care of my relatives, they are women totally dependent on me." As Frank opened the cell door Röhm pressed his hand. "All revolutions," he said, "devour their own children."

No sooner had Frank returned to his own office than Sepp Dietrich entered with a colleague to announce that he had orders to shoot a number of SA leaders. He produced a list checked personally by Hitler. Stunned, Frank said the executions could not take place under any circumstances. Dietrich insisted that the Führer himself had ordered it but was persuaded to telephone the Brown House. First he talked to Hess. After a pause Dietrich extended the receiver to Frank. "Hitler wants to speak with you."

Hitler began shouting: "You refuse to carry out an order from me? Are you in sympathy with that criminal scum? I'm going to destroy those boys, roots and all!"

Frank protested that there was no written authorization, just a list of six names. "I marked that list myself," said Hitler in more controlled language. "These gentlemen are criminals against the Reich. I am the Reich Chancellor. It is a matter of the Reich, which is never under your jurisdiction."

At Stadelheim the first six victims were led out into the courtyard, each guarded by two policemen. "The Führer and Reich Chancellor has condemned you to death," an SS officer droned out. "The sentence will be carried out forthwith." When the head of the Upper Bavarian Brownshirts, August Schneidhuber, realized the chief executioner was Dietrich, he cried out: "Sepp, my friend, what on earth's happening? We are completely innocent!" With set face Dietrich clicked his heels. "You have been condemned to death by the Führer," he said. "Heil Hitler!"

The first man was placed before the firing squad. He refused to have his eyes covered. Shots reverberated in the courtyard walls. The next victim and the next also disdained blindfolds. Dietrich witnessed the first few shootings but before it was Schneidhuber's turn he had to walk off. "I had had enough."

It was dark by the time Hitler's car started for the airfield. "I have pardoned Röhm," he promised General von Epp, who was seeing him off, "because of his services." Hitler took his place in the front of the plane and he sat silently as Baur headed the Junkers 52 toward Berlin.

For the average Berliner there was little on the surface to indicate that the nation was undergoing an upheaval. True, sinister rumors were beginning to circulate and there were traffic tie-ups on the Charlottenburger Chaussee, what with police barriers and the stream of army trucks. It was also known that house arrests were taking place but the violence was under cover. Few citizens knew that General von Schleicher and his wife had been murdered or that Gregor Strasser had been seized at his lunch table and put into Cell 16 of the Gestapo prison. There he was peppered with shots by unseen assailants from the cell window while he dodged around like a rat in a cage until wounded. Then one of the gunmen entered to finish the job. Thus the enemy of Goebbels and Göring perished, still faithful in his own fashion to the Führer.

The ringmaster of the purge in Berlin was Göring, who briefed foreign correspondents in the Ministry of Propaganda late that afternoon. "Göring arrived in one of his full-dress uniforms," wrote a Gestapo official. "Once again he did not walk; he strutted up to the platform with slow, mincing steps. He began the session with a long, impressive pause, leaning forward slightly, his chin propped in his hand, and rolling his eyes as if he feared his own revelations." When he mentioned Schleicher in connection with the Röhm-Strasser plot, someone asked what had happened to the former Chancellor. "He was foolish enough to resist," said Göring with what one chronicler described as a wolfish smile. "He is dead."

Later in the day DNB published another excuse for the purge in the form of a telegram the Führer had sent to Viktor Lutze appointing him Röhm's successor. In it he listed a dozen "tasks" for the new SA commander and his leaders and the first was: "I demand from the leader of the SA just as he demands from each SA man, blind obedience and absolute discipline." He also condemned "official journeys in costly limousines or cabriolets," sumptuous feasts, intoxication and brawling in public. "It is my special desire that every mother can give her son to the SA, to the party, or to the Hitler Youth, without fear that he might be morally injured there." In the future, therefore, all Brownshirt leaders who misbehaved would be immediately drummed out of the SA and the party. "I want my SA leaders to be men, not ridiculous apes." Such words, coming at such a time, were received with derision by most foreign observers, but the average German read them with approbation, relieved to know that the Führer shared their own revulsion of the Brownshirt rowdies.

He further called on every SA chief to show "completely honest, loyal and true fealty to the Reichswehr" and "prove himself a real leader, friend and comrade." Finally, after praising the old SA fighters—"the ones who have conquered Germany and not the clever latecomers of the year 1933, and subsequently"—he made the first mention of his personal bodyguard troops: "I desire that the SS man shall be educated mentally and bodily to be the most highly-trained National Socialist."

By evening the death toll was appalling. General von Bredow, a friend of Schleicher, was gunned down at his front door. The acting police president of Breslau was disemboweled by a shotgun and an SS cavalry leader murdered in his own smoking room. The ghost writer of the recent controversial Papen speech lay lifeless in an underground cell of the Gestapo prison in the Prinz Albrechtstrasse. Other executions were taking place, under the supervision of the SS, at the Lichterfeld Barracks. Here died an official of the Ministry of Transport, the president of Catholic Action as well as Karl Ernst, who had been brought back from his honeymoon. His last words were: "Heil Hitler!"

The Brownshirts were in a state of confusion. Some units were alerted, issued revolvers and ordered to catch traitors—only to be rounded up themselves by SS troops and carted off for detention. Others were beaten up in the streets by roving Himmler men and some shot out of hand. Still others were marked for arrest or death but spared by friends in the SS. For thousands, who felt they had sacrificed everything for the party, it was a night of terror and disillusionment.

It was not until 10 P.M. that the Hitler plane finally touched down at Tempelhof airfield. Waiting was a tight little group—Göring, Himmler, Frick, a few Gestapo officials and a police escort. The first to step out of the plane was the Führer, clad in brown shirt, black bow tie, leather jacket and black army boots. "He wore no hat; his face was pale, unshaven, sleepless, at once gaunt and puffed," recalled a Gestapo official. After shaking hands, Hitler drew Göring and Himmler aside and listened attentively to their reports. While Hitler perused a list given him by Himmler, a finger slowly moving down the page, his two companions whispered to each other. As the trio slowly headed for the car followed by an escort at a discreet interval, Hitler revealed that Röhm himself was not to be executed. He had given his word to General von Epp. Göring and Himmler were vexed. If the leader of the revolt was spared it would make a mockery of the day's massacre. The argument continued as they drove away.

4

President von Hindenburg took the executions calmly. His first reaction was a cranky "I told you so" to Meissner. "For months I have been telling the Chancellor to lock up this immoral and dangerous Röhm; unfortunately he did not listen to me; now see how much blood has been spilled!"

The next morning, the first of July, was pleasantly warm and Berliners were strolling the streets with their children as if it were any ordinary Sunday. Few realized the import of the curt announcement of half a dozen executions for treason or the continued transport of SS troops. Those who were privileged to see the Führer knew that he was going through one of the most traumatic crises of his turbulent career. It reached a climax that afternoon when he finally was forced to approve the execution of Röhm. Even Hitler's sentence of death was marked by affection. He instructed Brigadeführer Theodor Eicke to give Röhm the chance to commit suicide.

It was still light by the time Eicke and two subordinates arrived at Stadelheim with Hitler's verbal order. At first the prison governor refused to hand over the prisoner without something in writing but he wilted under Eicke's shouts and ordered a warder to escort the three SS men to Cell 474 in the new prison block. There slumped Röhm on an iron cot, bare to the waist and sweating heavily in the sweltering heat.

"You have forfeited your life," said Eicke. "The Führer gives you one more chance to draw the right conclusions." He placed a pistol loaded with a single bullet on a table, then left the cell. Eicke waited in the passage for almost fifteen minutes, then he and his deputies drew their own revolvers and pushed back into the cell. "Chief of Staff, prepare yourself!" shouted Eicke. And, when he saw his deputy's gun quivering, said, "Aim slowly and calmly." Two shots reverberated deafeningly in the little cell. Röhm collapsed. "My Führer!" he gasped. "My Führer!"

"You should have thought of that earlier; it's too late now," said Eicke. It was 6 P.M. The man who should logically have been the first to die was among the last to perish. With his demise those who remained on the death list in the Berlin area—at Lichterfeld Barracks and Columbia House, a former prison converted into an SS torture chamber—were prepared for execution.

Papen was still alive because influential friends and foreigners would drive slowly past his house every so often. That Sunday Ambassador Dodd left a card at the door with a handwritten message: "I hope we may call on you soon." Dodd considered Papen a devious coward but he couldn't help liking him personally and his card had been left "as a protest against the brutality of the Nazis."

The people still knew little of what was happening, nor was the truth well served by Göring's long version of the killings issued later in the day. "The purge will now be carried on ruthlessly," said Göring after assuring the citizenry that the nation was now at peace and the Führer in complete control. The unruly elements of the SA would be eliminated. "The people must know that we are in earnest to do everything for them." Like most communiqués from any nation, it was a hodgepodge of truth and fiction, and gave the public the opportunity to believe what it was eager to believe: that there was nothing to worry about and a nasty but necessary job had been done in the most honorable way for the good of the state.

This announcement was followed almost immediately by publication of an order issued to the Reichswehr by General von Blomberg expressing complete loyalty to the Führer. Despite protestations about remaining "outside the inner political struggle," it was graphic proof that the army was irrevocably bound in blood to Adolf Hitler.

Even as Blomberg was assuring the populace that the crisis was over, the killings continued into the early morning hours of July 2. At Columbia House Gruppenführer Karl Schreyer was called out of his cell by a non-com who said, "You will be shot on the Führer's orders." Schreyer had seen three comrades precede him to execution at half-hour intervals. "Put your head under the tap like the others, so that you'll look fresh and make a good impression." Schreyer was then led down the stairs to a small sports car which would take him to Lichterfeld for execution. A Mercedes roared up and an officer of the Leibstandarte leaped out, signaling violently. "Stop! Stop!" he shouted. "Nothing more is to happen; the Führer has given Hindenburg his word that the shooting is now finally over."

It was 4 A.M. A hundred men, perhaps two hundred—the exact number will never be known—had been murdered without trial.

Throughout the Reich that hot Monday the average German was congratulating himself with grim satisfaction that the roughneck Brownshirts were at last under control. "No one loved Röhm and his parvenu officers," recalled correspondent Delmer, "the ex-waiters, ex-hotel porters and ex-plumbers, who had been bossing the common people more arrogantly than any Prussian Guards Officers in the days of the Kaiser. They and their brand-new, elegant motorcars, roaring ruthlessly about the streets, were feared and hated by the German little man." By eliminating these ruffians Hitler had become his hero.

Hindenburg was having second thoughts. The brutal murder of General von Schleicher and his wife upset him deeply enough to demand an investigation. He simply could not accept the official version that the couple had been shot resisting arrest. At the same time he was incapable of putting his indignation into effect and he dutifully signed a congratulatory telegram to Hitler drafted by the Nazis. It read:

> FROM THE REPORTS PLACED BEFORE ME, I LEARN THAT YOU BY YOUR DETERMINED ACTION AND GALLANT PERSONAL INTERVENTION, HAVE NIPPED TREASON IN THE BUD. YOU HAVE SAVED THE GERMAN NATION FROM SERIOUS DANGER. FOR THIS I EXPRESS TO YOU MY MOST PROFOUND THANKS AND SINCERE APPRECIATION.

With this certificate of support, Hitler now had the uneasy sanction of almost the entire nation.

5

Approval of the purge did not extend beyond Germany's borders and scathing articles and editorials flourished abroad. Much as he flinched from foreign attack, Hitler's primary concern was a faint but growing suspicion among his own people that they might have been deceived. These misgivings were fostered by whispered revelations: for example, that one of the victims was Hitler's old nemesis, Bavarian State Commissar von Kahr, of the triumvirate which had "broken its word" in the Beer Hall Putsch; and that Dr. Willi Schmid, a music critic, was arrested in his apartment while playing the cello, then murdered under the impression that he was Wilhelm Schmid, the local Brownshirt leader.

Tiny as was this seed of doubt, it aggravated Hitler's own distressed state of mind. Genuinely shaken by the liquidation of old friends and comrades, he hid from the public. Privately he commissioned Hess, now his closest friend and associate, to embark on a number of missions of mercy (occasioned by remorse) to widows and relatives of the victims. Hess did his best to comfort the widow of the music critic by counseling her to look upon her husband's death as that of a martyr for a great cause. He also assured her a pension from the Reich. Frau Strasser and Röhm's mother were also offered pensions. The latter, still unable to believe that her son could be a homosexual (to this day his older brother and sister-in-law vehemently deny it), curtly turned down the offer. She would not take a pfennig from the murderer of her son.

Hitler also attempted to make amends to Papen, inviting him to attend an emergency session of the cabinet on July 3 just as if he had never been held in custody. All affability, Hitler invited the Vice-Chancellor to take his usual place at the table. Nettled, Papen said that was out of the question and demanded to see Hitler alone. The two moved into the next room where Papen told about his own house arrest and the murder of his press officer. He requested an immediate judicial inquiry into the matter, then insisted that his resignation be announced immediately. Hitler's polite refusal sent Papen directly to the Bendlerstrasse to see his old friend General von Fritsch. The army commander-in-chief stared as if facing a ghost. "As you can see, I am alive," said Papen. "But this *Schweinerei* has got to be stopped." Why, he asked, hadn't Fritsch prevented the purge in the first place? The army chief sheepishly explained that it had been impossible to act "without explicit orders from Blomberg or Hindenburg." The former had "rigidly opposed any intervention" and the latter could not be reached.

In the cabinet meeting General von Blomberg was congratulating the Führer on behalf of the armed forces for acting so expeditiously against traitors. This gave Hitler a felicitous opportunity to justify such harsh actions. "When a mutiny takes place," Schwerin von Krosigk recalls his saying, "then the captain of a ship cannot wait until the ship reaches shore to take court action. He must take things in hand at the time and place it happens."

Not a single member of the cabinet protested (including the Minister of Justice, a number of whose right-wing friends had perished), and this group then proceeded to do what it had been brought together to do: promulgate a law legalizing the "measures taken on June 30 and on July 1 and 2" as an "emergency defense of the state."

Papen was not the only official who wanted to resign. Bavarian Minister of Justice Frank also offered to step down. "Does one desert a ship in the middle of the ocean?" said Hitler caustically. "I have quarrels with many but I must hold everything together. We are a troop in battle." Justice and revolution, he argued, were incompatible. "Don't forget that every revolution has its victims!" Hitler could understand Frank's feelings of revulsion at the purge but nothing could be done about that now. "I have too many deadly enemies. Everything now hinges on my authority." When Frank protested that the police were assuming too much power and that too many party members were taking the law into their own hands, Hitler replied: "Justice and jurists serve the community best when they leave all political necessities to other organs."

He even had an answer for the growing number of concentration camps. "If I had a spacious Siberia at my disposal as Moscow has, then I wouldn't need any concentration camps. . . . Who in the world talks about the millions of victims of Bolshevism? The Jewish press of the world pursues me because I am an anti-Semite. Herr Stalin is their darling." Frank tore up his resignation.

Papen was not so easy to bring around. He insisted on getting the remains of his press officer—ashes in an urn—and arranging a proper burial at Schönberg cemetery despite warnings from Himmler against provoking any public demonstration. Papen not only delivered a moving oration at the funeral but kept bombarding the Führer with letters protesting against the continued imprisonment of four of his subordinates and pressing for a public inquiry into his press officer's death. A model of patience himself for a change, Hitler urged Papen to be patient. A special meeting of the Reichstag to explain the purge fully was to be held in forty-eight hours. At the time he, as Führer, would take full responsibility for everything that had happened, including those unfortunate events committed "in an excess of zeal."

The thirteenth of July was a Friday. Security measures at the Kroll Opera House were such that one veteran diplomat commented: "I have often seen governments in other countries in hot water, but even in the most dangerous period under the Czars I never saw anything like this." Hitler's path from the chancellery to the stage was flanked on both sides by heavily armed police and SS troops, and there were repeated searches of the opera's anterooms. Detectives were planted throughout the auditorium while soldiers in steel helmets and armed with swords guarded entrances. "No one present—and the American, French, and Russian Ambassadors made a point of not attending—could fail to recognize that a period of wild, hostile fear had begun among the men who wield power."

At 8 P.M. a grim-faced Führer stepped to the podium clutching the lectern as if for balance. Extending an arm in stiff salute, he began speaking in a voice harsher than usual, as if giving assurance that he was once more in control of events. He gave a lengthy, emotional account of the purge which, he explained, was necessitated by the treasonous actions of various groups which he described as "destructive elements" and "pathological enemies of the state." He could have been describing himself in earlier days—as well as his present role in world politics. With the skill of a born storyteller he gave his version of the events leading up to the dramatic decision to put down the rebellion in person. Except for the foreign observers, almost everyone in the opera house was spellbound by his performance, and throughout Germany enthralled crowds clustered around radios. At the American Embassy Ambassador Dodd, who had vowed never again to attend an address of the Chancellor or seek an interview except upon official grounds ("I have a sense of horror when I look at the man"), was listening with disbelief to Hitler's claim that only seventy-four plotters—including a few civilians and party members—had died for their infamy; and that he had executed three SS men who had "scandalously ill-treated" those taken into protective custody. The last was an apparent attempt to convince Papen that the murders of innocent victims like his press chief had been punished. And this spirit of conciliation was extended with an emotional offer of amnesty to those not yet punished who had shared in the guilt of treason. "May we all feel responsible for the most precious treasure that there can be for the German people: internal order, internal and external peace, just as I am ready to undertake responsibility at the bar of history for the twenty-four hours in which the bitterest decisions of my life were made, in which fate once again taught me in the midst of anxious care with every thought to hold fast to the dearest thing which has been given us in this world—the German people and the German Reich!"

The hand-picked audience rose as one to applaud enthusiastically. Almost as an anticlimax, the main purpose of the meeting was promptly accomplished: the Reichstag unanimously approved the bill legalizing the executions as "emergency defense measures of the state." Hitler had been given, ex post facto, a license to murder. There was not a single word of protest. The legislators had enshrined the Führer as the sole source of law.

Minister of Defense von Blomberg was not alone among the military in his endorsement of Hitler's ruthless cleansing of the SA and the liquidation of Generals von Schleicher and von Bredow. The officer corps accepted the death of two comrades with surprising equanimity, shutting their eyes to Hitler's methods on the grounds that suppression of the Putsch was a guarantee of internal peace. "Our verdict on the affair," recalled Karl Dönitz, "was decisively influenced by the cabinet resolution, which, by citing a state of national emergency, gave legal sanction to all the measures taken."

The sentiments of the officers drifted down to the enlisted men, who greeted Hitler with cheers when his open car drove past an infantry column on maneuvers a few days later. "This type of spontaneous demonstration," reported the French military attaché, "is not usual in the German army."

Only a handful of officers were bold enough to speak out in protest and their leader was almost as old as Hindenburg. Field Marshal August von Mackensen, an officer of distinction, had tried to reach the President by telephone in hopes of stopping the purge but he was always told the Old Gentleman was too sick to talk. Balked, Mackensen finally went directly to the Führer and made a plea for the re-establishment of common decency in public life. His words moved Hitler to such an extent that it took a moment before he could say: "It may be as you say, Herr Feldmarschall, but I cannot help myself. I cannot go back."

Determined to inform Hindenburg of the truth, Mackensen helped compose a memorandum outlining the details of the Schleicher-Bredow assassinations and demanding punishment for those responsible. It also urged the President to drop Blomberg, Goebbels, Ley, Neurath and two other Nazis from the cabinet and hand over control of the nation to a small directorate. Hitler was not named; presumably he was to remain as Chancellor under a military dictatorship.

The memorandum concluded on an emotional note: "Your Excellency has thrice before saved Germany from foundering: at Tannenberg, at the end of the war and at the moment of your election as President of the Reich. Excellency, save Germany for the fourth time! The undersigned generals and senior officers swear to preserve to their last breath their loyalty to you and to the Fatherland." Mackensen had persuaded twenty-eight other senior officers of the General Staff, many of whom were members of the regiment to which both Hindenburg and

Schleicher belonged, to affix their signatures. It was dated July 18 and arrived in Neudeck on the twentieth. But this gallant effort was of no avail. If the ailing field marshal ever read the memorandum, which was probably kept from him by his entourage, he took no action.

It appeared as if all influential segments of German society had either been intimidated or won over, and what could have been a personal disaster for Hitler turned out to be a victory of sorts; the purge had at least brought a sweeping conclusion to the factionalism which had long wracked his party. With a stroke the SA was castrated.

The SA's loss was Himmler's gain. On the same day Mackensen's memorandum arrived in Neudeck, Hitler promoted the SS to the status of an independent organization and permitted it to form armed units. It was a body blow to the military, which had compromised its honor to approve of the bloody elimination of the Brownshirts, only to be faced with an even more formidable rival.

The cost to the party was considerable, with the loss of many of its most ardent members, the idealists of the SA. "You have to realize that we sacrificed everything," said Hein Ruck, who later became a trusted lieutenant of Hitler's favorite commando, Otto Skorzeny. "We slept on a mattress in the kitchen and in the morning three of us would buy a bouillon cube for ten pfennig; that was our breakfast." Ruck himself was arrested twenty times during the struggle for power and his experience was not exceptional. "Then, to put it bluntly, we were betrayed. We wanted a new society and we suddenly had to face the fact that reaction was with us. Hurray, patriotism! No more revolution. And June 30 was the logical consequence of the movement which was now being destroyed by Hitler." Men like Ruck were convinced that Röhm had merely attempted to bring Hitler back to the old road of revolution—and socialism. "And here it was that Hitler really made his first true enemies, enemies in his own camp. For me and my friends, Hitler as a human being was finished."

Another young SA leader, Werner Naumann, was also disillusioned and angry. Although he would become Goebbels' private secretary, he too could never forget. "The Röhm affair," he recently said, "was important to the development of the Third Reich because here for the first time we had an unlawful, illegal action, one sanctioned by the Reichswehr, as well as the entire bureaucracy and legal body of the nation. It was totally unlawful and illegal, and nobody stood up to say, 'So far and no further.' Not even the Church. And none of these groups could say they knew nothing about the matter. Everyone knew what happened. And, in my opinion, this was the beginning of the end, because from now on the move was from the lawful and legal to the illegal and unlawful, and from now on there could be no turning back the clock."

And so, while Hitler appeared to be at the crest of his popularity, there remained a deep and bitter schism within his own movement. Thousands of the most motivated Nazis would never forget the weekend of shame. A state of underground war was declared by those SA leaders who felt betrayed by Hitler. Their resentment against his elite SS erupted into the open several weeks later in the restaurant of Stettin's Preussenhof Hotel where Viktor Lutze was drinking beer with about twenty fellow Brownshirts and three SS commanders. "One of these days," declaimed the new commander of the SA, his tongue loosened by beer, "the unjust and arbitrary action of 30 June will be avenged." Lutze openly intimated that it was Himmler and his SS who had egged on Röhm. "Who is up to their necks in what Röhm was supposed to have done? Was it the SA? These bestialities were not the SA's work or, at least, not the SA alone; the other side was much worse. Shall I give you names? I can produce names straight away!" One of the SS men tried to quiet tipsy Lutze but he had the last word. "I shall go on saying this, even if I am dismissed tomorrow and sent to a concentration camp!"

6

A month earlier, during his frustrating excursion to Italy, the Führer had promised Mussolini to respect Austrian independence. It was a considerable concession since *Anschluss*, incorporation of his homeland into a Greater Germany, had been one of Hitler's first goals. Despite this promise his own SS did not cease sending considerable financial and moral support to Austrian Nazis, who carried on a compaign of terrorism, blowing up railways and power stations with German dynamite and murdering supporters of Chancellor Engelbert Dollfuss with German weapons. Ironically the diminutive Dollfuss was a nationalistic, authoritarian reactionary who was countering the threats of both Nazism and socialism with suspension of parliamentary government. Earlier in the year Dollfuss had put down revolt from the left by bombarding socialists entrenched in a huge housing development until they surrendered. Since then he had concentrated on wiping out the local Nazis, reinforced by assurance from Mussolini that he would restrain Hitler from retaliation.

Perhaps the Austrian Nazis were inspired by the hubbub following the Röhm affair to take direct action. More likely, though there is no proof, Hitler approved it. At any rate, on July 25 they suddenly launched their own Putsch, under the code name Operation Summer Festival. At noon a secret striking force of 150 local Nazis in the uniforms of the Austrian army broke into the chancellery on the Ballhausplatz to seize Dollfuss and his advisers. The plot had already been discovered and all but two of the cabinet had fled, but the plucky Dollfuss had remained. He was shot in the throat from a range of six inches. As he lay on the floor, ignored and bleeding profusely, other rebels were broadcasting the lie that the Chancellor had resigned.

In Berlin the news of the uprising was welcomed in official circles and DNB prepared a statement to the effect that the people had revolted in righteousness. "The inevitable has happened. The German people in Austria have risen against their oppressors, jailers, and torturers." Hitler—in Bayreuth attending the Wagner festival—pretended indifference at first but as the afternoon wore on he became concerned over the possible repercussions of the revolt. Would Mussolini assume he had broken his word and bring his own superior military force into play? (Il Duce, in fact, was furious, not only because the word given in Venice had been broken but for personal reasons: Frau Dollfuss and her children were his house guests and it had been his painful duty to inform them Dollfuss was dying.) Hitler appeared in his box with the Wagner family that evening for the performance of *Das Rheingold*, but it was doubtful if he enjoyed it since he was often interrupted by whispered communiqués from Schaub or Brückner who were getting telephoned reports in the anteroom. These included a disturbing one that Mussolini had ordered a concentration of troops and aircraft on the Austrian border in line with his promise to aid Austria. By the time the curtain fell it seemed obvious that the Vienna Putsch was headed for failure, and when Hitler arrived at the Wagner home young Friedelind noted that he was "extremely" nervous and somewhat incoherent. His chief aim seemed to be to rush to a nearby actors' restaurant so he could mingle with the celebrities and create the impression he had nothing to do with the Austrian Nazi fiasco.

Later in the evening word arrived from Berlin that Chancellor Dollfuss had died at 6 P.M. but the Putsch had been quelled. Hitler telephoned the Wilhelmstrasse and asked State Secretary von Bülow for more details. When Bülow replied that Minister Rieth, German representative in Austria, was bargaining for the safe conduct of the arrested assassins to the German border, Hitler shouted that Reith had no business at all playing the part of mediator. At 11 P.M. the Führer rang up Bülow again for further information on the captured Putschists. "The Reich Chancellor," so Bülow noted in his official memorandum, "replied that he would have the expelled conspirators taken into protective custody and transferred to a concentration camp."

In his extremity, Hitler turned to Papen, whom he had recently humiliated with house arrest, and requested him to replace Rieth. Papen was in no mood to comply but Hitler persisted, appealing in the name of patriotism. The least Papen could do was to talk over the matter in person. Why not fly in the Führer's personal plane to Bayreuth? Papen could not resist such insistence and early the next morning took off from Tempelhof with his son. On the trip south his mind was in a turmoil. Why had Hitler turned to him of all people? Was it because he had protested against the terrorist methods of the Nazi underground in Austria and was a personal friend of Dollfuss? Papen found the Führer in "a state of hysterical agitation, denouncing feverishly the rashness and stupidity of the Austrian Nazi Party for having involved him in such an appalling situation." At first Hitler refused Papen's terms for acceptance: the dismissal of his own appointee as inspector of the Austrian Nazi Party. But when Papen said it was a choice "between him and me," Hitler finally acceded and Papen accepted the post.

In the waiting room he met an old friend, Hjalmar Schacht, president of the Reichsbank, who was next in line to see the Führer. He too was offered an important assignment, as head of the Ministry of Economic Affairs. Schacht was unhappy with the course of the Nazi Reich, particularly the excesses of the recent purge, but, like Papen, he convinced himself—so he later wrote—that he must help the country by acceptance. "There remained the one and only possibility of working from within outward, of making use of those very governmental activities in an attempt to combat the excesses of the system and direct its policies along decent lines." Like Papen, he too claimed to have accepted his post provisionally. His condition was put in the form of a question: "Before I take office I should like to know how you wish me to deal with the Jewish question."

"In economic matters," said Hitler, a master at handling opportunists, "the Jews can carry on exactly as they have done up to now."

Assured of Papen's help on the diplomatic front and with Schacht as master mind of accelerated rearmament, Hitler felt prepared to weather the criticism from abroad raised by the Dollfuss murder. The most scathing attacks were coming from Mussolini. He had not only wired Austrian Vice-Chancellor Prince Ernst Rüdiger von Starhemberg that Italy would fight for Austrian independence but traveled to Vienna to express his feelings in person. "It would mean the end of European civilization if this country of murderers and pederasts were to overrun Europe," he told Starhemberg, then charged Hitler with instigation of the revolt in Vienna. He became so emotional, according to Starhemberg, that his eyes rolled. "Hitler is the murderer of Dollfuss, Hitler is the guilty man, he is responsible for this." He called the Führer "a horrible sexual degenerate, a dangerous fool," and described Nazism as a "revolution of the old Germanic tribes in the primeval forest against the Latin civilization of Rome." Nor could one compare Nazism to Fascism. "Certainly there are outward similarities. Both are authoritarian systems, both are collectivist, socialistic. Both systems oppose liberalism. But Fascism is a regime that is rooted in the great cultural tradition of the Italian people; Fascism recognizes the right of the individual, it recognizes religion and family. National Socialism, on the other hand, is savage barbarism; in common with barbarian hordes it allows no rights to the individual; the chieftain is lord over life and death of his people. Murder and killing, loot and pillage and blackmail are all it can produce." He began to shout. "This abominable and repulsive spectacle that Hitler showed the world on the thirtieth of June would not have been tolerated in any other country in the world. Only these primitive Germans, prepared even for murder, will put up with such things." Hopefully, he added, the assassination of Dollfuss might do some good. Perhaps the Great Powers would recognize the German danger and organize a grand coalition against Hitler. A common front was the only answer, he said. "Hitler will arm the Germans and make war—perhaps even in two or three years. I cannot stand up to him alone. We must do something, we must do something quickly."

Mussolini's disgust at Hitler and Germany was such that he began expressing similar feelings in public. "Thirty centuries of history allow us to regard with supreme indulgence certain doctrines taught beyond the Alps by the descendants of people who were wholly illiterate in the days when Caesar, Virgil and Augustus flourished in Rome," he announced from the top of a tank at the inauguration of the fifth *Fiere del Levante*. His private epithets, such as the one describing Germans as pederasts and murderers, also began to be echoed in the Italian press.

7

The shock of the purge, followed so quickly by that of the Dollfuss murder, had a perceptible effect on Hindenburg. He declined rapidly and was confined to his bed. It was a spartan iron bed but he refused to get a more comfortable one on the grounds that he had always slept on a field cot. Nor would he buy a robe despite his chills. Soldiers don't have robes, he grumbled. He had no money for such things and besides he was about to die.

The Führer was still at Bayreuth when he learned that the Old Gentleman was sinking fast. He rushed to Neudeck on the first day of August with a small party including two public relations experts. The group was coolly received. Oskar von Hindenburg led the Führer into the President's bedroom. "Father," he said, "the Reich Chancellor is here." Hindenburg, lying with eyes closed, did not react and Oskar repeated the words. Without opening his eyes, the marshal said, "Why did you not come earlier?"

"What does the President mean?" Hitler whispered to the son.

"The Reich Chancellor could not get here until now," Oskar told his father, who only muttered, "Oh, I see." After a silence Oskar said, "Father, Reich Chancellor Hitler has one or two matters to discuss."

This time the Old Gentleman opened his eyes with a start, stared at Hitler, then shut them again and clamped his mouth shut. Perhaps the President had expected to see *his* Reich Chancellor, his Franzchen— Papen.

Hitler emerged "tight-lipped" and would not discuss the scene. That night his party stopped at the Finckenstein estate where Napoleon had carried on a romance with Countess Walewska. The host suggested Hitler sleep in the Little Corporal's bed but he curtly declined the honor.

The next morning, even while Hindenburg was expiring, Hitler's cabinet passed a law combining the offices of President and Chancellor. The vote was unanimous, with the absent Papen's signature affixed by proxy. The measure was to be effective with the death of Hindenburg and this occurred within minutes. The Old Gentleman died with the words: "My Kaiser . . . my Fatherland" on his lips. He was laid out on the iron cot with a Bible in his hands.

Thanks to a legal coup, Hitler now carried the title of Führer and Reich Chancellor. This meant he was also supreme commander of the armed forces and his first act was to summon General von Blomberg and the three commanders-in-chief of the three armed forces. "We were in his study," Admiral Erich Raeder later testified, "and Hitler asked us to come to his desk without ceremony or staging. There we took the oath which he, as Chief of State and Supreme Commander of the Armed Forces, read to us."

The four men repeated this oath: "I swear before God to give my unconditional obedience to Adolf Hitler, Führer of the Reich and its people, Supreme Commander of the Armed Forces, and I pledge my word as a brave soldier to observe this oath always even at the risk of my life."

It was unprecedented. The previous oath had demanded loyalty and obedience to the constitution and the President. This one to a specific individual established a personal link between Führer and every soldier, sailor and airman. Yet not one officer made the slightest protest or even questioned the unique wording, and before the end of the day every serviceman in the land had taken the same oath of personal fealty.

The first stage of Hindenburg's funeral ceremonies took place at the Kroll Opera House on August 6, where his coffin was carried past the ranks of army field gray and brown and black of the SA and SS. These diverse groups were at last united by similar oaths of loyalty to the Führer. It was symbolic that the music for the occasion was the funeral march from *Götterdämmerung*.

Burial took place the next noon not, where Hindenburg had wished, at Neudeck but, on Hitler's insistence, at the scene of the marshal's greatest triumph, Tannenberg. The body was placed on a catafalque in the center of the monument to the battle, an impressive structure with eight square towers some sixty feet high with fires flaming at the top of each. It reminded Ambassador François-Poncet of a castle built by the Teutonic Knights.

Hitler strode forward to face the coffin. At the podium he discovered that an adjutant had laid out the wrong speech and there was an embarrassing pause that must have puzzled radio listeners all over Europe. But he quickly collected himself and began extemporizing one of the shortest speeches correspondent Lochner, for one, had ever heard him deliver. Hitler ended with fulsome praise of Hindenburg's military and political achievements in words befitting a Wagnerian hero, not an orthodox fundamental Lutheran: "And now enter thou upon Valhalla!"

At the end of the services, Hitler kissed the hands of Hindenburg's daughters. Moved by the solemnity of the moment, if not by opportunism, General von Blomberg impulsively suggested that the armed forces should henceforth address him not with the customary "Herr Hitler" but as "Mein Führer." Hitler accepted the proposal and returned to Berlin. Here he sought further consolidation of his power by phoning Papen and asking if the Old Gentleman had left a political testament. Papen replied that he would ask young Hindenburg. "I should be obliged," said Hitler, "if you would ensure that this document comes into my possession as soon as possible." Papen promptly sent his private secretary to Neudeck. He returned with two sealed envelopes which Papen turned over to the Führer. It was obvious to Papen that Hitler was displeased with the contents of the envelope addressed to him when he said frostily, "These recommendations of the late President are given to me personally. Later I shall decide if and when I shall permit their publication." Rumors that Hitler intended to suppress the testament became so insistent among foreign correspondents that Hanfstaengl brought up the subject at teatime. "Tell your foreign friends to wait until the document is published officially," retorted Hitler irritably. "I don't care what that pack of liars thinks."

Finally on August 15 the testament was released for publication. It praised the achievements of Hitler and his government while stressing the importance of the army as the "symbol of, and firm support for," the new state. There was talk in the capital that the document had been doctored by the editor of Hindenburg's memoirs and that Oskar von Hindenburg and his father's adviser, Meissner, were co-conspirators in the deception. A measure of credence was given this rumor when Oskar swore in a radio speech to the nation that his father had always supported Hitler. The cynics notwithstanding, the son was not lying. Despite Hindenburg's repugnance for some aspects of the Hitler regime, he *had* seen the Führer as his direct successor.

Oskar's words were not necessary, for Hitler already had massive support on all levels of German society. Even the Association of National German Jews issued an appeal in his favor. And so, on August 19, almost 90 per cent of the German people freely voted their approval of Adolf Hitler as Hindenburg's successor. In doing so, they also sanctioned his program and leadership, and propelled him another step closer to dictatorship.

Chapter Thirteen

TRIUMPH OF THE WILL
1934–1935

1

After victory in the plebiscite Hitler retreated to Berchtesgaden for a late summer holiday. He spent hours strolling around his beloved Obersalzberg, engaging in one of his favorite pastimes, conversation. But he was also making preparations for the impending Party Day Congress in Nuremburg, which could be blighted by bitter memories of the Röhm purge. He was determined to prevent this through his usually reliable combination of threat, promise and conciliation. The nation was still in a state of unrest and a number of intellectuals like Spengler, who had given grudging approval of National Socialism, were now enemies.

He was also concerned by foreign journalists eager for material that would damn or ridicule his regime. Dorothy Thompson had found such a story for an article in *Harper's Bazaar*. "This is not a revolution," an American visitor at the Passion play in Oberammergau (which blamed the Jews for the death of Jesus*) reportedly told her, "It's a revival. They think Hitler is God. Believe it or not, a German woman sat next to me at the Passion play, and when they hoisted Jesus on the cross, she said, 'There he is. That is our Führer, our Hitler!' And when they paid out the thirty pieces of silver to Judas, she said: 'That is Röhm, who betrayed the

---

* Only in 1975 was the text revised to place the blame instead on Lucifer, the fallen angel of evil.

Leader.'" Thompson's story was almost identical to the August 23 entry in Ambassador Dodd's diary describing the same drama: "When Jesus was tried before the angry Jewish court, a well-dressed German, looking very solemn, said to me: '*Es ist unser Hitler* [He is our Hitler].' Ida Horne, a distant kinswoman of mine, sitting in another part of the hall, told me as we came out together: 'A woman near me said, as Judas received his thirty pieces of silver, '*Es ist Röhm!*' I suspect half the audience, the German part, considers Hitler as Germany's Messiah."

A contrary opinion, that Hitler was more Judas than Messiah, ran deep among many Brownshirts who had remained, if reluctantly, in the party. One such, Max Jüttner, Röhm's former subordinate, could not help praising his dead chief while discussing the coming Party Day with the Führer. Hitler lost his temper. "Why are you bringing up that subject?" he shouted. "This matter is closed. Röhm has been adjudged." Alarmed, Jüttner protested that the Führer would not have made Röhm chief of staff if he had lacked good qualities. With one of his lightning changes, Hitler patted Jüttner on the shoulder. "You are right," he said, "but you couldn't possibly know the whole story. Röhm and Schleicher intended to make a Putsch against me and it had to be averted. I wanted to have these matters examined before a regular court, but events overwhelmed me and many SA leaders were shot without my consent. Because of all the world publicity I took the blame."

Hitler chose young Alfred Speer as stage manager of the pageant at Nuremberg that was to consolidate his gains and bring back unity to the party. Speer tore down the temporary bleachers on Zeppelin Field and, inspired by the Pergamum altars, erected a stone structure 1300 feet long and 80 feet high. Crowning the stadium was a giant eagle with a 100-foot wingspread and on all sides were hung thousands of swastika banners. Positioned around the field at 40-foot intervals were 130 anti-aircraft searchlights with a range of 25,000 feet. Göring had resisted loaning these since they were the greater part of his strategic reserve but Hitler backed Speer. "If we use them in such large numbers for a thing like this," he reasoned, "other countries will think we're swimming in searchlights."

His imagination went beyond propaganda of the moment. Envisaging a permanent record that could be exported, he asked Leni Riefenstahl, the noted actress and director, to produce a commemorative film. He admired her work, particularly *The Blue Light*, and assured her she would have complete co-operation if she made a feature-length film of the 1934 Party Day. She yielded despite qualms, but once out of his sight decided she was not qualified to do a documentary. She turned over the direction to an associate and left for Spain to work on a film of her own. By the time she returned the Nuremberg Rally was only two weeks off. Awaiting her was a letter from Hess: the Führer was shocked to find she had delegated the assignment to someone else and wanted to see her at once.

Hitler was not angry, only persuasive. "You'll only have to give up six days of your life," he argued and, when she retorted that with cutting that meant six months, said, "Ah, but you are so young!" She insisted that she was the last person in the world to do such a film. "I'm not a member of the party and I don't even know the difference between SA and SS."

"That is why I want you to do it," said Hitler. "That will give it a fresh approach." She took over the difficult task herself and, to bring additional interest to the six-day program, devised shots from planes, cranes, roller skates and a tiny elevator platform attached to the tallest flagpole. Upon arrival in Nuremberg a week before the opening day, with a crew of 120, including sixteen cameramen, she got all the assistance Hitler had promised. The city's fire-fighting equipment as well as public utilities were turned over to her.

The participants were already flooding into Nuremberg. Carefully selected months in advance, each had a number, a designated truck, a designated seat in the truck, and a designated cot in the vast tent city near Nuremberg. By the time the ceremonies began on September 4 the thousands of party members had been rehearsed to perfection. That evening the Führer made a short welcoming speech at the old Rathaus, followed by Hanfstaengl's long one urging the foreign press to "report on affairs in Germany without attempting to interpret them." Afterward at least ten thousand enthusiasts crowded around Hitler's hotel, the Deutscher Hof, repeating the chant "We want our Führer!" until he at last came out on the balcony. Their fanatical faces reminded William L. Shirer (then with Universal Service) of the crazed expressions on Holy Rollers in Louisiana.

The next morning Hitler appeared at the Luitpold arena, more as an object of reverence than as an orator. He entered dramatically, followed by Göring, Goebbels, Hess, Himmler and several aides, to the strains of the "Badenweiler March." After a stirring rendition of the *Egmont* Overture, Hess came forward and slowly read the names of those who had died in the 1923 Putsch. To the audience of 30,000, if not to the foreign correspondents, it was a moving experience. The most important words were spoken by Gauleiter Wagner, who read a proclamation of Hitler's in a voice so similar to the Führer's that some correspondents listening on the radio thought it was he. "The German form of life is definitely determined for the next thousand years," read out Wagner. "For us, the unsettled nineteenth century has finally ended. There will be no revolution in Germany for the next thousand years."

Intoxicated as he was by the almost constant ovation from admirers, Hitler was nevertheless nagged by anxiety. Many Brownshirts had brought their resentment and disillusionment to the festivities, and the possibility of an embarrassing or even dangerous episode made him so tense that occasionally his own resentment flared up. During one meal at the restaurant frequented by party officials he suddenly turned on Hans Frank. "You certainly annoyed me by delaying things on the thirtieth of June in Munich!" he exclaimed and, when Frank again offered to resign, cut him off impatiently. "In a few weeks this whole joke of state justice will end." The Reich would command and Bavaria and the other states would obey, he said, then, after an uncomfortable silence, walked out.

In the rising excitement of the rally Hitler regained his mood of exultation. This was particularly evident on the evening of the seventh when 200,000 party faithful with more than 20,000 unfurled flags crowded into Zeppelin Field and lined up with military precision. The effect of Speer's 130 giant searchlights was more breath-taking than imagined. "The floodlit stadium gave the impression of a giant hall ringed by titanic gleaming white pillars," Speer recalled, "with an occasional cloud floating surrealistically through the majestic wall of light, like a translucent anemone drifting through the sea." In the awesome silence, Hitler's voice came across the field from loudspeakers with eerie effect. "We are strong and will get stronger!" he said, and made it as much a threat as a promise.

Leni Riefenstahl and her cameramen were filming the scene from a dozen angles, despite interference from officious Brownshirts who, at Goebbels' instigation and unbeknown to the Führer, kept harassing her cameramen, pushing them from the best vantage points and even dismantling several of their camera stations.

Hitler himself was threatened by possible SA reaction and was prepared to meet it when he faced 50,000 storm troopers en masse two days later. "There was considerable tension in the stadium," recalled Shirer, "and I noticed that Hitler's own S.S. bodyguard was drawn up in force in front of him, separating him from the mass of the brown-shirts." He wondered if one in the huge crowd would draw a revolver throughout the Führer's "carrot and club" harangue in which he finally absolved them all of complicity in Röhm's plot.

The session ended without incident, insuring the success of the concluding event on the following day, September 10. This was designated as Army Day and mobile units with the most modern equipment maneuvered flawlessly on the great meadow. It was the first public display of military might in Germany since the war and the audience of 300,000 was raised to a state of almost uncontrollable excitement at the sight of a realistic sham battle. Militarism, wrote Shirer in his diary, was not just a product of the Hohenzollerns. "It is rather something deeply ingrained in all Germans. They acted today like children playing with tin soldiers."

Hitler appeared to be as intoxicated as the crowd and after his final speech the cheering could not be quelled for some time. At last Hess could make himself heard and he bade farewell to the Führer on behalf of the NSDAP. "The party is Hitler," he said. "Hitler, however, is Germany just as Germany is Hitler. Heil Hitler! Sieg Heil! Sieg Heil! Sieg Heil Hitler!" The frenzied crowd joined in the chant of "Hail Victory!" It was exhilarating, inspiring, thrilling, but to those not under Hitler's spell it was bone-chilling, an animal roar, a shriek from the cave.

Nothing could have better symbolized the wedding of the Führer and the army and he decided to make a conciliatory gesture to the senior generals. After a tattoo held by massed bands in front of his hotel that evening, he invited them to dinner. "I know that you accuse me of many wrong things which exist in the party," he said, according to General von Weichs, who was taking word-by-word notes. "I admit that you are 100% correct, but you must remember that in the time of struggle, the intelligentsia deserted me, so that I still have to work primarily with personnel of low quality. I am constantly endeavoring to rectify this defect. But just as the construction of the officer corps for the new Armed Forces will take years to complete, so will the creation of a good corps of leaders for the party require even longer time." His words were effective for, as Weichs noted, "he knew how to fit his speech to his audience with masterful skill."

Later Hitler visited the soldiers' bivouac where he, the veteran corporal, mingled familiarly with the men, joking and reminiscing about old times. He returned to the hotel in a relaxed mood and, during a late snack with intimates, described the reunion in detail. It was a fitting end to the eventful week.

Hitler's high spirits were in evidence two days later at the reception in his honor at the presidential palace. All those diplomats who had been avoiding him were forced to be on hand to pay formal respects to the new president. Never had Ambassador Dodd seen him "quite so happy-looking as while he went down the line greeting the representatives of all foreign countries." Despite some annoyances and a few anxious moments, he had succeeded in accomplishing at Nuremberg what he had set out to do. The party was reunited, and the people and the armed forces were with him.

Nor had the memorial to the party been blighted by Goebbels' interference. Leni Riefenstahl and her cameramen came away with thousands of feet of extraordinary material. While the film was being edited she was deluged by protests from party leaders who had not been included or others who complained that there wasn't enough propaganda. When she refused to make any changes Hitler suggested a compromise: fit into the film pictures of the disgruntled leaders. This was an offense to Riefenstahl's artistic principles and she refused. Hitler just as heatedly persisted. According to her version, she stamped her foot and shouted, "I won't do it!" "Are you forgetting whom you are talking to?" he replied but such was her conviction and such was Hitler's appreciation of her talent that she completed the film without any changes. She did allow it to be called *Triumph of the Will* because she had no better title. At the premiere she was greeted coolly by party officials but even Goebbels, her greatest critic, realized it was an outstanding achievement and, in its way, far more effective propaganda for the Führer and National Socialism than any other film yet made. It was awarded the May Day "cultural achievement" award for best film of the year and was later recognized universally as one of the most important documentary films ever made, eventually winning a gold medal at the 1937 World Exhibition in Paris, for its artistry, if not its message.

2

There was gossip that Leni Riefenstahl was Hitler's mistress. This charge was as unfounded as those that he was sleeping with other famous actresses such as Olga Tschechowa, Lil Dagover and Pola Negri. It was not sex that Hitler sought from such charming women but the stimulation that his suppressed bohemian nature craved.

Unity Mitford, daughter of Lord Redesdale, had just come out in England. She was in Munich attending art classes and was caught in the excitement of the new Germany. From the moment Hitler kissed her hand she became a dedicated advocate of National Socialism. Hitler had never met anyone like this gay, irrepressible, golden-haired girl who would make the bluntest and most surprising remarks. Her freedom of expression, original outlook on life and lively humor, which she shared with her five sisters, was a new and refreshing experience to Hitler and his delight in her company soon generated a rumor—as unfounded as the others—that she was his mistress.

With Hitler's rise to power, he found an increasing number of women eager for his company. Perhaps it was his widening range of interest which soured his long-standing relationship with Frau Bechstein. She began to criticize him openly and upbraid him for some of his reforms. According to Friedelind Wagner, she would usually begin by asking the

Führer if he were crazy and then shower him with such a deluge of abuse that he was unable to defend himself. "During these violent scoldings, Hitler would stand there like an abashed schoolboy who had committed a misdemeanor."

Eva Braun was even more distressed at Hitler's broadening horizon. A few days after he came to power he had given her a matching ring, earrings and bracelet of tourmalines for her twenty-first birthday. But this was no indication that he planned to marry his mistress. She saw less of him than before. Occasionally he would phone her from Berlin—usually from a public booth. To prevent her parents from finding out how intimate were her relations with the Führer, she had persuaded them to let her have a private phone in her bedroom. Whenever he came to Munich he would invite Eva to his apartment but in Berchtesgaden she stayed at some hotel for appearance's sake.

By the autumn of 1934 Eva was stricken with long spells of melancholy. She had no hope that Hitler would marry her. As head of the Third Reich, he told her, he must devote himself to the nation with no family distractions. He was, in fact, like the Pope. His excuse to Captain Wiedemann was more blunt. Yes, he confided one evening, he did miss family life but if he got married he would lose many female votes. "So," he concluded, "I have a girl at my disposal in Munich." Hitler was even more revealing to his secretary, Christa Schröder. "Eva is very nice," he said, "but, in my life, only Geli could have inspired in me genuine passion. I can never think of marrying Eva. The only woman I could have tied myself to for life would have been Geli."

Hitler's relationship with his sister-in-law from England was also becoming an embarrassment. Brigid Hitler, former wife of his half brother Alois, was in desperate financial straits and made a second effort to get some aid from her famous relative. She returned to Germany with her son William Patrick and approached Hitler in hopes he "might be willing to pay something to keep her quiet." Hitler invited mother and son to Berchtesgaden where the latter was astounded (so he told the OSS years later) to be "roundly upbraided" by the Führer's sister Angela, who repeated the fiction that Hitler "was not even his uncle."*

In the meantime Hitler was devoting much of his time to foreign policy. Since success in this field almost always depends on power, Hitler was doing his best to rearm the Reich overnight. Behind the smoke screen of

* William Patrick Hitler eventually moved to America with his mother and served in the U. S. Navy during World War II. At present he lives in the New York metropolitan area under a different name and has a son, Adolf.

the disarmament negotiations at Geneva he was hastily building up Germany's armed forces on every level. Heartened by public reaction to the impressive military display at Nuremberg, Hitler issued a secret order three weeks later trebling the size of the 100,000-man army. That same day 70,000 recruits were enrolled. The defense budget rose to 654 million marks.

The sudden activation of nine corps headquarters, fourteen infantry divisions and seven motorized combat battalions even under tight security generated alarming rumors of infringements of the Versailles Treaty. These, combined with a deterioration in Anglo-German relations, were a real concern to Hitler. It was becoming obvious, moreover, that Britain and France were moving closer to military unity in view of German expansion. On the other hand, there were indications that England was not ready to take any great risks. "No country, and especially not England," the private secretary to the British Foreign Secretary confided to Otto, Prince von Bismarck, that autumn, "would ever go to war for the interests of other nations outside its own territory." And since Hitler had no designs on the British Empire and his entire foreign policy was based on Britain's forbearance if not friendship, his campaign to win back their sympathy was straightforward.

One step in this courtship was a formal party on December 19. Of the twenty-five guests there were four from Britain—a well-known member of the Anglo-German Fellowship, Lord Rothermere and his son, and Ward Price, the editor of the *Daily Mail*, the most influential Rothermere newspaper. For the occasion Hitler wore full evening dress rather than the party uniform. As the guests sat down to a simple meal of roast chicken he said, "It is ten years today since I was released from prison at Landsberg." He told how almost the entire staff of the prison, including the chief warder, had been converted to National Socialism. "The Bavarian Government was furious, and sent most of the warders to the Police School as punishment. Before they had been there six months the place had become a National Socialist recruiting center, and had to be closed."

After dinner Hitler invited the non-smokers to accompany him to a special room. Lord Rothermere, along with Ribbentrop and some of the ladies, joined Hitler. He had been introduced to the newspaper magnate by the Princess Stephanie von Hohenlohe, a half Jew. What attracted Rothermere to Hitler was a common hatred of Bolshevism and several weeks later the *Daily Mail* roundly applauded when more than 90 per cent of the Saar electorate (at the urging of the Catholic Church) voted for union with Germany. Late in January 1935 Hitler received two more friendly guests from England: Lord Allen of Hurtwood, who brought a message of good will from Prime Minister Ramsay MacDonald; and the Marquess of Lothian, a left-wing liberal who became so impressed by Hitler's assurances of peaceful intentions that he helped persuade Foreign Secretary Sir John Simon of the Führer's sincerity.

Even France was relieved by the peaceful return of the Saar to Germany and formally presented to Germany a joint proposal for a general settlement which included equality of armaments and an Eastern Locarno.* Hitler replied cautiously on February 14 that he welcomed the armament negotiations but wouldn't it be better if Germany and England had preliminary discussions before the general talks?

Sir John Simon agreed to come to Berlin early the following month. The prospect of his visit at first generated an aura of optimism in the Berlin foreign community but on March 5 Shirer noted in his diary: "Something has gone wrong with the drive for a general settlement. Simon was supposed to arrive here day after tomorrow for his talks with the Germans, but this morning von Neurath told the British that Hitler had a cold and asked Simon to postpone his trip. A little investigation in the Wilhelmstrasse this afternoon revealed it's a *'cold diplomatique.'*" The Führer had been provoked by publication of a British White Paper decrying the acceleration of the German arms program. What had particularly alarmed the English was the unbridled enthusiasm shown by the inhabitants of the Saar upon Hitler's arrival to help celebrate formal occupation of that contested territory.

Hitler made the next move in this diplomatic chess game on March 10 and did it by revealing exclusively to Price of the *Daily Mail* that the Luftwaffe had recently become an official branch of the armed forces. As Hitler hoped, there was no official outburst of condemnation from either England or France. Instead, Sir John Simon, who probably already had this information, informed Commons that he still planned to go to Berlin once the Führer recovered from his cold; the French reaction was merely a proposal from the War Ministry to extend the period of military service.

Hitler trumped this feeble rejoinder without benefit of counsel from his own generals. On the morning of March 15 he ordered his chief adjutant to meet him in Munich at the Four Seasons, the hotel which once had been the headquarters of Sebottendorf's anti-Semitic activities. He instructed the adjutant to announce the reintroduction of conscription and another enlargement of the armed forces. That evening the Reich Defense Council convened to discuss Hitler's disconcerting conscription plan. General von Blomberg's expressions of concern over possible reaction from the

* The crux of the agreements made at Locarno ten years earlier was a treaty of mutual guarantee binding the signatories to respect the frontiers between Germany, France and Belgium—including the demilitarized Rhineland.

major powers were minimized by Ribbentrop: There was nothing at all to worry about. "What you say is all stuff and nonsense!" retorted Blomberg irritably, and continued throughout the night to attack the measure. But by the time he and Fritsch reported to Hitler next morning his objections had been stilled.

That afternoon, a Saturday, some hundred foreign correspondents crowded into the conference room of the Propaganda Ministry. Nobody knew why they had been called so suddenly and there was an air of excitement. At last Goebbels entered, "looking very important and grave," and read out in a loud voice the text of a new decree proclaiming universal military service and raising the peacetime army to 300,000 men. Although everyone had expected as much, it came as a shock. Lochner and several other correspondents raced for the telephones in the hall even while Goebbels was answering questions.

At that moment the French ambassador was getting the news first hand from the Führer in his study at the chancellery. François-Poncet protested that this notification was a flagrant violation of the Treaty of Versailles, and he expressed regret that Germany had presented France with a fait accompli without previous contact or discussion.

Hitler's confident, solemn retort was that his intentions were purely defensive. France had nothing to fear. His main enemy was Communism, he said, and launched into such a diatribe against the Russians that François-Poncet left feeling almost confident that Hitler had no desire to wage war against either France or Britain—only the determination to destroy the Soviet regime.

The French answer to Germany's new show of power was a meaningless appeal to the League of Nations and on the morning of March 25 the official British delegation met Hitler in an atmosphere of amiability. Paul Schmidt, acting as the Führer's interpreter for the first time, noticed his smile was "especially friendly" when he greeted Sir John Simon, Anthony Eden and Ambassador Sir Eric Phipps. They grouped themselves around a low table at the Reich chancellery together with Neurath and Ribbentrop.

Simon announced that both the government and people of Britain wanted peace above all and earnestly wished Germany could co-operate with other European nations toward that objective. The British public, the decisive factor in England, he said, "was very disturbed" by such events as German "withdrawal from the League of Nations, Austria and certain unilateral announcements." England as a whole "was not at all anti-German, but she was strongly opposed to anything which was liable to disturb the peace."

"Hitler's reply," recalled Eden, who understood enough German to realize that Schmidt was interpreting ably, "was a skillful piece of special pleading which was none the less threatening in its undertones." In his second encounter, Eden was "most unfavorably impressed," by the Führer's personality. He seemed "negative to me, certainly not compelling," and was, moreover, "rather shifty." At the same time Eden admired the way Hitler conducted the meeting, "without hesitation and without notes, as befitted the man who knew where he wanted to go."

He explained each of his acts credibly without being convincing. He brushed off the accusation of violating the Versailles Treaty, for example, with the argument that he had never signed it. Fixing Sir John with his blue eyes, he added that he would rather have died than do so. Nor was Germany a violator of treaties—except at the time the Prussian army arrived to help the English during Waterloo. And on that occasion Wellington had made no protest. "This must have been the nearest to humour Hitler ever approached," observed Eden. "I thought it a good thrust, delivered without a flicker of a smile."

During the morning session Hitler astonished not only the British but his own interpreter by arguing calmly and politely. But after lunch he lost his poise when the subject of the proposed Eastern Pact, which involved Lithuania, arose. "We will have nothing whatever to do with Lithuania!" Hitler exclaimed. A conspiracy trial of minority Germans was presently in session there. His eyes blazed, his voice became hoarse and he rolled his r's. "In no circumstances shall we make a pact with a state which stamps upon the German minority in Memel!" he raged. In a moment the storm subsided and once more he was the polished negotiator. This time he argued against the pact on ideological grounds. "Between National Socialism and Bolshevism," he said quietly but with force, "any association is out of the question."

That evening at a banquet a relaxed Hitler engaged Eden in a lively discussion of their wartime experiences. They had fought opposite each other on the river Oise and together they drew a map of the battle lines on the back of a dinner card.* Some of the conversation was overheard by François-Poncet and after the meal he asked Eden if it was true he had fought Hitler. When Eden replied it seemed so, the French ambassador wryly remarked, "And you missed him? You ought to be shot." That night Eden wrote in his diary, "Results bad; whole tone and temper very different to a year ago, rearmed and rearming with the old Prussian spirit very much in evidence. Russia is now the bogey."

---

* Winston Churchill fought nearby as a lieutenant colonel in the 6th Royal Scots Fusiliers from November 1915 to June 1916.

At ten the next morning Sir John proposed that they take up the key question of armaments. Britain, he said, had recently been engaged in separate discussions with other powers in preparation for a great naval armaments conference which would revise existing naval treaties. He invited Germany to take part in similar informal discussions in London. Hitler readily accepted. He repeated a previous offer to Ambassador Phipps to limit German tonnage to 35 per cent of that of the British fleet. At the same time he did not see "any heavenly or earthly authority" which could force him "to recognize the superiority of the French or Italian fleets."

At this point Hitler dramatically produced a telegram and began reading it with impassioned indignation. Again the abrupt change from moderate statesman to fanatic was startling. The message announced the guilty verdict on those minority Germans accused of treason in Lithuania. What would Britain do, asked Hitler angrily, if the Treaty of Versailles had ripped off part of her territory and turned it over to a country like Lithuania; what if Englishmen were then tortured and imprisoned merely because they acted like Englishmen?

His rage soon ran its course and he resumed his role as man of moderation, asking only for military parity with England and France. Refreshments were served at the British Embassy at noon. It was the second time the Führer had entered a foreign embassy. Afterward the conferees returned to the chancellery where Hitler complained about Soviet attempts to push westward and in this connection he scathingly referred to Czechoslovakia as "Russia's thrust-out arm." He also reiterated his demand for German equality of rights in armaments and Schmidt was impressed that Simon and Eden listened patiently and placidly. "Only two years ago the skies would have fallen if German representatives had put forward such demands as Hitler was now doing as though they were the most natural thing in the world. Nor could I help wondering whether Hitler had not got further with his method of the *fait accompli* than would have been possible with the Foreign Office method of negotiation."

That evening Hitler was host at a dinner in the chancellery. From his simple brown tunic and red swastika armband he had changed into tails. To his interpreter he was "a charming host, moving amongst his guests as easily as if he had grown up in the atmosphere of the great house." Afterward Hitler exulted over his diplomatic success to a party of friends, including Winifred Wagner. He slapped his knee and clapped hands like a schoolboy, she recalled. "Great fellows, the English," he said. "Even when they lie they do it on a magnificent scale, not a bit like the niggardly French."

The day after the talks Hitler told Chief of Naval Command Raeder about the 35 per cent ratio with England and instructed him to build up the navy according to plan—but with "no big public announcements, so as to avoid complicating England's difficult situation vis-à-vis the other Great Powers." Hitler was determined to work in harmony with the British and continued his courtship of those influential citizens who showed sympathy for Germany's plight. In April he gave a luncheon in his Munich apartment for Sir Oswald Mosley, who had resigned from the Labour Party to become leader of the British Union of Fascists. Mosley observed that Hitler's "hypnotic manner was entirely absent; perhaps I was an unsuitable subject; in any case, he made no attempt whatever to produce any effect of that kind. He was simple, and treated me throughout the occasion with a gentle, almost feminine charm."

In London a far more important adherent to the German cause was reaffirming earlier sympathies. The occasion was a long conversation between Ambassador Hoesch and the Prince of Wales, during which the heir to the throne "once again showed his complete understanding of Germany's position and aspirations."

3

In Berlin, preoccupation with the international scene was briefly overshadowed by preparation for the wedding of Hermann Göring and Emmy Sonnemann, an actress. (His first wife, Carin, had died after a long illness in 1931.) They were inundated with presents donated by organizations and individuals seeking favor. Museums sent paintings on permanent loan, the most valuable being two priceless oils by Cranach. In addition to oriental rugs, tapestries, silver candelabra and jewels were pepper cake from Saxony, Kirsch from the Black Forest, cheese and cattle. The smaller items were on display in the Berlin residence, the bulkier transported by truck to Karinhall, the country estate near the capital named after his first wife but misspelled.

The wedding on April 10 could have been produced in Hollywood, and a play-by-play account was given by radio to the nation. The pomposity of the ceremony—performed by a bishop and witnessed by the Führer himself—was relieved when two storks were observed circling around the Evangelical Cathedral. An irreverent flying comrade had swooped down and released them over the *Dom*. As the bride and groom left the church a military band thundered out the march from *Lohengrin*. Passing under a long arch of extended swords, they were greeted outside by ecstatic cheers and a mass Roman salute.

The next day Göring invited Lochner and five other correspondents to see the presents at the Minister President's palace. "Gentlemen," he told them, "I have asked you to come here in order that I may show you the gifts which *mein Volk* have given me. Just like Majesty, *nicht wahr?*" "Anyway," Lochner wrote to his daughter, "Göring need not starve. If he ever gets in a pinch, the hocking of all the gifts will bring in a million or more."

The Göring circus was relegated to the background that same day when the British, French and Italians opened their conference at Stresa. Contrary to Hitler's expectations that French suggestions would not win the support of the other two powers, the meeting led to the issuance of a joint communiqué condemning Germany's illegal rearmament and reaffirming loyalty to the principles of Locarno. The presence of Laval, MacDonald and Mussolini gave force to the announcement. Hitler, hoping to isolate the French, found himself in danger of being isolated himself. This was emphasized several weeks later by a Franco-Soviet pact of mutual assistance, which was so unsettling to the Führer's basic strategy that he made new efforts to reassure his friend Lord Rothermere that England had no reason at all to fear the Reich. From the earliest days of the party, Hitler wrote on May 3, he had envisaged co-operation with Great Britain. "Such an agreement between England and Germany would represent the weighty influence for peace and common sense of 120,000,-000 of the most valuable people in the world. The historically unique colonial aptitude and the naval power of Britain would be combined with that of one of the first military nations of the world."

While Rothermere needed no convincing and continued to present a picture of a benign Germany in his papers, the general reaction in England was one of apprehension. When the MacDonald government leaders learned that Hitler would make a major political announcement after mid-May, they became concerned enough to schedule a Commons debate on rearmament to follow it.

The dreaded speech was delivered on May 21 and once more Hitler surprised the world. Earlier in the day he had promulgated a secret defense law which placed Schacht in charge of war economy and reorganized the armed forces: The Reichswehr officially became the Wehrmacht (Armed Forces) and Hitler was named its supreme commander; Blomberg's title was changed from Minister of Defense to Minister of War and he was given the title of commander-in-chief of the armed forces; and Beck's unrevealing title of *Chef des Truppenamtes* was changed to Chief of the General Staff. In private at least, a spade was being called a spade but when Hitler faced the microphone that evening, relaxed and confident, he was the model of moderation. His chief aim was peace nor had he any dream of conquest. All war ever did, he proclaimed, was destroy the flower of the nation.

After reiterating that "Germany needs peace and desires peace," he offered to make bilateral non-aggression pacts with all his neighbors (perfidious Lithuania excepted, of course!) and promised to observe the Locarno Treaty. All he wanted was a fleet 35 per cent the size of Britain's navy. That, he promised, would be the end of his demands. "For Germany," he vowed, "this demand is final and abiding."

In many influential quarters abroad his words were taken at face value, the London *Times* calling his address "reasonable, straightforward and comprehensive." In a stroke Hitler had reversed the trend of isolation and prepared the way for a sympathetic reception of German demands at the forthcoming naval conference. It opened exactly two weeks later at the British Foreign Office with Joachim von Ribbentrop as head of the German delegation. He seated himself at the conference table armed with good advice from the Japanese naval attaché in London. Captain Arata Oka informed his German counterpart that the Japanese had come to the Washington Conference in 1921 under the false impression that one could make "a deal" with the English. "Consequently we were unprepared when the English quickly drove a wedge between our diplomats and our naval experts, separating them into almost hostile groups." He recommended that the Germans concentrate on one clear demand—such as the 35 per cent ratio—and hold to it tenaciously even if it threatened to wreck the conference. Once the English realized the Germans were firm they would slowly give in—and have greater respect for their antagonists.

Simon opened the session at 10 A.M. with his usual amiability, pointing out that it was the task of the conferees to prepare the ground for the forthcoming conference of all major naval powers; otherwise the armaments race would continue at a greater pace. It was not enough to limit tonnage; certain types of dangerous vessels, for example, should be eliminated.

Following Oka's advice, Ribbentrop refused to discuss anything but Germany's demand for a 35 per cent ratio. "If the British government does not immediately accept this condition," he said, "there is no point at all in continuing these negotiations. We must insist upon an immediate decision." Once the British accepted this ratio, he promised, the technical details regarding the program of naval construction could be settled promptly.

Schmidt was interpreting, though Ribbentrop spoke good English, and was startled that his principal had immediately brought up—and so undiplomatically!—the most difficult question on the agenda. Schmidt wondered if it was Ribbentrop's lack of experience or blind obedience to instructions. What Ribbentrop was doing, besides following Oka's shrewd advice, was to implement the disconcerting tactic that Hitler had been using so successfully for years. The speech a fortnight ago was the carrot, this was the club.

As Schmidt translated Ribbentrop's words, he could see Simon flush. It was not usual, he replied stiffly, to make such conditions at the beginning of negotiations and he could, of course, make no statement on the subject. So saying, he bowed frigidly and left the room. After a moment's embarrassment Sir Robert Craigie took Simon's place and firmly presented Britain's objections. But the dogged Ribbentrop could not be moved. They met again in the afternoon without progress and Schmidt was sure the talks had been torpedoed. He had begun to wonder what the weather would be like on the flight to Berlin when, to his surprise, the British suggested they meet again next morning, this time in the historic board room of the Admiralty.

It was a large paneled chamber dominated by a long table surrounded by red leather chairs. Schmidt's surprise at the friendly atmosphere was raised to astonishment ("I scarcely believed my own ears") when the redoubtable Craigie opened the proceedings with the announcement that the British were prepared to meet Herr von Ribbentrop's demands. Complete victory was achieved the next day, June 6, when Sir John returned, beaming as if nothing had happened. Full agreement was reached so amicably that Ribbentrop, dropping his "rather awkward manner," became outright sociable. The British not only allowed Germany to fix her naval tonnage at 35 per cent of their own fleet but conceded a 45 per cent ratio for submarines. Ribbentrop returned to Germany as a conquering hero. The attainment of all of Germany's secret naval aims by negotiation had transformed Hitler from a man of force to a statesman. France, stunned at such unilateral action (made incidentally on the anniversary of Waterloo) by a so-called ally, sent an angry note to London but British public opinion was almost universally favorable and (except for Winston Churchill, who damned the agreement as damaging British security) even those politicians generally hostile to Hitler supported the agreement.

The Prince of Wales, predictably, was pleased by the pact and on the day of its signing reported to Ambassador Hoesch (the occasion was a luncheon with the Queen at Ascot) that his own enthusiastic approval of contact between German and British veterans, made recently in a controversial speech, had been done "entirely on his own initiative." (He didn't mention that his father had reprimanded him for it. "How often have I told you, my dear boy, never to mix in politics, especially where foreign matters are concerned. The views you expressed yesterday, however sensible, are, I happen to know, contrary to those of the Foreign Office." Never must he again speak on such controversial matters without consulting the government. The royal rebuke, while disturbing, had not inhibited the Prince, who promptly made another controversial speech attacking the London County Council for banning the use of weapons, including wooden guns, in the Cadet Corps of the schools within their jurisdiction.) The Prince of Wales added that "the timidity and hesitation which, as is well known, were characteristic of politicians, were much slower in achieving results than a frank word spoken at the right moment, even though it might exceed the bounds of reserve normally maintained." His remarks were sent by airgram to the Wilhelmstrasse where they gave impetus to the exaggerated views of pro-German feelings in England and contributed to the Führer's unwarranted assumption that from now on there would be no limit to British concessions.

The Soviet Union reacted almost as violently to the London pact as the French. It confirmed suspicions that elements of Britain's ruling class, including the heir to the throne, were helping Germany strengthen its navy in the Baltic Sea for an attack on the U.S.S.R. while supporting Japanese ambitions in the Far East. Despite such apprehensions the Soviets signed a new trade treaty with Hitler, who advanced their credit to 200 million marks and was preparing to boost that figure to 500 million over a ten-year period. This was no abandonment of his dream of Lebensraum but another devious move in the international game of diplomacy. For, while he talked peace with the West and did business with the East, rearmament in Germany continued as secretly as possible at a rate exceeding the estimates of most foreign observers.

4

As the political life of Adolf Hitler expanded so did his personal life. Two inner circles had formed around him—one composed of top associates like Goebbels, Göring, Hess (and their wives) and another on a more personal level: the chauffeurs, secretaries, servants and other intimates. This innermost circle, which included such disparate members as an architect, Speer, and a pilot, Baur, was also taking in some of the younger military adjutants, like Navy Lieutenant von Puttkamer and the representative of the Luftwaffe, Nikolaus von Below. A few belonged to both circles. The most notable was Martin Bormann, who had been working for Hess since the early days and now, as his representative in Berlin, was given the opportunity of assiduously devoting himself to the daily needs of the

Führer. Although unknown to most Germans, the indefatigible Bormann had become Hitler's shadow, remaining at his shoulder most of the day ready to jot down on cuff or notebook his slightest whim.

Hitler himself moved easily between the two circles as well as among a constellation of top military and civilian circles. What he could not do was conduct the affairs of high office in a businesslike manner. A night person, he usually arrived at his desk shortly before noon. He would glance through the press dispatches that Otto Dietrich had selected for him and then rush off to lunch. Upon returning, he would postpone matters that bored him to retire in privacy and consider those that did not. For hours he would discuss the rebuilding of Berlin, Munich and Linz with architects Speer and Giesler, while State Secretary Hans Lammers and Otto Meissner, whom the Führer had inherited from Hindenburg, impatiently waited for decisions that only the head of state could make.

His working methods were a constant concern to Captain Wiedemann. Rarely could his personal adjutant get him to read a file before making an important decision. "He was of the opinion," wrote Wiedemann, "that many matters took care of themselves as long as one didn't stir them up. And he was not often wrong about this. The question was merely how such matters took care of themselves." He was similarly bohemian in his selection of visitors. Some officials would wait for days in the anteroom but if an acquaintance of the old days showed up he was as likely as not to be invited at once to lunch where he could voice problems which were often solved on the spot.

Preoccupation with the international scene disrupted Hitler's already erratic schedule and consequently he found almost no time for his mistress. The love of Adolf Hitler had become Eva Braun's whole life, even though he had made it plain that they could never marry while he was Führer of the Reich. "For me marriage would have been a disaster," he explained to his inner circle seven years later. "There's a point at which misunderstanding is bound to arise between man and wife; it's when the husband cannot give his wife all the time she feels entitled to demand." A woman lived only for her husband's sake and expected him to live for hers. Whereas the man, a slave to his thoughts, was ruled by duty. "I'd have had nothing of marriage but the sullen face of a neglected wife, or else I'd have skimped my duties. . . . The bad side of marriage is that it creates rights. In that case, it's far better to have a mistress. The burden is lightened, and everything is placed on the level of a gift." Noting the crestfallen expressions on the faces of his two middle-aged spinster secretaries, Johanna Wolf and Christa Schröder, he hastily added, "What I've said applies only to men of a higher type of course!"

Eva had sunk into a deep depression that was momentarily relieved by one of her lover's rare visits. "Yesterday he came quite unexpectedly," she wrote in her diary on February 18, "and it was a delightful evening. . . . I am so endlessly happy that he loves me so much, and pray that it will always be so." Within two weeks she wrote: "I am again deathly unhappy. Since I cannot write him, this diary has to be the depository of all my tales of woe." He came on Saturday but after spending "a few wonderful hours" with her he left and sent no word when he would return. "I am sitting on hot coals thinking every moment he might come."

A week later she wrote disjointedly as if in great haste or under emotional stress:

I wish that I were very sick since I have not heard from him for 8 days. Why doesn't something happen to me, why do I have to go through all this. I wish I had never seen him. I am desperate. Now I am buying sleeping pills, at least I will be half dazed and don't think about it so much any more. . . . Why does he torment me like this and not just put an end to the whole thing.

A few days later she made excuses for him: he had "so much to do politically." But her resolve to "wait patiently" dissolved even though he invited her to the Four Seasons Hotel.

I had to sit next to him for 3 hours without being able to say a word. At parting he handed me, as he did once before an envelope with money. How nice it would have been if he had written a greeting or a nice word with it, it would have made me so happy. But he does not think of such things.

By the end of the month loneliness turned to bitter jealousy upon hearing gossip that Hitler had found another woman, nicknamed the Walküre.

. . . I think it is unconscionable for him not to tell me. He should know me well enough to realize that I would never get in his way if he suddenly discovered his heart belonged to another.

In desperation she sent him a letter late that May which was an entreaty of sorts. Then she wrote in her diary:

. . . If I don't have an answer by 10 tonight, I will simply take my 25 pills and gently slumber to the other side.

Is this the enormous love he so often promised me when he doesn't send me a comforting word in three months?

Granted that he has had his head full these days with political problems, but there must be time for some relaxation. What about last year?

Didn't Röhm and Italy give him a lot to handle and still he found time
for me. . . .
     I am afraid there is something else behind it.
     I am not to blame. Certainly not.
     Maybe it is another woman—but not the Walküre girl, that is not plau-
sible; but there are so many others.
     What other grounds could there be? Can't find any.

A few hours later she made a final pitiful entry:

Dear God, I am so afraid he won't answer today.* If only someone
would help me, everything is so terribly hopeless. Perhaps my letter
reached him at an inopportune time. Perhaps I shouldn't have written at
all.
     Whatever the case, this uncertainty is harder to bear than a sudden end.
     Dear God, please help me so that I can speak to him today. Tomorrow
will be too late.

What Eva Braun did not know was that at the time Hitler received
her letter of desperation he was undergoing an operation. For some
months he had been troubled by a sore throat. His voice, abused by
numerous speeches of interminable length delivered in all kinds of
weather, had become hoarse and discovery of a growth on his larynx revived an old fear; for months, according to Speer, he had been talking of
Emperor Frederick III, who died of throat cancer. The throat irritation
was accompanied by stomach pains—perhaps similar to those he suffered
as a youth in Vienna—for which he took Neo-Balestol. Apparently he took
excessive amounts of the drug, which contained fusel oil, and at least once
he was so stricken with a form of intoxication that he summoned Dr. Grawitz to complain of headache, vertigo, buzzing in the ears and seeing double. On May 23, two days after his important foreign policy speech, Professor Karl van Eicken, head of Berlin University's otolaryngology
department, removed a one-centimeter polyp from the Führer's vocal cord.
It was an easy operation which took place in Hitler's chancellery apartment, requiring only a small amount of morphine as a sedative. Even so
Hitler slept deeply for fourteen hours. "I was quite concerned," Eicken
later revealed. After the operation Eicken warned him to speak softly for a
few days, and in the future not to let his emotions "lead him to shout and
scream loudly. . . . He admitted he had been told that before, but forgot
himself during a speech.†

----

* The translation of the diary in the National Archives is crude: *"Mein Gott"* in this
sentence, for example, emerges as "Goddammit."
† From November 14, 1938, issue of *Time*, which also reported that Hitler had
previously requested Professor Heinrich von Neumann of Vienna, the world's foremost
otolaryngologist, to examine his larynx. Neumann, an Orthodox Jew, refused.

Eicken assured his patient that what he had removed was a "simple polyp," that is, a small benign growth. But Hitler still worried that he might have cancer like his mother. Perhaps his absorption by morbid doubts (and the affairs of state) might explain why he had not bothered to answer Eva's letter of desperation or instructed an aide to phone a few words of consolation.

Feeling hopeless and abandoned, she swallowed twenty tablets of Vanoform, a narcotic, in the early hours of May 29. She was found in a coma by her sister Ilse. After administering first-aid treatment, learned while working as a receptionist for a surgeon, she phoned her employer, Dr. Martin Marx, whose discretion she trusted. While he was treating Eva she found the notebook containing the diary. Determined to keep the second suicide attempt a secret, she ripped out the incriminating pages so as not to involve Dr. Marx, a Jew. Ilse also feared her father might react violently and the Führer might question the mental stability of his mistress; she suggested the suicide was part theater. After all, Eva had only taken twenty pills of a type milder than Veronal—aware that one of her sisters would say good night to her after returning home.

Dr. Marx obligingly recorded the case as excessive fatigue resulting in an overdose of narcotics. Hitler accepted this explanation (although Ilse Braun remains convinced that he had guessed the truth). In any case the "accident" accomplished what words of entreaty had not. That summer he found Eva a place of her own. On August 9, 1935, she and her younger sister, Gretl, moved into a three-room apartment in the quiet residential Bogenhausen section—a short walk from the Führer's Munich apartment. He paid the rent indirectly through Hoffmann and furnished the place with furniture bought on sale.

The master of the establishment was seldom there, and when he did come it was after the neighbors were asleep. Even then his trysts with Eva were scarcely private since secret police kept watch on the stairs and outside the building. Moreover, his larynx was still bothering him and he was continually clearing his throat loudly. He consulted a doctor at Berchtesgaden the day before Eva moved into her new flat and complained that some foreign body was in his throat. While accepting a bouquet from an admirer, a thorn had impaled itself under a fingernail, and he feared he'd swallowed the thorn inadvertently after withdrawing it with his teeth. The doctor found nothing and simply brushed Hitler's pharynx with a 2½ per cent solution of silver nitrate but the patient expressed renewed concern about cancer to Professor van Eicken, who submitted a series of preparations (calling his patient Adolf Müller) to a colleague at the university. Finally on August 21 came confirmation that "Adolf Müller" had nothing to fear; the polyp *was* benign.

Hitler's anxiety was eased—at least for the moment—but he still found little time to visit Eva, involved as he was in preparations for the forthcoming Nuremberg Party Day of 1935. Moreover, his nocturnal visits to Eva's apartment were occasioning rumors that could damage him politically. Eva's new-found freedom had raised another problem. Her father felt disgraced at an illicit relationship, even one with the Führer of all Germany. On September 7 Fritz Braun nerved himself and sent a letter urging Hitler to return his Eva "to the bosom of her family." Braun was prudent enough to have Hoffmann deliver the letter in person, and the photographer with even more prudence turned it over to Eva. She tore it up but gave her father the impression that the Führer had read it without deigning to reply. A similar letter was written by Frau Braun, unbeknownst to her husband, and sent directly to Hitler. It was never answered.

Hitler's first major speech at Nuremberg came on September 11. It turned from a plea for cultural development into another attack on Jews. He charged that they had never produced an art that was characteristically their own and never would. It was such a mild rebuke that foreign observers wondered if it was true that his anti-Semitic program was being muted as reassurance to the other Great Powers. On the contrary, the growing agitation in the West for a boycott of German goods had convinced him that the time had come to enact some of those legal measures against Jews which had been suggested in his first recorded anti-Semitic declaration almost exactly sixteen years earlier. On September 13 he ordered that a decree be drafted within forty-eight hours under the title "The Law for the Protection of German Blood and Honor."

No sooner had those assigned this task completed a draft prohibiting marriages and extramarital intercourse between Jews and citizens of "German or related blood" than a messenger arrived with new orders from Hitler. They were also to write up a Reich citizenship law. The harried authors soon ran out of paper and were reduced to using old menu cards. It was 2:30 A.M., September 15, by the time it was agreed that only those of "German or related blood" could be citizens.

The other provisions were acceptable and at 9 P.M. Hitler addressed an extraordinary session of the Reichstag in Nuremberg. Passage of these laws, he said, was actually to the advantage of the Jews. It might possibly "create a level ground on which the German people may find a tolerable relation towards the Jewish people." These moderate words were immediately followed by threatening ones: "Should this hope not be fulfilled and the Jewish agitation both within Germany and abroad continue, then the position must be examined afresh."

5

Fortunately for Hitler, the attention of the world was suddenly turned from this new assault on the rights of Jews as well as his illegal expansion of the Wehrmacht by a foolish act of Benito Mussolini, his one-time model. On the third of October Italy invaded Ethiopia. Moral indignation was almost universal. How could a civilized nation attack a weak foe forced to battle planes and tanks with tribesmen on horseback? Britain and America, with conveniently short memories of their own pacification programs, were particularly abusive, and the former led the campaign in the League of Nations to invoke limited economic sanctions against Italy. Despite numerous anti-Italian and pro-Ethiopian sympathizers in Germany, Hitler publicly refused to help Emperior Haile Selassie, while secretly sending him some military aid. At the same time Hitler gave Mussolini raw materials so as to embroil Italy (and, hopefully, England) in a debilitating campaign that would leave Germany more freedom of action. His public support of Il Duce was also a test case to see how Britain would react to German defiance of the League of Nations. It was soon evident that the English would do nothing in reprisal and this must have strengthened his conviction that they were going to come to an agreement with him.

Hitler went into seclusion to regain control of the situation and himself. He was not seen in public during the last four weeks of autumn; Rosenberg assumed that the Führer was ill but it was just as likely that he was suffering one of his pre-Christmas moods of despondency. What is more, he was faced with another crucial, and unpleasant, decision that involved the future of the NSDAP and the course of National Socialism itself. Hitler had reached his Rubicon. While he and the party had gained control over all aspects of public life in Germany, the Brown Revolution remained at a standstill. He had let everything in the domestic scene slide at the expense of foreign policy and was reacting rather than initiating. Public interest in the party as a consequence was at a low level. There were fewer applications for membership and the members themselves were showing less devotion to party activities.

On the third day of January 1936 Hitler summoned his Gauleiters and Reichsleiters to a conference in hopes this group could reconcile the issues that had arisen. He opened his talk with the full revelation of the plans to rearm the nation, hinted at the grand future he envisioned for Germany and then, with an air of desperation reminiscent of the black days of late 1932 when the party seemed about to split apart, begged his listeners to realize that all this could not be achieved unless the party leadership "formed a single community, loyal to him." This plea was followed by an emotional demand for absolute devotion, which was succeeded—as in 1932—by a threat to kill himself. The audience was stunned and Chairman Hess promptly assured Hitler that everyone in the room would follow him wherever he went with unquestioning loyalty.

The Führer's spirits were abruptly revitalized and by mid-January he was prepared to take his next step forward—seizure of the demilitarized Rhineland zone which encompassed all German territory west of the Rhine as well as a thirty-mile strip east of the river that included Cologne, Düsseldorf and Bonn. He was heartened in this ambition by the death of a monarch. On the evening of January 20 King George V died and was succeeded by Edward VIII, a man of individuality and independence who had made no secret of his sympathies with many of Germany's aspirations. In his first broadcast as King he made it clear that he would not change. Confirmation came the following day from Washington when Ambassador Hans Luther cabled the Wilhelmstrasse that the chief of the Western European Affairs Division of the U. S. State Department had recently been informed by the new King in an "extremely frank" conversation that he "disapproved of France's efforts to revive the *entente cordiale* and to hitch Britain to the French wagon. . . . He further deprecated the French desire to force Germany to her knees and declared that he had much sympathy for Germany's difficult position." In three talks with the King during his first month of reign the Duke of Coburg got personal reassurance from Edward. "To my question whether a discussion between [Prime Minister] Baldwin and Adolf Hitler would be desirable for future German-British relations," reported the duke, "he replied in the following words: 'Who is King here? Baldwin or I? I myself wish to talk to Hitler, and will do so here or in Germany. Tell him that please.' "

Such encouraging words from England, together with the weak half measures of the League of Nations against Italian aggression, strengthened the Führer's resolve to reoccupy the Rhineland. If England could not even bring herself to make an all-out effort to check Mussolini, surely she would never do more than formally protest if he followed in Il Duce's footsteps. On February 12 he summoned his chargé d'affaires in Paris for a conference regarding possible French reactions to remilitarization of the Rhineland. That same afternoon he spoke to General von Fritsch about military action. The army chief of staff was not at all enthusiastic. Why not negotiate? Hitler argued that a conference would take weeks and explained that he was only thinking of a symbolic operation. How long would it take to put nine battalions of infantry and some artillery into the Rhineland? Two days, said Fritsch, but warned that it should not be undertaken if there was the slightest risk of war.

Hitler agreed in principle but recalled his ambassador to Italy, Ulrich von Hassell, and said he was "at present considering an extremely far-reaching question." Should Germany take the Paris ratification of the Franco-Russian pact as grounds for denouncing the Locarno Treaty and stationing troops in the Rhineland? At that point, according to Hassell's official memorandum, the Führer revealed that until then he had always envisaged the spring of 1937 as the right moment to seize the Rhineland but political developments made him wonder whether the psychological moment had not already arrived. "He was now asking himself whether he should not approach Mussolini with the suggestion that he, for his part, should make use of the violation of the Locarno obligations, which the inclusion of Russia represented, as a pretext for denouncing the Pact, whereupon Germany would follow suit."

In any case Hitler had just about made up his mind to act in the near future even while assuring the French of his peaceful intentions. "Is it not plainly to the advantage of both our countries to keep on good terms?" he told journalist Bertrand de Jouvenel on February 21. "I wish to succeed in making a *détente* with France . . . It is extraordinary that you should still consider German aggression possible." Those Frenchmen who were tranquilized by such words should have heeded the significance of the Führer's subsequent answer to Jouvenel's criticism of certain Francophobic passages in *Mein Kampf*: "You want me to revise my book as if I were a writer preparing a new edition. But I am not a writer. I am a politician. . . . I enter my revision into the great book of history!"

It was not until the following day that Ambassador von Hassell informed Mussolini of the Führer's grave concern about possible ratification of the Franco-Soviet pact. Mussolini replied that, while he disapproved of this treaty, it did not concern Italy directly. At least it was an indication that Mussolini would stand aloof if Germany denounced the Locarno Treaty, and so the Führer gave the word to set in motion Operation Winter Exercise. On March 2 Blomberg issued preparatory orders to the chiefs of the three services to transfer units on Z-Day (D-Day) into the demilitarized Rhineland zone. Three days later Blomberg fixed Z-Day as the seventh of March, a Saturday. The stage was set but for some reason Hitler lost his nerve and asked his Wehrmacht adjutant, Colonel Friedrich Hossbach, if the operation could still be stopped. The answer was yes. Hitler's next words were even more revealing: Find out the very latest moment Winter Exercise can be called off.

By that afternoon Foreign Secretary Eden had returned to London. He reported to the cabinet in the evening that the French wished to invoke their authority over the Rhineland. "To the British people this was a much more doubtful cause," he observed in his memoirs. "There was not one man in a thousand in the country at the time prepared to take physical action with France against a German occupation of the Rhineland."

It was indeed France, not England, that concerned the Führer, and he was unable to "sleep a wink" that night. "Again and again," he later confided to Hoffmann, "I asked myself the same question: What will France do? Will she oppose the advance of my handful of battalions? I know what I would have done, if I'd been the French: I should have struck and I would not have allowed a single German soldier to cross the Rhine."

On Friday, Z-Day minus one, it was announced that the Reichstag would meet the following noon and the diplomatic community in Berlin guessed something momentous was afoot. That evening reporters and photographers of the leading German newspapers were invited to a conference in the Ministry of Propaganda. The mystified journalists were informed by Goebbels that they were to be taken on a journey next morning so secret that they were being held in custody until then. For the second straight night the Führer tossed sleeplessly on his simple white iron bed, fretting over the possible course of France. England did not worry him; he had selected Saturday to move since no English officials would be in their offices. "They will only be back on Monday," he told Wiedemann, "and by then the excitement will be over!"

Early on Saturday morning the special press group was driven to Tempelhof where a Junkers transport was waiting. When the plane took off the reporters still had no idea where they were going. The pilot himself did not know his destination; at a specified time he was to open a sealed envelope that would direct him to the Rhineland.

At 10 A.M. the German ambassador called on Eden. After some discussion regarding another Anglo-German naval agreement, Hoesch abruptly said: "I have a communication of very great importance to make. I am afraid that the first part of it will not be to your taste, but the later portions contain an offer of greater importance than has been made at any time in recent history." He began to read a memorandum charging that the Franco-Soviet pact violated the Treaty of Locarno. Consequently Germany was taking back the demilitarized zone of the Rhineland. Hoesch hurriedly read on that Hitler offered to sign separate non-aggression pacts with Eastern countries as well as those in the West. He also was willing to re-enter the League of Nations.

Eden expressed deep regret over the Rhineland move but said he would give careful consideration to the German proposals. Her attitude toward the League, he added, was most important. At this point Hoesch said he must make it clear that there were no conditions attached to his country's return to the League, then added casually that as for the Rhineland only a few small German detachments would move into that zone. Once Hoesch left, Eden summoned the French ambassador to express his deep regret at Germany's action. The denunciation of Locarno was "deplorable," said Eden, but it would require consideration by the British cabinet. This could not be done until Monday since most of its members were at their country homes.

After short interviews with the Italian and Belgian representatives, Eden telephoned Prime Minister Baldwin and then set off at once for Chequers to brief him. "Though personally friendly to France," recalled Eden, "he was clear in his mind that there would be no support in Britain for any military action by the French. I could only agree. I told him of the earnestness with which Hitler had spoken to me of Locarno. I could not believe him anymore." Neither did Baldwin but he agreed all they could do was await the French reaction.

At about 11:30 A.M. the Junkers carrying the German press landed at Cologne and half an hour later the reporters were standing with thousands of other patriotic Germans at the Hohenzollern Bridge which stretched across the Rhine. Here eighteen years earlier dejected German soldiers had retreated from France, leaving their guns behind. Suddenly the crowd could hear the tramp of feet, the rumble of iron-clad wheels and the clop of horses' hoofs. There was fervent cheering as the first soldiers moved onto the bridge. Other units were crossing at least five other bridges as a handful of fighter planes flew cover overhead. Only three of the nineteen infantry battalions in Operation Winter Exercise crossed the Rhine but the fervor (for Germans) and fear (for French) inspired by this handful of troops was momentous.

At the Kroll Opera House Hitler was addressing the Reichstag. He had been greeted with tremendous applause, except from the diplomatic section, and his words were received with rapt attention. The UP correspondent, Richard Helms, a recent graduate of Williams College, was watching Hitler "like a hawk." After a long preamble on the inequities of the Treaty of Versailles and the dire need for Lebensraum, the Führer's delivery seemed to slow down. He began nervously passing a handkerchief from hand to hand behind the lectern. He was unnaturally pale and seemed under a strain. Then in a low, controlled voice he announced, "At this moment, German troops are marching."

The opera house went berserk.

The three battalions were, in fact, across the Rhine—with orders to stage a fighting withdrawal if challenged by French troops.

Part 5

WAR IN MASQUERDAE

"Such subtle covenants shall be made
Till peace itself is war in masquerade."

Dryden

Chapter Fourteen

"WITH THE ASSURANCE OF A SLEEPWALKER"
MARCH 1936–JANUARY 1937

1

London never seriously considered taking action when German soldiers marched into the Rhineland on that Saturday morning, March 7, 1936. From Berlin François-Poncet urged "energetic reaction." Perhaps this sparked a spirit of resistance in the French government, which called on its General Staff to act. Like most such groups, it was conservative to the point of timidity. General Gamelin warned that "a war operation, however limited, entailed unpredictable risks and could not be undertaken without decreeing a general mobilization." He did agree to rush thirteen divisions to the Maginot Line.

A pusillanimous gesture, it panicked Gamelin's opposite number in Berlin. On Sunday morning General von Blomberg begged Hitler to at least withdraw troops from Aachen, Trier and Saarbrücken. If the French attacked, he said, the Germans would have to pull back without a battle, thus suffering a moral and military defeat of the first order. Hitler remained resolute despite misgivings. He told Blomberg to wait. If necessary they could retreat tomorrow. Nor did he waver when the French Premier broadcast a message of stern defiance: Never would France negotiate while Strasbourg was threatened by German guns.

By Monday more than 25,000 German troops, greeted by censer-swinging priests conferring blessings on them, were established in the Rhine zone. While there were still only words from the French, Hitler was consumed by anxiety. He couldn't, he later confessed, endure another such strain for ten years. "The forty-eight hours after the march into the Rhineland," he told his interpreter, "were the most nerve-racking in my life." If the French had retaliated "we would have had to withdraw with our tails between our legs, for the military resources at our disposal would have been wholly inadequate for even a moderate resistance." He made a triumphal tour of the reoccupied area without incident and on the trip back home in his special train relaxed. "Good Lord, am I relieved how smoothly everything went!" he said and turned boastful from relief. "Yes, the world belongs to the courageous. God helps him." He asked that a record of Wagner's *Parsifal* be played and, as he listened, remarked that he had built his religion out of that opera. "You can serve God only as a hero," he said.

In Paris the Locarno powers convened with results so inconclusive that French Foreign Minister Flandin flew to London for help. The attitude there was typified by Lord Lothian's remark: "The Germans, after all, are only going into their own back garden." Neville Chamberlain, being groomed to succeed Baldwin as Prime Minister, emphasized to Flandin that public opinion was against enforcing any sanctions and then wrote in his diary, "His view is that, if a firm front is maintained by France and England, Germany will yield without war. We cannot accept this as a reliable estimate of a mad dictator's reaction."

Surprisingly, this general feeling of helplessness was overridden the very next day, March 12, when the Council of the League of Nations met in London and unanimously passed a resolution condemning Germany as a treaty-breaker. This occasioned an alarmist telegram to Berlin from the three Wehrmacht attachés. Blomberg rushed with it to the Führer, who jammed the message into his pocket without reading it. He refused to consider Blomberg's pleas to make concessions and gruffly told him to refrain in the future from attempting to influence political matters. Policy, he said, was made in the Reich chancellery and not in the War Ministry. His Foreign Minister was far more bellicose than the generals. Neurath opposed any concessions at all, advising the Führer to await official reactions abroad before pulling out of the Rhineland.

This was the advice taken by Hitler, who then told an audience in Munich, "I go the way that Providence dictates with the assurance of a sleepwalker." Within hours word came from Ribbentrop in London that the crisis was over and Eden seemed interested only in negotiations.

The Führer was ecstatic. What would have happened if anybody else had been Germany's leader at that time? he later boasted to his inner circle. "Anyone you care to mention would have lost his nerve. I was obliged to lie, and what saved us was my unshakable aplomb. I threatened unless the situation eased in twenty-four hours to send six extra divisions into the Rhineland. In fact, I only had four brigades."

Holding the weakest hand in the game, Hitler had bluffed England and France, proof that words of condemnation from international bodies were futile without force behind them. At the same time he had learned that his own political instincts were sounder than those of his generals. It was a victory of far-reaching import, reinforcing faith in his own destiny. He had discovered how far a resolute man, unafraid of using force, could go against adversaries terrified by the thought of another world war.

He was also shrewd enough to capitalize on the Rhineland to further solidify his power at home. He dissolved the Reichstag and submitted this policy to plebiscite. Rather than an election campaign, it was a triumphal parade from city to city with the majestic new dirigible, *Hindenburg*, painted all over with swastikas, flying escort overhead. "I have not usurped this office," he told the people of Karlsruhe. "What I have done, I did according to my conscience, and to the best of my knowledge, filled with concern for my people, realizing the necessity of protecting its honor, in order to lead it again to a position of honor in this world. And should unnecessary sorrow or suffering ever come to my people because of my actions, then I beseech the Almighty God to punish me."

On March 29, without benefit of guns, 98.8 per cent of the electorate voted for Hitler.

No head of state in the world enjoyed such popularity. Moreover, he had maneuvered his country in little more than three years from supplicant to challenger. Nowhere was this rise of status more recognized than in England, and Thomas Jones, a Welsh Liberal with important connections, came to Germany as an unofficial ambassador. His first stop was at Dahlem where Ribbentrop, knowing of his intimate relationship with Baldwin, urged him to act as go-between with the Prime Minister.

"I want Mr. Baldwin to meet Hitler," said Ribbentrop according to Jones's diary. "He is not the dictator in conversation. He is like Mr. Baldwin. The issues we have to discuss will decide the fate of generations . . . Baldwin should hear Hitler's view straight from the Chancellor with no intermediary. Hitler would speak with him with complete candor." Ribbentrop did his utmost to make the Führer appealing: he was conservative at heart, lived the life of an artist and was devoted to music and painting. "In foreign policy," added Ribbentrop, "only Hitler counts and von Ribbentrop's advice."

"What about the General Staff?" asked Jones.

"The Junkers as an influence have ceased in the government of the Reich," replied the Foreign Minister. "The reintroduction of conscription was not an army decision, but Hitler's own. The fundamental idea of National Socialism is not to conquer and dominate others but to be ourselves."

The following morning, May 17, they flew to Munich to see the Führer and took with them Schmidt, the interpreter. These four met that Sunday just after noon in the spacious sitting room of Hitler's apartment, which struck Jones as solid and Victorian. "We might have been in Park Terrace, Glasgow, in a shipowner's drawing-room in 1880." Jones said that Baldwin hoped to co-operate with Germany but "there was a long way to go." Although the recent victory of Italy in Ethiopia had shocked supporters of the League of Nations, there remained a deep and widespread faith among Englishmen in this organization.

It was apparent, Hitler replied, that the British were divided between strengthening the League as presently constituted and transforming it into a consultative body. He himself favored the latter policy and opposed undertaking vast undefined commitments which were unrealizable. The Ethiopian affair had taught that there would have been a better solution without an international organization. "The effect of the League," he said, "had been to raise the hope of the Ethiopians, to delude the other nations into imagining something effective was being done at Geneva, and to let Italy 'get away with it.'" He could have been talking about his own gamble in the Rhineland, but if Jones perceived this he did not note it in his diary. The hour-and-a-half interview ended on an exchange of personal confidences. "I pointed out that Mr. Baldwin was a shy and modest statesman who had never entirely got over his astonishment at finding himself Prime Minister and when this was translated, the Führer smiled and interjected: 'And I also.'"

It was a particularly trying time for Hitler. His chauffeur Schreck had recently been killed in a crash and he himself was having trouble sleeping. Several days after the Jones interview he complained to Dr. Brandt of a high, metallic buzz in the left ear. Brandt advised him to stroll before retiring, then have a hot and cold foot bath and several mild sleeping pills.

The Führer did take the pills, and he settled into a more regimented schedule at the new Reich chancellery which had been rebuilt according to his own design. At night he would invariably lock himself in his spartan bedroom. The only decoration was an oil portrait of his mother copied from an old photograph. On the right of the bed was a night table; Karl Krause, one of his valets, had strict instructions to have a similar table in the same position wherever he slept. In the morning the Führer insisted on shaving himself and getting dressed without help. Only when he was putting on his jacket would he emerge from his room, greet Krause and proceed to the library for a breakfast of two cups of milk, up to ten pieces of zwieback and several pieces of semi-sweet chocolate. He would eat erect while examining reports from DNB. Breakfast was over in five minutes and, without pause, he set off for the office.

About his only recreation in these busy days was an almost nightly movie in the enormous drawing room. Krause would give him a list of five or six films and he would select several. If one bored him, he would exclaim, "Trash!" and call for another. "His favorite actress was Greta Garbo," according to Sir Ivone Kirkpatrick, "and one of his favorite films *Lives of a Bengal Lancer*, which he saw three times. He liked this film because it depicted a handful of Britons holding a continent in thrall. That was how a superior race must behave and the film was compulsory viewing for the SS." He preferred French productions since, he said, they recorded the life of the petite bourgeoisie so faithfully. "I'm sorry they can't be shown to the public," he told Friedelind Wagner, although it was he who had taken over the responsibility of censoring films not cleared by the Goebbels office.

When Hitler's health showed no improvement, Dr. Brandt advised him to go on vacation, preferably to Berchtesgaden, where he always slept better. He took this advice and spent as much time as possible the next few months at Haus Wachenfeld. That summer he again attended the Wagner festival. Since Unity Mitford and her sister Diana were also on hand, Frau Wagner suggested inviting them to luncheon. Hitler was delighted. "You know Unity lives on little more than a mark a month," he said, according to Friedelind Wagner. "Her parents have cut off her allowance to force her back to England. She has returned once or twice but always runs away again."

The idyl at Bayreuth was disturbed on the night of July 22 when he was visited by two Germans residing in Morocco who belonged to the foreign organization of the NSDAP. They brought a letter from a Spanish general named Franco, leader of a military revolt against the republican government. He desperately needed planes to ferry troops from Africa for action against the "Reds." Hitler immediately summoned Göring, who happened to be at the festival. He urged Hitler to support Franco for two reasons: to prevent the further spread of Communism and "to test my young Luftwaffe." Hitler approved sending part of the transport fleet along with a number of experimental fighter units, bombers and antiaircraft guns—but no more. It was to Germany's advantage to prolong the Civil War in Spain and keep Mussolini, who was already giving extensive aid to Franco, from establishing better relations with France and England. An isolated Mussolini would have to turn to Germany.

Ribbentrop advised Hitler to keep out of the Spanish affair. No laurels were to be won there and he feared "fresh complications with Britain, which would undoubtedly dislike German intervention." But Hitler argued that it was his duty as a National Socialist to support Franco. If Spain went Communist, France (already governed by a leftist regime) would also be Bolshevized. "Wedged between the powerful Soviet bloc in the east and a strong Franco-Spanish bloc in the west, we could do hardly anything if Moscow chose to attack us."

2

That summer the Olympics were staged in Berlin despite efforts by liberals in Great Britain, the United States and France to boycott them, largely because of Germany's anti-Semitic policies. In his eagerness to turn the Olympics into a showcase for Nazi achievements, Hitler made a number of concessions. Token Jews—notably Helene Mayer, the fencer, and Rudi Ball, the hockey star—were allowed to represent the Reich, and Captain Wolfgang Fürstner, another Jew, was charged with erecting and organizing the Olympic Village. More important, anti-Semitic posters along the highways as well as notices barring Jews from resorts were removed. In Berlin, Streicher's *Der Stürmer* disappeared from the newsstands. The entire anti-Semitic campaign, in fact, was muted. These marks of conciliation were given such international publicity that foreigners thronged to Berlin, where they were greeted enthusiastically.

The opening ceremonies on August 1 were blessed by a clear blue sky. That afternoon Hitler led the parade to the stadium down the Via Triumphalis. His car, followed by a long caravan, proceeded slowly down the ten-mile boulevard, protected from the crowds by 40,000 Brownshirts and other guards. When the procession reached the stadium Hitler, in the simplest uniform, and the two Olympic officials strode forward, followed by the King of Bulgaria, crown princes from Sweden, Greece and Italy, and Mussolini's sons. They marched through the tunnel into the world's largest stadium to be greeted by a brassy voluntary from thirty trumpets. The orchestra, led by Richard Strauss and assisted by a chorus of 3000, broke into "Deutschland über Alles" followed by the "Horst Wessel Lied" and the "Olympic Hymn," composed by Strauss for the occasion. The crowd of 110,000 cheered as Hitler took his place in the official stand. Some of the delegations used the Olympic salutation, a stiff right arm extended to the side but, to the delight of the audience, Austrians modified this to the Nazi salute. The Bulgarians outdid them by adding a smart goose step. The greatest applause came for the 250-member French team, whose salute was more Roman than Olympian. They were followed by the British in straw hats who, by merely executing an "eyes right," offended numerous onlookers. The Americans got the least applause, and some derogatory stamping of feet, as they passed the Tribune of Honor, eyes right, without even dipping their flag.

The next day Hitler was present to congratulate Hans Wölke, a German, for breaking the Olympic record for the shot-put. He also congratulated the three Finns who swept the 10,000-meter run as well as the German women who placed first and second in the javelin throw. By the time the German entrants in the high jump were eliminated it was dark and so he was not there to shake hands with the three American winners, two of whom were black.

This led the President of the International Olympic Committee to inform the Führer that, as guest of honor, he should henceforth congratulate all victors or none. Hitler chose the latter course and so did not meet Jesse Owens, who won four gold medals. That the Führer publicly turned his back on the great black athlete was denied by Owens himself, who further claimed that Hitler did pay him a tribute. "When I passed the Chancellor he arose, waved his hand at me, and I waved back at him. I think the writers showed bad taste in criticizing the man of the hour in Germany."

To the surprise of his entourage, the Führer attended almost every track and field event. Face contorted, he would watch the Germans perform with the passionate interest of a boy. (During the hockey game at the Winter Olympics in Garmisch-Partenkirchen he had been too nervous to stay till the end and had to have someone give him a brief account later.) The games ended on August 16 with Hitler on hand for the final ceremonies. As the orchestra played "The Games Are Ended," the crowd joined in the emotional farewell of the athletes, who rocked in time to the music. There were isolated shouts of "Sieg Heil!" for Hitler, who had been given no role at all in the final exercises. Others took up the cry and soon the stadium reverberated with the chant, "Sieg Heil! Unser Führer, Adolf Hitler, Sieg Heil!"

The games had been an almost unqualified Nazi triumph. Germans had won the most gold medals (33), as well as the most silver and bronze; and, surprisingly, defeated the second-place Americans by 57 points. More important, many of the visitors left Germany pleased by their hosts' cordiality and impressed by what they had seen of Hitler's Reich. The success of the games was further enhanced by a two-part documentary filmed by Leni Riefenstahl that won world-wide acclaim, despite Goebbels' attempted sabotage. He even tried to keep her from setting foot in the stadium.

In the paeans of self-congratulation that followed there was a tragic note. Captain Fürstner, replaced at the last moment as commandant of the Olympic Village because he was Jewish, attended the banquet honoring his successor, then shot himself.

3

After the Rhineland coup the Führer became ever more engrossed in the problems and opportunities of foreign policy at the expense of domestic matters. Content to leave things as they were, he forced party and state to accept an uneasy coexistence. He also began to isolate himself from old party comrades. "He became markedly less ready to receive political visitors unless he had expressly sent for them," recalled Otto Dietrich. "At the same time he contrived to erect barriers between himself and his associates. . . . Hitler could no longer tolerate objections to his ideas, or in fact anything which cast doubt on his infallibility."

When Ignatius Phayre, a writer for *Current History,* came to Haus Wachenfeld for an interview that summer, he found the Führer had aged perceptibly the past year. While he talked at length of music and painting, of his days in Vienna and even of the Röhm purge, he refused to answer questions about his future in politics. Instead he rhapsodized at length on the beauties of the Obersalzberg. Here and here alone he could "breathe and think—and live! . . . I remember what I was, and what I have yet to do—if only my strength lasts, and God and Fortune remain with me to the end!"

He mused in the same melancholy vein to his sister Angela as they sat on the porch looking out toward Salzburg. He was upset over a story that he had cheated a neighboring farmer of a thousand marks on the sale of a piece of property. "Look, Adolf, it is not that bad," she said. "A thousand marks more or less won't seem so important when you become 'The Old

Man of the Obersalzberg' in a few decades!" Hitler was silent, then put an arm around her shoulder. "First of all, a thousand marks more or less *is* the point and secondly, dear Angela, I shall never become the Old Man of the Obersalzberg. I have so little time."

Their close relationship changed later that summer, largely because of her growing disapproval of his liaison with Eva Braun, whom she privately referred to as *die blöde Kuh* (the stupid cow). But her attempts to turn Hitler against his mistress failed. Since Eva's second suicide attempt he had been more attentive and had recently bought her a snug two-story house near the apartment she shared with her sister. Hoffmann had paid 30,000 marks for the villa, turning it over to Eva and Gretl ostensibly as payment for photographs the two sisters had taken. Hitler also brought Eva to Obersalzberg so often that Angela now refused to shake hands with her and frigidly addressed her as "Fräulein" rather than the more polite "Gnädiges Fräulein." Angela usually saw to it that there was no room at Haus Wachenfeld so that Eva had to seek lodging at the Platterhof.

The relations between Angela and her half brother had become so strained by autumn that she decided to give up her post as housekeeper. It was rumored that she had been dismissed by Hitler over Eva, but according to the family their principal argument concerned her plans to remarry. Hitler wanted Angela to stay on as chatelaine of Haus Wachenfeld but she was as stubborn as he and left to wed Professor Martin Hammitzsch, director of the State School of Building Construction in Dresden.* The Führer was "too busy," according to the official news release, to attend the wedding.

So Eva became the undisputed mistress of Haus Wachenfeld, which was already undergoing total reconstruction. As official summer residence

---

* Another bone of contention, according to Hans Hitler, the Führer's second cousin, was Angela's insistence on making public appearances. "She liked to make herself important . . . and Hitler could not tolerate that." Another relative on his mother's side, Fritz Pauli, was much more of an embarrassment. He not only married a Jewess but, having a peculiar sense of humor, delighted in publicizing it. He printed up postcards of the Hitler family tree with his wife's maiden name (Rosenthal) as the bottom branch, then passed them out with the remark that this was the Jewish side of Adolf Hitler.

The story that Hitler treated his younger sister badly was denied after the war by Paula herself. When Hitler's notoriety spread to Vienna she changed her name to Wolf. Even so, she was dismissed from her job. "I went to Munich and described my difficult position in life to my brother. With full understanding he assured me that he would provide for me in future." He gave her 250 marks a month, raising that figure to 500 in 1938. In addition he gave her a present of 3000 marks every Christmas and helped her buy a villa. She would occasionally visit him in the Obersalzberg but rarely for more than two weeks.

it had to be enlarged to accommodate high-level diplomatic negotiations —and provide Eva with a bedroom, boudoir and bath adjoining his own room and studio. The construction of this show place, which was renamed the Berghof, as well as an expansive complex on the mountainside was turned over to Martin Bormann, who was doing his utmost to make himself absolutely indispensable in small as well as large matters to the point of absurdity. Once at lunch Hitler seasoned his food with sauce, then wondered what was in it. Bormann left the table and several hours later, after several hectic phone calls to Berlin, announced to a bemused Hitler: "Mein Führer, the ingredients of Maggi are as follows . . ." Less amusing was his treatment of subordinates. One day while dictating to Hildegard Fath, Hess's private secretary, he ordered her to take off her glasses. When she protested, he simply snapped them in two and said: "You're far prettier without them."

As Bormann rose, others were dropping out of favor. Esser was transferred to a minor position as a glorified travel agent, Rosenberg was shoved into the background and Hanfstaengl was treated with marked coolness. The latter's uninhibited comments were making him suspect in party circles and there were rumors that he was on a black list. Moreover, one of his last links to Hitler was broken in 1936 when Helene was granted a divorce. Informed of this, Hitler blurted out, "Well, I'll have to send her a telegram right away and wish her luck." But he quickly added, "No, that wouldn't do after all," and concluded, "Frau Hanfstaengl is one of the few real ladies in Germany." He continued to send her flowers on her birthday.

Hanfstaengl conveyed his concern to Egon—now fifteen—late that summer when their yawl lay becalmed in Lake Starnberg. "Boy, listen to what I have to say, and don't forget a word of it. Things are not well. We all believed in the movement, didn't we? I'm still trying to believe in it." He said he had found much corruption and that Hitler was listening to a number of despicable criminals and perverts. "At the rate we're going, we'll have a war—a war in which England and America will be against us. It's dangerous for Germany, and for the world." The country was in a foul state internally because of the blackguards sitting behind official desks. "I've tried, God knows, to get at Hitler and warn him." But he would not listen. "It's no use saying that he just doesn't know what goes on. He must know. And if he knows, he must be held responsible." Hanfstaengl revealed that his own enemies had tried to frame him for embezzlement. "Well, they failed and I cleared myself completely. But they are not through. I expect to be fighting for life itself before long. They're almost certain to get around to liquidating me sooner or later."

The youth was not surprised, for he too had felt the change in Hitler and wondered why his father didn't flee at once. Hanfstaengl replied it wasn't as easy as that. He had helped bring the party into power and saved the Führer several times from physical and political danger. "We're all responsible," he said. "The foundation, 95 per cent of the original aims are good. There is still a chance."

In the meantime they made contingency plans for escape, agreeing on a code word, the name of the little yawl. A message beginning with "Perhaps" would be the signal for Egon to board a train for Switzerland. He should leave without talking to anyone, not even his mother. Nor need he worry about reprisals against her now that she was divorced. Hitler undoubtedly was fonder of her than ever. "Pretend you notice nothing, but quietly walk out of the picture, and keep walking without delay."

The crisis came within six months. Hanfstaengl was ordered to fly at once to Spain, purportedly to protect the interests of German correspondents in that country, but once in the air, the pilot informed him that he was to parachute over the Red lines between Barcelona and Madrid. Hanfstaengl shouted that it was a death sentence. The sympathetic pilot explained he had been given orders signed by Göring, just before take-off, but before long one of the engines clattered and he called back that there was something wrong. He added with a meaningful look at Hanfstaengl that he had to land at a small airfield. Once on the ground, Hanfstaengl pretended to call Berlin for instructions, then came out of the phone booth and informed the pilot that the Führer had ordered him to return to Uffing. He took the night train to Munich and the following morning took another to Zurich, from where he sent his son a message with the code word. Egon packed a few clothes and an autographed picture of the Führer, slipped an automatic into an overcoat pocket, then boarded the Zurich train and hid in a toilet for several hours. Just before midnight he was reunited with his father.*

4

Distracted as he was by personal problems, Hitler did not break stride in his drive for German supremacy. In the summer of 1936 he composed a long memorandum on war economy written in foreboding language and typed in triplicate with one copy each for Göring and Blomberg and a

* Until recently it was generally believed that the plane incident was simply a cruel practical joke to punish Hanfstaengl for making adverse remarks about the fighting spirit of Germans fighting in Spain. But in Hanfstaengl's book *Zwischen Weissem und Braunem Haus*, published in 1970, the author has included a letter from Luftwaffe General von Schoenbeck which indicates that it may indeed have been a murder plot.

third for his personal file. In it he stated that military strength must be raised to the limits of Germany's potential. Nor did the urgency of the task permit any "gentle scruples." Germany not only lacked raw material but was overpopulated and could not feed itself from its own soil. "To keep on saying these things is absolutely pointless. We must now put measures into effect which can bring the future a final solution, and for the interim a temporary relaxation. The final solution lies in expanding the living space or the raw material and food resources of our people." It was the problem of the government, he continued, to eventually resolve the shortages of raw materials. "It is better to consider and solve these problems in peace than to wait until the next war before attempting to carry out these economic investigations and experiments in the midst of other demands." Autarchy (a self-sufficient economy) must be established as rapidly as possible with the following aims: "I. The German army must be ready for war in four years' time. II. The German economy must be ready for war in four years."

At the same time he was attempting to solidify connections with the British. They, in turn, were demonstrating persistent ineptitude in coping with a leader of such determination and cunning. They were convinced that Hitler could be brought into line with understanding and concessions; and he had kept this misinterpretation alive the past year with conciliatory talk and vague offers of treaties. The parade of dignitaries from England bearing messages of hope and good will continued. Historian Arnold Toynbee returned from Germany convinced of Hitler's peaceful intentions. He was followed by one of the authors of the Versailles Treaty, David Lloyd George, the wartime Prime Minister who had campaigned with the slogan, "Hang the Kaiser!" On the afternoon of September 4 Hitler greeted him warmly on the steps of the Berghof. "I have always been interested in promoting good relations between our two countries," said Lloyd George, "and I renewed my efforts after the close of the Great War." Action must be taken, he said, to bring about agreement within the next few months, otherwise the two nations would drift apart.

"I agree with all my heart," replied Hitler. He also had dreamed of such an alliance as a young man. Both nations came from common racial stock and mutual understanding was essential. The menace to the future of civilization was Bolshevism. This was no fanatical obsession, he hastened to elaborate, but a real danger and Western Europe must stand together as a bloc against it. He was also concerned about the Spanish Civil War and the extraordinary extent of the hold which Bolshevism had on that country. "Why have I so much anxiety? It is not that I fear an attack from Russia. But if all the countries around me go Bolshevik, what is to become of my country from an economic point of view? All here is on the razor's edge."

After the guest left, Hitler confided to Heinz Linge, his other valet, that the former Prime Minister had told him there was a considerable period during the Great War when England was on the point of surrendering. "I told Lloyd George I believed this and that the disaster for Germany was that we surrendered at 'five minutes to 12.'" His guest agreed that Germany had surrendered too soon. "But I told him that if ever there is another war between Germany and England, Germany will fight until 5 minutes after 12, so long as I am the Führer."

Schmidt accompanied the Prime Minister back to his hotel. At the entrance they were greeted by Lloyd George's daughter, who laughingly called out, with mocking salute, "Heil Hitler!" The old man did not smile. "Certainly, Heil Hitler!" he said in all seriousness. "I say it too, for he is really a great man."

Lloyd George was predictably impressed by the 1936 Party Day at Nuremberg. More spectacular than ever, it was marked by the launching of two new campaigns: the Four-Year Plan for economic self-sufficiency and an anti-Bolshevik crusade against "the powers of disorder." On a bright Sunday morning, Hitler spoke of the Bolshevik menace to 160,000 massed Brownshirts and SS men in the huge Nuremberg stadium, then drove back to the city in an open Mercedes acknowledging the plaudits of the multitude who jammed the narrow streets and hung from the dormer windows. In the car behind rode Richard Helms of UP, along with half a dozen other foreign correspondents who had been invited to have lunch with the Führer at the storied Nuremberg Castle. "By the time we got there," remembered Helms, "I was suffering from megalomania too. I decided I must be ten feet tall, even if the cheering wasn't for me."

The guests were taken to the parapet of the castle where they met a far less impressive Hitler. What struck Helms was his commonplace manner. Ill at ease, displaying none of the pyrotechnics he had shown earlier that morning, his knees would sway back and forth. It was difficult to believe this was the person who shortly before had thrown back his arms, proclaiming to an army of roaring, hypnotized storm troopers, "The wonder of this age is that you have found me—an unknown man among millions." Yet when someone mentioned Bolshevism the words began gushing out and Hitler was once more the orator. Moscow, he charged, was seeking to dominate Europe and Germany would not permit it. "People wonder why we are fanatics against Bolshevism. It is because we— Italy too—have lived through the same sort of thing which is happening in Spain." From the street down below came such an insistent chant of

"We want to see our Führer" that he stepped to the parapet to acknowledge his admirers.

Helms left, more impressed by what he had observed at the castle than at the stadium. Here, he thought, was a very "rational man with what to him was a very rational program."

On the last day of the rally the crowd was treated to an impressive military display. After a mock aerial fight and a demonstration of the efficiency of late-model anti-aircraft guns, a mechanized battle was fought in the arena with frightening reality. So ended the Party Day with assurance of peace, proclamations of new aims and a threatening display of military strength. Not only the faithful left convinced of their Führer's infallibility. Lloyd George had been overwhelmed by almost everything he saw and heard in Germany. In an article for the *Daily Express* he wrote that Hitler had singlehandedly raised Germany from the depths. He was a born leader of men, a dynamic personality with resolute will and dauntless heart who was trusted by the old and idolized by the young.

Before he could resume the course that would make a fool of Lloyd George, Hitler sought an understanding with Italy. He sent Hans Frank to Rome with an invitation to Mussolini to visit Germany not only as dictator of Italy but as leader of the original Fascist revolution. Now Il Duce showed genuine interest in liaison with Germany, and on October 21 his Foreign Minister and son-in-law, Count Galeazzo Ciano, arrived in Berlin to make preliminary arrangements. First Ciano talked to his opposite number, Neurath, who (so reported the Italian) ridiculed Ribbentrop's illusions of a meaningful Anglo-German friendship. Ciano was equally skeptical of a new Locarno and suggested Italy remain in the League of Nations to perform "a work of sabotage useful for our common ends." Three days later Ciano met Hitler at the Berghof. In a mood to captivate, Hitler began by saying, "Mussolini is the first statesman of the world with whom no one else has the right even remotely to compare himself." The Germans and Latins, he continued, complemented each other. Together they could unite in an invincible coalition against Bolshevism and the Western democracies.

Having charged his son-in-law with the task of driving a wedge between England and Germany, Il Duce had given him a document fallen into Italian hands: a telegram from the British ambassador in Berlin to London referring to the Hitler government as one of dangerous adventurers. Upon reading this, the Führer angrily exclaimed, "According to the English there are two countries in the world today which are led by adventurers: Germany and Italy. But England too was led by adventurers when she built her Empire. Today she is governed merely by incompetents." He assured Ciano that there was no need to be concerned about England since rearmament was proceeding at a far more rapid rate in both Germany and Italy. By 1939 Germany would be ready for war, in four or five years much more than ready.

Their new relationship, providing for co-operation over a wide range, was sealed in a secret agreement and signed in Berlin by Ciano and Neurath. A few days later Mussolini referred to it in a speech delivered in the Piazza del Duomo in Milan, using a term that would come to have an ominous ring in Western ears: ". . . this Berlin-Rome line is not a diaphragm but rather an *axis*, around which can revolve all those European states with a will to collaboration and peace."

For the remainder of the autumn of 1936 one of Hitler's concerns was Spain. Small but significant quantities of German supplies and personnel had already been delivered to Franco, and the Führer considered giving more substantial aid. A special air unit capable of providing vital tactical air support for the insurgents, was operational by November, and on the eighteenth Hitler, in concert with Mussolini, finally recognized the Franco regime as the legal government of Spain.

While the Foreign Ministry urged Hitler to proceed with caution, Göring, now in charge of the Four-Year Plan, regarded the Spanish conflict as a prelude to a genuine conflict. "We are already in a state of war," he told a conference of air officials on December 2—though not an official shot had yet been fired. Even so, beginning with the new year, "all factories for aircraft production shall run as if mobilization had been ordered." A few days later he was as frank with a group of industrialists and high officials in Berlin. He revealed that war was in sight and Germany was on the threshold of mobilization. "The battle we are now approaching," he said, "demands a colossal measure of production capacity. No limit on rearmament can be visualized. The only alternatives are victory or destruction."

Göring's announcement was followed by a disturbing report from General Wilhelm Faupel, the new representative to Franco: unless at least one German division was sent without delay to Spain along with a cadre of training officers, the war might be lost, and when this suggestion was ignored by the Wilhelmstrasse, he returned home to present his case to the Führer in person. They met in the chancellery on December 21 along with Göring, Blomberg, Hossbach, Fritsch and Lieutenant Colonel Walter Warlimont, who had just returned from his post as military representative at Franco's headquarters. After Faupel requested three divisions to avert a prolonged encounter, Hitler turned to Warlimont. It was a civil war, Warlimont pointed out, and had to be won with Franco's men alone. Successful co-operation between Spanish and German troops was impossible. The aid already given was sufficient to save the insurgents from defeat. Moreover, Franco was the right man in the right place and would make the best of the situation. The other military men backed Warlimont.

Hitler liked what he heard. Germany would *not* send troops on a large scale, he concluded; his reason was not military but political and he proceeded frankly to reveal that the last thing he wanted was a quick Franco victory. A bitter, lengthy war in Spain would divert world attention from Germany's ambitious rearmament program. He did promise to continue sending the anti-Communists help and if a military disaster seemed likely aid would be increased. His last words were a lesson in cunning; he would leave the honor of sending troops in force to Mussolini. The deeper Il Duce became involved in Spain the closer he would be driven to Germany, and if the conflict continued long enough he would be committed in fact as well as in words to the Axis.

Diplomatically 1936 was a successful year for Hitler and at minimal cost. England had been charmed and Italy brought to the threshold of an unequal partnership. He also had persuaded Japan to sign an Anti-Comintern Pact with Germany which contained secret agreements (vague to be sure) that each should help the other against the Soviet Union. Admittedly spineless, the agreement was important as a propaganda ploy to justify German rearmament.

The only setback of the season was the constitutional crisis in England caused by the King's determination to marry Mrs. Wallis Warfield Simpson. He told Prime Minister Baldwin, "If I can marry her as King well and good," but if the government opposed the marriage, as Baldwin had given Edward to believe it would, "*then I was prepared to go.*" A large segment of the public sympathized with Edward VIII but the Church and the Prime Minister remained adamant.

Ribbentrop was driven to distraction by the crisis since the Führer was counting on the King's support in the coming negotiations. "He's our greatest hope!" Ribbentrop told Fritz Hesse, a representative of DNB who doubled as press agent in the German Embassy. Considered an expert in British affairs, he also had a covert mission as special representative of the Foreign Office to deal unofficially with British officials, particularly Sir Horace Wilson, the industrial adviser to the Prime Minister. "Don't you think the whole affair is an intrigue of our enemies to rob us of one of the last big positions in this country?" Shortly Ribbentrop again sent for Hesse. He had just spoken on the telephone to the Führer, who refused to take the talk of abdication seriously. It was a piece of make-believe and he had ordered the German press not even to mention the matter. Hitler's confidence gave Ribbentrop assurance. "You'll see," he predicted, "the Führer will be proved right, the whole affair will go up in smoke and the King will be grateful to us for having treated the crisis with such tactful reticence."

On the evening of December 9 Edward signed the Instrument of Abdication to become the first monarch in British history to give up the throne voluntarily. That evening he told his subjects and the world in a moving broadcast that he was unable to "carry the heavy burden of responsibility and to discharge my duties as King, as I wish to do, without the help and support of the woman I love."

Hitler could not understand how any man could give up rule for romance. He telephoned Ribbentrop and (according to Hesse) dejectedly informed his ambassador he might as well pack his trunks and give up the game for lost. "Now that the King has been dethroned, there is certainly no other person in England who is ready to play with us. Report to me on what you've been able to do. I shan't blame you if it amounts to nothing."

5

This disappointment notwithstanding, 1936 had brought Hitler such success that the Yuletide season was his first happy one "in long years," so he told Frau Göring. "It was, I believe, my most beautiful Christmas." This despite severe stomach cramps, insomnia and eczema. On December 25 he selected a personal physician recommended by Hoffmann, the photographer. Dr. Theo Morell was a skin specialist with a lucrative practice in Berlin's Kurfürstendamm, his patients including the leading film and stage personalities. He was fat, swarthy, with a full round face and peered nearsightedly through thick glasses. His hands were large, hairy, his nails often dirty. In practice too he was occasionally careless. He was known to have wrapped a patient's arm with a bandage he had just used to wipe a table; and to inject the same needle without sterilization into two patients.

For some reason, perhaps out of the friendship that had sprung up between Frau Morell and Eva Braun, Hitler chose him from among all the doctors in Germany. And for the first time since his army days Hitler removed all of his clothes for a complete physical examination. Morell diagnosed the pains and cramps in the epigastric region as gastroduodenitis, for which he prescribed Mutaflor and Gallestol. Hitler also suffered from meteorism, uncontrollable farting, a condition aggravated by his vegetarianism for which Morell prescribed Dr. Köster's Antigas pills. These contained nux vomica but Morell, unaware that this was a seed containing strychnine, instructed his patient to take two to four at every meal. In addition, Morell supplemented Hitler's vegetarian diet with large doses of vitamins, often administering them intravenously together with glucose for energy.

The most prestigious specialists in the country—including Dr. Grawitz, head of the German Red Cross, and Professor Dr. Bergmann of the Berlin Charity Hospital—had failed to cure Hitler's stomach cramps or clear up eczema so painful he couldn't wear boots. The skin specialist from the Kurfürstendamm promised to do both within a year. It took him little more than a month and Hitler jubilantly announced that the miracle doctor had saved his life. "Both Grawitz and Bergmann let me go hungry. I was only allowed tea and zwieback. . . . I was so weak I could hardly work at my desk. Then came Morell and made me well." The Führer insisted all his new-found health came from Morell, claiming that improved gum conditions had come through Mutaflor injections, not the conscientious massaging and brushing prescribed by his dentist, Dr. Hugo Blaschke.

By the time Hitler addressed the Reichstag on January 30, 1937, to commemorate his first four years in office, he was in good spirits and looking younger than his age. He reasserted his divine mission. "Today I must humbly thank Providence whose grace has enabled me, once an unknown soldier in the war, to bring to a successful issue the struggle for our honor and rights as a nation." It was a speech of promise rather than of threat and made an impact because its boasts had a basis in reality. Hitler's achievements in the first four years had truly been considerable and impressive. Like Roosevelt, he had paved the way to social security and old-age benefits. And, like Roosevelt, he had intuitively divined that the professional economists, whose thinking was hobbled by accepted theory, had little understanding of the depression. Both leaders, consequently, had defied tradition to expand production and curb unemployment.* Hitler also was changing the face of the land with a network of *Autobahnen* that would help unite the nation in peace and mobilize it

---

* "Hitler also anticipated modern economic policy," commented economist J. Kenneth Galbraith in 1973, ". . . by recognizing that a rapid approach to full employment was only possible if it was combined with wage and price controls. That a nation oppressed by economic fear would respond to Hitler as Americans did to F.D.R. is not surprising." Perhaps he understood economics too little to know what he was doing. "But in economics it is a great thing not to understand what causes you to insist on the right course."

in war. To put the population on wheels, he was developing a "People's Car" so compact and inexpensive that the average German could afford it. He asked Ferdinand Porsche to design a vehicle that would get some forty miles per gallon, accommodate four passengers and have an air-cooled engine that would not freeze up in winter. He envisaged other innovations for the future. In large cities there would be automated underground parking, traffic-free centers, numerous parks and green areas, and strict pollution control. In line with his personal obsession with cleanliness (perhaps in connection with his recurring poison-cancer phobia), the problem of pollution so concerned him that he encouraged industry to work toward the complete elimination of noxious gases. Anti-pollution contrivances were already installed in some factories in the Ruhr basin, and new plants were required to construct preventive devices to avoid pollution of the waters.

His interest in city planning extended to towns and villages. Space (another obsession) was essential, he told intimates, "and I am delighted to see our architects planning on broad and spacious lines. Only thus shall we avoid the springing up of more towns in which the houses are cluttered up almost on top of each other, as one sees in Zwickau, Gelsenkirchen and so on. If I were banished to a town of this kind, devoid of all beauty, I should lose heart and happiness just as surely as if I had been banished from my Fatherland. I am therefore determined that some measure of culture and beauty shall penetrate even into the humblest of our towns, that, step by step, the amenities of all our towns will reach a higher level."

The welfare and training of the youth of the nation were also given priority. Drastic changes had already been made in the educational system, with high schools specializing in natural science and non-classical curriculum placed on the same level as the humanistic Gymnasia. With five hours a day for physical training, compulsory courses in racial biology and emphasis on German history and literature, subjects such as ancient languages and science suffered. "The goal of our education is formation of character," wrote one Nazi pedagogue. "We don't intend to educate our children into becoming miniature scholars. . . . Therefore, I say: Let us have, rather, ten pounds less knowledge and ten calories more character."

The character-building process was accompanied by semi-deification of Hitler. Before lunch the children of Cologne were required to recite this invocation:

> *Führer, my Führer, bequeathed to me by the Lord,*
> *Protect and preserve me as long as I live!*
> *Thou hast rescued Germany from deepest distress,*

I thank thee today for my daily bread.
Abide thou long with me, forsake me not,
Führer, my Führer, my faith and my light!
Heil, my Führer!

British Ambassador Phipps reported back to London: ". . . the German schoolboy is being methodically educated, mentally and physically to defend his country . . . but I fear that, if this or a later German government ever requires it of him, he will be found to be equally well-fitted and ready to march or die on foreign soil." This ominous development began in the training of the *Jungvolk*, the organization preparing boys of ten to fourteen to become Hitler Youth. "The Young Folk is the newly won element of eternity in inexorable truth," wrote the author of a booklet on the subject. "For us an order and an imperative are the most sacred duties. For every order comes from the responsible personage, and that personage we trust—the Führer. . . . So we stand before you, German Father, German Mother, we, the young leaders of the German Youth, we train and educate your son, and mould him into a man of action, a man of victory. He has been taken into a hard school, so that his fists may be steeled, his courage strengthened, and that he may be given a faith, a faith in Germany."

Upon graduation into the Hitler Youth each boy was given a dagger on which was engraved "Blood and Honor" and informed that now he could not only wear the brown shirt but defend it by force of arms. "We took this to mean that we were not to put up with anything from anybody," commented one member of the Hitler Jugend, recently escaped to England, "that we were superior to all civilians and could beat them up if they gave themselves airs."

Before 1933 the aim of Hitler Youth was to bring together young people from all walks of life, to break their ties with Communist organizations by persuasion and propaganda, and to indoctrinate them in the Fight for Power. Afterward, the mission was to build them physically, educate them politically and train them to work for Führer and nation. Contrary to popular belief, however, they were not given formal military training and the uniform, according to Hartmann Lauterbacher, Schirach's deputy, "was more in the nature of a national costume which was worn by members of youth organizations before the existence of the Hitler Jugend, not only in Germany but in other countries as well."

While preparing the nation mentally and physically for the future, Hitler had managed in four years to raise the standards of health to such a degree that many foreigners were impressed. "Infant mortality has been greatly reduced and is considerably inferior to that in Great Britain," wrote Sir Arnold Wilson, M.P., a seven-time visitor since the take-over. "Tuberculosis and other diseases have noticeably diminished. The criminal courts have never had so little to do and the prisons have never had so few occupants. It is a pleasure to observe the physical aptitude of the German youth. Even the poorest persons are better clothed than was formerly the case, and their cheerful faces testify to the psychological improvement that has been wrought within them."

Working conditions were improved with more windows, less crowding and better washrooms. Under the slogan "Beautification in Every Place," all offices and workrooms were kept clean and neat; there were abundant flowers so that those who labored could also enjoy their surroundings. Such gains were not illusory. Never before had the worker enjoyed such privileges. The *Kraft durch Freude* (Strength through Joy) program initiated by Robert Ley's Labor Front provided subsidized concerts, theater performances, exhibitions, dances, films and adult education courses for the workers. The most revolutionary project was subsidized tourism. The humblest laborer and his family could now travel aboard luxury liners for undreamed-of holidays.

"The worker sees that we are serious about raising his social position," said Ley. "He sees that it is not the so-called 'educated classes' whom we send out as representatives of the new Germany, but himself, the German worker, whom we show to the world." Single-class ships were constructed with employers and white-collar personnel placed on an equal basis with the workers. This spirit of social democracy was what Hitler meant when he told the Reichstag on January 30, "A radical transformation has taken place and has produced results which are democratic in the highest sense of the word, if democracy has any meaning at all."

He strove to unite people of all social levels—except, of course, the Jews—and his brand of socialism excluded neither the wealthy nor the middle class. "The bourgeois must no longer feel himself a kind of pensioner of either tradition or capital, separated from the worker by the Marxist idea of property," he told one interviewer, "but must aim to accommodate himself as a worker to the welfare of the community." In practice, this concept glorified the worker while underlining Hitler's theory of social equality. He himself was publicized as construction worker, artist and student; as a man of the people who sat next to his chauffeur and ate simple meals. He refused to accept any honorary doctorates and would address workers in plants with the intimate plural form *Ihr*, boasting that he too was without estates or stocks—but neglecting to note that *Mein Kampf* had made him a millionaire.

The spirit of equality was even felt in the armed forces. There was far more camaraderie than formerly between officers and enlisted men in the regular service and the elite SS units were models of democracy. Here there was no differentiation between ranks but a brotherly spirit of all for one and one for all that would have been frowned upon by most British and American officers. Nowhere was egalitarianism more evident than in the Youth Labor Service where young men and women of all classes between the ages of seventeen and twenty-five were obliged to work for a period as farm hands and laborers for *Volk und Vaterland*. This service had been instituted to alleviate unemployment but went far beyond Roosevelt's Civilian Conservation Corps, which had a similar aim, to become the manifestation of socialism. The walls of the labor camp barracks were hung with flags, pictures of the Führer and other leaders and inspirational slogans such as: "Germany needs you, as you need Germany," "Thy people is everything; thou art nothing," and "Labor service is honor service of the German youth." An American visitor, G. S. Cox, found a pair of remarkable slogans in one camp, a quotation from Hitler: "The Jew is not a German but merely a trader; not a citizen but an exterminator," side by side with another from Kant, "Have the courage to use your reason." Cox found the trainees a cheerful lot. "They were in splendid health, with plenty to eat—a luxury some of them had not experienced for years—and they were kept too busy to have time to criticize."

Of all of the achievements of Hitler's first four years, perhaps the most consequential was his unification of the nation. Hitler had not set the clock back, diplomat George Kennan warned a superior. "Germany has simply been unified and thoroughly so. What Bonaparte and Napoleon III left undone in this direction, Versailles completed, and Hitler is now stamping out the last vestiges of particularism and class differences. That he is doing this by reducing everything to the lowest and most ugly common denominator is neither here nor there. German unity is a fact. Hitler may go but the unity will remain, and with it, barring outside interference, will remain—must remain—the jealousy, the uncertainty, the feeling of inferiority, the consequent lust to dominate Europe which are all that most Germans really have in common."

No objective observer of the German scene could deny Hitler's considerable exploits and, while labor had lost its unions, so had management lost its right to organize politically. Every individual, in fact, had lost his rights, his liberty, while the nation was gaining in equality and prosperity. But loss of civil liberties was not the only price paid for Hitler's program: although he had lifted the country out of depression and ended unemployment by original means, his insistence on speeding up rearmament at all costs was forcing the nation into a potentially disastrous economic crisis. The brilliant Schacht had done his best to oppose the efforts of Hitler and the military to make Germany economically independent, first, by vetoing plans of the War Ministry and I. G. Farben to produce artificial rubber, and then by refusing Blomberg's request for expansion of fuel oil production for fear it would upset the peacetime balance of the economy. But by early 1936 Schacht's influence had waned and the economy had been thrown off balance by Hitler's order to increase the army to thirty-six divisions. There were two primary reasons: import prices had risen 9 per cent while export prices were falling 9 per cent; and with two successive bad harvests, German agriculture was unable to supply the needs of the nation. Existing raw material stocks were shrinking. There was already a disturbing shortage of food and fuel. This latter crisis was precipitated by a Russian embargo on German exports combined with a Romanian demand for higher prices. Heating, light, lubricating and diesel oil supplies were at a dangerously low level and could not be replaced by home production.

It was this emergency which had occasioned Hitler's aforementioned memorandum in the midsummer of 1936 on war economy. His answer to the oil crisis had been one repeated years later in the United States—autarchy. He knew, of course, that Germany could not possibly produce enough raw materials within her present borders to attain complete self-sufficiency yet insisted that the nation do its best. He held out the assurance that absolute autarchy *was* possible once Germany expanded to the east. Against Schacht's advice, he demanded increases in the production of synthetic rubber, iron ore, fats, textiles and light metals and then called for a solution of the fuel crisis within eighteen months.

He ignored the warnings of experts that the production costs of such a program were exorbitant, nor did he heed the cries of outrage from industrialists when he maintained the production of arms rather than stockpiling raw materials. Instead he counterattacked by threatening big business with state intervention if it refused to join in the battle for autarchy. He declared that "finance and economics and all theories are there to serve the struggle of a people to assert itself." To Hitler it was simply a question of will power and he demanded an economic mobilization "comparable to the military and political mobilization." Nor did he care how it was achieved so long as the Wehrmacht was operational in four years.

This was the Four-Year Plan he had announced at the 1936 Nuremberg rally. The following month he chose Göring to administer it and, significantly, his choice of collaborators included but one old party member, the top posts going to co-operative civil servants, representatives of industry and General Staff officers. This meant that the NSDAP, except for Göring, whose loyalty was to himself and Hitler, had been virtually excluded from the decision-making process in the nation's economic life.

In a speech calling for national mobilization, Göring declared that workers and peasants must apply their full strength, inventors must place themselves at the disposal of the state, and business must "think not of profit, but of a strong, independent national German economy." In words that would be paraphrased a generation later by an American President, he adjured all Germans to serve their nation. "Each one of us should ask himself every day what he can do, how he can contribute to the success of the common effort."

Two months later Hitler himself made a pressing appeal to an important group of industrialists to trust Göring as executor of this urgent mission: "He is the best man for this job, a man of iron will and determination. Therefore march in serried ranks behind him." At the same meeting Göring told the industrialists it was no longer a question of producing economically but of producing. He was not at all concerned how foreign exchange was brought in. Only those who broke the law *without success* would be prosecuted.

"It was incumbent on me to denounce this economic nonsense," wrote Schacht, "and to oppose this irresponsible and wanton flouting of the law, as openly as possible." He did so in a speech to the Chamber of Commerce on his sixtieth birthday, and his audience was almost the same as Göring's. He also decried Göring's claim that the only important thing was to produce. "If I sow a hundred-weight of grain on a certain area of land and harvest only three-quarters of a hundred-weight, then that is the most utter economic nonsense imaginable." It was a declaration of war by an official already out of favor and within a few months Schacht was forced to resign as Minister of Economics. This left Göring free to carry out his Führer's plan to transform the German economy into a barefaced instrument for rearmament—and war.

If Hitler had died in 1937 on the fourth anniversary of his coming to power—the great economic crisis notwithstanding—he would undoubtedly have gone down as one of the greatest figures in German history. Throughout Europe he had millions of admirers. Gertrude Stein (who found Roosevelt boring) thought Hitler should get the Nobel Peace Prize. In magazine and newspaper articles George Bernard Shaw defended Hitler and other dictators; Shaw's speeches on Fascism infuriated fellow Fabians and brought a spate of passionate letters from anti-Fascist exiles. Another outspoken adherent was Sven Hedin, the renowned Swedish explorer, who wrote that Hitler was endowed with an indomitable passion for justice, breadth of political vision, unerring foresight and "a genuine solicitude for the welfare of his fellow citizens." Hedin, himself one sixteenth Jew and proud of it, defended Hitler's anti-Semitism while disapproving of its harsh methods. An impartial investigation of the conduct of the Jews in the years after the armistice, he said, showed why Germans loathed Jews. "Wherever the policy of subservience and defeatism was preached, its leading protagonists were Jews. And as a rule they were the same Jews who formed the vanguard of Communism and Bolshevism." His summary of Hitler's accomplishments could have been written by Goebbels: "A man who within the space of four years has raised his people from the very lowest depths to self-consciousness, pride, discipline and power deserves the gratitude of his fellow citizens and the admiration of all mankind."

Beyond inspiring individual foreigners, Hitler, by example, stimulated the growth of similar movements throughout Europe. The most important was the British Union of Fascists, the Blackshirts, and Hitler had recently honored their leader, Sir Oswald Mosley, by attending the luncheon reception following his wedding to Diana Mitford. In France—where anti-Semitism had long been an aspect of nationalism, royalism and, at times, Catholicism—the Action Française under Charles Maurras flourished and was influencing such gifted authors as André Malraux. There was also the Croix de Feu, an extreme right-wing veterans' organization, under the leadership of Colonel François de la Rocque, and half a dozen similar groups. While Fascism in practice was repugnant to such non-conformists, the accomplishments and words of both Hitler and Mussolini had mobilized them against the liberal state, democracy and parliamentarianism.

In Belgium young Léon Degrelle, who would come to regard himself as the spiritual son of Hitler, founded his Rexist movement as a bulwark against Communism. "Our movement," he commented years later, "was more Falangist than Fascist, more spiritual than political." Rexism to him was a reaction against the corruption of the times; a movement of political renovation and political justice; a battle against disorder, incompetence, irresponsibility, uncertainty and, above all, Bolshevism.

The Fascist influence extended to the United States where the German-American Bund members openly wore a Nazi uniform of white shirt, black tie, jack boots and swastika emblems; and to China, where Chiang Kai-shek had secretly organized an elite group known as the Blue Shirts. "Fascism is now thought to be backward," one of its members remarked many years later. "But then it seemed to be a very progressive means of resurrecting the country." Its primary goal apparently was preservation of the nation. "Fascism is the only tool of self-salvation of nations on the brink of destruction," stated a contemporary editorial in the Blue Shirt publication, *She-hui hsin-wen.* "It saved Italy and Germany. . . . Therefore there is no other road than imitating the Fascist spirit of violent struggle as in Italy and Germany." Chiang Kai-shek was equally enthusiastic. "Can Fascism save China?" he asked a group of Blue Shirts and provided the answer: "Yes! Fascism is what China now most needs." Despite public disclaimers to Westerners, he too loathed democracy. ("In the last several decades we have in vain become drunk with democracy and the advocacy of free thought") and subscribed to Hitler's Führer principle. "The most important part of Fascism," he told a group of party cadres eight months after Hitler took power, "is absolute trust in a sagely able leader." Unless the nation completely trusted this one man, it could not be reconstructed. "Therefore, the leader will naturally be a great person and possess a revolutionary spirit, so that he serves as a model for all party members. Furthermore, each member must sacrifice everything, acting directly for the leader and the group, and indirectly for society, the nation, and the revolution. From the day we joined this revolutionary group, we completely entrusted our rights, life, liberty, and happiness to the group, and pledged them to the leader. . . . Thus for the first time we can truly be called Fascist."

The accomplishments of Hitler in his first four years of power had done much to encourage others of a like mind. The appeal of Fascism was not only to the disgruntled and disenfranchised but to responsible men of good will. It drew unto itself youthful elements as well as intellectuals who found it a refreshing alternative to bourgeois liberalism. And while each country had its own particular brand of Fascism, all its adherents (including Hitler and Mussolini) believed that, come what may, the spiritual unity of their nation would solve all problems. This end, they believed, justified the means.

Chapter Fifteen

"SUCH A LITTLE HUMAN WORM"
1937–FEBRUARY 1938

1

Hitler followed the speech of January 30, 1937, with another, three months later, that was far more revealing. This address to 800 district leaders at the dedication of the elitist political education school in Vogelsang was a private, frank, often repetitious monologue. His purpose was twofold: to instruct these leaders, the cream of the movement, in their duties, and to memorialize the beginning of the political instruction of 3000 carefully selected young men, one of whom hopefully would follow in his footsteps.

He was like some Metternich or Machiavelli instructing his sons in political and diplomatic tricks and dispensing practical and cynical advice on how to manipulate the masses. "An organization only has a future if it subdues in a natural manner the freedom of the individual so that the whole benefits." That was why they could never tolerate any authority above that of nationhood: "No matter what it is, not even the Church." He compared their totalitarianism with democracy, describing the latter as an anthill with everyone scurrying off in different directions. These democrats had freedom to do what they wanted and consequently were worthless as individuals. "They are soft, they are not worth anything, they have no resistance." How ridiculous it would be to concern the average man with problems that gave headaches to better heads. Imagine burdening "such a little human worm" with the final decision, for example, of the Rhineland crisis! What if the Four-Year Plan had to be first presented to a democratic parliament? "Only the Jew could have thought up and introduced such idiocy."

He then turned to the problem of finding the leaders of tomorrow, and when he declared that rank and wealth were of no consequence he might have been talking of his own boyhood. "It is only necessary to have ability. It matters not who their fathers are, what their mothers were. They only must have the stuff of leadership in them. Pure abstract thinking is of no value. The Führer must be able to lead. He must be able to say, 'This has to be done. I recognize it.' He must consult with those men responsible for carrying out his plan but in the final analysis it is he who must stand up for his ideas and decisions. He must make the decision." What more beautiful kind of genuine democracy was there?

After giving practical advice on a variety of subjects, he abruptly turned to the Jewish menace, talking in the private, obscure terms everyone in the hall understood. "The question to me is never to take a step that might have to be retracted and bring harm to us. You know, I always go to the very brink of boldness but not beyond. One has to smell out: 'What can I get away with and what can't I?'" There was laughter and applause, and he responded by immediately turning emotional. "I am not going to challenge my opponent immediately to a fight. I don't say, 'Fight,' just for the pleasure of fighting. Instead I say, 'I will destroy you. And now cleverness helps me to maneuver you into such a corner that not a blow will be struck until you get a thrust into your heart! That is it!'" His last words, leaving no doubt that he meant to solve the problem by killing the Jews, were drowned out by a spontaneous mass scream of blood lust. This flesh-creeping roar was preserved on tape, a reminder to posterity of man's primal brutality and how like the shrieks of the mob in the Roman Colosseum for the death of a fallen gladiator it must have been!

When the uproar died Hitler reverted to his quiet, reasonable catalogue of pragmatic advice as if what he had just said was to be filed in secrecy. He concluded with a call for all-out national rearmament: "I want the German people to emerge as the strongest people in Europe, not the second or third!" Exultant waves of applause swept the hall. "And even if this sacrifice fails, it will not be, in my eyes, the last chapter of German history, but the next to last chapter. We shall write the last chapter!"

Except to his closest adherents, Hitler had never been so candid. The very informality of the speech, its almost total absence of emotional appeal—except for the brief, terrifying revelation of his plan for the Jews—

were themselves fearsome. Stripped of pretense, this was a cold and calculated soliloquy by a man enjoying almost absolute power.

2

On the brink of total dictatorship, Hitler remained the artist. Art and politics to him were inseparable. One of his first steps to inaugurate Nazi art and architecture was to disband the Bauhaus, an institution founded immediately after the World War by architect Walter Gropius to create a functional experimental architecture by utilizing the resources of painting, sculpture and industrial design as well as architecture. This school had drawn to it some of Europe's most talented architects and painters— Klee, Kandinsky, Feininger and Mondrian—and was the epitome of modernity. Consequently it was anathema to the classically and romantically minded Hitler.

The architect he admired above all was Professor Paul Ludwig Troost. "I could no longer bear the things I had drawn up to then," Hitler later confessed to Speer. "What a piece of luck that I met this man!" He was so impressed, in fact, that he confided to Troost's young wife "that once he came to power and became the leader of the German people," he would call on her husband, whose work had "clarity, strength and nobility."*

Perhaps his most memorable project for Hitler was a modern art museum for Munich, the Haus der Deutschen Kunst, to be built from voluntary public contributions. The Führer himself had participated in laying the cornerstone in the fall of 1933. Prior to the ceremony thousands of Brownshirts, SS and Hitler Youth paraded along the Prinzregentenstrasse to the building site. The Führer was greeted by the mason's foreman and other workmen in medieval costumes. After an orchestra played the prelude to *Die Meistersinger*, Hitler once more proclaimed his theory of Germany's cultural mission, then bestowed on Munich the title of "the capital city of German art." Moments later, however, a chill came over the proceedings when he struck the cornerstone with a silver hammer so energetically that it broke. There was an awkward silence because of a superstition that the architect would die if the hammer broke. Goebbels tried to make light of it: "When the Führer strikes, he strikes mightily." But it was no joke to Hitler, who was convinced that it was a bad omen. So

* In his memoirs Speer claims he often accompanied Hitler to the Troost studio and considered the professor his "second teacher." Theirs, he asserted, was a "close relationship." Frau Troost denies this. Speer, she said in a 1971 interview, never met her husband and was brought to the Munich atelier only after Troost's death.

feared Troost and within a few days he was hospitalized by angina pectoris. He died a few months later of pneumonia.

Frau Troost carried on her husband's work and Hitler would visit her studio every time he came to Munich. Their relationship extended beyond architecture. A lady with a mind of her own, she expressed it forthrightly. When someone asked one day what she thought of Speer, she turned to the Führer and said that if Herr Hitler had asked her husband to design a building of 100 meters, Professor Troost would have thought it over and reported back next day that the building could only be 96 meters for structural and aesthetic reasons. "But if you said to Speer, 'I need a building of 100 meters,' he would immediately reply, 'Mein Führer, 200 meters!' and you would say, 'You are my man.'" Not at all offended, Hitler joined in the laughter. "He always liked to laugh," she recalled. "Hitler really had a good sense of humor—from the heart and not, as Speer says, sarcastic."

To the surprise of his aides, Hitler did not resent Frau Troost's candor. Argument with her only stimulated him—except on one memorable occasion. For the grand opening of the Haus der Deutschen Kunst in the summer of 1937 an ambitious exhibition of German art was scheduled. The judges, including Frau Troost, made their selection according to artistic standards and therefore a good many modern paintings were chosen. Since Hitler considered such art degenerate, he and Frau Troost had a violent argument at the museum just before the opening day. She argued that the selection was good since it embraced a representative cross section. Pointing to a pile of rejected paintings, she said, "These are gray. They have already been refused by our grandmothers." The colors had all faded into a dull brown. Hitler pointed to a huge painting of a man on a hill playing a violin. Why was that refused? "It's impossible," she retorted. "Too sweet for our exhibition." She asked Hitler why he accepted an artist only after his second stroke. As the quarrel grew more acrimonious the group following them hung back. Hitler never raised his voice but his manner became coldly formal. Ignoring the storm signals, she said she could not betray her artistic convictions. "And since you can't approve our selection and have a completely different opinion, I resign this moment as a member of the jury." The Führer bade her farewell with cool formality, delegating to Hoffmann, the photographer, the chore of selecting the best entries, but a few weeks later Hitler was back at the Troost studio as if nothing had happened.

The exhibition opened on July 18 with parades through the streets of Munich depicting two thousand years of German culture. Teutonic Knights with large swastikas on their chests hauled a huge sun while others carried aloft tinfoil-covered replicas of the cosmic ash tree Yggdrasill which, according to legend, held earth, heaven and hell together. The exhibition was not so much an evocation of the past as old-fashioned. The most modern paintings were those by artists such as Adolf Ziegler. Although there were good works, particularly in the field of sculpture, most of the paintings were soulful or heroic, idyllically pastoral or rhapsodies of rustic family life. Little of the stress and strain of life in postwar Germany was portrayed.

In his speech that day Hitler declared that this House of German Art had been designed for the art of the German people, not for an international art. It was not the function of artists, he said, to retreat into the past or to distort or make ugly. "The new age of today is at work on a new human type. Men and women are to be more healthy, stronger: there is a new feeling of life, a new joy of life." And what did the decadent moderns manufacture? "Misformed cripples and cretins, women who inspire only disgust, men who are more like wild beasts, children who, were they alive, must be regarded as cursed of God." If these "artists" really saw things this way, "then one has but to ask how the defect of vision arose, and if it is hereditary the Minister of the Interior will have to see to it that so ghastly a defect of vision shall not be allowed to perpetuate itself—or if they do not believe in the reality of such impressions but seek on other grounds to impose this humbug upon the nation, then it is a matter for a criminal court." Nothing could have more clearly outlined his conviction of the import of art than this threat to sterilize modern artists with defective vision and treat the others as dangerous criminals. He put the most prestigious German artists in this category—even Emil Nolde, a crusty genius of the Expressionist school who sympathized with National Socialism—and had already started the campaign to suppress such painters. Thousands of works by Nolde, Barlach, Feininger, Corinth and Grosz had been confiscated along with a number by foreign artists, including Picasso, Matisse, Van Gogh, Braque and Cézanne. Some 730 of these paintings were being concurrently exhibited in Munich as "Degenerate Art." They were hung haphazardly without frames with such crude comments as "Thus did sick minds view Nature" or "German peasants looked at in the Yiddish manner." There was one section illustrating the influence of Negro art, another that of Marxist ideology, and a large one devoted to Jewish artists.

The exhibit also included paintings by the insane to prove that the creations of the modernists were even more disordered. Two portrait sketches by Kokoschka were placed next to an impressionistic head created by a lunatic. "The artists ought to be tied to their pictures so that every

German can spit in their faces," exclaimed one outraged visitor. While such virulence was not uncommon, this exhibition, which later toured throughout the nation, attracted two million paying visitors, five times as many as those filing into the Haus der Deutschen Kunst to see Hitler's concept of the best in German art. Admittedly many of the two million had been drawn by the advertised lure of obscenity, but many of them had undoubtedly come to see for the last time the forbidden fruits of great art.

3

That year's Party Congress opened on September 6. Hitler arrived in Nuremberg that Monday afternoon and, after inspecting his personal body-guard, drove through the beflagged city to the ringing of church bells and the cheering of crowds. The following day he made his usual dramatic appearance at Congress Hall to the accompaniment of the "Badenweiler March." Once more it was his *alter vox*, Wagner, who read out the Führer's proclamation. After contrasting Bolshevik violence and bloodshed with the moderate National Socialist revolution, it charged that there had been a concerted attempt the past year to spread the Communist chaos to East and West. There was one comforting certainty: "The whole world may begin to burn about us but the National Socialist state will emerge from the Bolshevist conflagration like platinum." Germany had solved her social problems peacefully and equitably while other countries staggered under strikes and terrorism brought about by Jewish-Bolshevik agitators.

It was a speech designed to keep the populace complacent rather than inflame its warlike spirit, while he himself was preparing to woo an ally for the conflict he knew was inevitable. Benito Mussolini had agreed to come to Germany on two conditions: that he bring no civilian evening clothes and that he have the opportunity of meeting *mit der grossen Menge* (with the great multitude). He left Rome on September 23, attired in a chic new Fascist Militia uniform specifically designed for the occasion, and accompanied by a retinue of one hundred. He was met two mornings later at Munich's main station by a host dressed in simple party uniform. Hitler held out his arms in welcome as the drums rolled and the crowd shouted "Heil!" and "Duce!"

The party made its exit along a red carpet extending through the station and drove in state to the Führer's apartment on Prinzregentenplatz. Here they had their first conversation and, since Mussolini spoke German, interpreter Schmidt had the opportunity of comparing them. With his unruly lock of hair, Hitler had an untidy bohemian appearance. "His voice was rough and often hoarse as he flung out sentences full of rolling r's either at me or at Mussolini. Sometimes his eyes blazed suddenly, and then equally suddenly became dull as if in a fit of absent-mindedness." Il Duce was completely different. "Firmly erect, swaying from the hips as he talked, his Caesarian head might have been modeled from the old Romans, with its powerful forehead and broad, square chin thrust forward under a wide mouth. He had much more vivacious expression than Hitler when his turn came to thunder against the Bolshevists or the League of Nations. Indignation, contempt, determination and cunning alternately lit up his mobile face, and he had the histrionic sense native to Latins." Yet he never seemed to say a word too much. Schmidt was also struck by the difference in their laughs. Hitler's was marked by derision and sarcasm whereas Mussolini's was free and wholehearted.

In an hourlong talk they agreed in general to show friendliness to Japan, support Franco and thwart the ambitions of France and Britain. This, their only political discussion of the visit, was evidence that Hitler was beginning to realize there was little hope he would inveigle England into underwriting, even covertly, his program of expansion. From that moment on Mussolini was rushed through a series of ceremonies and appearances, including an impressive parade of goose-stepping SS men that he would never forget, army maneuvers in Mecklenburg and inspection of the vast Krupp works in Essen. The culmination of the tour came on the afternoon of September 28. As the separate trains of the two dictators approached their destination, the railway station near the Olympic Stadium, Hitler's pulled up alongside Il Duce's on an adjacent track and for the next fifteen minutes the two trains ran side by side. The operation, practiced by the engine drivers for days, was so smoothly executed that the Italians and Germans could carry on easy conversations through the open window. Then Hitler's train began to gain almost imperceptibly so that it reached the station platform a few seconds ahead of the other, giving him time to walk across the platform and greet Mussolini with outstretched hand just as his train pulled to a stop. It was a marvel of efficiency and, along with the goose-stepping troops and maneuvers, had the impressive effect Hitler hoped for.

There was more to come. Almost a million spectators, many brought in from the provinces by special trains, lined the triumphal avenue from the station to the center of Berlin, which had been decorated with Fascist and National Socialist flags. Long banners hung from rooftops to the street and at every square there were huge pylons displaying alternately the German and the fasces emblems. Work had been shut down at 4 P.M. so that the local population could swell the ranks. The enthusiastic crowd was held back by 60,000 SS men, recruited from all over Germany. Never before had there been such stringent security measures, numerous plainclothes men mixing with the crowd while armed launches patrolled the Spree.

The spontaneous cheers at the sight of the two dictators standing side by side in an open car delighted Il Duce. The reception was even warmer the following day when the two men drove back to the Olympic Stadium so that Mussolini could have his promised meeting with the masses. This time Hitler let Mussolini enter first to have a moment of private adulation. Then Hitler made a brief introductory speech broadcast to the "115 million citizens of our two countries who are sharing with deep emotion in this historic event." Theirs, he asserted, was a "community, not only of opinion, but also action. Germany is once again a world power. The strength of our two nations constitutes . . . the strongest guarantees for the preservation of a civilized Europe, true to her cultural mission, and armed against disruptive forces."

Il Duce strode to the microphones. Since he had insisted on speaking in German and became so excited by the spectacle that he talked faster and faster, his listeners could catch only a few words. "The Berlin-Rome Axis," he shouted, "was formed in the autumn of 1935, and during the last two years it has worked splendidly for the ever closer association of our two peoples and for European peace." His visit, he said, was not an ordinary diplomatic or political episode but a demonstration of unity between two revolutions with a common purpose.

All at once the skies dumped a torrent on the stadium and Mussolini's script began to disintegrate. "The greatest and most genuine democracies that the world knows today are Germany and Italy," he said in a voice distorted by the rain-soaked microphones and loudspeakers. He continued manfully and the audience sat stolidly to the end. "I have a friend, I go with him through thick and thin to the very end." What followed was even more chaotic. He was forced to make the slow trip back to the capital alone in an open car just so the population could take another look at him. He had no raincoat and arrived soaked and bedraggled at his quarters where there was no hot water for a bath.

While he did not catch cold, Mussolini slept poorly and awakened next morning exhausted and depressed. But by the time his train departed for home he had regained his spirits. He had come to Germany with a feeling of disdain for Hitler. How could you trust a man who was unmarried, childless and without even a mistress? He left deeply impressed by what he had seen. If he had not found out about Eva Braun, he had seen power far beyond what even he had dreamed; and from that moment on the role of the two dictators was reversed; it was Mussolini who was under the influence of his junior. Dr. Carl Gustav Jung, the Swiss psychiatrist, had personally observed the two dictators and noted startling differences. In contrast to Il Duce, Hitler was like a robot. "He seemed as if he might be a double of a real person, and that Hitler the man might perhaps be hiding inside like an appendix, and deliberately so hiding in order not to disturb the mechanism."

No specific agreements were signed in Berlin nor was a final communiqué issued, but the German Foreign Office informed all its missions that the two leaders had agreed that neither should draw closer to England without the other's approval and that Italy would henceforth have a free hand in the Mediterranean while Germany enjoyed the same privilege in Austria.

Hitler was as pleased with the arrangement as Mussolini, for he still held Il Duce in high regard. Their toasts at the chancellery banquet had been more meaningful than any communiqué, with Hitler reasserting that the two countries had been drawn together in sincere friendship by a common political purpose, and his guest replying that German-Italian solidarity was a living and active one and the two nations were "immune against any attempt to separate them." With the Axis a reality, Hitler was now in position to make his next move.

4

Late in October he confided to a group of Gau propaganda chiefs that people in his family did not live to a great age. Hence the great problems, particularly that of Lebensraum, must be solved as soon as possible. Those who followed him would no longer be able to do this since he alone was capable of it. "Now," he said, "I feel as fresh as a foal in the meadow."

A week later, on November 5, 1937, he summoned his military chiefs, his Wehrmacht adjutant, Hossbach, and Foreign Minister von Neurath. The ostensible reason was to resolve the growing competition between Blomberg and Göring for raw materials. The Minister of War deeply resented the latter's use of his position as chief of the Four-Year Plan to favor the Luftwaffe and had been pressing the Führer to forbid it.

Just before this conference Hitler privately told Göring that the main reason for calling the meeting, so the latter testified, was "to put pressure on General von Fritsch, since he was dissatisfied with the rearmament of the army. He said it would not do any harm if Herr von Blomberg would also exercise a certain amount of pressure on von Fritsch." When Göring

questioned Neurath's presence, the Führer replied that he "did not want
to make the thing look too military," and merely hoped "to make it very
clear to Commander-in-Chief Fritsch that the political situation required
a forced speed in armament."

It is probable Hitler did say something like this, for it was characteristic of him to avoid taking sides or offending either party in a dispute, and when everyone was assembled at 4 P.M. he began talking of foreign policy rather than of the quarrel. It was apparent from his sober mien
that this was no ordinary conference and, once he swore them to secrecy,
his listeners (with the possible exception of Göring) prepared themselves
for a shock. It came a moment later when he requested "in the interest of
a long-term German policy, that his exposition be regarded, in the event
of his death, as his last will and testament." So read the detailed notes
drafted a little later by Colonel Hossbach. Hitler went on to say that the
aim of German policy was to make secure, preserve and enlarge the racial
community. In fact Germany's future depended on acquiring sufficient
Lebensraum and this living space could only be found in Europe. "There
had never been spaces without a master, and there were none today: the
attacker always comes up against a possessor. The question for Germany
ran: where could she achieve the greatest gain at the lowest cost." Germany's problem, he informed his startled audience, "could only be solved
by means of force and this was never without attendant risk." The question was *when* and *how*.

German power, he said, would attain its peak within six years or so.
Thereafter her military equipment would be obsolete and the other
powers would have rearmed. They must take the offensive while the rest
of the world was still preparing its defenses. "If the Führer was still living
it was his unalterable resolve to solve Germany's problem of space at the
latest by 1943–45."

Hitler scarcely glanced at his notes, facts and figures rolling out in a
startling display of photographic memory, a gift reportedly shared by Caesar,
Napoleon and Lenin. Baron von Neurath sat stiffly, and the military leaders
fidgeted uncomfortably as Hossbach, no stenographer, feverishly scribbled
down what Hitler was saying. Germany's first objective, he continued, was
to secure its eastern and southern flanks by seizing Czechoslovakia and Austria. Undoubtedly both England and France had "already tacitly written
off the Czechs," and the former was having too many problems of its own
to wage war against Germany. He warned that the defense measures of the
Czechs were growing from year to year and the Austrian army was also getting stronger. At the same time he held out the promise of large quantities

of food for the Reich from both these countries once they were annexed. It would also mean "shorter and better frontiers, the freeing of forces for other purposes," and the possibility of creating new units up to a level of about twelve divisions, that is, one new division per million inhabitants. Italy certainly would not object to the elimination of the Czechs but he could not honestly estimate what her attitude would be to Austria; that depended essentially upon whether Il Duce was still alive. "The degree of surprise and swiftness of our action were decisive factors for Poland's attitude. [Significantly he had signed a minorities treaty with this neighbor earlier in the day.] Poland—with Russia at her rear—will have little inclination to engage in war against a victorious Germany." Similarly, Russian intervention would have to be countered by lightning operations.

It was growing dark by the time Hitler finished. He asked for comments. Both Blomberg and Fritsch opposed the Führer's blueprint for conquest; they urged him not to cast France and England in the role of enemies. The French army would certainly not be too distracted by war with Italy to be a formidable opponent on the western front. Blomberg also protested that it would be extremely difficult to break through the Czech defenses, which were as strong as the Maginot Line, then joined with Fritsch to elucidate all these points once more. The latter was so concerned that he offered to cancel his leave—he was planning to go to Egypt to recuperate from an attack of bronchial catarrh—but the Führer told him that was not necessary; possibility of conflict was not *that* imminent.

Hitler left most of the rebuttal to Göring, sitting back to listen attentively. The discussion became so heated that Hossbach was finding it almost impossible to jot down what was being said. "However," he recalled, "I do remember exactly that the sharpness of the opposition both in content and form did not fail to make its impression on Hitler, as I could see from his changing expression. Every detail of the conduct of Blomberg and Fritsch must have made plain to Hitler that his policies had met with only plain impersonal contradiction, instead of applause and agreement." Equally unenthusiastic, Neurath warned that a conflict between Italy and France was not as likely as the Führer seemed to think, and while Admiral Raeder did not join the argument, it was apparent that he too was skeptical.

The meeting finally ended at 8:15 P.M. After Hitler left, Göring took Raeder aside to allay his concerns. Surprisingly, Blomberg, who had so recently registered objections, also begged the admiral not to take the Führer seriously; his oration was intended only to spur Fritsch into accelerating the rearmament program. Nor was there the slightest danger of any naval conflict with the English. Raeder left the chancellery relieved that Hitler did not really mean to wage war. After all the navy did not have a single battleship in service and the army and air force were equally unprepared. "In no way were we armed for war, and a war against England," he recalled, "would have been sheer madness."

On the other hand, Neurath took the Führer at his word but it was not until reaching his office that the Foreign Minister really fathomed what he had heard. He became physically sick and had to summon a doctor. Within forty hours Neurath (who was to suffer several heart attacks over the matter) was so driven by conscience that he ignored his oath of secrecy. He met with Generals Beck and Fritsch at the Bendlerstrasse to discuss ways of inveigling Hitler to abandon his plans for war. These two promised to do what they could; they had no desire to fight without a better than even chance of victory. It was agreed that Fritsch would re-emphasize to the Führer the military folly of waging war, after which Neurath would argue the political case.

Fritsch did interview the Führer at the Berghof on November 9. While he left no record of the result, he wrote his good friend, the Baroness von Schutzbar, that day: "Again and again new difficult matters were brought before me which must be attended to before my departure. I am really very tired and exhausted, far more than you can tell from my appearance." Hours later he left for his holiday in Egypt, but his arguments must have made no impression. Hitler would not even see Neurath.

Did Hitler mean what he said at the momentous conference? Was it theater, as Göring suggested and both Blomberg and Raeder had come to believe? Or was it a rare glimpse into his mind? The Führer's unpublished book and the numerous speeches and observations made on Lebensraum and the Jews strongly indicate he was dead serious. So would a speech he made two weeks later warning the political cadets at Sonthofen that Germany could not survive without adequate living space and that war must be risked to attain this goal.

While his words at the fateful conference did not constitute a blueprint for war, they did suggest what he might do if diplomatic threats failed. He was resolved to wage diplomatic war even at the risk of a general conflict. Time was working against him. By 1943 he had to liquidate minor, preliminary obstacles one by one either by diplomatic blackmail or by a series of Blitzkriegs: first Czechoslovakia, then Poland and France. Hopefully England would be won over to neutrality but if not she too had to be taught a military lesson that would forcibly disinterest her in continental affairs. Thus by 1943 the way would be cleared to wage major warfare—and to knock out the primary enemy, Russia. In any case, he was seriously dedicated to a warlike course and, with a gambler's instinct for timing, he was prepared to embark on the ultimate course envisaged in 1928.

5

In England there was a new Prime Minister, set on a more conciliatory posture toward Germany. "Our objective," wrote Neville Chamberlain just before accepting the appointment, "should be to set out the political guarantees which we want as a general settlement; and if the discussions have to break down, we want the breakdown to be due to Germany's refusal to accept our reasonable requirements in the political field." Energetic, strong-willed and self-confident, Chamberlain promptly began moderating the foreign policy of his predecessor, Baldwin. "I believe the double policy of rearmament and better relations with Germany and Italy will carry us safely through the danger period," he wrote in a private letter, "if only the Foreign Office will play up." And since he ran his cabinet like a managing director, there was no doubt that he would override Foreign Secretary Eden, who doubted the possibility of agreement with Hitler on acceptable terms.

Chamberlain's announced willingness to work with Hitler was given a test that autumn when the Lord President of the Council, Lord Halifax, received a gilded card inviting him to attend a hunting exhibition in Berlin sponsored by Reich Master Huntsman Hermann Göring. As Master of the Middleton Hounds, Halifax was tempted to accept, and Chamberlain thoroughly approved since the promise was held out that Halifax would be able to see Hitler.

He left England intending to sound out the Führer on a possible understanding but as an envoy he was an unfortunate choice. Upright, religious and conventional, he knew little of German history and character, nor had he even read *Mein Kampf*. He found Göring "frankly attractive: like a great schoolboy, full of life and pride in what he was doing. . . . A modern Robin Hood: producing on me a composite impression of film-star, gangster, great land-owner interested in his property, Prime Minister, Party manager, head gamekeeper at Chatsworth." He had expected to dislike Goebbels intensely—but didn't. "I suppose it must be some moral defect in me, but the fact remains."

These impressions, along with his friendly reception by Berliners, who nicknamed him Lord Halalifax (Halali was the German equivalent of Tallyho!), favorably prepared him for a meeting with the Führer at the Berghof on the morning of November 19. As he looked out the car window Halifax saw a pair of black-trousered legs and assumed this was a footman descending to help him up the snow-swept steps, until he heard someone hoarsely whisper in his ear, "Der Führer, der Führer."

The tall, gaunt Briton hastily jackknifed out of the car to be met with a friendly smile from Hitler, who insisted on showing Halifax and Sir Ivone Kirkpatrick of the Berlin Embassy around the house before they settled themselves at an inconveniently low table in the study. "I have brought no new proposals from London," said Halifax, "I have chiefly come to ascertain the German government's views on the existing political situation, and to see what possibilities of a solution there might be."

At these words the Führer frowned so angrily that the interpreter Schmidt thought he would lapse into a silent sulk. Instead he launched into a series of "highly categorial demands." He railed at the British press, which he charged had tried to wreck the Halifax visit by publishing so-called German demands, and became overtly annoyed when Halifax stiffly defended the freedom of the press in England.

With gentle, stately courtesy Halifax tried to conciliate the peevish Hitler. He praised his host for keeping Communism out of Germany and expressed the hope that their two nations, along with France and Italy, could lay a very solid foundation for peace. Then he made a diplomatic blunder. Eden had warned him not to mention the situation in central and eastern Europe yet, in an effort to be conciliatory, he brought up the subject. Once he had naïvely revealed British intentions, Hitler began to list Germany's desiderata: a close union with Austria, end of suppression of Sudeten Germans in Czechoslovakia, and freedom to extend economic relations with southeastern and eastern Europe inasmuch as Germany was the principal importer of the products of those countries. His argument was consistent without being credible, so he abruptly changed to diatribe. "Obstacles are repeatedly being put in my way in southeast Europe by the Western powers," he shouted, "and political ambitions which I have never entertained are attributed to me!"

Halifax tactfully reiterated that England was always open to any solution not based on force, then added with no tact at all, "That also applies to Austria." It was as if he had touched an alarm button. Hitler excitedly retorted that force had never been considered in the case of Austria since it was the population itself that had demanded Anschluss with Germany.

By the time they adjourned for lunch Schmidt felt that a battle for peace had been lost. "Hitler was still in a bad temper," recalled Kirkpatrick. "Neurath was ill at ease and Lord Halifax could only talk through the interpreter. I made ineffective efforts to get a conversation going, but they all collapsed pitifully under Hitler's determination not to play."

When he did talk his sarcastic comments approached rudeness. "I can't see what there is in shooting," he observed when the subject which had brought Halifax to Germany arose; "you go out armed with a highly perfected modern weapon and without risk to yourself kill a defenseless animal." He sardonically suggested that they spare all the bother of the hunt and kill a cow in the slaughterhouse. "In short," recalled Kirkpatrick, "he behaved throughout like a spoiled, sulky child."

They went downstairs where the Führer was served a large cup of chocolate topped by a huge island of whipped cream, while the others had coffee. The mood became more relaxed, particularly when several SS men demonstrated how the huge leaded picture window could be lowered noiselessly into the floor, turning the room into a covered terrace.

On the night train back to Berlin, Neurath had tea with the two Britons. It was a pity, he said, that the Führer had been tired and out of sorts but it had been an excellent thing for him to meet foreigners. When they were alone, Halifax confided to Kirkpatrick that Hitler had bewildered him and "it was doubtful whether the conversation had done more than might have been achieved by a talk between two men of different nations neither of whom could understand the language of the other." For an envoy who had been so credulous, the day's entry in Halifax's diary displayed surprising insight. "He gave me the impression of feeling that, whilst he had attained to power only after a hard struggle with present-day realities, the British government was still living comfortably in a world of its own making, a fairyland of strange, if respectable, illusions. It clung to shibboleths—'collective security,' 'general settlement,' 'disarmament,' 'non-aggression pacts'—which offered no practical prospect of a solution of Europe's difficulties."

But by the time he returned to London (after another interview with Göring, who assured him, "Under no circumstances shall we use force") Halifax was convinced he *did* understand Germany—and fell into the appeasement camp. He assured his colleagues that the Führer was "very sincere," and then reported to the cabinet that "the Germans had no policy of immediate adventure. They were too busy building up their country, which was still in a state of revolution."

His private secretary was dismayed. "I am amazed," he wrote, "that Halifax with all his High Church principles is not more shocked at Hitler's proceedings, but he is always trying to understand Germans. He easily blinds himself to unpleasant facts and is ingenious and even jesuitical in rounding awkward corners in his mind."

Hitler's reasoning for bringing round Halifax was far different and peculiarly his own: "I have always said that the English will get under the same eiderdown with me; in their politics they follow the same guidelines as I do, namely, the overriding necessity to annihilate Bolshevism."

That Yuletide, like the previous, was not a period of depression for Hitler. He was positively jovial on Christmas Eve, according to valet Krause. While the two of them knelt on the floor of the Munich apartment wrapping gifts, Krause accidentally tied a knot on top of his master's thumb. Hitler laughed, clapped Krause on the back of the neck and then asked for his dinner jacket. He was bent on celebrating the night before Christmas in style and commandeered his valet as a companion. Avoiding SS guards, the two sneaked down the stairs like conspirators to a waiting taxi. "No one saw us and Hitler was quite relieved. I wanted to sit next to the driver but Hitler grabbed my arm and I got in the back with him." For the next two hours the taxi toured around Munich, constantly changing directions. Finally Hitler gave his destination: the Luitpold Café.

The driver, having no idea who his passengers were, seemed relieved to get rid of them and drove off rapidly once he had his fare. "He probably thought we were a couple of nuts," recalled Krause, "probably not too unjustifiably so; the whole thing struck me as pretty peculiar too." Instead of going into the café Hitler set off for the Königsplatz. Noticing that Krause kept looking around nervously, he said, "Don't be afraid. No one would believe that Adolf Hitler would be walking here alone in Munich." Even so he lowered his own head when someone approached. It began to hail and the Führer linked arms with his valet since his patent leather shoes were slippery. On and on they walked until they came back to the apartment. The Führer seemed as delighted as a boy that he had not only eluded his guards but managed to walk around the city unnoticed. But the next day Himmler reprimanded Krause for participating in such an escapade. Thereafter, he ordered, such plans must be reported even if the Führer forbade it.

6

By the end of the year Prime Minister Chamberlain had confirmed his conviction that only a policy of appeasement would bring lasting peace to Europe. Even Foreign Secretary Eden, despite qualms, expressed qualified hopes in his own recommendations for "The Next Steps Towards a General Settlement with Germany," which he submitted on New Year's Day, 1938. "The conversations between Lord Halifax and Herr Hitler showed that, if we wish for a general settlement with Germany, it will be for us, and not for the German Government, to take the next step by putting forward some concrete proposals. . . . The next step, therefore, lies with us. It is important, if we are really anxious to prevent the hopes created by the recent conversations from evaporating, that we should keep moving, that there should be no long delay. We must keep moving."

The "concrete proposals" Eden was referring to were such bribes as the offer to Hitler of what didn't even belong to England—a large section of Africa owned by Belgium and Portugal—and concessions to Sudeten Germans in Czechoslovakia. Hitler could not be bought so cheaply. His talk with Halifax had confirmed that the British would acquiesce in any expansion to the east and southeast as long as it was done with a show of legality. At the same time it was apparent that Fritsch, Blomberg and other senior military leaders feared his adventurous policy would lead to disaster. They blanched at the thought of using the threat of war as a diplomatic weapon, and a confrontation with their Führer seemed inevitable.

The crisis was precipitated by a onetime prostitute, Fräulein Erna Gruen, presently working in the office of Blomberg as a typist-secretary. After a brief acquaintance the field marshal, a widower of six years, decided to make her his wife even though marriage with a woman whose mother worked in a laundry was a violation of the officers' code.

On January 12 the field marshal and typist were married in a room of the War Ministry with Göring and Hitler as witnesses. But no sooner had the couple left on a honeymoon than rumors spread about the past of the young Frau Blomberg. From their dossiers the Berlin police found that she not only had a record as a prostitute but had posed for pornographic pictures. These revelations confounded Hitler and shock was followed by indignation. Convinced that Blomberg had inveigled him into being a witness at the wedding so he would be compelled to quash any rumors that might arise, Hitler ordered Göring to inform the field marshal of Erna's past. If he agreed to dissolve the marriage some way would be found to avoid a public scandal. If not Blomberg would have to be fired.

His logical successor was Fritsch, who was far more opposed to the Führer's policy. Göring had come to the chancellery prepared for this possibility with another dossier given him by Himmler and Heydrich. It purported to prove that Fritsch had committed criminal homosexual acts with two Hitler Youth and a male prostitute known as Bavarian Joe. Here was a timely excuse to rid himself of a most unco-operative commander-in-chief and Hitler readily availed himself of it.

When Göring left the room he must have been elated. In a single stroke Minister of War Blomberg and the best candidate to supplant him had apparently been eliminated, leaving Göring the most likely successor. The next morning he informed Blomberg of the Führer's ultimatum but the field marshal stonily refused to annul the marriage.

At the Bendlerstrasse generals were receiving roguish telephone calls from prostitutes delighted by the success of one of their number. The officer corps, which had winked at the murders of Generals von Schleicher and von Bredow, could not excuse this insult to their honor. The consensus was that Blomberg must resign at once and, unless he wished to be stricken from the officer list, divorce his wife. Fritsch was delegated to carry this demand to Hitler, who had about decided to do so on his own. Still the affair dejected him. "He walked up and down the room," recalled his personal adjutant, Wiedemann, "hand behind back—a brokenhearted man—while mumbling over and over, 'If a German field marshal marries a whore, then anything in this world is possible!' "

He called in Hossbach and they discussed a successor. His chief adjutant could see no objection to Fritsch; the evidence of homosexuality must have been manufactured. The two argued until late that evening and as Hossbach was leaving he asked permission to let Fritsch know of the charges against him. Absolutely not, said Hitler, and gave his adjutant a direct order not to do so. Hossback went directly to General von Fritsch's apartment. The general indignantly denounced the charges. "If Hitler wants to get rid of me," he exclaimed, "then he has only to say the word and I will resign!"

"What an influence a woman can exert on the history of a country, and thereby the world, without even knowing it," wrote Colonel Jodl in his diary the following day, January 26. That morning Hossbach had the grit to tell Hitler he had disregarded orders and seen Fritsch. Surprisingly the Führer did not lose his temper. He seemed to accept Fritsch's claim of innocence, remarking that there was now no reason why he shouldn't be named Minister of War. He went out of his way to praise the general and swear he had no desire to get rid of him. A few hours later, however, Hitler summoned Hossbach and began angrily assailing Fritsch. The adjutant begged him not to act until he had confronted the general in person. Reluctantly the Führer agreed to an interview that evening.

During the day Wiedemann also approached Hitler with another unwelcome proposal. Göring had persuaded Wiedemann to recommend him as Minister of War but Hitler said, "By no means! Göring doesn't even know how to hold an inspection. I know more about it than he does!"

Hitler heard the same proposition later in the day when he regretfully informed Blomberg of his dismissal and, out of courtesy, asked him to recommend a successor. Blomberg suggested the man who had helped ruin him. This time Hitler was even blunter: Göring was too impotent and lazy. In that case, said Blomberg, why didn't the Führer take over the post of Minister of War himself? Apparently Blomberg out of malice was willing to cripple the officer corps which had betrayed him by placing Hitler in charge of the armed forces.

Hitler neither accepted nor rejected this recommendation, only asked who could then take charge of the OKW Staff. When Blomberg offered no candidate Hitler asked who was in charge of *his* staff. General Wilhelm Keitel, replied Blomberg, hastily adding that the prospective father-in-law of his own daughter would not be suitable for such an important position. "He's nothing but the man who runs my office."

"That's exactly the man I am looking for!"

Blomberg returned to his office that noon and, appearing to be "absolutely shattered and near collapse," told Keitel what had happened. He confessed knowing all along of his wife's disreputable past, "but that was no reason for casting a woman out forever." He had parted from Hitler amicably, he said, with the assurance that if war should come he would once again be at the Führer's side. When Keitel suggested a divorce, "for their children's sake," Blomberg protested that it had been a love match on both sides and he would "rather put a bullet in his head than that." He rushed out of the office with tears in his eyes.

At 5 P.M. Keitel was shown into Hitler's study. The Führer complained of loneliness; Keitel would have to stand by him. With some agitation he spoke of his admiration for Blomberg and how much he owed him, then complained at being tricked into acting as a witness for the wedding. Would the officer corps ever have accepted such an impossible marriage? Keitel was forced to agree that they would not. The next question was on the succession. Whom did Keitel propose? Like Blomberg, he proposed Göring and Hitler again objected. Keitel's next choice was Fritsch. The Führer stepped to his writing desk and came back with an indictment signed by the Minister of Justice charging that officer with a criminal homosexual offense. Hitler admitted suppressing an earlier similar indictment since he could not bring himself to believe the charge, but the question of succession to the most important military post in the land made it necessary to clear up the matter once and for all. He was going to have a private conversation with Fritsch and ask him point-blank if he was guilty—then watch for his reaction.

This confrontation came late that evening in the Führer's library. Fritsch knew none of the details concerning the alleged homosexual acts with two Hitler Youth and Bavarian Joe. He thought he was being queried about a silly matter involving two other Hitler Jugend and was indignant that such an innocent affair was being taken seriously. He explained that occasionally he had invited the two boys to dinner and later given them lessons in map reading, and if one was not attentive he would administer a light tap on the rear with a ruler.

Hitler had never heard about *these* two youngsters, and fired Fritsch peremptorily. Before the dazed Fritsch was out of the chancellery Hitler was giving his personal adjutant an excited version of the scene. "Imagine, Wiedemann, all of a sudden it was not only two boys but *four* he was mixed up with! The case cannot be kept secret any longer."

Hitler was still agitated when Keitel reported to him the following afternoon and learned that Fritsch was confined to his apartment. The conversation again turned to a successor. This time Hitler said that he had decided to take over the supreme command himself. Keitel was to remain as his chief of staff. Along with the post went an unpleasant chore. He was to fire Hossbach for going behind Hitler's back to warn Fritsch. The Führer never wanted to see him again.

Wiedemann was almost as perplexed and angry as Hossbach at this dismissal. He approached the Führer, who was nervously pacing the floor of the winter garden. "Mein Führer," he impulsively exclaimed, "you have wronged someone grievously today." What did Wiedemann mean? "Colonel Hossbach!" "Yes, Wiedemann," said Hitler at last, "you are right. But it was only today that I saw the 'human being' Hossbach behind the General Staff 'machinery.' Tell him that I am sorry but I cannot reverse his dismissal now. He should take a trip to the Mediterranean and then join me for dinner in the future. I will also give him a letter of recommendation specifying his excellent qualifications." This mood of forgiveness soon passed, and he never sent the letter of recommendation. "That fellow did nothing but lie to me," he would say, "and I will make sure he never gets on the General Staff again!"*

In the following week the Führer addressed himself to the problems left in the wake of the Blomberg-Fritsch scandals. First he ordered a full Gestapo investigation of the latter, then concentrated on selection of a new army commander-in-chief. He settled on General Walther von Brauchitsch, an admirer though not a party member, but pretended that his first choice was Reichenau. General Gerd von Rundstedt, as representative of the army, indignantly disapproved. To the officer corps Reichenau was not only a rabid Nazi but a military radical not fit to hold any important command. Rundstedt in turn nominated Beck. Hitler would

---

* Hitler did approve Hossbach's subsequent appointment as commanding general of an army.

not accept him. His next choice, of course, was Brauchitsch. It had developed into a horse trade and this time Rundstedt said the Führer's candidate would be acceptable to the army.

This was not yet the end of the affair. Brauchitsch revealed that he could not accept the post unless a pressing personal problem was settled. He was in the midst of divorce proceedings but his wife was demanding a considerable settlement and he was already in debt. Hitler not only gave the general 80,000 marks but persuaded Frau von Brauchitsch to accept the terms. It was a good bargain for the Führer. He now had an army commander-in-chief indebted to him. Furthermore, the woman Brauchitsch planned to marry, Frau Charlotte Schmidt, was, according to Ulrich von Hassell, "a two hundred per cent rabid Nazi." Because of Hitler's manipulations and determination along with the vacillation of the most senior generals, the crisis was finally resolved.

Surprisingly, the abortive mutiny of the army hierarchy did not permeate to the field. Except for Fritsch's close friends, few officers knew of the scandals or that both he and Blomberg had been dismissed. And so it was with some mystification that many of the commanding generals of the Wehrmacht arrived in Berlin for a conference on February 4, 1938, and learned what had occurred from the morning newspapers. They were summoned to a large hall in the chancellery where Hitler informed them of the criminal charges against Fritsch and the need to dismiss Blomberg because of his unfortunate marriage. "We were flabbergasted," recalled Heinz Guderian. "These serious allegations against our most senior officers, whom we knew to be men of spotless honor, cut us to the quick. They were quite incredible, and yet our immediate reaction was that the first magistrate of the German state could not simply have invented these stories out of thin air."

The astounded officers meekly accepted Hitler's announcement of the reorganization of the Wehrmacht, and that evening Hitler legalized his takeover of the armed forces at a cabinet meeting. After presenting Keitel and Brauchitsch, he announced that he himself was now in command of the armed forces. It was the last time the cabinet would ever meet and it was fitting that its members merely sat and approved.

Just before midnight the people of Germany were informed by radio of the Führer's momentous decree. They also learned that Blomberg and Fritsch had resigned, sixteen high-ranking generals had been dismissed and forty-four more transferred to other posts. Finally, Hermann Göring was granted the baton of a Luftwaffe field marshal as a consolation for not being named Minister of War. The house cleaning also extended to the diplomatic service. Foreign Minister von Neurath was replaced by Ribbentrop, who believed that every hour not spent in preparing for war against England was an hour lost to Germany. There was no longer any possibility of an agreement with the British, he had recently told Hitler, since they would not tolerate a powerful Germany. "On that point they will fight."

It was a day to remember in German history. The most powerful dissidents in the Wehrmacht had been eliminated or curbed and the two leading military men in the land, Keitel and Brauchitsch, were both in Hitler's debt and little more than uneasy deputies.

Once he had delivered his monologue to the cabinet, Hitler set off for Berchtesgaden with Major Rudolf Schmundt, who had replaced Hossbach as chief military adjutant, and a new army adjutant, Gerhard Engel. Next morning he must have read the headlines of the *Völkischer Beobachter* with supreme satisfaction:

> STRONGEST CONCENTRATION OF ALL POWERS IN THE
> FÜHRER'S HANDS!

At last he was the supreme dictator of the German Reich. He was ready to embark on his final course.

Chapter Sixteen

THE RETURN OF THE NATIVE
FEBRUARY–APRIL 1938

1

The repercussions of Hitler's bloodless purge were felt almost immediately in Vienna. At the German Legation, Franz von Papen—once Chancellor and now merely a minister to a small country—was called on the telephone. It was Lammers, secretary of the chancellery. "The Führer wished to inform you," he said, "that your mission in Vienna has ended. I wanted to tell you before you read about it in the newspapers." Papen was almost speechless. He had been persuaded by Hitler to take the minor post to restore the dangerous situation created by the Dollfuss murder. "I had served my purpose, it seemed, and could now go," he recalled with some bitterness. To "obtain some picture of what was going on" he decided to go at once to Berchtesgaden where he found Hitler exhausted and disturbed. "His eyes seemed unable to focus on anything and his thoughts seemed elsewhere. He sought to explain my dismissal with empty excuses." The distracted Führer paid little attention to the conversation until Papen remarked that only a face-to-face meeting between Hitler and Austrian Chancellor Kurt von Schuschnigg could solve the numerous problems dividing the two countries.

"That is an excellent idea," said Hitler and told Papen to return to Vienna and arrange a meeting for the near future. "I should be very pleased to invite Herr Schuschnigg here and talk everything over with him."

Schuschnigg accepted Papen's invitation with some uneasiness, then confessed to his Foreign Minister, Guido Schmidt, that he did so "to forestall a coup and to gain time until the international situation should improve in Austria's favor." He added ironically that he only wished his place opposite Hitler at the conference table could be filled by a psychiatrist. Schuschnigg was, indeed, ill suited to face such a ruthless opponent. A devout Catholic, an intellectual, a decent man with little vanity or driving ambition, he would enter the contest at a disadvantage.

On the evening of February 11, accompanied by Guido Schmidt, he boarded the night express for Salzburg. Once the train reached the birthplace of Mozart the sleeping car was detached. The next morning the two men drove through the ancient city, past the airport and across the Salzach River to the German border. Papen was waiting with a Hitler salute. The German customs officials also smartly raised their arms, as did their Austrian counterparts in violation of the law. It was an alarming omen and moments later came another. Papen trusted the guests wouldn't mind that three generals had "quite accidentally" arrived at the Berghof. If he had been a Dollfuss, Schuschnigg might have protested, but he disliked scenes and had no desire to provoke Hitler. "No," he said, "I don't mind but it's strange."

On the outskirts of Berchtesgaden they turned sharply to the left, at the foot of the Obersalzberg where half-tracks were waiting to take them up the steep, icy road to the Berghof. They passed neat snowbound farmhouses and an old church, then came upon SS barracks, some still under construction. All at once there was a sharp turn and the tracked vehicle stopped below the large terrace of the Berghof.

Hitler advanced with outstretched hand, the genial host. After introducing the three generals behind him, he led the Austrian Chancellor into his study on the second floor. Here the Führer abruptly shed his affability, bluntly accusing Austria of following anything but neighborly policy. Was it friendly to stay complacently in the League of Nations after Germany withdrew? In fact, Austria had never done anything to help Germany. The whole history of Austria was one uninterrupted act of high treason. "And I can tell you right now, Herr Schuschnigg, that I am absolutely determined to make an end of all this. The German Reich is one of the Great Powers and nobody will raise his voice if it settles its border problems."

Determined not to lose his temper, Schuschnigg retorted that Austria's entire history had been an essential and inseparable part of German history. "Austria's contribution in this respect is considerable."

"Absolutely zero, I'm telling you, absolutely zero!" exclaimed Hitler, sounding like anything but a man born and raised in Austria himself, and, when Schuschnigg brought up Beethoven, reminded him that the composer came from the Lower Rhineland. "I am telling you once more that things cannot go on this way. I have a historic mission; and this mission I will fulfill because Providence has destined me to do so. I thoroughly believe in this mission; it is my life. . . . Look around you in Germany today, Herr Schuschnigg, and you will find that there is but one will." He had chosen the most difficult road that any German ever took and made the greatest achievement in the history of Germany, greater than any other German. And not by force! "I am carried along by the love of my people. I can go about freely and without guard at any time in Germany. And that because I am borne by the love and trust of my people."

He accused Austria of fortifying the German border and making ridiculous efforts to mine the bridge and roads leading to the Reich. "You don't seriously believe you can stop me or even delay me for half an hour, do you? Perhaps you will wake up one morning in Vienna to find us there —just like a spring storm. And then you'll see something! I would very much like to save Austria from such a fate, because such an action would mean blood."

When Schuschnigg replied that Austria was not alone in the world and an invasion of his country would probably mean war, Hitler scoffed. Nobody would move a finger for Austria—not Italy, nor England, nor France. "Think it over, Herr Schuschnigg," he said, lowering his voice. "Think it over well. I can only wait until this afternoon. If I tell you that, you will do well to take my words literally. I don't believe in bluffing. All my past is proof of that."

His tactics were getting on Schuschnigg's nerves. He longed for a cigarette but had been warned earlier not to light up in the Führer's presence. He asked Hitler exactly what he wanted. "That," replied Hitler, ending the session with dramatic abruptness, "we can discuss this afternoon." He rang a bell and the doors opened silently from the outside. They ate in the dining room, served by handsome young SS men in snow-white uniforms. In front of the others Hitler treated his guest politely; the conversation was relaxing and inconsequential.

Coffee was served in an adjoining walled-in winter garden. Suddenly the host excused himself and returned to his study with Ribbentrop. His departure was a relief to Schuschnigg, who began chain-smoking. It also gave him the opportunity of chatting with the three generals, none of

whom knew why they had been summoned to the Berghof. It was almost
4 P.M. before the Austrian was led to a small room for a meeting with Ribbentrop, who handed over a two-page typewritten draft of an agreement
that was essentially an ultimatum: Germany would renew its full support
of Austria's sovereignty if all imprisoned Austrian National Socialists,
including the assassins of Dollfuss, were set free within three days and all
dismissed National Socialist officials and officers were reinstated in their
former positions. In addition, Artur Seyss-Inquart, the leader of the moderate Pan-German faction, was to be appointed Minister of Interior with
full, unlimited control of the nation's police forces; a "moderate" Austrian
Nazi was to be Minister of Defense, and the incumbent propaganda chiefs
were to be removed as part of "the smooth execution of a press truce."

To Schuschnigg these concessions amounted to the end of Austrian
independence and, suppressing indignation, he began to contest the various points like a dispassionate lawyer. He had just managed to squeeze a
few minor concessions from Ribbentrop when word came that the Führer
was ready to see him upstairs.

Hitler was excitedly pacing up and down the study. "Herr Schuschnigg," he said, continuing to omit the *von*, "I have decided to make one
last attempt." He pushed another copy of the draft agreements at the
Austrian. "There is nothing to be discussed about it. I will not change one
single iota. You will either sign it as it stands or else our meeting has been
useless. In that case I shall decide during the night what will be done
next."

Schuschnigg refused to sign. Even if he did, he said, it would be valueless since by constitution President Miklas alone could appoint cabinet
members and grant amnesty. Nor could he in any way guarantee that the
time limits stipulated in the document would be observed.

"You must guarantee that!"

"I could not possibly, Herr Reichskanzler."

Schuschnigg's studied, courtroom rejoinders infuriated Hitler. He
rushed to the door and shouted, "General Keitel!" He turned back to
Schuschnigg. "I shall have you called later." The bellow was heard in the
winter garden and Keitel trotted upstairs like an obedient dog, entering
the study just as Schuschnigg was about to leave. Out of breath, Keitel
asked what commands the Führer had. "None at all! Just sit down."
Puzzled, the head of OKW perched in the corner dutifully and from now
on fellow officers would nickname him *Lakeitel*, for *Lakai* (lackey).

Unaware that Hitler was bluffing, Schuschnigg was badly shaken by
the time he reached the winter garden. He related what had happened to

Foreign Minister Schmidt, who said he would not be surprised if they were arrested "within the next five minutes."

Upstairs, another Austrian, a moderate Nazi, an art critic, was assuring the Führer that Schuschnigg was a scrupulous man who would honor his promises. Impressed, Hitler made one of his lightning tactical shifts and the next time Schuschnigg walked into the study he found a magnanimous Führer. "I have decided," he said, "to change my mind—for the first time in my entire life. But I warn you—this is your very last chance. I have given you three more days before the agreement goes into effect."

After the shock of the first two conversations, the minor concessions wrung out of Hitler seemed more important than they were and Schuschnigg agreed to sign the compact. Once the revised document was sent out to be retyped, Hitler again became the genial host—one who has just sold the guest an objet d'art for an exorbitant price and is assuring him it is a bargain. "Believe me, Herr Bundeskanzler, it is for the best. Now we can abide by this agreement for the next five years."

It was evening by the time the two copies of the agreements were signed. Hitler asked Schuschnigg and Schmidt to stay for dinner but they were anxious to get back to Salzburg. Accompanied by Papen, they proceeded in silence through the foggy night toward Salzburg. Finally Papen said, "Now you have some idea, Herr Bundeskanzler, how difficult it is to deal with such an unstable person." He quickly added that he was sure it would be different the next time. "You know the Führer can be absolutely charming." Schuschnigg wondered if there would be a next time.

At the Berghof Hitler was already engaged in another bluff. He instructed his generals to sham invasion maneuvers near the Austrian border for the next few days. Hopefully, the threat of attack would induce Austrian President Miklas to ratify the agreement. If Schuschnigg was having second thoughts, so was Hitler. "This Schuschnigg was a harder bone than I first thought," he jotted down in his notebook. "The appearance of Keitel seemed to impress him but I don't believe that his signature means a capitulation. One must be hellishly careful to see that no change of mood occurs. His Jesuit brothers are by no means to be trusted."

2

Schuschnigg had three days to get their agreement approved by his colleagues and President Miklas. It was Sunday when the Chancellor arrived back in Vienna and time would run out on Tuesday the fifteenth. He conferred at once with Miklas, who was willing to grant amnesty to those Austrian Nazis still in prison while vigorously objecting to the appointment of Seyss-Inquart. "I would give him any other post," he said, "but I refuse to give him the police and the army."

News of the secret meeting in Berchtesgaden soon spread to the coffeehouses, the unofficial parliament of Austria, and an uneasy spirit pervaded the nation. Bitter arguments sprang up among the cabinet members with one group complaining that Schuschnigg should publicly proclaim Hitler's brutal tactics at the Berghof and the other commending the Chancellor's policy of caution. Twenty-four hours before Hitler's ultimatum was to run out so much disagreement remained that an emergency conference was held in the office of the President. Present, besides the two principals, were the mayor of Vienna, the president of the National Bank and a former Chancellor. After reviewing the situation Schuschnigg presented three possible courses: select a new Chancellor who would be under no obligation to the commitments at the Berghof; carry out the agreements under a new Chancellor; or carry it out under Schuschnigg.

An atmosphere of desperation settled over the room due to more reports of German invasion maneuvers at the border, and the argument that followed was not only heated but digressive. The most unlikely proposals were made, including one that Braunau, Hitler's birthplace, be ceded to Germany. Schuschnigg felt sure that Hitler would invade Austria if a single one of his demands was turned down and at last Miklas bowed to pressure, reluctantly agreeing to the Chancellor's third proposal: to leave Schuschnigg in office and accept the Berchtesgaden pact.

The Führer's charade at the Berghof, along with his sham invasion, had intimidated the Austrians into capitulation. That evening a new cabinet was sworn in and the following day, February 15, some of the truth was transmitted secretly to Austrian representatives abroad. They were informed by ciphered telegram that there had been "sharp disagreements" at Berchtesgaden, owing to increased German demands and personal pressure from Hitler; only after hours of negotiations had a basis of agreement at last been found. Fearing even this language was too strong, the government hastily dispatched another telegram which ordered the recipients to "regard references in the previous telegram to difficulties connected with the Berchtesgaden conversations as for your personal information only."

In Vienna there was a rising demand that Schuschnigg reveal exactly what had happened in Berchtesgaden but, having promised to keep silent until after Hitler addressed the Reichstag on Sunday, he kept his word as a man of honor.

The German Legation phoned Berlin that there was "considerable agitation in Vienna because of the political and economic consequences" of the agreement, that the city "resembled an anthill," and that "quite a few Jews were preparing to emigrate." Secret SD reports confirmed this, one agent informing Heydrich on February 18 that the Chancellor was under heavy attack from both Jews and Catholics. "The Jews were attacking mainly through the stock exchange, to exert pressure on the currency. Since February 17, 1938 there has been an extraordinarily heavy flight of capital, which led to a substantial drop in Austrian securities in Switzerland and London, as well as in other foreign countries. Schilling notes are being taken over the border illegally in large quantities, so that they have not been quoted since last night."

On February 20 Hitler made his eagerly awaited speech to the Reichstag, which was also broadcast throughout Austria. After announcing that he and Schuschnigg had "made a contribution to the cause of European peace," he accused Austria of mistreating its "German minority." It was, he added, "intolerable for a self-conscious world power to know that at its side are co-racials who are subjected to continuous suffering because of their sympathy and unity with the whole German race and its ideology."

On and on he orated and, though quoting facts and figures at length, he managed to entrance most of the audience at the Kroll Opera House. "During the rhetorical passages his voice mounted to the pitch of delirium: he was a man transformed and possessed. We were in the presence of a miracle." These words came not from a German but from an English observer, Major Francis Yeats-Brown.

In Vienna journalist G. E. R. Gedye roamed the streets during the "interminable hours of that speech" to see how the populace was reacting. It was a city of the dead. He found only ten people at one of the busiest corners, all listening tensely under a loudspeaker. The local Nazis were delighted that Hitler was at last coming out into the open and, not long after he finished, began congregating and shouting over and over: "Sieg Heil! Sieg Heil! Heil Hitler! Heil Hitler!"

Gedye took a taxi to the German Legation, a focal point of activity. As he drew near another chant of "Sieg Heil!" could be heard. "As one first caught it in the distance it was just a rhythmic throb, like the beating of a feverish pulse, which as one approached seemed to change into the inarticulate but disciplined cawing of some militarised rookery—a-a-a-ah—Aaaah—Aah-A-a-a-ah—Aah! and finally into audible words. The dam of four years had been pierced by the Hitler speech and the Brown flood was beginning to trickle into the streets of Vienna."

While the oration was greeted in Rome with some sympathy and understanding, there was underlying concern since it did not confirm Austria's independence. The German chargé in Rome reported that the Italians were unhappy that Hitler, in violation of their 1936 pact, had not previously consulted them and if Berlin "should continue to use this method" it might mean the end of the Axis.

Schuschnigg's reply to Hitler came four days later at the opening session of the Federal Diet in a speech broadcast throughout both countries. The stage of the parliament was decorated with a mass of tulips in the Austrian colors of red-white-red. Near the rostrum was a bust of the martyred Dollfuss. Although the Chancellor walked erectly to the podium his restrained manner was that of a Jesuit scholar. He was greeted with shouts of "Schuschnigg! Schuschnigg!" for the word had gone out that he was going to make a fighting speech. "The one and only point on the order of the day," he said in a tired voice, "is: Austria." This brought renewed shouts. Inspired, he began to speak movingly of those who had fought for Austrian independence from the Empress Maria Theresa to Dollfuss. Never before had his delivery been so effective, so fervent. Gone were the restraints of the self-effacing intellectual who had allowed himself to be bullied at the Berghof. His tone hardened when he finally mentioned the Berchtesgaden agreements. "We have gone to the very limit of concessions, where we must call a halt and say, 'Thus far and no further.'" He went on to declare that "neither Nationalism nor Socialism is the watchword of Austria, but patriotism!" The nation would remain free and for this Austrians would have to fight to the end. He ended with a fighting motto: "*Rot-Weiss-Rot! Bis in den Tod!* [Red-White-Red! Until Death!] Austria!"

The members of the House stood to applaud frenziedly. Their shouts were picked up by the crowds outside. Someone started singing "*Gott Erhalte* [God preserve]" and it became a roaring chorus. They sang "Andreas Hofer," the anthem of revolt that came from the Tyrol, Schuschnigg's birthplace. The enthusiasm in the streets carried over to a general feeling of hope throughout the land and as far as Paris. In a debate on foreign affairs the next day at the Chamber of Deputies the French Foreign Minister declared that Austrian independence was "an indispensable element of the European balance," while one deputy went so far as to predict that "France's fate would be decided on the banks of the Danube."

Throughout Austria local Nazis began demonstrating. The center of the agitation was Graz where the swastika had been raised on the roof of the town hall during Schuschnigg's speech. Defying the government's ban on political meetings, the local Nazis subsequently announced a rally of 65,000 party members from all over Austria for the weekend. Schuschnigg reacted immediately by dispatching troops, bombers and an armored train to Graz. The Nazis backed down and canceled the meeting but it was little consolation to the Chancellor. The disturbance should have been quelled by Seyss-Inquart and his police, not by the army.

3

French indignation at Hitler's threat to Austria took the form of a proposal to London that the two big powers send a joint note of protest to Berlin. It arrived at an inauspicious time. Anthony Eden had just resigned and the Foreign Ministry was momentarily without leadership. The English public had not yet been aroused by the events in Austria and their Prime Minister remained devoted to the policy of appeasing Germany. Furthermore, Chamberlain was supported by the London *Times*, which consistently played down the importance of the events in Austria. "Fundamentally," it editorialized, "a close understanding between the two German states is the most natural thing possible." Goebbels could not have put it more convincingly. "Austria can never be anti-Germanic."

Not even Franklin D. Roosevelt's condemnation of all aggressors the previous autumn had affected Chamberlain's policy. Nor had he been moved by the President's practical suggestion, which followed his call to "quarantine" the Japanese, Nazis and Fascists from the community of nations. Roosevelt dispatched Captain Royal Ingersoll, chief of the navy's War Plans Division, to London with instructions to explore the implementation of a long-range naval blockade of Japan. The proposition found such approval in the British Admiralty that its members told Ingersoll they were "prepared to stop all Japanese traffic crossing a line roughly from Singapore through the Dutch East Indies, New Guinea, New Hebrides and around to the east of Australia and New Zealand." But Prime Minister Chamberlain put an end to the plan for mutual blockade early in 1938 by rejecting another proposal of Roosevelt's calling for Britain to join an international conference to discuss essential principles of international law that would, incidentally, awaken America to the true nature of the "bandit nations," as Roosevelt was privately calling them. At first the President did not grasp the full implication of Chamberlain's unexpected rejection, but it soon became clear that his refusal to join an international conference meant that the British government would take no part in any quarantine, either in the Orient or in Europe. Chamberlain's rebuff was such a blow to Roosevelt that it led him to abandon a vigorous foreign policy that might have stemmed further aggression all around the world—and so changed the course of history. Instead he allowed the United States to revert to isolation.

By the beginning of March, therefore, Great Britain was irrevocably bound to appeasement. On the third of the month the Ambassador to Germany, Sir Nevile Henderson, called at the chancellery to inform Hitler that His Majesty's Government was ready, in principle, to discuss all outstanding questions. Despite Henderson's obvious effort to be friendly and absolutely correct, "his general bearing, which was that of the perfect English gentleman," recalled interpreter Schmidt, "always somehow irritated both Ribbentrop and Hitler, who could not endure 'fine people.'"

It took Henderson ten minutes to state the object of his visit: a genuine desire to improve mutual relations between their two countries. Britain, he said, was prepared to make certain concessions to settle the grave problems of limitation of armaments and restrictions of bombing as well as a peaceful solution to the Czech and Austrian problems. What contribution to general security and peace in Europe was Hitler ready to make?

During this lengthy exposition the Führer crouched in his armchair scowling and when Henderson finally stopped he angrily replied that only a small percentage of Austrians supported Schuschnigg. Why did England persist in opposing a just settlement and interfering in "German family matters"? He abruptly went on the offensive, charging that the Franco-Soviet and Czecho-Soviet pacts were definite threats to Germany. That was why Germany had to be so heavily armed. In consequence any limitation of arms depended on the Russians. And this was a problem complicated "by the fact that one could place as much confidence in the faith in treaties of a barbarous creature like the Soviet Union as in the comprehension of mathematical formulae by a savage. Any agreement with the U.S.S.R. was quite worthless and Russia should never be allowed into Europe."

Theirs was a rambling conversation that, after two hours, left the case of Austria in limbo by begging the question "with a vague reply." The following day Hitler sent his chief economic adviser, Wilhelm Keppler, to Austria. Presenting himself to Schuschnigg as a personal representative of the Führer, he came bearing fresh demands which included everything deleted at Berchtesgaden. But Keppler's main interest was economic and, since he regarded Anschluss as a financial imperative for both countries, he acted more like a benefactor than a predator. "The Führer's wish at the time," recalled Schuschnigg, "was for an evolutionary development; in other words he wished to roll up Austria from within, if possible without any apparent German involvement." The time, concluded the amiable Keppler, had come to accelerate this process.

Schuschnigg reacted sharply to Keppler's new demands, such as the

Chancellor Hitler with President von Hindenburg and his son Oskar. BUNDESARCHIV

Propaganda poster. The grandparents: "That we should live to see this!" The grandchildren: "When will I see the Führer?" BUNDESARCHIV

Hitler campaigns for electoral approval of his policies in 1933. Ernst Hanfstaengl, his foreign press officer, is at the extreme right, mostly obscured.
BUNDESARCHIV

Above, a Brownshirt points to
the Führer's pistol shot in
the ceiling. STADTARCHIV, MUNICH

Right, re-enactment of the march,
November 9, 1933. Göring
to Hitler's right.
Dr. Schultze, who treated
Hitler's injury in 1923,
second row left. DR. SCHULTZE

Above, ceremony for those who died in the Putsch. Memorial designed by Troost. In row behind Hitler, extreme left, Göring and Keitel; extreme right, Dr. Schultze.
DR. SCHULTZE

Left, Brownshirt Chief Ernst Röhm.
SCHULZE-WILDE

Above, Party Day, Nuremberg, 1934. Dramatized by Leni Riefenstahl's documentary film, *Triumph of the Will.* BUNDESARCHIV

Right, Leni Riefenstahl. LENI RIEFENSTAHL

John Toland
herzlich gewidmet
Leni Riefenstahl
1971

my best wishes for
your work.

"Heil Hitler!" Berlin. BIBLIO. FÜR ZEIT.

The Berghof. Hitler's official residence at Berchtes-aden. The famed picture window could be lowered to the floor. Erich Kempka, Hitler's chauffeur, ok this and the following three candid photographs a typical pilgrimage to the Obersalzberg in the first ars of Hitler's regime. KEMPKA

Hitler greets admirer Viennese style. The two colorfully dressed youths are *Wander-vögel* (wandering birds), hippies of the day. KEMPKA

Above, in center, Bormann, face partially covered, appears in most unofficial pictures and yet was almost unknown to the German public. KEMPKA

Right, "Mein Führer!" KEMPKA

The Führer laughs at his critics. His first foreign press secretary, Ernst Hanfstaengl (Harvard graduate and acquaintance of Roosevelt), was allowed to publish two books of anti-Hitler cartoons under the title *Facts vs. Ink*. Hanfstaengl, against Goebbels' violent protests, persuaded Hitler that this kind of propaganda would impress Westerners, particularly Americans. HANFSTAENGL

Der Häuptling vom Stamm der wilden Kopfjäger nach der Schlacht von Leipzig — in vollem Kriegsschmuck

Right, Professor Gerdy Troost, widow of Hitler's favorite architect, objects to the exclusion of the best modern works at the first art exhibition in Munich's Haus der Kunst. One of the few who dared speak frankly to the Führer, she resigned moments later as judge. This is one of seventeen photographs in this book, most of them published for the first time, taken by Hitler's movie cameraman, Walter Frentz. He formerly worked for Leni Riefenstahl. FRENTZ

Below, March 1938. Hitler receives Reichstag ovation after announcing *Anschluss* of Austria: IMPERIAL WAR MUSEUM immediate appointment of a Nazi as Minister of Economics, cancellation of the ban on the *Völkischer Beobachter* and formal legalization of National Socialism. How, asked the incredulous Schuschnigg, could Hitler come along three weeks later with this fresh set of impositions? His government would co-operate with Austrian Nazis only on the basis of long-term recognition of Austrian independence. Schuschnigg recalled that the interview "ended inconclusively" but Keppler reported that it "began tempestuously but concluded in an entirely conciliatory manner," and that he "had the impression that Schuschnigg will by no means submit to force but that, if treated sensibly, he will come along to a great extent, if this is made possible for him without loss of prestige. We can rely on his loyalty as regards the Berchtesgaden agreements." He further reported that the Austrian party was making excellent progress, particularly in Graz where some 80 per cent of the people professed National Socialism. "At present we are inclined to apply the brakes to the movement, in order to wring more and more concessions from Schuschnigg."

Schuschnigg's concessions to the Nazis only incited new disturbances, placing Austria in a quasi state of undeclared civil war. In Vienna storm troopers and Nazi sympathizers would cross the Danube Canal to the Jewish quarter in Leopoldstadt shouting, "Sieg Heil! Sieg Heil!" one night and "Heil Hitler!" the next. They would be confronted by opponents shouting "Heil Schuschnigg!" and "Red-White-Red to the Death!" There were frequent clashes, usually brought to an end by truncheon-wielding police. Generally it was the patriots who got beat up, for the loyalty of the police extended more to Minister of the Interior Seyss-Inquart than to the Chancellor.

In desperation Schuschnigg dispatched an appeal to Mussolini on March 7 warning that he might have to hold a plebiscite to save the situation. Il Duce sent back words of reassurance. Professing to believe the pledge of Göring that Germany would not use force, he urged Schuschnigg not to hold a plebiscite. The message was cold comfort to a Chancellor threatened with invasion from abroad while under attack at home by workers for being too lenient and by Nazis for being too restrictive. He decided to ignore Mussolini's advice.

On March 9 he announced the plebiscite in a Tyrolean city, Innsbruck. He stepped onto the podium in the town square clad in the traditional Austrian gray jacket and green waistcoat and announced emotionally that the nation would go to the polls in four days to answer one question: "Are you in favor of a free and German, independent and social, a Christian and united Austria?" For the second time he spoke as orator rather than scholar. "Tyrolians and Austrians, say 'Yes' to Tyrol. Say 'Yes' to Austria!" he declared and then ended his speech in Tyrolean dialect with the famous words of Andreas Hofer, calling for volunteers to fight Napoleon: "*Marde, 's ischt Zut* [Men, the time has come]!" The audience of 20,000 shouted defiance. Most of those listening at radios were equally inspired. Prince Starhemberg, however, was dismayed. "This means the end of Schuschnigg," the former Vice-Chancellor of Austria told his wife. "Let us hope it is not the end of Austria. Hitler can never allow this."

As he feared, the announcement did force the Führer's hand. A vote for a free and united Austria—and this was the likely outcome—meant the delay, if not the end, of Anschluss. And since the union with Austria was a necessary preliminary to eastward expansion, the plebiscite threatened to wreck Hitler's entire program of Lebensraum. He could not tolerate such a challenge and on the morning of March 10 told General Keitel that the Austrian problem was so "acute" that he should make appropriate preparations. Keitel remembered that a General Staff plan, Operation Otto, had been drawn up in case Otto von Habsburg attempted to regain the throne of Austria. "Prepare it," ordered the Führer.

Keitel rushed to OKW headquarters in the Bendlerstrasse where he found to his dismay that Operation Otto was simply a theoretical study. Regretting his haste to please the Führer, he turned over to General Beck the task of submitting a report on the possible invasion of Austria. "We have prepared nothing," complained Beck, "nothing has been done, nothing at all." When Beck reported to Hitler and suggested using two corps and the 2nd Panzer Division for the military occupation of Austria, he was appalled to learn that these troops should be prepared to march across the border by Saturday the twelfth. The thought of preparing such an operation within forty-eight hours was inconceivable to a professional. Beck protested that it meant orders would have to go out to the various formations at 6 P.M. that same evening. Then do it, said Hitler the amateur strategist.

More concerned with Italian reaction to an invasion than with logistics, the Führer hastily dictated a letter to Mussolini. Austria, he wrote, was approaching a state of anarchy and he could not stand idly by. "In my responsibility as Führer and Chancellor of the German Reich and likewise as a son of this soil . . . I am now determined to restore law and order in my homeland and enable the people to decide their own fate according to their judgment in an unmistakable, clear and open manner." He reminded Il Duce of Germany's help in Italy's critical hour, the Abyssinian war, and promised to repay Italian support by recognizing the boundary between Italy and the Reich as the Brenner Pass. "This decision will never be questioned or changed." It was noon by the time he handed over the sealed letter to Prince Philip von Hessen with instructions to deliver it personally to Il Duce. As the prince boarded the special plane carrying a basket of plants for his garden in Rome, he had no idea how important his mission was.

Throughout Austria posters were being plastered on billboards announcing the plebiscite. Sound trucks circulated through towns and cities urging all Austrians to vote "*Ja*" on Sunday. In Vienna patriots were at last making more noise than the Nazis as groups ranged the streets shouting "Heil Schuschnigg!" "Heil Liberty!" and "Sunday is polling day; we vote *Ja!*"

Heartened by public enthusiasm, Schuschnigg continued to act resolute. "I am neither able nor prepared to play the role of puppet," he wrote Seyss-Inquart in reply to the Minister of the Interior's charge that the plebiscite was contrary to the Berchtesgaden agreements. "I cannot be expected to look on with folded hands while the country is ruined economically and politically." He concluded with an urgent request to Seyss-Inquart, as the minister responsible for security, to take measures to bring terrorism to an end. Otherwise he would not be able to hold the opposing forces in check.

Although Seyss-Inquart was generally regarded as Hitler's cat's-paw, he too was concerned for his country's independence, and while he sympathized with some of the policies of the Austrian Nazis, they did not regard him as one of their number. He was much closer in ideology and nature to Schuschnigg. Both considered themselves patriots; both were devout Catholics; both were intellectuals, shy men of culture with a deep love of music. Seyss-Inquart proved he was more patriot than Nazi by promising to appeal to his followers over the radio to vote affirmative on Sunday.

Schuschnigg went to bed that evening "fully satisfied" that the Nazi threat to the plebiscite had been scotched—unaware that Seyss-Inquart by now had little influence in his own party. The hard-core Austrian Nazis were already on the streets marching in columns of four toward the center of disorder, the official German Tourist Bureau which boasted a hastily painted larger-than-life oil portrait of Hitler. Their shouts of "*Ein Volk, ein Reich, ein Führer!*" were greeted at first with amusement by the patriots, who outnumbered them three to one. Then windows were smashed and the police, who had been standing by, formed cordons to prevent further damage. Making no move to subdue the howling mob of Nazis, they

concentrated on the patriots to such an extent that eventually the outnumbered wearers of the swastika dominated the streets.

4

At 2 A.M. on March 11 the improvised invasion plan, still bearing
the code name Operation Otto, was issued. In it, Hitler took personal control. "If other measures prove unsuccessful," it read, "I intend to invade
Austria with armed forces in order to establish constitutional conditions
and to prevent further outrages against the pro-German population." The
units involved were to be prepared by noon of March 12. "I reserve the
right to decide the actual moment of invasion. The behavior of the troops
must give the impression that we do not want to wage war against our
Austrian brothers."

At 5:30 A.M. Schuschnigg's bedside phone rang. It was his chief of
police reporting that the German border at Salzburg had just been closed
and all railroad traffic stopped. He hurried to the chancellery on Ballhausplatz where he learned that German divisions in the Munich area
had been mobilized, destination presumably Austria. Equally alarming
were the telegraphed texts of German newspapers alleging, for instance,
that Communist flags flew in Vienna while mobs shouted "Heil Moskau!
Heil Schuschnigg!"

At about 10 A.M. Glaise-Horstenau, Schuschnigg's minister without
portfolio, a Nazi, arrived at the Ballhausplatz with written instructions
from Hitler and Göring. He was accompanied by Seyss-Inquart, who had
met him at the Aspern airport. Badly shaken, Seyss-Inquart reported the
demands from Berlin: Schuschnigg must resign and the plebiscite was to
be postponed for two weeks so that a "legal poll," similar to the Saar plebiscite, could be set up. If Göring did not get a telephone answer by noon
he would assume that Seyss-Inquart was prevented from making the call
and would "act accordingly." It was already eleven-thirty and Seyss-
Inquart, a reasonable man, extended the deadline until 2 P.M. in the
Führer's name.

Schuschnigg used this time to assess possibilities of resistance. He
telephoned the chief of police, who informed him that Vienna remained
quiet. He had thrown a cordon—"in as far as that is possible"—around
the inner city but so many Nazi policemen had been restored to their jobs
that the government could no longer count on its police force. In this extremity Schuschnigg summoned the "inner cabinet," his closest advisers,
to discuss the emergency. He presented three alternatives: rejection of the

ultimatum followed by an appeal to world opinion; acceptance followed by his own resignation; and a compromise, accepting Hitler's demands for technical changes in the plebiscite but resisting all other demands. They decided upon compromise.

It was almost 2 P.M. and moments later the two reluctant messengers of doom, Seyss-Inquart and Glaise-Horstenau, were back. They could not accept the proffered compromise and Schuschnigg was faced with the unpleasant choice between complete submission or defiance. He hurriedly conferred with President Miklas and it was decided to call off the plebiscite. Returning to his office, he informed the inner cabinet members of the decision. They were momentarily struck dumb and in the silence could hear a sound truck announcing the plebiscite, then blasting out "*Oh, Du Mein Österreich* [Oh, You, my Austria]!"

Moments later the Chancellor was telling Seyss-Inquart and Glaise-Horstenau that Berlin's demands for postponement of the plebiscite had been granted. At the same time extensive security measures, such as an 8 P.M. curfew, would have to be taken. Concerned, the two men excused themselves to transmit this information to Göring by telephone.*

"These measures of Chancellor Schuschnigg are in no way satisfactory," replied Göring, who then hung up to think things over. He should have conferred with Hitler who, according to Papen, was currently "in a state bordering on hysteria," but instead acted on his own. A few minutes past 3 P.M. he was back on the phone with Seyss-Inquart. "Berlin cannot agree in any way to the decision taken by Chancellor Schuschnigg," he said, ruthless beneath a veneer of joviality. He demanded that Schuschnigg and his cabinet resign. He also repeated the demand to send Berlin a telegram asking for German help.

The two ministers solemnly marched back to the large room where their cabinet colleagues were assembled. Seyss-Inquart, "white in the face and agitated," read from his notebook Göring's ultimatum, and then quailed under a bombardment of questions. "Don't ask me," he replied bitterly, "I'm nothing more than an historic telephone girl." If he himself were not appointed Chancellor within two hours, he added, the German armies would move on Austria.

Life in Vienna was continuing as if nothing had happened. Planes circled overhead dropping clouds of leaflets urging the citizens to vote "Ja" on Sunday. On the streets truck columns of the "Fatherland Front" were greeted with patriotic shouts and waving handkerchiefs; strangers

---

* This and other telephone conversations between Berlin and various capitals during the next few days are from official transcripts found by Allied authorities in the Reich chancellery.

would welcome each other with: "Österreich!" For once the nation appeared to be united. All at once the gay waltzes and patriotic marches that had been coming from every radio station were abruptly changed by an announcement ordering all unmarried reservists of the 1915 class to report immediately for duty. Before long a stream of army trucks loaded with steel-helmeted troops headed for the German border.

In desperation Schuschnigg sought help from London. He told how he had given way to Hitler's demands rather than risk bloodshed and asked "for immediate advice of His Majesty's Government as to what he should do." This telegram ironically reached Prime Minister Chamberlain during a lunch at 10 Downing Street in honor of the Ribbentrops. Chamberlain frostily invited Ribbentrop into his study "for a private word" with himself and Lord Halifax, the new Foreign Secretary. "The discussion," as Ribbentrop reported it to Hitler, "took place in a tense atmosphere and the usually calm Lord Halifax was more excited than Chamberlain, who outwardly at least appeared calm and cool-headed." After the Prime Minister read out the telegram from Vienna, Ribbentrop "professed to be ignorant of the whole situation" and, in fact, expressed doubts about the truth of the reports. If it were true, he added, it might be the best way of achieving a "peaceful solution."

These words were enough to placate a man already determined to keep on good terms with Hitler; Chamberlain agreed with Ribbentrop that there was no proof of violent German action even when his own Foreign Secretary angrily charged that Schuschnigg had been "threatened with invasion." Then Chamberlain asked Lord Halifax to send off a reply to the Austrian government that must have made him wince: "His Majesty's Government cannot take responsibility of advising the Chancellor to take any course of action which might expose his country to dangers against which His Majesty's Government are unable to guarantee protection."

Schuschnigg had no illusion about getting any help from either England or Italy and about 4 P.M. tendered his resignation. President Miklas reluctantly accepted it but flatly refused to follow Göring's order to appoint Seyss-Inquart. Instead he selected the chief of police but he declined. So did the inspector general of the armed forces as well as the leader of a former Christian Social government. No one wanted the position and Miklas appealed to Schuschnigg to reconsider. He refused to take part "directly or indirectly—in the preparations for Cain once more to slay his brother Abel," but when Miklas replied in dismay: "I see that everyone deserts me," he reluctantly agreed to continue in office as ex-Chancellor until a new head of government was appointed. So saying, Schuschnigg returned to his own office and began clearing his desk.

As the afternoon wore on the emotional strain in the chancellery became almost unbearable. Pressure from Berlin, and particularly from Göring, who was in his element, was growing. At 5 P.M. the field marshal was shouting over the phone at a Nazi underground leader named Odilo Globocnik that a new cabinet must be formed by 7:30 P.M. At that time Seyss-Inquart was to telephone the Führer that it had been done, said Göring and dictated a list of the ministers that included his own brother-in-law. A few minutes later Seyss-Inquart himself was on the phone informing Göring that Miklas had accepted Schuschnigg's resignation but was insisting on replacing him with a former Chancellor. Göring roared out to tell Miklas to accept German demands. If not, "then the troops which are already poised all along the borders will march and Austria will have ceased to exist. . . . Tell him that we are not joking! If we are in possession of the report that you have been appointed Chancellor by 7:30 P.M., the marching orders will be stopped, and the troops will remain on our side of the border." In the meantime Seyss-Inquart was to send all National Socialists to the streets throughout the country. "If Miklas could not understand the situation in four hours," he concluded ominously, "he'll understand it in four minutes."

"Well, all right," said Seyss-Inquart dubiously.

Göring did not have to wait until seven-thirty for a report. In less than an hour he was informed that Miklas still refused to make the appointment. "Now listen here," Göring shouted at Seyss-Inquart, "I am willing to wait for another few minutes. I expect you to call me then immediately on the priority wire here in the Reichskanzlei. But you have to make it snappy. I cannot take the responsibility, in fact, I am not supposed to wait another minute." He gave the impression that he was under orders but more likely acted under his own authority since Hitler was not yet ready to press the issue. "If things don't happen within that time you will have to take over by force, all right?"

Nazis were already taking over the streets of Vienna in response to orders from Berlin. One mob sweeping toward the inner city shouted, "Heil Hitler! Sieg Heil! Hang Schuschnigg!" In the chancellery Schuschnigg heard the shouts and the tramp of feet. Convinced that this was a prelude to invasion, he went to the President's office to make a final appeal but Miklas remained adamant, stubbornly refusing to appoint a Nazi as Chancellor, and when Schuschnigg insisted, said, "You will desert me now, all of you." Still Schuschnigg saw no other possibility than Seyss-Inquart, a practicing Catholic with a reputation as an honest man, and suggested that he himself speak immediately on the radio to the Austrian people.

Shortly Schuschnigg entered the Corner Room on the first floor of the chancellery adjoining the grand staircase. Here in the middle of the room stood a microphone, barely five paces from the place Dollfuss had been murdered by the Nazis. There was a hush as Schuschnigg stepped to the microphone at 7:50 P.M. and told of the German ultimatum. Throughout Austria people were engrossed by a broadcast which William Shirer described as the most moving he had ever heard. "President Miklas asks me to tell the people of Austria that we have yielded to force. Because under no circumstances, not even in this supreme hour, do we intend that German blood shall be spilt, we have instructed our army to retreat without offering any resistance in the event of an invasion and to await further decisions." Shirer thought Schuschnigg's voice would break into sobs but he controlled himself. "Thus," he concluded, "I take leave of the Austrian nation with a German farewell which also expresses my heartfelt wish: God save Austria!"

There was not a sound in the Corner Room until the commissioner for cultural propaganda, who bore the old aristocratic German name of Hammerstein-Equord, lurched forward on crutches to shout into the microphone: "Long live Austria! Today I am ashamed to be a German." Hurriedly some technicians turned on a recorded version of the national anthem, composed by Haydn, and almost identical to "Deutschland über Alles."

Seyss-Inquart must have run from the Corner Room to a telephone because it was only 7:57 P.M. by the time he had Göring on the line. "The government has just put itself out of office," he reported. Austrian troops were being withdrawn from the German border. "The gentlemen here have decided to sit and wait for the invasion."

When Göring learned that Seyss-Inquart had not been nominated as Chancellor he lost his temper. "All right then. I am going to give marching orders now to the troops. And it is up to you to see that you will be in charge. Inform all leading personalities of what I tell you now: everybody who resists our troops or organizes resistance will be summarily dealt with by our tribunals." Seyss-Inquart's halfhearted protests were shouted down. "All right, now. You have got your official orders."

The crowd outside the Austrian chancellery, swollen to an estimated 100,000, was getting rowdy as Nazi supporters of both sexes chanted the name of the Führer and cavorted in the glow of smoking torches. Even more unruly groups ranged through the inner city singing Nazi songs and shouting, "Down with the Jews! Heil Hitler! Sieg Heil! Kill the Jews! Hang Schuschnigg! Heil Seyss-Inquart!"

Between delivering ultimatums to Vienna in an effort to force the situation, Göring had been urging Hitler to invade Austria come what may. The Führer hesitated until about 8:15 P.M. Then as he was reflectively strolling with Göring a police official saw him abruptly slap his thigh. "Now, get moving!" he cried. Half an hour later Hitler signed Instruction Order Number Two for Operation Otto which declared that German troops would march into Austria at dawn the next morning "to prevent further bloodshed in Austrian towns."

Three minutes after Hitler signed the order Göring was at a phone in the winter garden giving further orders to Keppler, the economic expert. Seyss-Inquart was to send a telegram in the name of the provisional Austrian government, urgently requesting that Germany help them restore law and order by dispatching troops to Austria. Seyss-Inquart was to take care of the matter at once. "He does not really have to send the telegram. He only has to say that he did. You get me?"

Neurath chanced to overhear this and brought the information to those in the anteroom. "For heaven's sake," exclaimed Papen, "see that it does not turn out to be a second Ems telegram. The request must be genuine and in black and white!"* Concerned, Papen turned to Captain Wiedemann. "What will this military march into Austria prove?" he said. "It will only get the whole world against us. A police action would have been sufficient." Wiedemann agreed but Neurath chided them both for taking the matter so tragically. Hitler, he said, had been dreaming for years of getting his best divisions into Austria. "Why don't you let him have that pleasure!"

His pleasure of the moment was the arrival of the telegram from the provisional government of Austria requesting the immediate aid of German troops in the exact words dictated by Göring, another case of legality after the fact. It gave Hitler the opportunity to masquerade his troops as liberators and, in high spirits, he ordered them to march in with bands playing and regimental colors flying. One thing was lacking, reassurance from Mussolini. And this arrived at 10:25 P.M. in the form of a long-distance call from Prince Philip von Hessen. "I have just returned from the Palazzo Venezia," he told Hitler, whose heart must have been pounding.

* The peremptory telegram sent in 1870 by the French Foreign Office to King Wilhelm of Prussia, who was taking the waters at Ems, was published in shortened form by Bismarck. The deletions made the French demands seem insulting and helped precipitate the Franco-Prussian War.

"Il Duce took the news very well indeed. He sends his very best regards to you." The Austrian question no longer interested him.

Elated, Hitler exclaimed, "Then please tell Mussolini that I shall never forget this." Words of gratitude spilled out. "Never, never, never! Come what may!" He could not restrain himself. "And listen—sign *any* agreement he would like. I feel no longer in that terrible position which we faced only a short while ago, militarily, I mean, in case I might have got into a conflict. You can tell him again: I thank him most heartily. I will never forget him!" He couldn't stop talking. "Whenever he should be in need or in danger, he can be sure that I will stick with him, rain or shine—come what may—even if the whole world would rise against him— I will, I shall—"

In Vienna, the new Chancellor's first significant act was to request Keppler to urge the Führer to cancel the invasion order. Then Seyss-Inquart turned his attention to Schuschnigg. He thanked his predecessor for services to Austria and, since the streets were still dominated by celebrating Nazis, offered to drive him home. "Or would you like to go to one of the embassies? Perhaps the Hungarian Embassy, which is just across the street?"

Schuschnigg preferred retiring to his own apartment. As he approached the grand staircase Schuschnigg noticed two lines of civilians wearing swastika armbands. Realizing for the first time that the chancellery had been occupied, he pointedly ignored their outstretched Nazi salutes and continued downstairs where the military guard saluted him properly. After a few words to them of thanks and farewell, he climbed into Seyss-Inquart's car. As it slowly drove off, young Nazis leaped on the running boards to protect the former Chancellor from the raucous crowd.

In Berlin, Seyss-Inquart's plea to restrain the German troops was just being relayed by telephone to the German Foreign Office. Then Keppler added a similar appeal. His petition was passed on to military headquarters and the chancellery. A three-way telephone argument ensued. Was this unexpected request from Vienna to stop the invasion based on reality? Should it be turned over to Hitler, who had retired two hours earlier in a state of euphoria after the call from Rome?

At 2:30 A.M. Hitler was awakened. After a moment's reflection he rejected the proposal and went back to bed. But his military leaders, deeply disturbed by the specter of invasion, kept mulling the question. About 4 A.M. the chief of the OKW Operations Staff, General von Viebahn, implored General Keitel by phone to "work on Hitler to give up the move into Austria." Keitel promised and called back shortly without having done so to say Hitler had again refused. "The Führer never knew anything about all this," Keitel later confessed. "If he had, his opinion of the Army Chiefs would have been shattering and I wanted to save both sides that experience."

The insistent telephone appeals from the army General Staff, Brauchitsch and finally Viebahn had turned that night into sheer "hell" for Keitel. Brauchitsch himself was most dejected, and Viebahn became so distraught that before long he was alternately praying out loud and predicting dire disaster before sinking into moody silence. When Jodl told him to get a grip on himself the general locked himself in a room, threw an inkwell against the door and threatened to shoot anyone who tried to come in.

5

Early that Saturday morning Hitler flew to Munich with Keitel to take part in the triumphal entry into his homeland. Before leaving, he signed a proclamation describing his version of the events that led to the crisis. "Since early this morning soldiers of the German armed forces have been marching across the Austro-German frontiers. Mechanized troops and infantry, German airplanes in the blue sky, summoned by the new National Socialist government in Vienna, are the guarantors the Austrian nation shall at an early date be given the opportunity to decide their own future by a genuine plebiscite." This was followed by a personal note, "I, myself, as Führer and Chancellor will be happy to walk on the soil of the country which is my home as a free German citizen."

At 8 A.M. his troops had begun streaming into Austria and at some points frontier barriers were dismantled by the inhabitants themselves. It was more like an improvised maneuver than an invasion. The 2nd Panzer Division, for instance, was advancing with the help of a Baedeker's guide and refueling at local gas stations. As the troops marched in they were bombarded with flowers by ecstatic women and children. Nazi tanks flew flags of both nations and were gaily decorated with greenery. "The populace saw that we came as friends," recalled General Heinz Guderian, "and we were everywhere joyfully received." Almost every village and town, houses decorated with swastika flags, greeted the Germans with jubilation. "Their hands were shaken, they were kissed, and there were tears of joy." All that delayed a rapid march to Vienna were the numerous mishaps that littered the roads with disabled tanks and trucks.

Hitler arrived in Munich about noon and led his cavalcade of cars to Mühldorf, less than an hour's drive from Braunau, where the commander of the invasion force, General von Bock, reported that his troops were meeting no resistance. The road to the Inn River was so clogged with cars and onlookers that Hitler's caravan did not cross it until midafternoon. His car inched its way into Braunau through a jubilant crowd struggling to touch the vehicle as if it were some religious relic. It slowly passed through the ancient town gate to the Pommer Inn where he had been born not quite forty-nine years earlier. The procession into familiar territory continued to the accompaniment of cheering crowds. At Lambach Hitler ordered the driver to stop in front of the old cloister (whose coat of arms was the swastika) where he had once taken singing lessons.

In London the cabinet was meeting in emergency session. Chamberlain's glum judgment was that the Anschluss had been inevitable, ". . . unless the Powers had been able to say: 'If you make war on Austria, you will have to deal with us.'" And that had never been a possibility. "At any rate," he concluded, "that question is now out of the way." He dismissed the fait accompli as a matter of little consequence.

It was dark when the first stage of Hitler's sentimental journey ended at Linz, whose streets he had wandered in solitude so many evenings. The crowd of 100,000 waiting in the market square engulfed the caravan in a display of joyous hysteria which amazed Hitler's aides and adjutants. When the Führer appeared on the balcony of the City Hall with the new Chancellor of Austria the people were in a frenzy. "The atmosphere of the whole demonstration was electric and excited beyond belief," recalled Keitel. Tears ran down Hitler's cheeks, and Guderian, standing next to him, was sure "this was certainly not play-acting."

After a brief, nostalgic speech Hitler returned to the Hotel Weinzinger. The proprietor had given up his own suite, whose main room was filled with stuffed animals. Hitler, who detested hunting, several times stumbled over the head of a polar bear, nor was the large double bed, over which hung a gaudily framed picture of Josephine Baker, to his taste. In this unlikely setting he and Seyss-Inquart conferred without even discussing Anschluss.

Hitler had not entered his homeland considering Anschluss in the fullest sense of the term, envisioning rather a loose union such as Austria had once had with Hungary. But the enthusiasm of the day was altering his concept and he confided to his valet: "It is fate, Linge. I am destined to be the Führer who will bring all Germans into the Greater German Reich."

Seyss-Inquart returned to the capital that evening to find Viennese Nazis gathered to greet the Führer. A torchlight procession awaited in place and the demonstrators had grown weary from cheering. General

Guderian's tanks had left Linz before dusk but it was snowing and the road, under repair, was torn up for miles. At least fifty tanks broke down and the advance guard did not reach Vienna until after midnight. Even at that hour Guderian found the streets filled with excited citizens who broke into "frantic rejoicing" on sighting the first German soldiers. Preceded by an Austrian military band, the invaders marched past the opera house. They were greeted with flowers and raucous friendliness. Enthusiasts tore off the buttons of Guderian's overcoat for souvenirs before hoisting him to their shoulders and carrying him to his quarters. What puzzled the citizens was the convergence at sunup of German officers on food stores where they bought up large quantities of butter, sausage and other food.

On Sunday morning Göring phoned Ribbentrop in London to tell of the wild reception Hitler had received. It was also a lie, he said, that Germany had issued an ultimatum to Austria or to President Miklas. Ribbentrop swallowed all this and replied that the average Englishman didn't really care what happened in Austria. Still a note of concern moderated Ribbentrop's own jubilation. *If* there should be any sort of threat or trouble, he asked, would the Führer stand firm?

Göring had already sent a courier by plane to urge Hitler to press beyond their original plan. "If the enthusiasm is so great," he suggested, "why don't we go the whole hog?" Perhaps Hitler was unaware of all Göring had been doing the past few days but it was just as likely that he was letting his field marshal proceed as if on his own so that he would have to take the blame if something went wrong. In either case, their minds ran in the same channel and Hitler himself had already ordered an official of the Ministry of the Interior to draft a law for the reunification of Austria and Germany. By noon it was ready, approved and dispatched in final form to Seyss-Inquart in Vienna with orders to have it passed within the day.

Shocked at first, the more the new Chancellor thought about the proposed legislation the better he liked it. Moreover, Hitler promised that a free and secret vote would be held within a month to confirm the law. After convincing himself that the decree was not only inevitable but "valuable and useful," Seyss-Inquart urged his cabinet to approve it on the grounds that Anschluss was "the will of the people." The cabinet unanimously agreed to turn over the country to Hitler but once more President Miklas showed his intransigence by refusing to sign the document and declared himself "hindered in the exercise of his office," thus giving him the constitutional right to turn over his functions to the Chancellor.

While Hitler was confident that Anschluss would be enacted, there remained one concern. Ever since the telephone call from Prince von Hessen, he had fretfully awaited Mussolini's formal approval. Almost two days had passed without a word from Rome. Mussolini, in fact, had been "floored" by the news of the Anschluss, exclaiming, "That damned German!" At last he regained his composure and that Sunday sent off a brief telegram:

I CONGRATULATE YOU ON THE WAY YOU HAVE SOLVED THE AUSTRIAN PROBLEM. I HAD ALREADY WARNED SCHUSCHNIGG.

The Führer's joy was complete. In gratitude he sent an even briefer reply:

MUSSOLINI, I SHALL NEVER FORGET THIS.

Feeling a need to share his triumph with Eva Braun, he phoned her to join him in Vienna.

Earlier in the day he had treated himself to a visit to nearby Leonding. Together he and Linge walked to his parents' grave in the churchyard across from the old homestead. Hitler took a wreath from his valet, told him to retire with the rest of the staff so he could meditate. After placing the wreath against the marker he stood silently for several moments. Afterward, still quiet and thoughtful, he revisited the scenes of his childhood, concealing his emotions even from intimates. He recognized an old schoolmate named Hagemüller and they chatted briefly. Later he held a reunion in Linz at the hotel for other friends, including a watchmaker and his former history professor, Dr. Hümer.

That evening Seyss-Inquart, more lackey than head of state, returned to Hitler's suite. The Führer was so deeply moved upon learning that the law making Austria a province of Germany was passed that he wept. "Yes," he finally managed to say, "a good political action saves blood." So ended Austria's independence and so ended Sunday, March 13, the day on which Schuschnigg had hoped his nation would affirm its independence by plebiscite.

6

Sigmund Freud had promised his family to leave Austria once the Nazis took over. Now he told an English colleague, Dr. Ernest Jones, "This is my post and I can never leave it." This reminded Jones of the officer on the *Titanic* who, when asked why he abandoned ship, replied: "I never left the ship, she left me." Freud got the point. He admitted Austria no longer existed and agreed to depart for England, "the land of his early dreams." He escaped none too soon. The restructuring of Austria in line with the NSDAP's notion of relationship between party and state was already in process under the personal supervision of Rudolf Hess. More sinister was Himmler's administration of the purge of the police and the neutralization of political opposition. Gestapo Chief Heydrich was installed on the Morzinplatz where his agents were examining statute books and records seized from the chief of the Austrian Secret Service. At least one political murder had already been perpetrated, that of Papen's closest adviser, the German Embassy councilor.

Local storm troopers began the persecution of Jews, dragging them from their homes and offices and forcing them to scrub Schuschnigg's propaganda slogans from walls and pavements with acid. Others were rounded up to wash toilets in the SS barracks and sweep the streets. Such bullying was distasteful to many of the Wehrmacht officers, and journalist Gedye watched two of them "kick over the bucket of two very old Jews who were scrubbing the pavements and tell them they could go, cursing the Nazi stormtroopers who were supervising."

Such scenes did not dampen the fervor of most Viennese, intoxicated as they were by the events of the past forty-eight hours. "It is impossible to deny enthusiasm with which both the new regime and last night's announcement of incorporation in the Reich have been received here," telegraphed the British ambassador to Viscount Halifax on Monday. "Herr Hitler is certainly justified in claiming that his action has been welcome by the Austrian population." There was good reason. Anschluss would probably end unemployment. There were 600,000 Austrians out of work, and particularly hard hit were professional men; some doctors were seen begging from door to door.

Later than morning Hitler set out for Vienna. He could average only twenty miles an hour, impeded partly by the crowds, partly by the stalled trucks and tanks. It was almost 5 P.M. by the time his cavalcade reached the outskirts of the capital. Every building, including churches, flew the Austrian and German flags. Masses lined the streets, shouting themselves hoarse at the sight of Hitler in his open car, erect with arm outstretched. The ovation was frantic, spontaneous. His car stopped before the Hotel Imperial and, upon entering, it was another dream come true. As a youth he had always longed to go inside. Now it was bedecked in long red banners, bearing his mark, the swastika.

The crowds kept shouting a variation of an old German drinking song: "We won't go home, we won't go home till the Führer talks!" until he stepped out onto the balcony of the royal suite. After acknowledging their frenzied yells with a salute and wave, he withdrew. But the mob tirelessly kept up its chant hour after hour, forcing him to show himself again and again.

At first he was quiet as if numbed by the endless ovation, but as the evening wore on (so intimates of the Führer told Pierre Huss of INS), he began reminiscing of the nights he used to walk past the Imperial Hotel. "I could see the glittering lights and chandeliers in the lobby but I knew it was impossible for me to set foot inside. One night, after a bad blizzard which piled up several feet of snow, I had a chance to make some money for food by shoveling snow. Ironically enough, the five or six of us in my group were sent to clean the street and sidewalk in front of the Imperial Hotel." On that particular evening the Habsburgs happened to be entertaining inside. "I saw Karl and Zita step out of their imperial coach and grandly walk into this hotel over the red carpet. We poor devils shovelled the snow away on all sides and took our hats off every time the aristocrats arrived. They didn't even look at us, although I still smell the perfume that came to our noses. We were about as important to them, or for that matter to Vienna, as the snow that kept coming down all night, and this hotel did not even have the decency to send a cup of hot coffee to us." The cheerful music inside not only made him wish to cry but made him boil with the injustice of life. "I resolved that night that someday I would come back to the Imperial Hotel and walk over the red carpet in that glittering interior where the Habsburgs danced. I didn't know how or when, but I have waited for this day and tonight I am here."

He awoke Tuesday morning without the stomach cramps he had felt in Linz. He made a spirited address to the huge crowd of 200,000 which gathered in the Heldenplatz to honor him. Now, he said, they had a new mission and their country a new name, *Ostmark*. But both mission and name came from their own history since assaults from the east had been broken on the frontiers of the old East Mark. Neither the new mission nor the new name cooled the ardor of his listeners, who shouted as enthusiastically as any Munich audience. At the end of his speech Hitler turned to the radio announcer and said in an undertone, "Announce that *Reichsstadthalter* [keeper of the Reich's city] Seyss-Inquart will now speak." No one was more surprised than the Chancellor to discover he had been transformed into a sort of provincial viceroy. He accepted the demotion in good grace as the crowd cheered. At that hour Adolf Hitler could do no wrong.

Then came the parade, past the Winter Palace and its tall spearlike iron fencing with Austrian generals trailing General von Bock on horseback; the Austrian army had just been absorbed into the Wehrmacht. During the pause in the impressive procession the good Catholic Papen turned to Hitler with a warning that the Anschluss would evaporate if he subjected the Church here to the attacks it had suffered in Germany.

"Have no fear," said Hitler, "I know that better than anyone."

Later in the day Cardinal Innitzer greeted him with the sign of the cross and gave assurance that so long as the Church retained its liberties Austrian Catholics would become "the truest sons of the great Reich into whose arms they had been brought back on this momentous day." According to Papen, Hitler was delighted with the cardinal's patriotic words, shook his hand warmly and "promised him everything."

Eva Braun also experienced the exultation of the moment and wrote on a postcard to her sister Ilse *"Ich bin verrückt* [I am crazy]." She had come to the city chaperoned by her mother and her best friend, Herta Schneider. She was lodged in a separate room just across the corridor from her lover's suite and their private meetings were so discreet that none of the Führer's aides or adjutants was aware of her presence. Late that afternoon the Führer flew back to Munich without her.

The next day he was greeted in Berlin as a conquering hero. "The city seemed simply delirious with joy," Lochner wrote his family. "The kids and girls are especially hysterical." Hitler spoke triumphantly of the Anschluss. "Germany has now become Greater Germany and will so remain." He was happy, he said, that he had been chosen by Providence to bring about this great union with Austria—"the land which had been the unhappiest is now the happiest."

But all was not well at home. The court-martial of General von Fritsch, abruptly postponed when Schuschnigg announced his plebiscite, was finally convened and in short order Fritsch was found innocent. The incident was an embarrassment to Hitler but he had discovered the political trick that would never go out of fashion—he drew attention from it with boasts of victory. He hurriedly assembled the Reichstag so he could report on the great events in Austria. Within three days, he said, the entire population of Austria had welcomed him "without a single shot having been fired." For the first time in history, he said, the entire German nation, the Greater Reich, would go to the polling booth on April 10 to testify to its allegiance. All he wanted was another four years to consolidate internally an Anschluss which had just been accomplished externally. The immediate response throughout Germany was almost total approval for everything the Führer had done or was about to do, and it was with the utmost confidence that he began the election-plebiscite campaign in Königsberg on March 25. "This National Socialist idea," he said, "goes far beyond the bounds of a small Germany."

He spent the last ten days of electioneering in his homeland where Himmler and Heydrich had almost completely reorganized the Austrian security system.* The wave of his popularity had not subsided. A declaration signed by Cardinal Innitzer and five other prelates had been sent to the newly appointed commissioner of Austria instructing Austrian Catholics how to vote: "On the day of the plebiscite, it is the obvious national duty of us bishops to declare ourselves as Germans for the German Reich, and we expect all faithful Christians to recognize where their duty to the people lies."

Wherever Hitler went he was greeted as savior and Führer. His return to Linz on April 8 was greeted with renewed frenzy. The lobby of the Weinzinger was jammed with citizens who clamored to see him. One was the best friend of his youth, Gustl Kubizek. He was told by Hitler's "office manager," Albert Bormann, that the Führer was not well enough to receive anyone that day. Would he come tomorrow for lunch? Hitler greeted Kubizek on the ninth with the joyful cry: "Gustl!" then took his outstretched right hand and held it firmly. Hitler said he no longer had a private life as in the old days. He gazed out a window at the Danube and the iron bridge that had offended him as a boy. "That ugly thing, still there! But not much longer, you can be sure of that, Kubizek!" He began to enlarge on the ambitious plans he had for Linz. There would be a great new bridge as well as a new opera house along with a modern concert hall worthy of Bruckner. Talk of the new symphony orchestra he would establish in Linz reminded Hitler of Kubizek's ambitions. What had he become? The embarrassing answer was: town clerk of Eferding. The war, explained Kubizek, had forced him to abandon his musical ambitions or starve. But he did direct an amateur orchestra and his three sons were musically gifted. This brought a spontaneous offer from Hitler to assume responsibility for the training of the three boys. "I don't want gifted young people to have such a hard time of it as we had. You know best what we had to go through in Vienna."

---

* The latter was also involved in discreet but assiduous research for any personal information concerning the Führer. Dollfuss and Schuschnigg had reportedly collected numerous documents indicating that Hitler's grandfather might have been Jewish, that Geli Raubal might have been murdered, and that his service in the war was nowhere as heroic as party propagandists said. The revelation of such material, even if based only on rumor, could seriously damage the Führer's reputation at one of the most critical periods of his career. Some postwar charges against Hitler are equally unfounded. It is widely believed, for example, that he turned the village of Döllersheim into an artillery range soon after taking over Austria for the purpose of obliterating the birthplace of his father and the grave of his grandmother along with any incriminating records. It is true that Döllersheim today is a decaying mass of rubble. It was destroyed, however, not by Hitler but by the Russians after the war. A German military training area was established in and around the village in 1941 but its farms and houses were practically intact by the time the Russians arrived.

They had been talking for an hour when the Führer rose. Kubizek assumed the interview was over but Hitler was only summoning an adjutant so he could give instructions for the musical education of the three Kubizek boys at the Bruckner Conservatory. Nor was this the end. After examining all the drawings, letters and postcards Kubizek had brought along, Hitler suggested his old friend write a book about him. Finally he gripped Kubizek's hand and said they should meet more often.

Later in the day Hitler proceeded to Vienna, the city of their youthful dreams, where he made the final speech of the campaign. He was proud, he said, to have been born in Austria. "I believe that it was God's will to send a boy from here into the Reich, to let him grow up, to raise him to be the leader of the nation so as to enable him to lead back his homeland into the Reich."

The elections the following day exceeded his hopes. In Austria 99.73 per cent of the voters approved Anschluss. In Germany 99.02 per cent voted in favor of union, while 99.8 per cent approved his list of candidates for the new Reichstag. Hitler's bold action (the result of considerable pressure from Göring) had been confirmed almost unanimously by the peoples of Austria and Germany. "For me," he said, "this is the proudest hour of my life." It also confirmed the conviction that his was the correct path and that he should continue along it to the next station— Czechoslovakia.

Chapter Seventeen

"ON THE RAZOR'S EDGE"
MAY–OCTOBER 1938

1

Even before Hitler marched into Austria he had suggested that he would no longer suffer the "severe persecution" of the German minority in Czechoslovakia. While this was in line with a vow to return lost people and land to the Reich, his main concern was Czechoslovakia's threatening geographical and political position. Here, he reasoned, was an artificial country created by the Allies after the war, a peninsula thrust into what remained of the Reich as a perpetual threat from the east.

Hitler was not alone in regarding it as a dagger aimed at the heart of Germany. The specter of simultaneous drives from east and west into the waist of the Reich inspired a counter German military plan known as Case Green: a surprise attack on Czechoslovakia. For about two years, however, Case Green was little more than a staff study; the easy seizure of Austria changed all that. Overnight Hitler had been given the opportunity to upset the balance of power in Europe; a thrust into Czechoslovakia, neutralizing her formidable defense system, would position his army for a drive against Poland or the U.S.S.R. All he needed was an excuse to invade and he had a ready-made one: three and a half million Sudeten Germans, inspired by the absorption of Austria, were now demanding a similar Anschluss, on the debatable grounds that they were a cruelly repressed minority. Their grievances, along with a traditional hostility to all things Czech, had plagued the tiny republic since its foundation. For the past three years Hitler had been covertly subsidizing the Nazi Sudeten Party led by Konrad Henlein and it now controlled the entire German minority movement. In late March 1938 German support took a more ominous character when the Führer named Henlein as his personal representative with instructions to make demands that could not possibly be accepted by the Czech government. This strategy, he hoped, would create a constant state of unrest that would finally "necessitate" German armed intervention to prevent civil war and protect the lives of its nationals in the Sudeten.

With an excuse at hand, Hitler was still restrained by apprehension that France, England and perhaps Russia would resist any effort to seize Czechoslovakia. Before facing such odds he needed the blessing of his sole ally. And so on May 2, 1938, he set out for Rome to get it, accompanied by a retinue of five hundred, consisting of diplomats, generals, security agents, party leaders and journalists, all wearing uniforms of one type or another.

It was with mixed feelings that Hitler left Berlin. Elation over the bloodless conquests of the Rhineland and Austria was tempered by recurrence of the gastrointestinal pains "miraculously" cured by Dr. Morell's Mutaflor. Concern over his health spurred him to spend several hours on the train bound for Rome writing out a will; from *Mein Kampf* alone he had amassed a fortune.*

The five trains of the Führer's party were met at the Brenner Pass by flowers, banners and formations of Italian soldiers and Fascist troops. A band played the national anthems of both countries as the Duke of Pistoia welcomed the Germans in the name of the King. The German railway cavalcade proceeded into Italy past guards of honor posted on both sides of the tracks. Houses were decorated with placards and banners acclaiming the Führer and Italian-German friendship. As the delegation neared Rome, Hitler summoned an adjutant and—within hearing of Linge —ordered him to go through the train informing everyone that a very little man would greet them in Rome but they were to behave themselves and not laugh. "That is an order. The little man is the King of Italy."

It was dark when they arrived at the beflagged San Paolo station

---

* By 1943 his accumulated royalties with Eher Verlag would amount to 5,525,811 R.M. To the party he left all his personal possessions, the Berghof, his furniture and his pictures. To Eva Braun and his two sisters he left the same amount, 12,000 marks a year for life. Alois was granted a lump sum of 60,000 marks and there were further bequests to relatives in Spital, Frau Winter and his valets. He also ordered the party to "worthily take care of my adjutants Brückner and Wiedemann for life."

specially constructed for the occasion. It annoyed Hitler that he was met by King Victor Emmanuel, not Mussolini, and he annoyed His Majesty by seating himself first in the state carriage. Drawn by four horses, it proceeded past illuminated fountains along the old Roman triumphal way. A profusion of searchlights and torches turned night into day; the gaudily lit Colosseum seemed on fire. Cheering crowds lined the route and at one point African cavalry charged down the avenue at the guest of honor like something out of *The Desert Song*. But Hitler felt demeaned by riding in such an ancient vehicle. Hadn't the House of Savoy ever heard of the automobile? Nor did he find his accommodations in the Quirinal at all to his taste. The palace was uncomfortable as well as gloomy and reminded him of a museum.

From the very beginning he and Victor Emmanuel were on bad terms. Hitler resented the sovereign's open coolness and kept complaining that Mussolini himself should have served as host. The reception banquet at the Quirinal did nothing to ease the situation. Hitler, eyes moving nervously, slowly led the Queen, a majestic figure taller than himself, on his arm. Behind came the diminutive King leading the governor's tall wife. The foursome made a comical sight and Hitler knew it. As the Queen entered the great reception hall the Italians either bent very low or kneeled down. Several kissed the hem of her gown. After the ordeal, Hitler confided to his pilot that it had been "a frightful hour. Such ceremonies are terrible for me. I shall never get used to such things."

During the meal he and the Queen did not exchange a word. Hitler was particularly annoyed by the huge crucifix the Queen wore around her neck. She had done it deliberately, he thought, to annoy him. The royal family was going beyond the bounds of being ungracious. The King was spreading malicious stories about his guest, including one that the Führer demanded a woman on his first night at the Quirinal. "Boundless amazement," wrote Ciano in his diary. "The explanation: it seems he cannot go to sleep unless a woman turns down the bed before his eyes. It was difficult to find one, but the problem was solved by recruiting a chambermaid from a hotel. If this were really true it would be weird and interesting, but is it? Isn't it just a piece of spite on the part of the King, who also alleges that Hitler has himself injected with stimulants and narcotics?" Part of the last charge was only too true and there was reason to believe the bed-turning routine was also accurate. But it was still malice on the King's part and it continued a few days later at a performance of *Aida* in Naples. After the first act the audience politely held applause, looking toward the distinguished guest in the royal box to give him the opportunity of starting it. In embarrassment Hitler turned to the King for his cue. "The monarch, with a disdainful sneer," wrote Louis Lochner, "professed not to notice his guest's discomfort."

After the opera Hitler was scheduled to review a formation of Nazis from the German colony. Since he wore tails, he had instructed Linge to bring along a military cap and coat for the occasion but the King's adjutant warned him that the train back to Rome was due to leave in a few minutes. Rather than disappoint the waiting party members, Hitler hurried to the street as he was and trooped the line of civilians as military commander with right hand raised in salute. Normally he hooked left thumb in belt but these trousers had no belt and he pressed hand against hip. It was a comical sight as he raced along, bareheaded, like a Teutonic Groucho Marx, the long tails of his coat fluttering. "The German Führer and Reich Chancellor," wrote the amused Wiedemann, "looked like a head waiter at the peak of business in a restaurant and he himself must have realized what a ridiculous figure he made." Once on the train he vented his rage on Ribbentrop, who loudly charged the chief of protocol with disloyalty to the government and the Führer.

By the time Hitler returned to Rome he had regained his composure and, at the Palazzo Venezia banquet on May 7, he made an effective speech that, according to Count Ciano, "was extremely successful in melting the ice around him." In effect, he offered the South Tyrol as a present to his host, a most generous gift since it would infuriate his own countrymen, particularly those from Bavaria. He had made the same offer through Göring back in 1924 while in Landsberg prison. In that case he had agreed to support Italy's claim to this hotly contested area for two million lire and to his chagrin got not one lire for his pains. Perhaps tonight's offer was some sort of signal to Il Duce that *this time* a substantial quid pro quo must be forthcoming.

This speech was the first event of political significance since Hitler's arrival. Satisfied to stay in the background and let the King play host, Il Duce had cleverly evaded any serious discussion by submitting his guests to a program that kept them busy day and night. Ribbentrop did eventually manage to present to Ciano a draft treaty of an alliance which he scanned without comment. Mussolini's son-in-law, in fact, had already written in his diary: "The Duce intends to make the pact. We shall make it, because he has a thousand and one reasons for not trusting the Western democracies."

More important, Hitler eventually succeeded in broaching the question that most concerned him—Czechoslovakia. Almost offhandedly, Mussolini gave the impression that this little country was not at all important to him and he would look the other way. This assurance was worth all the real and imagined insults Hitler had been subjected to and he now felt free to take the next step in his program.

President Beneš and other Czech leaders were under the illusion that Hitler would never risk an attack on their country for fear of setting off a general war. And if he did, wouldn't France, England and Russia somehow manage to restrain him? But these three were in no mood to act as protectors. "You only have to look at the map," Chamberlain had recently written his sister, "to see that nothing that France or we could do, could possibly save Czechoslovakia from being overrun by the Germans if they wanted to do it. . . . Therefore, we would not help Czechoslovakia—she would simply be a pretext for going to war with Germany. That we could not do, unless we had a reasonable prospect of being able to beat her to her knees in a reasonable time and of that I see no sign. I have therefore abandoned any idea of giving guarantees to Czechoslovakia or the French in connection with her obligations to that country." The Prime Minister's continuing lack of resolve disturbed the French leaders and, though they continued to make bold statements, perceptive observers were convinced that France, whose foreign policy had been in tow of the British since the Rhineland seizure, would not spring to the Czechs' defense. The third potential defender was publicly taking every opportunity to urge England and France to stand up to the Germans, while privately doing nothing. Stalin wanted Hitler controlled by the West, not himself, and on May 6 the Soviet chargé d'affaires in Prague admitted to the American ambassador that his country definitely would not supply Czechoslovakia any military aid unless France did so. Besides, how could they get the troops there? Poland and Romania stood between them and both these countries had understandably refused to allow passage of the Red Army. At the same time Stalin was assuring Beneš in private that the Soviet Union was ready to assist him militarily "even if France does not do so and even if Poland and Romania refuse to permit Soviet troops to pass in transit to Czechoslovakia."

This was all part of the attempt to convince liberals of the world that the Soviets were the true defenders of a brave little beleaguered nation when, in fact, they were no more willing to fly to its aid than England or France. Hitler had guessed as much and now that he had Mussolini's tacit approval of a march into Czechoslovakia he ordered Goebbels to intensify the press campaign against that hapless country. Activity among the Sudetenland Germans increased with assurance that *Der Tag* was at hand. This rumor was given credence by alarming reports on May 19 and 20 that Hitler's troops were mobilizing on the Czech borders: eleven in-

fantry and four armored divisions were already converging on the Bohemian frontier while German and Austrian troops were poised for attack in
southern Silesia and northern Austria.

On the afternoon of Friday, the twentieth, Beneš called an emergency meeting of the cabinet and the Supreme Defense Council. Shortly
after 9 P.M.—without consulting their French allies—a "partial mobilization" was ordered. By dawn of Saturday, Czech troops occupied the border fortifications and the Sudeten territories—and Europe was swept by a
crisis fever not experienced since 1914. A small power had taken the initiative against a powerful one, making known that she would not be a pawn
in the game of European power politics. In so doing, Czechoslovakia was
also forcing her reluctant sponsors, France and England, to back her up.

As a consequence, French Premier Daladier summoned the German
ambassador and showed him a mobilization order lying on his desk. "It
depends upon you, Excellency," he said, "whether I sign this document or
not." And in Berlin British Ambassador Henderson warned Foreign
Minister von Ribbentrop that "France had definite obligations to
Czechoslovakia and that, if these had to be fulfilled, His Majesty's Government would not guarantee that they would not be forced by events to
become themselves involved." Convinced that England was the prime
enemy, Ribbentrop decelerated from outright rage to righteous indignation, stoutly denying that German troops threatened the Czech borders. If
France and Britain were "crazy enough" to use armed force against Germany, "then once again we should have to fight to the death."

Ribbentrop left Berlin by special plane that evening to meet Hitler in
Berchtesgaden. He was as incensed as his Foreign Minister, for not a single major military movement or concentration aimed at Czechoslovakia
had taken place. Who then had started the rumor? It could have been the
Communists, the Czechs or the anti-Hitler group which included such disparate elements as Schacht, the self-styled financial wizard, and Admiral
Canaris, chief of the German intelligence service. More likely, panic itself
was the villain.

The Western press spread the story that the Führer had been forced
by foreign pressure to call off his invasion and by so doing made the mistake of humiliating him. "Hitler had embarked on no military enterprise,"
wrote Weizsäcker, "and could not therefore withdraw from one. But unfortunate provocation by the foreign press now really set Hitler going.
From then on he was emphatically in favor of settling the Czech question
by force of arms."

Before the week was out Hitler acted with dramatic suddenness. On
May 28 he summoned his top military leaders, officials of the Foreign

Office and other important functionaries to a special conference. As this unusually large group was gathering outside the chancellery winter garden, the general assumption was that Hitler was about to call for new military measures. An agitated Göring drew Captain Wiedemann aside. "Doesn't the Führer realize what he is doing? This will mean war with France!" The army was not combat-ready, he said, and promised to tell this to the Chief.

Hitler began speaking calmly but his words were explosive: "It is my unshakable will to wipe Czechoslovakia off the map. . . . We shall have to use methods which, perhaps, will not find the immediate approval of you old officers." This attack, he explained, was but part of a much broader strategy to acquire living space. When Germany made its inevitable drive to the east for Lebensraum, Czechoslovakia would be a threat to the rear. Consequently, she had to be eliminated and this was the propitious moment since neither Britain nor France wanted war, Russia would not intervene and Italy was uninterested.

When Hitler finished, Göring pushed forward, eyes agleam, and grasped his hand. "Mein Führer," exclaimed the man who had vowed to stop him an hour earlier, "let me congratulate you wholeheartedly on your unique concept!"

There were no protests, not even discussion. Hitler walked over to Keitel, Brauchitsch and Beck, who were standing together in one corner. "So," he said, "we shall just tackle the situation in the east [Czechoslovakia]. Then I will give you three or four years' time, and then we will tackle the situation in the west."

The three generals said nothing but the following day Beck wrote another critical memorandum. Germany, he claimed, was no stronger than in 1914 and far more vulnerable to air attack. She was confronted, furthermore, by a coalition comprising Czechoslovakia, France, Britain and America. "Germany's opponents," he concluded, "have time and space at their disposal and their resources of men and materials are superior to those of Germany and her allies."

On May 30 Beck delivered this grim appraisal to Brauchitsch, who asked Keitel how best to bring it to the Führer's attention. He was advised to delete the political section lest Hitler toss aside without reading it the part discussing the balance of military strength in case France intervened. Brauchitsch followed this counsel and the same day a truncated version was presented during a conference in the School of Artillery at Jüterbog. The Führer objected strenuously: the report was not objective and overrated French military strength. "It was another disaster for the army," wrote Keitel, "and resulted in a further lack of confidence in Brauchitsch, which I bitterly regretted, although the Führer did not hold Brauchitsch responsible as much as Beck and the General Staff."

Brushing aside all objections, Hitler concluded that Czechoslovakia must be dealt with by force and gave the army until October 1 to do it. Thus the fourth version of Case Green was put into motion. Work on the Westwall, the defense system on the French border, was accelerated under the direction of Fritz Todt, who had built the Autobahn complex. Within weeks more than a half million men were working on fortifications designed to hold off France with a minimum of troops while forces in the east seized Czechoslovakia in a lightning stroke. At the same time an intensive program of propaganda warfare was inaugurated, its purpose, in the Führer's own words, "to intimidate the Czechs by means of threats and wear down their power of resistance; and on the other hand it must give the national racial groups indications as to how to support our military operations and influence the neutrals in our favor."

Hitler's determination to drive forward was solidified by a dispatch from his ambassador in Moscow, sent on the day of the Jüterbog conference. Count von der Schulenburg reported that Czechoslovakia, intent on avoiding a conflict, was ready to make concessions within the bounds of reason. "Here the view prevails that the Soviet will for the present avoid being drawn into the war at all costs. The reasons for this attitude are to be found in strained internal conditions and in fear of a war on two fronts."

The stage was set for a European crisis that would make the events in May seem inconsequential.

2

Although Hitler had put Case Green in motion, his intent was primarily to use it for bargaining. The question was how close to the precipice of war he would go, and early that summer he himself probably did not know. Relying on intuition as he had in the Rhineland and Austrian crises, he allowed his personal adjutant, Wiedemann, to go to London in July for an informal talk with Lord Halifax. It was an extraordinary mission of exploration privately arranged by Wiedemann's close friend, Princess Hohenlohe, half Jewish by birth, which completely circumvented Ribbentrop. Wiedemann's official commission was to explore the possibilities of a state visit to England by Göring, but Hitler had also personally instructed him to inform Halifax that the crucial question of the moment was the mistreatment of the Sudeten Germans. "If there is no satisfactory solution in the near future, I will simply have to solve it by force. Tell this to Lord Halifax!"

Wiedemann repeated his warning in mid-July and Halifax replied cordially that much could be settled before that deadline. He also agreed in principle to a visit by Göring and extended a vague invitation to the Führer himself as a guest of the King. Wiedemann flew back to Germany in high spirits. He was kept waiting at the Berghof for several hours while the Führer strolled outside with Unity Mitford, and upon his return Hitler impatiently interrupted Wiedemann's report of British approval of the Göring visit to London. "By no means, no longer!" he exclaimed and refused to hear another word about Halifax. "I do not know," recalled Wiedemann, "whether this change in Hitler had come from something Unity Mitford had told him or whether he feared the possibility of Göring gaining too much political power by such a step. In any case, there was no opportunity for me to inform him of something he did not want to hear about."

Several weeks later Fritz Hesse, the covert representative of the Wilhelmstrasse, was recalled from London and chastised by Ribbentrop for sending a report indicating that Chamberlain was prepared to consider the cession of the Sudeten territories to Germany. "What's the good of sending me this kind of stuff?" said the Foreign Minister according to Hesse's account. The Führer, it seemed, was convinced the English planned to smash Germany to pieces once they had completed their own rearmament and had recently told Ribbentrop: "There is no international morality left, everybody snatches whatever booty he can. I shall take this as a lesson." Before he allowed the English to encircle him, he would strike first.

Hesse explained that Chamberlain's personal adviser had asked him to inform Hitler unofficially that a London *Times* editorial suggesting Britain was prepared to accept a solution favorable to Germany had been planted by the Prime Minister himself. With this in mind, wasn't it likely that Hitler could obtain autonomy for the Sudeten Germans without even a threat of military action? "Autonomy!" exclaimed Ribbentrop. "There can be no question of autonomy any longer." Before the lying reports of German troop movements, he said, Hitler might have been satisfied with autonomy. But now that was not enough. Hesse "went cold all over" when he heard this. For the first time he realized how real the danger of war was. He begged the Foreign Minister to assure Hitler that he could obtain the cession of the Sudetenland peacefully. Impressed, Ribbentrop promised to talk to Hitler but the following day he summoned Hesse to report that the Führer had ridiculed the idea of the Czechs surrendering their military bastion. "I simply don't believe it," he said. "They can't be that stupid!"

While Hitler's position hardened, his generals continued to resist his policy of expansion. Beck began openly to circulate gloomy predictions: the question of guilt in a new war would be a greater factor than it had been in the World War; and the aftermath of defeat would be far more disastrous than in 1918. That July he composed a third long memorandum for Brauchitsch declaring that he was positive an attack on Czechoslovakia would bring about another great conflict. "The outcome of such a war would be a general catastrophe for Germany, not only a military defeat." The people, he went on, did not want this war, nor was the Wehrmacht prepared for it.

When Beck presented this document on July 16 he spoke even more courageously, urging Brauchitsch to organize resistance among military leaders. "History will burden these leaders with blood-guilt," read his notes for this discussion, "If they do not act in accord with their special-ized political knowledge and conscience. . . . If they all act with resolu-tion, the execution of a policy of war is impossible. . . . Extraordinary times demand extraordinary measures."

In early August Brauchitsch was persuaded to convene the senior army commanders. It was he, in fact, who read a memorandum prophesy-ing that a Czech invasion would lead to a general war that Germany was doomed to lose. Was the Sudetenland worth risking the existence of the nation? The consensus was that citizens and soldiers alike were against war. The generals also agreed that the training and equipment of their troops might be up to defeating the Czechs but certainly not the com-bined powers of Europe. There were only two objections and these rather mild ones. General Busch repeated the cliché that soldiers should not in-terfere with politicians and Reichenau, the first general to go Nazi, warned his colleagues to confront Hitler singly rather than en masse. Brauchitsch decided to take his advice and faced the Führer alone. It is doubtful if he stated the case as forcefully as he had done to his peers, but even in milder form it brought a verbal explosion that promptly brought him back in line.

Discouraged by the commanders' negative attitude, Hitler invited their chiefs of staff to dinner at the Berghof on August 10. He regaled them for three hours with his political theories, but they too were not impressed. Universal opposition only made the Führer more determined and five days later, after witnessing artillery exercises near Jüterbog, he gathered his senior officers in a mess hall to announce that he had decided to solve the Czech problem by force that fall. He assured his listeners that so long as Chamberlain and Daladier were in power there would be no widespread war, and concluded with a reminder of his own prophetic powers.

Two days later Soviet Ambassador Maisky told Halifax that German policy was "at least 50 per cent bluff," and that the irresolute stance of the French and British "constituted a real danger for peace," since it gave an exaggerated impression of Germany's strength both at home and abroad. Additional pressure was brought to bear upon the British the following afternoon by a gentleman farmer from Pomerania. Ewald von Kleist-Schmenzin, a descendant of the great poet and a monarchist, had long been an enemy of Hitler. Using a passport provided by Admiral Canaris, he was in England as a representative of the moderates in the German General Staff who hoped to stop Hitler's aggression. Late that afternoon he was in private conversation with Sir Robert Vansittart, chief diplomatic adviser to Halifax. Kleist began with the sober announcement that war was a certainty unless the British stopped it. There was only one real extremist in Germany, he said. "Hitler has made up his mind for himself. All the generals in the German army who are my friends know it and they *alone* know it for a certainty and know the date at which the mine is to be exploded."

"Do you mean that such people as Goebbels and Himmler are not pushing Hitler in that direction as well?" asked Vansittart.

"I repeat that I discount them. Hitler has taken this decision by himself." All the generals were "dead against war but they will not have the power to stop it unless they get encouragement and help from outside. As I have already told you, they know the date and will be obliged to march at that date."

When asked the date, Kleist laughed. "Why, of course you know it," and it took some time to convince him that the British leaders did not have this information. "After the twenty-seventh of September it will be too late," he said, and the latest time to stop the operation was the middle of September. Hitler must be made to understand that England and France were not bluffing. A leading British statesman should make a speech aimed at the German public emphasizing the horrors of war.

Vansittart immediately wrote a detailed account of the meeting for Chamberlain. But he was too dedicated to appeasement to take Kleist seriously, and his position was reinforced the next day by a telegram from Henderson in Berlin. In the ambassador's opinion the chief danger of war lay not in Hitler himself, who stood to lose most, "but in the forces working for war, namely German and Czech extremists, communists, and other influences and the universal hatred abroad of Nazism." He advised London "not to drive Herr Hitler into a situation where his prestige being at stake he would feel himself obliged to yield to his extremists."

Kleist had come much closer to the truth. At home Hitler was surrounded by disapproval. The generals were still unconvinced by his arguments. The prime mover, Beck, once more offered his resignation and, when Brauchitsch continued to decline it, refused to serve any longer. Hitler solved the problem by accepting the resignation and ordering Beck to keep it secret from the public "for reasons of foreign policy." As a loyal German, Beck agreed but continued to support the anti-Hitler group which was secretly plotting to arrest the Führer once he gave the final order for execution of Case Green. Rarely in history had so many leading military and civilian leaders plotted to overthrow a government by force. Among the conspirators were General Erwin von Witzleben, commander of the Berlin area military district, Admiral Canaris, who had provided the passport for Kleist, former Commander-in-Chief of the Army Kurt von Hammerstein-Equord, and Beck's replacement as chief of staff, Franz Halder. It was the last who sent a second secret negotiator to London to repeat Kleist's warnings—again to no avail. The plot also involved Hjalmar Schacht and many other civilians, including Professor Haushofer's oldest son and other key Foreign Office officials such as Theodor Kordt who was spreading false stories about Ribbentrop to foreign diplomats.

At the same time open pressure on the Führer intensified. Late in August Weizsäcker took Hess aside after a private dinner and cautioned that if the Führer attempted to solve the Sudeten problem by force war between Germany and the West would inevitably follow. Hess passed on this warning to Hitler. Another came a few days later from his Minister of Finance, Schwerin von Krosigk. "After many years' acquaintance with England and the Englishman," wrote the Oxford graduate, "I am of the opinion that their repeatedly announced attitude, that is expressed in the cautious English manner, makes it crystal clear that their resolution to intervene does *not represent a bluff*. Even if Halifax and Chamberlain should not want war, behind them stand as their eventual successors the warmongers Churchill/Eden."

He urged Hitler to be patient. Time, he said, was working for Germany. Her rearmament and economic progress were steadily outdistancing those of the Allies. Further, France was showing an increasing willingness to break with Czechoslovakia and in America there were also signs of a reaction to the Jewish propaganda directed against the Reich. "That means we can only win by waiting. And that is why the Communists, Jews and Czechs are making such frantic efforts to push us into a war *now*."

All these admonitions had little effect on the Führer. He seemed set on war. After watching infantry maneuvers late that summer, he slapped a thigh with his gloves and remarked to two adjutants that war was the father of everything. "Every generation must experience war once," he said.

On September 3 he summoned Brauchitsch and Keitel to the Berghof to discuss the latest version of Case Green and learned to his dismay that the main thrust was to be made into the center of the Czech defense system by the Second Army. An attack on such a strongly fortified area, he complained, would mean bleeding to death uselessly. Another Verdun. Such an assault corresponded to Czech expectations. One should be launched instead by the Tenth Army into Bohemia. Brauchitsch protested somewhat mildly, citing the poor state of the motorized divisions, the paucity of reinforcements and the inadequate training of leaders, but Hitler brushed aside these objections as defeatist and ordered motorized and armored divisions added to the Tenth.

It was Hitler, the former corporal, who was the warrior, not his generals and observers feared that Hitler would declare himself openly at the impending Nuremberg Rally. "The anxiety is no less great in Germany than elsewhere," Henderson wrote in a personal letter. "And dictators can and must speak more clearly than the leaders of a democracy."

The Party Congress at Nuremberg that year served as a dramatic prelude to the developing political crisis by its impressive display of Nazi power and discipline. The title of the 1938 festivities was appropriate: "First Party Rally of Greater Germany," as were the trappings. Hitler had brought from Vienna, after a hundred and forty years, the insignia of the First Reich—the Imperial crown, the Orb of Empire, the Scepter and the Imperial Sword. At the presentation of these symbols of imperialism he solemnly vowed that they would remain in Nuremberg forever. But he made no mention of war during his opening address or the following afternoon when he received the entire diplomatic corps. He was graciously thanked by the spokesman, François-Poncet, who concluded with the observation that the greatest glory of a statesman was to attain his goal without making one mother weep. According to Wiedemann, Hitler responded with "a malicious smile."

Hitler's refusal to discuss international politics at Nuremberg inspired conjectures and rumors, including one directed to Henderson, that Hitler had become "quite mad" and was bent on war at all costs. In the next twenty-four hours Henderson spoke to a number of Hitler's close advisers, urging Anglo-German co-operation in a Sudeten settlement. Göring said he planned to go hunting the end of the month and "hoped to goodness the Czechs wouldn't upset his shooting plans by starting trouble in the middle of them," and Goebbels expressed the pious hope that the Führer would refer to co-operation with the English in his final speech. "He appeared to me anxious," reported a suspicious Henderson, "and I begin to doubt whether he is egging Hitler on to extremes."

In the midst of these interviews, Henderson received instructions to deliver a personal warning to Hitler that England "could not stand aside" in the event of a general conflict. Henderson protested: the Führer was on the borderline of madness and a second crisis could push him over the edge. The matter consequently was dropped.

Since Hitler was already convinced England had no intention of risking war over Czechoslovakia, he was going ahead with his invasion plans come what might. It was a decision combining shrewd calculation, intuition and an irresistible impulse. "You know I am like a wanderer who must cross an abyss on the razor's edge," Hitler told Frank. "But I must, I simply must cross." A few hours after the British decided not to transmit a warning, he summoned Keitel, Brauchitsch and Halder to Nuremberg. They met in the Deutscher Hof just before midnight of September 9, and it was the new chief of staff who outlined the revised version of Case Green. Surprisingly, it still entrusted the main thrust to the Second Army but did involve a pincer movement that had not been mentioned in the previous discussion. Hitler admitted that it was a clever idea. "But its success is nevertheless too uncertain for it to be depended on. Especially as a rapid success is necessary from a political point of view. The first week is politically decisive, within which a far-reaching territorial gain must be achieved." German howitzers, he pointed out, could not smash the Czech fortifications. More important, this plan ruled out the element of surprise.

Hitler kept lecturing Halder and Brauchitsch to the dismay of Keitel, who already agreed with everything the Führer proposed. By three o'clock Hitler had lost his patience, and he categorically ordered his generals to do as he proposed, then coldly and sullenly dismissed them. As the three men stopped in the vestibule for a drink, Halder indignantly asked, "What is he really after?"

"If you haven't found out," replied the irritated Keitel, "then you have my sympathy."

Brauchitsch intervened before another argument started and the trio set about to meet Hitler's demands. While Halder was busy writing out the new orders, Keitel took Brauchitsch aside. "Why do you fight with him [Hitler] when you know that the battle is lost before it's begun? Nobody thinks there is going to be a war over this, so the whole thing wasn't worth all that rear-guard action." It was the kind of practical advice that gave increasing currency to his nickname "Lakeitel." Afterward Keitel expressed his bitter disappointment in Brauchitsch to his own chief of operations. Jodl seconded the motion and wrote in his diary: "There is only one undisciplined element in the army—the generals, and in the last analysis this comes from the fact that they are arrogant. They have neither confidence nor discipline because they cannot recognize the Führer's genius." They still looked upon him as a corporal of the Great War "instead of the greatest statesman since Bismarck."

It was not Hitler but Göring who made the first public announcement on Czechoslovakia the following day. "A trifling piece of Europe," he said, "is making life unbearable for mankind. The Czechs, the vile race of dwarfs without any culture—nobody even knows where they came from—are oppressing a civilized race; and behind them, together with Moscow, there can be seen the everlasting face of the Jewish fiend!"

If such words had been uttered by Hitler, Europe would have trembled but even President Beneš ignored Göring's diatribe. "I firmly believe that nothing other than moral force, good will, and mutual trust will be needed," he broadcast in both Czech and German. Afterward William Shirer encountered the President in the hall of Broadcasting House. The American correspondent wanted to warn Beneš he was dealing with gangsters but didn't have the nerve. He observed that Beneš's face was "grave, not nearly so optimistic as his words, and I doubt not he knows the terrible position he is in."

Publicly Chamberlain did not. On September 11 the Prime Minister told a group of journalists: "Herr Hitler has repeatedly expressed his own desire for peace and it would be a mistake to assume that those declarations were insincere." At the same time he was expressing apprehension in a private letter: "I fully realise that if eventually things go wrong and the aggression takes place, there will be many, including Winston, who will say that the British government must bear the responsibility and that if only they had had the courage to tell Hitler now that, if he used force, we would at once declare war, that would have stopped him." But it was wrong, he felt, to let the vital decision of war and peace "pass out of our hands into those of the ruler of another country, and a lunatic at that."

The final ceremony of the Nuremberg Rally came on September 12. It was the last chance for Hitler to deliver the speech the world dreaded he might make. He arrived at the huge outdoor stadium just before 7 P.M. to the concerted roar of "Sieg Heil!" and slowly walked toward the rostrum in the glare of a spotlight, looking to neither side, right hand raised in salute. He spoke at first only of the party's struggles and at such length that some foreign observers began to hope he was not going to bring up the question of the day. Suddenly he began to condemn the Czechs. "I am in no way willing that here in the heart of Germany a second Palestine should be permitted to arise. The poor Arabs are defenseless and deserted. The Germans in Czechoslovakia are neither defenseless nor are they deserted, and people should take notice of that fact."

The audience roared, "Sieg Heil! Sieg Heil!" This was the moment the world had been waiting for all week, but instead of following such stridency with an ultimatum, he merely demanded justice for the Sudeten Germans, then concluded with bluster rather than threat: "We should be sorry if this were to disturb or damage our relations with other European states, but the blame does not lie with us!"

The French, English and Czechs had feared so much that such words were reassuring; it was generally believed that the sound and fury were for the benefit of German extremists and that Hitler was ready to work for a peaceful solution. Mussolini shared this belief, for he observed as he turned away from his radio, "I had expected a more threatening speech. . . . Nothing is lost."

3

This sense of well-being was brief. Hitler's oratorical condemnation of injustice inspired scenes of protest among the Sudeten Germans. By morning Eger was blanketed with swastika flags. Ten thousand protesters jammed the streets shouting, "We want self-determination!" State police opened fire, killing one demonstrator and wounding a score more. Within twenty-four hours bloody disorders spread through the Sudetenland and the death toll rose to twenty-one. Aroused by Henlein's call for freedom, the Sudeten Germans went on strike and refused to pay taxes. Prague declared a state of siege. Martial law was proclaimed in the border districts and more Sudeten Germans were shot down. Throughout Europe there were renewed rumors of an ultimatum by Hitler—or an outright invasion. Paris and London panicked. That evening Daladier sent an urgent message to Chamberlain. An invasion of Czechoslovakia, he said, had to be avoided at all costs or France would be forced to fulfill the obligations of her treaty. He proposed that they immediately invite Hitler to meet with them and work out a reasonable settlement.

The cryptic reply he got from Chamberlain kept Daladier perplexed for hours: "Some time ago I came to a resolution. I believe it to be useful. . . . I cannot tell you anything yet, but I will let you know about it a little later." That same evening Chamberlain telegraphed Hitler suggesting a man-to-man conference. Hitler was delightfully taken by surprise and described his feeling with a colorful idiom that would have perplexed Milton: "I fell from Heaven!" That afternoon he sent a reply placing himself at Chamberlain's proposal and suggesting that they meet the next noon at Berchtesgaden.

In England the first reaction of relief was followed by enthusiasm that their Prime Minister was making such an original move to keep peace. In Prague newsboys shouted out: "Extra! Read how the mighty head of the British Empire goes begging to Hitler!" The Czech citizens spontaneously massed in the streets to demonstrate that they stood behind their President's efforts to resist. In Rome Mussolini remarked to his son-in-law, Count Ciano, "There will be no war. But this is the liquidation of English prestige."

Early that morning, September 15, Chamberlain left 10 Downing Street to the cheers of an extraordinarily large crowd for that hour. Before boarding his plane at Croydon, in the presence of Halifax and other dignitaries, he paused to speak into the BBC microphones. "My policy has always been to ensure peace. The prompt acceptance of my suggestion encourages me to hope that my visit today will not be without results."

At about 8 A.M. the Lockheed Electra took off. It was the first long flight for the sixty-nine-year-old Prime Minister and he was as excited as a boy. But it would be wrong to assume he was an aging innocent proceeding to the slaughter. Chamberlain was a hard bargainer. "My method is to try and make up my own mind first on the proper course, and then try and put others through the same course of reasoning." Like his father, a successful businessman who became an outstanding statesman, he was a devout Unitarian, the very embodiment of Victorian virtues. His spare, ascetic figure, his chilling manner and his sardonic smile reminded many of a headmaster. Only his intimates knew that this austere exterior emanated from painful shyness and that beneath the armor lay warmth and sensibility.

The question was whether such an individual, convinced as he was that the Führer was half mad and needed to be handled cautiously, could cope with the situation. As he flew over London Chamberlain himself experienced "some slight sinkings," yet was buoyed by the thought that he too held strong cards and that, as long as he could keep negotiating with the Führer, Czechoslovakia would be safe.

He sat through the flight to Munich, according to one fellow passenger, "as always, aloof, reserved, imperturbable, unshakeably self-reliant." Henderson greeted him as he descended from the plane at 12:30 P.M. and was surprised how remarkably fresh he looked for a man of his age. "I'm tough and wiry," explained Chamberlain.

Despite the drizzle, enthusiastic crowds were waiting all along the route to the Munich railroad station shouting "Heil!" and lifting arms in salute. It was after four o'clock by the time the Chamberlain party started up the steep, winding road to the Berghof. The sky was dark and clouds hid the mountains as rain began to pelt down. Hitler, the polite host, waited at the head of the long flight of steps to the terrace. After exchanging stilted pleasantries over tea, Hitler abruptly asked what procedure his guest proposed for the meeting. Chamberlain said he preferred a tête-à-tête. Hitler led the Prime Minister and interpreter Schmidt upstairs to his study, leaving behind a patently annoyed Ribbentrop.

In this simple, wood-paneled room, almost bare of ornament, Hitler began quietly listing complaints against his neighbors as he presented a history of events leading up to the present crisis. Chamberlain listened attentively, answered questions with a friendly smile, then looked the Führer full in the face and said he was prepared to discuss the possibility of righting any German grievances so long as force was not used.

"Force!" said Hitler, excited for the first time. "Who speaks of force?" Wasn't it Beneš who was applying force against the Germans in the Sudetenland? As the mountain wind howled, rain slashed against the window, and he himself poured out such a torrent of words that Chamberlain asked him to stop so he might have a chance to understand what he was talking about. "I shall not put up with this any longer," exclaimed Hitler. "I shall settle the question in one way or another." It was the first time the alarmed Schmidt had heard him use such a phrase with a foreign statesman. "I shall take matters into my own hands."

Chamberlain was startled but answered resolutely, "If I have understood you right, you are determined to proceed against Czechoslovakia. If that is so, why did you let me come to Berchtesgaden?" This trip was a waste of time, and under the circumstances, he said, it was best to return to England at once. "Anything else seems pointless."

Hitler hesitated before this unexpected counterattack. Now, thought Schmidt, was the moment if he really wants to come to war. The interpreter stared at the Führer in agonized suspense: the question of peace was poised on the razor's edge. To Schmidt's astonishment, Hitler backed down. "If, in considering the Sudeten question," he said calmly, "you are prepared to recognize the principle of the right of peoples to self-determination, then we can continue the discussion in order to see how the principle can be applied in practice."

Then came a second surprise. Chamberlain did not immediately assent, objecting that a plebiscite in the Sudentenland held immense practical difficulties. Amazingly, Hitler did not flare up at this rebuff. Perhaps, thought Schmidt, the Führer had been frightened by Chamberlain's threat to go home. The Prime Minister said that he could not give Hitler an answer on the question of self-determination without first consulting his colleagues. "I therefore suggest that we break off our conversation at this point, and that I return to England immediately for consultation, and then meet you again."

Hitler looked uneasy as Schmidt translated the first words but, once he realized that Chamberlain would see him again, could not hide his relief. He expressed immediate agreement and, when Chamberlain asked "how the situation was to be held in the meantime," unhesitatingly promised that he would not give the order to march unless some "particularly atrocious incident occurred."

This ended the three-hour talk. They chatted cordially on the way downstairs, Hitler hoping that his guest would see some of the scenic beauties before he left. But Chamberlain could not spare the time "since lives were being lost." He left the Berghof pleased with the talk. "I had established a certain confidence, which was my aim," he wrote his sister, "and on my side, in spite of the hardness and ruthlessness I thought I saw in his face, I got the impression that here was a man who could be relied upon when he had given his word." At home he was greeted with encomiums of praise, including a poem composed in his honor by England's poet laureate, John Masefield:

> As Priam to Achilles for his son,
> So you, into the night, divinely led,
> To ask that young men's bodies, not yet dead,
> Be given from the battle not begun.

In Washington, Roosevelt was concerned. Fearing that such talks would only postpone the inevitable conflict, he lamented at a cabinet meeting that the Prime Minister was for "peace at any price," and bitterly observed to Harold Ickes that apparently England and France were going to leave the Czechs in the lurch, then "wash the blood from their Judas Iscariot hands." Before the weekend was over, further opposition to Chamberlain began to appear within his own cabinet but he stood firm. American Ambassador Joseph Kennedy had sent the Prime Minister an ominous report by the noted aviator, Charles Lindbergh, of overwhelming German air power based on a recent inspection of the Luftwaffe. Chamberlain had been as impressed as Kennedy and so England, which was poorly prepared for war, remained committed to appeasement.

On September 18 Chamberlain told the French delegation headed by Daladier which had come to England to discuss the problem: "There must be some cession of territorial area to the Reich. But it would be very difficult for us to carve up Czechoslovakia, unless the Czechoslovakian Government themselves were prepared to admit the necessity for frontier rectifications."

Daladier agreed that a little "friendly pressure" might persuade the Czechs to cede "some portions of Sudeten territory." At the same time, they had to be assured "of some sort of international guarantee of what remained." And Germany must participate in such a guarantee. Chamberlain hesitated but after a break in the proceedings agreed. If the French returned home still apprehensive, he was quite pleased with himself. "I have still many anxious days before me," he wrote his sister, "but the most gnawing anxiety is gone, for I feel that I have nothing to reproach myself with, and that on the contrary up to now things are going the way I want."

At the same time there remained the unpleasant job of telling the Czechs that they must give up the Sudetenland, and when Beneš was informed the next day after lunch by the British minister, he was so agitated he refused to discuss the matter at first. The embarrassed Sir Basil Newton stressed that a quick ratification must be forthcoming since Chamberlain hoped to resume talks with Hitler within forty-eight hours. Beneš bitterly charged that his country had been abandoned. The guarantees he already possessed, he said, had proven valueless. He feared the proposed solution would not be final, only a stage in the eventual domination of his country by Hitler. These words notwithstanding, Newton reported that he believed Beneš was "more likely to accept than refuse and is receptive to any reason which will help him justify acceptance to his people."

While Chamberlain anxiously waited all that Monday for an answer, Beneš was desperately searching for help from another quarter. On Tuesday he summoned the Soviet minister and asked two questions: Would the U.S.S.R. fulfill her treaty obligations if France did likewise? In the event of a Hitler attack would the Soviets support Czechoslovakia in an appeal to the League of Nations even if France refused to do so? Affirmative answers finally arrived from Moscow at 7 P.M. and forty-five minutes later Czech Foreign Minister Krofta was telling Newton that his government must reject the British-French proposal.

A little later, however, Newton's French counterpart, Victor de Lacroix, was hastily summoned to see Czech Prime Minister Hodža. He begged Lacroix to get a telegram from Paris stating that France would back out of the treaty if it came to fighting. "It was the only way of saving the peace," he said and assured Lacroix that he was acting with the consent of Beneš—which was a lie.

Lacroix transmitted this information to Paris while Newton was doing the same to London. In his message, Newton concluded with the suggestion that Halifax send Beneš an ultimatum to accept the proposal "without reserve and without further delay failing which His Majesty's Government will take no further interest in the fate of the country."

Despite the late hour, Halifax rushed to 10 Downing Street. He returned to the Foreign Office after midnight and instructed Newton to urge the Czechs to reconsider, otherwise Chamberlain would be forced to postpone or cancel his second meeting with Hitler.

It was two o'clock in the morning by the time Newton, accompanied by his French colleague, arrived at Hradschin Castle to see the President. Wakened from a fitful sleep, Beneš collapsed at Lacroix's first words "as if he had hit him with a club," and burst into tears. Shaken, the betrayed Beneš promised to give a final reply by midday.

The first word of acceptance came from the devious Hodža, who informed Newton that the Czech reply was affirmative and an official answer to that effect would be delivered as soon as possible. But the argument continued until late afternoon when Newton and Lacroix were summoned to the Ministry of Foreign Affairs. Each minister was handed a note stating that the Czechoslovakian government "sadly" accepted the Franco-British proposal.

That evening the Beneš government publicly announced its surrender in a communiqué that brought shame to many Westerners.

> We relied upon the help that our friends might have given us; but when the question of reducing us by force arose, it became evident that the European crisis was taking on too serious a character. Our friends therefore advised us to buy freedom and peace by our sacrifice, and this in proportion to their own inability to help us . . . The President of the Republic and our government had no other choice, for we found ourselves alone.

Hitler had won a victory by proxy.

4

The next morning, September 21, just before boarding a plane for his second flight, Chamberlain told newsmen: "A perfect solution of the Czechoslovakian problem is an essential preliminary to a better understanding between the British and German peoples; and that, in turn, is the indisputable foundation of European peace. European peace is what I am aiming at, and I hope this journey may open the way to it."

This time the two leaders would meet at Bad Godesberg on the Rhine. When the Prime Minister's plane landed at Cologne he was greeted by dignitaries and a guard of honor while an SS band played "God

Save the King." The British were driven to quarters in the Petersberg Hotel located on the heights across the river from Godesberg. Hitler greatly admired the view from the restaurant—he often came up at coffee time—and he wanted to impress the visitors with the vista of the spectacular country of the Drachenfels; less than fifty miles up the Rhine was the fabled rock of the Lorelei.

From his balcony Chamberlain could look across the river at the Dreesen Hotel where the first meeting would take place at 5 P.M. Late in the afternoon he was driven down the steep road to the river and onto a ferry. Thousands of onlookers lined both banks, intent on the progress of the little vessel as it plowed across the river in a scene reminding Henderson of the varsity boat-race day.

It was a short trip from the landing to the Dreesen on the west bank. Always the affable host, Hitler first inquired about the accommodations at the Petersberg. But it was all business once they adjourned to a conference room and seated themselves at the end of a long baize-covered table. Chamberlain began with a recital of the concessions he and the French had wrung out of the Czechs. After outlining the comprehensive and complicated plan to carry out the turnover of territory, he mentioned the guarantee the British and French had given the Czechs, then leaned back with an expression of satisfaction as if to say, thought Schmidt: "Haven't I worked splendidly during these five days."

To the interpreter's surprise, Hitler quietly, almost regretfully replied, "I am exceedingly sorry, Mr. Chamberlain, but I can no longer discuss these matters. This solution, after the developments of the last few days, is no longer practicable."

The Prime Minister bolted upright. Schmidt noticed that his kindly eyes gleamed angrily under bushy brows. Chamberlain indignantly exclaimed he could not understand. This solution answered the very demands the Führer had made at Berchtesgaden. After hedging on the grounds that it was impossible to make a non-aggression pact with the Czechs before the claims of Poland and Hungary were satisfied, Hitler retaliated by criticizing the British-French proposal point by point, then peremptorily demanded that the Sudetenland be occupied by the Germans "forthwith."

Chamberlain replied that he was both disappointed and puzzled at such an attitude. This was a brand-new demand, going far beyond what Hitler had proposed at Berchtesgaden. He had returned to Germany with a plan that gave the Führer everything he wanted, doing so at the risk of his political career. At this point Sir Ivone Kirkpatrick handed the Prime Minister a note that German troop formations had just crossed the frontier at Eger. Chamberlain seized on this. There were bound to be such incidents, on both sides, he said and urged the Führer to join him in an effort to do "all that was humanly possible to settle matters in an orderly, peaceful way, and not to allow the work for peace to be disturbed by shootings and incidents." What proposal, he asked, could Hitler make so they could reach agreement in principle?

The answer chilled Chamberlain: immediate occupation of the Sudetenland by German troops with the frontier to be determined later by a plebiscite. Since this amounted to almost complete capitulation by the Czechs, an acrimonious, tedious debate followed which was spiced by the arrival of another message from Eger, this one to Hitler that twelve German hostages had been shot. The result, of course, was a dissertation by the Führer on the iniquity of the Czechs, followed by an avowal that, "if Prague fell under Bolshevik influence, or if hostages continued to be shot, he would intervene militarily at once."

After three hours the first conversation ended in complete discord but with the understanding that they would meet again on the morrow.

Despite a calm visage, the Prime Minister was still angry and indignant as he recrossed the Rhine and was driven up the mountain to his own hotel. Only then did he wonder if he had made a mistake by not breaking off the talks and going home. Was Hitler actually on the edge of madness, or a sort of Dr. Jekyll and Mr. Hyde? If so, it was Chamberlain's responsibility to break through the deadlock. The question was how to do it.

He was not the only one at the conference who doubted Hitler's sanity. At the Dreesen several newsmen were circulating a story that the Führer was so distraught over the Czech crisis that he would fling himself to the floor and chew the edge of the carpet. This report had been inspired by a remark of one Hitler aide that the Chief had become so furious that he was "eating the carpet." This slang expression was taken literally by some American correspondents, who should have translated it into "climbing the walls." Such naïveté amused Hitler's adjutants, who had seldom seen the Führer lose his temper. When he did, he occasionally went into a tirade for half an hour but usually his outbursts were brief. "I was present at quite a few such 'fits,' " wrote Wiedemann, "and all I can say is that they were no different from the displays of others with a hot temper and little self-control."

Some intimates believed the Führer displayed anger for effect. If so, his outbursts that afternoon had surely placed his opponent on the defensive. Chamberlain was already writing him a conciliatory letter. In it he suggested that he himself ask the Czechs whether they thought there could be an arrangement by which the Sudeten Germans themselves could maintain law and order.

After breakfast on the twenty-third this letter was sent across the river. In no mood for reconciliation, Hitler took it as a flat rejection of his ideas and, after long and "feverish" discussions with Ribbentrop and other advisers, composed an unfriendly reply which was a repetition of what he had said at the conference table. It was too long for a written translation and Hitler instructed Schmidt to deliver it in person and translate it verbally. The interpreter left the Dreesen about 3 P.M., a large brown envelope under his arm. On approaching the Petersberg Hotel, Schmidt noticed newsmen crowding around the entrance. One called out: "Do you bring peace or war?" Schmidt was careful to give no hint, not even a shrug of his shoulders. He was taken immediately to Chamberlain, who was waiting on the balcony. Moments earlier he and Henderson had been worriedly pacing but, in a remarkable exhibition of self-control, the Prime Minister greeted Schmidt as if it were only a casual occasion.

Upon the interpreter's return, Hitler's first words were anxious ones: "What did he say? How did he take my letter?" But he visibly relaxed upon learning that Chamberlain had shown no excitement or anger. Within the hour the ferry brought two emissaries from Chamberlain who solemnly delivered the Prime Minister's answer. It was a model of diplomacy, being simultaneously conciliatory and ominous. First Chamberlain promised to put Hitler's proposals before the Czechs and therefore requested a memorandum detailing Hitler's demands. Upon receipt of this document, he proposed returning to England.

The threat of departure must have spurred a second meeting. It was agreed that Chamberlain should return to the Dreesen that evening not only to pick up the memorandum but to listen to Hitler's explanation of it. Their conversation started about 10 P.M. and, since more participants were on hand, took place in a small dining room. Henderson, Kirkpatrick, Ribbentrop and Weizsäcker sat informally in a semicircle around Hitler and Chamberlain while Schmidt translated the memorandum. Hitler demanded withdrawal of all Czech armed forces from an area shown on an accompanying map. Evacuation would start on September 26 and the territory would be formally ceded to Germany on the twenty-eighth.

"But that's an ultimatum!" exclaimed Chamberlain, lifting his hands in protest.

"*Ein Diktat!*" chorused Henderson, who liked to display his German. Chamberlain refused to transmit such a document to the Czechs. Its tone, not to mention its content, would cause indignation among neutrals, he said, and began to scold Hitler as if he were a recalcitrant member of his own cabinet. It was one of the rare occasions when Hitler was placed on the defensive, and was followed by a concerted attack by the three British statesmen on the timetable of the proposal, which allowed the Czechs an impossibly short period to evacuate and turn over the Sudetenland. Impracticable and dangerous, it could lead to a European war.

During the ensuing deadlock an adjutant entered with a message for the Führer. After glancing at it he handed it to Schmidt, who translated it out loud in English: "Beneš has just announced over the wireless general mobilization of the Czechoslovak forces."

It was Hitler who finally broke the silence. "Despite this unheard-of provocation," he said in a barely audible voice, "I shall of course keep my promise not to proceed against Czechoslovakia during the course of negotiations—at any rate, Mr. Chamberlain, so long as you remain on German soil." This remark, misleading by being softly spoken, was followed by a statement that could not be misinterpreted. The Czech mobilization, he said tersely, settled the whole affair. Chamberlain hastily pointed out that mobilization was a precaution, not necessarily an offensive measure, but the Führer replied that so far as he was concerned mobilization was a clear indication that the Czechs did not intend to cede any territory. Again Chamberlain dissented. The Czechs, he argued, had agreed to the principle of self-determination in the Sudetenland and would not go back on their word.

Then why mobilize? persisted Hitler

Germany mobilized first, said the Prime Minister.

You call that mobilization? retorted the Führer sarcastically and made another threat: the crisis could not drag on very much longer. He quoted an old German proverb: "An end, even with terror, is better than terror without end." The memorandum, he said, represented his last word.

In that event, said Chamberlain, there was no purpose in further negotiations. "He would go home with a heavy heart, since he saw the final wreck of all his hopes for the peace of Europe. But his conscience was clear; he had done everything possible for peace. Unfortunately, he had not found an echo in Herr Hitler."

A walkout was the last thing Hitler wanted and he hastily reassured the British that he would not invade Czechoslovakia during the negotiations. It was as if a thunderstorm had cleared the atmosphere. "To please you, Mr. Chamberlain," he said after a short recess, "I will make a concession over the matter of the timetable. You are one of the few men for whom I have ever done such a thing. I will agree to October 1 as the date for evacuation."

After negotiating a number of other minor alterations, Chamberlain agreed to transmit the memorandum to the Czechs. It was one-thirty in the morning and the meeting adjourned. The Führer thanked the Prime Minister for his work on behalf of peace, assuring him that "the Czech problem was the last territorial demand which he had to make in Europe."

Chamberlain left with a hearty "Auf Wiedersehen!" and those who watched him stride out of the hotel could not discern the slightest strain of displeasure on his face.

5

After a few hours of needed sleep, Chamberlain flew back to England and the following day met with the full cabinet. It was necessary, he explained, to appreciate people's motives and see how their minds worked if one would understand their actions. Herr Hitler "would not deliberately deceive a man whom he respected and with whom he had been in negotiation." Consequently it would be a great tragedy if they "lost this opportunity of reaching an understanding with Germany on all points of difference between the two countries."

He told of his apprehension as he was flying home up the Thames, imagining a German bomber taking the same course: "I asked myself what degree of protection we could afford to the thousands of homes which I saw stretched out below me. And I felt that we are in no position to justify waging a war today in order to prevent a war hereafter."

Never had there been such opposition from the cabinet. First Lord of the Admiralty Duff Cooper could place no confidence in the Führer's promises and proposed an immediate general mobilization. Chamberlain urged his colleagues to postpone any such decision and it was agreed to first consult the French, who had already ordered a partial mobilization.

When the cabinet met again Sunday morning there was opposition from a new source. "I cannot rid my mind of the fact," confessed Foreign Secretary Halifax, "that Herr Hitler has given us nothing and that he is dictating terms, just as though he had won a war but without having had to fight." So long as Nazism lasted, peace was uncertain.

Lord Hailsham, an earlier supporter of Chamberlain, agreed with Halifax. An argument ensued. Lords Stanhope and Maugham wanted pressure put on the Czechs to accept the Hitler memorandum while Lord Winterton urged rejection of the proposals on the grounds of morality. In an effort to restore order in his deeply split cabinet, Chamberlain argued that it was wrong to talk of accepting or rejecting Hitler's terms, or even of feeling humiliated. It was up to the Czechs to accept or reject.

No sooner had this meeting ended in discord than Chamberlain was subjected to another harrowing experience. Jan Masaryk, the Czech ambassador, arrived with a bitter protest. His government, he said, was "amazed" at the contents of Hitler's memorandum. It was a de facto ultimatum which deprived Czechoslovakia of every safeguard for its national existence. "Against these new and cruel demands my government feels bound to make their utmost resistance and we shall do so, God helping."

That evening the French delegation was back in London to discuss the situation. Its leader, Daladier, declared that France could not recognize Hitler's right to seize the Sudetenland but would give only a vague response to Chamberlain's question: would France declare war if Hitler simply imposed on Czechoslovakia a frontier based on strategic considerations? When Chamberlain pressed for a more specific answer Daladier replied that France might "try a land offensive, after a period of concentration."

This meeting was adjourned for half an hour so that Chamberlain could consult with his cabinet. "I am unwilling to leave unexplored any possible chance of avoiding war," he told his colleagues. "Therefore I suggest that, basing myself on the personal conversations I have had with Herr Hitler, I should write a personal letter." It would be delivered to the Führer by Chamberlain's closest adviser, Sir Horace Wilson, and would contain a last appeal suggesting a joint commission to determine how to put into effect the proposals already accepted by the Czechs. "If the letter fails to secure any response from Herr Hitler, Sir Horace Wilson should be authorized to give a personal message from me to the effect that if this appeal was refused, France would go to war and if that happened, it seemed certain that we should be drawn in."

The following morning, September 26, Wilson, who shared some of Hitler's apprehension about Jews, set off for Berlin with the letter.* The Führer listened quietly but with growing restlessness until he heard how shocked the British public had been by the terms of his Godesberg memorandum, then he burst out, "It is no use talking any more!"

This did not stop Sir Horace, who—despite "gestures and exclamations of disgust and impatience" from Hitler—insisted that Schmidt continue reading the Chamberlain letter. When the interpreter came to the words "the Czechoslovakian government . . . regard as wholly unacceptable the proposal," Hitler leaped to his feet and started for the door, muttering again that it was useless to keep talking.

"It was an exceptional scene," recalled the interpreter, "especially as

* In 1968 Wilson told journalist Colin Cross that "he could understand Hitler's feelings on the Jews and put the question: 'Have you ever met a Jew you liked?'"

Hitler seemed to realize when he reached the door how impossible his behavior was, and returned to his seat like a defiant boy." He barely controlled himself so that Schmidt was able to finish the letter but then let himself go more violently than the interpreter had ever witnessed during a diplomatic interview. Hitler shouted that Germans were being treated like niggers. One wouldn't even treat Turks like that. "On 1 October I shall have Czechoslovakia where I want her!" he exclaimed, and if France and England decided to strike, let them. He didn't care a pfennig. Finally calm was restored and Hitler agreed to negotiate with the Czechs. He insisted, however, that they agree to accept the Godesberg memorandum within forty-eight hours. Come what may, he added, German troops would occupy the Sudetenland on the first of October.

The fury of the afternoon carried over that evening to the Sportpalast. Rarely if ever had Hitler spoken with such abandon or venom. His principal target was Beneš. "It is not so much a question of Czechoslovakia, it is a question of Herr Beneš!" It was he who was set on destroying the German minority; it was he who was putting his nation at the service of the Bolsheviks. "He now holds the decision in his hand. Peace or war! Either he will now accept this offer and at last give Germans their freedom, or we will take this freedom for ourselves!" All Germany— "a people vastly different from that of 1918!"—stood united with him. "We are determined! Let Herr Beneš choose!"

Hitler sat down. Up sprang Goebbels shouting, "One thing is sure: 1918 will never be repeated!" This brought the Führer to his feet again. Slamming right hand on the rostrum, he roared, "Ja!" then slumped to his seat, hair plastered to his forehead with sweat, exhausted.

The speech brought despair to those hoping for peace. In London workmen dug trenches near Buckingham Palace; air raid posters were pasted up. From Paris, Ambassador Bullitt, a personal friend of Roosevelt's, phoned Washington: "I believe the chances are about ninety-five in a hundred of war beginning midnight Friday." The President, who had also been getting words of appeasement from his ambassador in London, Joseph Kennedy, cabled Hitler an appeal (his second in two days) to continue the negotiations.

Chamberlain too issued another appeal to the Führer in the form of a statement to the press. The British, he said, would guarantee that the Czechs kept their promise to evacuate the Sudetenland so long as the Germans abstained from force. His envoy, Wilson, was back in the Reich chancellery late the next morning with this new proposal, but Hitler refused to discuss it. There were only two possibilities open to the Czechs: accept or refuse the German proposal. "And if they choose to refuse I shall smash Czechoslovakia!" He threatened to march into the Sudetenland if Beneš did not capitulate by 2 P.M. the next day.

Sir Horace suddenly rose and read out a short message which Schmidt translated as slowly and emphatically as possible so that Hitler could mark its purport: "If France, in fulfillment of her treaty obligations, should become actively involved in hostilities against Germany, the United Kingdom would deem itself obliged to support France."

Hitler was furious. "If France and England strike, let them do so. It's a matter of complete indifference to me. I am prepared for every eventuality. It is Tuesday today and by next Monday we shall all be at war."

Wilson wanted to continue the conversation but Henderson signaled him against doing so. Sir Horace did get one moment alone with the Führer before leaving and reiterated that a catastrophe must be avoided at all costs. "I will still try to make those Czechs sensible," he promised.

"I would welcome that," said Hitler and repeated emphatically that England could wish for no better friend than he.

Despite the fervor of last evening's crowd at the Sportpalast, William Shirer (broadcasting from the balcony) had noted in his diary that there was no war fever. "The crowd was *good-natured*, as if it didn't realize what his words meant." This was illustrated again late Wednesday afternoon when a motorized division rolled through Berlin. Rather than cheer, most of those leaving their offices ducked into subways and the few that remained at the curb watched in silence.

Captain Wiedemann also noticed this lack of public enthusiasm and when he walked into the chancellery loudly remarked: "It looks like a funeral march out there!" "Shh!" whispered an adjutant. "He is sitting right here by the window." Hitler pensively watched the procession. Finally someone heard him mutter: "I can't wage war with this nation yet." Perhaps it was with this in mind that he sent off a message to Chamberlain, one that, for him, was conciliatory.

In England, which was far less ready for war than Germany, the Prime Minister was preparing himself for a broadcast to the nation. Criticism of appeasement was on the rise and he too was assailed with doubts. "I am wobbling about all over the place," he remarked just before he walked up to the microphone at 8 P.M.—the same moment the order for mobilization of the British fleet was issued—and bared some of his apprehension to the public. "How horrible," he said, "how fantastic, how incredible it is that we should be trying on gas-masks here because of a quarrel in a faraway country between people of whom we know nothing! It seems all the more impossible that a quarrel which has already been settled in principle should be the subject of war." He proceeded to prepare the people for more concessions. "I am myself a man of peace to the depths of my soul. Armed conflict between nations is a nightmare to me; but if I were convinced that any nation had made up its mind to dominate the world by force, I should feel that it must be resisted. Under such a domination, life for people who believe in liberty would not be worth living: but war is a fearful thing, and we must be very clear, before we embark on it, that it is really the great issues that are at stake."

Two hours later the Prime Minister's hopes were raised by the latest letter from Hitler. After opening with the usual diatribe against the Czechs, it concluded with an oblique suggestion that Chamberlain continue his efforts to "bring the government in Prague to reason at the very last hour." To the despairing Chamberlain it seemed the gap was narrowing and he hastily scribbled a draft reply inviting himself to another rendezvous. "I feel convinced that we could reach agreement in a week. . . . I cannot believe that you will take the responsibility of starting a world war, which may end civilization, for the sake of a few days' delay in settling this long-standing problem."

He then composed a personal message to Mussolini telling of this last appeal to the Führer. "I trust Your Excellency will inform the German Chancellor that you are willing to be represented and urge him to agree to my proposal, which will keep all our peoples out of war." And so, with reborn hope, he worked till long after midnight preparing the speech he was to make to Parliament in the morning, the day on which Herr Hitler's ultimatum would expire.

That dreaded day, Wednesday, September 28, started in frenzy at the core of the crisis, Berlin. At 8 A.M. French Ambassador François-Poncet phoned Weizsäcker urgently requesting an audience with the Führer so that he could present new suggestions. Weizsäcker hastened to the Kaiserhof Hotel where his own chief was staying. But Ribbentrop was so annoyed "at the prospect of his game being upset, this time from Paris," that a violent scene resulted.

"It is a monstrous thing," said the subordinate, according to his account, "that you should want to start a war when the real differences between the two sides are so small and are concerned only with the method by which the Sudetenland should be incorporated."

"You should leave that to the Führer!" exclaimed Ribbentrop, and in this mood the two set off for the chancellery.

At 10 A.M., four hours before Hitler's ultimatum would end, François-Poncet telephoned Henderson to report that he feared the worst. His request to see Hitler was still unanswered; apparently the Führer was not receiving ambassadors today. Henderson promised to do what he could. First he phoned Göring to inform him of Hitler's refusal to see François-Poncet, who had fresh proposals on which war or peace depended. Göring cut him short. So recently the aggressor in Vienna, he was now playing the role of peacemaker. "You need not say a word more," he said, "I am going immediately to the Führer."

Never had Schmidt seen such hectic activity at the chancellery. "Ministers and Generals, with their train of Party members, aides-de-camp, officers and heads of departments, who had hurried round to consult Hitler, were sitting or standing everywhere." Hitler wandered from group to group expounding his views at length but not listening to a word of advice. He had retired to the winter garden for privacy when Göring finally arrived to make his appeal for reason. Noticing Neurath in the anteroom, the Reichsmarschall persuaded the former Foreign Minister to join him, but once in the conference room it was Neurath who carried the burden of argument. "Mein Führer," he began, "do you wish to start a war under any circumstances? Of course not!"

Ribbentrop was hovering outside the winter garden, hoping to be invited in. Then Göring came out and belligerently strode over to him shouting, "Herr von Ribbentrop, if war should break out, I will be the first one to tell the German people that you pushed things to this end!" To the edification of the adjutants and aides, these two high officials began exchanging threats and insults. At one point Ribbentrop accused his opponent of fearing combat and Göring roared back that as soon as the Führer said "March!" he would take off in the leading airplane—on condition that Ribbentrop sat beside him! "If the situation had not been so serious," recalled Wiedemann, "it would have been comical to see the two insulted 'primadonnas' clawing at each other as often happens on stage before the final rehearsal."

A little after 11 A.M. Ribbentrop was finally admitted into the winter garden so that he could be present during the delayed interview with François-Poncet. Flourishing a map, the French ambassador prophesied that an attack on Czechoslovakia would spread throughout Europe. "You are naturally confident of winning the war just as we believe that we can defeat you. But why should you take the risk when your essential demands can be met without war?"

It was apparent that François-Poncet's arguments were gradually tilting the balance in favor of peace. No longer did Hitler flare up nor could he answer the Frenchman's logic. All at once an adjutant interrupted. Ambassador Attolico was outside with an urgent message from Rome. As soon as Attolico saw the Führer emerge from the winter garden he shouted unceremoniously from a distance that he had an urgent message from Mussolini! "Il Duce informs you that, whatever you decide, Führer, Fascist Italy stands behind you." Catching his breath, he added, "Il Duce is, however, of the opinion that it would be wise to accept the British proposal, and begs you to refrain from mobilization."

"Tell Il Duce that I accept his proposal," said Hitler, then returned to the winter garden to inform François-Poncet that Mussolini had just asked whether he would accept his counsel—failing, however, to add that he had agreed to do so. The two continued their conversation but Hitler's attention kept wavering. It was obvious that he was still pondering Il Duce's message and before long he got to his feet, indicating the interview was over. François-Poncet asked whether he should advise his government that the Führer was inflexible. Distractedly Hitler replied that he would give an answer early in the afternoon.

The parade to the winter garden continued. A few minutes past noon Henderson made his way through the crowd in the reception room. "It is going better," a German friend whispered to him. "Only stick to it." In the conference room Hitler listened patiently while Schmidt translated Chamberlain's offer to come to Berlin at once for a conference; he then replied that he must first communicate with Mussolini.

Il Duce seconded the idea. He suggested that they all meet in Munich. Hitler agreed and invitations were hastily dispatched to Daladier and Chamberlain. The one to the latter arrived while he was addressing the House of Commons and Queen Mary, who was in the gallery with Halifax, Baldwin and other notables. Chamberlain had just announced Hitler's acceptance of Mussolini's suggestion to delay mobilization and during the resultant mutter of approval the Chancellor of the Exchequer passed him a slip of paper. The Prime Minister's face was transformed. In a broken voice he continued: "That is not all. I have something further to say to the House yet. I have now been informed by Herr Hitler that he invites me to meet him at Munich tomorrow morning. He has also invited Signor Mussolini and M. Daladier." Some unidentified member shouted: "Thank God for the Prime Minister!" thereby touching off an unprecedented demonstration of hysterical shouting. Queen Mary, a symbol of self-control, wept without restraint as did the Duchess of Kent and Mrs. Chamberlain. "From all sides," wrote Sir John Simon in his memoirs, "there was impetuous cheering, in which few failed to join, and we adjourned almost at once by common consent. I saw men, some of whom have since spoken slightingly of what Chamberlain was trying to do, cross the floor in tears and with unrestrained emotion grasp him by the hand." One of the few members of Commons not overcome by the moment was

Winston Churchill. "And what about Czechoslovakia?" he was heard to mutter bitterly. "Does no one think of asking their opinion?"

With few exceptions the people of the democracies shared the relief. In the streets of Paris, London and New York jubilant crowds read the extras proclaiming the end of the crisis. From Paris, Ambassador Bullitt wrote his friend Roosevelt, "I am so relieved this evening that I feel like embracing everyone and wish I were in the White House to give you a large kiss on your bald spot." And from Washington the President dispatched a two-word cable to Chamberlain: GOOD MAN.

From another President, Beneš, the Prime Minister received a longer message, this a plea: "I ask Mr. Chamberlain very earnestly for help because it is our real desire to contribute to peace. I beg therefore that nothing may be done in Munich without Czechoslovakia being heard."

While most Germans were equally relieved, the anti-Hitler group was dismayed. The news scotched their latest scheme to seize Hitler by force and set up a military regime. When Halder learned of the Munich meeting he could "no longer see his way clear to set the Putsch apparatus in operation under such circumstances."

At 6 P.M. Il Duce's luxurious train left Rome to enthusiastic cheers. He was in an expansive mood, for he was not only being hailed around the world as the savior of peace but had managed to win Hitler's gratitude by supporting him through the crisis. Mussolini also felt he had scored a diplomatic victory over the British and ridiculed them good-naturedly at dinner with Ciano. "In a country where animals are adored to the point of making cemeteries and hospitals and houses for them, and legacies are bequeathed to parrots, you can be sure that decadence has set in. Besides, other reasons apart, it is also a consequence of the composition of the English people. Four million surplus women. Four million women sexually unsatisfied, artificially creating a host of problems in order to excite or appease their senses. Not being able to embrace one man, they embrace humanity."

6

Early the following morning, September 29, the Führer met Mussolini between Munich and the border. Beyond being a mark of courtesy to an ally, it gave Hitler an opportunity to bring Il Duce up to date on the latest developments. As the two dictators headed for the Bavarian capital in the Führer's train, Hitler revealed that, with the Westwall completed, he feared no attack from that quarter. If England and France were foolish enough to make an assault, the war would be over before the enemy could complete mobilization. "I have no need to mobilize. The German army stands ready and asks only to be allowed to realize my aims."

The other two conferees were Munich-bound by air. Chamberlain left Heston in a slight rain after telling journalists, "When I was a little boy, I used to repeat, 'If at first you don't succeed, try, try again!' This is what I am doing. When I come back I hope I may be able to say, as Hotspur says in *Henry IV*, 'out of this nettle, danger, we pluck this flower, safety.' "

To the shouts of "Long live Daladier!" and "Long live peace!" the French Premier boarded his plane at Le Bourget. It took off in a milky fog. At 11:15 A.M. the twin-motored plane set down at Munich's airport. François-Poncet watched Daladier descend, brow deeply furrowed with wrinkles. He had left a tense, fearful city and was surprised to find the Germans exuberant. They greeted him as a hero with enthusiastic hails.

Chamberlain landed a few minutes before noon and he too got a joyous reception on his trip to the Regina Palace Hotel. He was there only for minutes before taking off in an open car for the newly built Führerbau where the conference would take place. In the complex of National Socialist buildings clustered around the Königsplatz, it was a compact but monumental stone structure with a spacious central hall, sixty-five feet high and a hundred feet wide, from which two impressive stone staircases curved up to the conference room.

Chamberlain and his two colleagues, all in black suits, arrived first. Next came Mussolini, advancing with lively step, his chest thrown out, completely at ease, and patronizing, as if he were the host. The last to arrive was the Führer. The hard, strange look in his eyes impressed Daladier. The conferees and their aides congregated around a buffet set up in a salon, shaking hands courteously but coldly as they surveyed each other. Hitler did his best to be affable but his brows were furrowed with concern since most of his guests spoke no German and he was unable to communicate with them freely. At last the stilted buffet was over and Hitler led the way into a large rectangular room overlooking the Königsplatz. It was an impressive room with leather-covered walls, a profusion of green plants and paintings and a huge marble fireplace over which hung the imposing portrait of Bismarck by Lenbach.

Hastily prepared and poorly organized, the conference began in confusion and became increasingly muddled. With no chairman, no agenda or agreed procedure, it splintered into a series of involved individual discussions. At one point Hitler became so restive at Chamberlain's nagging concern over the matter of compensating the Czechs for property in the

Sudetenland that he shouted, "Our time is too valuable to be wasted on such trivialities!"

Mussolini brought some degree of order into the proceedings by submitting a written proposal for the solution of the Sudeten question which he presented as his own even though the Germans had drafted it. By then it was 3 P.M. and there was a recess for lunch. The proceedings were even more chaotic after the bolted meal. Often three or four would talk at once, making Schmidt's task almost impossible. He would have to insist that the preceding translation be heard first and, to friends watching in amusement through glassed doors, he looked like a schoolmaster trying to keep an unruly class in order. To complicate matters, outsiders began to invade the room. One by one Göring, François-Poncet, Henderson, Attolico and Weizsäcker wandered in with legal clerks, secretaries and adjutants. They all crowded around the principals, who were grouped in a semicircle before the huge fireplace, until it looked like a high-stake game of chance.

Il Duce had taken command of the proceedings. The other three principals could speak only their own language, while he held forth in all four. Although his English was laborious, his French Italianate, and his German questionable, he took over as interpreter-general, a dictatorial but amiable director of an undisciplined chorus. He would ask Hitler a question in German, get the answer and then summarize the meaning rather than the exact words for the French and English delegations. "That was my great day," he later told SS Captain Eugen Dollmann, whom he had brought along as an interpreter. "All eyes were on me, not on Mr. Daladier or Mr. Chamberlain. It was an occasion worthy of the Caesars—do you remember?"

As the evening approached the atmosphere in the room grew thicker. Finally the British introduced their own proposal, generally acceptable except on the plebiscite in the Sudetenland and an international guarantee of Czechoslovakia's new borders. At the height of this prolonged but not particularly caustic discussion Dollmann was summoned from the room: a mysterious veiled woman demanded his presence. In the guardroom he found the wife of Ambassador Attolico, who demanded that he "immediately and without delay" ask Herr Hitler how the conference was going. She explained that she had promised the Madonna in the Pilgrim's Church at Loreto to bring back a fat golden candle if the conference went well and world peace was preserved. Her train was leaving in half an hour. Dollmann said he could not possibly accost the Führer but would ask Il Duce or Ciano. They would not do; she instructed him to find out from Himmler, who knew everything. Left with no alternative, Dollmann

finally located the Reichsführer. "His initial surprise gave way to amusement. He authorized me to announce that peace was assured."

Agreement did seem assured but there were still a number of points
to clarify. It was already 8 P.M. and Hitler was becoming impatient. He
had arranged an elaborate banquet to conclude the conference and the
food was getting cold. He suggested they adjourn for dinner since the discussion would probably go on for several hours more. The British and
French turned down the invitation on the grounds that they had to telephone their governments but Schmidt felt it was because they were in no
mood to attend a banquet. "They had secured peace, but at the price of a
serious loss of prestige." The British hurried off to the Hotel Regina, while
the French returned to the Four Seasons where they had food sent up to
their rooms. In the meantime the Germans and Italians were celebrating a
victory at the Führerbau with champagne and a variety of delicacies.

It was a few minutes past ten by the time the four principals and
their advisers were again seated at the fireplace. After extensive redrafting
and tedious delays that continued until past midnight, agreement was
finally reached. "Actually the whole thing was a cut-and-dried affair,"
Göring later told an American psychologist. "Neither Chamberlain nor
Daladier was the least bit interested in sacrificing or risking anything to
save Czechoslovakia. That was clear as day to me. The fate of
Czechoslovakia was essentially sealed in three hours. Then they argued for
hours more about the word 'guarantee.' Chamberlain kept hedging.
Daladier hardly paid any attention at all. He just sat there like this."
(Göring slumped down and assumed a bored expression.) "All he did was
nod approval from time to time. Not the slightest objection to anything. I
was simply amazed at how easily the thing was managed by Hitler. After
all, they knew that Skoda, etc., had munition plants in the Sudetenland,
and Czechoslovakia would be at our mercy. . . . When he suggested that
certain armaments which were across the Sudeten border should be
brought into the Sudeten territory as soon as we take it over, I thought
there would be an explosion. But no—not a peep. We got everything we
wanted; just like that." (He snapped his fingers.)

At 1:30 A.M. an acceptable document was ceremoniously placed on a
mahogany table next to a huge, elaborate inkwell. The pact provided for a
four-stage evacuation of the Sudetenland to begin on October 1. An international commission would determine which districts were to hold plebiscites and make final determination of the borders.

Hitler appeared satisfied. The first to sign, he found the pretentious
inkwell empty and a substitute had to be hastily provided. The last to arrive, the Führer was the first to leave and William Shirer was struck by

"the light of victory in Hitler's eyes as he strutted down the broad steps" of the Führerbau.

It was some time before Chamberlain and Daladier left and it was their painful duty to inform the two Czech representatives, anxiously waiting off stage throughout the long day, of the fate of their country. They were brought to Chamberlain's room at the Regina about 2:15 A.M. The atmosphere was oppressive as the Czechs waited for sentence to be passed. Chamberlain made a long introductory speech, then, as Daladier was handing over a copy of the agreement, he began yawning. One of the Czechs was in tears. "Believe me," François-Poncet consoled him, "all this is not final. It is but one moment in a story which has just begun and which will soon bring up the issue again."

Daladier wakened to the cheers of a delirious and vocal crowd outside his hotel. They sang songs and called for "dear little Daladier" until he came out to the balcony.

Later in the morning Chamberlain was given an ovation by the Müncheners as he drove in an open car to Hitler's apartment for a final informal talk. The Prime Minister had come on a personal mission of vital import. He had composed a short statement hopefully to be signed by himself and Hitler. It went far beyond the documents promulgated at the Führerbau and expressed a determination never to go to war with one another again. "If he signs it," he told his Parliamentary Secretary at breakfast, "and sticks to it that will be fine, but if he breaks it that will convince the Americans of the kind of man he is."

When Hitler heard a translation of the memorandum, he exclaimed, "Ja! Ja!" and without ado the two affixed their signatures. Chamberlain handed over one copy and kept another, convinced that Hitler was as enthusiastic as he. But Schmidt had the feeling that he had agreed to the wording with a certain reluctance and signed it only to please Chamberlain. Hitler, it seemed, made a practice of spreading conflicting impressions. Once alone with his valet, he exulted that the Prime Minister, an old man, had traveled all the way just to see him. "I gave him a noseful. He won't be visiting me again soon." Yet a moment later he gave Major Gerhard Engel, his army adjutant, the impression that he "liked the old gentleman and wanted to continue negotiations with him." Hitler assured Engel that he himself was "not considering taking any steps that would be potentially dangerous. First gains had to be digested. The solution to the Polish question would not run away."

It was 5:38 P.M. when Chamberlain's plane touched down at Heston. He stood in the open doorway, smiling as he waved the document he and Hitler had signed. "I've got it!" he shouted at Halifax. "I've got it!" With the roar of the crowd in his ears, Chamberlain read a letter from the King asking him to "come straight to Buckingham Palace, so that I can express to you personally my most heartfelt congratulations on the success of your visit to Munich."

On the trip from airport to palace he was given a hero's welcome, rare in the history of England. The streets, as he described in a private letter, "were lined from one end to the other with people of every class, shouting themselves hoarse, leaping on the running board, banging on the windows, and thrusting their hands into the car to be shaken." It seemed that all England wanted to congratulate and thank him. "No conqueror returning from a victory on the battlefield," commented the London *Times*, "had come adorned with nobler laurels."

He was engulfed in front of 10 Downing Street and when the screaming throng refused to disperse he came to an open window. The cheering intensified, finally turning into a raucous rendition of "For he's a jolly good fellow!" Chamberlain stood beaming at the window, the same one at which Disraeli had announced "peace with honour" on returning from the Berlin Congress of 1878. "This is the second time in our history," he said, "that there has come back from Germany to Downing Street peace with honour. I believe it is peace for our time."

The weeks of crisis were at last over and the English, with few exceptions, were unrestrained in their joy but there was no celebration in Prague when the new premier, General Jan Syrovy, announced over the radio that his government had been forced to accept the Munich Diktat since they had been deserted and stood alone. It was a choice, he said, "between a reduction of our territory and the death of the nation."

7

Mussolini also received an ovation, perhaps the greatest, in his own opinion, of the entire twenty years of Fascism. At every station and grade crossing multitudes awaited his train, many on their knees, to acclaim him. He was given a Caesar's welcome in Rome as his open car traveled down the Via Nazionale, passing under a triumphal arch of leaves and branches. Upon entering the Palazzo Venezia the mob in the piazza began chanting "Du-ce! Du-ce!" The spontaneous roar, when he at last appeared on the balcony, indicated that perhaps never before had he enjoyed such popularity.

Still, through the world Chamberlain was the most honored of those who met at Munich. His lean figure and hawk nose had become a household symbol of peace. Former Crown Prince Wilhelm sent him a secret letter of thanks "for saving the peace," and the ex-Kaiser wrote Queen Mary with indelible pencil that he had not the slightest doubt that the Prime Minister "was inspired by heaven and guided by God" in averting "a most fearful catastrophe." Most Germans shared the sentiment and awoke on the first of October with the prayer that no incident impede the march of their troops into the Sudetenland. The Führer's train arrived at the Czech border before dawn and Reichenau, the first of the generals to pledge allegiance to Hitler, reported with words that astounded Wiedemann: "Mein Führer, the army today is making the greatest sacrifice that soldiers can make to their supreme commander, namely to march into enemy territory without firing a shot."

Wiedemann could not believe that a German general could make such a ridiculous remark. Then another general chimed in: "Yes, mein Führer, I was with my old regiment this morning. The men were weeping for being forbidden to attack the Czech bunkers!"

"And all along," said Hitler, "those defeatists tried to tell me that my politics would lead to war!" This, delivered in a sharp tone, alarmed Wiedemann, who stood directly behind him. Whom did he mean by defeatists?

At Chequers the tension and exhaustion of the past hours were just catching up with Chamberlain. "I came nearer there to a nervous breakdown than I have ever been in my life," he confessed in a letter. "I have pulled myself together, for there is a fresh ordeal to go through in the House." It came on Monday, October 3. By then the high emotion had worn off for many and relief at deliverance from war was being replaced by humiliation. Duff Cooper opened the debate over Munich in the Commons by tendering his resignation from the cabinet. A European war would follow the invasion of Czechoslovakia, he said. "The Prime Minister has believed in addressing Herr Hitler through the language of sweet reasonableness. I have believed that he was more open to the language of the mailed fist."

Obviously tired and irritable, Chamberlain rose to reply that the agreement he had signed with Hitler in the Führer's flat was extremely significant. There was sincerity and good will on both sides and it would be extremely difficult for Hitler to take back the emphatic declarations he had made. He was applauded but without enthusiasm, for a feeling of guilt pervaded the House. The debate continued for three days with the denunciations climaxed by an eloquent damnation from Churchill. "All is over," he said. "Silent, mournful, abandoned, broken Czechoslovakia recedes into the darkness." He did not begrudge the loyal, brave people of Britain their natural and spontaneous outburst of joy and relief on learning of the pact. "But they should know the truth. They should know that there has been gross neglect and deficiency in our defences. They should know that we have sustained a great defeat without a war, the consequences of which will travel far with us. . . . And do not suppose that this is the end. This is only the beginning of the reckoning."

Chamberlain and his co-appeasers had sought a new revisionist settlement in East Central Europe which Hitler would underwrite. But now it was obvious that the Führer's program ran counter to this and no accommodation had ever been possible. Already Chamberlain and his umbrella were becoming the symbol of pusillanimity, and such was his concern that he sought help from Adolf Hitler. He dispatched a secret message wondering if the Führer, who was to make a speech at the Sportpalast that evening, "could give the Prime Minister some support in forming public opinion in Britain." Hitler obliged, launching a blistering attack on Chamberlain's detractors in the House. But aid and comfort from such a dubious source were not necessary. The following day, October 6, the House of Commons hastily approved Chamberlain's policy "by which war was averted in the recent crisis." The vote was 366 to 144 with some 35 dissidents—including Cooper, Eden and Churchill—abstaining.

The attack of those three had far greater effect in Berlin where every word launched at Chamberlain was taken as a personal insult by Hitler. He had come out of the Führerbau after signing the pact pleased—so agreed his adjutants and aides—convinced that the Czech problem was solved once and for all, and he intended to keep his part of the bargain.

The chorus of condemnation in England changed all that. There were already whispers in the Wilhelmstrasse that Ribbentrop and Himmler were taking advantage of Hitler's annoyance to persuade him that Germany had not fully exploited the Western democracies' fear of war at Munich and that England only negotiated to gain time so she could strike later when better armed.

Aware of this discontent, François-Poncet did his best "to calm Hitler down" by suggesting he sign an agreement with France similar to the one concluded with Chamberlain. "I wished to flash before his eyes the possibility of further agreements, economic and financial, which might lead to a future organization in Europe; I hoped to direct his mind toward prospects and in directions other than those of violence."

But Hitler was convinced, or allowed himself to be convinced, that he had been deceived by perfidious Albion. On October 9 he publicly displayed these feelings in a bitter speech at Saarbrücken comparing the British attitude to that of a governess. He went on to attack that malevolent trio of Churchill, Cooper and Eden, far surpassing the acidity of the Sportpalast speech.

The effects of his diatribe were felt three days later when the International Commission selected to implement the Munich agreement voted unanimously to dispense with plebiscites. Its members had already bowed to German demands that the 1910 census be used in determining those districts to be ceded to the Reich and it was becoming increasingly obvious that the original pact was being contorted to strip Czechoslovakia of her last defensive line of fortifications.

François-Poncet made a final appeal for reason to Hitler in mid-October. The occasion was his farewell to the Führer, he was being transferred to Rome. Hitler had always liked him and showed his appreciation for seven years' service in Berlin by inviting the French ambassador to his mile-high mountain tea house atop the Kehlstein. Built under the direction of the indefatigable Bormann at a reported cost of thirty million marks, it was a remarkable engineering feat. Equally so was the five-mile winding asphalt road from the Berghof which had been blasted out of the side of the mountain at the cost of several lives. François-Poncet was driven up this road to an undergound passage dug into the peak. At the end of the corridor he was escorted into a copper-lined elevator, its shaft hacked out of solid rock. After a ride of about four hundred feet, François-Poncet found himself in a gallery of Roman pillars. Beyond was an immense glassed-in circular hall. Great logs were burning in a huge open fireplace. On all sides extended such an immense panorama of mountains that it gave the Frenchman a sensation of being suspended in space. The entire view, bathed in the autumn twilight, was grandiose, almost hallucinating.

In this fantastic setting—which was already palling on Hitler after several visits because of its grandiosity—ambassador and Führer held their last interview. Pale and drawn, the latter confirmed his disappointment with the aftermath of the Munich agreement. The crisis was far from over; in fact, threatened to worsen if the situation did not improve. Great Britain, he complained, was "sonorous with threats and calls to arms."

The ambassador pointed out that a reaction was inevitable after the excess of joy following the preservation of peace. Furthermore, Hitler's own harsh speech at Saarbrücken had spread the impression that the sacrifice of Czechoslovakia had only increased Germany's appetite and thereby strengthened the position of the adversaries of the Munich pact.

Hitler protested. It was the British who had started the present trouble. Nor had he uttered a word against France. As he went on to defend his treatment of the Czechs, François-Poncet interrupted, urging him not to linger over the past. The future was more important. The democracies and the totalitarian states must now demonstrate that they could live side by side in peace "and gradually lead Europe towards more normal and enduring conditions." Hitler objected neither to the interruption nor to the concept. He was quite prepared, he said, to do this.

As they descended the mountain François-Poncet reviewed the conversation. "I know that he is changeable, dissembling, full of contradictions, uncertain," he reported to Paris. "The same man with the debonair aspect, with a real fondness for the beauties of nature, who discussed reasonable ideas on European politics around the tea table, is also capable of the worst frenzies, of the wildest exaltations, and the most delirious ambitions. There are days when, standing before the globe of the world, he will overthrow nations, continents, geography and history, like a demiurge stricken with madness. At other moments, he dreams of being the hero of an everlasting peace, in which he would devote himself to the erection of the most magnificent monuments."

These apparent conflicts within the Führer were leading many foreigners to conclude that he was simply insane. One was Sigmund Freud, now safely established in London. "You cannot tell what a madman will do," he told an American admirer. "You know he is an Austrian and lived for years in great misery." When Hitler took over that country it seemed to go to his head.

A former disciple had a far different theory and that October in Zurich expounded it to H. R. Knickerbocker, who had just come from Prague. "Hitler belongs in the category of the truly mystic medicine man," said Dr. Carl Gustav Jung, who had spent hours discussing the Führer with Ernst Hanfstaengl immediately after the latter's escape from Germany. "His body does not suggest strength. The outstanding characteristic of his physiognomy is its dreamy look. I was especially struck by that when I saw pictures taken of him in the Czechoslovakian crisis; there was in his eyes the look of a seer." This prompted Knickerbocker to ask why Hitler made nearly every German fall down and worship him, yet made little impression on foreigners. "He is the first man to tell every German what he has been thinking and feeling all along in his unconscious about German fate, especially since the defeat in the World War, and the one characteristic which colors every German soul is the typically German inferiority complex, the complex of the younger brother, of the one who is always a bit late to the feast. Hitler's power is not political; it is *magic*." Hitler's secret was that he allowed himself to be moved by his own unconscious. He was like a man who listens intently to whispered suggestions from a mysterious voice and "then *acts upon them*. In our case, even if occasionally our unconscious does reach us through dreams, we have too much rationality, too much cerebrum to obey it—but Hitler listens and obeys. The true leader is always *led*." Hitler sang a purely Teutonic song which rang true to Germans and they chose him as their representative. He was the demagogue appealing to the primitive, an echo from their own tribal past.

Jung predicted that England and France would not honor their new guarantee to the Czechs. "No nation keeps its word. A nation is a big, blind worm, following what? Fate perhaps. A nation has no honor, it has no word to keep." Therefore, why expect Hitler to keep his word? "Because Hitler is the nation."

Notes

BA	Bundesarchiv, Koblenz
BFP	*Documents on British Foreign Policy*
BH	Bayerisches Hauptstaatsarchiv, München
CAB	British Cabinet Papers
CIC-PH	CIC interview with Paula Hitler, June 5, 1946. U. S. Army Military History Research Collection, Carlisle Barracks, Pa.
EGD	*The Early Goebbels Diaries*
GFP	*Documents on German Foreign Policy*
HA	Hauptarchiv der NSDAP
HBN	Maser, *Hitlers Briefe und Notizen*
HH	Fritz Hesse, *Hitler and the English*
HSB	OSS *Hitler Source Book*
HSC	*Hitler's Secret Conversations*
IMT	International Military Tribunal, Nuremberg
MK	*Mein Kampf*, Houghton Mifflin edition
MY	Hanfstaengl, *The Missing Years*
NA	National Archives, Washington
ND	Nuremberg Document
NSR	*Nazi-Soviet Relations, 1939–41*
OCMH	Office, Chief of Military History, U. S. Army, Washington, D.C.
PHP	Protokoll des Hitler-Prozesses
TAH	*The Testament of Adolf Hitler*
TMWC	*Trial of the Major War Criminals before the International Military Tribunal*
VB	*Völkischer Beobachter*

Prologue STAB IN THE BACK

page xii
"It caught him by the throat . . ." Heinz 83.
page xii
"It was still stinking of the stuff . . ." Heinz 83.
page xii
"with pride I can say our regiment . . ." Letter to Josef Popp, Dec. 4, 1914.
page xiii
"the poison of the hinterland . . ." Interview with Ignaz Westenkirchner by
    Julius Hagemann in Harry Schulze-Wilde Collection.
page xiii
"If my attack on Rheims succeeds . . ." Chambers 84.
page xiv
"the piercing in my sockets . . ." MK 203.
page xv
Information on Dr. Forster comes from a Restricted U. S. Navy Intelligence
    Report, declassified for the author in 1972, from the OSS files at the Na-
    tional Archives. Entitled "A Psychiatric Study of Hitler," it was written in
    1943 by Dr. Karl Kronor, a former Viennese nerve specialist. Apparently
    present at the original medical examination of Hitler at Pasewalk, he re-
    ported Dr. Forster's findings along with a definition of a psychopath as
    "mental inferiority usually conditioned by hereditary disposition, and dis-
    tinguished especially by weakness of will and inability to adapt oneself to
    society. It produces in consequence a tendency to misdemeanor and crime."
    Further information on Dr. Forster from Dr. Rudolph Binion: Letters and
    article in *History of Childhood Quarterly* 203–6.
page xv
"Now they raised the red rag in the homeland." MK 203.
page xv
"I lay there broken with great pain . . ." Record of Hitler's trial in Munich,
    Feb. 16, 1924. PHP.
page xv
"seemed all a-tremble . . ." MK 203–4
page xv
"But now I could not help it . . ." Ibid. 204.
pages xv–xvi
"The great vacillation of my life . . ." PHP, Feb. 16, 1924.
page xvi
"a psychopath with hysterical symptoms." U. S. Navy Intelligence Report
    31963, NA.
page xvi
Hitler's "supernatural vision." HSB 901; Karl H. von Wiegand, "Hitler Fore-
    sees His End," *Cosmopolitan*, Apr. 1939, 152; *Frankfurter Zeitung*, Jan.
    27, 1923, 1; Ludwell Denny, "France and the German Counter-Revolu-
    tion," *The Nation*, Mar. 14, 1923, 295; Adolf-Viktor von Koerber, *Adolf
    Hitler. Sein Leben und seine Reden* (Munich, 1923), p. 6–7.

Chapter One. DEEP ARE THE ROOTS

page 4
"laced his tiny knapsack." MK 5.

pages 3–5
Information on Schicklgruber birth register from documents in Ph. D. dissertations, University of Vienna, at Institut für Zeitgeschichte, Vienna.

page 7
"my husband was already on duty again." Jetzinger 41.

page 8
"He was very strict . . ." from interview with Fräulein Schichtl in NA, HA, File 17, Reel 1.

pages 8–9
"shabby and primitive . . . in exemplary order." Jetzinger 57.

page 9
"It was at this time . . . a little ringleader." MK 5–6.

page 9
"unmercifully with a hippopotamus whip . . . dog would cringe and wet the floor." HSB 924 and 913.

page 9
"He was imperious . . . over any triviality." Gilbert, *Psychology*, 18.

page 10
"solemn splendor of brilliant church festivals," MK 6.

page 12
"as a small boy it was his most ardent wish . . ." Interview with Helene Hanfstaengl, 1971.

page 13
"who challenged my father to extreme harshness . . ." CIC-PH.

page 13
"Toga boy" incident: Interview with Helene Hanfstaengl, 1971.

page 13
"I then resolved never again to cry . . ." Zoller 55.

page 14
"It was not long before . . ." MK 6.

page 14
"Woods and meadows were the battlefields . . ." Ibid. 9.

page 15
"I thought that once my father saw . . ." Ibid. 10.

page 15
"We all liked him . . ." Heinz 25.

pages 15–16
"Bismarck was for us a national hero . . ." Ibid. 26.

page 16
"You are not German . . ." Interview with Josef Keplinger, 1971.

page 16
"Let the Reich's enemy now appear . . ." Remak 14.

pages 16–17
"The sharp words that fell . . ." Jetzinger 53.

page 17
"a great artist," Bradley Smith, *Adolf Hitler*, 100.
page 17
"Why, Adolf, what on earth do you suppose you are doing?" Heinz 26–27.
pages 17–18
Hitler's play with the Schmidt children, including all quotes: Interviews with
    Maria Schmidt Koppensteiner and Johann Schmidt in Oct. 1938, HA, File
    17, Reel 1.
page 18
"complete waste of time." HSC 625.
page 18
"He had definite talent . . . not uncommon amongst immature youths." Jet-
    zinger 68–69.
page 19
"Even today I think back with gentle emotion . . ." MK 14.
page 19
"none was so sulky and surly . . . a fearful row!" Jetzinger 74–75.
page 19
"I often used to practice shooting rats from the window." HSC 201.
pages 19–20
Footnote: Poem in BA, R43 II/957 p. 71, courtesy of Dr. Eberhard Jäckel.
page 20
"I've completely forgotten what happened . . ." HSC 202.
pages 20–21
Hitler's health: CIC-PH
page 21
"What a horror of a film!" HSC 202.
pages 21–22
Kubizek-Hitler quotes: Kubizek 11–13, 26–27.
page 22
Life at the Humboldtstrasse: CIC-PH.
pages 22–23
Hitler postcards: Kubizek's *Erinnerungen* as quoted in Jetzinger 98–99.
page 23
"sitting for hours at the beautiful Heitzmann grand piano . . ." CIC-PH.
page 23
"a strange almost hostile glance . . . a special mission one day would be en-
    trusted to him." Kubizek 99–100.
page 24
"Very often he used to give lectures . . ." CIC-PH
page 24
"those dull, monotonous finger exercises . . ." Jetzinger 94.
page 24
"poor people's doctor." Kubizek 119.
page 24
Frau Hitler examination: Dr. Bloch article in *Collier's*, 1941.
pages 24–25
Hitler's romance with Stephanie. Kubizek 59–60.

page 25
"Adolf never took painting seriously . . . was completely carried away by it."
    Ibid. 84.
page 26
"When it was pointed out that he lacked . . ." HA, File 17, Reel 1, "Adolf
    Hitler in Urfahr."
page 26
Hitler as baker's apprentice: Interview with Fräulein Johanna Mayrhofer,
    1971.
page 27
"Have you heard from Adolf? . . . this crazy trip to Vienna?" Kubizek 114.
page 27
"showed my unfitness for painting . . ." MK 20.
page 27
"there were already metastases in the pleura." OSS interview with Dr. Bloch.
    HSB 21.
page 28
"so deeply engrossed." Kubizek 122.
page 28
Many historians believe that Hitler did not arrive until after his mother's
    death. Franz Jetzinger, for example, bases his conclusions on testimony
    from people who interviewed Frau Presenmayer, the postmaster's wife,
    after 1938. According to Jetzinger: "she told them all she could remem-
    ber: how she and Frau Klara's sister, Johanna, had nursed her together
    and how—the old woman stressed this particularly—it was only after Frau
    Klara's death that her son, Adolf, had arrived from Vienna, and how sorry
    she had been for him that he was too late to see his mother alive." In the
    article, "Adolf Hitler in Urfahr!" HA, File 17, Reel 1, the same woman
    testified that it was she who informed Hitler of his mother's condition and
    that he "interrupted his studies and rushed to the sickbed of his mother."
    She also corroborated Dr. Bloch's statement about the sketch—"He drew
    a picture of his mother on her deathbed." Moreover, in 1938 she told a re-
    porter that Hitler had come home before his mother died and nursed her
    with the solicitude of a loving son. (HA, Folder 17A.) Jetzinger has cho-
    sen to discount completely the accounts of both Dr. Bloch and Kubizek.
    It is true that Dr. Bloch's story in *Collier's* is filled with mistakes, particu-
    larly about those events where he was not present. It is also true that
    Kubizek's account of Hitler, both in his *Memoirs* and *The Young Hitler I
    Knew*, contains a number of errors, particularly in dates. Kubizek should
    be read with care; he has a tendency toward exaggeration, overemphasis
    and occasional flights of imagination. Most of Jetzinger's criticisms of
    Kubizek, I believe, are justified, but he himself has a tendency to accent
    events that make Hitler look bad. (He had been imprisoned in Vienna by
    the Hitler regime.) His own well-documented book borrows extensively
    from Kubizek's account, which is admittedly the best firsthand source on
    Hitler as a young man.
    A new piece of evidence, which corroborates the accounts of Dr. Bloch
    and Kubizek regarding Hitler's ministrations to his mother at the end, is
    from Paula Hitler's interview with a CIC agent in 1946: "Assisting me,

my brother Adolf spoiled my mother during this last time of her life with overflowing tenderness. He was indefatigable in his care for her, wanted to comply with any desire she could possibly have and did all to demonstrate his great love for her." Further corroboration comes from Dr. Rudolph Binion, who recently deciphered Dr. Bloch's casebook for 1907 and thereby reconstructed the case history it contains. The casebook indicates that on October 22, 1907, Dr. Bloch consulted Hitler in Linz.

page 28
Klara's iodoform treatment: Article by Binion, *History of Childhood Quarterly*, 197–201.

page 28
"The pleasure of having her son back . . . meanwhile realized his own faults," Kubizek 124–25.

page 28
"She bore her burden well . . ." Bloch, *Collier's*.

page 29
"Gustl, go on being a good friend to my son . . ." Kubizek 126.

page 29
"In all my career I never saw anyone so prostrate . . ." Bloch, *Collier's*.

Chapter Two. "THE SCHOOL OF MY LIFE"

page 30
"stern and composed." Kubizek 127.

page 31
"a young man who had failed at school . . ." Kubizek 139.

page 31
"turn their part of the inheritance over to the girls." OSS interview with William Patrick Hitler. HSB 925–26.

page 32
"In his dark, good-quality overcoat . . . something else special." Kubizek 143–45.

pages 32–33
"I had no idea I had such a clever friend . . . Never mind." Kubizek 149, 152–53, 157–58.

page 34
"so he would not be tempted again": Interview with Albert Frauenfeld, 1971.

page 34
"For days on end he could live on milk . . . Isn't this a dog's life!" Kubizek 150–51.

page 35
"And still I don't succeed." Kubizek 189.

page 35
"What would these Italians do . . . Can you imagine Lohengrin's narration on a barrel organ?" Ibid. 191.

page 35
"developing a taste for symphonic music." Ibid. 204.

page 35
"Swamped for long centuries by the Slavs . . ." Arthur J. May, *The Hapsburg Monarchy* (Cambridge, Mass., 1951), 308.

page 36
"the dubious magic of the national melting pot . . ." MK 23–24.

pages 36–37
Hitler's lectures on "conscientious planning": Kubizek 166–68.

page 37
"Holy Mountain in the background, before it the mighty sacrificial block . . ." Kubizek 154.

page 37
"I'm going to work up Wieland . . ." Jetzinger 121. On writing the opera: Kubizek 193–202.

page 38
Hitler letter to Kubizek, Apr. 18 or 19, 1908: Maser, HBN, 20–22.

page 38
"depraved (sexual) customs": Kubizek to Jetzinger, May 6, 1949, Oberösterreichisches Landesarchiv, Folder 64.

page 38
"We must see the Sink of Iniquity once." Kubizek 235–36.

page 39
"The more anything touched him . . ." Ibid. 255.

page 39
Postcard Hitler to Kubizek about July 15, 1908: Jetzinger 125–26.

pages 39–40
Letter Hitler to Kubizek, July 17, 1908: Jetzinger 126–27.

page 40
Letter Hitler to Kubizek about Aug. 17, 1908: Jetzinger 127–28; Kubizek 260–62.

pages 40–41
"last attempt to persuade him . . . and yet each spoiled each other's pleasure of living together." CIC-PH.

pages 42–43
"Even now I shudder . . ." MK 28.

page 43
"an enchantment out of *The Thousand-and-One Nights*" Ibid. 19.

page 43
"I am sorry to say, merely the living memory . . ." Ibid. 21.

page 44
"We met every night and kept up our spirits . . ." Hanisch 240.

pages 48–49
Hitler by no means anti-Semitic in Vienna: Ibid. 297, 272.

page 49
"the practical application of anthropological research . . ." Hanser 31.

page 49
Footnote: Freud castration theory: Ernest Jones, I, 292–93, 330; II, 261.

page 49
Hitler's hatred of Jews a "personal thing": Interview with Helene Hanfstaengl, 1971.

page 49
Hitler's "failure in painting" caused by Jews: CIC-PH.
page 50
Footnote: The Hitler letter appears on p. 195 of Müllern-Schönhausen's book,
  Die Lösung des Rätsels Adolf Hitler, a confusing hodgepodge of fact and
  fantasy. At the same time I am convinced that his collection of original
  Hitler documents, artifacts and paintings is, for the most part, genuine.
  Although he took me to the Vienna bank where the documents are stored
  and made photo copies of a number of them, he did not show the originals. He said he was given the items by Hans Bleyer-Härtl, an Austrian
  Nazi who was the lawyer for the Dollfuss murderers. After the Anschluss,
  Bleyer-Härtl became disenchanted with the Nazis and volunteered in the
  army "as a form of suicide." After turning over the collection to Müllern-
  Schönhausen, he died in battle. Professor Ernst Deuerlein of the University of Munich, shortly before his death, told me he had authenticated a
  number of the documents and urged me to see Müllern-Schönhausen. The
  interview was set up by Dr. Wilfried Daim of Vienna, who had seen some
  of the items.

page 51
An orphan's pension: Jetzinger 1938; interview with Johanna Mayrhofer.
page 52
"I, Anna Csillag, with the very long Lorelei-hair . . . There is no end of stupid
  people." Greiner 41–42.
page 53
"in a disdainful way that he was only a dilettante . . ." Statement by Karl
  Honisch, HA, File 17, Reel 1.
page 53
"an honor seldom granted to an inmate." Ibid.
page 53
"I learned to orate less . . ." MK 68.
page 53
"This place is occupied . . . a pity for every word wasted on you, you won't
  ever understand." Honisch, op. cit.
page 54
"I had set foot in this town . . ." MK 125.

Chapter Three. "OVERCOME WITH RAPTUROUS ENTHUSIASM"

page 55
"The city itself was as familiar . . ." MK 126.
page 55
"for this city more than any other place . . ." Ibid. 126.
page 56
"The young man and I soon came to terms," Heinz 50.
page 56
"achieve the goal I had set myself." MK 126.

page 56
"The nomads, which was how the Munich citizens . . ." Richard Seewald, *Der Mann von Gegenüber* (Munich, 1963).

page 57
"this doctrine of destruction . . ." MK 154.

pages 57–58
"an Austrian charmer . . . You couldn't tell what he was thinking," Maser, *Hitler*, 74.

page 58
"He just camped in his room . . . what isn't likely to be of use to him in life?" Heinz 51–52.

page 58
"the happiest and by far the most contented . . ." MK 126.

page 58
"If today I am more attached to this city . . ." Ibid. 127.

page 59
Hitler letter to Linz: Deuerlein, *Der Aufstieg* 76–77; Jetzinger 149–56; Maser, HBN, 40–42.

page 60
"unfit for combatant duties, too weak . . ." Jetzinger 155.

page 60
"a state of imminent threat of war." Fritz Fischer 86.

page 61
"Heil the Kaiser! Heil the Army!" Sayers 91.

page 61
"If only the King has already read my application . . ." Julius Hagemann interview with Ignaz Westenkirchner in Schulz-Wilde Collection.

page 62
"looked at it with the delight that a woman . . ." Mend 15.

page 62
"turned tail and ran," Heinz 53.

page 62
"I was put up in a stable . . . I hope we get to England." Maser, HBN, 55–57.

page 63
Hitler letter to Hepp, Feb. 5, 1915, BA, NS 26/4.

page 64
"What I noticed first was his unmilitary manner . . ." Wiedemann 13 (translation).

page 65
Hitler letter to Popp: Maser, *Hitler*, 83–84.

page 65
"He is just an odd character . . ." Mend 24–25.

pages 65–66
Postcard Hitler to Popp, Jan. 22, 1915: Maser, HBN, 68.

page 66
"With exemplary patience (he didn't understand a word of German), I gradually . . ." HSC 236.

page 66
Letter Hitler to Popp, Jan. 26, 1915: Maser, HBN, 73.
page 66
Letter Hitler to Hepp, Feb. 5, 1915: BA, NS 26/4.
page 66
"Amen in the prayer," Westenkirchner interview, op. cit.
page 67
"I learned a great deal from him," HSC 662.
page 67
Footnote: "I never really caught him lying . . ." Wiedemann 40 (tr.).
page 67
"It's more important to bring our messages . . ." Julius Hagemann interview
   with Ernst Schmidt in Schulze-Wilde Collection.
page 67
"like a race horse at the starting gate." Mend 124.
pages 67–68
"I was eating my dinner in a trench . . ." Price 40.
page 68
"I often go on bitter nights . . ." Müllern-Schönhausen 210.
page 68
"quietly spent holidays." Mend 165–66.
page 68
"in the face of almost certain death . . ." Heinz 70, 71.
page 69
"How many times at Fromelles . . ." HSC 235.
page 69
"It isn't so bad, Lieutenant, right?" Wiedemann 13 (tr.).
page 69
"for the first time in two years . . ." MK 191.
page 70
"Nearly every clerk was a Jew . . ." Ibid. 193.
page 70
"If all Jews were no more intelligent . . ." Westenkirchner interview, op. cit.
page 70
"It really seems impossible for me to believe . . ." Schmidt interview, op. cit.
page 70
One of the most quoted incidents of Hitler's wartime anti-Semitism appears on
   p. 161 of Mend's book, *Adolf Hitler im Felde*: Hitler refuses to salute a
   Jewish officer, Hugo Gutmann, and, after Gutmann angrily leaves, says,
   "I'll only acknowledge this Jew on the battlefield. Here he struts with Jewish arrogance but at the front he'd hide in a mouse hole and wouldn't concern himself with a salute." The veracity of this incident is lessened by
   later issuance of a "Mend Protocol," in which the author contradicted material in his own book. In the case of Gutmann, Westenkirchner testified
   that the lieutenant was generally disliked by the men. "Our dislike, however, had nothing to do with anti-Semitism." Once he heard Hitler say,
   "Gutmann is an ass-crawler and a coward." Westenkirchner interview, op.
   cit. Lieutenant Gutmann later initiated the award to Hitler of the Iron
   Cross, First Class.

The 16th Regiment, in fact, was known for its courageous Jewish officers. Two are commended in Wiedemann's book. Reserve Lieutenant Kuh, an assault leader, a painter like Hitler, had a reputation for fearlessness. "The most beautiful thing to me," Kuh told Wiedemann, "is the night before an assault!" One of the battalion physicians, Dr. Georg Kohn, was decorated with the Bavarian Military Medical Order, the highest decoration awarded doctors for extreme bravery in the performance of their duties. The Great War was the first major opportunity which had been given German Jews to demonstrate their patriotism to a nation which had given them legal if not social equality. Almost unanimously they supported the Fatherland in its hour of peril. The Jewish soldier consequently often did more than his duty as a retort to anti-Semitic propaganda that the Jew was a coward by nature. (Perhaps Hitler's own eager attitude was also to prove that he was a better German than his German-born comrades.)

page 70
Letter Hitler to Wiedemann: Wiedemann 30 (tr.).

page 70
"he hurled himself on me in frenzy." HSC 236.

page 70
"turned out an extra special mess . . ." Heinz 75.

page 71
Footnote: On Dec. 31, 1940, Sylvia Beach, of Shakespeare and Company, wrote Heinrich Heim, who took down Hitler's table conversations and occasionally bought paintings and sketches for him, the following letter: "Gordon Craig is going to thank you himself for your kindness to him and his family. You have not only saved his life, as in his present feeble health he would not have lived many weeks in those circumstances I am told, but the tribute you paid to his art has given him an immense joy. It is indeed a miracle that you have performed!"

pages 71–72
"You could give me 200,000." HSC 236.

page 72
The theft of the art case was the virtual end of Hitler as an artist although he did several other pictures after the war. One, a woodland scene in the Müllern-Schönhausen Collection, dated "about 1919," has an artistic quality not seen in previous pictures. Years later the stolen art items were discovered in a Munich curiosity shop and presented to the Führer.

page 72
"This has nothing to do with art . . ." Schmidt interview, op. cit.

page 72
Postcard to Schmidt: Maser, HBN, 106–7.

page 72
"War forces one to think deeply . . ." Frank 45–46.

page 73
"the biggest piece of chicanery . . ." MK 194–95.

page 74
"We must draw only one conclusion . . ." Goodspeed 207.

page 75
"more vigorous conscription of the young Jews . . ." Ibid. 209.
page 75
"became furious and shouted . . ." Schmidt interview, op. cit.
page 75
Dr. Rudolph Binion of Brandeis University believes that Hitler's vision at
Pasewalk released his unconscious resentment against Dr. Bloch, a Jew.
"Hitler was then nearly nineteen, and intellectually and emotionally re-
tarded after having lived idly with his widowed mother for some years past
at suffocatingly close quarters. Consciously, he loved Bloch like a kind father; unconsciously, he blamed Bloch for his mother's cancer, for the toxic
treatment, for the huge terminal bill paid on Christmas Eve. This blame
surfaced after 1918 as a burning rage against the Jewish profiteer, the Jewish poison, the Jewish cancer. On balance, the evidence that he was not an
anti-Semite until after World War I, despite his own account in *Mein
Kampf*, is compelling. At all odds, his deadly hate for 'the Jew' along with
his political vocation itself can be dated quite precisely from his hospi-
talization of October–November 1918 for a gas poisoning that blinded
him temporarily. The gas—mustard gas—was actually a liquid spray that
burned through the skin just like iodoform. Hitler associated his gas
poisoning with his mother's iodoform poisoning as he felt himself succumbing. By the time he was hospitalized at Pasewalk (north of Berlin)
he must have been raving, as he was assigned to psychiatric care. The chief
psychiatrist took his blindness to be hysterical—wrongly. But just when he
was recovering his vision in the normal course, he relapsed at the news of
the Revolution and Armistice. This relapse *was* hysterical. It may have
been prompted by the false diagnosis that governed his treatment. . . .
In that hallucination Hitler was summoned from on high to undo, and
reverse, Germany's defeat. The Germany that he was to restore and
avenge was transparently his mother: this is graphic in one of the accounts
of the hallucination that Hitler himself gave in the early 1920s and especially in an official party version of it that he must have approved. In his
trance he was not expressly called upon to kill the Jews; nonetheless he
emerged from his trance resolved on entering politics in order to kill the
Jews by way of discharging his mission to undo, and reverse, Germany's
defeat." Binion, unpublished article, "Hitler's Concept of *Lebensraum*:
The Psychological Basis."
page 78
"no longer complained of anything . . ." Ibid.
page 78
"The medical records at the hospital . . ." Deuerlein, *Hitler*, 68.
page 78
"Their whole activity was so repellent . . ." MK 207.
page 78
"The laziest and most impudent . . ." Heinz 89.
page 79
"parental religion was largely sham . . . shot through with hypocrisy." Howard
  Becker, *German Youth: Bond or Free* (London, 1946), 51.

page 79
"messages from the forest . . . and do the deed." Peter Viereck, "Stefan George's Cosmic Circle," in *Decision*, Oct. 1941.

page 80
"To them he was not their commanding officer . . ." W. Hoeppener-Flatow, *Strosstrupp Markmann Greift an!* (Berlin, 1939), 95.

page 80
"monastery with walls of flame," McRandle 63.

page 82
"Like the French in 1793 . . ." Spengler 69–70.

page 82
"to gain a fatherland for myself," Rosenberg, *Memoirs*, 29.

page 82
"Can you use a fighter against Jerusalem?" Alfred Rosenberg, *Dietrich Eckart: Ein Vermächtnis* (Munich, 1927), 45.

page 84
"who bears arms against government troops . . ." *Vorwärts*, Mar. 10, 1919.

page 84
Ben Hecht cable: Hanser 182.

page 84
"The Jewish Mafia." David Mitchell 119.

page 85
"because those dogs have not at once loaned me sixty locomotives," Gustav Noske, *Von Kiel bis Kapp* (Berlin, 1920), 136.

page 85
"Those who say we should remain neutral . . ." Thor Goote in *Aus der Geschichte der Bewegung*, Deutsche Arbeitsfront, Nov. 1934; also letter from Ernst Schmidt to Werner Maser, Aug. 16, 1962.

page 85
"even when a local or momentary success might be possible." Allan Mitchell 319.

page 86
"The liberated working class is celebrating . . ." Ibid. 329.

page 87
"It would require a volume . . ." Ambroise Got, *La Terreur en Bavière* (Paris, 1922), 269–86.

page 87
"The result of the Soviet episode in Munich . . ." David Mitchell 190.

page 87
"This is the New Man, the storm soldier . . ." Ernst Jünger, *Der Kampf als inneres Erlebnis* (Berlin, 1933), 76–77.

page 88
"When I first met him he was like a tired stray dog . . ." Mayr 194.

page 88
"Involuntarily I saw thus my own development . . ." MK, Eher edition, 296.

page 88
Throughout the whole world others besides Hitler saw Jews as the fountainhead of revolution and Communism. That July, at a meeting of the

Anglo-Russian Club in London, Winston Churchill had called for support of White General Denikin against Lenin, Trotsky "and the sinister gang of Jewish anarchists around them," and a few months later told the House of Commons, "No sooner did Lenin arrive than he began beckoning a finger there to obscure persons in sheltered retreats in New York, in Glasgow, in Bern, and other countries, and he gathered together the leading spirits of a most formidable sect, the most formidable sect in the world." (Lacquer 313–14.) Churchill called for a fourteen-nation anti-Bolshevik crusade to support the White forces in Russia battling the Soviets, and declared it was a delusion "to suppose that all this year we have been fighting the battles of the anti-Bolshevik Russians. On the contrary, they have been fighting ours: and this truth will become painfully apparent from the moment they are exterminated and the Bolshevik armies are supreme over the whole vast territories of the Russian empire." D. Mitchell 236–37.

The anti-Bolshevik crusade had also crossed the Atlantic with the U. S. Attorney General, A. Mitchell Palmer, persuading Congress to finance a Red hunt to be directed by J. Edgar Hoover. Throughout the Western world a whispering campaign spread to the effect that it was Jewish money which had started the Russian Revolution: one German primarily responsible for financing Lenin was Max Warburg, whose brother was Paul Warburg, a director of the U. S. Federal Reserve System; and wasn't the father-in-law of brother Felix Warburg the same Jacob Schiff of Kuhn, Loeb and Company who had financed the Bolshevik revolution? This charge was repeated years later on Feb. 3, 1939, in the New York *Journal-American:* "Today it is estimated by Jacob's grandson, John Schiff, that the old man sank about 20,000,000 dollars for the final triumph of Bolshevism in Russia."

page 88
"For me the value of the whole affair . . ." MK 208.
page 89
"Right after listening to Feder's first lecture . . ." MK 120.
page 89
"and now for the first time . . ." Ibid. 215.
page 89
"The men seemed spellbound by one of their number . . ." Karl Alexander von Müller, *Mars und Venus* (Stuttgart, 1954), 338.
page 89
"I started out with the greatest enthusiasm . . ." MK 215–16.
page 89
"Tell me, did they shit in your brain . . ." Oskar Maria Graf, *Wir sind Gefangene* (Munich, 1927), 114.
page 90
"talked and walked in his sleep . . ." Mayr 194.
page 90
"Herr Hitler, if I may put it this way . . ." Remak 25.
page 90
"spoke very well." Heinz Zarnke, in letter to his parents, BA, NS 26/107. "I came to a meeting once by choice," he continued. "23 people were present

and just think: Herr Gottfried Feder, whose wife is a Richter, was there too. A Herr Hitler also spoke very well, he is said to be a 'construction worker,' but he is probably a colleague of Herr Feder's, for only an educated man can speak like that. Herr Hitler served through the whole war and was badly wounded. He was even blinded for a short time and took a lively interest in my eye ailment."

pages 90–91
"an artist rather than a pedant." Ellic Howe, *Rudolph von Sebottendorff*, 38.
pages 91–92
"Our meetings were private . . ." Heinz 106–7.
page 92
"sprang out of the ground . . ." MK 218.
page 92
"left the hall like a wet poodle . . ." Ibid. 219.
page 92
"watching the droll little beasts . . ." Ibid. 219–20.
page 93
"Involuntarily I saw my own development . . ." Ibid. 220.
page 93
"Now we have an Austrian with a big mouth!" Lotter interview, HA, Feb. 17, Reel 1.
page 93
"Terrible, terrible! This was club life . . ." MK 222.
page 93
"frozen into an 'organization,' but left the individual . . ." Ibid. 222.
page 94
"to please Ludendorff, whose wishes were . . ." Mayr 195.
page 94
"He burrows into the democracies . . ." Deuerlein, *Der Aufstieg*, 91–93.

Chapter Four. BIRTH OF A PARTY

page 97
"Our small committee which in reality . . ." *Illustrierter Beobachter* ⌗31, Aug. 3, 1929.
page 97
"When we were assembled . . . in our hands as a 'walking stick.' " Ibid.
page 98
"We were again seven men . . ." MK 354.
page 98
"and what before I had simply felt . . ." MK 355.
page 98
"flew down the stairs with gashed heads." Ibid. 358.
page 99
"The misery of Germany . . ." Deuerlein, "Hitlers Eintritt," 207.
page 99
Police report: Deuerlein, *Der Aufstieg*, 99.
page 99
"a funeral vault than an office." MK 390.

page 100
"My little girl used to climb on Hitler's knee . . ." Heinz 140.
page 100
"We cracked our brains over it . . ." Heinz 141.
page 101
"swift as greyhounds, tough as leather . . ." MK 356.
page 101
"The first thing you felt was that there was a man . . ." Frank 39.
page 101
"made things understandable even to the foggiest brain . . ." Ibid. 41.
page 102
"if anyone could master the fate of Germany . . ." Ibid. 52.
page 102
"When I closed the meeting . . ." VB, Feb. 22, 1922.
page 103
"Since I am a wicked and immature man . . ." Ernst Röhm, *Die Geschichte
    eines Hochverräters* (Munich, 1928).
page 103
"I prefer a vain monkey . . ." Eckart quoted in MK 687.
page 104
"This is the man who will one day . . ." Dietrich, *Hitler*, 163.
page 105
"C'mon, boys, let's all go . . ." This very free translation of the "largely un-
    translatable" verse comes from Richard Hanser, who queried Mehring on
    his accurate prophecy. "At those times, and under the circumstances I
    wrote," replied the poet, "I could not help being aware of coming turmoil
    and terrors." Hanser's conclusion to this vague explanation was that
    "poets are often prophets without knowing how they do it." Hanser
    338–39.
page 105
"Germany must become a Republic of Soviets . . ." Hans Spethmann, *Zwölf
    Jahre Ruhrbergban*, II (Berlin, 1928), 133–34.
page 105
"If I were to tell you everything . . ." Maximilian Scheer, ed., *Blut und Ehre*
    (Paris, 1937), 43.
page 106
"Come on, Adolf, we have no further business here." Dietrich 164.
page 106
"Some lodgers who've rented it since . . ." Heinz 240.
page 107
"I would be lying if I said . . ." BA, NS8–177.
page 108
Footnote: "I often encountered him on the stairway . . ." Heinz 240.
page 108
On speech in general: Phelps, "Hitlers Grundlegende"; Franz-Willing 150,
    152.
page 109
"The Jewish race is the source of all dangers," Sayers 91.

page 109
"The bloody Jew. Butchering of spiritual leadership . . ." Maser, HBN, 229–353.

page 109
"We are tied and gagged . . ." Phelps, "Hitler als Parteiredner," 314.

page 109
"For us the enemy sits on the other side of the Rhine . . ." Maser, HBN, 305.

page 110
"We wanted something red enough . . ." Heinz 143.

pages 111–12
Quotes from Strasser-Hitler meeting: Otto Strasser, *Mein Kampf*, 16–19.

page 112
Ulrich Graf quote: Egon Hanfstaengl's unpublished memoirs, 101.

page 112
"in the style of a witty newspaper article . . ." MK 481.

page 113
Drexler quote: Deuerlein, *Der Aufsteig*, 128.

page 114
"With this the cord of my patience . . ." MK 498.

page 115
"Like a giant shell this hall . . ." Ibid. 500.

page 115
"Then you could hardly hear . . ." Ibid. 501.

page 115
"We recognized that this movement . . ." Hanser 285.

page 116
Footnote: E. J. Gumbel, *Vier Jahre politischer Mord* (Berlin, 1923).

page 116
"I make these demands not because . . ." Franz-Willing 110.

page 117
"The King of Munich." Deuerlein, *Der Aufsteig*, 138–40.

page 117
"your exceptional knowledge . . ." Maser, *Die Frühgeschichte*, 270.

page 117
"We do not wish to unite . . ." Ibid. 273.

page 118
"intended to serve as a means . . ." Konrad Heiden, A *History of National Socialism* (London, 1936), 73.

page 118
"It's all right. We got what we wanted." Ibid. 31 Ballerstedt incident in general: Deuerlein, *Der Aufsteig*, 46.

page 119
"One heard nothing but yells . . ." Heinz 119.

page 121
"Two thousand years ago the mob of Jerusalem . . ." Heiden 117.

page 121
"to blind the driver." HSC 428.

pages 122–23
Hitler speech, July 28, 1922: Baynes 28–41.

page 122
Footnote: Hell's notes for 1922 at Institut für Zeitgeschichte, Munich, ZS 640,
     Folio 6, Josef Hell.

page 123
Lüdecke quotes: Lüdecke 22–25.

page 124
Lüdecke quotes. Ibid. 60–61.

page 124
"You have everything I lack . . ." Hamilton 125.

page 125
"We shall *be* the State . . ." Lüdecke 74.

page 125
"His eyes grew thoughtful . . ." Ibid. 81.

page 126
"Seeing that one brawls as well in an English suit . . ." Ibid. 90.

page 127
"That's typical of your bourgeois world . . ." Hitler to Jurgen von Ramin.

page 127
Indicative of the wave of approval in western Europe and the United States for
the Mussolini coup d'état was a poem which appeared in Jan. 1923 in the
Wall Street Journal:

> On constitutional technique
> And precedents he's lame,
> On grace and glamor rather weak.
> Such lacks don't cramp his game!
> Instead they're assets for his job,
> Rough, rude, plain word and act,
> To mold a nation through a mob,
> To make a dream a fact!
> Red nonsense had its mischief proved:
> His black-shirts curbed and quelled,
> Perhaps in ways not graced or grooved,
> How the reins be held?
> A blacksmith's son to purple Rome
> A brusque command he brought;
> Italia, cleansed and rescued home
> But more than her he's taught!
> Word-froth and demagogues and drones
> Banned; sweat and service praised;
> Desks manned when A.M. intones,
> Languorous Italy dazed!

Chapter Five. "SUCH A LOGICAL AND FANATICAL MAN"

page 129
"wipe out the disgrace of Versailles . . ." Gilbert, *Psychology*, 93.

page 129
"I remember a meeting at which they were discussing . . . I'll tell the world it was military!" Ibid. 91–92. Unpublished entry in Gilbert's Nuremberg diary, dated Feb. 3, 1946.

page 130
"precisely because it was revolutionary . . ." Ibid. 93.

page 130
Quotes from the Hess essay: Heiden 98–99.

page 131
"restlessly wandered from place to place . . ." Philipp Bouhler, *Kampf um Deutschland* (Munich, 1938), 83.

page 132
"More than once Dietrich Eckart told me . . ." HSC 168.

page 132
"Today, when I happen to meet . . ." Ibid. 223–24.

page 132
"In the wintertime the anteroom . . ." Bouhler, op. cit., 78.

pages 133–35
Captain Smith's trip to Munich: Truman Smith report.

page 135
"the unmistakable soldier in mufti . . ." MY 33.

page 135
"There was honesty, there was sincerity . . ." HSB 891.

page 136
"His technique resembled the thrusts . . ." MY 35.

page 136
"Our motto shall be . . ." Prange 122.

page 136
"The muffled restlessness of the masses . . ." Hanfstaengl, *Out of the Strong,* unpublished.

page 136
"as though in some devotional . . ." MY 35.

page 136
"Whenever I make a speech . . ." HSC 534.

page 136
"Captain Truman Smith asked me . . . we will have to talk about that." HSB 892.

page 137
"I am sure we shall not have to quarrel . . ." HSB 892.

page 137
"My prognostication on the general . . ." NA, U. S. Embassy, Berlin report, State Dept. file.

page 139
"neither during the war nor during the revolution . . ." Karl Alexander von Müller, *Im Wandel einer Welt* (Munich 1966), 144.

page 139
"He is an extraordinary person . . ." Denny, *The Nation,* 295.

page 140
"Sometimes weeks go by . . ." MY 48.

page 140
"There are stupid dogs . . ." HSC 249.

page 140
"When your mother has grown older . . ." Rehse Collection, 791, Library of Congress.

page 141
"What a wonderful atmosphere . . ." HSC 22.

page 141
"And you should have seen the bathroom . . ." MY 43.

page 141
"This music affected him physically . . ." Ibid. 49.

page 142
"absolutely by heart and could whistle . . ." Ibid. 49.

page 142
"Whereas he otherwise kept the different groups . . ." Hanfstaengl, *Out of the Strong.*

page 142
"He was respectful, even diffident . . ." MY 39.

pages 142–43
"He was at the time a slim, shy young man . . . 'Please, Uncle Dolf, spank the naughty chair.'" Helene Hanfstaengl, *Notes,* 281–83. Helene Niemeyer (the former Frau Helene Hanfstaengl) agreed to write a book for Lippincott in 1940. "Got to the end of the Putsch story," explained her son Egon, "and told Lippincott she didn't want to go on. She never showed them what she'd written. . . . Today said that, in 1940, she was sick of the whole Nazi business and it also occurred to her that if she published the story, the Nazis might take it out on her relations." Letter to author, Feb. 16, 1973.

page 143
"It is imposing to think . . ." CIA files: Hanfstaengl, OSS Biography, 48.

page 143
"Someone who does not understand . . . bite off your head." Ibid. 31–32.

page 144
"Putzi, I tell you he is a neuter." MY 52.

page 144
"We chased girls together . . . and admire the ballet dancers." Gun, *Eva Braun,* 8, 59.

page 144
"If it is not the fashion now . . ." Hanfstaengl, OSS Biography, op. cit., 12.

page 145
"They would have had my head . . ." MY 57.

page 145
"in spite of the many pictures . . ." Ibid. 60.

page 145
"at least it was better than this duelling . . ." Ibid. 61.

page 145
"When he was in a good mood . . ." Ibid. 65.

page 146
"The most important thing . . ." Ibid. 64.

page 146
Hitler's speech: Baynes 51–53.
pages 146–47
"It had something of the quality of . . . annihilating his supposed adversary."
MY 68–69.
page 147
"When I talk to people . . ." Ibid. 267–68.
page 147
"I'd read the description . . ." HSC 183.
page 148
"Don't forget, this building belongs to a Jew . . ." Hanfstaengl, *Out of the Strong*.
page 148
"At six o'clock gangs of Reds . . ." HSC 270.
page 149
"I reject Hitler completely!" F. W. Heinz, *Sprengstoff* (Berlin, 1930), 222.
pages 149–50
Murphy report: NA. U. S. State Dept. file.
page 150
"I have fallen in love with the landscape." HSC 218.
page 150
Eckart story: Hanfstaengl OSS Biography, op. cit., 35–37.
page 151
"such enthusiasm as had not been seen . . . so overcome were they by emotion." Deuerlein, *Der Aufsteig*, 181–82.
page 151
"In a few weeks the dice will roll . . ." Hanser 321–22.
page 151
"The task of our movement . . ." VB, Sept. 7, 1923.
page 152
Hitler trip to Switzerland: According to Wilhelm Hoegner, who conducted an extensive investigation of the NSDAP's financial sources from 1924 to 1928, Hitler went to Switzerland in 1921 and 1922 to collect money so he could lead the fight against the Catholic Church in Germany. (Hoegner interview, 1971.) Nov. 25, 1924, two Geneva newspapers claimed that the previous September Hitler had stayed at the Hotel St. Gotthard in Zurich where he received donations of 33,000 Swiss francs, some of it from French sources. Other money came from Frau Gertrud von Seidlitz, who owned shares in Finnish paper mills, the Bechsteins, a locomotive manufacturer named Borsig, and a Munich industrialist, Hermann Aust. Reputedly, the largest single contribution, 100,000 gold marks, came from Fritz Thyssen of the United Steelworks. At this time there were approximately 170,000 gold marks in the NSDAP treasury.
page 152
"If nothing happens now the men . . ." BH, MA 103476, 1020.
page 152
"We must compromise these people . . ." MY 88.
page 152
"Absolutely no one could ever persuade . . ." Helene Hanfstaengl, *Notes*.

page 152
"Hitler now had definite Napoleonic . . ." BH, MA 103476, 1151.

Chapter Six. THE BEER HALL PUTSCH

For information on the Putsch I am particularly indebted to Prof. Ernst
Deuerlein, Richard Hanser, and Dr. Harold J. Gordon, Jr.

page 153
"an old member and fanatic member . . ." Letter from Maria Heiden,
Munich, Sept. 30, 1923.

page 153
"A man of action born on April 20 . . ." Ellic Howe, *Urania's*, 90–91.

page 153
"violence with a disastrous outcome . . ." Wulff 39.

page 154
"psychological astrology . . ." Howe, *Urania's*, 98.

page 154
"His sharp cheekbones . . ." F. Wagner 8.

page 154
"his voice took on a tone . . ." Ibid. 9.

page 154
"Don't you feel that he is destined . . ." HSB 933.

page 154
"With one blow you have transformed . . ." Röhl 52–53.

page 155
"I noticed you were not at all frightened . . ." Helene Hanfstaengl, *Notes*,
301.

page 155
Hemingway story: New York *Times*, Oct. 4, 1974.

page 156
"I can only take action . . ." Stein 97–98.

page 156
"For us this man was a whirling dervish . . ." Carl Suckmayer, *Als wär's ein
Stück von mir* (Frankfurt am Main, 1966), 384.

page 157
"There are decent emotions . . ." Eduard Hamm to Theodor Wolff, Jan. 3,
1922, BA, R431, 2681.

page 157
"until an adjustment between Bavaria . . . and is Bavaria's duty to right it."
NA, U. S. Embassy, Berlin, report, Oct. 22, 1923.

page 157
"as a result domestic politics are purely . . ." *Münchener Zeitung*, Oct. 22,
1923, BA, R431, 2264.

page 158
Footnotes: From TV tapes, "Der Frühe Hitler," Bayerische Rundfunk.

page 158
"We must think first of a march . . ." MY 90.

page 158
Footnote: "he never confided a single plan . . ." Helene Hanfstaengl, *Notes*, 295.

page 159
"The German problem will be solved . . ." E. Röhm, *Die Geschichte eines Hochverräters*, 229.

page 159
"Our people are under such economic . . ." BH, MA 103476, 691.

page 159
"The atypical way must be prepared . . ." PHP.

pages 159–60
"I am ready to support a rightist . . ." Gordon 256.

page 161
Hitler toothache: Egon Hanfstaengl, *Memoirs*, 101.

page 161
"Where is Captain Göring? . . . Tonight we act!" MY 91.

page 162
Hitler-Esser meeting: Interview with Esser, 1971.

page 162
"Hansl, if things don't go right . . ." BH, MA 1042221, Aigner Bericht.

page 164
"out of the way—you there!" Heinz 154.

page 164
"Take your hand out." NA, EAP, 10517, I, 97.

page 164
"Komödie spielen . . . but I had no other means." Ibid. 98.

page 165
"There are five rounds . . ." Idem.

page 165
"What followed then was an oratorical . . ." Müller, *Im Wandel*, 162–63.

page 165
"The task of the provisional . . ." Bullock 80.

page 165
"provincial bridegroom . . ." MY 100.

pages 165–66
"such a change of attitude in a few minutes . . . dead by dawn!" Müller, op. cit., 163.

page 165
One listener not converted by Hitler's speech was the man next to Müller, Dr. Max von Gruber, professor of "racial hygiene" at Munich University. Himself an ardent nationalist, he was not impressed by this first close look at Hitler: "Face and head: bad race, mongrel. Low, receding forehead, ugly nose, broad cheekbones, small eyes, dark hair; facial expression, not of a man commanding with full self-control, but betraying insane excitement. Finally, an expression of blissful egotism." Heiden 190.

page 166
"amazed and far from pleased." Goodspeed 239.

page 166
"I am going to fulfill the vow . . ." Bullock 81.
page 167
"the only thing missing is the psychiatrist . . ." Bavarian State Document ⋕72 from Allgemeine Staatsarchiv, Munich.
pages 169–70
Schwander story: Gordon 293–94.
page 170
Murphy telegram: NA, State Department documents.
page 170
Footnote: Murphy 22.
page 171
"Crush this movement at any cost . . ." Hanser 356.
page 172
"What? Still negotiating here? . . ." BH, MA 104221, Wilde Bericht.
page 172
Message "to all German wireless stations": Hanser 356.
page 173
"It came like a blow from a club," Hanser 359.
page 173
"If we get through, very well . . ." Heiden 193.
page 173
"March to Berlin! . . ." Frank 61–62.
page 174
"This is no revolution . . ." BH, MA 104221, Goebel Bericht.
page 174
"We're going to try the whole thing over again." Hanser 362.
page 175
"Greeted the appearance of the councillors . . ." Heinz 159.
page 176
"We march!" Ludendorff 65.
page 176
"We would go to the city to win the people . . ." PHP.
page 176
"the most desperately daring decision in my life . . ." Hitler speech, Nov. 11, 1935.
pages 176–77
Eckart story: BH, MA 104221, Eckart Bericht.
pages 177–78
Eckart story: BH, MA 104221, Eckart Bericht.
page 178
"If Ludendorff is marching that way . . ." Ludendorff 67.
page 178
Godin account: BH, MA 104221, Godin Bericht.
page 179
Footnote: "both Ludendorff and Hitler behaved . . ." Murphy 22.
page 179
Dr. Schultze account: Interviews with Dr. Schultze, 1974–75.

pages 179–80
Frankel account: Memorandum, undated, by Frankel, BA, NS 26/115.
page 180
"Pfui! Jew defenders! . . ." BH, MA 104221, Salbey Bericht.
page 181
Aigner account: BH, Aigner Bericht.
pages 181–82
Dr. Schultze account: Interviews, 1974–75.
page 182
Ilse Pröhl account: Interview with Ilse Hess, 1971; letter to author, 1975.
pages 182–83
Haushofer account: Karl Haushofer testimony, Nuremberg, Oct. 7, 1945.
pages 183–85
Helene Hanfstaengl account: *Notes* 322–27.
page 183
Dr. Schultze account: Interviews, 1974–75.
page 185
"He refused a bite or soup . . ." Heinz 170.
page 185
"There are many things that can be said . . ." Fritz Stern, *The Politics of Cultural Despair* (Univ. of Calif., 1961), 237–38.
page 186
"our history has gone astray . . ." Möller, *Das Dritte Riech* (Hamburg, 1931), 3, 7–8.
page 186
"The first period of the national . . ." BH, Generalstaatskommissariat, 575.

Chapter Seven. IN LANDSBERG PRISON

page 189
"She loves, and always has loved . . ." Helene Hanfstaengl, *Notes*, 333.
page 190
"These are the papers . . ." Helene Hanfstaengl interview, 1971.
page 190
Dr. Brinsteiner report, Jan. 8, 1924: Otto Lurker, *Hitler hinter Festungsmauern, ein Bild aus trüben Tagen* (Berlin, 1933), 9–11, 68. Dr. Walter Schultze, who treated Hitler on Nov. 9–11, stated in 1974 that a break such as Dr. Brinsteiner described was impossible; and that Dr. Brinsteiner was either incompetent or a liar. Interview with Dr. Schultze, 1974.
pages 190–91
Drexler account: BH, MA 104221, Drexler Bericht.
page 191
Knirsch account: Schlabrendorff 345–46.
page 191
"Her advice turned the scale . . ." MY 113.
pages 191–92
Ehard account: Interview with Ehard, 1971.
page 192
Angela Letter: Hans Hitler Collection.

page 192
Wagner letter: Edward Whalen Collection.
page 193
Rosenberg account: *Memoirs* 74.
page 193
"I was howled down in derision," Lüdecke 186.
page 194
"Adolf Hitler in Prison," Hoffmann 57.
page 194
Schacht account: *Old Wizard*, 181–83.
page 195
"Hitler was at all times . . ." Brinsteiner report, op. cit.
page 195
"From its failure I learned . . ." Hitler speech, Prange 160.
page 195
"It was the greatest good fortune . . ." Gordon 408–9.
page 195
"Landsberg was my college education . . ." Frank 47.
pages 195–96
Hitler-Hanfstaengl meeting: Interview with Hanfstaengl, 1971.
page 196
Frau Ebertin account: Howe, *Urania's*, 92–93.
page 196
Carin Göring letter: Bewley 56–57.
page 197
"These things undoubtedly satisfy . . ." Spengler, *Politische Schriften* (Munich, 1932), 148.
page 197
"You have one classic example . . ." PHP.
page 197
Ludendorff quote: Frank 52.
page 198
Rosenberg quote: Rosenberg 77.
pages 198–99
Hanfstaengl's visit: Egon Hanfstaengl *Memoirs* and interviews, 1971; MY 113.
page 199
Quotes from trial: PHP.
page 199
"I can never think without melancholy . . ." Hans von Hülsen, *Zwillings-Seele* (Munich, 1947), I, 207ff.
pages 200–1
Trial quotes: PHP.
page 201
"on the evidence of my defense . . ." HSC 282.
pages 201–2
The sentence: BA, NS 26/114.
page 202
Hemmrich quote: Heinz 171.

page 202
Hitler's diary: Müllern-Schönhausen 117.

page 203
Hemmrich quotes: Heinz 182, 174. The prison routine as described in follow-
ing pages by Heinz was corroborated by Hans Kallenbach, *Mit Adolf
Hitler auf Festung Landsberg.*

page 203
"Upstairs with him were the elite . . ." Interview with Dr. Weber, Schulze-
Wilde Collection.

pages 203–4
Hemmrich quotes: Heinz 183–84.

page 204
Carin Göring letter: Bewley 58; Countess von Wilamowitz-Moellendorff, *Carin
Göring* (Stockholm, 1933).

page 205
"pioneers and forerunners . . ." NA, Microcopy T-81, Reel 116, Frame
136437.

page 205
Drexler quote: Frank 48–49.

page 205
"The various groups quarreled . . ." Lüdecke 210.

page 206
Hemmrich account: Heinz 185, 188, 189.

page 207
Hitler quotes: HSC 46.

pages 207–8
Hemmrich account: Heinz 179, 181–82.

page 208
Hitler quotes: MY 114–15.

page 208
Ilse Pröhl account: Interview with Ilse Hess, 1971.

pages 208–9
Haushofer statement; Karl Haushofer testimony at Nuremberg, Oct. 7,
1945, p. 7.

page 209
Hess letter to Heinrich Heim, who would later become Bormann's secretary
and, in that capacity, copy down Hitler's table conversations.

pages 209–10
Kugler-Hitler meeting: *Der Nationalsozialist*, a Leipzig news magazine, Aug.
17, 1924. Bibliothek für Zeitgeschichte, Stuttgart, Flugblattsammlung,
Karton: Deutschland IV.

page 210
Leybold report, Sept. 22, 1924: BH, State Ministry of Interior file.

pages 210–11
Hemmrich account: Heinz 185, 192.

page 211
Göring-Negrelli correspondence: Ben E. Swearingen Collection.

page 212
Hitler account: HSC 282.

page 212
Hoffmann account: Hoffmann 61.
page 212
Hitler-Müller quotes: HSC 282–83.
page 212
Hitler quote: HSC 284.
page 213
Hitler quote: HSC 284.
pages 213–14
Hitler at the Hanfstaengls': MY 119–22; HSB 893; interviews with Helene and Egon Hanfstaengl, 1971.

Chapter Eight. HITLER'S SECRET BOOK

page 215
Hoffmann account: Hoffmann 145.
page 216
"This wild beast is checked . . ." Strasser, *Hitler and I*, 71.
page 216
Rosenberg quote: Lüdecke 257.
page 217
Lüdecke article: Lüdecke 249–50.
pages 217–18
Feb. 27, 1924 meeting: Müller, *Im Wandel*, 301.
page 219
"Fight Marxism and Judaism . . . reports will be circulated . . ." BH, Munich police report, Nov. 1929.
page 219
Haushofer account: Interview with Heinz Haushofer, 1971; correspondence, 1975.
page 221
Röhm letter to Hitler: Ernst Röhm, *Die Memoiren des Stabschefs* (Saarbrücken, 1934), 160.
pages 221–22
Röhm to Lüdecke: Lüdecke 265.
page 222
Hitler quote: HSC 586.
page 222
Hanfstaengl to Hitler: MY 133, 134, 129.
page 223
Mitzi Reiter story: Gun, *Eva Braun*, 61.
page 223
Hitler at Wahnfried: F. Wagner 30, 41.
page 224
Hitler quote: *Mein Kampf*, Eher, 69.
page 225
"the bridge from left to right . . ." Richard Hunt, *Joseph Goebbels*, Ph.D. thesis, Harvard Univ. 1960, 101.

pages 226–27
Diary entries: EGD 47, 50. The Goebbels diaries of 1925–26, for all their self-dramatization and exaggeration, present a revealing self-portrait of the author. They were discovered only after the war and turned over to ex-President Hoover. They were much more valuable testimonials than Goebbels' *Struggle for Berlin*, which was probably based on his journals.

page 226
"the servant of capital and interest . . ." EGD 62.

page 227
"was the foundation of our religion . . ." Orlow I, 70.

page 228
Goebbels quotes: EGD 78.

page 229
Hanussen story: Müllern-Schönhausen, 118.

pages 229–30
Goebbels quotes: EGD 91, 95, 100–1.

page 231
Hitler letter: Deuerlein, *Der Aufsteig*, 264–65.

page 232
Freud quotes: Tell 136.

pages 232–33
Hitler quotes: MK 652, 651.

page 233
Haushofer quote: E. A. Walsh, *Total Power* (Garden City, Garden City Publishing Co., 1948).

page 233
Hitler to Frank: Frank 46.

pages 233–34
Hitler speech, Dec. 18, 1926. BH, Sonderabgabe I, ⚔1762.

page 233
Footnote: Interview with Erich Kempka, 1971.

page 235
"There is complete confusion . . ." Riess 32.

page 235
Goebbels quotes: Bramsted 20.

page 235
"What record must I use . . ." Strasser, *Mein Kampf*, 31.

pages 235–36
Pharus Hall meeting: Heiber 51–52; Riess 33–36.

page 236
Goldschmidt story: Riess 36.

page 237
"What a miserable provincial sheet . . ." Ibid. 40.

page 238
Krebs account: Albert Krebs, *Tendenzen und Gestalten der NSDAP* (Stuttgart, 1959), 131ff.

page 239
Strasser account: Strasser, *Mein Kampf*, 39–41.

pages 239–40
"Socialism and nationalism . . ." *Der Angriff*, Apr. 2, 1928.

page 240
"I immediately rang up my sister . . ." HSC 221.

pages 240–41
On Geli: Interviews with Ilse Hess, Ernst and Helene Hanfstaengl, 1971; Hoffmann 48; Schirach 178–79.

page 240
It was Hitler who suggested that Hess and Ilse Pröhl get married. At first Hess had not appreciated the Führer's intervention. But then he was amused. "Hitler took a personal interest in all of us who were with him in the beginning," Frau Hess revealed in a 1971 interview. "We were a very close circle. We were also intimate friends of Geli. As far as my husband and I were concerned, we were too busy to get married; he was always away and I was working. He devoted his time more to political matters, and he didn't have much of a private life."

page 240
Ilse Hess account: Interview 1971.

page 241
"The compulsion to engage . . ." *Hitler's Secret Book*, 6.

pages 241–42
"Then the Jew can make . . ." Ibid. 29.

page 242
"It is not my task . . . exactly so with Jewry too," Ibid. 211–12.

page 242
"Never before had Hitler gone quite that far in his equation of the Jews with other peoples. But what, then, was the difference? Was it only the absence of a territorial state? No, the difference was found in the struggle for life." Jäckel 103. The author is indebted to Professor Jäckel for information on this subject.

page 242
"His ultimate goal . . ." *Hitler's Secret Book*, 213.

page 243
Hitler quotes: Ibid. 29, 79, 23, 76, 41.

page 243
Dr. Schwenninger story: Interview with Prof. Ernst Deuerlein, 1971.

Chapter Nine. A DEATH IN THE FAMILY

page 244
Goebbels quote: *Der Angriff*, Nov. 19, 1928.

page 245
Hitler speech: Prange 40–41.

page 245
Goebbels quote: *Der Angriff*, Nov. 19, 1928.

pages 245–46
Lochner account: Lochner, *What About Germany?*, 102–3.

page 246
Speer account: Speer 15–16.
page 247
"he hovered at her elbow . . ." MY 162.
page 247
Hoffmann account of Geli: Hoffmann, 148, 150.
pages 247–48
Henriette Hoffmann account: Schirach 73.
page 248
"She was a terror . . ." Gun, *Eva Braun*, 21.
page 248
First meeting Hitler-Eva Braun: Ibid. 42–43.
page 249
"fading into oblivion . . ." G. M. Gathorne-Hardy, *A Short History of Inter-national Affairs* (London, 1950), 357.
pages 249–50
Wessel story: Heiber 68–69.
page 249
Footnote: MY 149.
page 250
"His spirit has risen . . ." *Der Angriff*, Feb. 27, 1930.
page 250
"If anything goes wrong . . ." MY 149.
page 250
Burial of Wessel: Heiber 70.
page 251
Hitler-Strasser meeting: Strasser, *Ministersessel*.
page 252
Hitler letter to Goebbels: Kühnl 374.
page 252
"they were united behind . . ." Ibid. 253.
page 252
"The departure of my brother . . ." BA, Slg. Ach. folder 313: Letter, Gregor Strasser to Rudolf Jung, July 22, 1930.
page 253
August Wilhelm letter: unpublished letter, dated Apr. 7, 1930, from Ben E. Swearingen Collection.
page 254
"Do it jokingly, do it seriously . . ." *Der Angriff*, Sept. 14, 1930.
page 254
Hitler-Müller conversation: HSC 179.
page 255
"Great things are before us . . ." MY 151.
page 255
"Then the November 1918 revolution . . ." *Frankfurter Zeitung*, Sept. 26, 1930.
page 255
Hitler article in London *Sunday Express*: Baynes 994–95.

page 256
Hitler in London *Times:* Baynes 192.
page 256
"This was the élite of the 'Aryan' race . . ." Sender 276.
pages 256–58
On William Patrick Hitler and his mother: Interview with Hans Hitler, 1971; OSS interview with W. P. Hitler, HSB 926–27; *Paris-Soir*, Aug. 5, 1939.
pages 258–59
Frank investigation: Frank 330–31.
page 259
"suffered all his life . . ." Correspondence between Dr. Hans Dietrich Röhrs and Rittmeister von Schuh; correspondence between Dr. Röhrs and the author, 1972.
page 259
"Hitler was not often there . . ." Frank 93–94.
page 261
"I understand your distress . . ." Heiden 409.
page 261
Stennes Putsch: Höhne, *Order of Death's Head*, 67–68; interviews with Hein Ruck, 1971.
pages 261–62
"I found him a very decent fellow . . ." MY 157–58.
page 262
"When a mother has many children . . ." Interview with F. K. Florian, 1970.
page 262
"We were not loved everywhere . . ." Leaders' Conference, June 13–14, SS HQ Report, Berlin Documentary Center, Microfilm 87.
page 262
"I am the SA and SS . . ." *Münchener Post*, Apr. 11/12, 1931.
page 262
"The SA is a collection . . ." Feb. 3, 1931; NA, German Documents, Reel 85.
page 263
Delmer account: *Trail*, 106–7, 115–17.
page 264
Maurice account: Gun, *Eva Braun*, 8
page 264
Winter account: Ibid. 9.
page 264
"her life was very hard . . ." OSS interview with William Patrick Hitler, HSB 929–30.
page 264
Hanfstaengl's quotes: Interviews with Ernst and Helene Hanfstaengl, 1970, 1971.
page 264
Winter quote: Gun, *Eva Braun*, 10.
page 265
Geli to Frau Hoffmann: Hoffmann 151.

page 265
Hoffmann account: Hoffmann 154.
page 266
Frau Reichert account: Interview with Frau Reichert, Schulze-Wilde Collection.
page 266
Eva letter to Hitler: Gun, *Eva Braun*, 13.
pages 266–67
Hoffmann account: Hoffmann 153.
pages 266–67
There are conflicting versions of the discovery of the body. According to Frau Winter, she knocked on the door and when Geli didn't respond she summoned her husband and together they forced their way in. Frau Hess informed the author that her husband was summoned by Frau Winter and *he* broke down the door.

Eva Braun told her two sisters that Hitler himself had said Geli had wrapped the gun in a face cloth to muffle the explosion, then fired it in her mouth. There was also a report of an unfinished letter from Geli to a professor of music in Vienna stating that she wanted to take lessons from him. A fortuneteller (so Hitler told Friedelind Wagner) had once prophesied that a revolver bullet would end Geli's life, and since then she had a "hysterical fear" of guns. Wagner OSS 938.
page 267
Frank account: Frank 98.
pages 267–68
Frauenfeld account: Interviews with Frauenfeld, 1971; correspondence with Frauenfeld, 1975.
page 268
"So. Now let the struggle begin . . ." Hoffmann 159.
page 268
"It is like eating a corpse!" Gilbert, *Psychology*, 62.
page 268
Footnote: Interview with Frau Hess, 1971.

Chapter Ten. "IT IS ALMOST LIKE A DREAM"

page 271
"The movement is today so united . . ." VB, Oct. 31, 1931.
page 272
"An interesting man with exceptional . . ." Werner Conze, in *Vierteljahreshefte für Zeitgeschichte*, 1 Jahrg. (1953) 261ff.
page 272
"the chess game for power . . ." Goebbels, Vom *Kaiserhof zur Reichskanzlei* (Munich, 1936), 19–20.
pages 272–73
Hitler speech in Düsseldorf: Schweitzer 100, Prange 253.
page 273
"I know that I shall come to power . . ." Frank 101.

page 274
"Berlin was in a state of war . . ." Isherwood 86.

page 275
"dream of power was temporarily over . . ." Goebbels, *Vom Kaiserhof*, 55–56, 62.

page 275
"The first election is over . . ." Dietrich 15.

pages 275–76
Frank account of Röhm's homosexuality: Frank 88–89.

page 276
Delmer account: *Trail*, 155–56.

pages 276–77
Krebs account: Krebs, *Tendenzen*, 136–37.

page 277
"Hitler is a fool . . ." A. M. Koktanek, *Oswald Spengler in seiner Zeit* (Munich, 1968), 246.

page 277
"When one has a chance . . ." Hamilton 142–43.

page 278
"I very much doubt if I'm the right man." Papen 152.

page 278
"Well, my dear Papen, I hope . . ." Dorpalen 333–34.

page 279
"Just look, Baur, there is a beautiful . . ." Baur section in Ziegler; interview with Baur, 1970.

page 280
Egon Hanfstaengl account: *Memoirs*, 95.

page 282
"The President is not prepared . . ." Papen 196.

pages 282–83
Hitler-Hindenburg meeting: Memorandum by Meissner in Walther Hubatsch, *Hindenburg und der Staat* (Göttingen, 1966), 338–39.

page 283
Hanfstaengl account: HSB 911.

page 283
"Mind you, if it amuses you . . ." MY 188.

page 284
"Now that the National Socialists . . ." Rudolf Olden, *Hitler* (New York, 1936).

page 284
"The decision was right . . ." Dorpalen 356.

page 284
Hanfstaengl account: HSB 911.

page 284
"Only we ourselves can finish . . ." Dietrich 31.

page 285
Ribbentrop quote: Stein 111.

pages 285–86
Lochner-Kaltenborn—Wiegand interview with Hitler: *Wisconsin Magazine of History*, Summer 1967, 286–90.

page 286
Habsburg account: Interview with Otto von Habsburg, 1971.

page 287
Eva's attempted suicide: Hoffmann 161–62.

page 288
"If we held ourselves aloof . . ." Goebbels, *Vom Kaiserhof*, 181.

page 288
Delmer-Hitler meeting. *Trail*, 173–74.

page 288
"Open the windows quickly . . ." Interrogation of Crown Prince Frederick Wilhelm of Prussia at Nuremberg. This sentence was deleted from the stenographic text at his request, but noted in prefatory remarks.

page 288
"We must endeavor to put aside . . ." Papen 213.

page 289
"His entire manner of handling . . ." Hegner 16.

page 289
"Not long ago at Tannenberg . . ." HSC 226–27.

pages 289–90
Hitler-Hindenburg meeting: Dorpalen 379–81; Hegner 18–19.

page 291
Footnote: H. A. Turner, "Fritz Thyssen and 'I Paid Hitler'" in *Faschismus und Kapitalismus in Deutschland*, 25.

page 291
"I am ready to leave at any time . . ." Dorpalen 386.

pages 291–92
Hindenburg meeting with Papen and Schleicher: Meissner memo, Dec. 2, 1932, in *Vierteljahreshefte*, VI, 1958, 105–7. Papen 217–18.

page 292
Papen-Hindenburg meeting: Dorpalen 395–406.

page 293
"Along comes Hindenburg, a man of honor . . ." Frank 108.

page 294
"It is difficult to be cheerful," Goebbels, *Vom Kaiserhof*, 206.

page 294
"stabbed him in the back . . ." Orlow I, 293.

page 294
"Such contemptible behavior . . ." Goebbels, *Vom Kaiserhof*, 206.

pages 294–95
Strasser quote: MY 190–91; Heiber 104.

page 295
Strasser to Rosenberg: Rosenberg, *Memoirs,* 148.

page 295
"burst into a spontaneous ovation . . ." Goebbels, V*om Kaiserhof,* 209.

page 295
"most familiar with [Hitler's] basic ideas . . ." VB, Dec. 18–19, 1932.

page 295
On Hitler and Christmas decorations: Krause 52.

pages 295–96
Hitler letter to Frau Wagner: Wagner 73.

page 296
Bullitt report: Bullitt 23.

page 296
Hanussen prediction: Müllern-Schönhausen 155–56.

page 297
Hanfstaengl account: MY 195.

page 298
"success whose importance . . ." HSC 467.

page 298
"break the necks of all . . ." Dorpalen 416.

page 299
Hitler at Ribbentrop's: Ribbentrop, *Memoirs,* 23.

pages 299–300
Oskar Hindenburg-Hitler meeting: Meissner, IMT, XXXII, 152; same, Case
   No. 11 transcript, 4494; Hans Otto Meissner and Harry Wilde, *Die Mach-
   tergreifung* (Stuttgart, 1958), 161–64. Papen's account of the January negotiations in his memoirs is inaccurate. He states, for example, that
   he "had no contact whatever with Hitler between January 4 and 22," a
   palpable lie; nor does he mention his abrupt switch to Hitler on the evening of January 22.

page 301
"Joachim proposes link-up with Hugenberg . . ." Ribbentrop, *Memoirs,* 24.

page 302
"Whether what I am going to do . . ." Unsigned memorandum on Hinden-
   burg-Schleicher conference, Jan. 28, 1933, in Thilo Vogelsang, *Reichswehr, Staat und NSDAP* (Stuttgart, 1962), 490–91.

page 302
"After this breach of trust . . ." Hammerstein Memorandum in John
   Wheeler-Bennett, *Nemesis,* 280.

page 302
"It is my unpleasant duty . . ." Papen 239.

page 303
"If the new government . . ." Dorpalen 440.

pages 303–4
"Gentlemen, it is five minutes past . . . And now, gentlemen, forward with
   God!" Dorpalen 441–42.

page 304
Hoffmann account: Hoffmann 68.

pages 304–5
Egon Hanfstaengl account: *Memoirs*, 191.
page 305
"How on earth did he conjure . . ." Hoffmann 69.
page 305
Hitler-Papen: Papen 264.
page 305
Frank quote: Frank 111.
page 306
"Everyone felt the same . . ." Interview with H. Ruck, 1971.
page 306
Maschmann quote: Maschmann 10–13.
page 306
"The river of fire . . ." François-Poncet 48.
pages 305–6
Frank account: Frank 129–30.
page 306
Heine quote, 1834. From Louis Untermeyer, *Heinrich Heine, Paradox and Poet* (New York, 1937), I, 230.

Chapter Eleven. AN UNGUARDED HOUR

page 307
Frau Goebbels story: Frau Goebbels section in Ziegler.
pages 307–8
Papen quote: Ewald von Kleist-Schmenzin, *"Die Letzte Möglichkeit," Politische Studien,* X, 1939, 92.
page 308
New York *Times*, Jan. 31, 1933.
page 308
Schacht quote: NA, U. S. Dept. of State file, Berlin Embassy Report, Feb. 2, 1933.
page 309
Party at Hammerstein's: Institut für Zeitgeschichte, ZS 105–5, Horstom Mellenthin; O'Neill 125–26.
page 311
"to avoid at all costs . . ." Heiden, A *History of National Socialism*, 216.
page 311
"Every comrade a commander . . ." Bewley 97–98.
pages 312–13
Hanfstaengl account: Interview, 1970.
pages 313–14
Hitler at Reichstag fire: Delmer, *Trail*, 187–88; Papen 268–69; Tobias 84.
page 314
Conference after fire: Tobias 84–87; Holborn, *Republic*, 168.
page 315
"It took half an hour before I could find . . ." HSC 604.

page 314
"That's sheer rubbish! . . . if you sign it officially," Tobias 89–91.
page 315
"a ruthless settling of accounts . . . documents of the German people," Holborn, *Republic*, 183.
page 317
"I may say to the Communists . . ." Bewley 100–1.
page 317
Delmer–Hitler: *Trail*, 192–94.
page 318
Göring speech: Bullock 223–24.
page 318
"pragmatic, decent men . . ." Interview in 1971 with Kurt Schuschnigg, who was the visiting Austrian.
page 318
Göring quote: Bullock 219.
page 318
Schacht quote: Interview with Schacht, 1963; Manchester 407.
page 319
"He rants much less . . ." Eich 92.
page 320
"Munich is *the* city of Germany . . ." Frank 137–38.
page 320
Hitler to Ehard: Interview with Ehard, 1971.
page 320
"Authority is only a springboard . . ." Frank 156.
page 321
"like a timid newcomer . . ." François-Poncet 62.
page 321
"We consider it a blessing . . ." Dorpalen 466.
pages 321–22
Hitler speech: Baynes 426.
page 322
"We want the bill . . . your death knell has sounded," Bullock 229.
page 322
"I wish to assure you . . ." John Wheeler-Bennett, *Wooden Titan* (New York, 1936), 449.
page 323
"He stretched the truth . . ." Interview with Schwerin von Krosigk, 1971.
pages 323–24
Binding quote: R. Binding, *Die Briefe* (Hamburg, 1957), 182.
pages 324–25
Isherwood account: Isherwood 180–81.
page 325
Hitler quote: E. De Felice, *Storia degli ebrei italiani sotto il fascismo* (Turin, 1961), 113.
page 325
"Little knots of passers-by . . ." Isherwood 183.

page 326
Hindenburg-Hitler correspondence: Walther Hubatsch, *Hindenburg und der Staat*, op. cit., 375–78.
page 326
"It is precisely for these young Germans . . ." Baynes 729.
page 326
"nothing but pernicious enemies . . ." GFP, C, I, 347.
page 327
François-Poncet account: François-Poncet 69–70.
page 328
"The German government wishes . . ." Prange 349.
page 328
State Historial Society of Wisconsin: Lochner letter, May 28, 1933.
page 328
Footnote: New York *Times*, July 10, 1933.
page 328
"Within three weeks we had progressed . . ." HSC 470.
page 329
"We must now eliminate . . ." VB, July 6, 1933.
page 329
"When we discussed the measure . . ." Papen 304.
pages 329–30
"The revolution is not a permanent . . ." Speech, July 6, 1933, in Baynes 865–66.
page 330
"To gain political power . . ." Speech, July 13, 1933 in Baynes 848–85, 867–68.
page 330
"German socialism is directed by Germans . . ." Heinz 232.
page 331
Hitler to Spengler: *Spengler Letters* 290.
page 331
Richard Strauss received by Hitler: Koehler 67–68.
page 331
Pope welcomes Papen: Papen 279.
page 332
"It was like a country fair . . ." Interview, Stütz, 1971.
page 332
Hitler quote: F. Wagner 89.
pages 332–34
Hanfstaengls' trip to Obersalzberg: Egon Hanfstaengl, *Memoirs*, 216–29.
page 334
Literary Digest, Aug. 26, 1933, 13.
page 334
Lord Lothian quote: J. R. M. Butler, *Lord Lothian* (London, 1960), 206.
page 335
Dirksen quote: Herzstein 24.

page 335
"We must make a break . . ." Papen 297–98.

pages 335–36
Lord Allen quote: Martin Gilbert, *Plough My Own Furrow* (London, 1965), 340–41.

page 336
Heidegger quote: *Freiburger Studentenzeitung,* Nov. 10, 1933.

page 336
"very much upset over our step . . ." GFP, C, II, 28–29.

page 336
Cardinal Faulhaber quote: Amtsblatt Passau, ℀25, Nov. 10, 1933.

pages 336–37
Hitler speech at Siemens plant: Berlin, Nov. 10, 1933.

page 337
"Tomorrow show your national . . ." Dorpalen, 474.

page 337
"the representative of the German state idea . . ." Bracher 231.

page 338
"We wish thus to conform to the spirit . . ." *Jahresbericht der Deutschen Mathematiker-Vereinigung* (Leipzig, 1934), XLIII, 81–82.

page 338
Shaw quote: Tobias 124.

page 338
"grave grounds exist for suspecting . . ." Ibid. 126–27.

pages 338–39
Göring-Dimitrov exchange: *Neue Züricher Zeitung,* Nov. 6, 1933.

page 339
Hitler quote: MY 203.

page 339
Hanfstaengl quote: Martha Dodd 58.

pages 339–40
Dodd account: Ibid. 58–60.

page 340
Eden account: Eden, *Facing,* 61–65.

pages 340–41
Neurath cable: GFP, II, 611.

page 341
"The British were eager to get . . ." François-Poncet 122–23.

page 342
Hitler letter to Mussolini, Nov. 2, 1933; GFP, II, 63–64.

page 342
Hanfstaengl to Mussolini: Hanfstaengl, *Out of the Strong.*

page 342
Mussolini quote: Bojano 30–31.

page 343
"They were not over three yards from me . . ." Knickerbocker, 5–6.

page 343
"Mussolini stepped forth superbly . . ." Sisley Huddleston, *In My Time* (London: 1938), 309.

page 343
Wiedemann account: Wiedemann 32 (tr.).

page 344
Bojano account: Bojano 31.

page 344
Neurath's circular: GFP, C, III, 18.

page 344
"could not foresee any closer . . ." Weizsäcker 101.

Chapter Twelve. THE SECOND REVOLUTION—
"ALL REVOLUTIONS DEVOUR THEIR OWN CHILDREN"

page 345
"The Reichswehr is the sole bearer . . ." Schweitzer 244.

page 346
"Anyone who thinks that the tasks . . ." Heiden, *Der Führer*, 724.

pages 346–47
Conference, Feb. 28, 1934: Unpublished memoirs of Field Marshal von
  Weichs in O'Neill 39–41; Höhne, *Order*, 96. "What that ridiculous cor-
  poral . . ." Helmut Krausnick, "Der 30 Juni 1934," in *Das Parlament 30
  Juni*, 1954, 320.

page 347
"The SA is the heroic incarnation . . ." Röhm speech, Apr. 18, 1934.

page 348
"I implored him for the last time . . ." Baynes 315–16.

page 349
"He had some feeling that there was . . ." Interview with Röhm's sister-in-law,
  1971.

pages 349–50
Papen speech: Papen 305–7.

page 350
"If during these months I hesitated . . ." Baynes 309.

page 350
"He led me to his study . . ." The Lutze diary, in *Frankfurter Rundschau*,
  May 14, 1957.

page 351
"square accounts," Höhne, *Order*, 109.

page 351
"Woe to him who breaks faith . . ." VB, June 26, 1934.

page 351
"Now we are in the middle . . ." Delmer, *Trail*, 231–33.

page 352
"I had a feeling . . . would now have to take action . . ." Lutze diary, op. cit.

page 352
Hitler phone call to Röhm: Holborn, *Republic*, 235.

page 353
"That may be true . . ." Unpublished affidavit of Field Marshal Ewald von
  Kleist at Nuremberg, 1946. Institut für Zeitgeschichte, Munich.

page 353
"making a fatal error." *The Answers of Ernst von Salomon* (London, 1954), 273–74.

page 354
"The Reichswehr is against us!" Höhne, *Order*, 112; Case against Josef Dietrich, Munich Provisional Court I, July 4, 1956, 58, 80.

page 354
"It was at last clear to me . . ." Baynes 321.

page 354
"*Red of the morning* . . ." Lutze diary, op. cit.

page 355
"This is the blackest day . . ." Case against Dietrich, op. cit., 77.

page 355
"Lock him up!" Gallo 207.

page 355
"You are under arrest . . ." Lutze diary, op. cit.

pages 355–56
Kempka account: Interviews with Kempka, 1971.

page 356
"somewhat tense but not visibly excited." CIC interview of Wilhelm Brückner.

page 356
Lutze account: Lutze diary, op. cit.

pages 356–57
Brückner account: CIC interview, op. cit.; Kempka interview, 1971.

page 357
"I gave the order . . ." Baynes 321–22.

page 357
Epp account: Judgment on Josef Dietrich, Munich, May 14, 1957, 60.

page 357
"In a voice frequently . . ." Letter from Gruppenführer Karl Schreyer to Munich Police HQ, 4; Höhne, *Order*, 116.

page 358
Papen account: Papen 315.

page 358
Delmer account: *Trail*, 234.

page 359
Dietrich account: Interview with Dietrich, 1963.

page 359
"Select an officer and six men . . ." Höhne, *Order*, 117.

pages 359–60
Frank account: Frank 149–51.

page 360
Execution of the six men: Judgment on Dietrich, op. cit., 15–16; Case against Dietrich, op. cit., 69–70, 72.

page 360
"I have pardoned Röhm . . ." Judgment on Dietrich, op. cit., 61.

page 360
"Göring arrived in one of his . . ." Gisevius 156.
page 361
"He was foolish enough . . ." Wheeler-Bennett, *Nemesis,* 323.
page 361
DNB report: NA, Report, U. S. Embassy, Berlin, July 2, 1934.
page 361
Reference Karl Ernst: He was rumored to be involved in the mysterious murder of Hanussen, the astrologer, whose body was found in a forest near Stahnsdorf several weeks after his prediction of the Reichstag fire. There was some speculation that Hitler, reportedly incensed at the murder, took vengeance on Ernst. Hegner 21.

Curiously, another well-known astrologer was a victim of the Röhm purge: Dr. Karl-Günther Heimsoth, a close friend of Gregor Strasser, whose correspondence with Röhm about homosexuality and astrology was given wide publicity in the 1932 attempt to discredit the SA and the party. Dr. Heimsoth's death could also have been related to the recent ban on all forms of professional fortunetelling in the Berlin area. The predictions of Hanussen and his successors were becoming an embarrassment to the Third Reich. In the horoscope published by Frank Glahn in February 1933, for instance, it was predicted that the Führer would not be able to form a viable government.

Hitler's horoscope, however, continued to fascinate many Germans and a number were circulated surreptitiously. Soon after the Röhm purge, Hans Blüher, a founder of the *Wandervögel* movement, met an astrologer friend, Count Finckenstein, in a Berlin restaurant to discuss a horoscope of the Führer. "My friend Ulrich looked cautiously around to see if anyone was listening to us," wrote Blüher in his diary. "Then he leaned towards me and whispered in my ear through a cupped hand: 'He's a homocidal maniac!' Ever since then I knew that Germany had sold herself into the hands of a murderer." Howe, *Urania's,* 109.
page 362
"He wore no hat . . ." Gisevius 160–61.
page 362
"For months I have been telling . . ." Dorpalen 479.
pages 362–63
Death of Röhm: Statement by Lippert, *Stuttgarter Zeitung,* May 7, 1957; VB, July 1, 1934; *Süddeutsche Zeitung,* Mar. 30–31, May 11, May 14, 1947; *Frankfurter Rundschau,* May 8, 1957; Höhne, *Order,* 126–27.
page 363
"I hope we may call . . ." Martha Dodd 136.
page 363
Göring statement: NA, U. S. Embassy, Berlin, report, July 9, 1934.
page 363
Blomberg statement: Ibid.
pages 363–64
Schreyer account: Höhne, *Order,* 127.
page 364
Delmer statement: *Trail,* 235.

page 364
Hindenburg telegram: Wheeler-Bennett, *Nemesis*, 325–26.
page 365
Papen account: Papen 318.
page 365
"When a mutiny takes place . . ." Interview with Schwerin von Krosigk, 1971.
page 366
Frank–Hitler: Frank 152–54.
pages 366–67
"I have often seen governments . . . among the men who wield power."
   Anonymous source from *Das Neue Tage-Buch* in Paris.
page 367
Hitler speech: Baynes 290–328.
page 367
"emergency defense measures of the state," Orlow II, 115.
page 368
"Our verdict on the affair . . ." Dönitz 304.
page 368
"This type of spontaneous . . ." Gallo 289.
page 368
"It may be as you say . . ." Heinz Assmann 289ff.; also Assmann article,
   "Adolf Hitler—Genius and Demon."
pages 368–69
Mackensen Memorandum: Wheeler-Bennett, *Nemesis*, 329–31.
page 369
Ruck statement: Interview with Ruck, 1971.
pages 369–70
Naumann statement: Interview, 1971.
page 370
Lutze story: Report by Robert Schulz, Aug. 21, 1935, RFSS microfilm 33 at
   NA (Group T-175).
page 371
"The inevitable has happened . . ." Ivone Kirkpatrick 297.
page 371
Friedelind Wagner account: OSS interview, HSB 934.
page 371
Bülow account: GFP, C, III, 235–41.
page 372
Papen account: Papen 337–41.
page 372
Schacht account: *Old Wizard*, 292.
pages 372–73
Mussolini quote: Starhemberg 164–68.
pages 373–74
Hitler at Hindenburg's: MY 262.
page 374
"We were in his study . . ." Raeder testimony at Nuremberg, 1946.

page 374
Oath: Wheeler-Bennett, *Nemesis,* 339.
page 375
Lochner account: *What About Germany?,* 120.
page 375
Papen account: Papen 333.
pages 375–76
Hitler to Hanfstaengl: MY 263–64.

Chapter Thirteen. TRIUMPH OF THE WILL

pages 377–78
Thompson account: *Harper's Bazaar,* Dec. 1934.
page 378
Dodd account: William Dodd 154.
page 378
Jüttner account: Interrogation of Max Jüttner, Provincial Court I, Munich, Apr. 8, 1949.
page 378
Speer account: Speer 58–59.
pages 378–79
Leni Riefenstahl account: Interviews, 1971.
page 379
"The German form of life . . ." Shirer, *Berlin Diary,* 19.
page 380
Frank account: Frank 154–55.
page 380
"The floodlit stadium gave the impression . . ." Speer in *Playboy* 78.
pages 380–81
Shirer account: *Berlin Diary,* 22.
page 381
Hitler to generals: Unpublished memoirs of Field Marshal von Weichs; BA, H 07-19/1, 19/14.
page 381
Dodd comment: William Dodd 164.
pages 381–82
Riefenstahl account: Interviews, 1971.
page 383
"During these violent scoldings . . ." OSS interview of Friedelind Wagner: HSB 939.
page 383
Hitler to Wiedemann: Wiedemann 35 (tr.).
page 383
Hitler to Schröder: Zoller 101.
page 383
Brigid Hitler and son account: HSB 927; Brigid Hitler manuscript.
page 383
Footnote: Interview with Hans Hitler, 1971.

page 384
"No country, and especially not England . . ." Weinberg 202.
page 384
"It is ten years today . . ." Price 31.
page 385
"Something has gone wrong . . ." Shirer, *Berlin Diary*, 27.
page 386
"looking very important and grave," Ibid. 29.
page 386
François-Poncet account: Interview, 1971.
page 386
"withdrawal from the League of Nations . . ." GFP, III, 1043–44.
page 387
Eden account: *Facing*, 134, 133, 135.
page 387
"We will have nothing whatever . . ." Schmidt 19–20. The quotes from
    Schmidt throughout this book have been illuminated by two interviews
    with Dr. Schmidt in 1963.
page 387
Eden account: *Facing*, 138–39.
page 388
"Only two years ago the skies . . . atmosphere of the great house." Schmidt
    25.
page 388
"Great fellows, the English . . ." F. Wagner 129.
page 389
Mosley account: Mosley, 365; interviews, 1971–72.
page 389
"once again showed his complete . . ." GFP, C, IV, 49.
page 390
Lochner account: Letter to his daughter, Apr. 1935. State Historical Society
    of Wisconsin.
page 391
Oka's account: Robert Ingrim, *Hitlers glücklichster Tag* (Stuttgart, 1962).
page 391
"If the British government . . ." Schmidt 32–33.
pages 392–93
"How often have I told you . . ." Windsor 254.
page 393
"the timidity and hesitation . . ." GFP, IV, 331.
page 394
"He was of the opinion . . ." Wiedemann 35 (tr.).
page 394
"For me marriage would have been . . ." HSC 247–48.
page 396
Speer on Hitler's fear of cancer: Speer 104.
pages 398–99
Hitler to Reichstag: Baynes 732.

page 400
"formed a single community . . ." Orlow II, 138.
page 400
Luther cable: GFP, IV, 1017.
page 400
Coburg report: Ibid. 1063. Hassell's memorandum: Ibid. 1142–43.
page 400
Hitler to Jouvenel: Maser, *Hitlers "Mein Kampf"* (Munich, 1966), 47–48.
page 402
"To the British people . . ." Eden, *Facing*, 337–38.
page 402
Hitler to Hoffmann: Hoffmann 84.
page 402
Hitler to Wiedemann: Wiedemann 111 (tr.).
pages 402–3
Hoesch to Eden: *Facing*, 338–39.
page 403
Eden to Baldwin: Ibid. 343.
pages 403–4
Helms account: Interviews, 1971.

Chapter Fourteen. "WITH THE ASSURANCE OF A SLEEPWALKER"

page 408
Hitler to Schmidt: Schmidt 41.
page 408
"Good Lord, am I relieved how smoothly . . ." Frank 204ff.
page 408
"The Germans, after all, are only . . ." Shirer, *Rise*, 293.
page 408
"His view is that, if a firm front . . ." Feiling 279.
pages 408–9
"I go the way that Providence . . ." Hitler speech, Munich, Mar. 14, 1936.
page 409
Hitler quote: HSC 259.
page 409
Hitler speech: Prange 110.
pages 409–10
Ribbentrop-Jones meeting: Thomas Jones 197–98.
page 410
Hitler-Jones meeting: Ibid. 198–201.
page 411
Kirkpatrick comment: Ivone Kirkpatrick, *The Inner Circle* (London, 1959), 97–98.
page 411
Hitler to Frau Wagner: F. Wagner 127.
page 412
"Wedged between the powerful Soviet bloc . . ." *Ribbentrop Memoirs*, 59–60.

page 413
Owens quote: Mandell 227.

page 414
Dietrich comment: Dietrich, *Hitler*, 30–31.

page 414
Phayre article: *Current History*, July 1936.

pages 414–15
"Look, Adolf, it is not that bad . . ." Section on Ilse Hess in Ziegler.

page 415
Footnote: Interview with Hans Hitler; CIC-PH.

page 416
Maggi story: Interview with Dieter Allers, 1971.

page 416
Bormann-Fath: Interview with Hildegard Fath, 1971.

page 416
Helene Hanfstaengl divorce: Interview, 1971; correspondence with Egon Hanf-
     staengl, 1973.

page 416
Lake Starnberg incident: Egon Hanfstaengl, *Memoirs*, 362ff.

page 418
"It is better to consider and solve . . ." Gerhard Meinck, *Hitler und die
     Deutache Aufrüstung* (Wiesbaden, 1959), 234.

pages 418–19
Lloyd George-Hitler meeting: Thomas Jones 245–46.

page 419
Lloyd George-Linge: Linge, Installment ⚡12.

page 419
Lloyd George-Schmidt: Schmidt 59.

page 419
Helms account: Interview with Helms, 1971.

page 420
"Mussolini is the first statesman of the world . . ." Wiskemann 90.

pages 420–21
"According to the English there are . . ." *Ciano's Diplomatic Papers* (Lon-
     don, 1948), 60.

page 421
"this Berlin-Rome line is not a diaphragm . . ." Ivone Kirkpatrick 347.

page 421
"We are already in a state of war . . ." IMT, IX, 40.

page 421
"The battle we are now approaching . . ." Shirer, *Rise*, 300.

page 422
"If I can marry her as King . . ." Windsor 332.

pages 422–23
Ribbentrop to Hesse: HH 31–32.

page 423
"carry the heavy burden of responsibility . . ." Windsor 411.

page 423
Hitler to Ribbentrop: HH 33.

page 424
"Both Grawitz and Bergmann . . ." Interview with Dr. Giesing, 1971.

page 424
Hitler speech: Baynes 1334–47.

page 424
Footnote: New York *Times* Book Review, Apr. 22, 1973.

page 425
Hitler quote: HSC 425.

page 425
"The goal of our education . . ." *Hans Schemm spricht: Seine Reden und sein Werk* (Gauverlag Bayerische Ostmark, 1935), 175–78.

page 426
Phipps report: CAB 27/599.

page 426
Hitler Youth: Siemsen 145, 154; interview with Lauterbacher, 1971; Lauterbacher testimony at Nuremberg, May 27, 1936, 534.

page 427
Wilson quote: Santoro 416.

page 427
Ley quote: David Schoenbaum, *Hitler's Social Revolution* (Garden City, 1966), 105.

page 427
"The bourgeois must no longer feel . . ." Ibid. 58.

page 428
G. S. Cox article in New York *Times Magazine*, Oct. 28, 1934.

page 428
Kennan comment: *Memoirs*, 118.

page 429
On autarchy: Carr 52–61.

page 430
Göring quote: Speech, Oct. 28, 1936, reprinted in *Der Vierjahresplan*, Jan. 1937, 33–35.

page 430
Hitler quote: Santoro 423.

page 430
Schacht comment: *Account*, 98–99.

page 430
On Shaw: "His defense of 'Bosses' in the Preface of *The Millionairess* and in numerous magazine and newspaper articles, included Hitler . . . Mussolini . . . Lenin . . . and Trotsky . . . and, above all, Stalin, whom he regarded as the world's greatest man." Archibald Henderson, *GBS*, 311.

page 431
Hedin quotes: Hedin 71, 99.

page 431
Degrelle comment: Interview, 1971.
pages 431–32
Chiang Kai-shek quote: Eastman 4–5. The philosophy from Europe was accompanied by military assistance from Germany and, significantly, the adviser sent by the Weimar Republic to Chiang in 1929 was Colonel Hermann Kriebel, who had served time with Adolf Hitler in Landsberg for his
involvement in the Beer Hall Putsch. See "The Development of German-
Chinese Military Relations, 1928–1936," by Thomas M. Williamson, thesis for Department of History in the Graduate School of Arts and Sci-
ences, Duke University, 1967.

Chapter Fifteen. "SUCH A LITTLE HUMAN WORM"

pages 433–34
Hitler speech to the Kreisleiters: *Es spricht der Führer,* edited by Hildegard
von Kotze and Helmuth Krausnick (Gütersloh, 1966), 123–77. A German
farmer found the tapes in a ditch where they had been dumped in the last
days of the Third Reich. Now at the Bundesarchiv.
page 435
Hitler to Speer: Speer, *Inside,* 41.
page 436
Frau Troost account: Interviews, 1971; correspondence, 1975.
page 437
Hitler speech: Baynes 584–92.
page 437
"Thus did sick minds view Nature . . ." Grunberger 426.
pages 437–38
"The artists ought to be tied to their pictures . . ." Ibid. 425.
pages 438–39
Schmidt comments on Mussolini and Hitler: Schmidt 71.
page 440
Hitler and Mussolini speech: Schmidt 73.
page 441
Jung on Hitler: Knickerbocker 49–50.
page 441
"Now I feel as fresh as a foal . . ." Fest, *Face,* 48.
pages 441–42
Hitler to Göring: IMT, IX, 307.
pages 442–43
Hossbach Minutes: GFP, D, I, 29ff.; Hossbach, *Zwischen Wehrmacht und
Hitler* (Hannover, 1949), 207–20.
page 444
Raeder comment: Testimony at Nuremberg, May 16, 1946, 35.
page 444
"Again and again difficult matters . . ." Adolf von Kielmansegg, *Der Fritsch
Prozess 1938* (Hamburg, 1949), 586.

page 445
"Our objective should be set out . . ." CAB 27-626, FP (36) 23.

page 445
"I believe the double policy . . ." Feiling 319.

page 445
Halifax comment on Göring: London *Times*, May 28, 1973.

page 445
Halifax on Goebbels: Lord Birkenhead, *Halifax* (London, 1965), 373.

page 446
Halifax-Hitler meeting: Schmidt 76–77.

pages 446–47
Kirkpatrick account: Kirkpatrick, *Inner Circle*, op. cit., 94–98.

page 447
"Under no circumstances shall we use force." Schmidt 78.

page 447
Halifax to cabinet: CAB 43 (37).

page 447
"I am amazed that Halifax . . ." London *Times*, op. cit.

page 448
"I have always said that the English . . ." Günsche testimony to Russians:
   Bezymenski 16.

page 448
Krause account: Krause 53–55.

pages 448–49
Eden recommendations: CAB 237, 626, FP (36) 41.

page 450
Wiedemann account: Wiedemann 58 (tr.).

page 450
Wiedemann account, Wiedemann, idem.

pages 451–52
Keitel account: Keitel, 45–47.

page 452
Wiedemann account: Wiedemann 62 (tr.).

page 453
Guderian comment: Guderian 28.

page 454
"On that point they will fight," Annelies von Ribbentrop, 80.

Chapter Sixteen. THE RETURN OF THE NATIVE

page 455
Papen account: Papen 406–8.

page 456
"to forestall a coup . . ." Guido Schmidt interrogation, IMT, XVI, 152.

pages 456–58
Schuschnigg-Hitler first interview: Schuschnigg, *Austrian*, 12–19; interview
   with Schuschnigg, 1971.

page 459
Second interview: Ibid. 24–26; Keitel 57; IMT, X, 505.
pages 459–60
Third interview: Schuschnigg, *Austrian*, 25–27.
page 459
"Now you have some idea . . ." Papen 420; Schuschnigg, *Austrian*, 27.
page 459
Hitler notation: Müllern-Schönhausen 162.
page 461
"The Jews were attacking . . ." Schuschnigg, *Brutal*, 225.
page 461
Hitler speech: Gedye 232.
page 461
Yeats-Brown comment: *Living Age*, August 1938, 512–14.
page 461
Gedye account: Gedye 233.
page 462
"should continue to use this method." Schuschnigg, *Brutal*, 230.
page 462
Schuschnigg speech: Gedye 238–39; interview with Schuschnigg, 1971.
page 462
"an indispensable element . . ." Brook-Shepherd 103.
page 463
"Fundamentally, a close understanding . . ." Ibid. 85.
page 463
Ingersoll incident: Toland, *Rising Sun*, 49.
page 464
Schmidt on Henderson: Schmidt 86.
page 464
Henderson-Hitler meeting: N. Henderson 115–16.
pages 464–65
Schuschnigg-Keppler meeting: Schuschnigg, *Brutal*, 250.
page 465
Keppler report: Ibid. 249.
page 466
Starhemberg comment: Starhemberg 272.
page 466
"We have prepared nothing . . ." Shirer, *Rise*, 335.
pages 466–67
Hitler letter to Mussolini: GFP, D., I, #352.
page 467
Schuschnigg letter to Seyss-Inquart: Schuschnigg, *Brutal*, 264.
pages 468–69
Glaise-Horstenau account: IMT, XIV, 131–32.
pages 468ff.
Telephone conversations between Berlin and other cities throughout the chapter: Schuschnigg, *Austrian*, Appendix 290ff.

page 470
"professed to be ignorant . . ." Cadogan 60.

page 470
Halifax to Schuschnigg: BFP, 3rd, I, 13.

page 470
"directly or indirectly—in the preparations . . ." Schuschnigg, *Austrian*, 48–49.

pages 470–71
Schuschnigg account: *Austrian*, 48–52; interview with Schuschnigg, 1971.

page 472
Schuschnigg speech: Shirer, *Berlin Diary*, 99; Guido Schmidt Trial Protocols, Nuremberg, 290.

page 473
"Now, get moving!" Grolmann affidavit, quoted in Eichstaedt, *Von Dollfuss zu Hitler* (Wiesbaden, 1955), 411.

page 473
Ems telegram: Papen 429. Papen-Wiedemann: Wiedemann 64 (tr.).

page 474
"Or would you like to go . . ." Schuschnigg, *Austrian*, 54–55.

pages 474–75
Viebahn incident: Keitel 58–59; W. Görlitz, *Keitel* (Göttingen, 1961), 179.

page 475
Hitler proclamation: Santoro 102.

page 475
Guderian comment: Guderian 32.

page 475
Keitel comment: Keitel 59.

page 475
Guderian comment: Guderian 37.

page 476
Hitler to Linge: Linge ⚡21.

page 477
Guderian account: Guderian 33.

page 477
"If the enthusiasm is so great . . ." Brook-Shepherd 193.

page 478
Mussolini telegram: Mussolini 190.

page 478
"Yes, a good political action . . ." Memorandum by Seyss-Inquart, Sept. 9, 1945; ND, 3254-PS.

page 478
Freud story: Ernest Jones 294.

page 479
Gedye account: Gedye 299.

page 479
Telegram to Halifax: BFP, I, 44.

page 480
Huss account: Huss 19–20. IMT, XV, 633.

page 481
On Cardinal Innitzer: Papen 432–33; Schmidt Trial Protocols, op. cit., 383.
page 481
Eva Braun account: Gun, *Eva Braun*, 127–28.
page 481
Lochner letter, Mar. 15, 1938.
page 481
Hitler speech: Baynes 1427.
page 481
Hitler to Reichstag: Santoro 108–10.
page 482
Footnote: Interview with Schuschnigg, 1971.
page 482
Innitzer proclamation: Brook-Shepherd 202.
pages 482–83
Kubizek-Hitler: Kubizek 277–81.
page 483
"For me, this is the proudest . . ." Baynes 1459.

Chapter Seventeen. "ON THE RAZOR'S EDGE"

page 485
Linge account: Linge ⚡22.
page 486
Baur account: Section on Baur in Ziegler; interview with Baur, 1970.
page 486
Ciano account; Ciano diary, May 7, 1938; interview with Dollmann, 1971.
page 487
Lochner account: *What About Germany?*, II.
page 487
"was extremely successful in melting . . ." Dollmann 110.
page 487
Ciano account: Ciano diary, May 5, 1938.
page 488
Chamberlain letter, Mar. 20, 1938; Private Collection to be available at Birmingham University Library.
page 488
"even if France does not do so . . ." Louis Fischer 311.
page 489
"It depends upon you, Excellency . . ." Wheeler-Bennett, *Munich*, 57.
page 489
Henderson-Ribbentrop: GFP, D. 11, 317.
page 489
Weizsäcker comment: Weizsäcker 135–36.
pages 489–90
May 28 conference: *Nazi Conspiracy and Aggression*, V, 3037-PS, 743–44; Wiedemann Testimony, Nuremberg, Oct. 24, 1945, 3; Braddick 22.
page 490
Beck memorandum: O'Neill 155–56.

pages 490–91
Keitel comment: Keitel 63–64.

page 491
"to intimidate the Czechs by means . . ." GFP, II, 359.

page 491
"Here the view prevails . . ." Ibid. 363.

pages 491–92
Wiedemann account: Wiedemann 94 (tr.).

pages 492–93
Hesse account: HH 40–51; letter, Hesse, 1974.

page 493
Beck memorandum: O'Neill 157–58; Wolfgang Förster, *Ein General Kämpft gegen den Krieg* (Munich, 1949), 98–102.

page 494
Maisky to Halifax: McSherry I, 63.

pages 494–95
Kleist-Schmenzin-Vansittart meeting: BFP, 3 II-683–86.

pages 494–95
Henderson telegram: Ibid. 118.

page 495
Schwerin von Krosigk letter to Hitler: SvK to author.

page 496
"Every generation must experience . . ." Wiedemann testimony at Nuremberg, Sept. 28, 1945, 23; Wiedemann 97 (tr.).

pages 496–97
Henderson letter: BFP, II, 257.

page 497
"You know I am like a wanderer . . ." Frank 320.

page 497
"But its success is nevertheless . . ." GFP, II, 729.

page 497
Keitel-Brauchitsch: Keitel 69–70.

page 498
Jodl comment: Jodl's diary, Sept. 10, 12, 13, 1938; Warlimont 116.

page 498
Göring speech: Nogueres 107.

page 498
Shirer account: *Berlin Diary*, 125.

page 498
Chamberlain to journalists: BFP, II, 680–82.

page 498
Chamberlain letter: Feiling 360.

page 499
Mussolini quote: Nogueres 116.

page 499
Chamberlain to Daladier: BFP, II, 314.

page 500
"I fell from Heaven!" L. B. Namier, *Diplomatique prelude* (London, 1948), 35.

page 500
Mussolini quote: Ciano diary, Sept. 14, 1938.
page 500
Chamberlain on BBC: Nogueres 124.
pages 501–2
Hitler-Chamberlain meeting: Schmidt 92–93; Feiling 366–67.
page 502
Masefield poem: London *Times*, Sept. 16, 1938.
page 502
Roosevelt quote: Ickes diary, Sept. 18, 1938.
pages 502–3
Chamberlain-Daladier: BFP, II, 387–96.
page 503
Chamberlain letter: Feiling 368.
pages 503–4
Newton report: BFP, II, 416–17.
page 503
Hodža to Lacroix: Nogueres 148.
pages 503–4
Newton report: BFP, II, 425.
page 504
Czech communiqué: Nogueres 155.
page 504
Chamberlain to journalists: MacLeod 242.
pages 504–6
First Chamberlain-Hitler meeting: Schmidt 96–97; GFP, II, 876; BFP, II, 472.
page 506
On Hitler's outbursts: Wiedemann 126 (tr.).
pages 507–8
Schmidt account: Schmidt 99–100.
pages 507–8
Second Chamberlain-Hitler meeting: Schmidt 100–3; BFP, II, 502; MacLeod 246; GFP, II, 907–8.
page 509
Chamberlain to cabinet: CAB 23/95, 42 (38); BFP, II, 510; Parkinson 41–42.
page 509
Sunday cabinet meeting: Parkinson 43; CAB 23/95, 43 (38); Barnett 540.
page 510
Daladier quote: Parkinson 47.
page 510
Chamberlain to cabinet: Parkinson 48.
page 510
Footnote: Colin Cross, *Adolf Hitler* (London, 1973), 268.
page 510
Hitler-Wilson meeting: Schmidt 103; GFP, II, 555–57.

page 511
Hitler speech: Prange 114–15; Parkinson 52.
page 511
Bullitt phone call: Bullitt 296.
pages 511–12
Wilson-Hitler meeting: BFP, II, 565; Schmidt 104–5; Bullock 410; GFP, II, 965.
page 512
Shirer comments: *Berlin Diary*, 141, 143.
page 512
Wiedemann-Schaub: Wiedemann 101 (tr.).
page 512
"I can't wage war . . ." Fest, *Face*, 43.
pages 512–13
Chamberlain broadcast: Feiling 372; Nogueres 212–13.
page 513
Hitler letter: BFP, II, 578.
page 513
Chamberlain reply: Feiling 373.
page 513
Chamberlain letter to Mussolini: Feiling 373.
page 513
Weizsäcker-Ribbentrop: Weizsäcker 153–54.
page 514
"You need not say a word more . . ." N. Henderson 167.
page 514
Schmidt account: Schmidt 105–7.
page 514
Wiedemann account: Wiedemann 104 (tr.).
page 515
Henderson account: N. Henderson 168–69.
pages 515–16
House of Commons scene: MacLeod 249–50.
page 516
Bullitt letter: Bullitt 297.
page 516
Beneš message: BFP, II, 604.
page 516
Mussolini quote: Ciano diary, Sept. 29–30, 1938.
page 517
"I have no need to mobilize . . ." I. Kirkpatrick, *Mussolini*, 383.
page 517
Chamberlain to journalists: Nogueres 250–51.
page 518
"Our time is too valuable . . ." Schmidt 110.
page 518
"That was my great day . . ." Interview with Dollmann, 1971.

pages 518–19
Dollmann account: Dollmann 131–32; interview with Dollmann, 1971.
page 519
Göring comment: G. M. Gilbert, *Nuremberg*, 88.
page 520
Shirer comment: Shirer, *Rise*, 418.
page 520
François-Poncet account: *Fateful*, 273.
page 520
Chamberlain-Hitler: Schmidt 112–13; Feiling 376–77.
page 520
"I gave him a noseful . . ." Linge ⌗13.
page 520
Hitler to Engel: Engel 40–41.
page 521
Letter from King to Chamberlain: Feiling 378–79.
page 521
Chamberlain letter: Feiling 377.
page 521
London *Times* comment: Oct. 1, 1938.
page 521
Chamberlain at 10 Downing St.: Feiling 381.
page 521
Syrovy announcement: Gatzke 214.
page 522
Kaiser letter: Nelson 447.
page 522
Wiedemann account: Wiedemann 108 (tr.).
page 522
Chamberlain letter: Feiling 377.
page 522
Duff Cooper quote: Parkinson 69.
pages 522–23
Churchill quote: Ibid. 70.
page 523
Chamberlain to Hitler: Irving, *Breach*, 50.
page 523
François-Poncet comment: *Fateful*, 275.
pages 523–24
François-Poncet report: *French Yellow Book*, 22–26.
page 525
Freud quote: Blanton 101–2.
pages 525–26
Jung quotes: Knickerbocker 45–56.

R